FERGUSON

CAREER RESOURCE GUIDE TO

INTERNSHIPS

AND

SUMMER JOBS

VOLUME 1

Carol Turkington

Ferguson

An imprint of Infobase Publishing

Ferguson Career Resource Guide to Internships and Summer Jobs

Ferguson
An imprint of Infobase Publishing
132 West 31st Street
New York NY 10001

Library of Congress Cataloging-in-Publication Data
Turkington, Carol.
Ferguson career resource guide to internships and summer jobs / Carol Turkington.
   p. cm.
  Includes index.
  ISBN 0-8160-6019-3 (set) (hc : alk. paper)
  ISBN 0-8160-6020-7 (vol. 1)— ISBN 0-8160-6021-5 (vol. 2)
  1. Internship programs—United States. 2. College students—Employment—United States. 3. High school students—Employment—United States. 4. Summer employment—United States. I. Title.
  LC1072.I58T87   2006
  311.25'922—dc22

Text design by David Strelecky
Cover design by Salvatore Luongo

Printed in the United States of America

VB FOF 10 9 8 7 6 5 4 3 2 1

This book is printed on acid-free paper.

CONTENTS

VOLUME 1

Acknowledgments xv

PART I: INTRODUCTION AND OVERVIEW

Introduction xix

PART II: ESSAYS

Internships, Summer Jobs, and Lifelong Job Skills 3

What Kind of Internship or Summer Job Is Right for You? 3

Locating an Internship 6

Creating a Terrific Resume 7

Writing a Snappy Cover Letter 10

Acing the Interview 13

Ten Ways to Succeed in an Internship or Summer Job 16

Finding a Mentor 17

So You Want to Work Abroad . . . 18

Government Internships 19

Finding Great References 21

Launching Your Career 22

PART III: DIRECTORY

ACTIVISM

Accion International Internship 27

Advocates for Youth Internship 27

American Civil Liberties Union Immigrants Rights Project Internship 28

American Civil Liberties Union Internship 29

Amnesty International— Washington, D.C., Internship 30

Beyond Pesticides Internship 32

Boston Environment Department Internship 33

Bread for the City Legal Clinic Internship 34

Brooklyn Parents for Peace Internship 34

The Carter Center Internship 35

Center for Women in Politics and Public Policy Internship 43

Common Cause Internship 43

Earthtrends Summer Internship 44

Friends Committee on National Legislation (FCNL) Internship 45

Government Accountability Project Internship 47

Greenbelt Alliance Internship 47

Habitat for Humanity—New York City Internship 49

Heifer International Internship 49

Initiative for a Competitive Inner City Internship 51

International Center for Tolerance Education Internship 51

International Diplomacy Council Internship 52

Mediarights Internship 53

Merck Family Fund Internship 55

National Campaign to Prevent Teen Pregnancy Internship 56

National Environmental Law Center Internship 57

National Organization for Women (NOW)
Internship   58

New American Dream Communications
Internship   58

The New Press Internship   60

Peaceworks Foundation Internship   61

Pendle Hill Social Justice Internship   61

Physicians for Social Responsibility
Internship   62

Population Services International Internship   63

Prison Activist Resource Center Internship   65

Public Leadership Education Network
Internship   66

Rainforest Action Network Internship   67

Robert F. Kennedy Memorial Center for
Human Rights Internship   68

Santé Group Internship   69

Seeds of Peace Internship   69

Share Our Strength Internship   70

The Sierra Club—Washington, D.C.,
Internship   71

Strong Women, Strong Girls Internship   72

20/20 Vision Internship   73

United Nations Association of the
USA Internship   74

Washington Food Coalition Internship   74

Women for Peace Internship   75

Women Work Internship   75

World Affairs Council Internship   77

ANIMALS

The AARK Wildlife Rehabilitation
Internship   81

Beaver Dam Farm Equine Internship   81

Best Friends Animal Society Internship   83

Big Cat Rescue Internship   84

Chicago Zoological Society Brookfield Zoo
Internship   85

Denver Zoo Internship   87

Disney's Animal Kingdom Advanced
Internship   88

Dolphin Institute Internship   91

Farm Sanctuary Internship   92

Fort Wayne Children's Zoo Vet Medicine
Internship   93

Fossil Rim Wildlife Center Internship   94

Genesis Animal Sanctuary Summer
Internship   95

Great Dog Obedience Training Internship   96

Hilltop Farm Inc. Internship   97

Houston Zoo Internship   97

Mystic Aquarium Internship   99

National Aquarium in Baltimore Internship   101

National Zoo Beaver Valley Internship   102

New England Wildlife Center Internship   103

Oregon Zoo Internship   104

Paws Companion Animal Internship   105

Philadelphia Junior Zoo Apprentice Internship   106

Philadelphia Zoo Internship   108

San Diego Zoo Internquest   109

SeaWorld Adventure Camp Internship   109

Strides Therapeutic Riding Center Internship   111

Tiger Creek Wildlife Refuge Internship   112

Wild Horse Sanctuary Internship   113

Wildlife Rescue and Rehabilitation Internship   114

Wolfsong Ranch Foundation Internship   114

World Bird Sanctuary Internship   115

Zoo Atlanta Internship   116

ART

Archives of American Art Internship   121

Art Institute of Chicago Internship   122

Art Museum of the Americas Internship   123

Center for Arts and Culture Internship   123

Chicago Historical Society Internship   124

Christie's Internship   125

Cooper-Hewitt, National Design Museum
Internship 126

Corcoran Gallery of Art Internship 128

Field Museum Internship 129

Freer Gallery of Art/Arthur M. Sackler
Gallery Internship 130

Getty Foundation Internship 131

Guggenheim Museum Internship 133

Hirshhorn Museum and Sculpture
Garden Internship 135

International Child Art Foundation Internship 136

Julia Morgan Center for the Arts Internship 137

Metropolitan Museum of Art Internship 138

Michael Perez Gallery Internship 140

Museum of Contemporary Art San Diego
Internship 140

Museum of Modern Art Internship 142

National Endowment for the Arts Internship 146

National Gallery of Art High School
Internship 147

National Gallery of Art Internship 148

National Museum of African Art Internship 150

National Museum of Women in the Arts
Internship 150

National Portrait Gallery Internship 152

New Museum of Contemporary Art Internship 155

Philadelphia Museum of Art Internship 157

Seattle Art Museum Internship 158

Very Special Arts Internship 159

Whitney Museum of American Art Internship 159

WVSA Arts Connection Internship 160

BUSINESS

Abbott Laboratories Internship 165

Amelia Island Internship 166

Axle Alliance Group Internship 167

Bechtel Corporation Internship 167

Boeing Internship 168

Cessna Internship 169

ChevronTexaco Engineering Internship 170

Chrysler Group Internship 172

DuPont Summer Internship 173

Ernst & Young Internship 173

Ford Motor Company Internship 174

General Electric Internship 177

Hallmark Cards Internship 178

Hewlett-Packard Summer Internship 179

IMG International Internship 179

Inroads Internship 181

Kraft Foods Internship 182

Lands' End Internship 183

Liz Claiborne Summer Internship 185

Lucent Technologies Summer Internship 185

Mattel Internship 186

Macy's Internship 187

Mercedes-Benz USA Internship 189

Merck Internship 189

Pfizer Internship 190

Random House Inc. Summer Internship 192

Raytheon Internship 193

Saks Incorporated Internship 193

Toyota Motor North America Internship 194

Tyson Foods Internship 195

Verizon College Internship 195

Walt Disney World Culinary Jobs 196

EDUCATION

Acadia National Park Education Internship 201

American Folklife Center Internship 201

American Geographical Society Internship 202

American School for the Deaf Internship 203

Anasazi Heritage Center Internship 204

Boston Museum of Science Internship 205

Brooklyn Children's Museum Internship 210

Chicago Children's Museum Internship 210

Children's Museum of Indianapolis Internship 211

Daughters of the American Revolution (DAR) Museum Internship 217

Historic Preservation Internship Training Program 218

Independence Seaport Museum Internship 219

Japanese American National Museum Internship 219

Literacy Partners Inc. Internship 221

National Air and Space Museum Internship 221

National Anthropological Archives Internship 222

National Building Museum Internship 223

National Museum of American History Internship 224

National Museum of the American Indian Internship 225

Portland Children's Museum Internship 226

San Diego Museum of Art—Education Internship 229

San Diego Zoo's Wild Animal Park Summer Camp Teen Internship 230

South Street Seaport Museum Internship 230

Teach for America National Internship 231

University of the Middle East Project Internship 232

U.S. Department of Education Internship 233

U.S. Holocaust Museum Internship 233

The Washington Center for Internships and Academic Seminars 234

ENTERTAINMENT

Academy of Television Arts and Sciences Foundation Internship 241

Actors Theatre Workshop Internship 245

American Conservatory Theater Internship 246

American Dance Festival Internship 250

Arena Stage Internship 251

Atlanta Ballet Internship 254

BalletMet Internship 254

Berkshire Theater Festival Internship 255

Boston Ballet Internship 256

Chicago Symphony Orchestra Internship 257

Children's Television Workshop Internship 258

Dallas Theater Center Internship 259

Dallas Theater Center SummerStage Internship 260

Dance Place Internship 260

Dreamtime Festival Internship 261

DreamWorks SKG Internship 263

E! Entertainment Talent/Casting Internship 265

Eugene O'Neill Theater Internship 267

Folger Shakespeare Library Internship 269

Geddes Talent Agency Internship 270

Glimmerglass Opera Internship 270

Jim Henson Company Internship 274

Juilliard School Professional Internship 276

Kennedy Center for the Performing Arts Management Internship 280

The Late Show with David Letterman Internship 282

Longwood Gardens Performing Arts Internship 283

Los Angeles Opera Community Programs Internship 284

Lucas Digital Internship 284

Lucasfilm Internship 286

Metro-Goldwyn-Mayer (MGM) Internship 287

MTV Networks Internship—Nashville 288

MTV Networks Internship—New York City 288

MTV Networks Internship—Santa Monica 289

MTV Networks Latin America Internship—Miami Beach 290

National Endowment for the Arts Internship 290

New York State Theatre Institute Internship 291

Nickelodeon Animation Studio Internship 292

One Reel Internship 292

Other Hand Productions Puppet Internship 294

Paramount Pictures/*Dr. Phil Show* Internship 295
Philadelphia Orchestra Association Internship 295
Radio Disney—Boston Internship 297
RKO Pictures Internship 297
Sacramento Music Circus Summer Musical
   Theater Internship 298
San Francisco Mime Troupe Internship 299
Second Stage Theatre Internship 300
Shakespeare Theatre Internship 302
Smithsonian Folkways Recording Internship 304
South Shore Music Circus Internship 305
Spoleto Festival USA Internship 306
The Studio Theatre Internship 308
Texas Film Commission Internship 309
Walt Disney World Summer Jobs 310
Wilma Theater Internship 312
Wolf Trap Internship 312

GOVERNMENT

American Enterprise Institute Internship 317
Arizona Legislative Internship 318
Asian Pacific American Institute for
   Congressional Studies Internship 320
California Governor's Internship 322
Capitol Hill Internship 323
Central Intelligence Agency Internship 324
Connecticut Governor's Prevention
   Partnership Internship 325
Democratic National Committee Internship 326
Federal Bureau of Investigation (FBI)
   Washington Internships for Native
   Students (WINS) 327
Florida Governor's Internship 328
Georgia Governor's Internship 329
Idaho Lieutenant Governor's Internship 330
Illinois Governor's Internship 330
Library of Congress Internship 331
Maine State Governor's Internship 335

Maryland Governor's Summer Internship 335
Michigan Executive Office Internship 336
New Jersey Governor's Internship 338
New York City Summer Internship 339
North Carolina Governor's Internship 344
Oklahoma Governor's Internship 345
Oregon Governor's Internship 345
Republican National Committee Internship 346
South Carolina Governor's Internship 347
U.S. Supreme Court Internship 347
Vermont Governor's Internship 349
Washington Internships for Native
   Students (WINS) 349
Washington Leadership Summer Internship
   Seminar for Native American Students 350
Washington State Governor's Internship 352
West Virginia Governor's Internship 352
White House Internship 353
Wisconsin Governor's Internship 357

INDEXES

Internships and Summer Jobs by
   Application Deadline 361
Internships and Summer Jobs by
   Education Level 373
Internships and Summer Jobs by Salary 395
Internships and Summer Jobs by
   Country (non-U.S.) 405
Internships and Summer Jobs by State 407
Organization Index 419

VOLUME 2

HEALTH

Abbott Laboratories Environmental, Health,
   and Safety Internship 5
Administration on Aging Internship 6
American Cancer Society Internship 6
American Foundation for the Blind Internship 7

American Lung Association Internship 8

American Public Health Association Internship 9

American Red Cross Internship 9

Boys Hope, Girls Hope Internship 13

Center for Adolescent Health and the Law Internship 14

Center for Food Safety Internship 15

CIIT Centers for Health Research Internship 15

Doctors Without Borders Internship 16

Elizabeth Glaser Pediatric Aids Foundation Internship 18

Frontier Nursing Service Internship 19

Gay Men's Health Crisis Internship 20

Gould Farm Internship 21

Harvard School of Public Health Minority Internship 22

Head Start National Internship 23

Healthy Mothers, Healthy Babies Coalition of Washington Internship 24

Injury Center Internship 24

National Healthy Mothers, Healthy Babies Coalition Internship 25

National Mental Health Association Internship 26

New England Healthcare Institute Internship 28

Pennsylvania Department of Health Public Health Internship 29

Population Institute Internship 30

Project HOPE (Health Opportunities for People Everywhere) Internship 30

Pulmonary Hypertension Association Internship 31

Silent Spring Institute Internship 32

Surgeons of Hope Foundation Internship 33

Wakemed Health and Hospitals Internship 33

Washington, D.C., Department of Health Internship 34

YAI National Institute for People with Disabilities Internship 35

HISTORICAL AREAS

Anacostia Museum and Center for African American History and Culture Internship 39

Buchanan/Burnham Internship 39

Buffalo Bill Historical Center Internship 40

Colonial Williamsburg Internship 43

D. C. Booth Historic Fish Hatchery Internship 46

Eisenhower National Historic Site Internship 46

El Pueblo de Los Angeles Historical Monument Multicultural Summer Internship 47

Georgia State Parks and Historic Sites Internship 48

Grey Towers National Historic Site Internship 49

Hermitage Foundation Museum Internship 51

The Hermitage (Home of Andrew Jackson) Internship 51

Historic Deerfield Summer Fellowship 52

Historic Preservation Internship Training Program 54

Living History Farms Internship 55

Minnesota Historical Society Internship 56

Mount Vernon Summer Internship 60

National Council for Preservation Education Internship 61

National Trust for Historic Preservation Internship 68

Old Sturbridge Village Internship 69

Preservation Action Internship 70

Smithsonian Architectural History and Historic Preservation Division Internship 71

U.S. Capitol Historical Society Internship 71

Vermont Folklife Center Internship 72

Wyckoff Farmhouse Museum Internship 73

INTERNATIONAL

AIESEC 77

American Friends Service Committee
International Internship 77

American Institute for Foreign Study—
Cannes Internship 78

American Institute for Foreign Study—
Florence Internship 79

American Institute for Foreign Study—
London Internship 80

American Institute for Foreign Study—
Sydney Internship 81

American-Scandinavian Foundation
Internship 82

Australian Embassy Internship 83

Boston University Internship Abroad—
Auckland Internship 83

Boston University Internship Abroad—
Beijing Internship 84

Boston University Internship Abroad—
Dresden Internship 85

Boston University Internship Abroad—
Dublin Internship 86

Boston University Internship Abroad—
Geneva Internship 87

Boston University Internship Abroad—
Haifa Internship 88

Boston University Internship Abroad—
London Internship 88

Boston University Internship Abroad—
Madrid Internship 90

Boston University Internship Abroad—
Paris Internship 91

Boston University Internship Abroad—
Sydney Internship 92

Camp Counselors USA—
European Day Camps 93

Camp Counselors USA—Russia 95

Camp Counselors USA—United Kingdom 96

Canadian Embassy Internship 96

Carnegie Endowment for International
Peace Internship 97

Center for World Indigenous Studies
Internship 98

Cooperative Center for Study Abroad:
Ireland Internship 99

Costa Rica Internship Institute 100

Council on Foreign Relations Internship 100

Council on Hemispheric Affairs (COHA)
Internship 101

The Economist Internship 103

Hansard Society Scholars Program 104

International Atomic Energy Agency
Internship 105

UNICEF Graduate Student Internship 107

Women's International League for
Peace and Freedom Internship 108

Work Canada 111

MEDIA

ABC *Good Morning America* Internship 117

ABC John Stossel Specials Internship 117

ABC News Internship 117

ABC News *Primetime Live* Internship 120

ABC News Radio Internship 120

ABC News Special Events Internship 121

ABC News Washington Bureau Internship 121

ABC-TV Channel 7 (Los Angeles) Internship 122

ABC *Weekend News* Internship 122

ABC *World News Tonight* Internship 123

The Ad Club (Boston) Internship 124

Advertising Club Internship 124

Akron Beacon Journal Internship 125

American Red Cross Media Internship 126

American Society of Magazine Editors
Internship 127

Anchorage Daily News Internship 128

Associated Press Internship 129

Associated Press Broadcast News Internship 130

Atlanta Journal Constitution Internship 131

Atlantic Monthly Internship 132

Atlantic Monthly Web Site Content Internship 133

Audubon Internship 133

Austin American-Statesman Internship 134

Baltimore Sun Two-Year Internship 135

Bangor Daily News Internship 135

Blethen Maine Newspapers Minority Summer Internship 136

Boston Globe Internship 136

CBS News Internship 137

Charlotte Observer Internship 141

Chicago Sun-Times Minority Scholarship and Internship Program 141

Chicago Tribune Internship 142

Chronicle of Higher Education Internship 142

Cleveland Plain Dealer Internship 143

CNN News Internship 143

Columbia Journalism Review Internship 145

C-SPAN TV (Washington, D.C.) Internship 145

Dallas Morning News Internship 147

Denver Post Reporting/Photography Internship 148

Des Moines Register Internship 148

Detroit Free Press Internship 149

Dow Jones Newspaper Fund Minority Summer Internship 149

Entertainment Weekly Internship 150

Eurekalert! Web Site Internship 151

Fresno Bee Internship 152

Harper's Internship 152

HBO Internship 153

Kaiser Media Minority Internships in Urban Health Reporting 155

KFSK-Southeast Alaska Public Radio Internship 156

Knight Ridder Internships for Native American Journalists 157

KOCE Public TV (Huntington Beach, Calif.) Internship 158

KPNX-TV (Phoenix) Internship 158

KTTV-TV (Los Angeles) Internship 159

Los Angeles Times Internship 159

Marvel Comics Internship 160

Miami Herald Internship 161

Modesto Bee Internship 162

Mother Jones Internship 163

MSNBC Internship 164

MSNBC Multimedia Internship 166

National Association of Black Journalists Summer Journalism Internship 166

NBC Internship 168

Newsweek Internship 168

New York Daily News Graphics Designer Internship 169

New York Daily News Internship 169

New York Times Copyediting Internship 170

New York Times Graphics, Design, and Photography Internship 171

New York Times Reporting Fellowship 172

Nightline Internship 172

Orlando Sentinel Internship 173

Philadelphia Inquirer Minority Internship 174

Philadelphia Inquirer Nonminority Copyediting and Graphics Arts Internship 175

Reuters Internship 175

Rocky Mountain PBS-TV Studio and Production Internship 176

Sacramento Bee Internship 177

San Francisco Chronicle Summer Internship 177

San Francisco Chronicle Two-Year Internship 178

Science Magazine Internship 179

Science News Internship 180

Seattle Times Internship — 181
Sierra Magazine Internship — 181
St. Petersburg Times Summer Internship — 182
St. Petersburg Times Yearlong Newsroom Internship — 183
Tampa Tribune Internship — 183
Teen People Summer Internship — 184
Time Inc. Summer Internship — 185
USA Today Summer Internship — 186
U.S. News & World Report Internship — 186
Wall Street Journal Internship — 187
Washingtonian Advertising Internship — 188
Washingtonian Art Internship — 188
Washingtonian Editorial Internship — 189
Washington Post Internship — 189

NATURE

American Farmland Trust Internship — 193
American Forests Internship — 193
American Rivers Internship — 195
The Antarctica Project Internship — 197
Arnold Arboretum of Harvard University Internship — 197
Aspen Center for Environmental Studies Internship — 198
Aullwood Audubon Center and Farm Internship — 199
Bay Nature Magazine Internship — 200
Callaway Gardens Internship — 201
Chincoteague National Wildlife Refuge Internship — 201
Friends of the Earth Internship — 203
Hawk Mountain Sanctuary Internship — 204
Jane Goodall Institute Internship — 206
Longwood Gardens Internship — 208
Morris Arboretum of the University of Pennsylvania Internship — 214
National Park Foundation Internship — 217
Student Climate Outreach Internship — 218
Student Conservation Association Internship — 219

SCIENCE

American Association for the Advancement of Science Internship — 225
American Association for the Advancement of Science Internships Entry Point Internship — 226
American Geographical Society Internship — 227
American Society for Microbiology Research Internship — 228
Bettis Atomic Power Lab Internship — 229
California Academy of Science A. Crawford Cooley Internship in California Botany — 230
California Academy of Science Internship in Biological Illustration — 231
California Academy of Science Robert T. Wallace Undergraduate Research Internship — 231
Center for Science in the Public Interest Internship — 232
Cold Spring Harbor Lab Summer Internship — 235
Cornell University Materials Science Research Internship — 236
Cornell University Plant Genome Research Program Internship — 237
Duke University Neurosciences Summer Research Program in Mechanisms of Behavior — 238
DuPont Engineering Internship — 238
Genentech Internship — 239
GlaxoSmithKline Internship — 240
Harvard University Four Directions Summer Research Program — 241
Harvard University Summer Honors Undergraduate Research Program — 242
Harvard University Summer Research Program in Ecology — 243

Howard Hughes Honors Summer Institute 245

Institute of Ecosystem Studies Internship 246

Jackson Laboratory Summer Student Program 250

Leadership Alliance Summer Internship 251

Lunar and Planetary Institute Internship 252

Marine Biology Lab at Woods Hole Marine
Models in Biological Research Internship 253

Mickey Leland Energy Fellowships 254

Mount Desert Island Biological Lab
Research Fellowships for Undergraduates 255

NASA Kennedy Space Center Space
Flight and Life Sciences Training Program 256

National Institutes of Health Summer
Internship Programs in Biomedical
Research 259

National Museum of Natural History
Internship 261

National Science Foundation Research
Experience for Undergraduates (REU) 263

Naval Research Lab Science and
Engineering Apprenticeship Program 264

New York University Center for Neural
Science Undergraduate Summer
Research Program 265

New York University School of Medicine
Summer Undergraduate Research
Program 266

Nuclear Regulatory Commission Historically
Black Colleges and Universities Student
Research Internship 267

Office of Naval Research Internship 268

Pfizer Research and Development Internship 273

Rockefeller University Summer
Undergraduate Research Fellowship 275

Rocky Mountain Biological Laboratory
Summer Internship 276

Roswell Park Cancer Institute Summer
College Internship 277

Roswell Park Cancer Institute Summer
High School Internship 277

Smithsonian Astrophysical Observatory
Internship 279

Stanford Linear Accelerator Center
Summer Fellowship 280

SUNY Albany Summer Research
Experience for Undergraduates 281

University of California-Davis
Undergraduate Summer Training in
Environmental Toxicology 282

University of Colorado at Boulder Summer
Minority Access to Research Training 283

University of Massachusetts
Undergraduate Research in Ecology
and Conservation Biology 284

University of Massachusetts Medical School
Summer Enrichment Program 287

University of Massachusetts Medical School
Undergraduate Summer NIH Research
Fellowship Program 288

University of Texas-Houston Health Science
Center Summer Research Program 288

U.S. Department of Energy's Science
Undergraduate Lab Internships (SULI) 289

Virginia Institute of Marine Science
Internship 294

Wellesley College Biological Sciences
Internship 296

Whitney Laboratory Marine Biomedical
Research Experience for Undergraduates 296

SPORTS

Boston Celtics Internship 301

CBS-4 (KCNC-TV) Sports Department
Internship 302

Chicago Bears Graphic Design Internship 303

Chicago Bulls Ticket Sales Representative
Internship 303

Colorado Springs Sky Sox Internship 304

Indiana Pacers Internship 306

Kansas City Blades Internship 311

Kroenke Sports Enterprises Internship 312
Los Angeles Lakers Internship 314
NASCAR Diversity Internship 314
NASCAR Internship 315
New York Rangers Internship 316
Orlando Magic Internship 316
Performance Research Internship 321
Philadelphia Phantoms Internship 322
Philadelphia 76ers Internship 323
San Diego Chargers Internship 324
Toledo Mud Hens Baseball Club Internship 325

TECHNICAL

Aerospace Corporation Internship 329
Agilent Technologies Internship 329
Amazon.com Software Development
   Engineer Internship 330
Apple Computer Internship 331
AT&T Undergraduate Research Program 333
Ball Aerospace Internship 334
Bechtel Internship 334
Callaway Advanced Technology Internship 335
Cisco Systems Internship 336
Dell Computer Internship 337
Dow Chemical Company Internship 338
Eastman Kodak Internship 338
Fermilab Summer Internships in Science
   and Technology 339
IBM Extreme Blue Internship 340
Intel Internship 342
Lam Research Internship 343
Lexmark Internship 343
Lockheed Martin Internship 344
Los Alamos National Laboratory High
   School Co-Op Program 345
Los Alamos National Laboratory Internship 346

Lunar And Planetary Institute Summer
   Intern Program 348
Marathon Oil Corporation Internship 349
Marathon Oil Corporation/UNCF
   Corporate Scholars Program 350
Microsoft Internship 350
Motorola Internship 353
National Instruments Internship 354
National Renewable Energy Laboratory
   Internship 355
National Semiconductor Internship 356
NCR Internship 357
Oracle Corporation Internship 357
Pacific Gas and Electric Company Internship 358
Packer Foundation Engineering Internship 359
Pratt & Whitney Co-Ops and Internship 360
Sante Fe Institute Internship 361
Silicon Graphics Inc. (SGI) Internship 362
Texas Instruments Internship 363
Xerox Internship 364

PART IV: FURTHER RESOURCES
APPENDIXES

Appendix A: Internet Resources 371
Appendix B: Further Reading 375
Appendix C: Governors' Offices 377

INDEXES

Internships and Summer Jobs by
   Application Deadline 385
Internships and Summer Jobs by
   Education Level 399
Internships and Summer Jobs by Salary 419
Internships and Summer Jobs by
   Country (non-U.S.) 429
Internships and Summer Jobs by State 431
Organization Index 443

ACKNOWLEDGMENTS

This book wouldn't have been possible without the help of Sara McGovern, Beth Otto, Brittany Formica, Kara Kennedy, and Michael Kennedy. Thanks also for painstaking and patient editorial help from Neil Romanosky, James Chambers, and Vanessa Nittoli.

PART I
INTRODUCTION AND OVERVIEW

INTRODUCTION

Students face a lot of pressure to decide what they want to be when they grow up. For some students, the decision is easy, but others have a harder time figuring it all out. Once you get your diploma, you may find yourself competing with hundreds of other recent graduates for a dwindling number of positions. Often, the difference between landing the job of your dreams and dreaming about a job you don't get comes down to one thing—experience. The difference between getting an interview and a three-sentence rejection letter is the experience you can list on your resume. But how do you get experience on a job if you don't have the experience to get that job in the first place?

One solution to this problem is to land an internship or summer job in a related area *before* you graduate. Getting an internship provides experience, but it also shows that you've had the gumption, the creativity, and the ingenuity to get out there and find a way to learn more about something you love. Although many students happily spend their summers flipping burgers or bagging groceries to earn spending money, an internship can provide valuable experience that you'll be able to use for the rest of your life. Admittedly, many internships don't pay much (or anything at all). But if you're approaching your junior or senior year in college, you should think seriously about trying to get some type of internship, even if it is unpaid. Perhaps you can take a second job, or maybe your parents will help out financially.

Let's say you dream of working in the theater when you graduate. While you're still in college, finding an internship in a local, state, or national company can be a real help not just in getting experience but in making professional contacts. If you've ever heard: "It's not *what* you know but *who* you know," you'll see the value in meeting as many people in the business as you can. Whether your dream career is in business, science, medicine, or teaching, almost any field offers internship opportunities.

Ferguson Career Resource Guide to Internships and Summer Jobs will introduce you to a number of terrific internships and summer jobs. Each entry will help answer your questions, let you know what to expect, and explain how to apply and what credentials you may need. Appendixes provide more information on internship Web sites. Indexes in both volumes list internships that pay (and those that don't), plus listings by state, country, deadline, and level of education required.

HOW TO USE THIS BOOK

Ferguson Career Resource Guide to Internships and Summer Jobs is divided into four parts.

Part I, "Introduction and Overview," contains this Introduction, which will help you navigate your way through the material.

Part II, "Essays," contains information on a wide range of topics that will help you prepare for, locate, and land the internship or summer job that's right for you. Topics covered include choosing an internship, writing winning resumes and cover letters, tips on interviewing, the benefits of having a mentor, and finding internships abroad.

Part III, "Directory," contains hundreds of listings for internships and summer jobs divided by subject area. See the following section, "About the Internship and Summer Job Entries," to better understand the breakdown of the information in this part of the book.

Part IV, "Further Resources," contains appendixes that provide additional online and print resources for internships and summer jobs, and contact information for state governors' offices. Indexes at the end of both volumes that list the internships in this book according to application deadline, education level, salary, and geographical location. There is also an index of all the organizations that appear in the book.

ABOUT THE INTERNSHIP AND SUMMER JOB ENTRIES

The internship and summer job listings in Part III are divided into chapters by subject area. The following is a general overview of the types of jobs you can find in each section:

- **Activism:** In this section, you'll read about internships and summer jobs with organizations deeply involved in making the world a better place for a variety of groups, including women, Native Americans, the sick or disabled, and citizens of the Third World, to name just a few.
- **Animals:** In this section, you'll find a internships and summer jobs related to working with animals. Organizations in this section include zoos, animal parks, rescue groups, veterinarian offices and hospitals, stables, kennels, dolphin preserves, marine shows, rescue organizations, and more.
- **Art:** Here you'll find lots of places looking for creative interns and summer employees to work in the art field, including galleries, major art museums, and national art organizations.
- **Business:** There are hundreds of internship and summer job opportunities in the business world, appealing to a wide range of personal and professional interests. This section lists internships and summer jobs available in companies ranging from Abbott Laboratories to Random House, from General Electric to Hallmark.

- **Education:** Here you'll learn about a wide variety of internship programs and summer jobs in the broad field of education, including nonprofit organizations, research programs, day care, educational stores, child care, museums, and more.
- **Entertainment:** This section includes information on internship programs and summer jobs for students interested in working in theme parks, films, summer stock, circuses, cruise ship entertainment shows, and resorts throughout the country.
- **Government:** In this section, you'll learn about opportunities with members of Congress, Congressional committees, and with local, district, state, and federal government offices. As a summer employee, the pay you receive will depend on the education and work experience you already have. Deadlines depend on the type of job you're applying for, but the earlier you apply, the better. College students generally have the best chance for landing summer jobs with the federal government. Typically, requirements include being a U.S. citizen. Male applicants between 18 and 25 are eligible for appointment only after registering with the Selective Service.
- **Health:** In this section, you'll learn about opportunities in a variety of medical areas, including hospitals, clinics, medical and nursing schools, rehabilitation hospitals, summer camps for disabled children, nonprofit health organizations, and a wide range of summer opportunities for working with physically or mentally disabled patients.
- **Historical Areas:** Here you'll learn about opportunities with historical sites, museums, historic research organizations, archaeological digs, state archives, historic preservation groups, and living history programs.
- **International:** This section includes information about working abroad, including internships and summer jobs with international policy organizations, government agencies, international trade organizations,

relief organizations, and other global and international organizations.

- **Media:** Many newspapers, radio and TV stations have noncredit, paid summer or extended internships for after graduation. In this section, you'll learn what's available, such as internships with ABC, NBC, CBS, the *Chicago Tribune*, HBO, the *New York Times*, and many more.
- **Nature:** In this section, you'll find a variety of nature/environment possibilities, including internships or summer jobs with environmental organizations, ranches, camps, outdoor guiding, and seasonal state park jobs.
- **Science:** This section includes information on a wide variety of internship programs and summer jobs in astronomy, engineering, archaeology, biology, and more. You can work for large corporate firms, university research programs, nonprofit organizations, government organizations, labs, museums, space camps, and engineering projects.
- **Sports:** This section includes information about internships with a wide variety of sports teams ranging from the Boston Celtics to the San Diego Chargers.
- **Technical:** This is the section for those of you who love technology, including engineering and computer science. This section focuses on some world-famous companies involved in cutting-edge research in technology in science, space exploration, undersea exploration, automotive research, computer science, and more.

Each entry in Part III starts out with a snapshot of important basic information to give you a quick glimpse of that particular internship, including contact information, what you can earn, education requirements, other requirements, and deadlines.

- **What You Can Earn:** Admittedly, it often isn't very much, and many internships don't pay at all. What many of the nonpay-

ing slots do offer, however, is college credit, and that actually translates into dollars. If you can accumulate 12 credits during your internship that your school will accept, and your school charges $500 a credit, that means you've just saved yourself $6,000! Not to mention the time it would have taken to accrue those credits.

- **Educational Experience:** What kind of education or experience does the internship require? Most stipulate only that you be enrolled in college or graduate school; some limit internships to juniors and seniors. A few allow high school students to apply. Many recommend certain majors or courses; others require certain degree programs and certain GPAs.
- **Requirements:** Are you qualified for this internship? Many internships, particularly those with the government, have strict age or citizenship requirements. You might as well make sure you meet any health, medical, or screening requirements before going any further with your internship pursuit.

The remainder of each internship entry consists of the following sections:

- **Overview:** Here's where you'll learn exactly what the organization, group, or company really does, so you can decide if you want to intern with them. It also outlines the departments or areas offering internships, what those duties may include, and any specific requirements that the internship may stipulate. This section also takes a more in-depth look at what to expect during the internship, including perks (such as free tickets, opportunities to meet national leaders, seminars and workshops, discounts, and more), job responsibilities, length of time, and so on.
- **Housing:** This section, which appears in some entries, lists housing and transportation information for some of the internships and summer jobs.

■ **How to Apply:** This is the all-important section detailing exactly what you need to include in your application packet. Most internships require not just the standard cover letter and resume but also college transcripts and letters of recommendation from your professors or deans. Some internships require portfolios or examples of your work (especially for the more creative internships).

One important note: All of the Web sites in this book have been checked and rechecked as close to printing as is possible. However, remember that some Web sites will change, so if you find one that doesn't work, try using a search engine with the name of the organization to locate an updated Web site.

By opening *Ferguson Career Resource Guide to Internships and Summer Jobs,* you've taken the first steps toward finding a fabulous internship that could have a profound impact on the rest of your life. Read through as many of the entries as you can; perhaps you'll discover an internship in an area you've never thought of before. The time and effort you invest now in locating an internship will more than pay off in the friendships you make, the professional contacts you forge, and the foundation for a new career you build. Good luck!

PART II
ESSAYS

INTERNSHIPS, SUMMER JOBS, AND LIFELONG JOB SKILLS

There are so many internships available in this country and around the world—how on earth do you choose one? Would you like to study space exploration with a NASA internship or band birds with a nature organization in the South? Do you have a yen to learn more about the Plains Indians or go on an archeological dig out West?

In this section, you'll learn everything you need to know about identifying an internship, landing one, and how to benefit from the experience. We'll start off helping you figure out how to identify what kind of internship you'd like to pursue, outline exactly what it is you're looking for, and then help you figure out how to find specific internships that will be just right for you.

Of course, just finding something you'd like to do is only part of the battle. Next, we'll show you how to put together a terrific resume and cover letter, along with some good letters of reference. Once you submit this application package, the next step is to prepare for the interview, so we'll help you understand how to anticipate some typical questions, what to wear, and how to handle yourself during the process.

Once you've landed the internship, there are still things to learn! We'll discuss 10 ways to succeed in an internship, how to work with a mentor, what to expect if you're interning with the government or abroad, and, finally, how to translate these experiences into the next step: launching your career!

WHAT KIND OF INTERNSHIP OR SUMMER JOB IS RIGHT FOR YOU?

If you're thinking about a summer internship, the first thing you need to do is figure out the general type of internship you'd like to pursue. Next, spend some time thinking about what's motivating you to get the internship. Do you want to get more experience in your major or explore a business or organization as a possible career? Do you want an internship or summer job that looks good on your resume or that will help you get into graduate school? Or maybe you're hoping the internship will help you meet some people who may be able to get you a job after you graduate. If you perform well at your internship, you may be offered a full-time job next summer or even a full-time job when you graduate. Internships can also provide you with valuable references that can help you land future jobs.

List Your Strengths and Weaknesses

Once you've thought about your motivations, make a list of your interests and strengths (as well as your weaknesses) and keep them in mind as you look for internships.

If getting into a boat makes you queasy, you probably don't want an internship in which you'll need to travel out on the ocean. If your allergies kick up whenever you head out into the woods, you probably won't want a nature internship. If looking after little kids drives you crazy or if you burn in the sun, you'll know to avoid child care or outdoorsy internships. Be honest about your shortcomings or your dislikes.

On the positive side, what excites you and gets you really involved? If you're fascinated with medicine or microbiology, you might want to check out science internships. Love wildlife? Check out jobs in nature or animal care. Can't get enough of photography, writing, or art? Take that into consideration when you're looking for an internship.

An internship should not only be enjoyable: you should learning something, too—about yourself and what you're capable of, about the type of career you may be suited for. Because it will demand so much of your time, try to find an internship that may help guide you toward your long-term goals. For example, if you want to study veterinary medicine after college, finding an internship at an animal-rescue organization would be a better bet for you than working in a sports organization or a TV station. Which internship sites are most likely to boost your career objectives? Will you get feedback and thoughtful criticism and direction from the professionals you'll be working with? Will you get real-world assignments or be a "go-fer"?

Paid Versus Unpaid

Once you've decided the general type of internship you're looking for, the next most important question is whether or not you need to earn money while you participate. You'll find that most better-paid internships are offered in the world of science and big business, because those organizations want to attract talented students at an early stage in their education and lure them away from the competition. Some of the best-paying of these internships are found in investment or commercial banking, accounting, information technology, venture capital, pharmaceutical firms, and marketing. You'll also find that the federal government underwrites many science-related internships (especially for minorities and women).

High-profile industries such as entertainment, TV, magazines, and book publishing tend not to pay interns, because so many students are clamoring to work there.

If you know there's no way you could work for free, you don't have to give up on the idea of an internship. There are some alternatives. More and more organizations realize that many students are willing to forego a big intern salary if they are given enough money to cover basic necessities. That's why you'll find that many internships that haven't paid in the past are now coughing up some small stipends (ranging from $300 to $2,500 or more for the entire season) to help students defray the costs of living. A few will provide housing or at least help you find housing. Some throw in subway vouchers or free parking or discounts on organization-

related items—everything from T-shirts to fancy pens or bookstore freebies.

But remember: High-paying internships at big-name employers make up only a fraction of available opportunities. The experience and portfolio material that you'll get out of an internship are *much* more important than the short-term financial rewards. There's nothing wrong with aiming high, but be prepared to accept a second- or third-level opportunity if it gives you a chance to earn some experience in a professional environment. In fact, smaller employers in an industry often offer a wider range of experiences for interns than do large ones. For example, a journalism internship at a big-city paper might relegate you to pouring coffee and writing obituaries. An internship at a very small daily paper or even a weekly could send you out to attend local meetings and write articles, pitch in with headline writing or paste-up, or even do some darkroom work on the side. It might be less glamorous and pay poorly (if at all), but you'll more than make up for that with what you learn.

Usually, internships that don't pay get away with it because they're offering you something a bit more intangible—the chance to make connections, get on-the-job training, and build an understanding of the field. Keep in mind that hosting interns isn't always a day at the beach—it can take up a lot of time and can cost the company money. They're willing to put up with this in exchange for getting some free help.

And really, you can't put a price on getting to know folks who will be able to open doors for you later in your career. In addition, most companies and organizations will gladly work with your school to offer you course credit, which can translate into quite a bit of savings when it comes to paying tuition. If you can graduate a semester early and save all that tuition because of the internship credits you racked up over the summer, that represents a considerable savings no matter how you slice it.

Mentor-Led Versus Self-Directed

When you're thinking about internships, give some thought to how independent you want the experience to be. Do you want to work with a mentor, or would you prefer to strike out on your own? It all comes down to how you think you work best.

If you prefer to structure, develop, and monitor your own work, then you're probably not going to be happy having a mentor peering over your shoulder all day, telling you what to do and when to do it. However, if you know you want to learn a particular technique or technology, but you don't have the foggiest idea of how to go about achieving it, it's probably best to seek an internship with a mentor. That mentor could be your academic adviser or a professor who specializes in your field of interest.

Age

It's true that most internships are offered for college students between their junior and senior years. However, that is *not* by any means the only time you can explore an internship. A few organizations in this book offer high school internships. Others are willing to take on anyone in college, and most will also include graduate students. A few opportunities are also available to recent college graduates or graduate students who have just obtained their advanced degrees.

Getting Credit

More colleges, hoping to steer students toward the real-world experience an internship provides, grant college credit for approved internships. In most cases, internship notices will tell you whether the organization is willing to work with your school to provide you with academic credit for your experience. If your internship will net you credits, go to your academic adviser and ask him or her to sponsor you. Work out with the adviser how many credit hours you'll earn based on how many hours you're going to work and what you'll be doing. Most advisers will also ask you to write a paper explaining how your internship experience relates to your academic experience. They also may ask you to provide a file of the work you completed on the internship, and have your internship mentor send a letter reporting on the type and quality of work you performed.

Some schools actually require an internship as part of the curriculum, and many companies and organizations also require that your school offer you credit in return for an internship. But remember that nobody is going to cut through all that red tape for you—it's up to you to fill out the paperwork, do the legwork, and line up university credit before you sign on. You'll have to get permission from the school, follow through with all the appropriate forms, and make sure the participating organization will agree to work with your school on granting you credit.

If you do wangle credit for your internship, that's just about as good as getting a stipend, because if your school accepts between six and 16 credits for your internship – that means you won't have to pay for those credits later. The internship may even enable you to graduate early, which could save an entire semester of tuition.

Summer, Fall, Winter, Spring?

Many internships are available only in the summertime, which means you can go back to school to get your degree the rest of the year. However, a few do offer internships all year long, and some offer long-term internships of a year or more. European students have been taking advantage of these year-long internships for a long time—they call it a "gap year." European students take time off either before or in the middle of their university education to volunteer or work in a totally different environment. This gives students a chance to refocus their career goals and align the rest of their education with those goals.

American students are starting to get the word about the usefulness of taking off a semester or a year from school, too, since these experiences can be rewarding and provide a break from the rigors of the academic world.

Although many parents may fear that if you leave school you'll never return, most students do find that taking some time off to intern gives them a chance to figure out exactly what they do want to do with their career. Most go back to school and eventually graduate. Alternatively, you can consider a part-time internship that extends through the academic year and into the summer. The beauty of a part-time internship is that you won't have to take time off from school, and you'll still graduate with your class. On the other hand, many internships are available only in the summer, because organizations want to ensure that they have enough work to keep students busy and don't want students to have trouble combining schoolwork and interning at the same time. Many companies like to use summer interns to take up the slack while their regular employees go on vacations.

Time It Right!

You can't expect to wake up the day after school's out and suddenly uncover a terrific internship. The best internships are competitive and take some time to scout out. Most internships also require you to submit transcripts and letter of recommendations—and that means some advance time spent on paperwork.

Many internship applications are due three to six months before the starting date. Some begin closing applications in January for a summer gig, and almost all stop accepting applications by February or March for a summer placement. Those that accept interns for fall, spring, and summer openings may have a "rolling" acceptance policy.

Be sure to check on the deadlines for any internships in which you're interested. Pay attention to deadlines on advertised job postings. To be on the safe side, you should probably start your internship search in mid-October to early November. This will give you plenty of time to research your options before you must begin applying. At the very least, start well before spring break so that you can use the break to interview for jobs. However, keep in mind that most organizations do offer internships throughout the year. If you've missed a deadline, you can always apply for next year.

If you're applying for a variety of internships (which is a good idea), you should create an effective recordkeeping system to keep track of all those deadlines, contact names, and details about when you spoke to someone, to whom you spoke, the place and time of your interview, and so on.

LOCATING AN INTERNSHIP

You've thought about the kind of internship you want, and you've lined up all the particulars that will matter to you. Now it's time to actually identify a list of potential employers to contact for your summer job or internship. There are a number of ways to do that. The first one, of course, is to leaf through this book to see what's out there.

Don't overlook your college adviser and career services department; they often have specific internship information. For example, if you're a communications major, your dean's office might gather information about possible internships. Other universities may post a more centralized college-wide internship program. Many colleges offer some kind of career service, and this department may also provide information about internships and summer jobs. This would probably be the best place to check for any on-campus internship or summer job recruiting schedules.

Don't overlook the Internet as a valuable resource for uncovering internships, although you'll need to be sure the Web sites are as up-to-date as possible. You can find lots of internship listings simply by entering the topic in which you're interested with the word "internship" in the search engine. Or you can try visiting a college or university career center home page or a company or organization's home page.

Next, try paging through phone books to find companies that look interesting. If you're dreaming of working away from home, try visiting your local library. It will typically have phone books or yellow pages from major cities around the country. You also can try contacting chambers of commerce to identify companies in your target area that may not have advertised for interns or thought about the possibility of using interns. College career fairs in fall and spring semesters can sometimes provide helpful contacts for internships. It's best to try a variety of methods to uncover the most interesting internships in areas you'd like to pursue.

Check with Your Counselor

Your school counselor may be able to help open other doors of opportunity via internships. Many companies and organizations travel throughout the country recruiting at universities and colleges. Those that do typically keep their schedules posted on their Web sites, so check these out. Be prepared to go out and visit organizations that come to your school or a nearby campus to learn more about potential internships there.

Network

As with any job or internship search, don't ignore the benefits of networking. Talking to your friends, family, neighbors, and so on can help you uncover all kinds of information about various career fields and companies, to hear about strategies other students have used, and to uncover potential internship opportunities. The Internet and the marvels of e-mail have really opened up networking possibilities. For example, let's say you live on a farm in Iowa, but you've got a yen to work in New York City for the summer. If you send an e-mail to 10 people you know asking about intern or summer job possibilities in New York City, and each of them sends your request on to 10 people *they* know, your e-mail has suddenly been seen by 100 people. Odds are, at least one of them may have a lead for a job in the big city.

Develop Your Own Internship

If you can't seem to find exactly the right internship, you might consider designing your own by recognizing opportunities in an existing business that the business owner may not see. For example, Sharon often heard her aunt complain that she never had time to take care of the business end of her art gallery, because she was always too busy with her customers. Although Sharon knew she didn't have enough experience to handle the business's finances, she offered to help her aunt after school by answering phones, handling the mail, filing, and copying—giving her aunt time to do other tasks. At the same time, she learned plenty about the ins and outs of running a big-city art gallery, handling customers, and marketing a business. If you're thinking of finding an internship on your own, you should contact your major department or college long before

you start, so you can find out if it's possible to get credit for the experience.

CREATING A TERRIFIC RESUME

Once you've decided what internships you'd like to apply for and what the criteria should be, the next step is writing a killer resume, because that's usually the best way to grab the attention of the interviewer at an organization. Almost every internship will require an application and your resume, if nothing else. The application is the easy part—you just have to download the form from their Web site and answer the questions.

Much more challenging is the resume. At this point in their young careers, many students wonder what they can possibly find to fill a page. Keep in mind that a resume is nothing more and nothing less than a selling tool—you're marketing *you*. You'll want to craft a document that will clearly show that you're the right candidate for the internship—and better than 99 percent of the other students applying for the same place.

To do that, the first thing you'll need to do is throw away the resume template you downloaded from the Internet. You want to highlight your strengths while focusing on the key skills the internship is calling for. Don't build your resume on somebody else's blueprint. Still, there are some general points you can keep in mind. (See p. 8 for a sample resume.)

Highlight Your Relevant Experience

As you begin to scribble some notes for your first draft, keep the internship description next to you, so you can target your information to match the internship requirements. Of course, you're not going to lie about your accomplishments. But there are many ways to package a person's experiences, and you'll want to tailor your skills in the right way. Let's say you spent your last two years of high school walking dogs and taking care of pets in the summer. Put that way, it may not sound so impressive. But let's look at it another way: What if you described it by saying that you built a viable pet-sitting service, with a 25 percent growth in sales each year for two years? If you were

SAMPLE RESUME

JANE DOE

10 Sandy Road   Anytown, NY 12345
(555-555-5555)   doejane@xxx.com

OBJECTIVE

An internship in journalism that would enable me to develop my ability to write well under deadline pressure while contributing to a newspaper's goals.

EDUCATION

Smith College, Northampton, MA
Major: English
Course work: News Writing, Journalism, Desktop Publishing
GPA = 3.8 out of a 4.0

Lancaster Country Day School, Lancaster, PA
Graduated *summa cum laud*e, 2003

EXPERIENCE

Reporter, *Reading Eagle* "Voices" high school student-run magazine insert for hometown daily newspaper. Wrote one article a week for two years in high school (2003, 2002)

Head lifeguard, Lancaster Swim Club, Lancaster, PA (Summers 2005, 2004)
Gave swim lessons, coached grade school swim team to victory (2004).

Server, Anyone's Restaurant, Anytown, PA (2003).
Won Employee of the summer award, new employee trainer.

ACTIVITIES

Served meals at Woman's Shelter (Fall 2004 to present)
Band (Fall 2004 to present)
College paper (Fall 2003 to present)

SKILLS

Both Mac and PC, MS Word, PowerPoint, Desktop publishing software, Photoshop looking at a public relations or advertising internship, you could focus on how you marketed the business and advertised your services to build your business base. If you were looking at an animal-related internship, you'd focus on what kinds of animals you cared for, endorsements from local vets, how many pets you handled at one time, and so on. You need to highlight those aspects of your experience that directly relate to the internship you want.

Contact Information

All your contact information should go at the very top of your resume. Be succinct and avoid nicknames. Use a permanent address—you want them to be able to find you. The best choice is to use your parents' address or the address you plan to use after graduation. Don't forget to add a permanent telephone number (including the area code) and your e-mail address—many employers will find it useful. However, consider getting a new, more professional e-mail address (your friends may think that "candybreath" or "cuteEjanie" is too clever for words, but potential employers will not be impressed). Include a Web site address only if the Web page reflects your career objectives.

Grab Their Attention Right Away

A representative should be able to tell with a quick glance at the top portion of your resume that you're the perfect candidate. This is where you should translate your skills into satisfying their internship description. You can do this by using a "qualifications" section or box at the top of your resume to describe how your skills match each of the internship requirements. Be specific—it could be something like: "To obtain an internship requiring strong analytical and organizational skills." Tailor your objective to each internship you seek. Another option is to include a "Relevant Experience" category at the top that details all of your related school, volunteer, and previous internship experience.

The Body of the Resume

Following your lead information, you can include sections on your schoolwork, volunteer work, and any other awards or experience you've had. Remember to keep it short—one page is ideal. In most cases, you'll want to put your most recent information first, under headings such as "Experience" and "Activities," or "On-the-Job Experience." However, if you don't have a lot of job experience, you can use more of a functional resume—just list the job title and contact addresses.

In the "Work" section, outline the work you've done that has taught you particular skills. Use action words ("drafted," "planned") as opposed to more passive words ("was," "has") to describe your duties. Remember to list your work experience in reverse, so that you list the most recent job you had first. Include your job title, the name of the organization, its location, your employment dates, and a description of your work responsibilities, emphasizing specific skills and achievements.

In the "Education" section, list your most recent educational information, including your degree, major, college, and any minors or concentrations. Only add your grade point average if it's higher than 3.0, and include any academic honors.

Depending on the internship, you may want to add extra information, such as special skills (maybe you speak German or are fluent in American Sign Language); experience in volunteer organizations or participation in sports.

References

You shouldn't add your reference information on your resume, but you can place a brief note at the bottom: References furnished on request. However, even this line is not mandatory. Most employers know and expect that you will provide contact information for references if your application/interview process proceeds to a higher level.

Choosing a Delivery Method

Once you've written your resume and proofread it several times, you need to decide how to submit it: fax, e-mail, regular U.S. mail, or special delivery. Often, the internship description will let you know exactly how they want you to submit. Read these guidelines closely. If they want you to send your materials by U.S. mail, they won't be amused to find your e-mailed submission complete with attachments sitting in their inbox. It takes time to download applications and print them. Some companies have filters blocking attachments because of the risk of viruses.

Letters of Reference

Many organizations ask for two or three letters of reference that must be submitted along with the resume. Ideally, you'll want to avoid choosing your dad's basketball buddy or your mom's pinochle partner. They may think you're cute as a button, but personal references aren't typically what an organization is looking for. Recruiters *expect* that a personal reference will have glowing things to say about you (otherwise, you wouldn't give those names).

Instead, select the dean of your college, a professor or two who really know your work and can speak intelligently about your qualifications, or a college adviser. A college-related reference can address your qualifications to perform the internship, and will probably be more likely to tell the truth. (See the section "Finding a Great Reference" later in this chapter.)

WRITING A SNAPPY COVER LETTER

A resume is an essential tool for any job search, but you need a good cover letter along with the resume to convey your personality and explain why you're mailing the resume in the first place. The cover letter is the first thing that an employer is going to see—even before your resume—so it's important to create a good first impression. It doesn't make sense to spend days on your resume and then dash off a cover letter filled with typos, food stains, and misspelled words. If you take the time to make your cover letter really great, you'll have a better chance of landing that dream internship. (See p. 11 for a sample cover letter.)

Match the Look of Your Resume

First of all, you want to aim for a professional look, so use the same letterhead style and paper for your cover letter and your resume. This makes you look more professional and will set you apart from those applicants who submit letters written by hand, with colored markers, or on bright pink paper—or who wrap the letter in a box like a Christmas present. (This really does happen sometimes!) Some students think they need to make their cover letter "stand out" by being wacky or really unusual, but going to such extremes usually backfires. (Unless you're trying for an internship with an innovative advertising firm or a very creative art firm, but even then it's usually a risk not worth taking). It's always better to err on the conservative side when approaching organizations and companies, unless you know absolutely that a more unrestrained style will find acceptance.

A cover letter gives your prospective interviewer the chance to hear your voice, so your cover letter should reflect your personality, your attention to detail, your communication skills, your enthusiasm, your intellect, and your specific interest in the internship for which you're applying. When you're thinking about what to say in your cover letter, it's most important that whatever you say, you say it briefly. A cover letter should be only one page, using a standard business letter format. There will likely be quite a few candidates sending applications, so you don't want to annoy the interviewer by droning on for four pages. Interviewers also know that it's far more difficult to write succinctly, crisply, and to the point than to prattle on at length, so take the time to condense, condense, condense!

Addresses

Your name, return address, phone number, e-mail, and today's date go in the upper right hand corner (in a standard format). Space down twice, and type the internship address flush left.

Salutation

Next comes your salutation. It's always best to address the letter to a specific person rather than "To Whom It May Concern:" or "Dear Sir/Madam." Never assume the gender of the person reading the letter. If you don't know to whom to address your letter, call the company and see if the receptionist can provide a name and title. If you have any company literature, check that out. Often, in the

SAMPLE COVER LETTER

Sue Smith
2 Hometown Way
Springfield, NJ 12345

Ms. Kara Kennedy
Internship Coordinator
XYC Animal Rescue Group
York, PA 01954

Dear Ms. Kennedy:

Your advertisement for the animal care internship in the October issue of *Pennsylvania Pets* caught my attention. I was particularly attracted to the ad because of my strong interest in companion animals and my intention to pursue a career in veterinary medicine.

I've worked with my home town vet for the past three years, caring for a wide variety of companion animals (dogs, cats, birds, fish, and gerbils). This has included bathing, caring for wounds under the guide of vet techs, post-surgery observation, feeding, and so on. With my varied experiences, I think I can make a direct and immediate contribution to your organization.

I have enclosed a copy of my resume, which details my qualifications and suggests how I might be of service to you.

The three vets with whom I have worked are all willing to provide professional references for me.

Thank you for your time and consideration.

Sincerely,

Sue Smith

Sue Smith

details of the internship the company provides, a contact person's name will be given. If you can't locate a name, a general salutation such as "Dear Internship Coordinator:" or "Dear Hiring Manager:" will suffice.

Body of the Letter

Once you know to whom you're writing, focus on the first paragraph (journalists call it the lead). You want to grab the employer's attention right away and make him or her keep reading. You need to distinguish yourself from the rest of the pack, so be lively and punchy while still sounding professional. Don't be gimmicky in an attempt to be clever. In the first paragraph, announce where you learned about the internship opportunity and why you're interested. Here is where you can make specific references to the company, explaining why you want to work at that specific organization, why you're a great fit for that company, and how you qualify for the internship. Follow that with a professional-sounding tone in the second and third paragraphs as you highlight your most important accomplishments and qualifications. Yes, you've got all that stuff in your resume, but here's your chance to give a brief summary in a narrative form. The resume will provide the follow-up details that the interviewer will just *have* to read, because you've piqued his or her interest in the cover letter.

Consider using bullet points in the middle paragraphs of the cover letter to further highlight your accomplishments; it will give your letter a nice, crisp, graphic *oomph*. It also makes the letter easy to scan. Clarify what you can contribute to the employer's organization rather than what you hope to gain.

And one word about confidence: There's a difference between simply stating your accomplishments and bragging. Don't say, "I'm the best darn student teacher in the state!" That's opinion. Instead, try this: "I won two awards for Outstanding Student Teacher in my school district." The first example is bragging, because you're offering an opinion about yourself ("Hey, I'm terrific!"). The second example is a simple fact, which speaks for itself, relieving you of the necessity of doing so.

In the concluding paragraph, remind the interviewer that your resume will further explain your qualifications, experience, and education. Request a personal interview (by phone or face to face) to chat further about your qualifications, and indicate the times you're available. Tell the interviewer you look forward to hearing from the company or organization, and restate your enthusiasm for learning more about the opportunity.

Closing

You'll need to sign your letter either "Sincerely" or "Yours truly," followed by four returns (this will provide the space where you'll sign your name in ink). Then type your full name. Space down once more and type "Encl." if you are including any enclosures with your cover letter—which you are (your resume at the very least).

Be Sure to Proofread

You're not finished yet! Now use your computer's spellchecker, and then check the letter yourself for spelling and grammar mistakes. (You might want to have a second person read it over to catch something you might have missed.) Remember that a spellchecker program won't flag a word spelled correctly but used incorrectly. (If you type "right" instead of "write," the computer may not notice, because it's still spelled correctly. A grammar checker might flag it, but you never can be certain.)

Carelessness makes a bad impression on interviewers. If you can't be bothered to get your cover letter right, how do they know you won't be sloppy when you're putting together their company report or writing a press release for them? There are so many others out there hungering for that internship, many interviewers actually use cover letter mistakes as a way of eliminating some of the competition.

If everything looks good, go ahead and print the letter (be sure to use a good ink-jet or laser printer). Never, never send a photocopied letter or use a form letter. The company will know. Writing an original letter tells your prospective recruiter that you cared enough to take the time to craft an individual piece of writing. Remember, recruiters read hundreds of letters, and they'll be able to spot a generic cover letter. Recruiters want to know why you're the best student for the internship—provide examples and be specific.

ACING THE INTERVIEW

You've written and submitted your resume and cover letter, added some dynamite reference letters, and made it through the first several cuts in the winnowing process. The next step in the internship marathon is handling the face-to-face interview. Not all companies or organizations insist on meeting their interns. Some just conduct an interview on the phone. But if you are asked to put in an appearance, it's your chance to really make an impression, so be sure it's a positive one.

The interview process is an opportunity for an organization to learn what your strengths are. How do you make someone want to hire you? By figuring out exactly what the recruiter needs and providing it. If you're interviewing for a shot as a Disney character at Walt Disney World, you know they're looking for outgoing, friendly, people-loving students. You won't want to sit there glumly slumped in your chair, silent, anxious, picking your fingernails and avoiding eye contact.

What's the Recruiter Looking For?

To figure out what the recruiter is looking for, find out as much as you can about the company beforehand. Get a general idea of what the organization does, what some of their challenges are, and what the company philosophy is. Every company has a style. For example, the atmosphere at Ben and Jerry's corporate headquarters will be a lot more informal than the atmosphere at the World Bank. Are employees expected to show up in three-piece suits and shiny lace-up oxfords? Or is the dress code blue jeans and a T-shirt? How is the organization performing? What is its mission statement and who are its customers? What are the interviewer's priorities and responsibilities? The more you know, the more you'll be able to ask informed questions about the job.

In the days before your interview, see if you can talk to anyone who's worked at the organization. Learn the name and title of the person you'll be meeting, and memorize some facts about the company that you can mention during the interview. If you want to impress your interviewer, you'll understand the company so well after doing some research that you can bring up points of interest when you get together.

Study the description of the job or internship for which you've applied. Make sure you know what's expected and whether you have the background and skills to do what's required. Take an inventory of your strengths, and write down specific examples that demonstrate these strengths.

Practice for the Interview

After you've done your homework, you should practice for the interview before the big day. Some students find it helpful to practice speaking fluently and intelligently in front of a mirror—or even better, a video camera. That's how lots of actors practice for an audition, and a job or internship interview is exactly that: an audition.

When you walk in for your interview, hold your head high, try to feel as confident as you can, look the interviewer right in the eye, smile, and offer a firm handshake. Practice this if you have the slightest doubt about your performance.

Even if you've never had an interview before, you may be surprised that many employers ask the same basic questions. They may want you to give them concrete examples of how you've handled specific situations in the past. They may ask you to describe a high-pressure situation you've been in and the steps you took to work through it. They may ask you what your best and worst points are. One favorite question: "What do you hope to be doing in five years?" or "in five years after you graduate?"

You can pretty much guarantee that one of the most important things you'll be asked is pretty obvious: why you want the internship. Be very clear exactly what it is you hope to gain and how important it is to you. The more passionate you can be about this, the better. It's a guarantee that the internship will go to the applicant who sounds as though he or she wants it the most, because the interviewer knows that desire will translate into hard work and dedication.

Because it's inevitable that the interviewer will ask you if you have any questions, try to come up with several intelligent queries that you can ask during your interview. There are lots of books and online resources that can help you prep for potential interview questions. It's probably a good idea to write some questions before the interview and practice asking them. You might consider role playing with a friend or family member. Asking questions helps make you look interested; the employer wants to see some initiative, some spark, some sense that you have a lively curiosity and intelligence. Questions demonstrate interest and enthusiasm for the position, and enthusiasm is important.

This doesn't mean you have to giggle or gush to show enthusiasm. What you should aim for is a confident smile, direct eye contact, and confident body language (don't sit curled up in a ball with your arms crossed over your chest). Sure, it can be intimidating, but if you just sit there in silence, you won't be showing the employer your best side. This kind of shared dialogue will give you the chance to demonstrate your best qualities and help the company learn more about you.

Depending on the internship you choose, you may even want to prepare a portfolio that includes relevant work or writing samples. Think of this interview in just the same way that you'll eventually approach an interview for an entry-level permanent job.

How to Dress for the Interview

Yes, appearances do count. You've probably heard your parents talk about making a good first impression with what you wear. It may sound like a lecture, but in this case they're right.

Remember that you have only one chance to make a first impression, so unless you know that the organization is extremely informal, it's better to dress too formally than to dress too casually. The usual advice: Dress one notch above what's expected for the position you're interviewing for. You want the recruiter to notice your talent and personality, not that leopard-skin miniskirt or the Hawaiian-print golf shirt. Save the bright colors, wild prints, and trendy fashions for another occasion.

For Women

Aim for understated, restrained professionalism in most cases—projecting the image of someone who can be relied upon and who looks the part. Generally, it's a good idea to wear something you like and feel comfortable in, because if your clothes pinch, ride up, or cling, you're not going to feel comfortable. This means no miniskirts, tight sweaters, sloppy overalls, or torn jeans. Choose pumps or loafers (with nylons, if you're wearing a skirt or a dress). Don't use too much makeup, hair spray, perfume, or jewelry. That means lose the eyebrow ring or tongue stud; it could cost you an internship, unless you're applying for a spot with a punk rock band. A silk scarf is a nice touch, unless you're not used to wearing scarves and doing so makes you feel silly. Carry a nice leather briefcase or portfolio, not a bulging, disorganized handbag.

Right before you walk out the door on the way to the interview, inspect your hair, nails, hems, and the shine on your shoes. Check for wrinkles, rips, tears, stains, or scuffs. If you have to travel some distance for the interview, it might be a good idea to keep a spare pair of nylons in your purse in case of a snag.

For Men

You can't go wrong if you wear a suit and tie to any company that's part of a more formal industry, such as banking or law. Choose a basic black, dark gray, or dark navy suit, a matching tie, and black leather lace-up shoes. Don't have any of this? Go ahead and borrow anything you need from your nattier roommate, but do so early enough so that if your friend is two sizes too big, you'll have discovered the problem in time.

If you know the organization doesn't expect suits, choose dressy casual attire. A safe choice would be neatly pressed khakis or slacks; a clean, ironed button-down shirt; a belt; and leather loafers. Remember to match the belt to the color of your shoes: black if your outfit is dark gray, navy, brown, or black. Choose dark brown if you're wearing tan, muted pastel, or medium tone colors.

The night before, clean and polish your shoes. The look you're aiming for is quietly professional, so it's okay to bring along a nice leather briefcase or vinyl-bound portfolio to carry your resume, references, and any other documents you may need. Folders emblazoned with your favorite cartoon character or college football team aren't appropriate. Remember that not every interviewer may appreciate a heavy dose of scent, so avoid heavy cologne or aftershave.

During the Interview

Now it's the big day, so try to remain calm. It's very important to be comfortable and relaxed in the interview yet still professional. You'll do your best if you're well-prepared and ready to speak about the information on your resume. If you've followed the preceding advice, you've already learned a lot about the organization and its products or mission, and you've prepared a list of questions. Be confident and be yourself; you'll make a positive impression and demonstrate what you can bring to the organization.

Arrive at least 10 minutes early to collect your thoughts. This also gives you time to visit the bathroom for a last-minute check of your appearance. If you know you look good, you'll be more confident. Take time to greet and acknowledge the secretary or administrative assistant; it's old-fashioned courtesy, and besides, you never know how much influence this person has.

Bring along an extra resume and letters of recommendation in case the interviewer doesn't have them handy. Walk in prepared with a few relevant questions and listen carefully. Because you've taken the time to learn the company's business, clients, market and direction, you're prepared for any questions the interviewer may throw at you.

Be open and upbeat. Face your interviewer with arms and legs uncrossed, head up, and hands and face at ease. Smile and look the interviewer in the eye. Look for common ground between the two of you to establish a positive connection and to make a bit of an impression. Perhaps you went to the same school (if you did, the recruiter is bound to mention this) or have the same hobby (if you notice a chess set in the corner and you're a master, go ahead and mention chess if you can do so gracefully). Most people keep at least some personal objects in their offices; if you notice something that could forge a link, you can mention it.

The Questions

Interviewers often ask very similar questions, so the more you can anticipate these and what your answers will be, the better. One favorite request is: "Tell me about yourself!" This can be really unnerving to anyone, since Americans are typically brought up to believe that talking about oneself is vulgar. Of course, you've got to say something, and you want to put your best foot forward. So what do you say?

Don't start at the beginning, providing a narrative about where you were born and grew up. And don't focus on hobbies or experiences that may not be relevant to the job. Focus on your internship-related experiences and your education. If you could tell the interviewer only five things about yourself, what would they be? Here's a good potential list:

- I graduated magna cum laude or number one in a class of 450 students.
- I was the senior class president.
- I opted out of four English classes with A's because of my performance on entrance exams.
- I commit three evenings a week to local charities while maintaining a 3.8 average at college.
- I'm passionate about physics and I believe I can make an important contribution to science when I graduate.

Another favorite: What do you want to be doing in five years? Try to be as specific with this as possible. Avoid a general beauty-pageant type of response:

"I want to work for world peace" or "I want to win the Nobel Prize." Instead, try for something such as: "I hope to be working as a health reporter for a midsized newspaper in an urban area."

Here's a scary one: "What's your greatest weakness?" You can't avoid the question. "I don't have any" is not the response the interviewer is looking for. Instead, give an honest answer, but include the methods you use to overcome it. If you're a hopeless procrastinator, you could say: "I tend to put off answering e-mails, so I've made it a habit always to do those tasks the very first thing in the morning to get them out of the way. Since I know I tend to procrastinate, I have learned to be hard on myself with projects I'm worried about. I always do those first."

Another common request: "Tell me about a time when you had to work with someone who was difficult." Try to come up with an example ahead of time. Choose a situation where you managed to deal with the person, and explain how you did it. Don't say, "I just made my boss transfer me." The interviewer wants to see how sensitive you can be to another person and how you handle adversity.

Handling Problem Areas

The interviewer will also be looking for potential problems in your resume, so it's a good idea to be ready to turn what could be seen as weaknesses into strengths. If the recruiter notices that you're applying for an internship with a PR firm but you haven't had any experience in public relations, you might point out: "While it's true that I haven't worked in a PR office, I handled all of the publicity for the college speaker series for the past year and a half, and we've had record-breaking attendance." Don't get rattled if any of these objections are brought up. Calmly and confidently point out what you *can* do. Make the interviewer feel good about hiring you by being enthusiastic, truthful, and friendly.

Race may be mentioned if the internship is designed specifically for minorities or underserved populations. Otherwise, questions about race, religion, gender, marital status, childcare issues, and sexual preference are against federal law. Interview questions should focus on the job at hand, not on your personal life.

As you talk, subtly give the impression that you're already part of the team by using "we" when asking how something is done. For example, ask, "How do we handle press releases?"

At the end of the interview, come up with a positive statement and a quick, firm handshake. Look the interviewer right in the eye, and ask when you might hear their decision. Get the recruiter's business card.

After the Interview

Your mother was right: Manners do count, and the better yours are, the greater your chance of landing an internship (and eventually, a permanent job). After your interview, be sure to write a brief, polite "thank you" note. It's one of most important things you can do in your internship search. Always be sure to send this out within 24 hours of the actual interview.

Don't know what to say? It doesn't have to be a three-page epic. Reiterate how you think your skills or experience fit with the position (it's not bragging if it's true), and mention specific topics covered in the interview to trigger the person's memory. Conclude by emphasizing your interest in the position.

Appearances count here, so go for high-quality paper with a good printer (no smudges, coffee stains, or wrinkles). In some cases, you can substitute an e-mail if you sense the interviewer won't be put off (especially if the internship is with a technology company), but it's generally better to opt for the standard mail approach.

Be aware, however, that while a brief thank-you is good, calling every day to find out if they've made a decision is not. It's hard, but be patient.

TEN WAYS TO SUCCEED IN AN INTERNSHIP OR SUMMER JOB

You've finally landed the internship of your dreams. Now what? The hard part is just beginning. The following are some time-tested ways of ensuring you get the most out of your internship or summer job.

1. Be responsible and dependable. Be someone your boss can count on.

2. Be enthusiastic; you're there to learn. Ask questions and keep your ears open.

3. Be willing to work hard and lend a hand doing anything, including running for coffee or making copies. Don't cop an attitude about a task being "beneath" you.

4. Be cheerful, professional, and honest. Integrity is something you can't barter; once it's lost, it's almost impossible to restore.

5. Punctuality is a virtue; try always to be on time. If you're going to be late, call.

6. Be flexible and adaptable; sometimes the job may change or you'll be asked to do something you hadn't counted on. Go with the flow.

7. Try to network and meet as many people in the organization as possible, not just the top brass but also the folks on the lowest end of the employee ladder.

8. Take advantage of every learning opportunity that comes your way, even if it's not exactly in your area. You'll never know what information will come in handy later.

9. If you run into a disagreeable boss or adviser, don't burn your bridges and tell the person off. Someday you may regret it.

10. Always remember that every job, no matter how marginal, and every person, no matter how seemingly inconsequential, has something to teach you. Be open to these lessons.

FINDING A MENTOR

When looking at internships and summer jobs, it helps to know a lot about yourself and how you best work. If you think you'll do better under someone's guidance, you really need a program that's going to provide close mentoring with established professionals. However, if you're the independent type who prefers to develop and monitor your own work, a self-directed experience will be better for you.

Formal training programs are not offered by all employers, but you should expect some training and regular supervision. There are a lot of other reasons why having a mentor makes good sense, which is why so many internships include one. Having someone show you the professional ropes is the best way to make progress in your chosen field. Remember, no matter how much you think you've learned in school, your mentor is the one with the solid on-the-job experience—probably years of it. Typically, everybody learns more tricks on the job than during four years of college. A good internship supervisor (often called a mentor or adviser) should be committed to offering you career advice and constructive feedback. If so, listen carefully! This is experience you can't get in any high school or college class.

If your internship does include guidance from an adviser or a mentor, be sure the person has a clear understanding of what you would like to achieve during your program and what your time frame is. It's also important that the mentor know how to structure an internship and track your progress throughout the project.

Your mentor also may be able to introduce you to some valuable contacts and perhaps offer you an invitation to some helpful organization functions. In the best situations, your mentor may become not just a work associate but a confidante and friend. Work hard on this relationship, but remember that the mentor-mentee bond is just like any human interaction; it takes time to build trust and a sense of shared personal interest. Try to make sure to talk to your mentor at least once a week (more often is even better) and to involve your mentor not just in your daily tasks but in the big picture of how this internship might fit in with your career. The nice thing about a mentor-mentee relationship is that it's pure—your mentor isn't trying to sell you a service or hoodwink you into buying something. As your relationship grows over time, the trust between you can grow stronger.

If your internship sets up formal meetings with your mentor, come to each session with a tape recorder, a laptop, or at least a pad and pen to take notes. Also bring along a list of goals so you can discuss them with your mentor. Especially in the beginning, try not to take up too much of your mentor's time. Bring a few salient, direct questions you'd like to have answered rather than an hour's worth of interrogation. For example, ask: "Right now, I'm dealing with this problem. How would you handle that?"

Keep in mind that while you certainly can ask your mentor questions, it's your job to make the most of the information and take it from there. Your mentor is only supposed to give you some guidance as you make your own way. Your responsibility is to make the connection between what you're told and how you apply it to the job.

Also keep in mind that a true mentor relationship is a two-way street. Obviously, your mentor is the one with most of the experience, and you're there to learn from this person. That doesn't mean you've got nothing to offer, however. If your mentor is wise, he or she knows that every single person, no matter how young or inexperienced, has something to offer, something to teach. If you see an article you think your mentor would enjoy or learn from, clip it out and send it over. If you have a unique skill, offer to help your mentor out. (Maybe your mentor is a whiz at statistics but can't figure out some of the latest software; if that's your specialty, offer to help program his PDA.) Even if your mentor never takes you up on your offers of help, he or she will probably appreciate your willingness to share. If an employer doesn't seem to have a formal plan for you, see if the person will sit down with you and develop a *learning contract*—a set of goals and knowledge you'd like to achieve. This will structure your experience and help the employer know how to utilize your best capabilities.

SO YOU WANT TO WORK ABROAD . . .

Landing any internship takes work, but securing a good international internship really requires a significant amount of research. The first big question, of course, is to figure out *where* in the world you'd like to go. Some brave souls are willing to go anywhere, but many students have a preference for where they'd like to start. Internship programs may not exist in the areas that interest you, so it's

important that you approach your search with this information in mind. If you're not fluent in any foreign language, you might want to stick to an English-speaking country for your first visit abroad.

When you have an idea of where you would like to intern, you should do some investigating into the business culture of that region or country. Job strategies may vary from country to country. For example, some western European countries ask for passport-style photographs to be attached to resumes and letters. Make sure you're familiar with local-industry practices.

If you know of a specific company or organization you're interested in interning with, do some Internet research. It may be easier to start your search by going through domestic offices of international corporations. Some U.S. companies, such as Ernst & Young, may have internship programs that also include international opportunities. A U.S.-based human resources officer may be able to suggest ways for you to contact the hiring office in the country of your choice.

Never underestimate the power of input from others. Talk to your families, their friends and colleagues, and previous employers, plus any contacts you may have at domestic offices of international companies, your professors, alumni, and other professional contacts. Let people know that you're interested in working abroad or doing an internship outside the country.

Can You Handle It?

You need to be very honest with yourself about whether you can handle the extra stress of working in an international job or assignment far from home, in another country whose culture or language may be unfamiliar to you. It takes a special type of person to be able to handle this—someone with plenty of maturity, flexibility, adaptability, tolerance, and friendliness. You should feel comfortable leaving your friends and family for a relatively long period of time and be able to commit yourself 100 percent to the success of the assignment and company for whom you're working.

The single most important factor in your success in working in another country on an international assignment is your ability to accept and work within the culture, customs, beliefs, and attitudes of that country. You must not be judgmental of other people's ways of living and doing things. This is especially important if you've never traveled outside the United States. People in other countries can be different in many ways. They may have a different sense of permissible physical interaction than you're used to, such as kissing your cheeks, patting your back, or standing much closer to you than you're normally comfortable with. "I was walking down a street in Marseille," recalls one international intern, "and suddenly my French friend grabbed my hand! My first reaction was to jerk away, but then I noticed lots of other girls our age were walking around holding hands, too." Other cultures may be far more formal and reserved, which may initially make you feel isolated.

Dealing with the unexpected is common in many countries and can be especially challenging for U.S. students who go overseas, since they are generally accustomed to modern conveniences. Can you handle it if the power goes out regularly, if there isn't a bathroom in your room, if you have the chance to shower only once a week? Can you cope with fluctuating electronic equipment, unusual foods or unclean water, and roads and cars that might not be in the best repair? Although such conditions can provide a world of rich experience, different people have different levels of tolerance. Make sure that you have a good sense of your own limits before you travel for an extended period of time.

Safety Issues

In the current political climate, it is vital for American students to be aware that negative attitudes toward Americans exist in some countries. Safety is not a minor issue these days. When you're walking down the street, project a confident attitude. Walk as if you know exactly where you're going and what you're doing, even if you don't have a clue. Women, in particular, should learn about the customs, religion, and appropriate dress before visiting another country. Internet sites about the country are another good resource. Follow examples of culturally appropriate dress and behavior,

and avoid putting yourself in situations where you are alone or unable to easily ask an official or other authority figure for help.

Know Before You Go

Once you've got your internship, be sure to find out from that country's consulate if you need any specific vaccinations. Pack a medical kit to take with you, and be sure to obtain prescriptions for any medications you require. You may need to obtain a letter from your doctor if you have asthma or allergies and you must carry an Epi-pen on board the plane. Because of recent security crackdowns, carrying an hypodermic needle on board a plane is allowed in medical necessity cases, but you'll need that letter from your doctor.

GOVERNMENT INTERNSHIPS

The federal government has a lot to offer when it comes to offering internships and summer jobs. Most agencies offer student jobs and internships as part of the Student Temporary Employment Program (STEP). Some student jobs, such as science and engineering co-ops at the National Aeronautics and Space Administration and internships at the National Institutes of Health, relate to students' career goals. Students often get school credit as well as pay. Other jobs provide experience.

To qualify for a student job in the government, you need to attend a high school, college, or vocational school, with at least a half-time schedule. In addition to the government jobs in this book, you can find government internships, co-ops, and other jobs by checking the online database at http://www.studentjobs.gov. This site is run by the U.S. Office of Personnel Management and the U.S. Department of Education and lists lots of internship opportunities. But keep in mind that agencies aren't required to post opportunities on the site.

You also might want to check for government jobs with the career guidance office at your school or call federal or state agencies directly. If you are looking for a summer job, start your search in the fall, because some agencies begin advertising positions in October, and jobs often fill quickly.

However, just because the federal government offers a huge employee pool doesn't mean it will be easy to land a temporary position. These summer jobs are quite competitive, and the number of jobs available is relatively small in comparison to the large number of applicants for summer employment with the federal government. Only a small percentage of applicants who apply are hired. This is why you shouldn't limit your efforts to obtain summer work solely to the federal government.

To get started, check out the government's official summer job Web site at http://www.usajobs.opm.gov. On the Web site, you can find current job vacancies, employment information fact sheets, applications and forms, and in some instances apply for jobs online. Complete job announcements can be retrieved from the Web site. The USAJOBS Web site also has an Online Resume Builder feature. Using the resume builder, job seekers can create online resumes specifically designed for applying for federal jobs. Resumes created on the USAJOBS resume builder can be printed from the system for faxing or mailing to employers and saved and edited for future use.

For many of the vacancies listed on the site, you can submit resumes created through USAJOBS directly to hiring agencies through an electronic submission process.

If you have questions about your application after it's been submitted, you should contact the agency directly. Be sure to give the agency enough information to easily locate your application (name, social security number, summer job vacancy announcement number, job title, and date submitted).

Sometimes, a person who worked for a federal agency during a previous summer may be reemployed by the same agency without having to compete with other applicants. To find out about reemployment possibilities, contact the agency where you previously worked.

Recent Grads

The federal government also offers special programs for recent college graduates. Participants usually receive special training and assignments and yearly promotions. You can find out more about these programs, which often are specific to particular agencies, by attending career fairs, contacting agencies that interest you, and searching the USAJOBS database. There is also an interactive telephone system at (703) 724-1850 or TDD (978) 461-8404, where you can access worldwide current job vacancies, employment information fact sheets, and applications and forms, and in some instances apply for jobs by phone.

Once you've found a summer job listing you like, and you're sure you meet the work experience and education requirements, you'll need to complete the application forms in the agency's vacancy announcement. Contact any of the sources identified above to obtain the required application forms. You should submit a separate application for each job for which you are interested and qualified.

Remember, don't wait until June 1 to start your search. Application filing dates vary with each agency, so be sure to check vacancy announcement deadlines. You'll also want to remember to specify the title of the job and the vacancy announcement number on your application. If more information is needed, it will be included in the agency's vacancy announcement and should be submitted at the time you apply. Incomplete applications won't be considered.

Presidential Management Fellows (PMF) Program

This program for students with a graduate degree has been attracting outstanding master's, juris doctor (J.D.), and doctoral-level students to the federal service for the past 27 years. PMFs may work in a variety of fields, including domestic or international issues, technology, science, criminal justice, health, or financial management.

A qualified student who has completed the required thesis for a graduate degree can be nominated by his or her university after demonstrating breadth and quality of accomplishments, capacity for leadership, and a commitment to excellence in the leadership and management of public policies and programs. If you want to be considered for the PMF Program, you must apply to your school by October 14 and be nominated by your school's dean, chair, or program director of your graduate program. The online application is made available on the PMF Web site (http://www.pmi.opm.gov) from September 1 through October 14 of each year. This online application and resume builder contains a format for entering all the information you need for the initial application process, including a resume component that includes education and work history.

Each school conducts a competitive screening process to evaluate its graduating PMF applicants and makes its final determination of nominees by October 31. You'll be notified of your acceptance status via e-mail by November 1.

If you're nominated by your school, the selection process then moves to the Office of Personnel Management (OPM), which will select PMF semifinalists based on the online applications and resume builders, including the accomplishment records. Once your electronic application is received by OPM, a preassessment will be conducted based on documentation provided in the accomplishment record portion of your application. After this initial review process, semifinalists are invited to participate in a structured assessment center process during the months of January and February. Based on these scores, and any veterans' status, nominees are ranked and notified of their PMF finalist status in March. You can then select the agency for which you'd like to be appointed. Positions are posted to an online job bank (the PMF Projected Positions System) on the PMF Web site each year.

As a PMF, you'll receive formal and informal on-the-job training and receive assignments designed to further their career goals. The two-year fellowship is available to anyone with a graduate degree in any subject.

Fellows usually start at the GS-9 level and are eligible for the GS-12 level at the end of the program. However, fellows who already have relevant experience can start at higher pay levels.

Being selected as a finalist makes you eligible for a PMF appointment by a federal agency, but you need to find the appropriate job. A job fair conducted exclusively for PMF finalists is held in the Washington, D.C., area in the spring of the year finalists are notified. Federal agency representatives attend the job fair and discuss their PMF hiring opportunities with the finalists. You don't have to attend the job fair to land a PMF appointment, but the job fair is a great way to make federal agency contacts for finalists.

FINDING GREAT REFERENCES

Whether you're looking for an internship, a summer job, or a full-time job, having a couple of great references is always a must. But what sort of people should you ask to provide you with this all-important letter?

First of all, you should be thinking of asking someone who knows you from school or from another job you've held. Your Great Aunt Tillie or your mom's best friend's lawyer, even if they know you well, won't do. If your dad's work colleague happens to be a state senator and you figure a fancy letterhead will help you, you'll only be half right. The letterhead might grab the interviewer's attention, but once he or she actually reads the letter, it will become obvious that the person barely knows you or doesn't know you in the right way.

The interviewer wants to see a recommendation from someone who knows what you can do and who's really seen you in action. Ideally, that would be someone at school—and the higher the position, the better, as long as the person has observed you or has firsthand knowledge of your work. So, if you've worked with the dean of your college on a public relations project, by all means, ask the dean for a recommendation. Or ask a professor who knows you well.

When you ask the person for a reference, it can really help the person providing the reference if the two of you sit down together briefly to think through how your internship may help you reach your career ideals. For example, if you've taken a marine biology course with a professor and you're applying for a dolphin communication internship, letting the professor know this will remind her to mention the fact that you worked with dolphins during a summer course the professor taught.

Bring along a copy of your resume that outlines your latest accomplishments. If you're asking for a reference from a college administrator or professor, remember that the person has taught hundreds of students. He or she may have forgotten some of your skills or accomplishments. Include a list of courses you've taken with this instructor, outstanding papers you've handed in, and grades you earned.

If you've worked in a summer job that in some way would relate to your career or the internship, it's also a good idea to see if you can get a recommendation from your boss. That will carry a lot of weight with the interviewer, because the boss has seen exactly how you work in a job situation. An official at a volunteer organization would also be appropriate, if the person can link your skills and performance in the volunteer work with the internship in some way.

Whomever you choose, be sure to ask people you think will give you a good reference. If you've had an unpleasant experience with a professor or a business associate, save yourself a lot of grief and don't approach that person for a reference. If you have any doubt, you should come right out and ask the person if he or she would feel comfortable in giving you a positive recommendation. You might feel a bit uncomfortable doing this, but it's much better to find this out ahead of time, before an uncomplimentary letter is sent.

And don't forget: Make sure the person knows the deadline for providing the reference letter.

Most likely the people you're asking for references are very busy professionals who may have other reference letters to write as well. You'll need to give the person lots of advance notice (and maybe even send a reminder as the closing date approaches).

LAUNCHING YOUR CAREER

As you prepare to begin your internship or summer job, think of it as your first major career step—so make the most of it. A summer job or internship is a terrific chance to network, because almost every person you work with is a potential reference for the future. Look for opportunities to mingle with employees professionally and socially. Soak up every bit of detail about the culture of the workplace. Don't be intrusive, but don't be shy about making suggestions or showing initiative if you have a good idea. Think about ways that you may share technical skills that are more advanced than those currently being used. If you have a great idea for a better way to do something, offer it tactfully.

Ideally, when you first start, you'll be given an overview of all departments and functions within the organization. If you aren't given the opportunity to interact with people outside your department, take it upon yourself (when you can) to make appointments with other people within the company, to interview them for information and gather a broader picture of the organization's operations.

PART III
DIRECTORY

ACTIVISM

ACCION INTERNATIONAL INTERNSHIP

ACCION International Internship Coordinator
56 Roland Street, Suite 300
Boston, MA 02129
Fax: (617) 625-7020
oscoville@accion.org
http://www.accion.org

What You Can Earn: $10 an hour.
Application Deadlines: May 30.
Educational Experience: None specified.
Requirements: Interest in writing, marketing, and public relations; excellent verbal, writing, and organizational skills; excellent computer skills (including MS Word, Excel). Spanish is helpful but not required

OVERVIEW

ACCION International is a private nonprofit organization that gives people the financial tools they need (microenterprise loans, business training, and other financial services) to work their way out of poverty. By providing "micro" loans and business training to needy individuals who want to start their own businesses, ACCION helps people work their own way up the economic ladder, with dignity and pride. With capital, people can build their own businesses, earning enough to afford running water, better food, and schooling for their children. The organization's goal is to bring microlending to millions of people to truly change the world.

A world pioneer in microfinance, ACCION was founded in 1961 and issued the first microloan in 1973 in Brazil. ACCION International's partner microfinance institutions today are providing loans as low as $100 to poor entrepreneurs in 20 countries in Latin America, the Caribbean, and sub-Saharan Africa, as well as in the United States. ACCION was among 25 organizations awarded the 2005 Social Capitalist Award by *Fast Company* magazine for "using business excellence to engineer social change."

Interns can work three or four days a week from June to August with ACCION in the communications department, helping primarily with administrative support, maintaining ACCION's photo archives, researching online outlets, writing and organizing borrower success stories, and tracking media clips and information pertinent to ACCION and the microfinance industry. Interns also help research local and international media pitches, compile targeted media lists for local pitches, produce materials and a newsletter (print and electronic), produce weekly reports on ACCION Web site traffic, and cover the front desk for about an hour a day. Intern tasks tend to change depending on public relations and media opportunities.

HOW TO APPLY

Mail, fax, or e-mail a cover letter and resume to the preceding address.

ADVOCATES FOR YOUTH INTERNSHIP

Director of Internships
Advocates for Youth
2000 M Street, NW, Suite 750
Washington, DC 20036
(202) 419-3420
http://www.advocatesforyouth.org

What You Can Earn: Stipends based on the District of Columbia's minimum wage for each hour worked; unpaid internships are also available to students who receive credit for their work. Unpaid interns will receive an expense stipend of $200 per month to cover expenses.
Application Deadlines: Rolling.

Educational Experience: None specified.
Requirements: Desire to learn more about fundraising and grant writing, in addition to some interest in adolescent reproductive and sexual health issues; attention to detail, solid organizational skills; good to excellent writing skills; familiarity with Internet research; ability to work independently; have the ability to work on multiple projects independently; sense of humor.

OVERVIEW

Advocates for Youth is an organization interested in creating programs and working for policies that help young people make informed and responsible decisions about their reproductive and sexual health. Advocates provides information, training, and strategic assistance to youth-serving organizations, policy makers, youth activists, and the media in the United States and the developing world. Advocates for Youth is founded on the belief that society should view sexuality as normal and healthy and treat young people as a valuable resource.

Interns at the Advocates for Youth will work in the development department 20 hours a week. As the development intern, you'll support the director of development, helping on foundation prospect research and writing initial letters of inquiry. You'll also help with general office administration, including organizing files, processing thank you letters, and packaging and sending grant reports and proposals. This organization is committed to youth development, and provides interns with a flexible and supportive work environment in which each intern can find ways to pursue his or her own interests.

HOW TO APPLY

Interested students should submit a resume with a cover letter to the preceding address (no phone calls). In the cover letter, specify the internship period: summer (June to August), fall (September to December), or spring (January to May).

AMERICAN CIVIL LIBERTIES UNION IMMIGRANTS RIGHTS PROJECT INTERNSHIP

American Civil Liberties Union
125 Broad Street, 17th Floor
New York, NY 10004
(212) 549-2621
Fax: (212) 549-2654
egrimsley@aclu.org
http://www.aclu.org

What You Can Earn: Unpaid.
Application Deadlines: May 31.
Educational Experience: Undergraduate students in all majors; Spanish fluency is preferred but not required.
Requirements: Must be committed to civil liberties and should have a strong interest in social justice and legal issues, excellent writing and communication skills, and the initiative and energy necessary to see projects to completion. Must be comfortable with research and writing as well as administrative tasks.

OVERVIEW

The American Civil Liberties Union (ACLU) Immigrants Rights Project conducts the largest litigation program in the country dedicated to enforcing and defending the constitutional and civil rights of immigrants and to combating public and private discrimination against noncitizens.

The Immigrants Rights Project maintains offices in New York and California with a combined staff of 15, plus interns and volunteers. Cases have included lawsuits against Donald Rumsfeld and military commanders for torture of detainees in Iraq and Afghanistan; litigation challenging unconstitutional detention of immigrants; challenges to discriminatory "special registration" policies; protecting the fundamental right of access to the courts for immigrants; protecting the workplace rights of immigrant workers; and challenging the improper application of deportation laws.

Interns with this project may work during the school year or in the summer and will be responsible for a variety of tasks, including handling written correspondence and inquiries from immigrants in detention centers, searching for newspaper and press articles related to immigrants' rights, maintaining press files, and other administrative projects. Interns will be exposed to the legal aspects of public-interest work. Interns will be under the direct supervision of the project's paralegals and will also have an opportunity to work on assignments related to the project's cases.

The internship will last about 10 to 12 weeks with the option to continue into the next semester.

HOW TO APPLY

To apply, send a cover letter and resume via either mail or e-mail to the preceding address.

AMERICAN CIVIL LIBERTIES UNION INTERNSHIP

ACLU Washington Office Internships
1333 H Street, NW, 10th Floor
Washington, DC 20005

ACLU National Headquarters
Internship Coordinator
125 Broad Street
New York, NY 10004
(212) 549-2610

What You Can Earn: Unpaid.
Application Deadlines: July 15 for fall semester; October 1 for winter/spring semester.
Educational Experience: Some grasp of current civil liberties issues before Congress is helpful but not required.
Requirements: None.

OVERVIEW

The American Civil Liberties Union (ACLU) is the nation's foremost advocate of individual rights and offers a selective, semester-long legislative internship program in the nation's capital, designed to give students the opportunity to delve into the workings of a full-service national legislative office.

(Many internships are available with other offices of the ACLU; for information on other internships, contact the New York national office at the address above, or contact your local affiliate.)

The legislative internship program is designed to give you a realistic view of working in Washington. Interns are selected to work in one of the following areas:

- Legislative advocacy and research: Work to enact federal legislation to protect peoples' rights and liberties.
- Media relations, Internet advocacy/communications: Work to shape public opinion on key civil liberties issues.
- Field and campus organizing: Help organize grassroots movements to defend civil liberties on Capitol Hill.

The ACLU hosts interns throughout the academic year. If you're applying for an intern position, you should be able to show a strong interest in the legislative process and working for social justice. Excellent writing and research skills and the ability to work independently are essential. Because the ACLU can't provide a stipend, they offer flexible hours for internships but require a minimum commitment of 20 to 25 hours a week.

HOW TO APPLY

There is no application form. To apply, submit a detailed letter of interest with dates of availability, along with your resume and writing samples (5 to 10 pages) to the preceding Washington, D.C., address. Selection of interns is made on the basis of previous work, academic experience, grades, references, and writing samples. Face-to-face interviews are not required, but telephone interviews may be conducted.

AMNESTY INTERNATIONAL— WASHINGTON, D.C., INTERNSHIP

Internship Coordinator, Amnesty International USA
600 Pennsylvania Avenue, SE, 5th floor
Washington, DC 20003
Fax: (202) 546-7142
ic-dc@aiusa.org
http://www.amnestyusa.org/activism/volunteer.do

What You Can Earn: Unpaid but daily commuting and program-related expenses are reimbursed.
Application Deadlines: February 15 for spring semester; April 15 for summer semester; August 15 for fall semester; November 30 for winter semester.
Educational Experience: College juniors or seniors or graduate students.
Requirements: Possess strong written and verbal communication skills.

OVERVIEW

Amnesty International (AI) is a grassroots movement designed to ensure human rights for every individual throughout the world. Staffed largely by volunteers, AI works to release prisoners of conscience, to focus on targeted country campaigns, or to work on other human rights issues such as torture, refugees, and the death penalty.

Amnesty International USA (AIUSA) offers internships tin any of four sessions (spring, summer, fall and winter) throughout the country. Visit AI's Web site at http://www.amnestyusa.org/activism/volunteer.do for an up-to-date list.

This entry discusses the Washington Office Internships, which are granted for a 12-week period, but longer internship commitments are encouraged. Although business hours are 9:00 A.M. to 5:00 P.M. Monday through Friday, the internship program is flexible and can accommodate class and work schedules.

Interns are selected to work with one of 13 programs in the Washington office, helping organize projects and participating in a variety of other events.

Amnesty International is looking for interns who understand human rights concerns and current affairs and can articulate ideas. It's also important to be willing to learn from the internship experience, to take on a significant amount of responsibility, and to work well as a team or independently. Typically, interns work a minimum of 35 hours per week.

Campaigns

Each year AI conducts a major international human rights campaign focusing on specific issues or countries. This unit is responsible for AIUSA's participation in these major international campaigns and also for a number of smaller, ongoing country campaigns. You'll help with all aspects of these campaigns, including strategic planning, creating activist campaigning and education materials and tools, public events and actions, and campaign-related meetings. To intern in this program, you should have either a background or interest in organizing or in Amnesty International's human rights campaigns.

Communications

Here you'll raise public awareness through media relations, advertising/marketing, new media, artist relations, and the *Amnesty Now* magazine. You'll primarily support the media relations unit, tracking coverage of AIUSA placements, developing lists of relevant journalists, researching media outlets, supporting press conferences, writing internal documents, drafting external press releases, and participating in various projects.

Country Specialist (Co-Group)

This program recruits, trains, and services a corps of 120 volunteer activists to serve as AIUSA's country strategists and experts. You'll be responsible for supporting the human rights work of country specialists focusing on a particular world region (Africa, Americas, Asia, Europe, or the Middle East). You'll take an active part in the recruiting process, help develop training manuals, and help organize the annual training and strategy meetings.

Crisis Preparedness & Response

This unit mobilizes AIUSA membership, staff, and allies to prepare for and respond to human rights crises around the world. The CPR Unit has managed AIUSA's response to crises in Israel/Occupied Territories/Palestinian Authority, Iraq, Colombia, Liberia, and the Côte d'Ivoire. During times of crisis, AIUSA provides analyses of human rights abuses during crisis, offers solutions to prevent future abuses, and addresses past abuses. Your responsibilities include helping to write newsletters and conducting research projects on countries in crisis.

Domestic USA Program

This new national program focuses on monitoring human rights abuses in the United States and supporting communication among the national and regional programs. Special focus is placed on police brutality, racial profiling, and prison conditions. Your responsibilities include researching issue areas, tracking issues through the media, handling human rights complaints, conducting legal/nonlegal research, and drafting action and issue briefs. Ideally, if you want to intern with this program you should have a background or strong interest in criminal justice, civil rights, marketing, and/or community organizing.

Government Relations

Staff and interns work together in this program to influence U.S. policy on human rights issues. Interns are responsible for encouraging grassroots advocacy and helping staff monitor human rights developments in Africa, Asia, Latin America, Europe, or the Middle East. Interns also help distribute recently-released documents and cover hearings for the team.

Membership Mobilization

This department is in charge of recruiting new activists, building public awareness of Amnesty's work through outreach, enhancing public and formal education, and approaching local and regional media. You'll take an active part in helping with the overall support of the department, assisting the staff with the Special Initiations Fund (SIF) and resolutions-related projects.

New Media

This unit uses the Internet to promote human rights and to recruit, mobilize, and support activists and members. It is responsible for AIUSA's Web site, e-mail newsletters, and online action center, as well as for online discussion areas, online events, and audio and video content. To intern here, you should have Internet skills and experience or strong writing skills and interest in human rights. Intern projects have included creating new sections of the Web site, organizing online events, and writing for e-mail newsletters and the site.

Mid-Atlantic Regional Office

This office works with AIUSA members in Washington, D.C., Delaware, Maryland, Pennsylvania, Virginia, and West Virginia to mobilize and educate people, institutions, and organizations to end international human rights abuses. You'll help organize publicity efforts, work with community organizations, and design and implement public education programs, in addition to helping with day-to-day office work.

National Field Program (NFP)

This group focuses on national organizing opportunities and educational projects, coordinating national training programs and developing tools to educate, publicize and mobilize for human rights. Working with AIUSA's five regional offices, the NFP coordinates the National Student Program of AIUSA. You'll help create tools and resources such as the activist tool kit and the volunteer leadership workbook.

Program to Abolish the Death Penalty (PADP)

Abolition of the death penalty is a crucial part of AI's mandate, and this program coordinates international, state, and local activities, including mobilization around legislative issues and urgent actions. You'll be responsible for daily tasks such as responding to e-mails from the public, including general requests for information, maintaining the database for the abolition network, preparing clemency appeals on scheduled executions, and updating the Web site. Special tasks include helping with promotion, resource development, and outreach for the National Weekend of Faith in Action on the Death Penalty and working on the issue of juveniles on death row and attending legislative hearings on the Hill on death-penalty related bills.

The Refugee Program

This program helps people fleeing persecution in their home country. You'll be responsible for providing research and documentation to be used as evidence in asylum claims. Responsibilities include: researching computer and hard copy resources to substantiate individual claims and tracking allegations by detainees about mistreatment in INS detention. You'll also summarize the relevance of material to individual claims, and draft *Urgent Action* (UA) letters and articles for AI publications, including the AIUSA monthly Mailing and the Web page. Interns also field telephone, e-mail, and fax inquiries, and maintain database and resource files.

Women's Human Rights Program

You'll work with staff to promote and defend the rights of girls and women worldwide, working with AIUSA members, policymakers, and local and national women's organizations on a wide range of women's human rights issues. You'll represent AIUSA's Women's Human Rights Program at events, meetings, and networking opportunities as necessary (this may be during the weekend or evenings), conduct outreach to women's organizations who are potential coalition partners, compile a comprehensive events calendar for the program, and provide support in the coordination of training and conferences sponsored by the program.

HOW TO APPLY

Mail, fax, or e-mail a cover letter with your resume, a writing sample, and two letters of recommendation to the preceding address. In your cover letter, you should indicate the number of days a week that you'll be available for an internship, including start and departure dates, along with the programs you're interested.

Your writing sample does not have to be of any specific length or on any particular topic; it can be a recently written term paper or news article, for example. You should submit all of your materials at once, including your letters of recommendation (if possible), although recommendations can be mailed under separate cover. An incomplete application will not be considered.

BEYOND PESTICIDES INTERNSHIP

Project Director, Beyond Pesticides
701 E Street, SE, Suite 200
Washington, DC 20003
(202) 543-5450
Fax: (202) 543-4791
jkepner@beyondpesticides.org

What You Can Earn: Small stipend.
Application Deadlines: Rolling.

Educational Experience: None specified.
Requirements: None specified.

OVERVIEW

Beyond Pesticides is a nonprofit national grassroots organization founded in 1981 and dedicated to leading the transition to a world free of toxic pesticides. The organization advocates a policy to protect public health and the environment and carries out an extensive program of public education and advocacy on the toxic hazards of pesticides and the availability of safe alternatives. Beyond Pesticides' programs are focused on school pesticide use, lawn care, insect-borne diseases, organic agriculture, and documenting pesticide poisoning incidents.

Beyond Pesticides has historically taken a two-pronged approach to the pesticide problem by identifying the risks of conventional pest-management practices and promoting nonchemical and least-hazardous management alternatives. The organization's primary goal is to take local action, helping individuals and community-based organizations stimulate discussion on the hazards of toxic pesticides, while providing information on safer alternatives. Beyond Pesticides has sought to bring to a policy forum in Washington, D.C., state capitals, and local governing bodies the pesticide problem and provides information on pesticides and alternatives to their use. The organization offers a quarterly news magazine, a monthly news bulletin, a Web site service, and a bimonthly bulletin on school pesticides. The organization also publishes a wide variety of brochures, information packets, and reports.

The summer intern may help produce fact sheets, articles, report contributions, and online materials; update and develop Web pages at http://www.beyondpesticides.org; help field phone calls and e-mails from the public; research and answer information requests; and help the executive director and program staff with outreach, research, and administrative tasks. You'll be given tasks that match your interests, skills, and background with Beyond Pesticides' goals. In addition to working on specific projects, you'll learn about the importance of grassroots action, the complexities of environmental issues, and how nonprofits function. Internships vary from three months to a year.

HOW TO APPLY

To apply, send a resume and cover letter outlining what type of internship interests you, what you hope to gain from the experience, and what date you are available to the preceding address.

BOSTON ENVIRONMENT DEPARTMENT INTERNSHIP

City of Boston Environment Department
(617) 635-3850
bryan.glascock@cityofboston.gov
http://www.cityofboston.gov/environment

What You Can Earn: Unpaid; course credit may be obtained with prior approval.
Application Deadlines: December.
Educational Experience: None specified.
Requirements: Minimum of 10 hours a week.

OVERVIEW

The City of Boston's Environment Department aims to protect the built and natural environments and provide information on environmental issues affecting Boston. Sound management and environmental practices will help ensure the future of a livable city. The department protects Boston's wealth of historic sites, buildings, landscapes, and waterways through protective designation and review. The department is involved in all environmental review processes.

The department is seeking interns to assist a number of environment and historic-preservation commissions, including the conservation commission (wetland/water protection); air pollution control commission (air quality and parking freezes); environmental reviews, archeology, and landmarks; and historic districts.

HOW TO APPLY
Contact the department at the preceding e-mail address or number for more information and to apply.

BREAD FOR THE CITY LEGAL CLINIC INTERNSHIP

Bread for the City Internship
1640 Good Hope Road, SE
Washington, DC 20020
(202) 265-2400
Fax: (202) 745-1081
http://www.breadforthecity.org

What You Can Earn: Unpaid.
Application Deadlines: May 31.
Educational Experience: Applicants from legal internship and work study programs.
Requirements: None specified.

OVERVIEW
Bread for the City provides free legal assistance, medical care, social services, food, and clothing without cost to low-income residents of Washington, D.C. The legal clinic represents individuals in landlord-tenant law, family law, disability appeals, and other public-benefits issues.

The Legal Clinic of Bread for the City's SE Center has a full-time legal internship available for 10 weeks in the summer. The legal intern's duties will include interviewing clients; conducting legal research; drafting pleadings, correspondence, motion papers, and memoranda of law;

reviewing court files in Washington, D.C., Superior Court; reviewing official files at the Social Security Administration's Office of Hearing and Appeals and assisting with representation of individuals in administrative hearings; helping with representing tenants at grievance hearings before the D.C. Housing Authority; and helping with trial preparation.

HOW TO APPLY
To apply, send a cover letter and resume to the preceding address.

BROOKLYN PARENTS FOR PEACE INTERNSHIP

Program Coordinator
Brooklyn Parents for Peace
138 Court Street
PMB 416
Brooklyn, NY 11201
(718)624-5921
Fax: 718 624 5921
emilia@brooklynpeace.org
http://www.brooklynpeace.org

What You Can Earn: Small stipend for part-time weekdays with some evenings and weekends possible (minimum of eight hours a week) in the fall and spring.
Application Deadlines: Rolling.
Educational Experience: Students interested in advocacy and effecting social change.
Requirements: Excellent writing, communication and administrative skills, highly organized and detail-oriented, and computer literate.

OVERVIEW
Brooklyn Parents for Peace is a small community activist organization in Brooklyn that

has for more than 20 years offered analysis on international and domestic policies. The group consists of a network of Brooklyn residents (parents, neighbors, and educators) alarmed by the growing militarism of American society and its effect on their lives. The group tries to inform themselves and the community about issues of war and peace. Founded in 1984, the group has organized local opposition to the Staten Island home port for nuclear-capable Cruise missiles, the U.S. intervention in Central America, the Gulf War, and economic sanctions that penalized Iraqi children. They also fought to preserve the entitlement status of welfare and Medicaid, supported efforts to strengthen New York public education, and supported compensation to civilian victims of U.S. bombing in Afghanistan.

The intern at this organization would help coordinate community meetings, set up information tables, participate in phone and advertising campaigns, meet with elected officials, and participate in demonstrations.

HOW TO APPLY

Submit a cover letter and resume to the preceding address.

THE CARTER CENTER INTERNSHIP

The Carter Center
Educational Programs
One Copenhill
453 Freedom Parkway
Atlanta, GA 30307
(404) 420-5100
carter-intern@emory.edu
http://www.cartercenter.org

What You Can Earn: Unpaid, but college credit is possible. If your university offers academic credit for internships, the Center will work with your school to match academic requirements with the requirements of the intern's host program. Necessary forms from your college or university should be submitted upon acceptance to the intern's program supervisor.

Application Deadlines: Summer: March 15; fall: June 15; spring: October 15.

Educational Experience: Junior or senior college students, recent graduates (within two years of graduation), and graduate/professional students.

Requirements: Minimum 20-hour, four- or five-day a week commitment for at least 15 weeks (except summer, which is between 10 to 15 weeks).

OVERVIEW

The Carter Center is a nongovernmental organization founded in 1982 in Atlanta, Georgia, by Jimmy and Rosalynn Carter in partnership with Emory University. The Center seeks to wage peace, fight disease, and build hope in a world where people live every day under difficult, life-threatening conditions caused by war, disease, and famine. Interns are a vital presence at the center, which has gained an international reputation for nurturing interns' skills, knowledge, and commitment in shaping participants' educations and careers. Interns come to the Center from universities throughout the world to support the Center, where they learn through a series of educational programs, mentoring, and interaction with a group of intern peers.

At the Carter Center, you'll be working from 8:30 A.M. to 6:00 P.M., depending on program needs, but the program will make allowances for you if you must attend classes or work elsewhere. Depending on program and project needs, you may have the opportunity to travel, but you should arrive expecting to spend the duration of the internship in Atlanta. Although some former interns are currently working in temporary staff positions, these jobs are not usually offered after an internship.

President Jimmy Carter visits the Carter Center for about one week a month (yes, you'll see both the Carters walking through the building). President and Mrs. Carter meet the interns as a group at least once each semester, schedules permitting, to talk about Center-related issues and attend a photo session. They are genuinely supportive of the internship program and appreciate interns' work. When the Carters visit, you may have one or two books signed by President or Mrs. Carter (but the books must be written by one of them); you may have it signed for yourself, a relative, or friend.

The programs and offices of the Carter Center are divided into three main areas: peace, health, and operations. Peace programs include the Americas Program, China Village Elections Project, Conflict Resolution Program, Democracy Program, Development Office, Educational Programs (serves Peace and Health programs), Global Development Initiative, and the Human Rights Office (serves Peace and Health programs). Health programs include Global 2000, Health Development and the Mental Health Program. Operations programs include art services, development, public information, and special events.

Peace Programs

Americas Program
Recently, the emphasis has shifted from election monitoring, now led by the Democracy Program, to strengthening inter-American relations and democratic consolidation in the Western Hemisphere. This work includes efforts to foster productive relationships between civil society and governments and to promote accountability through improved access to information, campaign finance reform, and support to election monitoring. The Americas Program maintains the Council of Presidents and Prime Ministers of the Americas, a group of more than 30 current and former prime ministers and presidents who are regularly consulted on projects for their expertise and influence throughout the region.

The Americas Program offers conferences at the Carter Center in Atlanta and visits countries throughout the hemisphere. The program fosters dialogues that bring together politicians, policy professionals, scholars, media, business executives, and civil society leaders from across the Americas.

Recent projects included a major policy conference on financing democracy and crisis management in Venezuela.

You should be an upper-level undergraduate student or a graduate and professional student whose area of study is international relations, political science, history, or Latin American and Caribbean studies. A concentration on issues of development and democracy and a strong course background in social sciences are ideal. Being able to speak, read, and write Spanish or Portuguese is helpful; you must have strong writing and computer skills and the ability to use the Internet for research purposes. You also should have overseas experience and a strong academic record.

You'll be assigned to a particular issue, theme, or country, where you'll be responsible for providing research and logistical support for a relevant program activity. This often includes conference preparation and follow-up, staff travel abroad, writing regular updates, and periodically briefing program staff. Work commonly leads to contact with high-profile politicians and diplomats throughout the Americas. You also may opt to dedicate additional time to a mentored study for which you may be able to receive university credit.

You'll need a "can-do" attitude here, along with curiosity, resilience, flexibility, and resourcefulness. Past interns have gone on to work in positions at think tanks in Washington, D.C. (such as The Brookings Institution and Inter-American Dialogue), the U.S. Peace Corps, and government agencies such as the Foreign Service, U.S. Department of State, and USAID.

China Village Elections Project
This project is dedicated to providing help and advice to the Chinese government in standardizing electoral procedures at the village, township, and county levels. President Carter and Minister Duoji Cering of the Ministry of Civil Affairs reached an agreement in 1997 to allow the Center to cooperate with the MCA to help with village election data gathering, civic education, and election official training. After a pilot project in nine counties in three provinces from 1998 through

1999, a three-year project was signed in early 2000 to expand the project to four provinces. The project is also working with the National Peoples' Congress of China to help with elections at the township and county levels. Over the past three years, the Center sent several election observation delegations to China to observe village and township elections. Chinese elections officials were also invited to observe the American midterm elections, presidential primaries, and the presidential election.

For this internship, you should have a background and/or course work in international relations, political science, and other related fields, and you should be able to communicate at an advanced level of Mandarin Chinese. You need good writing skills in English and rudimentary Chinese reading and writing capabilities. You also must have good communication and computer skills (especially in the Internet, Web page creation, PowerPoint and Excel), be able to work independently, be willing to travel occasionally, and understand current Chinese affairs and U.S.-China relations.

Typically, you'll be expected to perform a variety of tasks, including administrative assistance, translating documents both into Chinese and English, monitoring the Western and Chinese media about political developments in China, and researching bibliographies of Chinese reports. You'll also be expected to provide logistical support and to accompany Chinese delegations visiting the United States.

Conflict Resolution Program (CRP)

This program is dedicated to the peaceful prevention and resolution of armed conflicts, including civil wars. Much of the work revolves around regularly monitoring many of the world's armed conflicts. When a situation arises where President Carter has a unique role to play, the CRP is directly responsible for supporting his intervention efforts. To accomplish this, CRP works closely with representatives of international organizations, governments, and nongovernmental organizations. The CRP has been involved in projects in the Baltics, Bosnia and Herzegovina, and the Great Lakes regions of Africa, Korea, Liberia, Sudan, Uganda, Fiji, and Ecuador.

You'll be expected to have a solid academic background in conflict resolution, international relations, and foreign policy courses, but the program will consider interns from a wide range of academic interests and fields. It's also important that you have relevant real-world experiences, such as jobs in related fields (conflict resolution or mediation); student internships; and study, work, or time spent living abroad. The ability to speak a second language (especially French) is desired but not required. In addition, you must have had some experience in volunteering or work activities at a local or national level.

While each CRP intern must spend at least 20 hours a week at the Carter Center, 40 hours a week is preferred. It's particularly important for you to have advanced research and writing skills and to be adept with computers and the Internet.

Between four to six interns will help CRP staff with projects designed to prevent or resolve armed conflicts throughout the world. You might monitor and research some of the armed conflicts the program regularly follows, helping to draft memoranda and reports, attend meetings, prepare briefing materials for meetings and trips, and organize conferences. All interns are responsible for writing, editing, and producing the weekly Conflict Updates, which focus on developments in the countries covered by the CRP.

You should be prepared to work independently and as a member of various teams in an irregular and fast-paced environment and be willing to do more than is required. You also should have a strong curiosity about the world and how it functions, as well as an avid quest for knowledge. Communication and research and writing skills are particularly important, as are patience, flexibility, and a good sense of humor.

Democracy Program

Because the Carter Center believes that reinforcing the process of democratization is the best means of promoting human rights, this program supports sustainable economic opportunity and focuses on resolving conflicts peacefully. The program's goals are to promote democratic transition and consolidation through projects involving election monitoring and mediation, technical assistance to strengthen civil society, and efforts to advance the rule of law and improve compliance with human rights standards. The program provides electoral assistance to countries around the globe that are undergoing first or second transitional elections or are at risk of backsliding in their democratization process. In the last several years, the program has organized election observation projects in Nigeria, Liberia, East Timor, the Cherokee Nation, Mozambique, and Zimbabwe and civil society building projects in East Timor, Liberia, and Guyana.

You can be either an advanced undergraduate or a graduate student, with course work in political science, international relations, democratization, human rights, or other relevant areas. In addition, you should have real-world experience, such as previous internships or work experience and overseas study, as well as strong foreign language skills. It's particularly important for candidates to demonstrate advanced research and writing skills and to be adept with computers and the Internet.

Three to four interns work in a variety of areas related to democratization, including projects on election observation and mediation, as well as technical assistance to promote democratic consolidation and human rights and civil society building. You'll monitor specific countries and/or projects and typically write regular country updates, conduct research projects, and often work directly on project planning and implementation. Responsibilities may include drafting memorandums, preparing briefing materials for meetings, and aiding staff in forming election observation delegations. In addition, you are expected to provide administrative support to staff. You should be flexible and able to adapt quickly to change, since you'll be working in an exciting and fast-paced environment.

DEVELOPMENT OFFICE

This office supports the mission and activities of the Carter Center Peace and Health programs by generating money and other resources from foreign governments, U.S. government agencies, foundations, corporations, and individuals. Much of the staffers' work involves maintaining long-term relationships with more than 150 program donors, such as the government of Norway, Merck & Co., the MacArthur Foundation, and so on. The department cultivates relationships with organizations such as UNICEF, helps brief President and Mrs. Carter, and plans fund-raising trips.

Development positions are available to support both the Peace and Health programs of The Carter Center.

Interns should be upper-level undergraduate or graduate students with course work in English, international development, international finance and economics, international affairs, public health, public policy, philanthropy, business, scientific and technical writing, library sciences, and/or nonprofit management. It's also helpful if you're interested in foreign aid, mental health, international health and disease control, sustainable agriculture, corporate philanthropy, democracy, civil society, human rights, and conflict resolution. It is extremely helpful if you have worked with a member of Congress or other policymakers (especially if you've helped write letters), or if you've worked in a foreign country and learned more about the European Union or the World Bank. Experience in research and technical writing for academic, business, or nonprofit proposals; work in government contracts; and work with university or nonprofit development is very helpful.

Exceptional writing and research skills are critical. Extensive experience with the Internet and electronic databases such as Lexis-Nexis, SSCI, and WorldCat are essential. Proficiency with Access or another contact database is nice, but not a requirement. While each intern must spend at least 20 hours per week at the Center, 30 to 40 hours a week is preferred.

Educational Programs

This is the area that works on the internship program itself; a two-person program staff, along with an intern, helps select, support, and provide learning opportunities to foster professional development. In addition to supporting the Internship Program, Educational Programs hosts forums for college and high school groups interested in learning about the Center's programs.

During each internship, the program conducts a series of educational and social programs designed to enrich the intern experience, such as a ropes course, retreat, excursion to Plains, GA (home of the Carters), and field trips to Atlanta sites such as the Martin Luther King, Jr. Center and the CNN Center. In addition, the program administers evaluations to make sure that interns are gaining the maximum benefit from their experience.

You should be an undergraduate, graduate student, or recent graduate with an interest in careers in student affairs administration, nonprofit management, or international affairs. Foreign language skills are helpful but not necessary, but you should have strong writing and computer skills and a strong academic record.

You may help develop an intern handbook and an intern supervisor's manual, help develop a supervisor's training session, measure program outcomes, and conduct an evaluation process. In addition, you may help with routine activities such as planning events and processing internship applications.

You should understand common developmental concerns facing undergraduate and graduate students, be creative and organized, enjoy socializing with college-age people, and be eager to pitch in with tasks ranging from complex problem-solving to simple paperwork. You should also be interested in the work of the program as well as the overall goals of the Carter Center.

Global Development Initiative

This program's aim is to promote sustainable development by addressing the social, environmental, and economic interrelationships of development issues. This program believes that the most appropriate development policies and strategies will come from within a country, not from without. The Global Development Initiative (GDI) also serves as the institutional base for the Carter Center's environmental activities.

You should be a college senior, or a graduate/professional student in such fields as international relations, international development, development studies, public policy, economics, political science, or related backgrounds. It helps if you're familiar with international development, foreign aid; democratization, economic reform; and sustainable human development. It also is helpful if you have some experience in a developing country, experience with an international development organization, or study abroad. You must have a good grade point average, strong recommendations, and excellent research and writing skills.

GDI has a small staff that travels frequently. You may be asked to act as junior support staff, so you'll need to be able to learn quickly and work independently. Generally, you'll help with memo writing, research, and internal/external communication. You are asked also to monitor and report on issues or countries of interest to GDI, and you are expected to assist with administrative support. Interest or experience in Guyana, Albania, Mali, and Mozambique is a plus.

Human Rights Office

The Carter Center is founded on a commitment to human rights, which are integral to all Carter Center activities. In this office, one staff member works in collaboration with staff from each of the Center's programs. Human rights initiatives at the Carter Center include work with the United National High Commissioner for Human Rights, technical assistance projects in one or more countries, and individual case interventions. If you're an intern here, you'll be able to make rewarding, substantive contributions in support of some or all of these aspects of the Center's work.

The human rights casework undertaken by the Center involves both staff interventions and President and Mrs. Carter's personal interactions with world leaders on behalf of victims of human rights abuse. You'll help with all case-intervention work, researching cases and sometimes communicating with clients, their families, nongovernmental organization partners such as Amnesty International and Human Rights Watch, attorneys, and government offices. You'll also draft detailed memos regarding cases as well as letters for the Carters' signatures.

You should be a law student, a recent graduate, or a college senior, with a solid human rights education and/or experience. Excellent writing and oral communications skills are essential, as is flexibility and self-sufficiency.

You can expect rewarding substantive research work as well as some administrative duties such as filing or correspondence. You may write reports of meetings on various subjects, memoranda to senior Carter Center staff (including President Carter), and may have the opportunity to draft letters for President Carter addressed to heads of state on human rights issues.

Interested college sophomores should try to gain valuable experience with human rights organizations over summer breaks before applying to The Carter Center, which may increase your chance of being accepted.

Health Programs

Global 2000

Global 2000 (G2000) works to improve the quality of life through health programs in disease eradication/control and agriculture and leads a worldwide campaign that has achieved a 99 percent reduction of dracunculiasis (Guinea worm disease) in Africa and Asia. Efforts also are underway to prevent and eventually eradicate onchocerciasis (river blindness) in Africa and Latin America and to test eradication strategies for lymphatic filariasis and schistosomiasis in Nigeria. In Africa, small-scale farmers are learning improved agricultural techniques to grow more food for their families and boost local economies

You should be an outstanding graduate student with some overseas health or agricultural experience in a developing country under hardship conditions.

Project opportunities may vary from studies of remote communities in a developing county to

developing maps of disease patterns; projects are directly relevant to Global 2000 programs.

Mental Health Program

This program is dedicated to promoting mental health and improving policies and services to improve the quality of life for people with mental illness, guided by the Mental Health Task Force chaired by Mrs. Carter. The priorities of the program include reducing stigma and discrimination against people with mental illness; promoting the equitable treatment of mental illness; promoting early childhood education and mental health; and promoting mental health and improved services for people with mental illnesses around the world.

You should have an interest in healthcare issues, with course work in psychology, public health, medicine, or a related field. Practical experience in a mental health setting is a definite plus, and strong writing and analysis skills are required.

The program has several annual events in which you may participate, including:

- The annual Symposium on Mental Health Policy, which convenes the leaders in the mental health community from around the country for a two-day meeting each fall
- An annual fellowship program, which provides grants to journalists to research and report on a specific area of mental health/mental illness
- The annual Georgia Forum, which offers a full-day spring meeting on a mental health issue of concern throughout the state
- The International Committee of Women Leaders for Mental Health, a committee of the World Federation for Mental Health consisting of first ladies, royalty, and heads of state, chaired by Rosalynn Carter

You may help prepare for and follow up after these large-scale meetings, preparing research, planning programs, and writing and editing follow-up reports. You also may prepare materials for the program director's presentations.

This program is ideal for self-starters willing to work independently and interested in mental health policy issues.

Operations

Art Services

This office is responsible for the professional care of the Carter Center's growing art collection, which includes a diverse range of items given to President and Mrs. Carter or to the Carter Center. Course-work in museum studies or art history is helpful here, along with an interest in museum registration and/or curatorial work. Computer skills are required, and experience working with databases is desirable.

You'll help register and manage the Center's art collection; maintain computerized and written records; catalog new acquisitions; help with inventory; and work on installation and maintenance of art. Possible projects could include labeling and collection research.

If you're able to work independently and be flexible and conscientious, this program offers a unique opportunity to experience all facets of collection management.

Conference and Special Events Office

This office supports the programs and departments of the Carter Center by planning and executing conferences, media events, and social events. This department also markets the Carter Center facility to outside organizations that host conferences, media, and social events and assists the host organization with planning and executing those events.

You should have a background in the hospitality industry (catering, hotel, or conference centers), with an interest in marketing or in event management. You must spend at least 15 hours a week at the Carter Center; because the events schedule is variable depending on the type of event booked, some of those hours can be evenings and weekends. Good communication and phone skills are important.

You may help staff events, deal with sponsors during events, conduct site visits, attend pre-conference meetings with programs and outside clients, and provide information for clients. You may help maintain events files or client and financial databases and update and disseminate event information.

You need a good attitude and the ability to learn quickly and work independently. You'll be working with every program and department at the Center and with outside clients during high-level, high profile events. Flexibility, resourcefulness, and a sense of humor will make the experience in this very service-oriented department useful.

Development Office

This office supports the Center's mission and activities by generating donations and financial support from foreign governments, U.S. government agencies, foundations, corporations, and individuals. Staffers research potential funding prospects and initiate relationships through letters, proposals, phone calls, and meetings and help maintain long-term relationships with more than 150 program donors, such as the government of Norway, Merck & Co., and the MacArthur Foundation.

You should be an upper-level undergraduate or graduate student with course work in English, international development, international finance and economics, international affairs, public health, public policy, philanthropy, business, scientific and technical writing, library sciences, and/or nonprofit management. You also should be familiar with at least one or more of the following issues: foreign aid, mental health, international health, disease control, sustainable agriculture, corporate philanthropy, democracy, civil society, human rights, and conflict resolution.

You should have relevant experience such as work with a member of Congress or other high-level policy-maker, particularly drafting correspondence for official signature; work in a foreign country (especially in financial institutions); research and technical writing for academic, business contracting, or nonprofit proposals; work in procurement/contracting with a government agency or contractor; and work with university or nonprofit development departments.

Exceptional writing and research skills are critical. It's helpful if your skills have been recognized by awards and/or publication. Extensive experience using Internet resources and electronic databases such as Lexis-Nexis, SSCI, and WorldCat to research program, country, corporate, and individual information is essential. Proficiency with Access or another contact database is desired but not required. While each intern must spend at least 20 hours per week at the Center, 30 to 40 hours a week is preferred.

You'll help staff in all aspects of donor research, solicitation, and cultivation, monitoring news for information about prospective and current donors; attending meetings and briefings; helping to draft reports, proposals, briefing materials, talking points, and correspondence, including letters from President and Mrs. Carter to heads of state and foreign government officials; maintaining record of all contact with donors in files and electronic database; and conducting in-depth research on foreign government agencies' development policies, U.S. and foreign companies, individuals, and issues related to specific programs.

You should be prepared to work independently and as part of a team in this deadline-driven environment. You should be creative at identifying potential new funding sources, and you'll be expected to provide some administrative and clerical support. If you have an interest in international development and foreign aid in a wide-ranging spectrum of countries, as well as in nonprofit management, you should enjoy interning here. If you intend to start or lead a nonprofit organization in the future, you'll benefit from the high-level fund-raising and grants-management experience that you'll get here.

Public Information Office

As you might imagine, the PR wing of the Carter Center is busy handling all sorts of communications. One internship is available for a student to work with the publications manager on a publication project; if you're interested in this opportunity, you should indicate your preference, since this internship focuses on publishing and writing as opposed to publicity and media relations.

You should have strong interest and experience in journalism or public relations, with strong writing and typing skills and good newswriting skills. You'll help with ongoing office projects and special projects or events, scanning newspapers, magazines, and Internet sites for news coverage of the Carter Center; maintaining databases of media contacts; writing short articles for the in-house newsletter *Centerpiece;* researching information for press releases or articles; responding to public requests for information; and maintaining office archives of print and photo coverage. The office handles media and publicity for all major events at the Carter Center, and you'll help with this planning and implementation.

A flexible attitude and the willingness to work hard will help you get the most from your exposure to a high-profile press office. Assignments vary from semester to semester, depending on the Center's changing agenda of activities, usually with a heavy clerical and research focus.

HOUSING

Although the Carter Center does not provide housing for interns, it will provide information on available housing in staff and neighborhood resident homes, local apartment complexes, and the like.

HOW TO APPLY

Download the application from http://www.cartercenter.org. (Click on "About Us" at the top of the page; then click on "internship program.") Submit your completed application together with your resume, two letters of recommendation, an official transcript, a short essay (why you want to apply as an intern), and a writing sample of fewer than 10 pages. Mail your application to the above address.

You can reapply if you aren't successful the first time. Unsuccessful applications are kept on file for a year, so to reactivate your file you should send a written request to the internship coordinator and submit updated transcripts and resume prior to the appropriate deadline.

CENTER FOR WOMEN IN POLITICS AND PUBLIC POLICY INTERNSHIP

Center for Women in Politics and Public Policy
University of Massachusetts at Boston
100 Morrissey Boulevard
Boston, MA 02125-3393
(617) 287-5541
Fax: (617)-287-5544
cwppp@umb.edu
http://www.mccormack.umb.edu/cwppp

What You Can Earn: $500 for the summer.
Application Deadlines: Rolling.
Educational Experience: None specified.
Requirements: Interest in women's issues and ability to work as part of a team.

OVERVIEW
The mission of the Center for Women in Politics & Public Policy is to promote women's leadership in politics and policymaking by providing graduate education, conducting research that makes a difference in women's lives, and serving as a resource for women from diverse communities across Massachusetts, New England, and the nation. Recognizing the talent and potential of women from every community and guided by the urban mission of an intellectually vibrant and diverse university in the heart of Boston, the center wants to increase the involvement of women in politics and the world.

The center was established with the support of the Massachusetts Caucus of Women State Legislators in 1994 at University of Massachusetts/Boston. The center provides education, research and pub-

lications, online information, public events, and collaboration.

A number of internships are available, including communications, general, library, and research interns.

Communications Internship
This intern will help develop an e-newsletter for the center and update the center's contacts database.

General Internship
In this internship, you'll help organize events, mailings, database updates, and so on.

Library Internship
In this internship, you'll catalogue the center's private library and develop an archive of historical documents.

Research Internship
In this internship, you'll help with research on a variety of projects of concern to women, including women and work, women in healthcare professions, and women elected officials. You'll also gather data for a national study of women of color who are elected officials, and you'll help maintain the research funding database.

HOW TO APPLY
E-mail a cover letter and resume to the preceding address.

COMMON CAUSE INTERNSHIP

Common Cause
150 Nassau Street
New York, NY 10038
(212) 349-1755
http://www.rpi.edu/~interns/work/internships/
  Gov/Common.html

What You Can Earn: Unpaid; students can receive academic credit and reimbursement for traveling costs.
Application Deadlines: Rolling.
Educational Experience: Not specified.
Requirements: None specified.

OVERVIEW

Common Cause is a national nonprofit, nonpartisan citizen lobby group dedicated to improving government. With more than 250,000 members around the country, the group believes that government should be more accessible and responsive to the average American citizen.

During the fall and spring semesters, Common Cause/NY offers a unique opportunity to college students to play an integral part in social change. Interns are given serious responsibilities that include working on media projects, organizing grassroots mobilization efforts, public speaking, and issue research. Common Cause internships are flexible and are adapted to a student's particular area of interest when possible.

The Common Cause internship provides an excellent opportunity for you to get an inside look at the world of politics and allows you to actively participate in politics. Internships may be full or part time, during the fall, spring, and summer semesters.

HOW TO APPLY

Students interested in a Common Cause internship should send a resume or call for more information.

EARTHTRENDS SUMMER INTERNSHIP

World Resources Institute
10 G Street, NE , Suite 800
Washington, DC 20002
Fax: (202) 729-7775

rsoden@wri.org
http://earthtrends.wri.org

What You Can Earn: $10 to $15 an hour, depending on experience.
Application Deadlines: May 15.
Educational Experience: An undergraduate or graduate student or recent graduate with knowledge of international environmental issues and understanding of the role that scientific information plays in formulating environmental policy.
Requirements: Strong quantitative abilities and experience in using statistics and math to interpret data; advanced knowledge of spreadsheet and database software; ability to manipulate large data sets while maintaining an eye for detail; knowledge of global and international geography and environmental issues; an affinity for graphic design and data visualization.

OVERVIEW

World Resources Institute (WRI) is an environmental think tank that goes beyond research to create practical ways to protect the planet and improve people's lives. Its mission is to urge humans to live in ways that protect Earth's environment for current and future generations. Specifically, WRI is concerned with biological resources, climate change, sustainable enterprise, and access. WRI is trying to reverse rapid degradation of ecosystems and assure their capacity to provide humans with needed goods and services, while protecting the global climate system from further harm due to emissions of greenhouse gases. WRI is also interested in developing markets and enterprises to expand economic opportunity and protect the environment and to guarantee public access to information and decisions regarding natural resources and the environment.

WRI accepts interns to help manage the Web site. The successful applicant will help to fulfill WRI's mission of guaranteeing public access to information and analysis related to sustainable development and the environment. Major responsibilities include helping to plan and maintain EarthTrends: The Environmental Information Portal. More specifically, the intern will work with the global information program to maintain and improve the EarthTrends Web site, help with research, and help with updating the EarthTrends database, a comprehensive collection of environmental, social, and economic indicators drawn from over 40 international data providers.

HOW TO APPLY

Candidates should send a cover letter and resume to the preceding address. No phone calls.

FRIENDS COMMITTEE ON NATIONAL LEGISLATION (FCNL) INTERNSHIP

Intern Coordinator, FCNL
245 Second Street, NE
Washington, DC 20002
(202) 547-6000
Fax: (202) 547-6019 (use only for sending references)
http://www.fcnl.org/intern.htm

What You Can Earn: $14,000 for 11 months of work; social security and taxes are taken out of paychecks. Interns also receive health benefits, paid sick leave and vacation, and mass-transit fare assistance. Most interns and junior staff share housing and other expenses.
Application Deadlines: Applications are accepted from January 10 to March 1.
Educational Experience: College degrees or equivalent experience, of any age; typically, recent college graduates who can afford to live on low pay fill these positions. Many different majors are considered.
Requirements: Computer literacy, good writing skills, research skills, and a solid command of Eng-

lish. Applicants with less than a 3.0 GPA will be at a stark disadvantage given the competitiveness of the selection process.

OVERVIEW

The Friends Committee on National Legislation (FCNL) is a public-interest lobby founded in 1943 by members of the Religious Society of Friends (Quakers) that brings the concerns, experiences, and testimonies of Quakers to bear on policy decisions in the nation's capital.

People of many religious backgrounds participate in this work with a nationwide network of thousands of people to advocate social and economic justice, peace, and good government. FCNL is a public-interest lobby, not a political-action committee nor a special-interest lobby. The group's multi-issue advocacy connects historic Quaker testimonies on peace, equality, simplicity, and truth, with peace and social justice issues

Over the years, FCNL's legislative goals have included eliminating nuclear weapons and other weapons of mass destruction; banning landmines and halting sales of weapons to human rights abusers; peaceful prevention of deadly conflict; abolition of the death penalty; advancement of civil rights and liberties; and ensuring that all Americans have access to the basic necessities.

As an intern, you'll have the chance to use your skills and knowledge to further FCNL's legislative goals. While your specific duties will depend on the issues you cover and the lobbyist with whom you work, you might advocate, encouraging constituents and members of Congress to take action by providing them with information. You may also help gather information, attending committee hearings and coalition meetings and analyzing documents and reports. You will also help write action alerts, letters, and background reports to keep constituents informed and to express FCNL's views to Congress and the government. You'll also be expected to encourage action, supporting and communicating with grassroots advocates. Also, FCNL sometimes has specific internship opportunities in the field or publications programs.

You'll work as a full-time member of FCNL's staff for 11 months, from early September through the end of July. Prospective interns should demonstrate a deep commitment to making their community a better place. Interns help where needed: on the Web site, in publications, answering inquiries from the public, and attending to requests for products. Although your tasks and responsibilities will vary with the type of internship you are given, each intern is given a great deal of responsibility and plenty of room to succeed. FCNL provides training, guidance, individualized instruction, and close supervision to new interns. Interns must be independent but always work with experienced professionals in their assigned field work, communications work, or legislative action.

FCNL interns don't do direct lobbying with U. S. senators and representatives, and there's no guarantee that you'll get to work on a favorite issue or have a particular supervisor. In fact, some interns work for two supervisors on two different organizational functions. However, an intern's interests and experience are taken into consideration in making ultimate assignments. Interns at FCNL have a great deal of responsibility and are held to high performance standards.

You also should decide if you'll be comfortable working for a small organization where many staffers are Quakers. You'll be working for an organization with religious traditions such as moments of reflective silence before important meetings; however, you don't have to be a Quaker to apply. Diversity in life experience is embraced by FCNL. They do ask about your knowledge of Quakers because interns communicate a great deal with FCNL supporters, many of whom are Quakers. Beyond religious and other types of diversity, the FCNL encourages people of color, people of Native American heritage, and others who are often not fully included in U. S. society to apply.

HOUSING

If selected, you'll be put in touch with other interns in case you want to share an apartment.

HOW TO APPLY

You must be able to let the organization know about what you have to offer on paper and on the telephone, because FCNL does not interview intern candidates in person. To download the intern application guidelines and information packet, visit this Web site: http://www.fcnl.org/pdfs/intern/preapp.pdf. Then visit this link to download the intern application: http://www.fcnl.org/pdfs/intern/NEWAPP05.pdf.

You may fill out the application by hand, although typing is appreciated, or you may download the forms and complete the application on your computer. Most applicants hand-print their answers on the form and type their essays on separate pages, which they attach.

References are important. You should ask each prospective reference if she or he is willing to write a letter about your qualities and qualification, in addition to sending in the reference form with the checklist. If the person can't take time, you'll be disadvantaged. It's best to select people as references who know your talents but who aren't family members and who don't have a business relationship with your family. While a friend can serve as a personal reference, it works best when that friend can describe your efforts as a volunteer or leader or how you furthered a social cause.

When complete, forward the application along with transcripts and four references directly to FCNL at the preceding address. Applicants who do get the entire package in on time (by March 1) are given preference. When an intern candidate's folder still lacks transcripts or references or other materials three weeks after the deadline, the candidate is no longer considered. By the second or third week of March, you should e-mail the intern coordinator (pat@fcnl.org) to make sure that everything has been received.

You should receive some type of formal response in six weeks. Those who make the first cut will receive a letter and will be more seriously considered. Any interviews with the intern coordinator or with possible supervisors will be by phone. Final decisions aren't usually made before the end of April.

GOVERNMENT ACCOUNTABILITY PROJECT INTERNSHIP

Government Accountability Project
1612 K Street, NW, Suite 1100
Washington, DC 20006
(202) 408-0034, ext. 156
Fax: (202) 408-9855
shelleyw@whistleblower.org
http://www.whistleblower.org

What You Can Earn: Unpaid.
Application Deadlines: Rolling.
Educational Experience: None specified.
Requirements: A team player with initiative, flexibility, and creativity. Organizational, writing, and research skills are a plus. Full-time applicants are preferred, but part-time interns will be considered.

OVERVIEW

The Government Accountability Project (GAP) is a nonprofit public-interest organization that seeks to protect the public interest by promoting government and corporate accountability through advancing occupational free speech and ethical conduct, defending whistleblowers, and empowering citizen activists.

GAP provides legal and advocacy support to employees who "blow the whistle" on unlawful conduct and other practices that endanger public health, safety, and the environment. Focusing on the areas of nuclear-weapons oversight, national security, food safety, environmental enforcement, and general whistleblower protection, GAP uses an activist strategy that combines litigation, policy advocacy, media and legislative outreach, and coalition building to both defend whistleblowers and seek reform around their underlying disclosures. GAP is a 27-year-old national organization with offices in Washington, D.C., and Seattle and the equivalent of 20 full-time staff. GAP's activities include policy advocacy, litigation, legislative outreach, media campaigns, and coalition building. Current areas of emphasis include nuclear safety, food and drug safety, environmental enforcement, worker health and safety, and international whistleblower policymaking.

The summer development intern in the GAP's D.C. office is ideal for an energetic self-starter seeking professional experience in the nonprofit field. If you're chosen as an intern, you'll research new foundations and funding opportunities; help launch a major donor recognition program; compile development materials; and perform other fund-raising tasks as needed.

HOW TO APPLY

To apply, e-mail a copy of your resume and a cover letter to the preceding address, putting "Development Internship Application" in the subject line.

GREENBELT ALLIANCE INTERNSHIPS

Volunteer Application
631 Howard Street, Suite 510
San Francisco, CA 94105
volunteer@greenbelt.org

What You Can Earn: Unpaid; college credit possible.
Application Deadlines: Rolling.
Educational Experience: A background in urban/regional planning, political science, or environmental studies.
Requirements: Must be self-motivated, eager to learn, and dedicated to smart-growth issues. Access to a car is helpful but not necessary.

OVERVIEW

The Greenbelt Alliance is the San Francisco Bay Area's leading land conservation and urban planning nonprofit. Founded in 1958, the alliance has worked in partnership with diverse coalitions on public-policy development, advocacy, and education to protect the Bay Area's Greenbelt of open space and promote livable cities.

There are a number of different areas in which you can intern for between five and 40 hours a week for three to six months (unless otherwise indicated in the specific internships below), including in the field offices of East Bay South Bay, Sonoma, Marin, and Solano/Napa field office interns; compact development endorsement team intern; and youth outings.

Compact Development Endorsement Team Internship

In this internship, you'll learn about smart-growth development and livable communities, communicating with local developers, helping with project reviews, maintaining the database of endorsed compact development projects, corresponding with the volunteer team, writing project summaries for the Web site, and helping with program administration. Interns in this office can choose to work between 10 to 20 hours a week for three to six months.

East Bay Field Office Internship

Interns here will work on a variety of key East Bay campaigns, including a Contra Costa County urban limit line, the Alameda County open space funding measure, and smart-growth research projects. Interns will help manage the East Bay office and learn about land-use patterns and policies in Contra Costa and Alameda Counties.

Ideal candidates will have a strong interest in land-use planning, good organizational and communication skills, and the ability to work well independently.

Solano/Napa Field Office Internship

At the Solano/Napa field office, you'll help protect open space and promote transit-oriented development in the Bay Area, conducting land-use and housing research, maintaining databases, helping with public outreach, and learning about grassroots organizing. You'll be trained and meet weekly with the Solano/Napa Field representative at the Greenbelt Alliance field office in Fairfield.

Sonoma/Marin Field Office Internship

In this internship, you can join the Sonoma/Marin field office in protecting open space and promoting transit-oriented development in the Bay Area. You'll conduct land-use and housing research, maintain databases, help with public outreach, and learn about grassroots organizing. Interns must be self-motivated, eager to learn, and dedicated to smart-growth issues. Interns will be trained and meet weekly with the Sonoma/Marin Field representative at the Greenbelt Alliance field office in Santa Rosa.

South Bay Field Office Internship

In this South Bay field office, interns will help protect open space and promote transit-oriented development in the Bay Area. You'll also conduct land-use and housing research, maintain databases, help with public outreach, and learn about grassroots organizing. Interns will be trained and meet weekly with the South Bay Field representative the Greenbelt Alliance field office in San Jose.

Youth Outings Internship

If you like working with kids and you're passionate about the outdoors, you can hone your skills in environmental education by working as a youth-outings intern for 15 to 40 hours a week for between three and six months, beginning in early June and ending in August.

In this internship, you'll work with the education program coordinator to plan, coordinate, and lead outdoor day trips with Bay Area youth. This internship also includes administrative support and one or more projects such as recruiting new youth groups, designing educational activities, or creating volunteer training materials.

HOW TO APPLY

To intern with Greenbelt Alliance, send a resume and cover letter to the preceding address.

HABITAT FOR HUMANITY— NEW YORK CITY INTERNSHIP

Internship Coordinator
334 Furman Street
Brooklyn, NY 11201
(718) 246-5656 ext. 305
Fax: (718) 246-2787
pavbuckley@habitatnyc.org

What You Can Earn: Unpaid.
Application Deadlines: Rolling.
Educational Experience: Have successfully completed one year of full undergraduate coursework and maintained a GPA of 3.0 or higher.
Requirements: Minimum age is 16; be willing to sign an internship agreement and commit to at least 10 hours a week for at least 100 hours of service.

OVERVIEW

Habitat-NYC's internship program provides opportunities for individuals enrolled in higher education to work with Habitat-NYC staff members to assist in the creation of new programs and systems. Habitat-NYC internships are excellent opportunities for students to gain practical work experience and learn new skills while earning academic credit. Habitat for Humanity-New York City transforms lives and the city by uniting all New Yorkers around the cause of decent, affordable housing for everyone.

Founded in 1984 as an independent affiliate of Habitat for Humanity International, Habitat-NYC builds in four boroughs: the Bronx, Brooklyn, Manhattan, and Queens. The group completes about 25 houses a year. Recent projects include 13 newly constructed row houses in the Mott Haven neighborhood of the Bronx and a 10-unit condominium building in Harlem. New projects will begin in Brooklyn, Harlem, and Queens.

Interns and volunteers build the homes with the "sweat equity" of family partner homeowners who work side-by-side with volunteers. Professional contractors build the exterior shells to code, and volunteers do the interior construction. Each year, more than 10,000 New Yorkers from faith institutions, corporations, schools, and civic groups come to build and learn more about how to help solve New York's affordable-housing crisis.

In addition to building homes, Habitat-NYC is a leading advocate for affordable housing. Its goal is to ensure that every New Yorker has a decent, affordable home by creating a social movement to end the housing crisis plaguing New York City and by calling on elected officials to make affordable housing a priority.

HOW TO APPLY

Contact the intern coordinator at the preceding address for an application.

HEIFER INTERNATIONAL INTERNSHIP

Heifer International, Internship Coordinator
PO Box 8058
Little Rock, AR 72203
(800) 422-0474; (800) 422-1311
Fax: (501) 907-2820
tim.ogborn@heifer.org
http://www.heifer.org

What You Can Earn: $7 an hour.
Application Deadlines: Mid-June.
Educational Experience: Bachelor's degree in an area relevant to the organization (international development, agriculture, community development, and so on); currently enrolled in a postgraduate

program in a relevant area; experience carrying out policy analysis, preferably in the area of Heifer's work.

Requirements: Ability to analyze and synthesize complex policy documentation; self confidence; self motivation; ability to write clear and concise reports; knowledge of international development, particularly in the areas of agriculture and community development; knowledge of Heifer's work both in the United States and internationally; and knowledge of the NGO/PVO approach and of global sustainable development essential. International knowledge of hunger organizations is desirable.

OVERVIEW

Heifer International has a unique and successful approach to ending hunger and poverty. Since 1944, Heifer has provided food- and income-producing animals and training to millions of resource-poor families in 115 countries. Giving microcredit in the form of livestock promotes self-reliance, which builds self-esteem and helps families lift themselves out of poverty. Milk, eggs, wool, draft power, and benefits from the animals provide families with food and income. Selected appropriately and managed well, animals improve nutrition and help families earn money for education, clothes, healthcare, better housing, and starting a small business.

Heifer's grassroots approach lets people make their own decisions about how to improve their lives. As partners work together to overcome obstacles, they strengthen their communities and foster democracy. By training partners in environmentally sound, sustainable agriculture practices, Heifer makes lasting change possible. At the heart of Heifer's philosophy is the commitment families make to "pass on the gift," by sharing one or more of their animal's offspring with other families in need. Helping others ensures dignity and multiplies the benefits of the original gift from generation to generation. Heifer's time-tested approach helps build stronger fami-

lies, gender equity, vibrant communities, and a healthier planet.

If you're a graduate intern intrigued by Heifer's program, you can apply as a summer intern to carry out research and analysis of federal government agricultural and foreign policy in relation to Heifer's priorities and identify potential federal money. The detailed work program will be coordinated and supported closely between the senior managing director in Washington, D.C., and the director of foundation relations in Little Rock. This four-month internship should take about six hours a week.

As an intern, you'll develop experience in policy research and writing of policy papers; an understanding of the federal government's farm and international development policies and departments; experience with and knowledge of other international development organizations in Washington, D.C.; and a good understanding of Heifer International and its work.

The work program will consist of a combination of Internet research and telephone or face-to-face interviews or meetings with agency and federal government staff. You'll help collate and analyze relevant key government policy and funding documentation, Web sites, and other information resources relevant to Heifer's programs; contact key government staff as appropriate to develop a better understanding of federal policies and programs; contact relevant InterAction and other PVO staff members as appropriate; and write an interim report after two months, identifying likely key areas for more detailed investigation. In addition, you'll develop two- or three-page documents identifying and describing key potential funding possibilities and write a final report providing overall analysis of relevant federal policy and potential money, identifying areas for future priority.

HOW TO APPLY

To apply, e-mail your resume and cover letter to the senior managing director at the preceding e-mail address.

INITIATIVE FOR A COMPETITIVE INNER CITY INTERNSHIP

Initiative for a Competitive Inner City
727 Atlantic Avenue, Suite 600
Boston, MA 02111
(617) 292-2363
Fax: (617) 292-2380
jpoulos@icicHR.org
http://www.icicHR.org

What You Can Earn: Paid.
Application Deadlines: May 31.
Educational Experience: A background in economic development is helpful but not necessary.
Requirements: Self-motivated individual with strong writing skills, a sense of humor, good organizational skills, and familiarity with basic office software. An interest in the health and vitality of America's inner cities is a plus; minimum commitment of 15 to 20 hours a week in a flexible schedule.

OVERVIEW

The Initiative for a Competitive Inner City (ICIC) is a national nonprofit organization founded in 1994 by Harvard Business School Professor Michael E. Porter. ICIC's mission is to build healthy economies in America's inner cities in order to create jobs, income, and wealth for local residents. The group tries to provide cities with a new vision of economic development and engage the resources of the private sector to accelerate inner-city business growth. ICIC changes perceptions and unites corporate and civic leaders to take action, believing that an inner-city renaissance is possible.

ICIC seeks to replace the traditional focus on urban blight and community deficiencies with a more constructive focus on market opportunities. Working from a distinctive market-based approach, ICIC has gained national recognition for generating cutting-edge solutions. ICIC also brings together community and business leaders to put ideas into practice.

The intern with ICIC will work from mid-June to the end of August and may help doing grant research and writing; donor database management; project management; filing; and donor follow-up. These tasks will vary week by week and are based on upcoming deadlines and events. The two members of the development department will supervise the position.

HOW TO APPLY

To apply, forward a cover letter and resume via e-mail (preferred), fax, or regular mail to the preceding address.

INTERNATIONAL CENTER FOR TOLERANCE EDUCATION INTERNSHIP

International Center for Tolerance, Internship Coordinator
25 Washington Street, 4th Floor
Brooklyn, NY 11201
(718) 237-6262
Fax: (718) 237-6264
icte@tmf-tolerance.org
http://www.seedsoftolerance.org

What You Can Earn: Unpaid.
Application Deadlines: Mid-May.
Educational Experience: None specified.
Requirements: Attention to detail and very organized, motivated, and self-directed, with solid writing, research, and computer skills. Good phone skills and program knowledge of Excel and Word

a must. An interest in human rights and child-oriented tolerance education and with basic office administration is important.

OVERVIEW

The International Center for Tolerance Education (ICTE) is a laboratory for innovative ideas in the field of tolerance education and human rights. The center promotes conferences and houses a scholar retreat. Special features are the Commons, where the ICTE guests collaborate, and the Human Rights Atelier for helping young activists and creating new ideas. The goal of ICTE is to promote the field of tolerance education on a global scale by encouraging individuals and projects that enable children and their families to participate in a vibrant and inclusive society.

Interns at ICTE will work either as an assistant to the director or in a technology internship.

Assistant to the Director

This intern will work with the director on short- and long-term projects, conducting research (such as for potential grantees or peer grant makers); processing grant proposals for guest offices, Incubator Projects, and other special projects; and maintaining files and assisting in correspondence and administration.

ComCon Internship

Interns in the ComCon program may help with evening events (panels, lectures, screenings, and so on) to one- to three-day conferences, video-teleconferences, and more. Students must commit to the full duration of the Commons event and attend a half-day center training orientation prior to the event.

Applicants should have strong social skills and the ability to think creatively and be problem solvers under pressure. It's also important to be organized, detail oriented, and self-directed. Some experience with project management or special events is highly desirable.

Technology Intern

This intern will help develop ICTE's technology on both physical and virtual levels to build community networks locally and globally. This includes working in one or more of the following areas: network management; research and planning (especially regarding the creation of knowledge networks); database development/administration; general technical assistance; and project-based tech support. Interns should be intuitive and thorough researchers and creative thinkers. Interns should also be able to document findings and be techno-lovers with sympathy for newbies. Basic design skills including knowledge of Photoshop and PowerPoint are a plus.

HOW TO APPLY

To apply for any of these three internships, e-mail copies of your resume, statement of interest, and references with the appropriate subject heading to the preceding e-mail address. Candidates for the assistant to the director internship should put "ASSIST INTERN" in the subject heading; candidates for the technology internship should put interns "TECH INTERN" in the subject heading; candidates for the ComCon internship should put "COMCON" in the subject heading.

INTERNATIONAL DIPLOMACY COUNCIL INTERNSHIP

Office Coordinator
155 Sansome Street, Suite 600
San Francisco, CA 94104
(415) 986-1388
Drice@diplomacy.org
http://www.diplomacy.org

What You Can Earn: Unpaid.
Application Deadlines: Rolling.
Educational Experience: None specified.
Requirements: Attention to detail; ability to work as part of a team.

OVERVIEW

International Diplomacy Council (IDC) is a 50-year-old nonprofit organization that advances citizen diplomacy by providing professional, cultural, and educational meetings between emerging foreign leaders and the San Francisco Bay Area community. These emerging foreign leaders are selected by American embassies overseas and travel to the United States under the auspices of the U.S. State Department. Among the prestigious alumni are nearly 1,000 cabinet ministers and 150 current and former heads of state, including Margaret Thatcher, Anwar Sadat, Indira Gandhi, and Tony Blair.

Global Voices Education Enrichment Program Internship

The Global Voices Program is a vital part of IDC's mission to promote understanding and respect between the people of the United States and other nations. As an intern here, you'll play a key role in providing Bay Area schools with the opportunity to meet with IDC's international visitors.

You should be prepared to spend at least two days a week (10 hours a week), but more time is even better. While you're here, you'll help arrange appointments for IDC's international visitors to speak in Bay Area schools, and attend school visits whenever possible. You'll also work closely with instructors to develop detailed presentation content to prepare both guest speakers and students for school visits, maintain relationships with schools already involved in the Education Enrichment Program, particularly in noting their visitor preferences and keeping them advised of upcoming visitors. You'll also track programs and record information regarding visits, continue outreach to introduce the EEP program to new schools and teachers, and research teacher interests and curriculum needs.

Candidates should be creative, articulate, dependable, well organized, comfortable working independently as well as with a team, with excellent communication skills and an interest in international affairs and education.

Marketing & Membership Internship

As an intern in this department, you'll help recruit members and increase the visibility of the International Diplomacy Council in the Bay Area. This position incorporates strategic development, marketing, and administrative duties, and you'll be responsible for developing and implementing projects that will help the marketing and membership department run efficiently.

You'll help maintain and track new member prospects; mail weekly prospect packets to prospective members; compile prospect packets for corporate/foundation prospects; and create reports demonstrating the progress of the prospect program. You'll also create summaries of the work by IDC; create IDC statistics' pages for Web site and marketing materials; and create one-page article summaries about IDC programs based on prior months' visitors. You'll also review returned evaluation forms, log reviews of meetings, and create marketing pieces for IDC newsletter and marketing materials; follow up with Bay Area program participants to solicit feedback; follow up via e-mail with international visitors on feedback; maintain a list of community organizations to contact for membership or professional resources; and help with events and programs. This internship requires a minimum of 12 hours a week (more hours are desirable) for three days a week, for at least three months.

HOW TO APPLY

To apply for the marketing/membership internship, e-mail a resume and cover letter to the development associate at Tim@diplomacy.org.

To apply for the education enrichment internship, e-mail a resume and cover letter to Drice@diplomacy.org.

MEDIARIGHTS INTERNSHIP

Internship Coordinator
104 West 14th Street, 4th Floor
New York, NY 10011

(646) 230-288
Fax: (646) 230-6328

What You Can Earn: Unpaid.
Application Deadlines: Rolling.
Educational Experience: None specified.
Requirements: Familiarity with Macintosh computers and programs; good communications skills; good organizational skills; ability to assist several different projects simultaneously. Also helpful to have media experience, good proofreading skills, be a fast learner, and have high energy. See individual tracks for specific requirements.

OVERVIEW

MediaRights is an innovative Internet-based company bringing together social activists and filmmakers, funded by the Ford Foundation. Launched in 2000, MediaRights was founded with the aim of encouraging new partnerships and collaboration, promoting innovative media about social issues, and finding new audiences for social issue documentaries. This nonprofit organization helps media makers, educators, librarians, nonprofits, and activists use documentaries to encourage action and inspire dialogue on contemporary social issues.

The nonprofit company helps members find films on certain topics, organize events around a specific film, or make more meaningful films about issues in members' communities. The group also helps social-activist documentary filmmakers find resources (everything from funders to equipment to viewers to buyers).

The site specializes in social-issue documentaries (nonfiction films or videos that address human rights or environmental issues) and advocacy videos (usually short formats produced by or for an organization working toward social change). Documentaries that feature dramatizations, poetical vignettes, or narrative voiceovers are also available.

If you're interested in learning about documentary filmmaking while you learn to use the media

to promote human rights, racial justice, and environmental protection, an internship at this company could be for you.

Interns work for two or three days a week for two to four months, learning how a Web-based nonprofit promotes social change through promoting and distributing social-issue documentaries. As an intern, you'll be assigned a specific track depending on your interests and skills. In general, interns help out with office tasks, public relations, marketing, research, outreach, maintenance of Web site databases, occasional errand running, proofreading, and writing. The specific internship tracks include the following departments: outreach; marketing and publicity; Web development; and membership.

Marketing/Publicity

In this department, you'll spearhead outreach and promotion, initiate online partnerships, and help with events planning and press kits. You'll be involved in every aspect of publicity, from planning to execution and evaluation of information and communications strategies that present the organization to the media, public, and members. You'll help write press releases and work on getting media coverage, and also develop ways to keep current members and attract new ones.

For this internship, you should have experience and interest in organizing public-relations activities from soup to nuts, along with excellent writing and communication skills and the ability to think creatively and strategically.

You also should be able to handle high-quality research and meet simultaneous demands while paying close attention to detail. You should be a highly motivated self-starter, able to work independently and as members of a team, and be committed to activism.

Outreach Development Internship

Interns in this department coordinate research and development for the filmmaker, educator/librarian, and workshops. You'll attend programs and offsite events and workshops, help coordinate the traveling "Media That Matters Film Festival," manage the conference database, and help with conference travel and itineraries.

To qualify for this internship, you should have excellent research, writing, and oral communication skills and be able to think creatively and strategically. You also should be able to handle high-quality research and meet simultaneous demands while paying close attention to detail. You should be a highly motivated self-starter, able to work independently and as a member of a team, and be committed to activism.

Membership

Interns in this department will be responsible for organizing publication of the monthly e-mail newsletter, analyzing site usability, and managing membership databases. You should have experience in writing/editing for a Web audience and be able to think creatively and strategically while meeting multiple simultaneous demands and paying close attention to detail. Ideal candidates will be highly motivated self-starters able to work independently and as members of a team. A commitment to activism is essential.

Web Development

If you like Internet work, you might be interested in this internship, where you'll help out the Web staff with office, publishing, and online duties. You'll also maintain hardware and develop the database, help develop the Web site and desktop publishing, and manage site traffic.

For this internship, you should have excellent research, writing, and oral communication skills and be able to think creatively and strategically. You'll also need experience in data gathering and analysis (traffic, e-mail opt-ins, and so on), with at least two years in Web site production, including experience with HTML, Photoshop, Flash, MYSQL, and content management systems.

HOW TO APPLY

Interested applicants should e-mail a resume and cover letter to the preceding address.

MERCK FAMILY FUND INTERNSHIP

Fund Administrator
303 Adams Street
Milton, MA 02186
(617) 696-3580
Fax: (617) 696-7262
http://www.merckff.org
merck@merckff.org

What You Can Earn: $1,400 per month for a four-day work week.
Application Deadlines: Rolling.
Educational Experience: Currently pursuing or have completed an undergraduate degree.
Requirements: A genuine committed to the fund's mission; excellent verbal and written communication skills; demonstrable ability to write clear, concise, meaningful reports and articles; comfortable with Macintosh computers, MS Word, Excel, PowerPoint, Adobe PageMaker, and FileMaker software and familiar with Internet research; highly organized; comfortable working in a small office; integrity, curiosity, and a sense of humor.

OVERVIEW

The Merck Family Fund is a private foundation that makes grants to U.S. nonprofit organizations in two areas: the environment and the urban community. Grants for the environment are designed to help restore and protect the natural environment and ensure a healthy planet for future generations. The fund supports projects that protect and restore vital eastern U.S. ecosystems (forests of TN, KY, SC, GA, VA, NH, ME, VT, and coastal wetlands of SC) and that promote sustainable consumption and sustainable economics by individuals, institutions, communities, businesses, and as public policies. Urban grants strengthen the social fabric and physical landscape of the urban community. The fund supports grassroots organizations in Boston, Providence, and New York City that create green and open space and support youth as agents of social change through youth organizing.

Full-time (four days a week) academic year internships are available from September to May. Based on the intern's interests and skills and the needs of the fund, the intern's duties will include helping with publications and grants. The intern will help compile research materials and write white papers, reports, and evaluations and newsletters and create charts, graphs, and maps for inclusion in publications and reports. The intern also will evaluate grant proposals and draft summaries for the board of directors.

The intern also will research issues dealing with program areas, including sustainable consumption and economics, protecting forest-based eastern U.S. ecosystems, creating green and open space, and youth organizing in underserved communities.

HOW TO APPLY

To apply, e-mail, mail, or fax your cover letter, resume, and a brief writing sample (preferably an article or research report) together with a list of three references to the preceding address.

NATIONAL CAMPAIGN TO PREVENT TEEN PREGNANCY INTERNSHIP

National Campaign to Prevent Teen Pregnancy
1776 Massachusetts Avenue, NW, Suite 200
Washington, DC 20036
(202) 478-8500
Fax: (202) 478-8588
research@teenpregnancy.org
http://www.teenpregnancy.org

What You Can Earn: Unpaid.
Application Deadlines: May 20.
Educational Experience: Coursework in basic statistics a plus.
Requirements: Strong computer skills; thorough command of written and spoken English; experience with word processing (WordPerfect or Word), spreadsheet (Excel or Quattro Pro), and presentation (PowerPoint or Presentations) applications, as well as Internet proficiency; demonstrable interest/background in teen pregnancy; ability to work independently; flexibility to handle multiple tasks; office experience.

OVERVIEW

The National Campaign to Prevent Teen Pregnancy, founded in February 1996, is a nonprofit, nonpartisan initiative trying to improve the well-being of children, teens, and families by reducing teen pregnancy. The campaign's goal is to reduce the teen pregnancy rate dramatically.

To reduce teenage pregnancy, the campaign tries to raise awareness of the issue and to attract new voices and resources to the cause. It provides concrete assistance to those already working in the field and tries to ease the many disagreements that have plagued both national and local efforts to address this problem. To reach the goal of reducing the teen pregnancy rate, the campaign tries to build a more coordinated and effective grassroots movement; influence cultural values and messages by working with the entertainment media; enlist the help of the media; support state and local action; build common ground and reduce conflict; and make sure that everyone's efforts are based on knowledge about what works.

The campaign takes a multidisciplinary approach to teen pregnancy prevention, viewing teen pregnancy as a problem related to maternal and child health, economic development, family strengthening, youth development, and crime prevention, among other issues.

Campaign interns will help the research department update fact sheets with new data on pregnancy, childbearing, sexual activity, and contraceptive use; write new fact sheets with existing statistics on sexual activity and contraceptive use; and help with administrative tasks such as mailings and meeting planning.

HOW TO APPLY

To apply for this internship, fax, e-mail, or mail your resume with a cover letter including your desired schedule (full time or part time, hours per week, and start/end dates) to the National Campaign to at the preceding address. (No phone calls.) Only individuals selected for an interview will be contacted.

NATIONAL ENVIRONMENTAL LAW CENTER INTERNSHIP

National Environmental Law Center,
   Internship Coordinator
44 Winter Street, 4th floor
Boston, MA 02108
(617) 422-0880
Fax: (617) 422-0881
nelc@nelconline.org
http://www.nelconline.org

What You Can Earn: Unpaid.
Application Deadlines: Rolling.
Educational Experience: Undergraduates.
Requirements: Flexibility; comfort in working in a campaign-style office; initiative; excellent writing skills; good judgment; a commitment to environmental protection; the capacity for outrage and a sense of humor are mandatory.

OVERVIEW

The National Environmental Law Center (NELC) is a nonprofit environmental litigation center dedi-

cated to enforcing antipollution laws and promoting long-term solutions to the nation's most pressing environmental problems. NELC works closely with state and local citizen groups, providing essential legal and scientific expertise. Founded by the State Public Interest Research Groups to take enforcement action against the nation's worst polluters, NELC scientists, lawyers, and policy experts have a proven track record of bringing corporate polluters to justice and translating innovative ideas into practical reforms. On behalf of citizen-plaintiff organizations, NELC obtains court orders to stop illegal discharges of pollutants and secures major penalties against violators of environmental laws. Money from fines and settlements is often directed to local environmental projects in and around affected areas. NELC has a five-person litigation staff, including four attorneys and a paralegal/administrative assistant.

Undergraduate Internship

This year-long intern position is designed to provide support in paralegal and administrative tasks that include maintaining organizational and case files, tracking billable staff hours, updating the legal library, assisting with production of documents and legal filings, handling citizen inquiries, and processing donations. Internships are for the academic year beginning in September, and interns are expected to commit at least 10 weeks during their tenure.

Undergraduate Summer Internship

This position is designed to provide support in paralegal and administrative tasks, including maintaining organizational and case files; tracking billable staff hours; helping to produce documents and legal filings; handling citizen inquiries; and processing donations. These summer internships begin in June. You'll be expected to commit at least 10 weeks from five to 12 hours a week, depending on your availability.

HOW TO APPLY

To apply, e-mail a resume and cover letter to the preceding address.

NATIONAL ORGANIZATION FOR WOMEN (NOW) INTERNSHIP

NOW-NYC Intern Coordinator
150 West 28th Street, Room 304
New York, NY 10001
(212) 627-9895
Fax: (212) 627-9891
http://www.nownyc.org

What You Can Earn: Unpaid.
Application Deadlines: Rolling.
Educational Experience: None specified.
Requirements: Applicants must be professional, responsible, and dedicated to achieving women's rights; requires a minimum of three to five full days a week in the summer and 12 hours a week during the fall and spring semesters.

OVERVIEW

The New York City chapter of the National Organization for Women works to win equality and justice for women and promote social change through action in several key areas, including reproductive rights; lesbian, bisexual, and transgender women's rights; the rights of older and younger women and girls; and the elimination of violence against women and racism, colorism, and ethnicism.

As a feminist intern, you'll have the opportunity to research and design fact sheets on a topic, write articles for the bimonthly newsletter, draft letters to governmental officials, and take on projects of vital importance to NOW-NYC's activism and infrastructure. Interns work with issue-action committees (Anti-Violence, Emergency Campaign for Judicial Justice, Eliminating Racism, Lesbian/Bi/Transgender Rights, Older Women's Rights, Reproductive Rights, and Young Women's and Girls' Rights) and chapter-development task forces (Web site development, newsletter, fund-raising, membership, and publicity).

HOW TO APPLY

To apply, submit a cover letter indicating where you learned about the internship, what you hope to gain from the internship, and what you can give to NOW-NYC, along with your resume and a two- to three-page page writing sample to the intern coordinator at the preceding address.

NEW AMERICAN DREAM COMMUNICATIONS INTERNSHIP

Center for a New American Dream
6930 Carroll Avenue, Suite 900
Takoma Park, MD 20912-4466
newdream@newdream.org

What You Can Earn: Paid internships earn $1,250 a month, plus medical insurance, four weeks paid vacation, and public transportation commuting reimbursement; unpaid internships may receive college credit.
Application Deadlines: End of May for paid internships; rolling application for unpaid internships.
Educational Experience: College graduate for paid positions; undergraduates for unpaid positions.
Requirements: Creative, highly organized, able to juggle multiple tasks; excellent verbal and written communications skills; some communications training and/or experience; persuasive; loves our mission; Internet literacy; an intuitive grasp of human motivations and needs; a quick learner.

OVERVIEW

This Washington, D.C., nonprofit organization helps Americans consume responsibly to protect the environment, conserve natural resources, counter commercialization, and promote positive changes in the way goods are produced and consumed. The group works with individuals, institutions, communities, and businesses to conserve natural resources, counter commercialization, and promote positive changes in the way goods are produced and consumed.

Internships are available in several different areas: a paid internship in the communications and institutional purchasing departments, an unpaid internship in the general internship.

Communications Internship

Interns in the organization's communications department work with from 9:00 A.M. to 5:00 P.M. Monday through Thursday to help with media outreach, marketing, membership recruiting, writing and proofreading, and a variety of other communications efforts. Interns also help conduct research to support media efforts, track media-related activities, provide administrative support, write and proofread the organization newsletter, and help with general administrative work.

Institutional Purchasing Internship

Interns for this paid position in the organization's communications department work for one year, from 9:00 A.M. to 5:00 P.M. Monday through Thursday, to help with cutting-edge work helping state and local governments and other large institutions buy environmentally preferable products and services. The intern will help gather and analyze the latest data to promote environmentally preferable purchasing in specific product areas. Current research areas include cleaning products, hybrid electric vehicles, paper, renewable energy, and computers. The intern also will contact constituents to generate involvement, gather information, and solicit feedback on various initiatives. These tasks include telephone research and participation in meetings. The intern also will help research and write about environmentally preferable products and services for the Web site, publications, newsletters, media pieces, presentations, and so on. Finally, the intern will help support staff, attend meetings, organize events, and perform administrative work and so on.

The ideal candidate should have a bachelor's degree (master's preferred); excellent research, writing, and verbal skills; basic quantitative skills; flexibility; the ability to juggle multiple tasks simultaneously; and the ability to work well both individually and as part of a team. Familiarity with environmentally responsible business practices and products, the automotive and paper industries, and/or renewable energy is desirable.

Unpaid General Internship

These interns help the center fulfill its mission of working with individuals, communities, and institutions to establish sustainable practices that will ensure a healthy planet for future generations. You should be interested or experienced in issues related to sustainable consumption, the environment, or social justice. Here you'll have some general administrative responsibilities (no more than one third of the time spent in the office), but you'll work largely in their respective area of assignment for eight hours a week in the fall or spring for college credit.

Unpaid internships are available throughout the year when appropriate projects are available.

HOW TO APPLY
Unpaid or Credit Internship

Review the program descriptions and then send a cover letter, resume, and a two- to four-page writing sample to the preceding address (attention: "Unpaid/Credit Internship.") In your cover letter, describe how much time you'd like to commit each week; what days and for how long you're available; and what specific areas you'd like to support or the staff for whom you'd like to work. The center will review your responses and application materials to see if there is a good match.

Paid Internships

To apply, send a cover letter, resume, and two- to four-page writing sample to the preceding address. You may e-mail applications for the purchasing internship to kelly@newdream.org or to robin@newdream.org for the communications internship.

THE NEW PRESS INTERNSHIP

The New Press, Internship Coordinator
38 Greene Street, 4th Floor
New York, NY 10013
(212) 629-8617
lkerobyan@thenewpress.com

What You Can Earn: $25 per day stipend, free books, plus a monthly Metrocard; academic credit can be arranged.
Application Deadlines: Rolling.
Educational Experience: None specified.
Requirements: Strong word-processing, communication, and office-management skills, as well as a strong interest in publishing.

OVERVIEW

Established in 1990 as a major alternative to large, commercial publishers, The New Press is a nonprofit publishing house operated editorially in the public interest. It is committed to publishing works of educational, cultural, and community value that, despite their intellectual merits, might not be considered profitable enough for commercial publishers. Like PBS and NPR, The New Press aims to provide ideas and viewpoints that are under-represented in the mass media. Since publishing its first book in 1992, The New Press has been widely hailed as a leading trade publisher.

The New Press relies heavily on the help of interns, treating them in many respects the way salaried assistants are treated at other publishing houses. This means far greater exposure to interesting work than is normally given to interns, but it also calls for a much greater degree of responsibility. The New York office is large and efficient enough to offer a wide spectrum of experience but small and casual enough for interns to form intimate and lasting bonds with the staff they'll be supporting.

As an intern, The New Press is guided by its nonprofit mission and not by earning a profit, but otherwise it functions in many ways as a commercial trade publisher: It identifies new authors, generally pays standard advances and royalties, and distributes its books nationwide. Many commercially successful authors (such as Studs Terkel, Howard Zinn, Marguerite Duras, and James Loewen) have published their books with The New Press to support nonprofit publishing principles.

Its internship program offers a unique opportunity to gain hands-on experience in book publishing through intensive work at a nonprofit, public-interest publisher. Interns spend one month in each of the following four departments (publicity, marketing/administration, development/finance, and editorial/production) and are expected to provide general clerical assistance throughout their stay. Each intern post comes with its own specific and challenging duties, so you'll become familiar with a wide array of skills and techniques.

In addition to providing general office assistance, you'll evaluate manuscripts, write reader's reports and press releases, and carry out specialized projects as assigned. Bi-weekly lunch seminars will provide you with an in-depth understanding of the book-publication process and expose you to the different career paths available in the industry. The four-month internships are full time, from 9:30 A.M. to 5:30 P.M. Monday through Friday. Summer work hours are in effect from Memorial Day until Labor Day and are 9:15 A.M. to 6:00 P.M. Monday through Thursday and 9:15 A.M.. to 1:00 P.M. on Fridays.

HOW TO APPLY

To apply, mail your resume and at least two references with phone numbers, a cover letter briefly describing your skills and interests, what you hope to gain from the internship, and your available dates to the preceding address. Appropriate candidates will be called for an interview. Applications submitted without a cover letter will not be considered. You also may e-mail your resume, cover letter, and references (as attachments in .doc or .rtf formats) to lkerobyan@thenewpress.com. No phone calls.

PEACEWORKS FOUNDATION INTERNSHIP

Peaceworks Foundation
PO Box 1577
Old Chelsea Station
New York, NY 10113
(212) 897-3985 ext. 233
Fax: (212) 897-3986
http://www.silentnolonger.org

What You Can Earn: Unpaid.
Application Deadlines: May 15.
Educational Experience: None specified.
Requirements: Proficiency in computers and Microsoft Office (Word, Excel, Access); good interpersonal skills; ability to work in a fast-paced environment; ability to self-motivate.

OVERVIEW

The PeaceWorks Foundation supports creative and innovative efforts to foster understanding, tolerance, and co-existence in regions of conflict through concrete and practical methodologies.

Currently, its major project is an initiative called OneVoice, a global undertaking to amplify the voice of Israeli and Palestinian moderates by empowering them to seize the agenda from violent extremists and achieve broad-based consensus on core issues.

OneVoice is the first undertaking to reassert the will of the people at the grassroots level through a constructive and educative approach, firmly built upon a neutral forum. Interns will help in the efforts of the OneVoice movement, a grassroots undertaking that focuses on the civic empowerment of moderate Israelis and Palestinians who wish for peace and prosperity. The communications and administrative internship is aimed at improving fund-raising, public outreach, event planning, and general organizational communication.

HOW TO APPLY

Submit your resume and cover letter to the program director at the preceding address.

PENDLE HILL SOCIAL JUSTICE INTERNSHIP

Pendle Hill
338 Plush Mill Road
Wallingford, PA 19086
(800) 742-3150; (610) 566-4507, ext. 137
bobbi@pendlehill.org
http://www.pendlehill.org/social_action,_social_
    witness_internships.htm

What You Can Earn: Tuition, room, board, health insurance, and local transportation costs.
Application Deadlines: Rolling.
Educational Experience: People of all backgrounds and levels of experience, from young adults to seasoned and skilled activists.
Requirements: Committed social-justice volunteers 18 and older.

OVERVIEW

Pendle Hill is a Philadelphia-area Quaker center for contemplation and study, which also offers a number of internships each year in social action and social witness. Committed social justice interns are expected to work 20 hours a week on a service/activist project, live in the Quaker retreat center called Pendle Hill, and participate in the resident program (taking classes, using the arts studio, hermitages, library, and so on).

Pendle Hill was founded in 1930 by members of the Religious Society of Friends (Quakers) and is open to people of all faiths. Their educational philosophy is rooted in four basic social testimonies of Friends: equality and respect for individuals; simplicity; inward and outward harmony; and community in daily life and in the seeking of the Spirit.

Internships provide for volunteers working with ongoing Pendle Hill projects in the areas of community and youth development, peace activism and service, criminal justice, and environment/food.

Pendle Hill's Chester project is a youth-development program serving at-risk youth. Interns will assist as program staff and may be involved in many different areas of this work according to their interests and abilities (interns have taught art, poetry, nutrition, and wood-working; they also work on nonviolent conflict resolution, issues of self-esteem, relationships, and restorative justice projects).

Interns may do relevant research for program development and evaluation or be engaged in social action around juvenile-justice issues. Depending on your experience and skill, you may develop new areas of programming for at-risk youth and/or families.

In addition, one or two experienced activists may be accepted on the basis of their proposals for off-campus volunteer work that is a continuation of a current project or that represents a leading not included among current site placements.

HOW TO APPLY

For information and to apply, contact the intern coordinator at the preceding address.

PHYSICIANS FOR SOCIAL RESPONSIBILITY INTERNSHIP

Internship Coordinator
1875 Connecticut Ave., Suite 1012
Washington, DC 20009
Fax: (202) 667-4201
mriley@psr.org
http://www.psr.org/home.cfm?id=internships

What You Can Earn: All internships offer a stipend, but PSR also accepts applications for unpaid internships.

Application Deadlines: Deadlines for applications are two months before the beginning of a term, although dates are flexible.

Educational Experience: Undergraduate and graduate students.

Requirements: Excellent interpersonal, oral, and written communications skills; computer proficiency; and an ability to work independently. Minorities and women are encouraged to apply.

OVERVIEW

Physicians for Social Responsibility (PSR) is a public-policy organization that represents health professionals and concerned citizens, working together for nuclear disarmament, the environment, and an end to gun violence. The group promotes public policies that protect human health from the threats of nuclear war and other weapons of mass destruction, global environmental degradation, and gun violence.

Founded in 1961, the group worked to end atmospheric nuclear testing and then broadened their efforts to educate the public about nuclear war. During the 1990s, PSR helped end nuclear-warhead production and won a ban on all nuclear tests.

Internships begin in three different sessions, in January, May, and September. Interns typically work 40 hours a week for at least three months, although six-month to one-year internships are also available (and are preferred by the health and environment program).

Interns typically help staffers with a full range of program activities, including outreach to members and other activists and developing fact sheets, position papers, and legislative alerts for health professionals and others. Interns also conduct research on PSR issues and attend coalition meetings and some congressional briefings and hearings as needed. Responsibilities may include some clerical and administrative tasks.

Health and Environment

Interns in this department will help with advocacy and public education regarding the health and environmental threats posed by global climate change and by persistent organic pollutants. PSR works through public education, citizen activism, Congressional outreach, participation in the United Nations treaty process, media advocacy, and educational publications.

Gun Violence Prevention Program

Interns here will help with public and physician education about gun violence as a public-health issue. PSR works through public education, citizen activism, Congressional outreach, media advocacy, and educational publications to support policies that prevent violence.

Security Program

In this area, interns will be working to help advocate and inform the public about nuclear arms reduction and elimination, key nuclear arms control treaties, and the impact of nuclear weapons on public health and the environment. Activities include citizen advocacy with Congress, speaker tours, media work, educational publications, and grassroots organizing.

HOW TO APPLY

Interested applicants should send a resume and writing sample with a cover letter stating their program area of interest and dates of availability to the preceding address.

POPULATION SERVICES INTERNATIONAL INTERNSHIPS

Population Services International
1120 19th Street, NW, Suite 600
Washington, DC 20036

(202) 785-0072
Fax: (202) 785-0120
http://www.psi.org

What You Can Earn: Stipend.
Application Deadlines: May 13.
Educational Experience: Currently in a masters program in a related area of study (MPH, MBA, international studies); fluency in English, as well as either French, Spanish, Russian, or Portuguese. Domestic internships are part-time positions, generally for students in the Washington, D.C., area.
Requirements: Two years experience working in a fast-paced office environment; excellent organizational and administrative skills, with special attention to detail; proven ability to manage large workloads and organize work efficiently with minimal supervision; ability to prioritize and perform multiple tasks within deadlines; excellent communication skills; advanced computer skills (MS Office application, including Word and Excel); flexibility, resourcefulness, and the ability to assume varied responsibilities with minimal supervision.

OVERVIEW

Population Services International (PSI) is a nonprofit organization based in Washington, D.C., that harnesses the vitality of the private sector to address the health problems of low-income and vulnerable populations in 70 developing countries. PSI, with programs in safe water/oral rehydration, malaria, nutrition/micronutrients, family planning, and HIV/AIDS, deploys commercial marketing strategies to promote health products, services, and healthy behavior that enable low-income and vulnerable people to lead healthier lives. PSI is now the leading nonprofit social-marketing organization in the world. It has created demand for essential health products and services by using private-sector marketing techniques and innovative communications campaigns to motivate positive changes in health behavior. On the supply side, PSI works with the commercial sector to increase the availability of these products and services at prices that are affordable to at-risk populations. With a bottom-line orientation that is rare among non-profits, PSI social markets products and services for family planning, maternal and child health, and the prevention of AIDS, malaria, and other diseases.

PSI was founded in 1970 to demonstrate that social marketing of contraceptives, managed entirely in the private sector, could succeed under differing circumstances and on different continents. For its first 16 years, PSI worked entirely in family planning (hence the name Population Services International), except for oral rehydration therapy, which it started in 1985. PSI's first HIV/AIDS prevention project (promoting abstinence, fidelity, and condoms) began in 1988. PSI entered the areas of malaria and safe water in the mid-1990s.

If you're committed to providing low-cost, high-quality health products and services to people around the world, PSI may be the place for you to gain valuable work experience while pursuing your studies. Two internships are available with PSI: one in financial services and one in program support for Nigeria, Uganda, and Eastern Europe divisions.

Financial Services

The financial services department intern will have a variety of duties and work on many different projects, including working with accounting software to restore and save field financial reports and help in verifying inventory-reconciliation reports. Interns also will help with monthly net-asset reconciliation, audit documentation and verification, and review inventory reporting and match it to donor or vendor-delivery schedules. Interns also may help with annual compilation of donated commodities, prepare journal entries, and help with monthly currency revaluations and correcting entries. In addition, interns may help the financial services manager with various analyses and special projects and provide administrative support to the financial unit, including photocopying, filing, and so on.

Some financial or accounting experience or a related degree is strongly preferred. The intern must be a detail-oriented self-starter; an interest in international relations, marketing, or public health is a plus.

Program Support in Nigeria, Uganda, and Eastern Europe

Summer interns in this area will help support program-management functions in its Nigeria, Uganda, and Eastern Europe divisions. You'll work with PSI staff in Washington and overseas, but the internship is based in Washington, D.C. You'll help research selected topics (such as health, marketing, and communications); edit and proofread reports; format charts, graphs, and presentations; help write and edit proposals; and create and maintain filing systems. You'll also help with travel arrangements and expense-report preparation; respond to requests for information; manage communications with overseas staff; help monitor contract compliance; help prepare and track budgets and expenditures; and help track procurement and logistics.

The position requires a minimum of 30 hours a week (negotiable) for the months of June, July, and August; demonstrated willingness and ability to work independently and on a team in a cooperative, problem-solving capacity; and research experience. Preference will be given to candidates with an interest in international health and development issues and to candidates who can start the last week of May.

HOW TO APPLY

For the financial internship, apply online at http://sh.webhire.com/servlet/resp/grf?acctid=624 (no calls or e-mails). For the program-support internship, submit applications to eeurope@psi.org.

PRISON ACTIVIST RESOURCE CENTER INTERNSHIP

Internship Coordinator
PO Box 339
Berkeley, CA 94701
(510) 893-4648
http://www.prisonactivist.org/?q=taxonomy_
   menu/9/27/38/40

What You Can Earn: Unpaid but you'll receive a PARC T-shirt, PARC e-mail account, and a transportation stipend.
Application Deadlines: May 15 for summer session (June through August); August 15 for fall session (September through December); December 15 for spring session (February through April); November 15 for January intensive session.
Educational Experience: None specified.
Requirements: Self-motivated; good people skills; attention to detail; good organizational skills; a desire to work in a truly collective environment; and a commitment to or interest in prison abolitionist politics.

OVERVIEW

Prison Activist Resource Center (PARC) is a nonprofit organization that provides support for educators, activists, prisoners, and prisoners' families, building networks for action and producing materials that expose human-rights violations while fundamentally challenging the rapid expansion of a prison industrial complex. This all-volunteer collective believes in abolitionist politics and a non-hierarchical collective structure.

PARC offers interns an opportunity to contribute meaningfully and to grow politically in a number of departments, including outreach and organizing, Web site maintenance, prisoner support, research and materials production, and grassroots fund-raising and development.

PARC interns must make a commitment to volunteer at least 12 hours a week for three months. Although each session has formal start and end dates, there is some flexibility with interns' schedules. The summer session runs for two months, from mid-June through mid-August, but there is also a January intensive session where interns commit to spending 25 hours a week in the office.

As a PARC intern, you'll work with committed and highly motivated organizers whose dedication to and knowledge of prison activism will help you become more effective in your activism for human rights and social justice. As an intern, you'll get valuable work experience and exposure to several Bay Area activist networks. On-the-job training will be provided as necessary. Unless otherwise stated, all internships are based in downtown Oakland, California.

All interns are required to participate in PARC's antiracist organizing work as well as other full collective meetings. The PARC Collective expects all interns to be willing to struggle with and develop with the Collective politically. The group is striving to conduct radical antiracist prison abolitionist work.

Grassroots Funding

This intern will assist in PARC's fund-raising efforts by helping with benefit events and helping to develop a donor base, writing grants, updating the grant database, and expanding the major donor base. Interns should have good phone skills, a desire to learn about and do fund-raising, and a creative approach to raising money.

Outreach and Organizing

The outreach and organizing intern will coordinate outreach events, including publicity for PARC events, and work at broader community events.

Major responsibilities will include: creating calendars of these events and distributing them in paper, e-mail, and voicemail format; organizing speaking engagements/community events; and preparing and maintaining materials and gear for community events. Interns should have experience coordinating volunteers and working with desktop publishing and have a social justice activism background. PARC will provide an orientation to the general landscape of Bay Area political activism and allied groups.

Prisoner Support Intern

This intern will help project coordinators run the program, reading, sorting, and responding to mail; updating prisoner-support directories; doing research for specific questions; writing alerts; and doing some office work. Interns should have good writing skills with an emphasis on sensitivity to people in need. The organization will provide training in answering letters, sorting mail, and gaining access to visiting programs.

Research and Materials

This intern will conduct research on targeted issues and will research antiprison groups nationally for PARC's Resource and Prisoner Support Directories. Some data entry and statistical analysis may be necessary. The intern will work with staff and volunteers to create, maintain, and update educational materials distributed to the public from literature tables and the PARC Web site. Interns also will help produce drafts and visually compelling final versions of publications and help distribute them to the public. Interns in this position should have good writing, research, and desktop publishing skills.

PARC will provide training in source-gathering, fact-checking, data compilation, and some targeted-issue writing.

Web Development

This intern will develop and thoroughly update the PARC Web pages, including re-evaluating the Web site overall design and developing systems for continued volunteer maintenance of the site. Interns should have experience with Web development and familiarity with the Linux operating system.

HOW TO APPLY

If you're interested, you can call for more information about what's available and request an application, or you can download an application at http://www.prisonactivist.org/internship/application.html. Complete the application, and on a separate sheet (no more than one page) describe why you're interested in prison-activist work in general and why you're interested in the PARC internship in particular. Submit your application and written sample to the preceding address.

PUBLIC LEADERSHIP EDUCATION NETWORK INTERNSHIP

Public Leadership Education Network
1001 Connecticut Avenue, NW, Suite 900
Washington, DC 20036
Fax: (202) 872-0141
plen@plen.org
http://www.plen.org

What You Can Earn: Unpaid.
Application Deadlines: May 15.
Educational Experience: Undergraduate or graduate students with a focus in women's studies, political science, government, or other liberal arts subject areas.
Requirements: A self-starter with the ability to work successfully with little supervision; excellent communication and strong writing skills; proficient with Microsoft Office, including Word, Excel and Access; experienced with Internet research methods; enthusiastic, detail-oriented, and eager to learn. Students with a demonstrated interest in women's leadership are strongly encouraged to apply.

OVERVIEW

This nonpartisan, nonprofit organization believes that women's participation is critical in the formation of public policy and strives to prepare the next generation of women leaders by engaging young women in politics and the policy-making process.

As an intern with this group, you'll work in a small office and help in the delivery of programs, getting a unique opportunity to meet women leaders from Congress, courts, the executive branch, and numerous advocacy groups. Responsibilities include helping to plan and deliver PLEN's summer internship seminar, implementing an outreach plan to identify PLEN alumni, and researching and completing outreach to investigate internship opportunities in international organizations. Administrative tasks may include copying, mailing, and answering phones, but no more than 25 percent of your time will be spent on administrative tasks.

A full-time or part-time schedule is negotiable for this internship, as are start and end dates.

HOW TO APPLY
To apply, send a cover letter, resume, and a two- to three-page page writing sample to the preceding address. No phone calls.

RAINFOREST ACTION NETWORK INTERNSHIPS

Rainforest Action Network
221 Pine Street, 5th Floor
San Francisco, CA 94104
(415) 398-4404
Fax: (415) 398-2732
rainforest@ran.org
http://www.ran.org/what_you/volunteer_info/
   intern.html

What You Can Earn: Unpaid, but a $7 daily commuting stipend provided, along with a complimentary year's membership to RAN, and a RAN T-shirt.
Application Deadlines: May 15.

Educational Experience: See specific internships below for details.
Requirements: Good public speaking and organizing skills a must! Must be willing to work in a dynamic team to achieve a great goal. See specific internships below for other details.

OVERVIEW
All interns will work at the Rainforest Action Network's (RAN) office in San Francisco for at least 12 hours a week for a period of three months. You'll be directly supervised by an experienced staffer who will design a special project for you to work on, and you'll also participate in the daily operations of a campaign or department. When your internship is over, you'll be given a letter of reference. Internships are available in three main areas: campaigns, communication, and development.

Campaign Internships
These internships are all about grassroots organizing and helping RAN's Old Growth team mobilize and expand its network to interact with lumber companies. The intern will help with telephone and e-mail outreach to grassroots groups, short speaking engagements with campus and community groups, and coordinating protests and demonstrations around the country against businesses' involvement with logging projects that harm endangered forests.

Interns also will help create online and printed materials to assist activists, including manuals, brochures, fact sheets, and newsletters. The intern also will be encouraged to propose additional projects. Interns should be familiar with Filemaker Pro, Word, Excel, e-mail and Web programs.

Communications
Interns here will help write press releases, letters, articles; update media lists; and place calls to media to discuss possible articles. Interns should have excellent communication and writing skills.

The Web site assistant intern in the communications department will help maintain the Web site; post press releases, action alerts and other updates; convert RAN reports to PDF format for uploading; archive digital photos; and identify new ways to use the Internet and increase multimedia on the site. This intern must be detail oriented with good writing and editing skills; a keen eye for good test layout designs a plus. Experience with Photoshop, Dreamweaver, and Acrobat is a help.

Development
Interns in the development department will help research foundations and donors, write proposals and letters, and help produce parties and events. These interns also will help with graphic design, research national polling data, and brainstorm promotional ideas.

HOW TO APPLY
To apply online, fill out the online application at: http://www.ran.org/what_you/volunteer_info/application.html and include an online cover letter and resume.

ROBERT F. KENNEDY MEMORIAL CENTER FOR HUMAN RIGHTS INTERNSHIP

Internship Coordinator, Robert F. Kennedy Center for Human Rights
1367 Connecticut Avenue, NW
Washington, DC 20036
(202) 463-7575
Fax: (202) 463-6606
shen@rfkmemorial.org
http://www.rfkmemorial.org

What You Can Earn: Unpaid.
Application Deadlines: May 15 for the summer legal internship.

Educational Experience: Must have completed at least one year of law school.
Requirements: A demonstrated interest in human rights. Ability in one of the following languages is helpful but not required: Arabic, Bahasa Indonesian, French, Haitian Creole, or Spanish.

OVERVIEW
The Robert F. Kennedy Memorial, founded in 1968, was established to promote Robert Kennedy's ideals of civic responsibility and social conscience, the importance of community involvement, and the pursuit of social justice and human rights. The Robert F. Kennedy Memorial Center for Human Rights implements the vision of RFK by promoting the full spectrum of human rights both in the United States and throughout the world. The center develops and carries out projects that enhance and complement the work of the Robert F. Kennedy Human Rights Award laureates and that promote social change.

As a summer legal intern, you'll help research legal issues related to international financial institutions, the United Nations, international law, and U.S. law as they pertain to various national and international programs. You may help conduct research and draft memoranda on the human rights situation in countries of interest to the center and on thematic issues (such as the right to health or the right to development). You may conduct legal research on the application of international human-rights norms to country conditions, developments in the domestic legal systems of specific countries and their implications for human rights, and other questions; or prepare documents for submission to government or U.N. officials. You may attend and report on briefings, Congressional hearings, symposia, and other meetings; monitor sources of information on countries and issues of concern to the center; and provide administrative support.

HOW TO APPLY
E-mail Gloria Shen at shen@rfkmemorial.org or fax a cover letter, resume, three references, and a brief writing sample.

SANTÉ GROUP INTERNSHIP

The Santé Group
700 Roeder Road
Silver Spring, MD 20910
(301) 589-2303, ext. 417
balbaneze@santegroup.org
http://www.thesantegroup.org

What You Can Earn: Parking reimbursement. Several summer interns are able to participate in the Everett Public Service Internship Program, which allows students currently enrolled in an undergraduate or graduate program to receive a stipend toward their university studies.
Application Deadlines: Rolling.
Educational Experience: Enrollment in a university; university credit is possible for this internship.
Requirements: None.

OVERVIEW
Students who want to make a difference in the lives of mentally ill or developmentally disabled people can intern with the Santé Group, a family of Maryland-based companies dedicated to providing mental health treatment, rehabilitation, and support to individuals and families. Together, the Affiliated Santé Group, Rock Creek Foundation, and Santé Medical Associates compose the Santé Group of companies.

Internship placements, which last for at least one college semester, include tutoring, mentoring, counseling, group leadership, public relations, marketing, community outreach, Web management, and research. Interns apply for this placement from colleges throughout the United States and abroad.

Founded in 1974, the Rock Creek Foundation was developed in response to longstanding gaps in the delivery and availability of rehabilitation, vocational, and treatment services for persons with both developmental disabilities and psychiatric disorders. Rock Creek's efforts were successful, and the company was considered to be a pioneer in the field of independent living and psychiatric treatment. The Affiliated Santé Group and Santé Medical Associates were formed during the early 1990s to reach a wider group of people with serious and persistent mental conditions who did not have developmental disabilities. The Santé Companies now operate programs at single-site and multiservice centers and housing are located in five Maryland counties, providing psychiatric treatment and rehabilitation services to more than 3,000 people each year. Target populations are children and adults with serious and persistent mental illness (SPMI) or those with SPMI and co-occurring developmental disabilities.

HOW TO APPLY
To apply, send a cover letter with your resume and a request for an application at the above address.

SEEDS OF PEACE INTERNSHIP

Internship Coordinator—Communications
Seeds of Peace
370 Lexington Ave., Suite 401
New York, NY 10017
Fax: (212) 573-8047
info@seedsofpeace.org
http://www.seedsofpeace.org

What You Can Earn: Stipend available; college credit is possible.
Application Deadlines: Rolling.
Educational Experience: Current college/university student or recent graduate.
Requirements: Experience working in a busy office environment; basic computer skills, including Web, Microsoft Word, Excel, and Outlook; excellent written and oral communications skills; creativity and flexibility. Experience with Photoshop, Quark, and HTML is preferred. Interest in nonprofit organizations, conflict resolution, and the Middle East is helpful.

OVERVIEW

Seeds of Peace is an internationally renowned nonprofit organization that brings young people from regions of conflict together to learn mediation and critical thinking skills for coexistence and conflict resolution. Seeds of Peace tries to reverse legacies of hatred by nurturing lasting friendships that become the basis of mutual understanding and respect. Seeds of Peace works with the next generation of leaders to make real peace by equipping them with the tools to end cycles of violence.

Seeds of Peace has been featured on "60 Minutes," the "Today Show," "Nightline," and many other TV programs and has close to 2,000 Israeli and Arab graduates from the Middle East, the Balkans, Cyprus, Greece, Turkey, India-Pakistan, and the United States. Seeds of Peace welcomed its first Afghan student in the summer of 2002.

Either part-time or full-time interns are needed to help the communications team for three months in the summer to work on specific projects. As an intern, you'll work with the communications department in the New York office, archiving media and press clippings; helping with public relations, promotions, and marketing including e-newsletters and printed materials; and providing event support.

HOW TO APPLY

Mail or e-mail your resume and cover letter to the preceding address. No phone calls.

SHARE OUR STRENGTH INTERNSHIP

Public Relations Coordinator
Share Our Strength
1730 M Street, NW, Suite 700
Washington, DC 20036
(202) 393-2925
Fax: (202) 347-5868
iedlow@strength.org
http://www.strength.org

What You Can Earn: Unpaid, but college credit is possible.
Application Deadlines: May 15.
Educational Experience: Sophomores, juniors, or seniors majoring in communications.
Requirements: A self-starter; excellent communications, writing, and research skills; proficient in Microsoft Office Suite; and a great sense of humor.

OVERVIEW

Share Our Strength, one of the nation's leading antihunger organizations, works toward ending childhood hunger in the United States and abroad. The group is committed to building a hunger-free generation in America by ensuring that all children have access to the nutritious food they need to learn, grow, and thrive. Share Our Strength believes that by working with others to create greater resources, better community-based systems, new partnerships, and targeted grants, they can end childhood hunger in America.

Share Our Strength meets immediate demands for food while investing in long-term solutions to hunger and poverty. To meet its goals, Share Our Strength mobilizes both industries and individuals to contribute their talents to its antihunger efforts and creates community wealth to promote lasting changes.

The organization is offering an internship in the communications department, which oversees all internal and external communications for Share Our Strength and its programs. The department implements all media-relations activities, develops graphic-design projects, produces all materials for Share Our Strength events and programs, crafts all message strategies for the organization, drafts editorials and speeches, and creates public-service campaigns. The department also is responsible for the publication of *The Dish,* an online monthly newsletter.

As a public relations intern, you'll conduct research for programs and events; handle administrative duties for the department; maintain media clips, the media database, videos, and Share Our Strength publications; submit articles for Share Our Strength's *The Dish;* help communicate grant-impact data; and help plan forums and gatherings.

HOW TO APPLY

To apply for this internship, e-mail your resume, cover letter, and writing samples to the preceding e-mail address.

THE SIERRA CLUB— WASHINGTON, D.C., INTERNSHIP

The Sierra Club Internship Program
408 C Street, NE
Washington, DC 20002
(202) 675-7905

What You Can Earn: Unpaid.
Application Deadlines: Rolling.
Educational Experience: Interest, education, and experience in political science, environmental studies, natural resources, history, law, journalism, computer science, or other related fields; especially important to have been directly involved in conservation work.
Requirements: Good communication and writing skills.

OVERVIEW

With more than 700,000 members, the Sierra Club is one of the nation's largest grassroots conservation organizations, dedicated to exploring and protecting the Earth's wild places through education and promotion of the responsible use of the planet's ecosystems and resources.

The Washington, D.C., office of the Sierra Club concentrates on educating Congress, the public, and members about the quality of the natural environment and monitors legislative activities of environmental concern.

To help do this, the Sierra Club Legislative Office sponsors internships throughout the year to provide a hands-on opportunity for you to gain an in-depth understanding of the field of environmental protection and the specific role that the Sierra Club plays in this field. This is also a great way to learn how Congress works and understand the roles played by other nongovernmental organizations in Washington.

Typical intern rotations are in the fall, winter/spring, and summer, but the organization is flexible with other starting dates. In Washington, you can work with the directors of the field, issue, media, or political programs.

Field Interns

The Sierra Club has one of the most effective national grassroots networks in the country, with field organizers in more than 40 states. As a field intern, you'll work directly with the national field director, national conservation organizer, and members of issue teams to coordinate and provide resources for national field staff.

You'll help coordinate national grassroots actions and report releases, provide field staff with legislative information, coordinate the production of materials with issue teams, attend coalition meetings, or help with grassroots training and strategy.

Issue Interns

Issue interns can select from areas including environmental quality, global warming and energy, international, lands protection, and environmental partnerships. Interns will work with a Washington legislative director and concentrate on a specific environmental issue area. Interns may conduct research, gather and analyze information, write summaries and fact sheets for educational purposes, help prepare Congressional testimony, and accompany staff on visits to Congressional offices. You also may attend meetings of other environmental groups, monitor Congressional hearings, help develop background information on a particular issue, and prepare briefing materials.

The Environmental Quality programs deals with issues including air and water quality, sprawl, and Superfund. The Global Warming and Energy team works on improving fuel economy, promoting the increased use of renewable energy sources, and reducing overall emissions as part of a comprehensive national energy plan. The International group includes areas related to responsible trade, global population and the environment, human rights and the environment, as well as the Beyond the Borders program.

Lands Protection focuses on protecting habitat, saving streams, and safeguarding communities by promoting policies that restore forests and protect wildlands and wildlife in America's public lands. The Environmental Partnerships team builds alliances with other constituencies such as labor, hunter/anglers, faith communities, and Latinos.

Media Interns

Media interns help promote the Sierra Club's mission and help produce press releases and fact sheets for Washington-based reporters, editors, and producers. You may write editorials and help with special projects or help with mailings, newspaper clipping, or library research. Also, you may help organize press conferences or monitor various publications for environmental coverage.

Political Interns

As a political intern, you'll gain first-hand knowledge of how a political program works. The political director manages the club's participation in elections, including making political endorsements and contributions, organizing local volunteer efforts in elections, conducting research on candidates, and training volunteers. As a political program intern,

you'll help the director by distributing information to club staff and leaders; monitoring election campaigns; attending meetings; conducting research on candidates, organizations, and issues; and helping with political training activities.

HOW TO APPLY

You should submit a resume, cover letter, and a two-to-five page writing sample to the preceding address, indicating your specific interest or experience, if any, in relevant environmental issues and your availability dates.

STRONG WOMEN, STRONG GIRLS INTERNSHIP

Executive Director Strong Women, Strong Girls
Executive Director
7 Temple Street
Cambridge, MA 02138
(617) 491-6050, ext. 244
lhyde@swsg.org
http://www.swsg.org
What You Can Earn: Unpaid.
Application Deadlines: June 1.
Educational Experience: College undergraduates.
Requirements: Proficiency in Microsoft Office programs suite (Word, Excel, PowerPoint, Access); excellent writing and verbal communication skills; ability to manage complex projects and multitask with ease while prioritizing a large number of disparate tasks; abundant enthusiasm and energy; strong interpersonal skills; and the ability to work both independently and as a part of a team in a small office. Experience working with or in student-led groups, campus service organizations, or community-based programs is helpful but not required.

OVERVIEW

The mission of Strong Women, Strong Girls (SWSG) National is to make use of the lessons learned from strong women throughout history to encourage young girls to become strong women themselves. By building communities of women committed to supporting positive social change, SWSG works to create cycles of mutual empowerment for women and girls. SWSG is a Boston-based nonprofit organization that emphasizes the study of contemporary and historic female role models, skill-building activities, and mentor relationships to help girls gain the skills they need to become strong and successful women. Featuring a community-based mentor model, SWSG puts together groups of undergraduate women who serve as program mentors and community leaders on their college campuses.

Interns with SWSG will help develop the *Student Director Handbook*, *Campus Coach Handbook*, and *Site Liaison Handbook*; work on the organization's Web site in conjunction with a Web designer; and develop a community-launch plan for the roll-out of new communities of SWSG. In addition, interns will help design program-evaluation materials and training in conjunction with SWSG evaluation consultants.

HOW TO APPLY

To apply, submit a resume and cover letter to the executive director at the preceding e-mail address.

20/20 VISION INTERNSHIP

Internship Coordinator, 20/20 Vision
1828 Jefferson Place, NW
Washington, DC 20036
(212) 833-20020
vision@2020vision.org
http://www. 2020vision.org

What You Can Earn: Transportation stipend.
Application Deadlines: For the fall semester, August 15; for the spring, December 15; for the summer, March 15.
Educational Experience: None required.
Requirements: None required.

OVERVIEW

If you're interested in environmental and peace activism, the 20/20 Vision organization may have the right approach for you. Their straightforward "$20 a year, 20 minutes a month" request has inspired Americans to contribute time and money to activism causes.

If you're selected, the organization will take you and one other intern a term and put you to work in legislation, media, development, promotion, and membership areas, doing everything from office work to hands-on nonprofit political work in downtown Washington, D.C. This is a young, progressive, energetic office with lots of fun activities and regular staff events.

The organization makes grassroots activism easy for busy people, giving citizens the information and tools they need to get involved on issues such as reducing air pollution from cars and power plants, keeping pesticides out of food, limiting nuclear arms, and making the country more secure. The group's "alerts" tell members how to contact politicians and corporate officials and quickly and easily tell them you're watching them on an urgent issue.

20/20 Vision watchdogs Congress and collaborates with dozens of groups and experts to make sure online actions and bimonthly postcards are focused on who, what, and where they will make the most difference.

HOW TO APPLY

If you're interested in saving the world and the environment, submit your resume with a cover letter and a writing sample to the above address.

UNITED NATIONS ASSOCIATION OF THE USA INTERNSHIP

United Nations Association of the USA
Internship Coordinator
801 Second Avenue
New York, NY 10017-4706
(212) 907-1300
Fax: (212) 682-9185
adrakulich@unausa.org
http://www.unausa.org

What You Can Earn: Unpaid.
Application Deadlines: May 30.
Educational Experience: Journalism majors or related experience required; graduate students preferred; knowledge of U.N. and international relations required.
Requirements: At least 21 hours a week.

OVERVIEW

The United Nations Association of the United States of America (UNA-USA) is a nonprofit, nonpartisan organization that supports the work of the United Nations and encourages active civic participation in the social and economic issues facing the world today.

As the nation's largest grassroots foreign-policy organization and the leading center of policy research on the U.N. and global issues, UNA-USA offers Americans the opportunity to connect with issues confronted by the U.N.—from global health and human rights to the spread of democracy, equitable development, and international justice. Through its work, UNA-USA educates Americans about the work of the U.N. and encourages public support for strong U.S. leadership in the U.N. UNA-USA is a member of the World Federation of United Nations Associations.

Interns with the publications department of the United Nations Association of the USA will write and publish articles for the association's quarterly magazine on U.S.-U.N. relations; research and help copyedit the annual textbook on the U.N.; help with marketing efforts; and more. A flexible schedule for this June to August internship is possible.

HOW TO APPLY

Send your resume and clips to the preceding e-mail address.

WASHINGTON FOOD COALITION INTERNSHIP

Washington Food Coalition
PO Box 95752
Seattle, WA 98145
(206) 300-3214
tracy@wafoodcoalition.org
http://www.wafoodcoalition.org

What You Can Earn: Unpaid but includes a Metro Flex-Pass to help with commuting costs.
Application Deadlines: Rolling.
Educational Experience: None specified.
Requirements: Excellent verbal and written communication skills; a minimum of 15 hours each week.

OVERVIEW

The Washington Food Coalition strives to alleviate hunger throughout Washington State. In 1992, emergency food providers throughout Washington recognized the need to develop a cohesive, unified network of antihunger programs and merged two regional networks to form the Washington Food Coalition. The coalition also advocates at the state and federal levels on issues relevant to emergency food providers and the clients that they serve.

Membership in the Washington Food Coalition includes more than 275 independent nonprofit community-based organizations trying to alleviate hunger. The Food Coalition includes agencies, community food banks, food voucher programs, soup kitchens, food distribution centers, antihunger advocates, nutritionists, and dietitians.

Summer interns will get the chance to work from June through August for up to 40 hours a week planning conferences, advocating, and recruiting members.

HOW TO APPLY

To apply for the position, send a resume to the preceding address.

WOMEN FOR PEACE INTERNSHIP

Women for Peace
2302 Ellsworth Street
Berkeley, CA 94704
(510) 849-3020
http://www.womenforpeace.org

What You Can Earn: Unpaid but college credit is possible.
Application Deadlines: None.
Educational Experience: None specified.
Requirements: None specified.

OVERVIEW

Women for Peace is a group of women dedicated to the cause of international disarmament and works to oppose military expenditures, urging that the country's wealth be devoted instead to meeting education, housing, healthcare, and environmental needs. The group was founded in 1961 to demand the banning of above-ground nuclear tests. Its work helped lead to the Partial Test Ban Treaty, which ended atmospheric nuclear tests. Today, Women for Peace continues to join with others all over the world in the struggle to achieve the complete abolition of nuclear weapons. The group works for a change in national priorities and for achievement and preservation of peace, justice, and human rights for all.

Women for Peace produces a bimonthly newsletter; maintains a library of books and videotapes; arranges public forums and cooperates with other groups in educational meetings and demonstrations; and works with local schools to develop peace-related activities for students.

The group also maintains an office in Washington, D.C., to monitor Congressional and administration activities, lobbying on behalf of peace, social justice, and a livable environment.

Interns with Women for Peace can get college credit, skills, knowledge, experience, hope, confidence, support, friendship, and a different perspective on the world, guided by peace, justice, and social responsibility. Women for Peace provides individual attention and support to interns working in its office.

HOW TO APPLY

No formal application is necessary. Instead, the group invites potential interns to stop by for a casual talk and meet some of the staffers.

WOMEN WORK INTERNSHIP

Women Work
1625 K Street, NW, #300
Washington, DC 20006
webmaster@womenwork.org
Fax: (202) 467-5366
http://www.womenwork.org

What You Can Earn: $200 a week stipend.
Application Deadlines: Rolling.
Educational Experience: None specified.

Requirements: See individual internships for specific requirements; in general, all interns must have excellent writing and computer skills; strong interest in women's education, employment, and economic issues; and the ability to meet deadlines, work on projects with minimal supervision, and remain focused.

OVERVIEW

For more than 25 years, Women Work has served as a vital link between programs, agencies, and educational institutions nationwide that provide education, job training, and support services to millions of America's displaced homemakers, single parents, and other women in transition. In addition to individuals throughout the country, network members include more than 1,100 education, training, and employment programs. Women Work! The National Network for Women's Employment is a membership organization rooted in the Displaced Homemakers Movement, dedicated to empowering women from different backgrounds and helping them achieve economic self-sufficiency through job readiness, education, training, and employment. The network is committed to ongoing comprehensive public education to build awareness of and support for the needs of midlife and older displaced homemakers and other women entering, re-entering, or training for the workforce.

The network collects data, disseminates information, provides training and technical assistance, and acts as a communication link to programs, agencies, and educational institutions. The network affects public policy by working with lawmakers, business leaders, and labor to create and strengthen programs and policies for women.

A number of internships are available in different areas, including fund-raising, network development, and public relations/communication.

Fund-raising Internship

If raising money sounds like fun to you, this part-time internship might be of interest. The intern will help cultivate and solicit prospective and cur-

rent donors; research individual, foundation, and corporate-funding prospects on-line; write letters of inquiry and make cold calls to prospective corporate funders; draft and edit the fund-raising resource section of the Women Work's Web site; and help with the fund-raising database entry.

Network Development and Services Internship

As a full-time intern in this department, you'll help keep current members and find new ones, do research, compile data, develop an online career center, and write newsletter articles. You'll also help with a variety of network projects and assist in developing network materials and manuals, membership mailings, and membership resources. Communication with members is also part of the job.

Public Relations/Communication Internship

This intern will be part of the communications and technology team, working full time (40 hours a week), although part time is possible. (Fall and spring internships are part time.)

If you choose this internship, you'll have the chance to design publications (such as tip sheets); write articles, press releases, and updates for the Web site; and interview "success stories." You'll help with newsletters, media outreach, and a variety of communications projects. Since you'll be working for a national women's organization, you'll also learn about issues affecting working women, misplaced homemakers, and low-income women.

Candidates should have specific experience creating publications, fliers, or brochures; using desktop publishing programs such as Pagemaker or Quark; excellent writing, editing, research, interviewing, and computer skills; and experience writing articles for newsletters and the Web, press releases, op-eds, and so on. Basic experience coding in HTML is a plus.

HOW TO APPLY

To apply for the public relations internship, mail, e-mail, or fax a cover letter, resume, and two or three relevant writing or design samples (such as press releases, op-eds, newsletter, or Web site articles and/or fliers/brochures/Web pages you designed) to the preceding address. If sending an e-mail, reference "communications intern" in the subject line.

Development candidates should fax a resume and cover letter to the preceding number or e-mail to rlusk@womenwork.org.

Fund-raising candidates should fax, e-mail, or mail a cover letter describing their interests and experience and resume to Lkmiller@womenwork.org.

WORLD AFFAIRS COUNCIL INTERNSHIP

Internship Coordinator, World Affairs Council
1800 K Street, NW, Suite 1014
Washington, DC 20006
ksimhan@worldaffairsdc.org
http://www.worldaffairsdc.org

What You Can Earn: Unpaid.
Application Deadlines: End of June.
Educational Experience: None specified.
Requirements: Background or strong interest in international affairs/education; excellent written and oral communications skills; strong computer skills; attention to detail; commitment to working some evening hours (6:30 P.M. to 8:30 P.M.)

OVERVIEW
The World Affairs Council of Washington, D.C., is a nonprofit, nonpartisan organization founded in 1980 and dedicated to increasing public awareness about global issues. The council offers programs and events featuring foreign dignitaries, American officials, legislatures, and other experts to foster public discussion and debate on the global challenges and policy choices facing the United States. It's an affiliate of the Foreign Policy Association in New York and is part of a national network of World Affairs Councils located in such metropolitan areas as Boston, Philadelphia, Chicago, Dallas, and San Francisco.

Its mission of expanding public knowledge and understanding of international affairs also extends to D.C.-area schools, where—through its educational workshops and travel programs—the council promotes international education in local schools.

As an intern here, you'll help conduct and prepare for the council's public events, including town hall meetings, book events, and panels on contemporary international issues. You'll also be responsible for preparing brief written reports on the council's events.

HOW TO APPLY
To apply, e-mail a cover letter, resume, and one- or two-page writing sample to the preceding address.

ANIMALS

THE AARK WILDLIFE REHABILITATION INTERNSHIP

Aark Wildlife Rehabilitation
107 Twining Bridge Road
Newtown, PA
(215) 968-4963

What You Can Earn: Unpaid but academic credit is possible.
Application Deadlines: February.
Educational Experience: None required.
Requirements: Interns must be at least 18 years of age.

OVERVIEW

The Aark is a wildlife rehabilitation center that sets broken bones, treats illnesses, and provides food and shelter for birds and mammals that have been injured or have been orphaned and are too young to care for themselves. The goal is to return these creatures to their natural environment as quickly as possible, able to fend for themselves. Every effort is made to avoid interfering with the development of those natural characteristics that each wild creature requires to survive in the wild.

Each year, more than 4,000 birds and mammals are treated at the Aark; if you intern here, you'll work at least one four-hour shift each week, gaining invaluable experience in the handling and care of wounded creatures and orphans. The Aark is accredited by many regional colleges that offer academic credit for the rigorous program under the guidance of the Aark staff.

The work of the Aark is divided into three major areas: rehabilitation, education, and training, each with the common goal of fostering the care and understanding of wildlife. Mary Jane Stretch, one of the nation's leading authorities on wildlife rehabilitation, is the founder and executive director; she holds federal and Pennsylvania wildlife rehabilitation permits and is a Master Bird Bander.

With more than 30 years of dedicated experience in aiding the care and rehabilitation of birds and mammals, Stretch is a frequent speaker before national, state, and local groups. Her work has been featured on "The Today Show" and her life has been chronicled in *The Swan in My Bathtub* and, more recently, *For the Love of Wild Things*.

The Aark is staffed by a cadre of professionals and dedicated trained volunteers who provide 24-hour service, seven days a week, 365 days a year. Depending upon age and/or injury, an orphaned or wounded creature may require attention every couple of hours around the clock.

HOW TO APPLY

If you are interested in a summer internship with the Aark, please call the Aark.

BEAVER DAM FARM EQUINE INTERNSHIP

Beaver Dam Farm
Carol and Arthur Rivoire
beaverdf@ns.sympatico.ca
http://www.beaverdamfarm.com

What You Can Earn: Unpaid but interns may get tips from farm guests.
Application Deadlines: Rolling.
Educational Experience: Must have experience caring for horses and an intermediate level of riding, preferably in dressage; intermediate level means being comfortable and confident on the horse at all gaits and able to ride correctly and influence the horse. Driving experience is helpful but not required.
Requirements: Medical insurance to cover all medical expenses while in Canada and sufficient pocket money for your stay in Canada. Interns

must be confident, sociable, and used to being away from home. Most interns are female.

OVERVIEW

Beaver Dam Farm specializes in two areas devoted to the versatile Norwegian Fjord Horse, one of the world's oldest and purest breeds. The farm offers internships to a small number of girls who help during the summer with the beginner driving vacations and horse care.

Beaver Dam Farm is a beautiful 350 acres of rolling fields and spectacular ocean views, with a lovely, six-mile beach 10 minutes from the farm. During the summer, if you choose this internship you'll have the opportunity to experience a successful horse breeding, training, and equine tourism business.

At Beaver Dam Farm you'll experience a learning vacation in a beautiful, friendly part of the world and get a chance to experience firsthand the Canadian way of life. You'll also be able to improve your horsemanship and make new friends with girls from Europe and Canada as well as across the United States. The farm is located in a tiny French Acadian village, 10 minutes from a university town with cinema, theatre, shops, restaurants, music, and sports. You'll have lots of opportunities to ride and to learn to drive, as well as time off to see the local area.

Owners Carol and Arthur Rivoire have been running Beaver Dam Farm Fjords II Limited for more than 25 years. Beaver Dam Farm has been in the business of breeding, importing, training, and selling Fjord horses for 26 years and also offers an equine tourism program called Nova Scotia Beginner Driving Vacations, now in its 14th season.

The internship program fulfills the requirements of most equine schools. At the farm, you'll be working with young horses from weanling through three years of age and riding horses to train and condition them, all under the supervision of a professional staff. There is also barn work (cleaning stalls and tack) as well as stable chores such as picking rocks out of the arena so the horses won't injure their feet, clearing the grass paddocks of weeds that are harmful to the horses, helping in the office, and helping to keep the house clean and in order. Interns are responsible for keeping their rooms clean and neat and also for daily cleaning of the shared bathroom. You'll also be asked to help with such chores as watering or picking vegetables in the garden.

Keeping the house and farm operation running efficiently is the work of everyone who lives and works on the farm; this means that everyone must be willing to do any task required to keep the farm and the house running smoothly. All interns must do some housework every day, which usually means 15 minutes per girl per day, including helping with food preparation and washing up.

Interns typically stay for *at least* six weeks, but if you can only stay less than six weeks, it is possible that your schedule will fit theirs. However, four weeks is the minimum stay, and preference will be given to girls who can stay the entire summer to the end of August.

HOUSING

Interns are the personal guests of the farm's owners and are treated like family, with all meals and lodging provided. Interns (most interns are girls) live together in the owner's home in three double bedrooms and one single room. The bathroom is shared, and sheets and towels are provided. Interns are expected to help with cleaning, dishwashing, and gardening. They eat all meals with the family. If at all possible, the owners will buy favorite foods for the girls. The pantry and refrigerator are well stocked at all times, and the girls are always free to help themselves. Sometimes meals will be prepared for the interns, but other times the interns will cook for themselves.

HOW TO APPLY

To apply, fill out the online application form at http://www.beaverdamfarm.com/pages/intern-program/intern-application.pdf and e-mail it to beaverdf@ns.sympatico.ca. You should include a letter from your parents granting permission to come to the farm for the agreed period of time and a letter from your family doctor warranting that you are in good physical and mental health. You should also include a letter from your riding instructor detailing your riding level and experience, as well as your work ethic.

BEST FRIENDS ANIMAL SOCIETY INTERNSHIP

Best Friends Animal Society
Humane Education Department
Dave Perry, Internship Coordinator
5001 Angel Canyon Road
Kanab, UT 84741-5000
(435) 644-2001, ext. 317
Fax: (435) 644-2078
dave@bestfriends.org

What You Can Earn: Unpaid.
Application Deadlines: Rolling.
Educational Experience: None specified.
Requirements: Must be age 20 or over and want to work with animals.

OVERVIEW

If the thought of working at a typical animal shelter leaves you queasy, this internship might be a good choice for you. Best Friends is the nation's largest lifetime care sanctuary for abused and abandoned animals, a no-kill shelter dedicated to helping homeless animals. "No-kill" means that animals are not destroyed except in cases of terminal and painful illness, when compassion demands euthanasia because there isn't any reasonable alternative. Most of the animals, about three out of four, don't stay long at Best Friends, but are soon ready to go to good homes with permanent or foster families, making way for the daily new arrivals.

As an intern here, you'll have hands-on experience in animal care, socialization, behavior, and rescue as you participate in the daily work of the sanctuary.

The sanctuary, at the heart of Southern Utah's Golden Circle of national parks, is home to about 1,500 dogs, cats, horses, rabbits, and other animals. The animals come from all over the country, mostly from shelters that don't have the resources to rehabilitate them and where they would otherwise be destroyed. In exchange, many of these shelters take back animals that are ready to be placed in good homes. Others, who are too badly traumatized through ill treatment or who are old, crippled or chronically ill, find a permanent home at the sanctuary. Best Friends Animal Sanctuary is located at Angel Canyon, a 33,000-acre ranch in the majestic red-rock country of southern Utah, just outside the town of Kanab. The sanctuary is at the heart of the Golden Circle of national parks, close to Zion National Park, the Grand Canyon's North Rim, Bryce Canyon, and Lake Powell.

In 1987, about 17 million homeless dogs and cats were destroyed in shelters and pounds in the United States. By 1998, fewer than 5 million were being killed each year. This remarkable achievement is a direct result of spay/neuter and adoption programs and a growing public belief that pets have value. Best Friends staff members provide free information and help to people with an animal problem, such as pets that need new homes, feral cats, or behavior problems. The staff currently responds to more than 20,000 requests for help each year. Best Friends was started when its founders rescued animals from shelters where their luck was about to run out, rehabilitated them, and found homes for most of them. Those who were still unadoptable kept growing, until Best Friends was established in the early 1980s as a unique sanctuary at Angel Canyon.

As the sanctuary grew, the founders realized that since Best Friends could never take in every homeless animal everywhere, their work would need to expand to include a nationwide No More Homeless Pets campaign. In Utah, Best Friends manages a model No More Homeless Pets campaign with shelters and humane groups statewide to ensure that every healthy dog or cat can be guaranteed a loving home. Best Friends also works nationwide to help humane groups, individual people, and entire communities to set up spay/neuter, shelter, foster, and adoption programs in their own neighborhoods, cities, and states. The mission of Best Friends is driven by the simple philosophy that kindness to animals helps build a better world for all. Through the generous work of workers and interns, Best Friends ensures that animals who come to the shelter will never again be alone, hungry, sick, afraid, or in pain.

The internship program lasts six weeks and is geared toward general animal care. For the first two weeks, you'll work in all animal areas, observing and learning general animal care techniques for domesticated animals. After the first two weeks, you'll be expected to come up with goals and objectives, which will be used to determine an area of concentration. For the rest of your internship, you'll be concentrating on an area of particular interest to you. You'll also have an opportunity to observe procedures in the spay/neuter clinic, to shadow a vet tech, and to perform weekly reflections and animal-area-experience reports.

Best Friends interns provide enormous help to the animals and staff at the sanctuary. At the same time, the internship program can help students with an interest in animal care get a head start on a life-long commitment to animals in need.

HOW TO APPLY

Contact the internship coordinator at the preceding address to discuss internship openings.

BIG CAT RESCUE INTERNSHIP

Big Cat Rescue Educational Sanctuary
12802 Easy Street
Tampa, FL 33625
(813) 920-4130
http://www.bigcatrescue.org/work_with_animals.htm

What You Can Earn: Unpaid.
Application Deadlines: Rolling.
Educational Experience: None specified.
Requirements: Good health and endurance; must be at least 18 years old and willing to work six days a week, some holidays, and follow strict safety guidelines. Strong work ethic and love of animals are more important than degree; the work is physical and occurs outdoors in all types of weather.

OVERVIEW

Big Cat Rescue is the world's largest sanctuary for more than 150 big cats that have been abused, abandoned, retired from performing acts, or saved from being slaughtered for fur coats, and they offer a formally structured intern program for six to 12 interns throughout the year.

The sanctuary houses more than 150 tigers, lions, leopards, cougars, bobcats, lynx, ocelots, servals, caracals and others, a total of 18 of the 35 species of wild cats, many of which are threatened, endangered, or now extinct.

Most big cats are abandoned as a result of the pet trade; breeders convince people that cubs can make good pets, but most people end up abandoning the cats, often leaving them with lifelong infirmities that result from not knowing how properly to feed and care for them. A number of the Big Cat Rescue cats were owned by drug dealers and confiscated by law enforcement when the owners were arrested. These wild cats should never have been pets, but most states don't forbid their sale or private ownership, so breeders thrive and the number of abused and abandoned cats continues to grow.

Other big cats are used for commercial purposes; for instance, people claiming to support conservation and preservation of species charge the public to have photos taken with the cats when they are young or charge to take them to schools or other venues under the guise of education, only to abandon the cats when they mature. Performing acts and roadside zoos use the cats, often abusing them to force them to perform and then discarding the cats when they are no longer useful.

Big Cat Rescue provides a good home for a limited number of cats, but they can save only a small percentage of those in need. The sanctuary turns away more than 300 cats a year. Because of this, the broader mission of the sanctuary is to reduce the number of abandoned or abused cats by educating as many people as possible.

As an intern here, you'll be responsible for cleaning enclosures, preparing food and feeding, and performing operant conditioning and behavioral enrichment for lions, tigers, leopards, cougars, lynx, servals, caracals, bobcats, and other exotic animals. You also may be involved in guest relations, helping with educational programs, fund-raising, legislation, and other tasks as required.

Full-time internships are available for three-month terms, although three-month extensions may be offered and long-term employment opportunities are available for exceptional performers.

HOUSING

Comfortable housing is available on the sanctuary or in a nearby riverfront home, where interns all have their own private bedrooms, access to phones, Internet service, shared computers and shared kitchen and living areas. You'll need to provide your own food and transportation.

HOW TO APPLY

E-mail your resume to intern@BigCatRescue.org. A background check will be performed and your references will be checked.

CHICAGO ZOOLOGICAL SOCIETY BROOKFIELD ZOO INTERNSHIP

Brookfield Zoo
3300 Golf Road
Brookfield, IL 60513
(708) 485-0263; (800) 201-0784

zookeeper_internships@brookfieldzoo.org (for more information on zookeeper internships)
interns@brookfieldzoo.org (for further information or application materials on nonzookeeper internships)
http://www.brookfieldzoo.org/0.asp?nSection=11&pageid=&nLinkID=32&sHTTPLink=search.asp

What You Can Earn: Unpaid.
Application Deadlines: Fall (September through December), August 1; winter (December through January), December 1; summer (May through August), February 1.
Educational Experience: Two years of college, 2.5 GPA, willingness to commit to a minimum six-week term (five days a week, 40 hours per week), and a sincere interest in the particular field in which you want to work.
Requirements: Proof of a current tetanus vaccination is required for zookeeping internships before the start of the internship assignment. In some animal areas, additional inoculations/tests may be required at your expense.

OVERVIEW

The internationally renowned Chicago's Brookfield Zoo has a long-standing internship program designed to help prepare students for eventual careers involving animal care and conservation. Zookeeper internships for 40 hours a week for between six and 12 weeks are available in a variety of animal areas featuring all aspects of management, including exhibit and enclosure maintenance, diet preparation and distribution, animal observation and documentation, animal handling, record-keeping, and informal educational interactions with the visiting public. The internship introduces students to the reality of a career as zookeeper, a physically demanding profession subjecting interns to a variety of physical demands and environmental factors. Zookeeper interns may be required to work outdoors in extreme weather conditions, including heat and cold, rain, snow, and humidity.

The internships for zookeepers include many different exhibit areas in which to learn, such as

Australia House, Children's Zoo and Hamill Family Play Zoo, Habitat Africa! The Savannah, The Fragile Kingdom, Seven Seas Panorama, The Living Coast, The Swamp, and Tropic World.

Australia House

One of the zoo's original exhibit buildings, Australia House features diurnal and nocturnal indoor exhibits as well as several large outdoor enclosures with Australasian animals including kangaroos, bats, echidnas, owls, parrots, snakes, frogs, tree kangaroos, feather-tailed gliders, bettongs, emus, and a cassowary. Here, you'll have the opportunity to work with some animals (such as the Southern hairy-nosed wombat) rarely kept outside of Australia. In fact, Brookfield Zoo is one of only three zoos in the United States to house these wombats. You'll get practical, hands-on experience in keeper duties and learn many aspects of captive animal management, including record-keeping, diet preparation, enclosure maintenance, and animal behavioral management.

Children's Zoo and Hamill Family Play Zoo

At this "zoo within a zoo," you'll have an opportunity to work with a wide assortment of native and nonnative wild and domestic animals, from tiny domestic hamsters to huge Clydesdales, including nearly 300 other animals representing numerous species of mammals, birds, reptiles, amphibians, and invertebrates. If you intern in the fall, winter, or spring, you'll participate in animal training programs, bird programs, and the dairy program. If you intern in the summer, you may get a chance to participate in Animals-in-Action demonstrations. This internship offers lots of hands-on animal contact as well as extensive interaction with visitors in the encounter area, walk-in-farmyard, pet play, zoo at home, and the keeper kitchen.

The Fragile Kingdom

In this unique exhibit spanning several continents, you'll get a chance to understand the survival of a delicate ecosystem. The Fragile Kingdom includes two multispecies exhibits: The Fragile Desert and The Fragile Rain Forest. At each, you'll have the chance to work with a wide variety of species, including small cats, reptiles, invertebrates, otters, bats, and naked mole rats. You'll prepare animals' meals, maintain the exhibit, learn more about animal behavior, keep records, observe animals, and interact with the public. As part of your Fragile Kingdom experience, you'll also complete a short research project related to any aspect of animal husbandry that interests you.

Habitat Africa!

Here you'll intern in two African habitats in this indoor/outdoor exhibit, featuring a variety of animals that share habitats on the open African plains, such as plated lizards, milky eagle owls, African wild dogs, and reticulated giraffes. You'll work closely with keepers as you acquire practical experience in keeper duties and learn many aspects of captive animal management. You'll be involved in diet preparation, exhibit maintenance, record-keeping, animal training, and animal observations, and you'll be required to complete a short research project related to some aspect of animal husbandry.

The Living Coast

In this exhibit, visitors tour the South American coastline of Chile and Peru, watching moon jellies, several species of sharks, sea turtles, sea horses, anemones, nudibranchs, and starfish. Then they are transported to one of the world's hottest deserts, home to animals such as Humboldt penguins, vampire bats, and Inca terns. Working with this exhibit, you'll get lots of experience in animal behavior and training and learn how to prepare varied diets and understand more about water and environmental quality and other aspects of animal management. You'll work closely with keepers in all areas and complete a short research project on a related topic of your choice.

Seven Seas Panorama

In this popular site featuring marine mammals, you'll care for Atlantic bottlenose dolphins, California sea lions, Northern fur seals, harbor seals, and Pacific walruses. All of the animals participate in daily training sessions and public presentations. Under the guidance of marine mammal staff, you may help prepare food, maintain enclosures, and offer presentations to zoo visitors. However, you won't have direct hands-on experience with these animals; instead, you'll learn how to manage and train marine mammals by working beside trainers, talking with zoo staff, observing training sessions, and reading suggested literature.

The Swamp

Here you'll be working with more than 60 species of animals that live in Southern cypress swamps and Illinois river habitats, in an exhibit that immerses visitors in the sights, sounds, and smells of wetlands. Mammals, waterfowl, wading and perching birds, reptiles, amphibians, fish, and invertebrates are all represented, many from wildlife rehabilitators requiring special exhibit design and care. The Swamp also presents a strong interpretive program of graphics and visitor interactive experiences regarding the benefits of wetlands. Here you'll gain hands-on experience working alongside keepers through the building's three areas, preparing food, helping with animal procedures and medications, monitoring water quality, and learning basic animal training and behavioral enrichment. You'll work with keepers who have a wide variety of experience and individual interests, allowing you the unique opportunity to delve further into areas of animal husbandry, behavioral enrichment, and public education.

Tropic World

One of the largest indoor mixed-species exhibits in the world, this facility represents the tropical rain forests of South America, Asia, and Africa and hosts many species of primates, birds, and mammals. Baboon Island houses a troop of Guinea baboons in a large outdoor habitat. The building's three sections (South America, Asia, and Africa) have eight different animal runs, including two off-exhibit breeding colonies of endangered primates. Here you'll work for 12 weeks with primate department keepers in all areas of Tropic World (interns working shorter terms will be assigned to fewer areas and work with fewer animal runs). You

may maintain enclosures, prepare food, make routine animal observations, and interact daily with the public. You'll also work closely with primate department staff to learn about animal husbandry, mixed-species exhibits, and tropical rain forest conservation.

Other Internships

Nonanimal internships are also available in areas such as marketing and special events, education, design/graphic arts, public relations, development, horticulture, water quality lab, and conservation biology. Interns in nonanimal areas must commit to a minimum term of six weeks.

HOW TO APPLY

You can download the zookeeper internship application (in PDF format) by visiting http://www.brookfieldzoo.org/0.asp?nSection=11&pageid=&nLinkID=32&sHTTPLink=search.asp.

Once you've filled out the application, you should submit it to the preceding address with a cover letter explaining your career intentions, a current resume, transcripts, and two letters of recommendation. Internships are available on a year-round basis. Applicants chosen to be interviewed will be notified by e-mail. Successful applicants will be advised of their selection and internship assignments by mail. A $15 program fee is required upon placement into the internship program.

DENVER ZOO INTERNSHIP

Denver Zoo College Internship Program
2300 Steele Street
Denver, CO 80205
cwhite@denverzoo.org
http://www.denverzoo.org/join/career/
    internships/Internships.htm

What You Can Earn: $9 an hour for paid internships; some internships are unpaid.

Application Deadlines: March for a summer paid internship; the Bird Department and Tropical Discovery accept applications year round for nonpaid internships.

Educational Experience: None.

Requirements: Candidates should have career goals consistent with the animal field and some related experience with animals.

OVERVIEW

The Denver Zoo's goal is to provide a wildlife conservancy that offers high-quality experiences in an urban recreational setting and provides environmental education that inspires public awareness of global conservation. The zoo also tries to offer scientific programs that make meaningful contributions to the conservation of animals and their ecosystems. The summer internships are a vital part of these goals.

Zookeeping internships are available in various areas within the animal department, including birds, mammals, and tropical discovery (fish/reptiles). As an intern with the Denver Zoo, you'll gain experience in the daily care of animals by working closely with zookeepers.

The Bird and Mammals Departments offer paid internships during the summer; Tropical Discovery offers nonpaid internships throughout the year. A bird-zookeeping internship is often available throughout the year.

Unpaid academic internships are usually available in the fall and winter, whereas summer internships last from May to August.

HOW TO APPLY

To apply for a summer internship in animal care, submit a resume and cover letter indicating the position for which you wish to apply, along with a letter of recommendation from an academic advisor, teacher, employer, or current or past volunteer manager/coordinator. (The letter may be sent separately or with your application.) The Bird Department accepts applications year round for nonpaid internships. Preference in selecting interns will be given either to residents of the seven counties of the metro Denver area or to students attending school within the same district. Mail your application to the preceding address.

DISNEY'S ANIMAL KINGDOM ADVANCED INTERNSHIP

Walt Disney World Animal Kingdom
PO Box 10090
Lake Buena Vista, FL 32830
(407) 828-1736
http://www.wdwcollegeprogram.com

What You Can Earn: Varies.

Application Deadlines: Rolling.

Educational Experience: Junior, senior, or recent grad (sophomores qualify for some internships) with major in biology, psychology, wildlife biology, zoology, or other related fields.

Requirements: Strong computer proficiency (Microsoft Word and Excel), excellent ability to speak in front of groups, direct research experience (assistance with established research programs) and a GPA greater than 3.0. You must have transportation.

OVERVIEW

There are about 20 different opportunities to work with animals in the Walt Disney World Advanced Internship Program at Walt Disney World's Animal Kingdom. These internships allow you to network with successful professionals in particular fields of study. In most instances, the Walt Disney World Advanced Internship program serves as a springboard in launching a successful career. Internship positions last for six months, starting either in January or June. Among the animal-related advanced internships are opportunities in animal behavior, animal nutrition, education, reproductive biology, marine biology, vet hospital, marine mammal, and aquatic vet services.

Animal Behavior

If you choose this area, you'll receive training in behavioral research at Disney's Animal Kingdom with the goal of preparing you for future work and training in this area. Behavioral research is used to add to the understanding of zoo animals and to facilitate their optimal care and well being, as well as to assess the effectiveness of Disney's educational programs and experiences for their guests. You'll participate in all aspects of behavioral research, including project development, data collection, date entry and analysis, library research, statistical analyses, and dissemination of results (including both written and oral presentations). You may collect data through direct observations of animals, through viewing videotapes, or through guest interviews.

Animal Nutrition

Under the supervision of both the animal nutritionist and the animal nutrition center management team, you'll be involved with the different aspects of the department, including helping with food preparation within the animal nutrition center, including "on-stage" food preparation in front of guests, as well as demonstrations to back-stage tour groups. You will be asked to interact with guests and share with them information about animal nutrition. Under the supervision of the nutrition laboratory staff, you'll help with nutrition research projects such as food-nutrient analysis (sample processing, data collection, and entry) and you'll conduct quality-control analyses on forages/browses using in-house laboratory equipment (such as ovens, freeze dryers, grinders, and near infrared reflectance spectrophotometers). You'll spend about 75 percent of your time preparing food and 25 percent conducting research.

Aquatic Vet Services

Assisting veterinary cast members in the daily operations of The Living Seas, your job as an intern here may include diet preparation; record-keeping; stocking medical supplies; data entry; laboratory assistance; cleaning; maintenance of surgical equipment; and other animal-related work. You may help develop and implement presentations that educate and inspire guests in areas of aquatic zoological medicine and wildlife conservation. You also must be a certified scuba diver.

Education Presenter

This is a great entry-level position for interns who love sharing their passion for conservation with others. Your primary responsibility is to engage guests of all ages in fun, interactive conversations focusing on conservation action and awareness. You need to be able to deliver presentations that are accurate, entertaining, and inspiring and that communicate the appropriate conservation messages on topics such as wildlife natural history, animal behavior, and conservation. You'll interact with Disney guests in a variety of settings at Disney's Animal Kingdom, including the park's main entrance and Kids Discovery Club sites.

Specifically, you'll be responsible for operating the Kid's Discovery Club locations throughout the park, involving large numbers of families with children. These interactive stations are designed to connect children (ages three to eight years) with the natural world by encouraging them to get involved. The Kids Discovery Clubs embrace strong education themes, which you'll convey through personal conversations that inspire conservation action. Most of your day will be spent staffing the Kids Discovery Clubs locations.

You'll also be responsible for the safety of live animals in containers while presenting them to guests. (Live animals include tarantulas, scorpions, spiders, snakes, and turtles.) Training on animal safety and welfare issues will be provided and conducted by animal keeper staff.

You'll be expected to participate in all required cast training programs and staff meetings in an effort to remain current on subject matter related to wildlife conservation and animal information. The internship experience includes a five-session seminar series that focuses on leadership, animal-related careers, and networking opportunities.

In addition to the requirements listed above for all Disney interns, if you work as an intern in this area, you must have a strong conservation and environmental knowledge in order to communicate the appropriate wildlife messages to all guests. You must be able to communicate biological information and make it personal and relevant to guests in an informal setting and understand proper safety measures for guests, animals, and cast during all animal presentations. Finally, you've got to be willing to work outdoors in all kinds of weather.

Marine Mammal

As an intern here, you'll help conduct educational presentations stressing marine conservation issues and marine mammal awareness. As an intern here, you'll give daily presentations at the West Indian Manatee exhibit. You'll help prepare daily food to satisfy nutritional requirements of marine mammals, help feed West Indian Manatees, and clean all animal areas each day. You may help observe various types of sessions with Atlantic Bottlenose dolphins, with an introduction to training basics, record-keeping, and research sessions and implementations. Topics could include but are not limited to behavioral development and animal observation and environmental enrichment. You must be a certified scuba diver for this position.

Marine Biologist and Aquarium

Interns here will work alongside resident biologists assisting with all areas of marine fish husbandry, working with animals ranging from large sharks to corals and jellyfish. Daily responsibilities include food preparation and maintaining cleanliness of all areas to USDA standards. You'll be expected to dive and feed on a daily basis in the 5.7 million gallon aquarium and maintain life-support systems for a series of smaller exhibits. Interns will work in quarantine systems, perform necropsies, analyze water chemistries, collect and record data, and interact with guests regarding all aspects of marine conservation and aquarium husbandry. You also must be a certified scuba diver.

Reproductive Biology

Interns here participate in a variety of endocrine projects that boost the reproductive success of captive endangered species. You'll work directly on the reproductive monitoring of elephants, okapi, and white rhinos to aid in the conservation of these captive endangered species. Other projects on black rhinos and hippos track reproductive cycles for management and husbandry purposes. You'll run the entire process of enzyme immunoassays and graph data for various animals. In addition, you'll have the opportunity to participate in projects such as working closely to monitor the success of contraceptives to manage captive populations of cotton-top tamarins, as well as tracking reproduction for samples of wild tamarins. You also may help monitor wildlife on Walt Disney World's 8,500 conservation areas, and you'll assist in the inventory of species to determine their population sizes. Field activities include surveys of birds, alligators, deer, gopher tortoises, and butterflies. Interns work closely with all members of the wildlife tracking center team and learn about projects including elephant communication and tracking of sea turtles, wood storks, and swallow-tailed kites. Interns also interact with guests to spread conservation messages and educate them about exciting scientific research.

In addition to the general requirements listed at the beginning of this entry, you must have strong laboratory skills (particularly chemical and biochemical techniques).

Vet Hospital

The Veterinary Service's advanced interns function in two roles: the primary wildlife case contact and assistant to the veterinary technicians. You'll be responsible for receiving all wildlife cases that come to the veterinary hospital from Walt Disney World property, including assessment, triage, giving necessary care as directed by the animal care staff and veterinarians, animal transport to rehabilitation facilities, and maintenance of all records and databases. You'll provide support to the veterinary technicians, including setting up supplies/equipment prior to procedures, maintaining supplies, clean up after procedures, clean/pack/sterilize instruments, helping with sample preparation, and completing related laboratory paperwork. You're also responsible for guest interaction and giving presentations in the on-show veterinary treatment window.

In addition to the general requirements listed above, you must have direct animal care experience at a vet clinic, a wildlife rehabilitation facility, or a zoo. Your experience should include cleaning and maintaining animal facilities.

HOW TO APPLY

First, you should apply online at http://www.wdw-collegeprogram.com. Once you complete this form, you must attend a presentation to be eligible for an interview. Presentations are held at colleges across the country at various times. (Visit the preceding Web site to find the nearest presentation site.) The presentation is your opportunity to have your questions answered and learn detailed information about the Walt Disney World College Program.

You should bring your completed application to the presentation. At the presentation, you will be able to sign up for an interview, which generally takes place within 24 hours of the presentation. Advanced Internship applicants will need to submit all of their interview materials after the presentation to the recruiter. You'll be given additional information on scheduling a telephone interview. You'll receive notification about two to three weeks after the interview.

If it's been longer than three weeks since you interviewed, you should send an e-mail to wdw.college.recruiting@disney.com with your full name, the school where you interviewed, and your complete mailing address.

DOLPHIN INSTITUTE INTERNSHIP

Kewalo Basin Marine Mammal Laboratory
Attn: Internship Program
1129 Ala Moana Blvd.
Honolulu, HI 96814 USA
kbmml@hawaii.edu
(808) 593-2211

What You Can Earn: Unpaid.
Application Deadlines: Spring (early January through July): August 15; fall (early July through January): February 15.
Educational Experience: Must be at least a junior in college.
Requirements: None specified.

OVERVIEW

Have you ever wanted to be involved in hands-on dolphin research and care? Would you like to learn about animal-training techniques? The Dolphin Institute offers internships to students who have completed at least two years of college.

The program offers qualified individuals from all over the world semester-long internships in dolphin research and education. Interns are an integral part of the staff, and they work with senior researchers and graduate students in this carefully designed apprenticeship program.

You'll work directly with dolphins and researchers to learn effective dolphin-teaching techniques and research skills and also gain valuable experience by helping to orient one-, two-, and four-week Dolphin Institute volunteers.

The internship begins as a full-time volunteer position from Monday through Friday and on alternate Saturdays until all initial training has been accomplished (usually this takes about half the semester). During the latter part of the semester, your required time commitment is reduced by 75 percent, which will allow you to get another job, if necessary. You must provide your own transportation, housing, and daily expenses.

After all the interns for a semester have been chosen, you're given contact information for other interns in your group so you can coordinate living arrangements. The length of this program will offer interns more opportunities to improve their skills in a variety of areas, including research, education, and training.

You'll participate in all aspects of the program, including exploring dolphin perception, intelligence, and communication; helping with dolphin husbandry and care; helping the staff to operate the research laboratory; acquiring hands-on experience in dolphin research, training, and husbandry; receiving an education in dolphin and whale behavior and natural history; and working with other interns, students, staff, and volunteers.

If you're currently enrolled in college, you can make arrangements for credit for the semester. Alternatively, course credit can be obtained by registering at the University of Hawaii, if arranged in advance. (In the latter case, you'll have to pay out-of-state tuition fees if you don't live in Hawaii.)

HOW TO APPLY

First, you'll need to download a PDF version of the application (http://www.dolphin-nstitute.org/education_programs/researchinternship/index.htm) or print an MS Word version from the same Web site. Alternatively, you can request an application by e-mailing, calling, or writing to the preceding addresses.

Submit the completed application with transcripts of all college courses, three letters of recommendation (preferably from college instructors who know you personally), your resume, and a statement of purpose that describes your background, skills, and what you expect to contribute to and gain from the internship. You also should demonstrate your familiarity with the type of research conducted at the Kewalo Basin Marine Mammal Laboratory. There is no application fee.

Specific starting and ending dates are flexible for each semester, and it's possible to change the dates if there are conflicts with school schedules. It takes about six to eight weeks before a decision on the internships are made; early submission will not result in early notification.

FARM SANCTUARY INTERNSHIP

Farm Sanctuary
PO Box 150
Watkins Glen, NY 14891
(607) 583-2225
Fax: (607) 583-2041
info@farmsanctuary.org
http://www.farmsanctuary.org

What You Can Earn: Unpaid.
Application Deadlines: Farm Sanctuary internships are available year round. Positions are filled on an ongoing basis as applications are received. Summers fill up quickly, so if you're interested in summer months, be sure to apply well in advance.
Educational Experience: Not specified.
Requirements: Must be age 16 or older, with a strong commitment to animal rights; interns are required to be vegan while on sanctuary premises (vegan living includes no meat, dairy products, eggs, honey, or other animal byproducts; personal care items must be cruelty-free with no animal byproducts; no leather, silk, or wool clothing).

OVERVIEW

Farm Sanctuary is the nation's largest farm animal rescue and protection organization, begun in 1986 when Gene and Lorri Bauston found a living sheep abandoned on a stockyard "deadpile." They rescued the sheep, named her Hilda, and created Farm Sanctuary. Most state anticruelty laws specifically exempt farm animals from basic humane protection, so abandoning a sick animal on a pile of dead animals is considered "normal animal agricultural" practice.

Farm Sanctuary is working to change the way society views and treats animals used for food production. With the active support of over 100,000 members, the organization operates coast-to-coast shelters and a national rescue and adoption network. Farm Sanctuary operates a 175-acre shelter in upstate New York and a 300-acre shelter in northern California, in addition to coast-to-coast shelters that provide rescue, rehabilitation, and lifelong care for cattle, pigs, chickens, turkeys, goats, sheep, ducks, geese, and rabbits.

All of the animals housed at Farm Sanctuary were victims of cruelty and neglect. Some of the animals are rescued during investigations of farms, stockyards, auctions, and slaughterhouses; others arrive from humane societies and SPCA cruelty cases.

Interns at Farm Sanctuary help care for hundreds of animals. It's possible that most of your time will be spent in the barn, cleaning and doing farm chores. While the work is physically demanding and repetitive, it is essential to the health of the animals. Other assignments may include animal care and feeding; staffing the Visitor Center and running educational tours; and bulk mailing and helping with administrative projects. Occasionally, interns may also assist with shelter tours and shelter outreach events and activities.

Here you'll volunteer a full-time, 40-hour-a-week schedule. The shelters are open seven days a week, and scheduling varies but generally includes weekends and holidays. Interns who live at the shelter are also responsible for helping with shelter security, which includes being on-call two to three nights during the week for after-hour shelter emergencies. If you are on call, you must stay at the intern house so you're available if needed.

All interns are welcome to volunteer any extra time they wish or to take part in extra activities such as animal healthcare and grooming, research and campaigns, and other programs (volunteer opportunities will vary depending on location). We encourage interns to make the most of their Farm Sanctuary experience. The more you put into the internship, the more you will get out of it.

Optional educational programs are provided for all interns. These may include but are not limited to History of Farm Sanctuary, Stockyard Investigations, Basics of Animal Care, How to Start and Operate a Farm Animal Shelter, and Vegan Resources. All interns will have the opportunity to give their preferences for topics, and Farm Sanctuary will try to accommodate as many of these choices as possible.

HOUSING

Housing is offered at no charge for all Farm Sanctuary interns and includes a shared bedroom, bathroom, and kitchen facilities. Interns are required to share in household cleaning chores and keep community areas clean for the comfort of everyone living together. Interns are responsible for buying and preparing their own food; weekly trips to the grocery store are provided for interns without cars.

HOW TO APPLY

Fill out the online internship application (http://www.farmsanctuary.org/join/internform.htm) or call the national office and ask for an internship application.

FORT WAYNE CHILDREN'S ZOO VETERINARY MEDICINE INTERNSHIP

Fort Wayne Children's Zoo Education Department
3411 Sherman Blvd.
Fort Wayne, IN 46808
(260) 427-6808
cheryl@kidszoo.org
http://www.kidszoo.org

What You Can Earn: Unpaid; priority given to those who can obtain college credit.
Application Deadlines: Rolling but submit application two months before expected start date.
Educational Experience: College student (those enrolled in vet medicine curriculum preferred but not required).
Requirements: Applicants should have a long-term interest in exotic animals and be experienced and comfortable with dealing with domestic species. Experience with exotic species is preferred but not required. Applicants must be available to work a flexible schedule, at least 30 hours a week (40 hours a week is preferred). A negative tuberculin skin test must be performed within one year of the start date. Current rabies, hepatitis B, and tetanus vaccinations are recommended.

OVERVIEW

The Fort Wayne Children's Zoo is internationally recognized for its innovative displays, award-winning animal exhibits, and well-manicured grounds. With more than 1500 animals, the zoo lets kids get up close and personal with a goat, explore a misty jungle trail, or watch giraffes roam a vast hillside.

As an intern here, you'll support the zoo's vet department by helping with animal care, procedures, and hospital maintenance as you learn more about the field of zoo/exotic veterinary medicine. You'll report directly to the zoo's veterinarian, helping with routine procedures (such as immobilizations, physical exams, and treatments), as well as emergency procedures. You'll also help vet techs with hospital and equipment cleaning and maintenance as needed and help the keeper staff with daily care of animals housed at the veterinary hospital or in quarantine. You'll also work on other tasks or special projects, depending on your experience and skills.

Internships are available all year, and the duration of your internship is flexible to meet your school requirements. However, you should plan to intern for at least four weeks.

HOW TO APPLY

To apply for the internship position, download an application at http://www.kidszoo.com/pdfs/internapp.pdf or call the education department at the number listed previously.

FOSSIL RIM WILDLIFE CENTER INTERNSHIP

Fossil Rim Wildlife Center
PO Box 2189
Glen Rose, TX 76043
(254) 897-2960
http://www.fossilrim.org

What You Can Earn: Unpaid.
Application Deadlines: Animal care internships: spring term: November 1; summer term: March 1; fall term: June 1; summer avian internship: January 1; animal care apprentice: February 1.
Educational Experience: Open to college juniors and seniors.
Requirements: At least two years of undergraduate college work in wildlife management, conservation biology, or a related scientific discipline.

OVERVIEW

Fossil Rim Wildlife Center is an 1,800-acre, award-winning conservation, research, and education facility nestled among the live oaks and junipers of the North Texas Hill Country. The Wildlife Center is dedicated to conservation of species in peril, scientific research, training of professionals, creative management of natural resources, and public education. A leader in propagation and management programs, scientific research, diverse public education initiatives, and training facilities for conservation professionals, the Wildlife Center offers several animal-related internships to college juniors and seniors.

The animals at Fossil Rim, with the exception of the carnivores, rhinos, and a few others, are free to roam 1,500 acres of Central Texas Hill Country savannas and juniper-oak woodlands. The Wildlife Center focuses on threatened species, protecting and preserving endangered animals through research, cooperative management, and public awareness. Fossil Rim was founded on the conviction that all creatures have a right to exist, that the natural world has intrinsic value apart from human perceptions and needs, and that this right and this value deserve our deep respect.

The Wildlife Center offers internship opportunities in animal care, petting pasture, rhino research, and avian and naturalist training in the education department.

Avian Internship

Avian internships are offered in spring and run through summer of each year. Avian interns will assist the avian supervisor with daily record-keeping, cleaning, and care of Attwater's prairie chickens and Japanese Red Crown cranes. Your responsibilities include observing specimens, compiling data, maintaining flights, preparing diets, helping with incubation procedures, and hand-rearing chicks for the annual release program.

Black Rhino Internship

Rhino Research internships are offered in the spring, summer, and fall each year; with this job, you'll be responsible for the daily maintenance of the black rhino herd. Other duties include observation and chute conditioning of the rhinos, keeping records, collecting samples, and participating in publishing scientific articles. Fossil Rim is currently involved in several research projects, both within and in cooperation with other facilities.

Children's Animal Center Internship

Children's Animal Center internships are offered in the spring, summer, and fall of each year. Here you'll help clean and care for the petting-pasture animals, including pygmy, Nubian and Angora goats; Navajo-Churro, Southdown, Hampshire, and Suffolk sheep; Vietnamese pot-bellied pigs; Aldabran and African spurred tortoises; cockatoos; macaws; and ocelots and maned wolves. You'll also be responsible for maintaining nature trail areas, along with interacting with children, talking to visitors about the animals, helping to develop educational displays and programs, and helping with outreach and youth volunteer programs.

The Whitfield Collins Carnivore Internship

If you land this internship, you'll be responsible for the daily feeding, cleaning, and health monitoring of a number of exotic species, including red, Mexican, and maned wolves and coati.

HOW TO APPLY

Apply online at http://www.fossilrim.org/learning/internships_form.php.

GENESIS ANIMAL SANCTUARY SUMMER INTERNSHIP

Warren Wilson College
Environmental Leadership Center
Campus Box 6323
PO Box 9000
Asheville, NC 28815
Fax: (828) 771-7092

What You Can Earn: A stipend of $100 weekly, with room and board included.
Application Deadlines: Completed application forms, cover letter, professional resume, and three recommendations are due by January 31; formal interviews will be scheduled in February. Notification of most internship awards will occur in March.
Educational Experience: Freshman, sophomores, and juniors with a commitment to graduate from Warren Wilson College are eligible to apply.
Requirements: Prior experience in rehab is not necessary, but the sanctuary requires an intense appreciation in wildlife and environment and a strong commitment.

OVERVIEW

Each year, the animal sanctuary handles about 500 birds/animals on a rehab status. We maintain a Conservation Center for the containment of those birds and animals unable to return to the wild; some of these are used in educational programs and many are used in display habitats. The sanctuary has two active sites for rehab with several outreach rehab programs funded by Genesis. While individual admissions make up most of the sanctuary's work, education and prevention is also important.

The live-in internship position includes two interns sharing responsibilities for the center's wildlife rehabilitation program. The center is fully staffed from 9:00 A.M. to 4:00 P.M. seven days a week. During those hours, the employees are experienced staff specializing in high-level emergency and rehabilitation care for wildlife. This is an excellent learning opportunity for the individual interested in any area of wildlife preservation. During off hours, an experienced rescuer is on call. You're encouraged to respond with a rescuer to any emergency so you might benefit from this learning experience.

The intern will learn wildlife rescue from the initial admission to release. You'll be involved in daily weight monitoring, dietary needs, care of wounds or splints, physical therapy, and giving medication. During the spring and summer months, orphans constitute the bulk of admissions. You'll learn the proper dietary needs of individual species, how to identify a featherless or furless orphan, and how to determine the proper diet for that species.

The senior intern will actively participate in both on-site and outreach educational programs, helping a permanent employee in the various functions and handling the raptors and mammals used in these programs. Self-motivation and high energy is a definite plus to Genesis.

You'll be expected to work 40 hours a week in a flexible time frame, so you'll have the time to enjoy mountain activities such as hiking, biking, rock climbing, white-water rafting, and boating.

HOW TO APPLY

Send a copy of your current resume, a cover letter, and three recommendation forms (one from your faculty advisor) along with an online application. Links to online application forms and recommendation forms can be found at http://www.warren-wilson.edu/~elc/internships/application.shtml. If you elect to fill out the form by hand, please mail completed application to the preceding address.

GREAT DOG OBEDIENCE TRAINING INTERNSHIP

Great Dog
11333 Roosevelt Way, NE
Seattle, WA 98125

(206) 526-1101
Info@gogreatdog.com
http://www.gogreatdog.com/contactus.htm

What You Can Earn: Unpaid.
Application Deadlines: August of each year.
Educational Experience: High school diploma or equivalent.
Requirements: Must be 18 years of age, interested in dogs, dog training, and dog care, comfortable demonstrating in a classroom setting. You should have a good command of the English language, enjoy dogs, have a wonderful sense of humor, enjoy working in a team environment, and be able to work 25 to 30 hours a week (plus homework).

OVERVIEW

Great Dog is more than just a doggy daycare. Since opening shop in 2001, Great Dog has offered a culture that places an emphasis on a pet's experience with a wide array of opportunities for dogs of all sizes, shapes, and temperaments. At Great Dog, staff tries to make the most of each dog's day by enriching each dog's life through a series of special group and individual projects, touch therapy, and obedience activities using positive methods. Some dogs even get a job, such as helping staff with various activities.

If you're a dog nut, you'll be happy to hear that Great Dog Obedience offers internships to students interested in starting a career in dog training. You'll work with experienced dog trainers in class rooms, help with developing training programs, and assist in monitoring and tracking the daycare pack environment. You'll also document canine behaviors, establish well-rounded activities for difficult dogs, and learn basic grooming and nutrition techniques. Internships range from six to 12 months depending on dedication, background, personal skills, and experience.

HOW TO APPLY

Call for more information about applying for an internship.

HILLTOP FARM INC. INTERNSHIP

Hilltop Farm Inc.
1089 Nesbitt Road
Colora, MD 21917
(410) 658-9898
info@hilltopfarminc.com
http://www.hilltopfarminc.com

What You Can Earn: Unpaid.
Application Deadlines: Rolling.
Educational Experience: Undergraduate students only.
Requirements: None specified, other than interest in horses and equine health.

OVERVIEW

At Hilltop Farm, you'll find a complete sporthorse center that provides training services for riders and horses of all disciplines. The farm is also actively involved in breeding horses (broodmares and young horses receive daily, individualized care) and hosting internationally known seminars and clinics for riders, veterinarians, and breeders.

In addition, Hilltop Farm offers training services for riders and horses of all sporthorse disciplines, with horses of all levels in dressage and jumping; the farm also successfully prepares stallions and mares for performance testings, develops riders from novice through the FEI-levels, and skillfully prepares and presents horses of all ages at breed competitions.

The training team includes committed, well-trained professionals with diverse talents to handle almost any training or instruction need for dressage, hunter/jumper, or three-day event interests. Because young fillies and geldings benefit from the natural socialization of herd life, just as young colts do, Hilltop also offers in-hand training, young horse starting services, and stallion inspections.

Sound like fun? One-year internships at the farm are offered in the "mare and foal care" or in a lab internship, but you should know that none of the internship positions involves riding. If you intern in mare and foal care, your responsibilities will include feeding the horses, cleaning stalls and grooming, and keeping the foaling barn clean inside and out. You may help check field horses, help with turnouts, and help the vet or farrier with field horses. You also may help with foal watching, treating, and handling; cleaning and organizing sheds; and doing an evening barn check.

The lab internship includes care of tease mares, grooming, and bringing in from the field every morning and turn out at end of collections. You may also hold the mare for collections when needed, put the mare in a holding stall between collections, prepare the collection area, remove manure, record collection data, package semen prepared by a technician, do paperwork, and handle daily chores in the lab.

HOW TO APPLY

Fill out an application online at http://www.hilltopfarminc.com/form_intern_application.htm and click to send online; then e-mail your resume to Gayle.Stike@hilltopfarminc.com. The application process takes four to six weeks; positions vary depending on the time of year and availability.

HOUSTON ZOO INTERNSHIP

Primate Supervisor
Houston Zoo Inc.
1513 N. MacGregor
Houston, TX 77030
(713) 533-6673
Fax: (713) 533-6755

What You Can Earn: Unpaid.
Application Deadlines: Rolling.
Educational Experience: Interns should be pursuing a career in some aspect of conservation,

animal/wildlife management, education, graphics, Web design, psychology, food preparation, marketing, operations, or zoo-related business. Check individual internships for specific requirements.

Requirements: Must be at least 18 years of age and have a current negative TB test.

OVERVIEW

Recently privatized and under new leadership, the Houston Zoo prepares to meet the challenges and responsibilities of a 21st-century zoo with exhibits habitat-based exhibits, presenting wildlife in naturalistic surroundings. Internships are typically available in different areas in the zoo, taking about 20 hours a week. A zookeeper internship in the bird department and the Golden Lion Tamarin area are two popular choices.

Golden Lion Tamarin Free-Range Program

The Houston Zoo is one of fewer than 10 zoos in the country that have free-ranging Golden Lion Tamarin monkeys. During warmer months, these monkeys are released from their enclosure and encouraged to forage for their food as they would in the wild. Volunteers observe, track, collect data, and describe to guests details about these monkeys. Obviously, the zoo must watch the monkeys to make sure they don't venture outside of the zoo. There are approximately 120 volunteers who help us make this happen.

As a Golden Lion Tamarin intern, you'll help with animal tracking, data collection, coordinating of volunteers, and public outreach. The internship is a four- or five-month (April through October) position, but a minimum three-month commitment is required. The position requires 15 to 20 (or more as desired) hours of work per week.

All interns must have completed at least two years of college in a related field such as anthropology, education, biology, zoology, or psychology. This internship offers an extraordinary experience in animal-behavior research, animal care, animal management, and volunteer management.

Zookeeper Internship: Bird Department

If you're a bird lover, you'll love working here, where you'll clean animal exhibits, prepare animal diets, maintain exhibits (raking, sifting, plant trimming, propping), observe and record animal condition, behavior, and responses, and interact with zoo guests. You also may help with veterinary care and treatments. This position can be a challenge; you may need to climb ladders, lift heavy objects up to 50 pounds, and assume awkward positions, all while being exposed to significant heat and humidity. At first you'll be supervised closely by a staff member, but as you gain confidence and experience you'll be given more independence.

For this internship, you'll need at least one year of animal experience (either in a vet, or at FFA, 4-H, private aviculture, volunteering, and so on). This internship requires 24 to 25 hours a week, in five five-hour days or three eight-hour days (all work days are available, but Saturday and Sunday availability is preferred). Work begins at 7:00 A.M. but may start as early as 5:30 A.M. if you like.

HOW TO APPLY

When applying for an internship, send your resume and a cover letter describing your career hopes, experience, and availability. This information helps the zoo find a potential internship that works best for you. Your internship application will be considered as soon as the zoo receives your cover letter and resume, which may take up to one month.

For information on the zookeeper internship, e-mail kfacker@houstonzoo.com.

To apply for the Golden Lion Tamarin internship, send cover letter, resume, an "adult volunteer" application (http://www.houstonzoo.org/Adult_Volunteers/Application_Process.aqf), and two references to the preceding address.

For information on all other internships, contact volunteer@houstonzoo.com.

To apply for other internships that may open, e-mail or fax your resume and application to the volunteer department at the number/address listed above.

MYSTIC AQUARIUM INTERNSHIP

Mystic Aquarium
College Intern Coordinator
55 Coogan Blvd.
Mystic, CT 06355-1997
(860) 572-5955 ext. 227
interninfo@mysticaquarium.org
http://www.mysticaquarium.org/divein/
    internships/internships.asp

What You Can Earn: Unpaid but college credit is possible.
Application Deadlines: Spring (January through May): October 31; summer (June through August): February 28; fall (September through December): June 30.
Educational Experience: Undergraduate, graduate student, or recent college graduate.
Requirements: None specified.

OVERVIEW

The Mystic Aquarium tries to make discovering the underwater world easy and fun for students and teachers. Through a wide variety of internships, the aquarium offers positions in the research and study of marine animals and veterinary internships. Interns also can work behind the scenes in the marketing and public relations departments or with graphic arts and communications technology.

The Mystic Aquarium is dedicated to the advancement of knowledge of the aquatic world for present and future generations. The internship program supports this mission by providing an opportunity to complete a project under the guidance of an intern supervisor while gaining career experience.

Husbandry and research internships are full-semester commitments with a minimum of 38.75 hours per week. Internships in departments that don't deal directly with animal care require a minimum of 16 hours a week. However, you should expect to devote time after work to research and completion of the internship project. (The total number of hours worked may be dictated by credit requirements.)

As a Mystic intern, you'll also develop an independent project in conjunction with your supervisor on a topic usually determined by current research or programs provided by the department. Once the topic of the project is defined, you'll be responsible for developing the project (including collection of data and data analysis for research projects), writing a project report, and giving a brief oral presentation of the project to aquarium staff. All materials and data remain the property of Sea Research Foundation and must be placed on file in both hard-copy form and on computer disc.

Internships are available in pinniped and penguin husbandry; beluga whale husbandry; fish and invertebrate husbandry; research and veterinary services; education; graphics; communications technology; visitor/member services; marketing; public relations; merchandising; development; and engineering/maintenance.

Beluga Whale Husbandry

Cetacean aquarists feed, train, and care for the Aquarium's collection of beluga whales. As an intern here, you'll help prepare diets for beluga whales, clean and maintain exhibits and back-up areas, help feed beluga whales, help with the training of husbandry behaviors, help husbandry staff and staff veterinarian with medical procedures, and help with stranded marine mammals when possible.

Recent projects have included a comparison of cetacean vocalizations before and after training demonstrations; quarantine procedures for stranded marine mammals; toy preference in beluga whales; and the ability of a beluga whale to discriminate between differentially rewarded stimuli.

Communications Technology

The Communications Technology Department designs, implements, and supports the computer, network, Internet, telephone, telecommunications, and audio/visual equipment for the aquarium. As an intern, you'll help staff maintain computer and telecommunications networks; help design, install, and maintain Web pages; and help design, install, and maintain audio/visual systems.

Recent projects have included Web development for the aquarium Internet site.

Education

The Education Department offers classes and activities to supplement an aquarium visit and enrich classroom learning. As an intern here, you'll help aquarium teachers teach classroom and field programs for students of all ages, travel with aquarium teachers to present outreach programs at local schools, present public programs within the aquarium, help with the design and preparation of class materials, and teach portions of aquarium classes. You'll also help maintain classroom aquaria and help summer staff with summer camp programs.

Recent projects have included developing various teaching units and activity kits; development of a "sharks" class for fourth-grade students, evaluating and upgrading elementary programs, and developing the concept and construction of a "touch box" to incorporate a tactile experience for visitors.

Graphics

Aquarium graphic artists produce materials for the aquarium to promote education and research. As an intern, you'll help graphic artist staffers produce posters, ads, brochures, signs, and educational materials and help with the illustrations and layout of the aquarium magazine. Recent projects have included the design and painting of a fish mural on a classroom wall, aquarium Web site design, and interpretive elementary graphic systems for aquarium exhibits.

Fish and Invertebrate Husbandry

Fish and invertebrate aquarists feed and maintain the exhibits and reserve holding tanks of the Aquarium's fish and invertebrate collection. As an intern, you'll help prepare food, feed the fish and invertebrates, maintain aquariums (algae scrubbing, water changes, water monitoring, filter maintenance, and H_2O chemical analysis) under aquarist supervision; clean food-prep and other back-up areas; and help with new-exhibit construction and collection of specimens.

Recent projects have included operant conditioning of an octopus, the effects of temperature on embryonic development and egg-laying behavior in chain dogfish, early growth and development of horseshoe crabs, and new exhibit and husbandry of the lined sea nettle.

Pinniped and Penguin Husbandry

Pinniped and penguin aquarists feed, train, and care for the aquarium's collection of northern fur seals, Steller's sea lions, and African penguins. Here, you'll help staff prepare food for pinnipeds and penguins, maintain exhibits and back-up areas, keep records, help feed pinnipeds and penguins, help with the training of husbandry behaviors, help husbandry staff and staff veterinarian with medical procedures, and help with stranded marine mammals when possible.

Recent projects have included shade utilization in northern fur seals and Steller's sea lions; quarantine procedures for stranded marine mammals; and dietary trends of Steller's sea lions.

Research and Veterinary Services

The Department of Research and Veterinary Sciences is responsible for conducting research in many aspects of marine sciences. In addition, the medical care of the exhibit collection is the responsibility of the veterinary staff with its advanced program of preventative medicine, diagnostics, and therapy.

As an intern here, you'll help with microbiological cultures, dissection of stranded marine mammal carcasses, medical assessment of stranded animals (seasonal), blood-cell counts and slide preparation, animal-record management, and field-sample collection. Recent projects have included tissue distribution and serum levels of selected enzymes in sharks, analysis of stranding and sighting patterns for seals in Connecticut and Rhode Island waters, and studies of marine-mammal parasites.

HOW TO APPLY

To apply to one of the areas listed above, obtain an application form at http://www.mysticaquarium.org/divein/internships/application.asp. Submit it to the preceding address, along with a cover letter stating your interests, goals, and relevant experience. Also, you should send a transcript, resume, and a letter of recommendation from a faculty advisor, professor, or instructor (additional letters of recommendation may be submitted by employers, coaches, other supervisors, or advisors.) Letters of recommendation should be sent directly to the preceding address.

If you apply in husbandry, research, or education, you'll be given a list of preselected topics from which to write a research paper, which you should include with your application. The written report should be 1000 words (two to five pages, double-spaced) and include a complete reference section. Applicants for other areas may suggest a topic to research or may submit portfolios or writing samples in lieu of the research paper.

If you're interested in interning in Visitor and Member Services, Marketing, Public Relations, Merchandising, Development, or Engineering and Maintenance, you should submit only a completed application form. The intern coordinator will contact you by phone to discuss possible internship projects within the department of your choice. If an opportunity is available, you'll be asked to submit all application materials.

NATIONAL AQUARIUM IN BALTIMORE INTERNSHIP

National Aquarium in Baltimore
Conservation Education Department - Internships
Pier 3/501 East Pratt Street
Baltimore, MD 21202

(410) 576-3888
intern@aqua.org

What You Can Earn: Unpaid but interns receive a 30-percent discount at the food court and gift shop.
Application Deadlines: Apply before November 1 to intern during the winter and spring semesters; apply before April 1 to intern during the summer and fall semesters.
Educational Experience: Undergraduate registered at a two- or four-year college or university; some areas require students to be juniors or seniors; must receive academic credit.
Requirements: Must be able to work a minimum of 120 hours within the chosen semester.

OVERVIEW

Clownfish, pufferfish, and hammerhead sharks — the National Aquarium in Baltimore has them all! If you're fascinated by fins and fish of all descriptions, you might want to consider an internship at the National Aquarium in Baltimore.

The National Aquarium tries to stimulate interest in and inspire stewardship of aquatic environments. A member of the Baltimore community, Maryland's leading tourist attraction, and an international icon, the aquarium provides cultural, recreational, and educational experiences. The aquarium strives to blend naturalistic exhibit elements with the most modern interpretive techniques, engaging visitors by focusing on the beauty of the aquatic world. Exhibits are designed to replicate natural environments and avoid the unnatural mixing of species. Specimens are chosen to give the best examples of biological concepts in an interesting and accurate way. The collections embrace diverse world-wide habitats to spark responsible actions in visitors.

Internships at the aquarium provide hands-on and minds-on experiences that will be a vital part of your college career. Applying classroom knowledge, interns obtain valuable job experience and establish professional contacts. The aquarium makes every effort to match interns to work that complements their studies, interests, and skills.

Animal Behaviorist

Juniors or seniors are preferred for this internship, in which students will help the aquarium animal behavior and husbandry staff with daily care of the aquarium's animals. Duties include tank maintenance and cleaning, food preparation and feeding, and special projects dealing with animal behavior modification and environmental enrichment.

Aquarist

Junior or senior interns are preferred for the aquarist area, caring for invertebrates and fish. Duties include tank maintenance and cleaning, food preparation and feeding, cleaning behind-the-scenes areas, and keeping records.

Aviculture

It might seem strange to have birds in an aquarium, but that's just what you'll find in this internship area. Interns assist in caring for birds in the Rain Forest exhibits, cleaning the exhibit and back-up areas, preparing and distributing food, keeping records, and performing general maintenance.

Herpetology

If snakes are more your style, you might enjoy this area. Interns help care for reptiles and amphibians in the Rain Forest exhibits, cleaning the exhibit and back-up tanks, distributing food, observing the animals, and keeping records.

Marine Animal Rescue Program

Juniors or seniors are preferred for this internship. Interns will help rescue, rehabilitate, and release stranded marine animals and sea turtles as part of the outreach efforts of the aquarium's Ocean Health Initiative.

Marine Mammal Training

Interns in this area will help with the daily care of the marine mammals. This internship is open only to juniors and seniors; summer and winter terms require 40 hours a week for three weeks. Spring and fall terms require eight hours a day, one day a week. For this internship, you'll prepare food, clean and maintain the exhibit and back-up areas, observe behavior, and keep records.

HOW TO APPLY

Fill out the online application at http://www.aqua. org/students_internprocess.html; click on "internship application."

Once you've printed and completed the application, have your academic advisor sign it, and attach brief responses to the three statements. Enclose a transcript or have the school's registrar send one to the preceding address (it does not have to be an official copy).

Applicants may apply for a maximum of two internships, but you should enclose a copy of the entire application for each position. Incomplete applications will not be considered. Applicants will be contacted by phone or mail approximately four to six weeks after the deadline has passed. Those chosen to be interviewed will be contacted by the supervisor of the area for which they applied.

NATIONAL ZOO BEAVER VALLEY INTERNSHIP

Beaver Valley Internship
National Zoological Park
3001 Connecticut Avenue, NW
Washington, DC 20008
smithki@nzp.si.edu
http://nationalzoo.si.edu/UndergradInternships/
    AnimalPrograms/Default.cfm

What You Can Earn: Unpaid but college credit is possible.
Application Deadlines: September 1 for spring session (January 15 to May 15); January 1 for summer session (May 15 to August 15); April 1 for fall session (August 15 to December 15).

Educational Experience: Undergraduate or grad students in an animal-related field.

Requirements: Negative TB test and completed rabies vaccination series or current rabies titre. You also must have strong communication skills and the ability to work as part of a team and in all weather conditions. You must be able to lift at least 50 pounds, be flexible, and have a good sense of humor.

OVERVIEW

The Smithsonian National Zoo is the nation's zoo, providing leadership in conservation science in a beautiful 163-acre urban park in the heart of Washington, D.C. The home to a diverse animal collection ranging from hummingbirds to elephants, the zoo connects people with wildlife through animal exhibits and science-based programs. The zoo brings visitors close to the animals with exhibits that stimulate natural behavior and well-being for the animals. Visitor experience is enhanced by creative educational materials, as well as by direct interaction with scientists, zookeepers, and volunteers. The National Zoo is a leading center for zoo-animal care, reproductive biology, and conservation research.

This internship centers on Beaver Valley, on the zoo's forested Valley Trail, home to many North American mammals, including American beavers, bald eagles, bobcats, brown pelicans, California sea lions, gray seals, hawks, Mexican wolves, and river otters.

As an intern at the zoo in Beaver Valley, you'll have an opportunity to participate in daily animal management and visitor education during the three internship sessions (spring, summer, and fall). You'll work 30 to 40 hours a week in Beaver Valley, which features North American avian and mammal species. Here you'll help animal keepers with daily food preparation, feeding, and cleaning and provide formal and informal interpretive educational programs for visitors. You'll also develop and implement animal-enrichment programs and observe animal behavior.

HOW TO APPLY

To apply, send a resume with your name, home and college addresses and phone numbers; e-mail address; name of university; current academic status; curriculum (major and minor); and degrees held or expected with institution names and dates conferred or anticipated date(s) of graduation. In addition, you should include a statement of your interest in pursuing this internship, mentioning relevant experience and career goals. Your statement is a very important part of the application evaluation. You should include college transcripts from all schools (unofficial transcripts are okay), along with two letters of reference and documentation of negative TB test and completed rabies vaccination series or current rabies titre.

NEW ENGLAND WILDLIFE CENTER INTERNSHIP

New England Wildlife Center
19 Fort Hill Street
Hingham, MA 02043-9905
(781) 749-5387
http://www.newildlife.com

What You Can Earn: Unpaid.
Application Deadlines: Rolling.
Educational Experience: High school graduate.
Requirements: Proof of being prevaccinated for rabies and tetanus.

OVERVIEW

If you have a passion for wildlife medicine and natural history, this internship could be for you! The nonprofit wildlife animal hospital is located in Bare Cove Park, Hingham, Massachusetts, about 15 miles south of downtown Boston. Between 40 to 50 student interns each year shoulder some demanding tasks at the center, which treats about

5,000 native and naturalized wild animals each year. Student interns are responsible for all aspects of the center's daily operation, and what you don't know when you get there is taught to you by full-time staff vets, a certified vet technician, an office manager, and a resource development officer.

At the center, you'll be responsible for foraging for wildlife foods, dietary design and preparation, cleaning, husbandry, giving medicine, helping with medical and surgical procedures, maintaining medical records, cleaning hospital rooms and cages, and releasing patients into appropriate habitats. In addition, you're required to answer citizens who call or write with questions about wildlife. You're also required to help with fund-raising and teaching educational programs to elementary and secondary students. Periodically, you may be expected to help in special public events, cable TV presentations, and in processing fund-raising materials.

You'll be given reading materials and classroom seminars in medicine; environmental public health; habitat protection; wildlife management and ethics; basic comparative anatomy and physiology; wildlife identification; wildlife medical procedures; diagnostics; and therapeutics.

You can expect to spend between 40 and 60 hours a week during this rigorous internship, beginning at 9:00 A.M., when the intern crew begins the day by cleaning each patient's cage (and sometimes the patient as well). Each animal is then fed and given its morning treatments. After lunch, the prerelease and educational animals are taken care of, and the clinic must be completely cleaned and sterilized before afternoon treatments are given.

The final chore of the day is to feed the educational raptors at the house, a task usually accomplished by whichever interns are currently living in the house. Although the schedule sounds straightforward, in fact no two days are ever the same. From the time the clinic opens until well after it closes, the phone rings constantly, and it's the interns' job to answer these calls about wildlife problems.

You will learn how to deal with the many medical situations as animals are brought in, including how to do physical exams and how to restrain and diagnose with blood and feces analysis and radiography methods. You'll also learn initial treatments for various ailments such as shock and dehydration and basic wing wraps for fractures.

Paperwork is also a constant chore, and you'll be responsible for each patient's records, with facts ranging from how and where a bird is perching to what it ate overnight. Initial information about where it was found and its final disposition information are also kept with this record. The details of where, when, and what time it was released or its death and necropsy information are also recorded.

HOUSING

Housing is available on a limited basis for a fee of $200 a month to out-of-state residents and to instate students whose permanent addresses are west of Worcester, Massachusetts.

HOW TO APPLY

You may download an application at http://www.newildlife.com/NEWC/Jmail/InternApplication.html. To apply, complete and e-mail or mail the application, your resume, and two letters of recommendation to the preceding address. You should be available for a follow-up interview. To check the status of your application, you can e-mail newcinternship@yahoo.com or call the clinic Monday through Friday between 9:00 A.M. and 5:00 P.M.

OREGON ZOO INTERNSHIP

**Zoological Curator, Living Collections
    Division**
Oregon Zoo
4001 SW Canyon Road
Portland, OR 97221
http://www.oregonzoo.org/Intern/animal_care.
    htm

What You Can Earn: Unpaid.

Application Deadlines: Fall term, August 1; winter term, November 1; spring term, February 1; summer term, April 1.

Educational Experience: None specified.

Requirements: Written documentation of current negative tuberculin skin test and tetanus vaccination; candidates should have career goals consistent with the field of animal care and some related experience with animals. Interns must be able to lift at least 50 pounds and may be required to work outdoors. Therefore, you must be able to tolerate extreme weather conditions, including heat and cold, rain, snow, and humidity.

OVERVIEW

Founded in 1887, the award-winning Oregon Zoo is the oldest zoo west of the Mississippi. Its 64 acres are home to animals from all corners of the world, including Asian elephants, Peruvian penguins, and Arctic polar bears (about 1,029 specimens representing 200 species of birds, mammals, reptiles, amphibians, and invertebrates). Of these, 21 species are endangered and 33 are threatened. The zoo is currently active in 21 species-survival plans. Committed to conserving endangered species and their habitats both locally and around the globe, the zoo is a center for wildlife preservation and field research.

The Oregon Zoo's award-winning education programs serve more than a half-million people both at the zoo, schools, and senior and community centers in the region. A summer concert series, seasonal events, and the zoo railway help this popular Oregon attraction draw more than 1 million visitors each year. The Oregon Zoo is also a safe place for families to share moments of discovery and fun.

Animal Care Internships help the zoo's staff with basic animal husbandry duties, including data gathering, analysis, and preparing a final report intended to increase the zoo's understanding of some aspect of the husbandry, nutrition, behavior, or welfare of wild animals in captivity. As an intern here, you'll work five days a week, eight hours a day, which may include weekends and holidays.

Depending on the nature of the assignment, routine daily tasks typically include cleaning animal exhibits, unloading hay, cleaning buildings and grounds, and retrieving or storing bags of grain or salt blocks. Zookeeping is a physically demanding profession that involves frequent bending, stretching, climbing into small spaces, and sometimes working in awkward positions. Tasks are occasionally strenuous; interns are also subjected to strong odors, dust, hay, and animal hair/fur/dander. If you've got a lot of allergies, this might not be the place for you.

Animal Care Internships are available in several areas within the Zoo's Living Collection Division, including Africa, Cascades Stream, Marine Life, Education Programs, Birds, Primates, and Butterflies.

HOW TO APPLY

Send your resume to the preceding address, along with a cover letter that discusses your career goals and how this internship would help you achieve them, what kind of course work and/or experience you have that would make you a valuable intern, and what areas interest you the most in attaining experience through this internship.

PAWS COMPANION ANIMAL INTERNSHIP

Hilary Anne Hager, PAWS CAS Intern Program
PO Box 1037
Lynnwood, WA 98046
hilary@paws.org

What You Can Earn: Unpaid.

Application Deadlines: Rolling.

Educational Experience: None required.

Requirements: Must be interested in animal-welfare issues and be able to work effectively with others and must have experience dealing with the public and providing customer service. Computer skills are a must; sheltering experience is preferred but not required. You should be flexible and willing to learn and try new things.

OVERVIEW

If you're passionate about animal rights and you care deeply about other creatures, this internship could be for you. PAWS advocates for animals through education, legislation, and direct care and serves as the leading voice for animals in Washington State and a recognized leader in the nation for its progressive outreach and education programs, legislative work, and premier wildlife rehabilitation and companion animal services. PAWS envisions the world to be a place where all people recognize the intrinsic value of animal life, are mindful of the impact of their daily behaviors and choices on animals, and consistently demonstrate compassion and respect.

This three-month internship addresses the companion animal needs for the greater-Seattle area through the operation of a limited-admission, high-placement shelter, where no healthy adoptable animals are euthanized. A satellite cat-adoption facility and spay/neuter clinic are also a part of the program. The PAWS companion animal shelter places over 4,500 animals in loving, responsible homes every year.

If you intern with the Companion Animal Services department, you'll help in many areas of shelter operations, managing the lost and found services to help reunite lost animals with their guardians, answering phones and responding to questions about companion animals, answering Web inquiries, and taking notes for PAWS's behavior-evaluation program. You'll also support the shelter management team. While the internship itself does not offer the opportunity to provide direct animal care, there are many opportunities for you to be trained for animal contact.

Puppies and kittens are usually in the shelter only for a matter of days, while some dogs and cats have been with PAWS for months. More than 300,000 animals have come through the doors since 1967, and this direct experience with animals gives PAWS the perspective on how best to advocate and educate for all animals.

If you're considering a career in animal welfare and you're interested in learning more about animal sheltering, want to learn more about companion animals and their behavior, and want to support the PAWS mission, this internship could be a great choice.

At the shelter, you'll be supervised by the shelter managers (especially in the beginning), and you'll work 15 to 20 hours a week during normal business hours. The exact schedule can be determined between you and the shelter managers.

HOW TO APPLY

Fill out an application at http://www.paws.org/cas/internships/casinternapp.html) and send it to the preceding address.

PHILADELPHIA JUNIOR ZOO APPRENTICE INTERNSHIP

Philadelphia Zoo
JZAP Coordinator
3400 West Girard Avenue
Philadelphia, PA 19104-1196
(215) 243-5310

What You Can Earn: Unpaid; however, students who complete the first year with satisfactory performance are helped to find paid summer jobs at the zoo the next year. Junior Zoo Apprentices are entitled to free zoo passes, discounts on food, beverages, and merchandise, and invitations to special recognition events.

Application Deadlines: A new JZAP class is recruited each spring, so it is best to apply at some point between December and March.

Educational Experience: Preference is given to freshman or sophomores in high school.

Requirements: High school students aged 14 to 18; applicants must still be in high school their first summer of the program and must be at least 14 years of age by July 1 of the summer in which they work. (Therefore, you could be 13 when you begin the program in June if you turn 14 by July 1).

OVERVIEW

The Philadelphia Zoo offers a special program for high school students (especially from low-income areas) in which you can intern one summer and then come back the next for a paid job. The Junior Zoo Apprentice Program (JZAP) is committed to fostering an interest in zoology, conservation, and the natural world for deserving youth, particularly from low-income communities. The program takes pride in providing these students with opportunities for career exploration, self-discovery, personal development, and community and conservation service.

JZAP is a work-based learning program for deserving Philadelphia-area high school students, gaining experience in the Children's Zoo, education, horticulture, and grounds. Students who complete the first year are helped to find paid summer jobs at the zoo. Program members also participate in monthly workshops that cover a variety of animal, job-skill, and life-skill topics such as animal behavior, veterinary science, college, conflict resolution, resume writing, and interview skills. Free field trips are offered throughout the year to participants, to various educational institutions such as the Academy of Natural Sciences, the Baltimore Aquarium, and the National Zoo.

Those who joined the program in 2005 traveled to Baltimore to meet and work with students in a similar program at the Baltimore Zoo. All third-year apprentices in good standing are eligible to compete for the opportunity to go on a 13-day safari to Africa.

One of the many benefits of JZAP is that students get to work with animals! JZAP participants are specially trained to handle many of the small animals in the Children's Zoo's collection. What's more, JZAP participation often fulfills student's community service requirements. Some participants have received community service credit for their work in the program. (Students should check with their schools to determine whether JZAP participation meets this requirement.)

All student program members must complete one full year of volunteer work in the zoo before being eligible to apply for a paid position. This involves working 12 full days a month in the summer and one day a month during the school year, in addition to attending workshops and special events. If you are hired for a paid summer job, you may be required to work both Saturdays and Sundays, since that is the zoo's busiest time.

Program members are expected to maintain excellent attendance, punctuality, and conduct. Uniform shirts and sweatshirts will be provided, but students must provide their own khaki pants and sturdy shoes.

The Junior Zoo Apprentice Program lasts up to four years. When a Junior Zoo Apprentice graduates from high school, he or she may also graduate from JZAP. At that point, the Junior Zoo Apprentice will be invited to join the alumni group and, if interested, may occasionally be asked to help with workshops and field trips.

HOW TO APPLY

JZAP is a very competitive program, and only 18 students are accepted each year. Early applicants have a better chance of acceptance into the program. To apply, download a printable form at http://www.philadelphiazoo.org/media/doc/jzap_application2005.doc.

You should send a copy of the completed application, along with a copy of your most recent report card, which must include information on attendance and behavior. If your school doesn't include these details, you must supply a contact number for a teacher or guidance counselor who can provide the information.

Also send a 150- to-250-word essay explaining why you want to be part of JZAP, what you hope to get from the program, and what you can offer the program. In addition, send a recommendation from a guidance counselor or current teacher, including a contact number for that person.

All applications must be received between February 1 and May 21; applications will not be accepted after May 21. All applications are reviewed, but only those candidates selected for interviews will be contacted directly. Interviews are usually conducted between March and May. Acceptance decisions are made by June 11, and orientation typically follows in about a week.

PHILADELPHIA ZOO INTERNSHIP

Philadelphia Zoo
Human Resources Department, Internships
3400 West Girard Avenue
Philadelphia, PA 19104-1196
Fax: (215) 243-5219
zoointerns@phillyzoo.org
http://www.philadelphiazoo.org

What You Can Earn: Unpaid but interns are entitled to free zoo passes, discounts on food, beverages, and merchandise, and invitations to special recognition events.
Application Deadlines: Two months before the start of the semester internship; internships are offered during spring, summer, and fall semesters.

Educational Experience: College freshmen through seniors as well as recent college graduates majoring in biology, zoology, environmental education, or a related field.
Requirements: A GPA of 2.5 or higher, demonstrated interest in working with animals, and basic biological knowledge; you should be professionally minded, motivated, and energetic.

OVERVIEW
The Philadelphia Zoo, America's first zoo, is reaching new heights in all areas of its mission as a conservation, education, and recreation organization. Its state-of-the-art animal exhibits and healthcare facilities, award-winning education and conservation programs, recreational opportunities, guest services, scientific accomplishments, and historically significant areas make the Philadelphia Zoo one of the world's most renowned zoological societies and gardens. The zoo is also the Philadelphia region's leading family attraction, welcoming more than a million visitors a year. The zoo includes more than 1,600 rare and exotic animals from around the world, 42 acres of picturesque Victorian gardens, and outstanding art and historical architecture.

The zoo's internships offer college students a chance to gain valuable work experience while caring for live animals. Interns who earn an animal care internship at the Children's Zoo help care for more than 60 exotic and domestic mammals, birds, and reptiles in the zoo's teaching collection. The zoo was the first in North America to open a special zoo just for children; today's Children's Zoo features a petting yard and daily live animal shows.

With the zoo's commitment to education and wildlife conservation, interns and apprentices experience a uniquely supportive, educational, and passionate environment. Zoo interns and apprentices are immersed in learning, dedication, and fun! Through internships, the zoo provides college students with practical, high-quality experience that enhances their academic work and helps them achieve their professional goals.

HOW TO APPLY

You should submit a letter of interest stating that you are applying for the animal care internship and why, along with a detailed resume, a reference letter or letter of recommendation, and a copy of your college transcripts. You should compile all the required documents and submit them as a complete packet to the preceding address.

SAN DIEGO ZOO INTERNQUEST

San Diego Zoo Internquest
PO Box 120551
San Diego, CA 92112-0551
http://www.sandiegozoo.org/zoointernquest/
   participate.html

Application Deadlines: Applications will be accepted in April for the succeeding fall and winter terms.
Educational Experience: Students must be in grade 11 or 12, attending San Diego County schools during the InternQuest school year.
Requirements: Minimum 3.0 GPA; a demonstrated commitment to conservation or the environment; two letters of recommendation (one from a science instructor and one from a teacher, career counselor, school administrator, or other adult); a well-written essay describing an interest in a zoo-related career or field.

OVERVIEW

If you've ever dreamed of a career in the life sciences (biology, zoology, human or veterinary medicine, wildlife management, or botany) this internship can provide you, while still in high school, with the opportunity to learn from zoo experts. In this program, you'll learn about conservation, pathology, genetics, veterinary medicine, animal behavior, reproductive physiology, ecology, and more.

You'll also have the opportunity to visit behind-the-scenes areas at the San Diego Zoo and San Diego Zoo's Wild Animal Park and meet researchers, veterinary staff, animal care managers/keepers, and trainers.

Typically, you'll meet at the San Diego Zoo or Wild Animal Park three days a week from 2:30 to 5:00 P.M. for about seven weeks. Wednesdays and Thursdays are spent with zoo experts, and Tuesdays are dedicated to creating the Web pages in the zoo's computer lab.

You'll also be trained to create Web pages that include journals of your experiences, illustrated with digital or scanned photos, and you'll communicate with "virtual interns" throughout the world on the online forum! On your own time, you'll keep a journal either on your home computer or in the Zoo's education computer lab.

HOW TO APPLY

Two terms are typically offered during the school year; the fall term usually lasts from September to November, and the winter term is from February to March.

If you're interested in Zoo InternQuest, you must complete an application and submit it with the required information and references. Selected candidates will be interviewed by zoo staff.

Students with a sincere interest in science or education careers who have good writing skills will be the strongest candidates for final selection. Applications may reopen in the fall for any remaining openings in the winter or fall terms.

SEAWORLD ADVENTURE CAMP INTERNSHIP

SeaWorld Orlando Education Department
Attn: SeaWorld Adventure Camp Internship
   Program
7007 SeaWorld Drive

Orlando, FL 32821
http://SeaWorld.org

What You Can Earn: Minimum wage, plus academic credit (with prior approval of your school).
Application Deadlines: March.
Educational Experience: Must have completed your sophomore year of college and be seeking a degree in education, science, or recreation.
Requirements: Undergraduates in good standing at a recognized academic institution. CPR and first aid certification are recommended; American Red Cross lifeguard certification required for resident camp counselors.

OVERVIEW

If you're interested in learning about animals and their habitats, SeaWorld Orlando might be the internship for you. You can apply to work as a counselor at either of their two types of accredited camp programs—a day camp and a resident camp—that last from May through August. Here, campers go behind the scenes to learn about the shows and attractions, along with creative crafts, games, and activities that reinforce animal information.

Resident camp programs are multiday, overnight trips to field locations such as Orlando, the Florida Keys, and Florida's diverse east coast. At resident camp, middle and high school students are immersed in the study of marine science through activities such as snorkeling, canoeing, and exploring the challenges and rewards of working with animals.

The camps aim to instill in students an appreciation for science and a respect for all living creatures and habitats and the desire to conserve our valuable natural resources. Another goal is to increase students' basic competencies in science and math.

Interns in both camps have certain separate responsibilities, although both will overlap in some duties. No matter which camp you are working for, you'll spend the first two weeks training on animal information and camp operations.

Day Camp

If you're accepted for the day camp internship, you'll be assisting with week-long day camp programs for campers in kindergarten through sixth grade. You'll also help other counselors prepare class materials, register campers, teach classes, and assist with daily operations.

Resident Camp

If you're selected for the resident camp internship, you'll help other counselors with off-site programs for campers in grades 6 through 12. Each of these programs are six to 11 days long and include staying with the campers the whole time, including safely escorting campers to and from Orlando International Airport. Resident camp interns will also help with daily operations of day camp and resident camp programs.

To maximize your chances of getting an internship, you might consider applying for both camps. A limited number of positions are available for both internships, and only a few candidates will be selected for the resident camp internship program.

You're responsible for finding your own housing and transportation. Once you're selected for the internship program, you'll receive a confirmation packet that includes information such as how to find housing, together with a contact list to help you find housing with fellow interns.

HOW TO APPLY

To apply, submit a completed application form along with your resume, an official copy of your college transcripts, an Anheuser-Busch employment form, and a completed recommendation form to the preceding address. You can get these forms via e-mail at swf-cswinterns@SeaWorld.com, or visit their Web site at: http://www.seaworld.org/career-resources/internship/pdf/packet.pdf.

If you would like to apply for internships at both the day camp and the resident camp, you should check both boxes on the application form. If you're applying for the resident camp internship, American Red Cross lifeguard certification materials must accompany your application.

Your completed application packet will be reviewed by the education department; qualified applicants will be contacted for phone interviews. All applicants should be notified of a job by the beginning of April.

STRIDES THERAPEUTIC RIDING CENTER INTERNSHIP

Strides
PO Box 572455
Tarzana, CA 91356-2455
strides@onebox.com
http://www.strides.org/internships.html

What You Can Earn: Unpaid; free riding lessons for those working more than 25 hours a week; college credit.
Application Deadlines: Rolling.
Educational Experience: None specified.
Requirements: Must be 18, must work at least 12 hours a week; love of horses; good communication skills; patience, good sense of responsibility, and ability and interest in working with handicapped riders.

OVERVIEW

The Strides Therapeutic Riding Center is one of the nation's top centers for teaching handicapped people how to ride. A premier accredited center of the North American Riding for the Handicapped Association (NARHA), Strides provides quality, professional therapeutic riding by certified instructors who offer physically, mentally, and emotionally challenged individuals an opportunity for emotional and physical growth through horsemanship. In addition to Strides' commitment to therapeutic riding, Strides also seeks to involve inner-city children, homeless children, and at-risk children in an activity that will improve their self-esteem and teach them tools they can use to make a living as an adult. Strides is strongly committed to community-outreach programs.

Each year, eight to 10 students from around the world intern at Strides Therapeutic Riding Centers. Classes are offered during the internship about teaching therapeutic riding and how to start a therapeutic riding program; an extensive library of books and tapes on therapeutic riding is also available to interns.

Typically, interns stay for an average of about three months and are usually at the ranch five days a week, with two days off each week to do sightseeing and enjoy the beaches and sights of Los Angeles. College credit usually requires about 150 hours per semester, depending upon the academic requirements of the department.

Interns may seek certification through the North American Riding for the Handicapped Association, beginning with the online self-study courses. Interns will receive a certified Instructor as a mentor and will be given hands-on education about all aspects of teaching therapeutic riding. In addition to a regular schedule of meetings, classes, and teaching opportunities, interns will have regular performance evaluations with written evaluations, opportunities for observation of other instructor's classes, and riding lessons on Strides program horses. If you work more than 25 hours a week, your lessons are free; if you work less than that, the fee is $30 per group lesson. Interns also receive guidance toward NARHA certification, including personal riding-skill evaluation, assistance with registered level exam, self-study, and CAT course. Interns also have the opportunity to help in other areas of the program, including recruiting and training volunteers, helping with special events and fund-raising, and caring for the horses.

HOUSING

Rooms are available for a minimal fee at the homes of Strides staffers.

HOW TO APPLY

To receive an internship application, write to Strides at the preceding address.

TIGER CREEK WILDLIFE REFUGE INTERNSHIP

Tiger Creek Wildlife Refuge
TMLF/Texas Field Office
Personnel Dept.
17544 FM 14
Tyler, TX 75706
http://www.tigercreek.org/internships.html

What You Can Earn: Unpaid.

Application Deadlines: September for winter term (November to February); December for spring term (February to May); March for summer term (May to August); June for fall term (August to November); check Web site for exact dates.

Educational Experience: Two years of college in a related field such as biology, zoology, wildlife management, or ecology, at least one year of job experience in a related field, such as a vet clinic or zoo, or three years of verifiable job experience in an unrelated field.

Requirements: Minimum age 20; proof of current tetanus shot (within three years); a 3.0 GPA, with some animal care experience preferred. You must be able to lift up to 60 lbs, be in good health, drug free, hardworking, dedicated, and self-motivated.

OVERVIEW

Because humans have moved into the habitats of tigers, lions, and many other big cats, most of these animals have lost their home in the wild. After these animals had their natural habitats destroyed and were taken to the brink of extinction from unmanaged hunting and habitat destruction, experts around the world are trying to raise these creatures in captivity. Tiger Creek Wildlife Refuge is a big-cat sanctuary founded in 1998 and officially opened to the public a year later. Begun by Brian and Terri Werner, the Refuge is a division of Tiger Missing Link Foundation.

Tiger Creek is nestled in the gentle rolling hills and valleys of the East Texas piney woods, where it is run by four employees, a small staff of volunteers, and board members. Tiger Creek currently is working toward creating larger natural habitats for the resident cats.

Three-month internships are available to provide experience in the zoological field. If you sign on as an intern here, you'll clean, prepare food, do light maintenance, and conduct education tours. Interns are responsible for the daily cleaning and health monitoring of a number of exotic feline species, including tigers, lions, leopards, and pumas. Big Cat Internship opportunities also include working in environmental education with schools and scout groups in a variety of learning activities, presenting short guided lessons on animal care techniques, conservation and rescue methods, backgrounds on the big cats, and much more. This wide variety of teaching opportunities and education training can provide you with an exciting array of new skills and experiences. Training is provided by the staff.

You'll be working full time Mondays through Saturdays, with light duties on Sundays, and all interns will undergo training on safety procedures, crisis management, and the rules of the road involving Class 1 Animal Care. You'll be involved in the daily care of the animals upon completing training, including food preparation, cleaning, light maintenance of the caging, grounds, compounds, and so on. In addition, you'll be involved in public tours and educational programs, and you'll be responsible for completing an individual project.

If you have a yen to wrestle with the big cats, you should know that this program does not include direct physical contact with adult big cats. These animals are not pets; only park management is authorized to allow any direct contact, which requires either direct supervision and/or training (including cubs).

HOUSING

Tiger Creek provides dormitory rooms (furniture, full kitchen, bedding, and towels provided), along with TV, DVD, VCR and satellite system, Internet access, local phone service (no long distance calls), uniforms, materials, curriculum and training, and an intern vehicle (if you don't bring your own car).

HOW TO APPLY

To apply, submit a completed application (http://www.tigercreek.org/application.pdf) along with a resume, a cover letter including an explanation of your experience, why you want to intern at Tiger Creek, your career goals, and a recent photo. You should hear about the status of your application within one to two weeks after the deadline.

WILD HORSE SANCTUARY INTERNSHIP

Wild Horse Sanctuary
PO Box 30
Shingletown, CA 96088
Telephone and Fax: (530) 335-2241
info@wildhorsesanctuary.org
http://www.wildhorsesanctuary.org/internships.
   htm

What You Can Earn: Unpaid but housing is included and meals are included on trail rides; college credit is possible.
Application Deadlines: Rolling.
Educational Experience: College students who have finished at least their sophomore year and have an interest in pursuing a career involving horses, veterinary medicine, animal behavior, wildlife management, or ethology. While it is preferable that a student is enrolled in the study of animal science, animal behavior, ethology, or preveterinary medicine, this is not required.
Requirements: None.

OVERVIEW

The government estimates that 47,000 wild horses are still roaming western public lands. To manage these populations, wild horses are rounded up annually by the U.S. Department of Agriculture and made available for public adoption. More horses have been taken from their homes on the public land than there are people willing or able to provide homes for them. Thousands have been removed from the range and held in crowded holding areas. Nearly 200 wild horses and burros live on the Wild Horse Sanctuary, running free in small bachelor bands or harems, a stallion and his mares. These horses are descendants of Spanish horses brought to the New World in the 1500s by the Conquistadors. In the 1800s, the Spanish stock began to mix with European horses, favored by the settlers, trappers, and miners, that had escaped or been turned out by their owners. The wild horses were in demand until tractors and other mechanical means replaced them. Then they were pushed back into the most arid, hostile public lands that remain. Yet they still survive!

As an intern here, you'll help with daily horse care and ranch operations, assisting with weekend horseback camping rides and participating in wild horse identification or contraception projects. Additional projects are available and will be tailored according to student interests and the needs of the sanctuary.

Internships are offered during summer sessions and entail 10 weeks of full-time work. Most internships are scheduled to begin the first week of June and end the second week of August. However, some flexibility is allowed to accommodate students' schedules.

Students should consult with their college advisors to determine if credit can be earned through a Wild Horse Sanctuary internship. As a guideline, three credit hours are typically awarded for completion of a full 10-week internship program. Wild Horse Sanctuary will coordinate with interns' advisors as needed to ensure that all requirements for students' programs are met.

HOUSING

Rooms are provided for all interns, and meals are provided on trail rides.

HOW TO APPLY

A general application form for Wild Horse Sanctuary's internship program is available on this site.

Fill out the online application at: http://www.wildhorsesanctuary.org/internships2.htm. College programs may have additional requirements for intern applicants. Students should first determine the requirements of their college and then complete both their college application (if applicable) and the Wild Horse Sanctuary application.

Completed applications should be sent to Dianne Nelson at the preceding address.

WILDLIFE RESCUE AND REHABILITATION INTERNSHIP

Wildlife Rescue And Rehabilitation Inc.
PO Box 369
Kendalia, TX 78027
(210) 698-1709
Fax: (830) 336-3733

What You Can Earn: Housing and a $50 per week stipend.
Application Deadlines: Rolling.
Educational Experience: None specified.
Requirements: Must be 18 years of age or older; must have rabies pre-exposure vaccinations before or upon arrival.

OVERVIEW

Established in 1977, Wildlife Rescue and Rehabilitation (WRR) receives more than 7,000 wild animals per year for rehabilitation and release as well as provides permanent sanctuary for 300 to 400 resident nonreleasable indigenous wildlife, exotic wildlife (large mammals, primates, reptiles, and birds), and farm animals rescued from the exotic pet trade, roadside zoos, or retired from research facilities.

The organization serves the cities of Austin and San Antonio, as well as the entire state of Texas, from its 187-acre site in Kendalia. WRR also provides assistance on a national basis to wild animals in need of rescue. Like all accredited sanctuaries, WRR is not open to the public, and the animals are never placed on exhibit. WRR works to increase public awareness through educational outreach programs that focus on wildlife protection and habitat preservation.

General animal care internship positions require a six-month commitment at 40 hours minimum per week. Interns will learn about animal husbandry and basic wildlife rehabilitation, provide care for a diverse range of animal species, provide rescue and transport of animals, and perform limited administrative duties. This is an excellent opportunity to learn about the many factors and issues regarding captive, free-ranging, and urban wildlife with an emphasis on humane ethics and solutions.

HOW TO APPLY

Complete the online application (http://www.wildlife-rescue.org/WRRInternApplication.pdf) and mail it to the preceding address.

WOLFSONG RANCH FOUNDATION INTERNSHIP

The Wolfsong Ranch Foundation
PO Box 138
Rodeo, NM 88056

(505) 557-2354
info@wolfsongranch.org

What You Can Earn: Room, board, and a small personal-expense stipend.
Application Deadlines: March of the year you want to intern.
Educational Experience: None specified.
Requirements: Ability to tolerate living in wilderness area; must be in excellent health with no medical conditions requiring regular doctor visits. People on certain kinds of medications would not find Wolfsong a safe environment due to desert heat, hard work, and extended hours working in the sun.

OVERVIEW

This private nonprofit organization is dedicated to the rescue, rehabilitation, and study of predator and raptor species at a 440 acre facility in Rodeo, New Mexico. At present, more than 160 animals (mostly wolves and wolf hybrids) live on the ranch. Wolfsong Ranch Foundation is committed to furthering the educational goals of anyone interested in the fields of animal behavior, zoology, wildlife biology, ecology, veterinary medicine, veterinary science, and all related fields.

Student internships are offered for periods of one to three months (longer stays are considered on an individual basis). The ranch lies in a very rural setting, with the nearest small store eight miles away and medical facilities an hour away. The nearest towns with small grocery stores are 45 and 50 miles away, and the nearest urban areas are more than 100 miles away.

HOUSING

Interns live in a travel trailer or camper and make their own meals.

HOW TO APPLY

Fill out and send the online application at http://www.wolfsongranch.org/interns.html#intern.

WORLD BIRD SANCTUARY INTERNSHIP

World Bird Sanctuary
Attn: Intern Coordinator
125 Bald Eagle Ridge Road
Valley Park, MO 63088
(636) 861-3225
Fax: (636) 861-3240
info@worldbirdsanctuary.org
http://www.worldbirdsanctuary.org

What You Can Earn: $200 stipend for food.
Application Deadlines: Rolling.
Educational Experience: A college degree or working toward a degree is recommended.
Requirements: At least 18 years of age, reliable, enthusiastic, motivated, and able work well independently and as part of a team. You must be capable of rigorous outdoor work in all types of weather and be able to lift at least 50 pounds. Your own transportation is recommended. A minimum 12-week commitment, except where otherwise noted, is expected.

OVERVIEW

The World Bird Sanctuary (WBS) is one of North America's largest facilities for the conservation of birds and strives to preserve the earth's biological diversity and protect threatened bird species in their natural environments through education, captive breeding, field studies, and rehabilitation. To do this, the WBS employs a full-time staff of 35 and hires about 25 part-time employees each year. In addition to captive breeding, its rehabilitation department treats more than 250 sick and injured raptors each year. The WBS also helps rescue and relocate smuggled and confiscated animals for the U.S. government.

General Internship

As a general intern, you'll help with avian captive management, education, and avian field studies.

You'll also participate in all aspects of the captive management of the resident birds from around the world used in education programs and captive breeding projects. This includes assisting the staff in daily husbandry duties and working hands-on with trained birds from around the world. You may also help rehabilitate injured birds and help the staff of the Office of Wildlife Learning present educational programs to the public. You'll interact with the general public on a daily basis and help in the visitor centers.

In addition, you may participate in the release, tracking, and monitoring of peregrine falcons and become experienced in the use of radio telemetry, field identification of birds, and documentation of behaviors. You may work very long hours and in all types of weather conditions.

Propagation

The Captive Breeding department of WBS has celebrated many significant achievements since its inception in 1977, including successful efforts to re-establish several endangered species. The WBS emphasizes the breeding of native and exotic species of raptors, and the successes have included many species of eagles, falcons, buzzards, vultures, condors, hawks, and owls. Propagation interns gain experience in managing breeding raptors and their support colonies, incubation techniques, and hand-rearing procedures. Applicants must be available from January 15 through June 15.

HOUSING

Coed housing and utilities are furnished.

HOW TO APPLY

Send your resume along with a cover letter stating your career goals and how this internship will help you achieve those goals, and state which position you are applying for, along with three letters of reference and an intern application (http://www.worldbirdsanctuary.org/volunteerapplication.txt) to the preceding address.

ZOO ATLANTA INTERNSHIP

Zoo Atlanta
Attention: Animal Care Supervisor
800 Cherokee Ave, SE
Atlanta, GA 30315

What You Can Earn: Unpaid.
Application Deadlines: Rolling; interns are accepted year round, but it's a good idea to apply as early as possible before the start of a semester or the summer season.
Educational Experience: Candidates must have completed at least one year of a college degree program, preferably in biology, animal behavior, zoology, or a related field.
Requirements: You must be able to provide proof of current negative TB test. You must have a strong desire to work with animals and interact with zoo visitors and be capable of performing vigorous physical activities.

OVERVIEW

Zoo Atlanta is a cultural institution engaged in the care, exhibition, study, and conservation of wildlife. Its mission is to establish superior environments and high-quality care for the animals in our collection and to provide patrons with an enjoyable educational experience. Internship possibilities offer hands-on animal experience. These internships allow qualified individuals the opportunity to gain professional hands-on experience while also creating a potential pool of qualified applicants to fill future openings in Zoo Atlanta or other zoos. Interns also help to provide support to the Zoo Atlanta staff.

If you join the petting zoo, you'll work with a variety of domestic animals (including goats, sheep, and pigs) in the "contact yard" and surrounding exhibits. You'll be supervised by education animal care staff as you care for animals and help with visitor interpretation activities.

You'll also have an opportunity to be involved with animal training and public presentations. Assignments and opportunities to participate in various animal care and training activities is based on your prior experience with animals, your animal care knowledge, and how much you progress while you're at the zoo.

HOW TO APPLY

Download and complete the application at http://www.zooatlanta.org/pdf/intern.pdf. Fax your application and resume to (404) 627-7514 and indicate "Petting Zoo Internship" in the subject line. Direct the fax to "Animal Care Supervisor." Or you can mail your materials to the preceding address.

ART

ARCHIVES OF AMERICAN ART INTERNSHIP

Archives of American Art
MRC 937 PO Box 37012
750 9th Street, NW, Suite 2200
Smithsonian Institution
Washington, DC 20013-7012
kirwinl@si.edu
http://www.aaa.si.edu

For information on the graduate archival internship, contact

Archives of American Art
Attn: Barbara Aikens, Chief, Collections Processing
PO Box 37012
Victor Building, Rm. 2200, MRC 937
Washington, DC 20013-7012
aikensb@si.edu

What You Can Earn: Unpaid.
Application Deadlines: Rolling for general internships; March 15 deadline for summer internships.
Educational Experience: Undergraduates and graduate students with a background in art history, American history, American cultural studies, historic preservation, or archival studies.
Requirements: Must work 10 weeks on a full-time basis; must have good research, analytical, computer, and writing skills.

OVERVIEW

The Archives of American Art (AAA) collects the personal papers of American artists, art dealers, critics, and others concerned with American art. Interns at the AAA encourage students to explore careers related to archival, information management, curatorial, and art history fields. Here, interns are given a chance to conduct research using primary sources, process archival collections, prepare written descriptions of collection contents, and help with registrarial duties. An internship at the Smithsonian Institution is a prearranged, structured learning experience scheduled within a specific time frame, under the direct supervision of Smithsonian staff. Internships, for the most part, are arranged individually.

Internships are structured around current and ongoing projects and may include the preparation of subject guides and collection finding aids; researching and planning archival exhibitions; archival processing and preservation; Web site development; special registrar projects; scanning historical documents and photographs; database management; and so on. Recent intern projects have included transcribing and auditing oral histories and conducting background research; archival exhibition research, label and text preparation, and installation; Web site enhancement projects, such as online archival exhibitions, document scanning, digital database management and maintenance, HTML document encoding; and processing and preserving archival and manuscript collections.

Graduate Archival Internships

AAA also has opportunities for graduate students in advanced archival tracks and programs. Depending upon the individual needs of the program and student, a professional and focused experience in archival work may be structured around processing and preservation; cataloging and Encoded Archival Description (EAD) descriptive practices and standards; collections management surveys and databases; and digital collections' access projects. Interns will work Monday thru Friday during regular business hours. Course credit can be given with the approval of the intern's university.

Graduate interns work under the supervision and guidance of senior-level professional archivists in either the collections processing department or the digital initiatives department. The archives has expanded facilities with large and bright processing areas, large climate-controlled storage areas, and a well-equipped digital collections' center. Facilities and offices of the Archives of American Art are located in the Smithsonian's Victor Building in downtown Washington, D.C., in the Gallery

Place/Chinatown neighborhood, easily accessible by metro.

HOW TO APPLY

To apply for the general and summer internships, send a cover letter and resume detailing your experience, career interests, and internship goals, along with a transcript and two letters of recommendation to the preceding address.

Inquiries about the graduate archival internships should be directed to the chief of collections processing at the preceding address.

ART INSTITUTE OF CHICAGO INTERNSHIP

The Art Institute of Chicago
Internship Program
111 South Michigan Avenue
Chicago, IL 60603-6110
aic.jobs@artic.edu

What You Can Earn: Unpaid but academic credit is available.
Application Deadlines: March 15 for summer; August 15 for fall; November 15 for spring.
Educational Experience: Junior- or senior-level college students, or graduate students; a major in art history or fine art is not essential.
Requirements: Must be earning academic credit at the time of the internship; a minimum of 14 hours per week is generally expected.

OVERVIEW

The Art Institute of Chicago, founded in 1879 as both a museum and school, first stood on the southwest corner of State and Monroe Streets. It opened on its present site at Michigan Avenue and Adams Street in 1893. Built on rubble from the 1871 Chicago fire, the museum housed a collection of plaster casts and dreamed of conducting educational programs and acquiring and exhibiting art of all kinds. The collection now includes more than 5,000 years of art from cultures around the world, and the school's graduate program is continually ranked as one of the best in the country. Within the next decade, a new complex will continue this process of growth.

It takes many diverse people with a wide range of skills and interests to successfully run the Art Institute of Chicago. Internships are available in a wide range of departments, including accounting; African and Amerindian art; American art; architecture; archives; Asian art; audience development and public affairs; conservation; development; European decorative arts; European painting; film center; human resources; imaging; installation and packing; contemporary art; museum education; museum registration; operations; prints and drawings; purchasing; Ryerson/Burnham libraries; student affairs; and video data bank. Open internships are updated at the institute's Web site once every other month.

HOUSING

Housing arrangements are not provided for interns; it is your responsibility to find your own housing. However, the institute does offer dorm rentals for summer interns. If you're interested in a dorm rental, you may contact the School of the Art Institute's Department of Student Life at (312) 899-7460 for more information.

HOW TO APPLY

To apply for an internship, you must fill out an application, which may be downloaded from http://www.artic.edu/aic/jobs/internap.pdf. Submit the application along with your resume and a cover letter in which you include the department in which you'd like to intern to the preceding address. (or send an e-mail). Open internships are updated once every other month. Application materials are accepted even if your department of interest is not listed. If you are selected as a candidate for a potential internship, the institute will call you to schedule an in-person or telephone interview. Students are responsible for their own travel arrangements.

ART MUSEUM OF THE AMERICAS INTERNSHIP

OAS Student Intern Program
Organization of American States
1889 F Street, NW
Washington, DC 20006
(202) 458-6016
Fax: (202) 458-6021
http://www.museum.oas.org/education/
internship.html

What You Can Earn: Unpaid.
Application Deadlines: November 1 for winter/spring session; March 15 for summer session; June 15 for fall.
Educational Experience: None specified.
Requirements: None specified.

OVERVIEW
Established in 1976 by the Organization of American States (OAS) Permanent Council, the Art Museum of the Americas is dedicated to boosting awareness and appreciation of the art and cultural traditions of the 34 OAS member countries, especially modern and contemporary art from Latin America and the Caribbean. The building housing the museum was originally designed by noted architect Paul Cret in 1912 as the residence for the Secretaries General of the Organization of American States. If you have a strong interest in a museum career, you're encouraged to apply to this internship. Interns have the opportunity to gain experience in various activities of the museum by participating in the ongoing work of the different departments.

HOW TO APPLY
Download the application at http://www.oas.org/en/pinfo/hr/intern-form2.doc, including a brief essay (between 75 and 100 words) explaining why you are interested in an OAS internship position and how this will help your academic or career goals. Submit the completed application, along with a description of relevant coursework and grades you received, an official statement from your program advisor (if you'll be receiving academic credit), and two letters of recommendation from a professor, academic advisor, or employer, to the preceding address.

CENTER FOR ARTS AND CULTURE INTERNSHIP

Aimee Fullman, Internship Coordinator
Center for Arts and Culture
4350 N. Fairfax Drive, Suite 950
Arlington, VA 22203
(703) 248-0430, ext. 13
Fax: (703) 248-0414
afullman@culturalpolicy.org
http://www.culturalpolicy.org/issuepages/
infotemplate.cfm?page=Internship

What You Can Earn: Unpaid during academic year, but academic credit is available; summer internship stipend may be available.
Application Deadlines: April 16 for summer internship; December 1 for spring session; August 15 for fall session.
Educational Experience: Graduate and undergraduate students who can assist the center with research, communications, and administrative projects.
Requirements: Knowledge and interest in public policy and the cultural sector; familiarity with Windows, data entry, and Web site maintenance; excellent research and communications skills; ability to work independently and with a team; positive attitude and willingness to help where needed.

OVERVIEW

The Center for Arts and Culture is a nonprofit, nonpartisan organization that tries to inform and improve policy decisions that affect cultural life. A consortium of foundations founded the Center for Arts and Culture in 1994 as a way of moving beyond public debates about government funding for arts and culture, in an attempt to provide a broader context for cultural policies in the United States. The guiding principles of that mission, according to the center, include freedom of imagination, inquiry, and expression, as well as freedom of opportunity for all to participate in a vital and diverse culture.

Founded in 1994 in Washington, D.C., the center is supported by foundations and individuals and commissions research, holds public roundtables, and publishes new voices and perspectives on the arts and culture.

If you're interested in art and culture, an internship here will provide you a unique opportunity to get administrative experience in a small, nonprofit think tank, to become familiar with policy options in arts and culture. At the center, you'll work as part of an informal, creative team to help provide support for all of the organization's activities. You'll work directly with staff members to support programs and communications under the supervision of the internship coordinator.

You may find yourself researching various topics related to the arts, culture, and public policy; editing and maintaining database-driven information for the center's Web site; preparing for conferences and other events; helping with communications and public relations; managing a variety of diverse project assignments; and performing clerical and administrative tasks. Hours are flexible and arranged based on the needs of the Center and of each individual's schedule.

HOW TO APPLY

Download an application at http://www.cultural-policy.org/pdf/internapp.pdf. Submit a completed application along with a resume, an unofficial transcript, two references, and a writing sample to the preceding address.

CHICAGO HISTORICAL SOCIETY INTERNSHIPS

Intern Coordinator
Chicago Historical Society
Clark Street at North Avenue
Chicago, IL 60614-6071
(312) 799-2274
Fax: (312) 266-4549

What You Can Earn: Unpaid but academic credit is available, along with a 30 percent discount on merchandise in the museum store; discounted prices to programs; invitations to special events, exhibition openings, and receptions; and a free copy of *Chicago History* magazine.

Application Deadlines: Rolling but applications for summer internships are generally considered between February and May, fall internships between June and September, and spring internships between October and January. Some winter session internships may be available depending upon institutional needs.

Educational Experience: Undergraduate and graduate students interested in pursuing a career in museum practice, archival administration, arts administration, or historical scholarship. Applications are encouraged from African American, Asian American, Latino, and Native American students.

Requirements: Ability to work between 15 and 35 hours a week.

OVERVIEW

As the historian of metropolitan Chicago, the Chicago Historical Society (CHS) collects, preserves, interprets, and presents the history of all Chicagoans in a collection of more than 20 million photographs, documents, and artifacts relating to Chicago and American history.

An internship at the Chicago Historical Society is a challenging educational experience in which you'll work alongside staff members in a tutorial arrangement, so you can learn valuable skills and training in your chosen field. Individuals participating in the summer internship program will also have the opportunity to participate in educational seminars and enrichment programs exploring current issues in the museum field.

Specific projects vary according to the institution's needs and priorities and your academic and professional goals, so check the Web site of the society frequently to see which internships are available. Typically, internship opportunities are available in the following areas:

Arts and Museum Administration

In this internship, you'll have the opportunity to learn vital skills in arts management and administration by helping with fund-raising and special-event planning and with other administrative projects.

Collections Care and Management

Here you'll work with CHS curators and collections managers to develop and implement plans for the proper storage, conservation, and exhibition of the society's priceless collection of prints and photographs, archives and manuscripts, costumes, architectural drawings and fragments, decorative and industrial arts, paintings, sculpture, and books.

Educational Programs and Planning

In this department, you'll help create youth-outreach programs, develop curriculum materials and gallery guides, and research and coordinate special events and public programs, working with CHS staff to develop new ways to present history to diverse audiences.

Exhibition Design

If you love art, this design internship can offer you the chance to hone your skills in design, drafting, or carpentry while working beside CHS designers as they design and create new exhibition spaces.

Exhibition/Project Research

Here you'll help with research for special exhibitions and projects, performing library, collection-based, and community-based research on a wide range of topics related to Chicago and American history.

Publications

If writing is more your style, this internship will allow you to help create a variety of CHS publications. Graphic design internships help produce *Chicago History* magazine, gallery guides, promotional materials, and other publications on a limited basis.

HOW TO APPLY

Download an application at http://www.chicagohs.org/internshipform.pdf. Mail your application to the preceding address, along with a one-page personal statement describing your reasons for seeking an internship and what you hope to gain from the experience; a resume outlining your educational, professional, and volunteer experiences; and two letters of recommendation from current or former professors or employers. Every effort is made to match your skills and interests with the needs and priorities of the department and the institution.

CHRISTIE'S INTERNSHIP

Christie's
Human Resources/Internship Program
20 Rockefeller Plaza
New York, NY 10020
Fax: (212) 636-4945
careers@christies.com
http://www.christies.com/careers/internship.asp

What You Can Earn: Unpaid with academic credit; paid (minimum wage) without academic credit.
Application Deadlines: Rolling.
Educational Experience: Should have a background in art history or decorative arts and knowledge of at least one foreign language.
Requirements: Interest in the art world; summer interns must work Monday through Friday from 9:00 A.M. to 5:00 P.M.

OVERVIEW

Christie's founder, James Christie, conducted his first sale in 1766. A levelheaded businessman famed for his eloquence and humor, Christie turned auctioneering into a sophisticated art as he conducted the greatest auctions of the 18th and 19th centuries. Among his most famous auctions were his negotiations with Catherine the Great, empress of Russia, for the sale of Sir Robert Walpole's collection of paintings, which would form the base of the Hermitage Museum Collection in St. Petersburg. Today, Christie's salerooms continue to be a popular showcase for the unique and the beautiful.

If you love art, Christie's offers spring (January to May) and fall (September to December) internships in specialist departments at its Rockefeller Center location in New York City. Successful applicants will be placed in available positions according to their interests and background, which will expose them to the operations of an auction house as they perform various administrative/clerical tasks.

HOW TO APPLY

E-mail, fax, or mail the following application materials to the preceding address. A resume of work experience with your home and school addresses, telephone number, and e-mail addresses; a letter describing what you hope to gain from an internship at Christie's, and an indication of whether your application is for academic credit or pay, together with a listing of art history courses you've taken and any foreign languages you know.

COOPER-HEWITT, NATIONAL DESIGN MUSEUM INTERNSHIP

Internship Coordinator
Cooper-Hewitt, National Design Museum
2 East 91st Street
New York, NY 10128
http://ndm.si.edu/EDUCATION/index.html

What You Can Earn: Both paid and unpaid internships (see details below).
Application Deadlines: February 1 for summer internships; March 1 for Kell-Muñoz Fellowship; July 1 for academic year internships (fall term); December 1 for academic year internships (spring term).
Educational Experience: Undergraduate students and graduate students currently enrolled in a degree-granting institution; students who have graduated from a degree-granting institution in the last six months or who have been accepted into a degree-granting post-graduate program within six months.
Requirements: See specifics below.

OVERVIEW

Cooper-Hewitt, National Design Museum of the Smithsonian Institution is the only museum in the nation devoted exclusively to historic and contemporary design and offers educational programs, exhibitions, and publications. The museum was founded in 1897 by Amy, Eleanor, and Sarah Hewitt (granddaughters of industrialist Peter Cooper) as part of The Cooper Union for the Advancement of Science and Art. A branch of the Smithsonian since 1967, Cooper-Hewitt, National Design Museum is housed in the Andrew Carnegie Mansion on Fifth Avenue in New York City.

The museum includes the Design Resource Center for collections study and storage; the Drue Heinz Study Center for Drawings and Prints; the Henry Luce Study Room for American Art; the Di Palma Center for the Study of Jewelry and Precious Metals; the Barbara Riley Levin Conservatory; the Agnes Bourne Bridge Gallery; the Nancy and Edwin Marks Masters Program Suite; the Lester and Enid Morse Garden Room; and the Arthur Ross Terrace and Garden.

With more than 250,000 objects, Cooper-Hewitt, National Design Museum is one of the largest design repositories in the world, dating from the Han Dynasty to the present. The collection is organized in four curatorial departments: applied arts and industrial design; drawings and prints; textiles; and wallcoverings. These departments are supported by design archives and a reference library with more than 60,000 volumes, including 5,000 rare books.

The internship program at Cooper-Hewitt, National Design Museum offers a variety of paid and nonpaid opportunities to encourage promising young students of art history, architectural history, museum studies, museum education, and design to explore careers in the museum profession.

This program is designed to acquaint participants with the programs, policies, procedures, and operations of the National Design Museum and of museums in general. Interns are assigned to specific curatorial, education, or administrative departments where they will assist on special research or exhibition projects, as well as participate in daily museum activities.

Subject to availability, internships are available in a number of departments, including communications, design (Quark required), development; drawings, prints, and graphic design; education; exhibitions; graphic arts; image rights; industrial design and decorative arts; IT (PC-based); library; textiles; textile conservation; and wallcoverings.

Academic Year Internships

A certain number of volunteer (unpaid) internships are available during the academic year, based on the projected workload of the host department.

Kell-Muñoz Education Fellowship

To promote diversity throughout the professional museum community, Cooper-Hewitt, National Design Museum offers a 10-month fellowship to a graduate student of Latino or Hispanic origin. The fellowship is sponsored by Kell-Muñoz Architects of San Antonio and gives a student a chance to work in the museum's education department for 10 months, earning $10,000. This internship requires a 24-hour a week commitment, plus some nights and weekends.

Summer Internships

There are two types of 10-week summer internships available each year: volunteer unpaid internships and paid Peter Krueger internships.

Unpaid Internships

About five unpaid internships are available each summer for 10 weeks beginning the second Monday of June at the National Design Museum.

Peter Krueger Internship

This internship honors the memory of former museum intern Peter A. Krueger. Eight Krueger internships, each of which includes a stipend of $2,500, are available each year, for a period of 10 weeks.

HOW TO APPLY

To apply, download a Smithsonian Internship Application form (SI-3954) at http://ndm.si.edu/EDUCATION/index.html. Send it along with a cover letter stating up to three museum departments where you hope to be placed. You also must clearly state the type of internship or fellowship to which you're applying (Krueger, volunteer or Kell-Muñoz). In addition, include a current resume with your permanent and current contact information and e-mail address (mandatory), along with your date of birth and social security number. Also include your official college transcripts, with seal/stamp from undergraduate and graduate universities, and two letters of recommendation (at least one must be from a recent or current instructor; the second may be from someone who knows you but who isn't a relative). Letters should be in a sealed envelope with signature across the seal. Finally, include a one- or two-page essay describing your career goals and specific areas of interest.

You should submit all materials in one envelope, postmarked by the application deadline, to the preceding address.

CORCORAN GALLERY OF ART INTERNSHIP

Coordinator of Education Programs
The Corcoran Gallery of Art
500 17th Street, NW
Washington, DC 20006
(202) 639-1852
interns@corcoran.org
http://www.corcoran.org/education/internship.
  htm

What You Can Earn: Unpaid but academic credit is available.

Application Deadlines: There is no official deadline for academic year internships, but priority is given to applications received two months before the start of the spring and fall semesters; summer internship applications must be postmarked by March 15.

Educational Experience: Academic year internships open to undergraduate and graduate students; summer internships open to juniors or seniors in college, graduate students, and students between academic degree programs interested in gaining firsthand museum experience or intending to pursue careers in arts administration.

Requirements: Must work at least 15 hours per week; summer interns must work regular staff hours, from 9:00 A.M. to 5:00 P.M. Monday through Friday.

OVERVIEW

The Corcoran museum presents, interprets and preserves art, while its college of art shapes new generations of artists and designers. Although the Corcoran's collection emphasizes American art, it also includes the art of other nations and cultures.

In addition to educating its own artists, the Corcoran also tries to reach out to citizens of all socioeconomic strata throughout the greater Washington, D.C., region through innovative exhibitions and educational programming, systematic research, and rigorous scholarship.

The Corcoran offers both complete academic year internships (from September to May) and summer internships. Based on a program of supervised learning, Corcoran internships provide students with an opportunity to learn about museum operations and to pursue academic and professional goals.

Academic Year Internships

To correspond with class schedules, interns can arrange flexible work hours for the internship period that lasts from September to May. Interns during the academic year work on a substantial research project that contributes to the Corcoran's programming.

Summer Internships

If a year-long commitment is too involved, a variety of summer 10-week internships are also available from early June through mid-August.

In addition to regular duties, you'll experience weekly brown bag lunch meetings with Corcoran department heads to offer you the chance to learn about all facets of the museum and to learn about the backgrounds of seasoned and successful museum professionals. In addition, you'll also visit other Washington, D.C., arts and humanities institutions to see special exhibitions, tour permanent collections, and meet museum professionals.

Internships are available with the following curatorial departments: American art; photography and media arts; prints and drawings; contemporary art; European art; and departments of education; public programs; public affairs; graphics; finance and administration; membership; development; and the museum shop. Your personal interests, capabilities, and future career plans are taken into account when assigning your department.

HOW TO APPLY

To apply to either the summer or full-year internship, send a resume, transcript, and two letters of recommendation, along with a cover letter listing three departments where you'd like to work, why you want an internship, and how such an experience will further your education and career plans. Since your letter is used instead of a personal interview, you also should outline your abilities, interests, and career goals. Send all materials by mail to the preceding address (do not fax or e-mail your application). For more information, you may contact the coordinator of education programs by phone or e-mail.

FIELD MUSEUM INTERNSHIP

The Field Museum
1400 South Lake Shore Drive
Chicago, IL 60605-2496
(312) 922-9410
http://www.fieldmuseum.org

What You Can Earn: Seventy percent of internships are paid; academic credit is also available; all interns also get free admission to the Field Museum and other Chicago Museums; discounts at museum restaurants and stores; invitations to museum member events, including members' nights; invitations to staff events and exhibition previews; free and discounted education classes; and staff and volunteer newsletters
Application Deadlines: Early March (check Web site for exact deadline).
Educational Experience: Open to undergraduate and graduate students of all majors, most of whom come from top colleges and universities throughout the nation.
Requirements: Detail-oriented self-starters with solid computer skills (Internet research, database, and Microsoft Office), good analytical skills, and excellent communication skills.

OVERVIEW

Located on Chicago's beautiful lakefront Museum Campus, the Field Museum is one of the finest natural history museums in the world. Established in Illinois in 1893 as the Columbian Museum of Chicago, its purpose was to accumulate and disseminate knowledge and to preserve and exhibit objects illustrating art, archaeology, science, and history. In 1905, the name was changed to Field Museum of Natural History to honor the museum's first major benefactor, Marshall Field, and to better reflect its focus on the natural sciences.

The Field Museum was founded to house the biological and anthropological collections assembled for the World's Columbian Exposition of 1893, which form the core of its collections, including more than 20 million specimens. The collections form the foundation of the museum's exhibition, research, and education programs, plus a world-class natural history library of more than 250,000 volumes.

Each summer, the museum hosts more than 100 internships representing every department. In addition, more than 40 internships take place during the academic year. Interns get extensive hands-on experience and an in-depth look at the requirements of a world-class institution, with access to educational activities and exposure to all areas of the museum.

The Field Museum focuses on dynamic new exhibitions, scientific research, and educational programs concerning the earth's environments and cultures. Once here, you can explore your skills and ambitions, as well as the collected fortunes of long-lost civilizations, examine meteorites, and study the very bones of history.

Many departments often host interns, including academic areas (anthropology, botany, environmental conservation, geology, and zoology); administrative areas (human resources, finance, and general counsel); business enterprises (museum stores and special events); education (program development and summer camp counselors); exhibitions (exhibition development, production, and graphic design); information services (desktop services, library, media services, photography, and Web development); and institutional advancement (auxiliary boards, development/fund-raising, marketing, publications, and public relations).

HOW TO APPLY

To apply for any Field Museum internships, complete the on-line application at http://www.bfound.net/detail.aspx?jobId=20951&CoId=45. Competition for internship opportunities is strong, and interviews are conducted for every position available.

FREER GALLERY OF ART/ ARTHUR M. SACKLER GALLERY INTERNSHIP

For volunteer internships, contact
Internship Coordinator
Education Department
Freer/Sackler Galleries
Smithsonian Institution
PO Box 37012
Washington, DC 20013-7012
(202) 633-0465
TTY: (202) 786-2374
http://www.asia.si.edu

For the Dick Louie Internship, contact
Dick Louie Internship Program
Freer and Sackler Galleries
Smithsonian Institution
Attn: Internship Coordinator
Department of Education
1050 Independence Avenue, SW
Washington, DC 20560

What You Can Earn: Volunteer internships are unpaid; Dick Louie internship carries a $1500 stipend.
Application Deadlines: March 15 for summer internships (or longer internships beginning in summer); July 15 for fall session; November 15 for winter/spring session; March 25 for Dick Louie internship.
Educational Experience: Volunteer interns (high school, undergraduate, and graduate students);

Dick Louie internship open to high school students of Asian descent entering or completing their senior year of high school.
Requirements: A working knowledge of pertinent Asian languages is suggested for curatorial internships; must live and attend high school in the Washington, D.C., metropolitan area.

OVERVIEW

The Freer Gallery of Art and its sister museum, the Arthur M. Sackler Gallery, are the national museums of Asian art at the Smithsonian Institution and are jointly administered. The Freer Gallery of Art houses one of the most distinguished collections of Asian art in the world today, as well as the largest collection of work by James McNeill Whistler. The gallery supports advanced research and disseminates the results through exhibitions and publications.

The Arthur M. Sackler Gallery's outstanding collection of Asian art complements the strong Asian holdings at the Freer. The Sackler supports advanced research and disseminates the results via exhibitions and publications.

A number of internships are available at the galleries, including a named and paid internship and volunteer internships at either the Freer Gallery or the Sackler Gallery.

Freer Gallery and Sacker Gallery

Internships are available to high school, undergraduate, and graduate students for special projects and general departmental work in the following 15 departments: administration; archives; collections management (registrar); conservation and scientific research; curatorial; design and installation; development; education (including public programs); library and archives; publications; photography; public affairs; and shops.

About 20 percent of applicants are accepted for internships ranging from one month to one year (the duration is based on arrangements made between the department and the intern).

Dick Louie Summer Internship

This summer internship honors Dick Louie, former associate director of the Freer Gallery of Art.

This memorial internship for Americans of Asian descent was established in 1994 to honor Dick Louie and is made possible by funds donated through the Richard Louie Memorial Fund. Its goal is to offer area high school students of Asian descent practical experience in a museum setting.

Here, you'll have an opportunity to accomplish a specific independent project, and the museum staff will try to include you in ongoing public and behind-the-scenes museum activities. You don't need to be planning a career in museum work or Asian studies, but you should be interested in learning about museum work and Asian art. Typically, the internship begins in late June and ends in mid-August. Each intern will be expected to report to work Monday through Friday from 9:00 A.M. to 4:30 P.M.

HOW TO APPLY

To apply directly to the Freer and Sackler galleries for unpaid internships, submit an online application or completed print-out of the online application (you can download the application at this Web site: http://www.asia.si.edu/education/internships. htm). Submit the application along with two letters of recommendation and a resume and/or high school or college transcript. You must hand deliver your application or send it via Fed-Ex or UPS. Do not send it through the U.S. Postal Service or your application may be delayed. Applications may not be faxed.

All applicants will be notified of the selection committee's decision by mid-May.

GETTY FOUNDATION INTERNSHIP

The Getty Foundation
Attn: Graduate Internships
1200 Getty Center Drive, Suite 800
Los Angeles, CA 90049-1685

(310) 440-7320
Fax (inquiries only): (310) 440-7703
gradinterns@getty.edu

What You Can Earn: $17,300 for eight months and $25,000 for 12 months; grants include health benefits.
Application Deadlines: December 15.
Educational Experience: Must either be currently enrolled in a graduate program leading to an advanced degree in a field relevant to the internship(s) for which you are applying or have completed a relevant graduate degree in 2002 or later.
Requirements: None specified.

OVERVIEW

Graduate Internships at the Getty support full-time positions. Programs and departments throughout the Getty provide training and work experience in areas such as curatorial, education, conservation, research, information management, public programs, and grantmaking.

Getty graduate internships are offered by several programs at the Getty Center, including the museum, research institute, conservation institute, foundation, and Web production.

J. Paul Getty Museum

This museum collects and exhibits Greek and Roman antiquities, European paintings, drawings, manuscripts, sculpture and decorative arts, and European and American photographs and offers a range of special exhibitions and educational programs. Interns participate in the daily activities of one of the museum's six curatorial departments. Projects may include assisting with the preparation of exhibitions and publications, research and writing on existing holdings and prospective acquisitions, cataloging objects, and other routine curatorial tasks.

The intern in the museum's exhibition design department uses elements of architectural, interior, graphic, and industrial design as each applies to the planning, interpretation, promotion, and installation of museum exhibitions. The intern in the museum's education department focuses on one of the many programs serving audiences ranging from students and teachers to families and adults, facilitating a variety of learning experiences centered on works of art in the collections and exhibitions.

The intern in the museum's department of exhibitions and public programs takes part in the overall coordination of selected museum exhibitions, helping to bring together the departments involved in developing an exhibition, and works on special projects as assigned.

Conservation internships generally require advanced conservation training on the part of applicants. Conservation internships are offered in the museum, where interns focus on the examination, care, and treatment of objects in the museum collections.

The intern in the museum's interactive programs department takes part in the production of materials for a range of resources for the public, including audio and media accompanying exhibitions and the permanent collection. The intern also works with GettyGuide, the Getty's interactive computer system for delivering information and interpretation of the collections, new acquisitions, and exhibitions to the public.

The intern in the Registrar's Office becomes acquainted with the museum's acquisition policies, registration procedures, and collections management practices. The registration intern assists with exhibitions, including loan, shipping, courier, installation, and de-installation arrangements.

The Getty Research Institute (GRI)

GRI promotes advanced scholarship in the visual arts through an international residential scholars' program, a growing 800,000-volume library, major archival collections, exhibitions, publications, lectures, and symposia. The GRI hosts a conservation intern who performs and documents treatment on the GRI library's collection materials (paper-based, photographic, and 3-D composite objects.)

The intern in the department of special collections and visual resources develops skills in cataloguing archival collections, including one consisting of photographs of Old Master draw-

ings. The intern in the GRI's Project for the Study of Collecting and Provenance contributes to the provenance databases, using training received in the methodology of provenance research, analysis of archival inventories, and auction catalogs from various European countries.

The Getty Conservation Institute (GCI)

GCI pursues a broad range of activities dedicated to furthering conservation practices and education to enhance and encourage the preservation, understanding, and interpretation of the visual arts. The GCI offers internships in the department of field projects, where interns participate in the organization and implementation of field campaigns that may include the development of site management plans and reference documentation. The GCI also offers internships in science, where interns learn to use instrumentation and perform tests to investigate the processes of material deterioration, to design and evaluate conservation solutions, and to conduct technical examinations of works of art in the Getty collections.

The intern in the GCI's education department contributes to the creation of curricula and didactic materials for specialized training of conservation professionals, the development of teaching skills and strategies for conservation education, and the exploration of Web-enhanced teaching.

The intern in the department of dissemination and research resources helps develop programs about conservation and create publications that inform general and professional audiences about the work of the GCI and benefit the conservation field. The intern also helps to develop methodologies to manage the institute's research resources, including the Web site, and make them available to professional communities around the world.

The Getty Foundation

This foundation supports institutions and individuals throughout the world by funding a diverse range of projects that promote learning and scholarship about the history of the visual arts and the conservation of cultural heritage. The intern participates in the administration of philanthropic programs in the areas of research, conservation, and education, from fielding inquiries through the awarding of grants and the evaluation of project results.

The Getty Leadership Institute (GLI)

GLI offers professional development opportunities for current and future leaders in the museum field. The Getty Leadership Institute intern helps with the administration and coordination of professional development programs and the convening of leaders to discuss current issues and opportunities in the museum field. The intern also assists in strengthening the organization and accessibility of the GLI's resource library.

Web Group

The intern here participates as part of a team and contributes to all aspects of developing and maintaining a Web site. Opportunities exist in concept development, storyboarding, writing, editing, programming, and content management for the Getty Web site.

HOW TO APPLY

Download application forms at the Getty Web site: http://www.getty.edu/grants/education/grad_interns.html. Mail your application to the preceding address. Getty cannot accept applications hand-delivered to the Getty Center or those sent by e-mail or fax. Application materials cannot be returned. All applicants will be notified of the Getty's decision in April.

GUGGENHEIM MUSEUM INTERNSHIP

Internship Coordinator
Solomon R. Guggenheim Museum
1071 Fifth Avenue
New York, NY 10128
http://www.guggenheim.org

What You Can Earn: Academic credit can be arranged; academic year and undergraduate summer internships are typically unpaid; summer internships for diversity in the museum profession carries a stipend of $2500 for nine weeks; Hilla von Rebay graduate interns earn $1000 for nine weeks.

Application Deadlines: February 15 for the summer internship; June 15 for the fall/spring internship and for the Hilla von Rebay International Fellow; November 1 for the spring internship.

Educational Experience: See specific internships below for details.

Requirements: Individuals interested in pursuing careers in the arts and museum field.

OVERVIEW

The Solomon R. Guggenheim Foundation was incorporated in 1937 as the basis of the Museum of Non-Objective Painting (as the Guggenheim was then known), which was established two years later. The museum, which was temporarily housed in a former automobile showroom on East 54th Street in New York, focused on radical new forms of art being developed by artists such as Vasily Kandinsky, Paul Klee, and Piet Mondrian. Philanthropist Solomon Guggenheim and artist-adviser Hilla von Rebay insisted the museum should concentrate on a new kind of art in a new kind of space, so the first permanent home for the museum was designed by Frank Lloyd Wright. It was Wright who designed its curving, continuous space as a "temple of spirit" where viewers could arrive at a new way of looking. Named the Solomon R. Guggenheim Museum in honor of its founder, the building opened in 1959, drawing huge crowds and stirring considerable controversy. It is still considered to be one of the great works of architecture produced in the 20th century.

The Solomon R. Guggenheim Museum offers a variety of internships for undergraduates, recent graduates, and graduate students in art history, administration, conservation, education, and related fields. Interns learn how a particular department functions within the context of a major museum, as well as skills related to a particular department. You may be assigned to a department based on your academic background, professional skills, interests, and career goals. Potential internships are available in the following departments: curatorial, education, public affairs, registrar, library/archives, photography, conservation, film and media arts, director's office, development, membership, special events, visitor services, finance, and information technology.

Academic Year Internships

Intended for upper-level college students, recent graduates, and graduate students, these unpaid internships are available throughout the academic year on a full- or part-time basis. National internships are six months. The fall/spring internship program corresponds to the academic semester and runs from mid-September through mid-April. Periodic field trips to cultural institutions, galleries, and auction houses, as well as lectures by museum staff, are offered weekly during the fall/spring semester.

Hilla von Rebay Foundation Research Award

The Hilla von Rebay Foundation awards two Guggenheim Museum graduate student summer interns a $500 grant for travel, research, and scholarship related to Hilla von Rebay, her friends, and the movement of Abstraction. Interested applicants who have been accepted into the Guggenheim summer program are invited to apply.

Hilla von Rebay Graduate Interns

In honor of the Guggenheim Museum's first director, Baroness Hilla von Rebay, the Hilla von Rebay Foundation offers funding for up to 12 summer interns who are currently enrolled graduate students.

Summer Internships

Rising college juniors and seniors, recent graduates, and graduate students in all areas of museum work may apply for a summer internship, which runs from mid-May through mid-August and requires a full time, five-days-a-week commitment. Every other week, the museum offers a culture seminar program involving field trips to auction houses, galleries, corporate collections, artists' studios, and other museums; discussions with staffers from other museum departments; and discussions of museum-related issues and publications.

Summer Internships for Diversity in the Museum Profession

The museum offers summer internship funding for two U.S. citizens who have demonstrated a commitment to museum careers and who are from African-American, Alaskan Native, American Indian, Asian American, Hispanic, or Pacific Islander cultures. Preference will be given to candidates from the New York City area.

HOW TO APPLY

There are no application forms. Instead, you must type your own application, specifying the internship and departments for which you'd like to be considered, and send it to the address above, along with the following:

- a cover letter including your name, addresses, telephone numbers, and e-mail address
- full resume of your education and job history
- two letters of recommendation (one academic and one professional, although two academic references are acceptable)
- official transcripts from all undergraduate and graduate schools attended
- a separate list of all relevant course work, including all art history, arts administration, studio art, education, marketing, and business courses

- a list of all foreign languages you have studied, specifying how well you speak, read, and write each

- an essay of no more than 500 words, typed and double-spaced, describing your interest in the internship program, museum work, and reasons for applying

- for Hilla Rebay International Fellows a piece of graduate writing, criticism, or thesis should be included

You'll receive the final notification in mid-April for summer, or mid-August for fall/spring internship programs.

HIRSHHORN MUSEUM AND SCULPTURE GARDEN INTERNSHIP

Hirshhorn Museum and Sculpture Garden
Intern Coordinator
Smithsonian Institution
PO Box 37012
MRC Code 350
Washington, DC 20013-7012
hmsgeducation@si.edu for more information
http://www.hmsg.si.edu/education/internships.
   html

What You Can Earn: Unpaid.
Application Deadlines: November 1 for spring internship; March 1 for summer internship; June 1 for fall internship.
Educational Experience: 15 semester hours of art history or equivalent academic preparation; a specialization in modern and contemporary art history is helpful; certain department internships require other college experience or majors (see below for details).

Requirements: A grade point average of 3.25 for undergraduates and 3.5 for graduate students.

OVERVIEW

Conceived as the nation's museum of modern and contemporary art, the Hirshhorn Museum and Sculpture Garden includes key artists of the 20th century, from Picasso and Giacometti to de Kooning and Warhol. The Hirshhorn Museum and Sculpture Garden has primarily focused on the post-World War II period, with particular emphasis on art created during the last 25 years.

Joseph H. Hirshhorn (1899-1981) gave his extensive art collection to the nation in 1966 and later contributed $1 million to the Smithsonian Institution toward the construction of the Hirshhorn building. Today it is primarily federally funded. The museum owns about 11,500 artworks, including paintings, sculptures, works on paper, photographs, collages, and some decorative art objects.

Each year a number of undergraduate and graduate internships are available at the Hirshhorn Museum and Sculpture Garden for the summer, spring, and fall/winter semesters. Academic credit may be arranged through the intern's school; international students are encouraged to apply.

While internships are unpaid appointments, they provide an excellent foundation for future museum work or art-related careers. You'll work extensively within specific departments, as well as interact with professionals in every area of the museum, learning how various departments realize particular and common goals. Today many former Hirshhorn interns are curators, educators, public affairs officers, and conservators at national and international museums. There are a variety of departments that use interns, including the following:

Conservation Department

If you have appropriate conservation training and prior approval from the department chief, you can work with the conservation department, learning about modern and contemporary materials in the lab. Summer interns also assist conservators in treating outdoor sculptures.

Curatorial Division

Here you'll help with research related to the permanent collection or temporary exhibitions and may provide editorial assistance on publications.

Education Department

You'll help with special projects, such as symposia and festivals, and you may lead tours of the permanent collection and temporary exhibitions.

Exhibition and Design Department

If you have had course work in studio art, you will be eligible for this department's internship, where you will help with exhibition installation, graphic design, and/or publications.

Public Affairs

For this internship you should have a background in English or journalism, as well as a working knowledge of art and art history, since you'll be preparing and distributing press materials and interact with members of the press at exhibition press previews. You also may be asked to write public service announcements for radio and TV.

Other Opportunities

Here you'll help with registration and collections management, documenting and photographing the collection and exhibitions and helping with a variety of library projects.

HOW TO APPLY

To apply, send a brief statement listing specific reasons for desiring an internship, including areas of greatest interest, along with three letters of recommendation from people familiar with your academic qualifications, official college or graduate transcripts, a resume detailing prior academic and work experience, and proof of citizenship, social security number, and date and place of birth. Incomplete applications will not be accepted. Noti-

fication of selection will be mailed about 30 days after the deadline.

INTERNATIONAL CHILD ART FOUNDATION INTERNSHIP

Volunteer Coordinator
International Child Art Foundation
1350 Connecticut Avenue, NW, Suite 1225
Washington, DC 20036-1702
(202) 530-1000
Fax: (202) 530-1080
childart@icaf.org

What You Can Earn: Unpaid but academic credit is available.
Application Deadlines: Rolling.
Educational Experience: High school seniors; college or university students in any accredited degree, undergraduate, or graduate program.
Requirements: Must work at least one full day per week for a semester or full academic year (preferred); summer interns work a minimum of 20 hours a week.

OVERVIEW

International Child Art Foundation (ICAF) is a small and creative nonprofit organization based in Washington, D.C., whose work is supported by a team of volunteers and interns. The only international children's art and creativity organization in the world, ICAF prepares children for a creative and cooperative future so they can lead us into a better and peaceful world.

ICAF's founder, educator, and award-winning child artist, Ashfaq Ishaqild, wanted to create an organization to nurture, sustain, and promote the artistic promise and creativity of children around the world. In addition to programs designed to actively engage children in the creation of original artwork worldwide, Dr. Ishaq envisioned an international children's art festival, to be held like the Olympic games, in a host city every four years. Schools in every country would participate, and creative children, along with their parents and teachers, would be invited to attend the festival's exhibitions, creativity workshops, seminars and ceremonies.

Before ICAF was established in 1997, there was no truly comprehensive national and international effort to promote child art and visual learning, particularly regarding the underserved group of 8-to-12-year-old children. ICAF is associated with the Department of Public Information of the United Nations and an extensive array of public, private, and governmental organizations worldwide.

The organization sponsors the international Arts Olympiad, the world's most prestigious and popular arts initiative for children. This four-year comprehensive art program includes a global art competition as well as local, regional, and international festivals and exhibitions. ICAF's Third Arts Olympiad (2005-2008) links art and sport to promote peace and development.

The Child Art Festival is held once every four years as the culmination of the Arts Olympiad competition and is traditionally held on the National Mall in Washington, D.C. Finalists from every participating country, U.S. state and territory, their parents, and their art teachers are invited to this one-week event.

Its Healing Arts for Tsunami Survivors is a program designed to help the children who survived the Asian tsunami overcome the psychological trauma through art therapy. American and international experts working with ICAF have developed the Healing Arts for Tsunami Survivors program to transfer the knowledge and experience gained from the treatment of the child survivors of the 9/11 tragedy and other recent disasters to help the tsunami child survivors.

The very successful internship program attracts students from a wide variety of programs, including communication, international studies, event management, and art therapy/human services. Interns may work either for a semester, a full academic year, or the summer, as either project or program assistants. Journalism or creative writing majors might also write articles for *ChildArt* magazine.

HOW TO APPLY

Download application at http://www.icaf.org/get-involved/intern-app.doc. Submit your application along with your resume and a cover letter to the preceding address.

JULIA MORGAN CENTER FOR THE ARTS INTERNSHIP

Intern/Volunteer Coordinator
Julia Morgan Center for the Arts Internship
2640 College Avenue
Berkeley, CA 94704
(510) 845-8542
Fax: (510) 845-3133
rebecca@juliamorgan.org
http://www.juliamorgan.org

What You Can Earn: Unpaid.
Application Deadlines: Rolling.
Educational Experience: Unspecified.
Requirements: Basic computer, organizational, or other office skills; research skills; classroom practice or coursework in child development; organizational and people skills. Interns who will be working with children must pass a security and sign an agreement to observe JMCA guidelines for the safety of children. Also, interns in the summer camps must attend an orientation in late May or early June.

OVERVIEW

The Julia Morgan Center for the Arts is a nonprofit arts center with a commitment to arts-based learning for all ages. It boasts a 350-seat theatre, an active after-school and holiday camp, and arts-based learning partnerships with 10 Bay Area schools.

Interns at the center can work in a variety of areas, including administration, education, theater management, technical support, and house management, for at least eight hours a week. Internships typically last for at least three months on a relatively regular schedule.

Dance Is Festival Internship

Interns assist with the preparation and development of the annual Dance Is Festival in March, but your help is needed at any time from the summer before March through the actual festival. As an intern here, you'll help work on publicity, communicate with the participating dance groups, and assist with choreography workshops and other jobs.

Kaleidoscope Arts Education Internship

These performing arts camps are offered both during spring break (early April) and during the summer, giving interns a great way to gain valuable experience working with kids in an arts-based setting by supporting professional teaching artists. As an intern here, you may find yourself helping to lead class activities and acting as a role model, helping students with independent work, and doing some minor office work. Camps, which last for one or two weeks, serve students in grades pre-kindergarten through 6.

Kaleidoscope Unlimited Camp

Interns will help the teaching artist at this summer camp designed especially for children with special needs, creating a supportive and caring environment to encourage relationships, creative self-expression, and imaginative play. As an intern here, you'll be a role model and work closely with teaching artists to help kids actively participate in group activities and have a lot of fun. This camp was developed by artists, teachers, and therapists for children with Asperger Syndrome or with similar behavioral problems.

HOW TO APPLY

To apply for the internships, fill out the form available at: http://www.juliamorgan.org/intern.shtml and submit it electronically; you should also send your resume to the address above. All applicants also will be interviewed and evaluated for placement.

METROPOLITAN MUSEUM OF ART INTERNSHIP

Internship Programs
The Metropolitan Museum of Art
1000 Fifth Avenue
New York, NY 10028-0198
mmainterns@metmuseum.org
http://metmuseum.org

What You Can Earn: Honorariums range from $2,500 for college students to $3,250 for graduate students
Application Deadlines: Mid-January (Check Web site for specific deadline).
Educational Experience: Cloisters summer internship is for any college student (especially first- and second-year students). The college internship is for undergraduates enrolled as juniors or seniors in a four-year degree program or recent graduates who have not yet entered graduate school. Current freshmen and sophomores are not eligible for this internship. The graduate internship is for individuals who have completed at least one year of graduate work in art history or in an allied field.
Requirements: Should be interested in a career in an art museum; strong knowledge of art history.

OVERVIEW

The Metropolitan Museum of Art was founded in 1870 by a group of American businessmen, financiers, artists, and philosophers who wanted to create a museum to gather together art for the

American people. Its first object was a Roman sarcophagus obtained in 1870, even before the museum was opened. This was quickly followed by three private European painting collections, including a number of Dutch and Flemish paintings, as well as those by great European artists. Today, the Metropolitan Museum of Art houses a vast collection of art from every part of the world and from the earliest times to the present, in every medium. The mission of the museum is to collect, preserve, study, exhibit, and stimulate appreciation for works of art that represent the broadest spectrum of human achievement at the highest level of quality.

To help with this vision, the museum sponsors a full-time summer internship (from June to early August, 35 hours a week). This includes a one-week orientation of the museum for graduate students, a two-week orientation for college students, meetings with museum professionals, and field trips to other institutions.

Basic College and Graduate Student Internships

The basic 10-week college internship is awarded each summer to interns who will work on various projects, give gallery talks, and work at the Visitor Information Center. The 10-week graduate student internship allows graduate students to work on projects related to the museum's collections or on a special exhibition. Based on interns' academic training and interests, as well as the availability of projects, they may work in either the curatorial, education, conservation, administration, or library departments at the museum. Selected candidates will be awarded one of the following internships:

Jack and Lewis Rudin Internships
This scholarship is awarded to three college students who will participate in the college program.

Roswell L. Gilpatric Internship
College juniors, seniors, recent graduates, and graduate students who are especially interested in museum careers may apply for this award (there

is no need to submit a separate application). Successful candidates can participate in the college or graduate program.

William Kelly Simpson Internship for Egyptian Art
A graduate student who has completed the course work for an M.A. degree in Egyptology or in art history with an emphasis on ancient Egyptian art may apply for this internship. The intern will work with the curatorial staff on projects related to the museum's Egyptian collection or a special exhibition.

The Cloisters Summer Internship for Younger College Students

This nine-week internship (mid-June to mid-August) is for younger undergraduate college students, particularly first- and second-year students who are interested in art and museum careers, who like working with children, and who are particularly interested in medieval art. As an intern here, you'll join the education office of The Cloisters, the branch museum of The Metropolitan Museum of Art devoted to the art of medieval Europe. After intensive training, you'll be able to conduct gallery workshops for New York City day campers and to develop a public gallery talk. This internship carries a $2,500 honorarium.

HOW TO APPLY

There are no application forms. Instead, you should send a typed application including the following information:

- internship(s) for which you are applying
- name, home, school, e-mail address, and telephone numbers
- full resume of education and employment
- two academic recommendations
- official transcript(s) (graduate students must supply both official undergraduate and graduate transcripts; Cloisters internship applicants must supply transcripts for at least the past two years)

- a separate list of art history or other relevant courses taken, as well as knowledge of foreign languages
- an essay (no more than 500 words) describing your career goals, interest in museum work, and reasons for applying.

After an initial review of the applications, a small number of students will be invited for an interview at the museum in March. Final notification for all candidates will be mailed April 15.

Application materials for all internships, except for The Cloisters Summer Internship, should be submitted to the address above.

Cloisters summer internships should be submitted to the address below. (Questions may be submitted via e-mail, but the application may not be electronically submitted.)

The Cloisters Summer Internship Program
The Cloisters
Fort Tryon Park
New York, NY 10040
cloistersinterns@metmuseum.org

MICHAEL PEREZ GALLERY INTERNSHIP

Michael Perez Gallery
8 Merrick Avenue
Merrick, NY 11566
http://www.MichaelPerezGallery.com

What You Can Earn: Small stipend available for lunch and transportation, plus commission for each painting you sell; academic credit available.
Application Deadlines: Rolling.
Educational Experience: Undergraduates enrolled as juniors or seniors in a four-year degree program, students who have completed their second year in a two-year program by spring before the summer internship, and graduate students.

Requirements: U.S. citizens only; outgoing, personable and responsible. Specific requirements for individual departments are described below.

OVERVIEW
This pop art gallery on Long Island is open from May through September, and internships are available at any point during this time. The gallery is owned and operated by New York artist Michael Perez and exhibits his work exclusively. His work is distinguished by the use of contrasting colors and shapes and typically involves faces, flowers, and figures. As an intern in this gallery, you would be responsible primarily for selling art, and for interacting with customers, opening or closing the gallery, answering the phone, helping arrange the art, handling credit card purchases, and keeping things organized. You would be working in the gallery mainly by yourself during semiflexible hours.

HOW TO APPLY
Mail your resume and a detailed cover letter with photo, which must include a discussion of when you would be available, your plans for living and transportation arrangements (including your monthly budget to cover these two things). Do not e-mail an attachment file of your resume.

MUSEUM OF CONTEMPORARY ART SAN DIEGO INTERNSHIP

Summer Internships
700 Prospect Street
La Jolla, CA 92037
(858) 454-3541
Fax: (858) 454-6985
education@mcasd.org

What You Can Earn: Unpaid.

Application Deadlines: End of March (check Web site for specific deadline).

Educational Experience: Undergraduates enrolled as juniors or seniors in a four-year degree program, students who have completed their second year in a two-year program by spring before the summer internship, and graduate students. Specific requirements for individual departments are described below.

Requirements: Comfortable using databases (Access, Excel, preferably some experience with Raiser's Edge); good general computer knowledge; familiarity with online research; meticulous when looking at data and lists; development and/or museum experience a plus; experience writing letters and/or proposals; outgoing personality is important in fund-raising.

OVERVIEW

The Museum of Contemporary Art San Diego internships provide hands-on experience within various departments of the museum, beginning in mid-June and ending in mid-August (check Web site for exact internship dates). Chosen applicants are trained by and work closely with museum staff and are given lots of different projects to provide meaningful experiences for students who want to pursue a career in museums or art-related fields. Different internships are available at different times, but the following are typical of the types of internships that may be available:

Curatorial Department

There are four interns in this department: the *La Jolla intern* reports to the curator and works closely with the curatorial assistant, helping with exhibition and permanent collection related research, writing, and planning. The *downtown curatorial intern* reports to the curator and curatorial coordinator, helping the curatorial staff with exhibition research and related programs. Both of these candidates should be fine arts or art history students with an interest in contemporary art and with excellent administrative and research skills.

The *education intern* is responsible for implementing public, family, and school programs related to all exhibitions. In addition, the education staff facilitates the training of volunteer museum docents and organizes daily museum tours. The education office also acts as a liaison between the museum and local schools, colleges and universities, and works closely with the curators in planning exhibition-related programs. As education intern, you'll be responsible for helping the staff in education program planning, as well as reporting on and archiving the past fiscal year's education programs. You'll also be expected to help with the Family Day event on the first Sunday of each month, as well as the monthly TNT downtown event. For this internship, you'll need good general computer knowledge of Microsoft Word, Excel, and Power Point; excellent research and organizational skills; museum/education experience; comfort with children; and a good grasp of contemporary art.

The *registration intern* will help out in the Registration Office, which is responsible for the care and preservation of artworks both in the permanent collection and on loan to the museum. This office organizes the shipping and crating of objects, loans of artworks, maintains the museum's vaults, handles rights and reproduction requests, maintains the museum's photographic archives, handles insurance, and houses all of the documents and paperwork related to permanent collection works. This office also ensures the safety and care of objects at both museum spaces. As a summer intern, you'll help catalog Rights & Reproduction text, exhibition histories, and provenance and published references information in the collection management database. You'll also work on the ongoing project to inventory and condition report objects in the permanent collection. For this position, you must be detail orientated, organized, and thorough. Familiarity with contemporary art is preferred.

Department of Institutional Advancement

Three internships are available in this department. The *membership intern* will work with staffers on projects related to the membership database and fund-raising. This is a great opportunity to learn about development in museums and the department's interaction with donors. You'll also gain firsthand experience with Raiser's Edge, the leading membership, fund-raising, and information database used by museums, as you work with the development team on major events, research, department projects, and fund-raising. You'll also help with incoming membership requests, payments, and distribution of benefits packages to new and renewing members. You'll also be expected to provide administrative support and to help at museum functions and education events. Applicants must be very detail oriented, with an excellent telephone manner and time-management and organization skills. Data entry experience is a plus.

The *gala intern* will work with the institutional advancement team on the museum's gala fund-raiser, a yearly event that involves months of planning and preparation. You'll learn the specifics of fund-raising through events including seeking sponsorship and support from companies and individuals; designing the look and the flow of the evening; and the writing and design of associated print materials. You'll be the project coordinator of the silent auction portion of the gala, researching companies for pro bono requests, updating and using the in-kind donor database, and creating auction packages. The candidate for this internship must be detail orientated, organized, and thorough. Familiarity with Microsoft Access is a plus. You should be available to attend and help at the gala.

The *corporate and individual giving intern* will work with staff on donor research, prospecting, and fund-raising. This is a great opportunity to learn Raiser's Edge, the leading membership, fund-raising, and information database used by museums, and to learn fund-raising techniques such as proposal writing, soliciting prospects, developing relationships, and programming based on corporate marketing needs as well as individual prospect development and solicitation. You'll research new and existing corporate and individual donors and prepare solicitations for exhibitions, education programs, and special events such as the museum's annual black-tie fund-raiser.

HOW TO APPLY

Submit one letter of recommendation from a college professor, preferably in a field related to the internship, a resume with a cover letter detailing why you'd like to intern at MCASD, and your preference of department placement, as well as an official college transcript, to the preceding address.

MUSEUM OF MODERN ART INTERNSHIP

The Museum of Modern Art
Attn: Internship Coordinator
11 West 53 Street
New York, NY 10019
internships@moma.org

What You Can Earn: Fall and spring internships are unpaid; 12-month internships pay $20,000 plus standard health benefits, two weeks paid vacation, and an additional $500 to cover travel expenses and registration fees for one approved professional conference; full-time spring and summer interns each receive $2,500 (award based on available funding). Academic credit is also available.

Application Deadlines: End of May for fall session; end of October for spring session; early December for *Carole Kismaric Mikolaycak Spring Internship* (February to April); early January for full-time *Helena Rubenstein spring session internship*; late May for *year-long internship* (check for exact deadlines, which change each year, by visiting the MoMA Web site).

Educational Experience: College juniors and seniors, recent graduates, graduate students, and beginning museum professionals; candidates from diverse backgrounds and academic disciplines are encouraged to apply.

Requirements: Fall and spring internships require a minimum commitment of two days a week (one day must be Tuesday) and are unpaid. Summer and 12-month internships are full time and provide a stipend.

OVERVIEW

College students and young professionals have been working as interns since MoMA opened in 1929; apprenticeships were transformed into a formal program in 1984 to give college juniors, seniors, and graduate students in-depth exposure to individual departments, practical and theoretical training in museum practices, and an idea of the role of museums in contemporary society.

During the internship, department heads, curators, educators, and administrators help students understand the museum's structure and collections. A lecture program complements the day-to-day museum experience, with talks in conjunction with the museum's exhibitions, and visits to specific departments to familiarize interns with all the behind-the-scenes activities at MoMA.

The Department of Education encourages interns to consider theoretical and practical questions about the art community. During the summer, in addition to lectures, the museum organizes field trips to artists' studios, collectors' homes, galleries, and alternative exhibition spaces. These visits provide interns with opportunities to examine and understand the diverse roles, functions, and practices of a wide range of arts institutions and professionals.

Typically, the museum hires five to 10 12-month interns each year and 25 to 30 interns for each of the spring, fall, and summer terms.

Summer and 12-month interns also can choose to participate in a new lecturer program that provides training in researching, writing, and delivering a gallery talk to the general public. Participants take part in weekly two-hour sessions in which they learn about pedagogical approaches, present research and writing on works in the collections, and deliver mock tours to internship colleagues. After a comprehensive training program, outstanding interns may deliver gallery talks to

the general public during regular museum hours. Internship projects are based on museum needs and requirements and are assigned to interns with the appropriate skills and interests.

Fall and Spring Unpaid Internships

Internships are offered during the school year, coinciding with the fall and spring semesters, and are assigned to interns with the appropriate skills and interests. These fall and spring internships are ideal for students registered in courses that require internship or practicum credits.

Carole Kismaric Mikolaycak Spring Internship

A 12-week, full-time, paid publishing internship in the spring allows interns to work within the Department of Publications to gain firsthand experience of how a museum publication is produced from its inception, from first-draft text and editing to design, printing, and final publication. A lecture series every Tuesday featuring museum staff in various departments will introduce the intern to the workings of the museum as a whole while considering the role of museums in a broader cultural context. This internship is full time, Monday through Friday from 9:30 A.M. to 5:30 P.M. Students must be at least rising juniors in college, recent graduates, currently registered as graduate students, or have recently completed coursework.

Helena Rubinstein Summer Internship Program

This full-time, 10-week, paid internship includes each Tuesday a full day of field trips to other museums, galleries, foundations, corporate collections, private collections, alternative spaces, nonprofit organizations, and artists' studios in New York City. You'll also have the opportunity to develop and deliver public gallery talks about the museum's permanent collection.

This internship is full time, Monday through Friday 9:30 A.M. to 5:30 P.M.

To be eligible, you must be at least a rising junior in college, have recently graduated, be currently registered as a graduate student, or have recently completed coursework as a graduate student.

Twelve-Month Internships

Full-time, year-long internships with stipends are offered for recent college graduates interested in pursuing a museum career whose academic or professional experience combines art history with either arts administration, museum studies, arts management, development, studio art, or related studies. In this internship, which begins in September, the departmental training is integrated with the fall, spring, and summer lecture series and also includes a paid attendance to a national conference of your choice. At the end of the internship, you may obtain career planning and job placement counseling from the internship coordinators and the human resources department.

These year-long internships provide training in specific museum fields with close work with a professional staff member, seminars and discussions, and an educational program that exposes interns to the workings of the museum as a whole and considers the role of museums in the broader cultural context. You'll also be given the opportunity to deliver public gallery talks about the museum's permanent collection.

Year-long interns must be able to work full time, Monday to Friday, from 9:30 A.M. to 5:30 P.M. Recent graduates of bachelor's and master's degree programs are eligible for the internship, which typically is paid.

DEPARTMENTS AT MoMA

The following is a list of departments that offer internships at MoMA. You may choose which department in which you'd like to intern; you should list your three departmental choices on the space provided in the application form. Those applying for fall, spring, summer, or 12-month internships must list specific departments, since MoMA tries to best match an intern's experience and skills with departmental needs. However, if you are accepted, the museum cannot guarantee that you will be placed in the department of your first choice.

Administrative Departments

Digital Media
This division designs and produces the museum's Web site and subsites, kiosks, digital displays, and other media.

Director's Office
This division oversees deputy directors, the building project, and ongoing museum activities.

Information Systems
This division researches and supports computer technology in the museum, including Macs, PCs, midrange systems, and networking.

International Program
Interns in this division help coordinate a wide variety of initiatives aimed at improving cultural and professional exchange with museums and other visual arts institutions, including specially organized traveling exhibitions from the MoMA collections, workshops for museum professionals, publications, education and conservation programs, professional assistance to museums, lectures and symposia, exchanges of library materials, and travel abroad by members of the museum's staff.

Finance
This division monitors the museum's revenues and expenses in order to facilitate the Museum's primary mission.

Government and Community Relations
This division develops and maintains close working relationships with political leaders, elected officials, government agencies and administrators at the city, state, and federal levels, as well as community members and neighbors. It also works closely with other museum departments to expand, enhance, and promote the museum's educational and outreach programs to the general public.

Operations
This division oversees building functions, housekeeping, and engineering.

Curatorial

Architecture and Design

This division collects, manages, and exhibits architectural drawings and models, design objects, and graphic design works.

Chief Curator-at-Large

This division organizes the museum collection and loan exhibitions; oversees the research and scholarly publications program.

Deputy Director for Curatorial Affairs

This division oversees all curatorial departments.

Drawings

This division collects, manages, and exhibits modern and contemporary drawings.

Film and Media

This division collects and exhibits film and media and includes the divisions of Film Archive, Film Study Center, Circulating Film Library, Exhibitions and Programming, and the Video Program.

Imaging Services

This division produces photographic materials of works of art in the collection.

Painting and Sculpture

This division collects, manages, and exhibits modern and contemporary painting and sculpture.

Photography

This division collects, manages, and exhibits modern and contemporary photography.

Prints and Illustrated Books

This division collects, manages, and exhibits modern and contemporary prints and illustrated books.

Publications

This division edits and produces all Museum books and exhibition catalogues, brochures, and wall text.

Education and Research Support

Education

This division offers programs to help audiences of all ages and backgrounds understand and enjoy modern and contemporary art and includes a variety of divisions such as school programs, family programs, adult and academic programs, and community access programs.

Library

This division supports the research needs of the museum staff and members of the public.

Museum Archives

This division organizes, preserves, and coordinates the historical records of the museum.

Exhibitions and Collection Support

Conservation

This division cares for collections and technical research on paintings, works on paper, sculpture, and design objects.

Exhibition Program

This division oversees all exhibition-related details such as budgets, planning, and coordination.

Registration

This division coordinates the packing, shipping, storage, insurance, and documentation of art in the permanent collection, as well as those on loan for temporary exhibitions.

Security

Just as it sounds, this division oversees the security of the building and its collections and maintains the safety of all visitors and staff.

External Affairs

Contemporary Arts Council and Junior Associates

This division supports the museum's ongoing activities and organizes special programs designed for its young members.

Development

This division finds sources of funding for operational budget and programs, including foundations, corporate, and government support as well as the capital campaign for the museum's building project.

Exhibition Funding

This division finds sources of funding for the museum's exhibition program.

Membership

This division designs and conducts programs that help members understand and appreciate the collections, exhibitions, and activities of the museum.

Special Programming

If you like to plan and coordinate exhibition opening receptions and internal and corporate events, check out this division.

Marketing and Communications

Communications

This division handles all media contacts.

Graphic Design

This division produces the museum's graphics, including exhibition and corporate graphics, signs, ephemera, and advertising.

Marketing

This division defines, develops, and places museum advertising and promotions.

Retail

Interns in this division help with the MoMA design stores, the MoMA bookstore, the online store, and the mail order gift catalog.

Visitor Services

This division works to try to improve and sustain the quality of the overall visitor experience.

HOUSING

The Internship Department does not provide housing but can offer a list of suggested housing (primarily hostels and student housing). It is up to you to arrange for your own housing.

HOW TO APPLY

There is one standard application form for all internship programs. You can download the application at http://www.moma.org/education/Internship_application.pdf. After completing the application, mail it to the museum along with the three essays as required in the application, a complete course list or transcript of records, your resume, and two letters of recommendation (academic or professional). Do not submit any extra materials, such as writing samples or artwork. If you are applying for a graphics internship, submit five design samples (color copies, on disc or via e-mail.)

The museum will review only complete applications. These materials (application form, resume/curriculum vitae, essays, two letters of recommendations, and transcript) should be mailed in one package by the application deadline to the preceding address. No exceptions will be made and incomplete applications will not be reviewed. If you need additional information about the Internship Program, e-mail internships@moma.org.

Select candidates will be called or e-mailed to set up an interview, which may be conducted either in person or over the telephone, depending on your proximity to New York. All candidates accepted to the Internship Program will be interviewed.

NATIONAL ENDOWMENT FOR THE ARTS INTERNSHIP

Office of Human Resources, Room 627
National Endowment for the Arts
The Nancy Hanks Center

1100 Pennsylvania Avenue, NW
Washington, DC 20506
(202) 682-5472
http://arts.endow.gov/about/Jobs/Internships.
   html

What You Can Earn: Unpaid.
Application Deadlines: At least four to six weeks
before your anticipated start date.
Educational Experience: Undergraduate and
graduate students.
Requirements: None specified.

OVERVIEW

The National Endowment for the Arts is a public agency dedicated to supporting excellence in
new and established art, bringing art to all Americans, and providing leadership in art education.
Established by Congress in 1965 as an independent agency of the federal government, the NEA
is the nation's largest annual funder of the arts.
The organization brings great art to all 50 states,
including rural areas, inner cities, and military
bases.

If you're interested in working at the NEA,
you'll receive a national overview of arts activities across the country as you help the staff with a
variety of tasks related to the process of awarding
federal grants. A variety of resources are available
for participants of the NEA Internship Program,
including an extensive arts library and meetings
of advisory panels and the National Council on
the Arts.

HOW TO APPLY

To apply, send a cover letter detailing the time
period you will be available (including days of
the week, if you won't be available for five days),
your interest areas, experience and typing ability, and whether you will be earning academic
credit. Letters of recommendation, references,
and college transcripts are suggested but not
required.

NATIONAL GALLERY OF ART HIGH SCHOOL INTERNSHIP

High School Summer Institute
Department of Teacher, School, and Family
   Programs
Division of Education
National Gallery of Art
2000B South Club Drive
Landover, MD 20785
(202) 842-6252
highschoolinstitute@nga.gov
http://www.nga.gov/education/highschool/
   index.shtm

What You Can Earn: $250 stipend.
Application Deadlines: Early April for the eight-
day internship beginning in late June (check Web
site for exact dates).
Educational Experience: Beginning and advanced
high school art students in grades 10, 11, or 12 (or
having graduated from high school immediately
before the internship).
Requirements: A Washington, D.C., resident, able
to attend all sessions of the program; responsibility; working as a team member; working independently; good listening skills; patience; creativity;
a willingness to learn; leadership; and being on
time.

OVERVIEW

The National Gallery of Art was created in 1937 for
the people of the United States by a joint resolution
of Congress, who voted to accept the gift of financier and art collector Andrew W. Mellon. During
the 1920s, Mellon had begun collecting art because
he wanted to create a gallery of art for the nation in
Washington, D.C. When he died in 1937, he gave
his collection to the United States. The paintings
and works of sculpture given by Andrew Mellon
formed the center of the art collections, which have

since been enlarged. Mellon hoped that the newly created National Gallery would attract gifts from other collectors, and soon others provided major donations of art.

The Gallery's East Building was built on land set aside in the original Congressional resolution. Opened in 1978, it showcases the gallery's growing collections with an expanded exhibition schedule and houses an advanced research center, administrative offices, a library, and a growing collection of drawings and prints. In 1999 the gallery opened an outdoor sculpture garden designed to offer year-round enjoyment to the public. Located in the 6.1-acre block adjacent to the West Building at 7th Street and Constitution Avenue, N.W., the garden provides an informal, elegant setting for works of modern and contemporary sculpture.

High school art students can participate in a brief summer internship at the National Gallery for eight days of fun and learning while they get to know the gallery from the inside out. During the internship, you'll meet a variety of museum professionals, create your own work of art for a local exhibition, and earn 20 hours of community service or service learning credits. The program is full day, from 9:00 A.M. to 5:00 P.M.

HOW TO APPLY

Print and complete the three-part application form: the main application (download at http://www.nga.gov/education/highschool/app-hsimain.htm); a sponsor form (download at http://www.nga.gov/education/highschool/app-hsispon.htm) and a signature form, found at http://www.nga.gov/education/highschool/app-hsisig.htm.

On a separate piece of paper, describe why you want to spend eight days at the National Gallery of Art and why you are interested in learning about museums. Choose two of these traits: responsibility, working as a team member, working independently, good listening skills, patience, creativity, a willingness to learn, leadership, and being on time, and describe ways you display them in the classroom or in an after-school activity.

Put all three parts of your application together in one envelope and mail it by early April (check Web site for exact deadline) to the preceding address.

NATIONAL GALLERY OF ART INTERNSHIP

Department of Academic Programs
Division of Education
National Gallery of Art
2000 B South Club Drive
Landover, MD 20785
(202) 842-6257
intern@nga.gov

What You Can Earn: $20,000 plus funds for public transportation for full-year interns; summer interns receive $3,600 plus a $1,000 housing allowance, along with partially subsidized funds for public transportation.

Application Deadlines: For full-year interns: Must be received by January 14 (check Web site to make sure deadline has not changed); for summer interns: mid-April (check Web site for exact date).

Educational Experience: Preference will be given to applicants enrolled in a graduate program or to recent graduates of an M.A., M.F.A., or M. Arch. Program, but outstanding recent undergraduates will be considered. Applicants from all backgrounds are encouraged to apply.

Requirements: Intern candidates must show a strong career interest in museum education; summer intern candidates must have experience teaching or working with children ages four through 12 and/or high school students.

OVERVIEW

The National Gallery of Art was created in 1937 for the people of the United States by a joint resolution of Congress, who voted to accept the gift of financier and art collector Andrew W. Mellon. During the 1920s, Mellon had begun collecting art because he wanted to create a gallery of art for the nation in Washington, D.C. When he died in 1937, he gave his collection to the United States. The paintings and works of sculpture given by Andrew Mellon formed the center of the art collections, which have since been added upon. Mellon hoped that the newly created National Gallery would attract gifts from other collectors, and soon others provided major donations of art.

The Gallery's East Building was built on land set aside in the original Congressional resolution. Opened in 1978, it showcases the gallery's growing collections with an expanded exhibition schedule and houses an advanced research center, administrative offices, a library, and a growing collection of drawings and prints. In 1999 the gallery opened an outdoor sculpture garden designed to offer year-round enjoyment to the public. Located in the 6.1-acre block adjacent to the West Building at 7th Street and Constitution Avenue, N.W., the garden provides an informal, elegant setting for works of modern and contemporary sculpture.

Since 1964, the National Gallery of Art has offered professional museum training to candidates from all backgrounds through a variety of internship programs, including both full-year and summer paid opportunities.

Full-Year Interns

Internships at the National Gallery of Art provide institutional training to students interested in a career in the museum profession. Working closely with professional staff at the gallery from September to May, you'll participate in the ongoing work of a department, complete a project, and attend weekly orientation sessions to learn more about gallery staff, departments, programs, and functions. You'll work in one of the gallery's departments, including curatorial, education, exhibition design, and the library, depending on your academic training, interests, experience, and the availability of projects.

Summer Interns

If you'd like to intern at the National Gallery for a shorter period, you can choose a summer internship from early June to early August. These internships provide opportunities to work on projects directed by a gallery curator or department head. Orientation sessions each week introduce interns to the broad spectrum of museum work. For example, summer interns may help with family and youth education programs for the summer, collaborating with staff on preexisting projects such as the Stories in Art series and the Children's Film Program. Additionally, you may help with the High School Summer Institute, working closely with 20 teenagers who will explore the gallery behind the scenes, learn techniques of printmaking and bookmaking, and organize an exhibition of their work.

HOW TO APPLY

Download an application form for the full-year internship at: http://www.nga.gov/pdf/intern_museum_2005.pdf; the summer internship application can be downloaded from http://www.nga.gov/pdf/summer_intern_2005.pdf. Applicants for either internship should send the completed application form to the preceding mailing address, along with contact information for three references (one must be a department chair or dean, the second must be a professor, and the third is an open choice). Your references will be contacted only if you make it to the second phase of the selection process.

Full-year interns should also include a letter (single spaced, about 750 words) to the selection committee explaining why you want to participate in the museum training program at this point in your education, including what you hope to achieve from the experience, what you feel you can contribute to the department in which you're interested, and how such an experience will help further your education and career plans.

If you're applying as a summer intern, you should include the same references, but in place of a face-to-face interview, add a letter (about

400 words) to the selection committee describing your abilities, interests, and career goals. You also should identify the departments in which you'd like to intern and state why you qualify for each position. Also explain how an internship would help further your education and career plans and why you want to participate in the internship program at this point in your education or career.

All applications will be reviewed by a selection committee composed of gallery staff and outside specialists. Interviews in Washington, D.C., will be with the selection committee and prospective mentors.

Semifinalists for the full-year internship will be notified of their status by the end of January; finalists for the summer internship will be notified by mid-April; at this point, all finalists for both internships will be asked to submit one original and five copies of a resume, five copies of a writing sample, and one copy of official transcripts from each undergraduate and graduate institution attended. By the end of February, finalists for the full-year internship will be notified and invited to Washington, D.C., for an interview; final selection for the full-year internships will be completed by mid-March.

Summer intern applicants are not scheduled for interviews; final selection for these internships will be made by early May.

What You Can Earn: Unpaid.
Application Deadlines: October 15 for spring internships, February 15 for summer internships, and June 15 for fall internships.
Educational Experience: Undergraduate and graduate students and individuals interested in exploring museum professions; specific training in African art or other aspects of African culture is desirable, particularly in education and curatorial departments.
Requirements: Ability to work for a minimum of 10 weeks, 20 hours a week, in the fall, spring, or summer.

OVERVIEW

The National Museum of African Art is dedicated to advancing an appreciation and understanding of Africa's rich visual arts and diverse cultures. This annual internship program allows undergraduate and graduate students an opportunity to work under the supervision of museum professionals and to explore aspects of museum professions. Intern opportunities are available in administration, conservation, curatorial, education, exhibition and design, photo archives, public affairs, and registration.

HOW TO APPLY

Download an application at http://www.si.edu/ofg/intern.htm and submit to the preceding address.

NATIONAL MUSEUM OF AFRICAN ART INTERNSHIP

National Museum of African Art
MRC 708 PO Box 37012
Washington, DC 20013-7012
(202) 202-357-4600
Fax: (202) 357-4879
ed@si.edu

NATIONAL MUSEUM OF WOMEN IN THE ARTS INTERNSHIP

National Museum of Women in the Arts
Manager of Volunteer and Visitor Services
Education Department
1250 New York Avenue, NW
Washington, DC 20005

(202) 783-7996
http://www.nmwa.org/about/volunteer_interns.
asp

What You Can Earn: Unpaid (however, two named internships described below are paid: $1200 for the Coca Cola Endowed Internship and $2,000 for the Southern California Council of the National Museum of Women in the Arts Internship).

Application Deadlines: Applications for both paid and unpaid internships must be postmarked by March 15 for the summer session, by June 15 for the fall session, and by October 15 for the spring session.

Educational Experience: Rising college juniors and above, graduate students, as well as recent graduates with a minimum 3.0 cumulative GPA; (Coca Cola and SCC interns must have a 3.2 GPA); in addition, applicants for the Southern California Council (SCC) of the National Museum of Women in the Arts endowed internship must be rising juniors at a design or art school in the Los Angeles County area.

Requirements: Part-time internships must be at least 2 ½ days or 20 hours a week; full-time internships are also available; applicants for the Southern California Council of the National Museum of Women in the Arts must be residents of Los Angeles County.

OVERVIEW

Have you ever wondered what takes place beyond the galleries at a museum? You can find out by being an intern at the National Museum of Women in the Arts! The nation's first museum dedicated to women artists began when Wilhelmina Cole Holladay and Wallace F. Holladay began collecting art in the 1960s, just as scholars and art historians were beginning to discuss the underrepresentation of women and various racial and ethnic groups in museum collections and major art exhibitions. Among the first to apply this revisionist approach to collecting, the Holladays committed themselves for over 20 years to assembling art by women. By 1980, Wilhelmina Cole Holladay began to devote her energies and resources to creating a museum that would showcase women artists, and the Holladay Collection became the core of the institution's permanent collection.

The National Museum of Women in the Arts opened in 1981 as a private, nonprofit museum that operated during its first five years with docent-led tours of the collection at the Holladay residence. Special exhibitions also were presented. In 1983, the museum bought a former Masonic Temple, a Washington, D.C., landmark near the White House. In the spring of 1987, NMWA opened the doors of its permanent location with the inaugural exhibition *American Women Artists, 1830–1930*.

Interns at this museum make significant contributions to its mission, whether they are providing visitors with information about the museum, giving a tour of the permanent collection, or working with staff behind the scenes. The National Museum of Women in the Arts' mission is to discover, document, and celebrate the achievements of women in the arts. In addition to exhibitions, NMWA conducts education programs, houses a library and archives, and publishes a magazine and exhibition catalogues.

As an intern at NMWA, you'll get the chance to work on a one-to-one basis with museum professionals and meet other interns with similar academic interests and career plans. Former NMWA interns have found jobs at many of the leading museums throughout the country. In addition to an unbeatable work experience in an arts organization, the NMWA offers you a chance to learn about women artists in college-level art history classes and through field trips to other cultural places in Washington, D.C., featuring work by women artists. In addition, you'll have access to the Library and Research Center, which houses one of the most extensive collections of materials about women artists in the world, providing a rare opportunity for primary research.

NMWA offers fall, spring, and summer internships in the following departments: accounting; administration (director's office and founder's office); development; communications and marketing; curatorial; education; exhibition design and production; information technology; library and research center; member services; national programs; publications; registrar; retail operations; and special events.

Coca-Cola Endowed Internship

This paid internship is offered every fall, spring, and summer for a full-time, 12-week period. To apply, you must be interested in pursuing a museum career; you must be an undergraduate who has completed at least the sophomore year in college, a graduate student, or a recent graduate with a cumulative GPA of 3.25. Application requirements are the same as for the unpaid internships, described below.

Southern California Council (SCC) of NMWA Internship

The Southern California Council (SCC) of the National Museum of Women in the Arts offers an endowed internship each summer for a full-time, 40-hour per week period. The SCC Intern may work in any department of the museum as determined by museum staff in consideration of the intern's experience and interests.

HOW TO APPLY

Applications for both the general, unpaid internship and the Coca Cola endowed internship must include a cover letter, stating how the internship program will further your personal and professional goals; the departments in which you're interested in working; and how you learned about NMWA's internship program. List several departments in which you'd like to work. Because internships at NMWA are very popular, you may not be assigned to your first choice. You also should include a resume (including your education and employment history, school, and permanent addresses) along with a most-recent transcript, one academic and one personal letter of recommendation, and a brief writing sample of one or two pages. Send three copies of all application materials to the preceding address.

Applicants for the Southern California Council (SCC) of NMWA internship should send a let-

ter of purpose stating your personal and professional goals and how this internship will help you reach those goals, along with your three preferred choices for placement in a department (not more that one page). Also include your most-recent college transcript, a personal recommendation and an academic recommendation; your resume, including current educational and employment history, school, and home addresses; and a brief one- or two-page writing sample. Send three copies of all materials to the preceding address.

NATIONAL PORTRAIT GALLERY INTERNSHIP

Intern Coordinator
National Portrait Gallery
Office of Education
PO Box 37012
Victor Building, Suite 8300, MRC 973
Washington, DC 20013-0712
(202) 275-1811
Fax: (202) 275-1904
NPGEducation@si.edu
http://www.npg.si.edu/educate2/educate10.htm

What You Can Earn: Unpaid.
Application Deadlines: March 31.
Educational Experience: Undergraduate and graduate students and individuals not affiliated with academic programs who have research or museum career interests.
Requirements: See individual departments for specific requirements.

OVERVIEW

Various departments at the National Portrait Gallery sponsor interns throughout the year. Intern projects are based on interests and needs of the department and are agreed upon by the mutual consent of the intern candidate and the supervisor. Various departments sponsor internships throughout the year. Projects are based on various interests and needs of participating departments within the Gallery.

Internships are available in the administration office, the Center for Electronic Research and Outreach Services; the offices of design and production; development; education; exhibitions; history; photographic services; photographs; prints and drawings; public affairs; publications; registrar; rights and reproductions; the department of painting and sculpture; the library; and the Charles Wilson Peale Family Papers.

Center for Electronic Research and Outreach Services/Catalog of American Portraits

The center administers research and electronic outreach programs, including the gallery's online sites and the Smithsonian's Intranet. The Catalog of American Portraits is a national archives and research database dedicated to portraits that gives researchers biographical information on subjects and artists, artist attributions, histories of ownership, and related works, as well as digitized images of the portraits. Interns should have good organizational skills and attention to detail, understand library research methods, be familiar with computer systems, and have an interest in American history or art history.

Charles Wilson Peale Family Papers

This department researches events, people, and ideas contained in the thousands of letters, documents, and paintings made by artists in the Peale family from 1735 to 1885 and in biographies of the individuals whose portraits were painted. An intern in this area should be interested in historical research and should be a good writer. Interns should be willing to learn to transcribe handwritten documents; to read broadly and deeply in historical materials; to discover the answers to historical questions posed by documents; and to write short, interesting, and accurate annotations or footnotes.

Department of History

This office is responsible for conducting biographical research on the individuals represented in the collection, creating history-based exhibitions, evaluating objects proposed for acquisition, and keeping records. An intern should have a background in American history.

Department of Painting and Sculpture

This curatorial department is responsible for acquiring, cataloging, and researching all paintings and sculpture in the gallery. Members of the department also do research for special exhibitions and for publications on the history of American portraiture and handle public inquiries. An intern should have a sound academic background in art history, American studies, or American history; good research and writing skills; and the ability to use a word-processing program.

Department of Photographs

This curatorial office takes care of the gallery's extensive collection of portrait photographs, handling exhibitions and acquiring, researching, cataloging, and storing objects. An intern should have a strong background in art history or American history and be familiar with the history of photography and various photographic processes. Legible handwriting and an understanding of library research techniques are helpful; some knowledge of word-processing and computer database systems is also required.

Department of Prints and Drawings

This curatorial office handles works of art on paper and the acquisition, documentation, research, storage, and conservation of these objects. An intern should have a strong academic background in art history or American history and be good at library research.

Library

The library offers more than 100,000 books, plus auction catalogs, microfilm, and vertical files on artists and institutions, for the use of gallery fellows, visiting scholars, the public, and the staffs of the National Portrait Gallery and the Smithsonian American Art Museum. Attention to detail and accuracy are important skills for an intern in the library, as well as general familiarity with libraries, including the Library of Congress classification system.

Office of Administration

This department handles the gallery's financial and administrative activities, overseeing budget and procurement and managing gallery operations. Interns in this office should have a good grasp of grammar, spelling, and writing, as well as an interest in financial functions. Knowledge of Microsoft Excel, Access, and Word are helpful but are not required. Because this internship involves interactions with staff, visitors, and vendors, the applicant should be tactful and diplomatic.

Office of Design and Production

This office is responsible for the design and installation of the gallery's public spaces, and must interpret the permanent collection and special exhibitions. This includes designing, building, and decorating exhibition spaces, and designing, building and installing cases, frames, mounts, and supporting graphics. Interns should have experience in at least one of the following areas: design, drafting, graphic design, cabinetmaking, computer assisted design (CAD), or graphic computer skills in VectorWorks, Illustrator, Photoshop, or InDesign. Any other exhibition-related experience, such as picture installation or art moving, would be useful.

Office of Development

This office is responsible for finding private funds to support the gallery, working closely with individuals, foundations, corporations, and government sources. As an intern, you would be able to help research, develop strategies, and write proposals for various projects. Interns should be detail oriented, be interested in research, and have strong writing and critical thinking skills. Knowledge of the Internet and of Windows-based word-processing and database programs is essential.

Office of Education

This department's responsibility is to make history come alive for its visitors through the art of portraiture. Department employees interact with daily visitors of all ages and abilities, providing gallery tours, public programs, and educational outreach programs to address the full range of American history and portraiture. An intern needs to have general knowledge of American history and art and be good at library research. Interpersonal and writing skills are essential and some knowledge of word-processing and computer database programs is required.

Office of Exhibitions

This department is responsible for administering the gallery's exhibition program, setting the exhibition schedule, establishing contracts with guest curators and museums, negotiating art loans, obtaining photographs of exhibition items, working with other gallery offices, and helping with the gallery's development program. An intern should have either an American history or American art background, good typing skills, and some experience with a word-processing system.

Office of Photographic Services

This department includes a photography studio, darkrooms, and a storage area for recording and editing video and audio tapes. An intern must know how to handle black-and-white developing and printing, plus understand basic photographic principles and photography.

Office of Public Affairs

This office is responsible for gallery public relations, including handling the news media, exhibition openings, and special events. An intern must be able to research, write, and work well with journalists and the general public.

Office of Publications

Employees in this department develop, edit, and produce books, catalogues, and brochures for the gallery. All material published by staff is handled by this office to ensure accuracy and uniformity of style. An intern should be interested in publishing and be detail oriented, with a background in American history, art history, or English. Facility with Microsoft Word is a must; knowledge of Excel and Access would be helpful.

Office of the Registrar

This department keeps records of the gallery's collection in a variety of formats, including files, catalog cards, and computerized databases. The office also oversees transportation, packing, and insurance, and processes legal custody agreements. An intern should be able to type and understand databases.

Office of Rights and Reproductions

This is the repository and sales office for photographs of objects in the gallery's collection, and it works closely with the gallery's photograph and curatorial offices and the public. An intern should be able to type and understand databases and have research and organizational skills. Some experience in photography is helpful.

HOW TO APPLY

To apply for an internship with the National Gallery, download a general application form at http://www.npg.si.edu/docs/applicant.pdf. Submit the completed application along with a copy of your resume, an official college transcript, a personal essay (500–1,000 words), and two letters of recommendation. To ensure proper consideration, be sure to indicate the departments in which you are interested in working.

You can submit your application materials either by mail or by e-mail at the preceding addresses, but your transcript should be sent via regular mail.

NEW MUSEUM OF CONTEMPORARY ART INTERNSHIP

New Museum of Contemporary Art
235 Bowery at Prince Street
New York, NY 10011

Administrative offices:
210 11th Avenue, 2nd Floor
New York, NY 10001
(212) 219-1222
newmu@newmuseum.org
http://www.newmuseum.org/info_internships.
 php

What You Can Earn: Unpaid.
Application Deadlines: December 1 for spring session (January 15 through April 30); April 15 for summer session (June 1 through August 31); August 15 for fall session (September. 15 through December 31).
Educational Experience: Some positions require a college degree or training.
Requirements: Some positions require professional experience.

OVERVIEW

The Internship Program at the New Museum of Contemporary Art offers participants hands-on training in the museum profession and a comprehensive overview of museum operations by participating in day-to-day activities and working on specific projects. If you're chosen, you'll work at least two full days a week (seven hours a day) for a full trimester.

Founded in 1977, the New Museum of Contemporary Art is the premier contemporary art museum in New York City and is among the most important internationally. Each year, the museum presents six major exhibitions and five media lounge shows. The program of dynamic solo exhibitions and landmark group shows defines key moments in the development of contemporary art, reflects the global nature of art today, and spans a vast array of cultural activities and media.

In spring 2006, the New Museum opened a new home at 235 Bowery at Prince Street. This 60,000 square foot facility, designed by the Tokyo-based firm Sejima + Nishizawa/SANAA, expanded the museum's exhibitions and programs and was the first art museum constructed in downtown New York's modern history.

Internships are available in a variety of museum departments, including administration, bookstore, curatorial, development, director's office, education, marketing/communications and registrar, operations, and information systems.

Administration

This department is responsible for the financial management of the museum, including budgeting, accounting, tax and audit preparation, and benefits and human resources. In addition, this department manages the day-to-day functions of the museum offices. Interns interested in developing their business and management abilities who choose this department will learn skills in program budgets and nonprofit financial administration.

Curatorial

The curatorial department researches and organizes upcoming exhibitions, including timelines, checklists, and signs; produces exhibition catalogues; manages the travel of selected exhibitions; corresponds with artists, curators, galleries and museums; and orchestrates a weekly slide review of artist's work. If you'd like to work here, you'll be introduced to issues related to contemporary art and will obtain administrative and curatorial skills in organizing art exhibitions.

Development

The development department is responsible for all grants from government, foundation, and corporate sources; the membership program; contributions to the museum; and the capital campaign for building and endowment needs. Interns in this department help research prospective donors, plan programs, organize membership events, and work on budgeting and solicitation for special projects and grants writing.

Director's Office

The director and deputy director manage the work of all the museum's departments. If you intern here, you'll be involved in all areas of museum operation, and you'll learn how a contemporary art museum is run.

Education

In this department, you'll help organize programs for high school students and teachers, public programs for adults (lectures, panel discussions, and performances), and group tours and internships and assist with the museum's Web site. This is a great way to develop an understanding of public education programs related to a contemporary art museum.

Information Systems

The information systems department is responsible for the museum's computer hardware and software, network, and database applications. If you choose to intern here, you should have some technical experience, since you'll be helping maintain the museum's computer systems.

Marketing and Communications

This department works to expand public awareness of the New Museum and increase attendance and revenue. The department produces the museum's media releases, circulates images for reproduction, places advertisements, produces newsletters and other promotional materials, organizes an annual art auction and exhibition openings, and coordinates the Limited Editions program. Interns will help produce media and marketing materials and coordinate special events.

New Museum Store

The bookstore complements the museum's exhibition schedule by providing an assortment of contemporary art books and objects for sale. If you choose this department, you'll gain experience in the day-to-day operations of a retail space, budgeting, visual merchandising, marketing, special events, and maintaining an online store, as well as getting an insider view into the world of fine art books.

Operations

This department maintains the physical space of the museum and provides security for the exhibitions and public safety. In conjunction with the registrar's office, it supervises construction of gallery space installation and exhibitions. If you choose this department, you'll learn about the physical maintenance of the museum and its operations, as well as become involved with any renovations of the museum's galleries and office space.

Registrar

With this internship, you'll have an opportunity to develop skills related to the installation, preparation, and shipment of works of art for exhibition. You'll also help maintain inventory and the documentation of the museum's semipermanent collection. Experience with collection maintenance is a plus; it also helps to have basic clerical and word processing skills.

HOW TO APPLY

All interested individuals are eligible to apply for an internship. Qualifications vary for each intern, and some positions may require college or graduate training and/or professional experience. To apply, submit an intern application with two letters of recommendation from professors and/or previous employers, along with a resume and a cover letter.

You'll be contacted if the department in which you're interested plans to interview you, and you'll be notified of acceptance at least two weeks before the start of each cycle.

PHILADELPHIA MUSEUM OF ART INTERNSHIP

Coordinator, Museum Studies Internship Program
Philadelphia Museum of Art
PO Box 7646
Philadelphia, PA 19101-7646
(215) 684-7397
Fax: (215) 236-4063
http://www.philamuseum.org/opportunities/internship.shtml

What You Can Earn: Unpaid but academic credit is available.
Application Deadlines: Mid-February.
Educational Experience: Must have completed your sophomore year by the spring before your internship begins in the summer; students from all backgrounds are encouraged to apply.
Requirements: None specified.

OVERVIEW

Located at the end of the Benjamin Franklin Parkway, the Philadelphia Museum of Art stands among the great art institutions of the world. Founded more than 125 years ago, the museum houses more than 300,000 works of art encompassing some of the greatest achievements of human creativity and offers a wealth of exhibitions and education programs for a public of all ages.

The Philadelphia Museum of Art was a legacy of the great Centennial Exposition of 1876 held in Fairmount Park, which served as the art gallery for the great fair. At the conclusion of the Centennial celebrations, Memorial Hall was to remain open as a Museum of Art and Industry for the improvement and enjoyment of the people of the Commonwealth. The founders imagined a museum similar to the great Victoria and Albert Museum in London but with an active school where craftsmen could be trained for the growing industries of the United States.

A year after the Exposition, Memorial Hall reopened as a permanent museum, followed by The Pennsylvania Museum School of Industrial Art in a separate location on North Broad Street, with an entering class of 100 students. Eventually, the school moved to a new Greek Revival building at Broad and Pine Streets, where students were taught drawing, painting, and modeling, with specialized courses in textiles, furniture design, pottery, wood carving, metalwork, and other crafts.

The Philadelphia Museum of Art is a leader in the training and mentoring of young museum professionals and future museum colleagues. The

Museum Studies Internship Program provides interns with exposure to the inner workings of a major metropolitan museum, promoting an awareness of museum careers through experiences not available in most academic settings. The museum selects a diverse group of talented undergraduate and graduate students from a highly competitive regional, national, and international pool of candidates.

The Museum Studies Internship Program offers internships each summer, from Monday through Friday for nine weeks. Interns participate in a museum studies curriculum including collection tours with curators, departmental orientations, field trips, and seminars, which take place on Mondays. Tuesdays through Fridays are spent in departmental placements. Interns are placed according to departmental needs that vary from year to year but that may include development, external affairs; library; marketing and public relations; registrar; American art; East Asian art; costume and textiles; European painting; Indian and Himalayan art; and modern and contemporary art and prints, drawings and photographs. Education placements are made in two divisions: public programs for adults and college students or programs for youth and family.

HOW TO APPLY

Download an application at http://www.philamuseum.org/opportunities/internapp05.pdf.

To apply, submit the completed application along with your official academic transcript; two letters of recommendation from college professors; your resume; and a one-page essay describing your interest in the internship, skills that would contribute to the program, and career goals. All materials need to be received by mid-February (check Web site for exact deadline).

Applications will be reviewed by the Summer Internship Advisory Committee. Finalists selected will be invited for interviews in person or by telephone. If you've been accepted, you will be notified by late April.

SEATTLE ART MUSEUM INTERNSHIP

Seattle Art Museum
Volunteer Program Manager
100 University Street
Seattle, WA 98101-2902
(206) 654-3168
volunteer@seattleartmuseum.org

What You Can Earn: Unpaid
Application Deadlines: Rolling.
Educational Experience: Undergraduate degree in any discipline, technical familiarity with information management systems and HTML.
Requirements: Proficiency with desktop publishing and Web site development software, PowerPoint, scanning and imaging software; familiarity with SharePoint or other server development environment; ability to communicate effectively and work with staff and volunteers in a professional manner.

OVERVIEW

The Seattle Art Museum strives to offer a welcoming place for people to connect with art and to consider its relationship to their lives. The museum actually offers three separate art experiences: the Seattle Art Museum downtown, the Seattle Asian Art Museum at Volunteer Park, and the Olympic Sculpture Park on the downtown waterfront.

Internships are available within the Curatorial Division at the Olympic Sculpture Park, which seeks a motivated and detail oriented intern to help museum staffers with design and implementation of intranet and public Web sites. This internship may require a commitment of at least 10 hours a week, during normal office hours, from August to December.

HOW TO APPLY

Send a volunteer application (available at http://www.seattleartmuseum.org/volunteer/volunteer-

Form.asp) along with a letter of interest, resume, and two letters of recommendation to the address above.

VERY SPECIAL ARTS INTERNSHIP

VSA Internship
Human Resources
818 Connecticut Avenue, NW, Suite 600
Washington, DC 20006
http://www.vsarts.org

What You Can Earn: Full-time assignments receive a monthly stipend of $650 and there is a pro-rated amount for part-time interns.
Application Deadlines: Rolling.
Educational Experience: College juniors and seniors or graduate students interested in pursuing arts education, arts administration, special education, and disability careers.
Requirements: Must be able to work a minimum of three full days a week, from 9:00 A.M. to 5:00 P.M. and have an interest in art and in working with people with disabilities.

OVERVIEW

This international nonprofit organization was founded in 1974 by Ambassador Jean Kennedy Smith as a way of helping to create a society where people with disabilities can participate in the arts. Today, 5 million people participate in VSA arts programs every year through a network of affiliates nationwide and in more than 60 other countries. Designated by Congress to coordinate arts programming for persons with disabilities, VSA arts is supported by its affiliate network to offer many different programs and events, such as training institutes and artist-in-residence projects, arts camps, and emerging artist award programs. Its innovative learning opportunities can be found at the local, national, and international levels. VSA is located just a few blocks south of Dupont Circle and just a block from the White House.

As an intern here, you'll be considered as one of the staff, as you help with administration, management, and outreach. Full- and part-time internships are available in the fall, spring, and summer semesters in arts administration, communications, educational research, event planning, exhibition design and fabrication, or information technology.

HOW TO APPLY

Interested, qualified candidates should e-mail a letter of interest, resume, references, and any curriculum requirements to the address above. Resumes sent via e-mail must be in text, RTF, PDF, or MS Word.

WHITNEY MUSEUM OF AMERICAN ART INTERNSHIP

Whitney Museum of Art, Internship Program
Human Resources
945 Madison Avenue
New York, NY 10021
(212) 570-1807
hr@whitney.org
http://www.whitney.org

What You Can Earn: $500 plus two monthly Metro-Cards (used on MTA, New York City Transit). Interns can attend most New York museums for free, receive a 33 percent discount at the Whitney Museum sales desk, a 10 percent discount at the museum's in-house gourmet restaurant, and free admission to museum talks held in the fall and spring.

Application Deadlines: Summer session: March 1; no deadlines for the academic year.

Educational Experience: College juniors and seniors.

Requirements: A strong interest and background in American art and/or museum studies.

OVERVIEW

The Whitney is the world's most comprehensive museum of 20th and 21st century American Art, with 17,000 permanent works of art, including Georgia O'Keefe, Charles Demuth, Edward Hopper, Max Weber, and George Bellows in its collection. Interns here gain firsthand experience in how a museum functions.

Under the supervision of a department head or curator, you'll help in regular departmental activities that range from research and special projects to routine administrative and clerical tasks.

Interns are placed in the following departments: curatorial, development, education, film and video, library, communications/public relations, publications, and new media.

Every week, the museum arranges a half-day presentation to give you an overview of the museum and career possibilities. Past seminars have featured lectures from department heads as well as films and panel discussions about art. In addition to attending the weekly seminars, you can take several afternoon field trips that include the Studio Museum of Harlem, Whitney's permanent collection storage facility, and other related sites.

HOW TO APPLY

If you're interested in applying for the academic year, submit the following to the preceding address:

- a resume
- a cover letter
- a one-page statement of purpose as to why you want to work at the Whitney and what you hope to gain and contribute

- a letter of recommendation from a college professor or employer
- college transcripts
- a list of three museum departments, in order of work preference
- proposed beginning and ending dates of internship
- housing arrangements
- availability for an in-person interview (give dates)

WVSA ARTS CONNECTION INTERNSHIP

WVSA Arts Connection
1100 16th Street, NW
Washington, DC 20036
(202) 296-9100, ext. 307
Fax: (202) 261-0200
flento@wvsarts.org

What You Can Earn: Unpaid, although a stipend may be possible in individual cases.

Application Deadlines: Rolling.

Educational Experience: Undergraduate (junior, senior) or graduate student.

Requirements: A positive attitude; sense of responsibility; accountability, punctuality, flexibility; reliability as a team player interest and experienced in fine arts; strong written and verbal communication skills; good attention to detail; and excellent organizational and interpersonal communication skills. Interest and experience in Macintosh and Wintel platforms is required; some experience with XP Professional and SQL Server may also be required pending project designs.

OVERVIEW

WVSA arts connection (formerly Washington Very Special Arts) is a unique nonprofit organization that has served Washington, D.C.-area children and young people with special needs for more than 20 years. Using the arts as an innovative method of education, WVSA provides the tools for success in school, adulthood, and life.

WVSA was founded by special educator Lawrence Riccio, Ed.D., in 1981, with two Trinity College graduate students, as a way of providing high-quality arts and education programming for children and youth with special needs in Washington, D.C. From modest beginnings in the basement of Trinity College with a part-time executive director operating an annual arts festival, WVSA has grown to include more than 40 staffers operating a range of year-round programs. Each semester, WVSA/SAIL provides a variety of internships for interested individuals.

ARTiculate Employment Training Program

This program provides professional arts instruction and vocational training in arts entrepreneurship to participating artist apprentices with special needs, from ages 14 through 25. The program helps participants develop the skills to move from school to the work force. ARTiculate gives participants experience in polishing their work skills.

As an intern here, you'll help curate exhibits and help in the ARTiculate Gallery, marketing clients' personal artwork. You also may set up studios for classes, provide hands-on support to participants with various art techniques such as acrylic/watercolor painting and printing. You'll also help monitor the participants' workplace behavior, including language, sign in/out, goal planning, implementing deadlines, and so on. You'll help with clean-up, dismissal, collecting materials after class, and help participants in the Information Technology component of the program, with word processing, digital photography and imaging, and Internet use). In addition, you may help with administrative tasks such as phone calls, filing, copying, and faxing.

ARTiculate Gallery

This full-functioning gallery is open to the public Monday through Friday 10:00 A.M. to 5:30 P.M. The gallery has six yearly openings, displaying and selling works created by ARTiculate artist apprentices.

You may be required to help with customers in the gallery, learn how to exhibit and hang artwork, help hang the show, take slides of art, learn how to frame artwork, prepare for the opening reception, and help the gallery director with Art On The Move, an art-leasing program.

Development and Outreach

This department focuses on raising money and increasing community awareness and involvement with WVSA. As a development intern, you may help manage grants, fund-raise, and work with direct mail appeals (including writing, mailing, tracking responses, and sending donation acknowledgements and thank you notes). You also may handle administrative tasks, such as answering phones, running errands, filing, faxing, copying, and pitching in whenever and wherever is necessary.

As an outreach intern, you might help write and distribute press releases, update press kits, and help write and distribute correspondence, including invitations, directions, volunteer instructions, thank you letters, and so on.

Applicants for these positions should have an interest in fund-raising, public relations, and development.

Finance

In this department, your duties may include organizing check requests, filing back-up documentation, processing financial records, working closely with the finance director to provide administrative support on all financial matters, and working with vendors and contractors.

Research and Program Development

This department conducts research and evaluation activities, managing arts-in-education and arts-in-healthcare programs, and developing and producing curricula, monographs, training manuals, and other publications. This department also provides design and editing services for all publications, brochures, and marketing and public relations materials; develops PowerPoint presentations; monitors reporting status for grants; and develops federal and local government grant proposals.

As an intern here, you may help with administrative tasks such as letter writing, faxing, photocopying, making phone calls, and word processing. As a member of the department, you'll have the chance to contribute to all activities, including writing for publications, developing grant proposals, and so on.

SAIL School for Arts In Learning

The school is a public charter elementary (K-6) school that encourages students to achieve their potential while becoming more aware of art in their daily lives. SAIL's mission is to provide individualized education for children with learning disabilities or special learning styles that make it difficult for them to succeed in traditional classroom settings. As a SAIL intern, you may work as a student teacher or artist. Your duties and responsibilities will be evaluated on a case-by-case basis, usually following guidelines given by your university. If you're a visual, dance movement, or music artist, your duties will vary depending on your expertise and the needs of the school. Individuals with a background in either the arts or education who seek to become proficient in the other may work as an arts educator intern.

Technology

Here, your responsibilities may include installing and maintaining the Local and Wide Area Network infrastructure to ensure efficient operation and high availability of servers, network hardware, and installing and maintaining desktops, laptops, scanners, printers, digital cameras, and so on. You also may help in the classroom, such as with Web site design by students, and in the multimedia lab. Interns in this area must have an interest in and experience with Macintosh and Wintel platforms; occasional experience of XP Professional and SQL Server may also be required pending project designs.

HOW TO APPLY

To apply for an internship, fill out an application and background-check form available at http://www.wvsarts.org/donate/howtoapply.asp. Then mail, fax, or e-mail the completed forms to the preceding address.

BUSINESS

ABBOTT LABORATORIES INTERNSHIP

Abbott Laboratories
100 Abbott Park Road
Abbott Park, IL 60064-3500
(847) 937-6100
https://jobs.brassring.com/EN/ASP/TG/cim_
  home.asp?sec=1&partnerid=281&siteid=50
http://www.abbott.com

What You Can Earn: $324 to $625 a week for undergraduates; $490 to $1,250 for grad students; round-trip travel expenses, plus housing for students living more than 40 miles away.
Application Deadlines: Rolling.
Educational Experience: Students must have completed at least one year of college and must be enrolled in school for the fall following the potential internship.
Requirements: A grade point average of 3.0 or higher, together with leadership ability, extracurricular activities, relevant course work, and proficiency in Abbott's core competencies (integrity, innovation, initiative, teamwork, and adaptability).

OVERVIEW

Abbott's national, highly popular internship program provides 250 to 350 college students with three months of supervised, practical work experience in areas directly related to their education and career goals. Rated for the seventh time as one of *Fortune* magazine's 50 best companies for minorities in 2004 (they came in 29th), Abbott doesn't offer this program lightly; their purpose is to identify and select talented undergraduate and graduate students with the intention of hiring them as full-time employees.

For this reason, it's not easy to land an internship here. Selection is competitive and based on grade point average, leadership abilities, communication skills, and relevant course work, the same criteria used for entry-level employee selection.

If you make the grade, the company will mail you a handbook filled with program info, maps, and descriptions of the company facilities. Included is a list of housing, details on what to bring, and lots of other helpful information. Once you arrive, you'll have the opportunity to work with Abbott's innovative technology and network both socially and professionally through organized activities. Although internship opportunities vary each year, past internships have included the following areas: engineering, environmental health and safety, finance and accounting, general business, information technology, manufacturing, quality assurance, and science. Abbott tries to provide an environment that nurtures your creativity and energy and inspires you to achieve.

Abbott Laboratories is a global, broad-based healthcare company devoted to discovering, developing, manufacturing, and marketing pharmaceuticals and medical products, including nutritionals, devices, and diagnostics. The company employs more than 55,000 people and markets its products in more than 130 countries. Some of their leading brands include Depakote, Ensure, Isomil (soy-based infant formula), Similac, and Synthroid (synthetic thyroid hormone).

Their longstanding commitment to workplace diversity has helped the company earn recognition as one of the top 10 in the "100 Best Companies for Working Mothers" by *Working Mother* magazine in both 2002 and 2003, *The Scientist* magazine's list of "Best Places to Work in Industry" and *Princeton Review's* "Best Entry Level Jobs." *Fortune* also has named Abbott as one of "America's Most Admired Companies" every year since the list's inception in 1983.

HOUSING

Interns are housed at the nearby Residence Inn in Waukegan and Deerfield, featuring full kitchens, complimentary housekeeping services, and a hot breakfast seven days a week. Hot dinners are offered four nights a week, along with complimentary grocery shopping, a pool and Jacuzzi, and a sport court.

HOW TO APPLY

You can chat with Abbott reps when they visit your university. Abbott visits several universities nationwide each year. Check with your career services office at school to see if the company will be at your campus soon or visit the Internet site "Abbott On Campus" at (http://www.abbott.com/career/abt_on_campus.cfm) to review scheduled recruiting events. You should consult with your school's career services office to learn how to sign up for an interview.

You can e-mail your resume ahead of time, along with a cover letter detailing your GPA and your areas of interest, to the preceding address. Applications are completed during the interview process on campus.

AMELIA ISLAND INTERNSHIPS

Amelia Island Internship Coordinator
PO Box 3000
Amelia Island, FL 32035-3000
(904) 277-5904
Fax: (904) 491-4345
intern@aipfl.com
http://www.aipfl.com

What You Can Earn: Students in most areas receive $250 a week plus two meals per scheduled shift, assistance in locating housing, extensive training, and many perks including use of amenities at a discounted rate. Golf Level 1 and turf management, culinary, club culinary, and pastry interns are considered "seasonal" employees and are paid minimum wage and tips without meals. Tennis interns are considered "seasonal" employees and will be paid minimum wage or a rate for teaching/tennis instruction completed. The teaching rate will be a percentage of the amount of lessons taught. Teaching may account for 15 to 25 percent of time worked.

Application Deadlines: Rolling.

Educational Experience: College students who must receive school credit for their experience. Students must be actively pursuing a degree in a related field. Preference is given to students who express the desire and have the ability to seek a permanent position with the company after their internship.

Requirements: Must be fluent in conversational English (speaking, reading, and writing); must provide transportation (a car is strongly recommended; housing is found at least six miles from the resort); a 16-week minimum commitment is preferred. Most areas require a valid driver's license as well as a good driving record.

OVERVIEW

Amelia Island Plantation is Florida's premier AAA-Four Diamond destination island resort. Located on Amelia Island, Florida, just 29 miles north of Jacksonville International Airport (JAX), the 1,350 acre property overlooks the Atlantic on the east and the green marshland and Intra-coastal Waterway on the west. Three 18-hole championship golf courses, 23 clay tennis courts, a health and fitness center, full-service spa, award-winning youth programs, a variety of fine shops, and a choice of dining options are among the many activities offered at Amelia Island Plantation.

The resort has more than 20 years of experience in offering a variety of internships in the following areas: commercial, corporate, and social recreation; aquatics/rentals; retail; environmental interpretation; lodging; housekeeping; food and beverage; marketing; sales; graphics; retail; Golf-Level I; turf management; tennis; and pastry and culinary.

In addition to salary, intern benefits include a 50 percent discount for dinners and 20 percent discount for breakfast/lunch in many outlets; 20 percent off merchandise in AIP outlets, Spa, and Retail; free golf (cart fee only) and discounted lessons/employee clinics; free tennis (up to three guests at an additional $6/person); discounted tennis lessons/employee clinics; Bausch & Lomb Tournament employee rates; free use of bicycles at Amelia's Wheels; discounted rates on Island Hoppers; beach service discount; use of facilities; employee room discount; employee aerobics, wellness walks, and tournaments; dry cleaning discounts; purchasing at cost from purchasing department; discount passes for SeaWorld, Busch Gardens, Wild Adventures, Islands of Adventures, and Six Flags; discounted room rates at participating hotels; Sam's Warehouse discounts; and free on-property nature tours.

HOW TO APPLY

Applicants can request information and an application via e-mail or phone or can download information from the Web site. Indicate your area of interest and the semester you are interested in, along with your name, e-mail address, and phone number. Mail or fax completed application forms, along with your resume and cover letter, to the Internship Coordinator at the preceding address.

AXLE ALLIANCE GROUP INTERNSHIP

Axle Alliance Group
13400 Outer Drive, West
Detroit, MI 48239
313.592.5894
http://career.daimlerchrysler.com/dc/wms/dc/
    index.php?re_gion=3&ci=241&language=2

What You Can Earn: Competitive compensation depending on education.
Application Deadlines: February/March for September, or August/September for March.
Educational Experience: College student in business management, industrial engineering, Mechanical Engineering, or Computer Science, or a graduate student with a degree in a related field.
Requirements: Strong communication and interpersonal skills, ability to work in a team, advanced computer skills in MS Office (PowerPoint, Excel, Access, Word, MS Project), ability to work with

minimum supervision, and ability to show initiative with assignments.

OVERVIEW

If it's front and rear axles you're interested in, you might consider the Axle Alliance Company (AAC), which is a wholly owned subsidiary of DaimlerChrysler. Bridging American and European technology, AAC develops and produces innovative axle systems for the commercial truck market and consults with the commercial car industry.

As an intern here, you might spend time with one of the following departments: finance/controlling, human resources, procurement/supply, logistics, quality, IT, program management support and marketing/communications.

HOW TO APPLY

Submit your application (retrievable from the URL above) and a cover letter with information about the department in which you're interested and your college major, along with your resume, college transcripts, and a letter of reference discussing previous internships or training.

BECHTEL CORPORATION INTERNSHIP

Bechtel Corporation Internship Coordinator
PO Box 36359
Phoenix, AZ 85067
staffpx@bechtel.com
http://www.bechtel.com

What You Can Earn: Varies depending on education and experience.
Application Deadlines: Rolling.
Educational Experience: College students who have satisfactorily completed at least one year of study in engineering or in a professional academic

discipline such as business, accounting and finance, or computer science.

Requirements: Only students from local colleges and universities near a Bechtel office will be considered.

OVERVIEW

Founded in 1898 with W.A. Bechtel's work grading railroad beds, Bechtel is one of the world's premier engineering, construction, and project-management companies. Its 40,000 employees are teamed with customers, partners, and suppliers on a wide range of projects in nearly 140 countries. Among Bechtel's projects are the Hoover Dam, the Channel Tunnel, Hong Kong International Airport, the San Francisco Bay Area Rapid Transit (BART) system, and the reconstruction of Kuwait's oil fields after the Gulf War.

Bechtel's internship program is designed to provide participants with practical, hands-on experience and exposure to the company, while giving Bechtel an opportunity to evaluate students' professional potential. Depending on the program needs, students may work at Bechtel a few days a week or full time for several months.

HOW TO APPLY

To apply for a summer internship, send a letter to the preceding address, explaining your interest in the summer internship program. Priority will be given to students within one year of graduation, to recipients of Bechtel scholarships, and to students who have previously worked for Bechtel and have been identified as high performing and/or having high potential.

BOEING INTERNSHIP

Boeing College Relations
Internship Coordinator
PO Box 37071, M/S 6H-PR
Seattle, WA 98124
http://www.boeing.com/employment/college/internshipDetails.htmlInternship

What You Can Earn: Varies with location but may include relocation fees, temporary lodging, mileage allowance, recreation, and employee benefits.
Application Deadlines: January 31 for summer.
Educational Experience: Engineering, engineering technology, computer science, mathematics, or business.
Requirements: None specified.

OVERVIEW

An internship at Boeing can provide a breadth of opportunities, from commercial aircraft to next-generation military aircraft, to spacecraft and beyond. In addition to competitive salaries and benefits, Boeing offers video facilities where you can continue your college attendance as you work.

As an intern at Boeing, you might help develop integrated circuits for a mission to Mars, sophisticated anti-tank weaponry, or microelectromechanical load sensors for commercial airliners.

You should possess a good understanding of engineering science fundamentals, math (including statistics), physical and life sciences, information technology, design and manufacturing processes, economics, and business. Prospective interns also should be able to think critically and creatively and work independently and cooperatively. You should have the ability to adapt to major changes, a desire for lifelong learning, the highest ethical standards, and excellent communication skills.

Boeing will work with you to figure out your area of expertise and match you with a program that suits your skills, which means you'll be working with employees and managers on real projects that affect the company and the world of aerospace science. You may be working with electrical engineers; industrial engineers; mechanical engineers; computer engineers; information systems analysts; technical designers; systems analysts and programmers; database administrators; procurement analyts; network designers; budget analysts; market analysts; and business systems analysts.

HOW TO APPLY

If you're interested in an internship, you should apply online at http://www.boeing.com/employment/ college/internshipDetails.html. Internship opportunities may be available in Alabama, Arizona, California, Florida, Illinois, Kansas, Missouri, Oklahoma, Pennsylvania, Texas, Washington, D.C., and metro Washington.

CESSNA INTERNSHIP

Cessna Aircraft Company
Intern Submission
2 Cessna Boulevard
Wichita, KS 67215
Fax: (316) 517-6157
jobs@cessna.textron.com
http://cessnajobs.com/resumeexpress.chtml

What You Can Earn: Varies (depends on experience and department) plus benefit package including holiday pay, vacation, and insurance.
Application Deadlines: Fall: July 1; spring: November 1; summer: April 1.
Educational Experience: An engineering, accounting, finance, marketing, or business student with at least 60 hours of course study toward a degree in aeronautical, mechanical, electrical, manufacturing, or industrial engineering; accounting; finance; marketing; or business.
Requirements: Engineering internship: minimum 2.8 GPA; finance internship: minimum 3.0.

OVERVIEW

Ever since the first Cessna took off from a makeshift airstrip in Wichita, Kansas, Cessna has been one of the country's top aircraft manufacturers, currently experiencing 14 straight years of growth producing aircraft ranging from the Citation X business jet that cruises near the speed of sound to classic single engine aircraft. Cessna routinely visits college campuses to discuss job opportunities with students and is committed to developing top college students and exposing them to different areas of work throughout the company, providing students with the opportunity to apply the theory learned at university and apply it in the workplace.

The intern program is designed to provide you with work experience in an area related to your chosen field of study, and the level of difficulty will correspond to your educational level. Your salary level will be developed in conjunction with the human resources department, and you may be offered a permanent position with Cessna after graduation if the need exists and you do well.

Engineering

If you're selected as a Cessna engineering intern, you'll work in one of the following areas: advanced design, project design, systems integration, structural integrity, or flight test. You may choose an internship either during the fall or spring semester of the school year.

Finance Summer Internships

Cessna's finance and accounting divisions offer full-time summer internships to college students majoring in accounting, finance, or related business fields. During the 10-week internship from May to August, interns work on projects in at least three of the following areas: internal audit, general accounting, accounts payable, service center accounting, financial analysis, cost accounting, payroll, and the aircraft completion center.

HOW TO APPLY

You can submit your resume and cover letter to the address or fax number listed previously, e-mail your resume (in the body of the message— no attachments), or post your resume online at the previously listed URL.

CHEVRONTEXACO ENGINEERING INTERNSHIP

ChevronTexaco Internship Coordinator
6001 Bollinger Canyon Road
San Ramon, CA 94583
(925) 842-1000
http://www.chevron.com/about/careers/internship_index.asp

What You Can Earn: Varies.
Application Deadlines: Rolling.
Educational Experience: College students working toward a degree in chemical, civil, electrical, mechanical, or petroleum engineering.
Requirements: Students who want hands-on experience and an opportunity to learn and contribute.

OVERVIEW

Chevron is the fifth-largest integrated energy company in the world. Headquartered in San Ramon, California, and conducting business in approximately 180 countries, this corporation is engaged in every aspect of the oil and natural gas industry, including exploration and production; refining, marketing and transportation; chemicals manufacturing and sales; and power generation.

The company traces its roots to an 1879 oil discovery at Pico Canyon, north of Los Angeles, a find that led to the formation of the Pacific Coast Oil Co., which later evolved into the Standard Oil Co. of California and, later, into Chevron Corp. The company's history also includes the 1901 formation of The Texas Fuel Co. in Beaumont, Texas. It later became known as The Texas Co. and, eventually, Texaco Inc. In 2001, these entities merged to form ChevronTexaco.

Chevron develops advanced energy technologies, including core hydrocarbon technologies, a global digital infrastructure and information technology.

The current business development portfolio includes hydrogen infrastructure, advanced battery systems, nano-materials and renewable energy applications. In 2004, ChevronTexaco produced more than 2.5 million barrels of oil per day, with two-thirds of the volume occurring in more than 20 different countries. With a global refining capacity of more than 2 million barrels of oil a day, the company also has a marketing network that supports approximately 25,700 retail outlets in nearly 90 countries.

Earth Science Internships

If you're an outstanding student working toward your master's or doctorate degree in geology, geophysics, or geological engineering, this internship could be for you. Chevron is looking for students who want hands-on experience and an opportunity to contribute to the oil business.

As an intern here, you'll usually focus on an oil field or exploration project, so your work has an immediate business application. You'll work in a team environment conducive to learning. In addition, you'll learn about petroleum geoscience (including geological and geophysical data and how they're obtained, interpreted, and applied), see how the business operates in oil field operations and exploration, and sharpen your computer skills by using the latest workstation hardware and interpretation applications.

Recent summer projects have included mapping reservoir sands in a California enhanced oil-recovery project, using well log and production data; constructing a set of cross sections, structure maps, and reservoir maps for a western Texas oil field to determine remaining oil potential; applying sequence stratigraphic techniques in the construction of cross sections to delineate favorable reservoir faces in southern Texas; and conducting velocity analyses to enhance migration techniques for improved seismic imaging of Gulf of Mexico deep water prospects.

Chevron's earth-scientists interns work at locations in Bakersfield and San Ramon, California; Houston and Midland, Texas; New Orleans and Lafayette, Louisiana.; Anchorage, Alaska; and Evanston, Wyoming.

Engineering Internships

An internship at Chevron provides excellent practical experience in engineering, as well as an opportunity to get to know the company. The internship program helps the company identify future Chevron employees and lets you check out the company as a potential employer. While most internships are offered during the summer, some six-month assignments are also possible. As an intern here, you'll work on marketing, exploration, production, or refinery projects, ranging from hands-on field support to detailed technology support. You'll work side-by-side with other engineers and disciplines in a team environment.

Chevron's engineers work at locations across the United States and around the world. Interns work at our locations in the United States, including Bakersfield, Brea, El Segundo, Richmond, or San Ramon, California.; Pascagoula, Mississippi; Atlanta, Georgia; or Houston or Midland, Texas.

Finance

Interns in this department will see firsthand how the oil and gas industry works and will gain finance and accounting experience at a Fortune 500 corporation. Your assignment during your internship will involve a challenging and rewarding project. Candidates should be working toward a bachelor's degree in business with an emphasis in accounting or finance; be a rising senior who's completed accounting and finance courses through the intermediate level while maintaining a 3.5 GPA overall, including accounting and finance courses; and have strong analytical, communication, and interpersonal skills. As an intern at Chevron, you'll probably work in the Chevron Financial Center, the Corporate Treasury Department, the Corporate Comptroller's Department, ChevronTexaco Shipping Company, or Chevron's operating company for domestic refining and marketing. During your internship, you'll have opportunities to build your professional network and participate in presentations and management luncheons. You'll interact with senior management, current program members, and alumni,

and you'll tour our facilities and socialize with other employees. Most finance interns work in the San Francisco Bay Area.

Finance MBA Development Program

First-year MBA students are also eligible for a special summer MBA internship program. Throughout the summer, you'll have an opportunity to work on a special project, just like those in the full-time finance MBA development program. You'll have opportunities to interact with senior management, current program members, and alumni and tour the facilities, attend learning-centered presentations, and socialize with other Chevron professionals. You might be assigned to work in the corporate treasury or comptroller's groups or in one of Chevron's major San Francisco Bay Area operating companies. All internships are located in the San Francisco Bay Area.

Human Resources

If you're working on your master's degree in human resources or industrial labor relations, or if you have an MBA in human resources, consider Chevron's internship program. It provides excellent practical experience in human resources, as well as an opportunity to get to know the company. If you excel during the internship, you'll be considered for regular employment in the HR development program.

As an intern here, you'll work in corporate human resources or with an operating company. Assignments are available in most human resources functions, including staffing, training and organizational development, compensation and organizational design, and benefits design; employee or labor relations, generalist roles in various lines of business, expatriate administration, or policy design. You'll work in the San Francisco Bay Area or Houston.

Information Technology

The co-operative education and INROADS internship programs at Chevron provide excellent practical experience in information technology. As an intern, you'll learn how to take full advantage of advanced technology to meet the challenges of the energy industry. Chevron is dedicated to using state-of-the-art equipment and software.

Interns usually work for six months: January through June or July through December (or you may work on a three-month or four-month summer assignment). You will work in a team environment conducive to learning in areas such as applications delivery, consulting, applications development, project management, NT infrastructure, and SAP business analysis.

Candidates should be working toward a bachelor's or master's degree in computer science or management information systems in a related technical or business field. You may work at one of many U.S. locations, including Anchorage, Alaska; Atlanta, Georgia; Bakersfield, Concord, Richmond, or San Ramon, California; Evanston, Wyoming; Houston, Texas; or Louisville, Kentucky.

HOW TO APPLY

To find out if Chevron will be recruiting at your college campus or at a special event, visit http://www.chevron.com/about/careers/recruiting_events.

CHRYSLER GROUP INTERNSHIP

Chrysler Corporation, Internship Program
1000 Chrysler Drive
Auburn Hills, MI 48326
(248) 576-5741
http://www.careers.chrysler-group.com

What You Can Earn: Up to $750 for undergraduates, up to $1,000 for graduate students.
Application Deadlines: Rolling.
Educational Experience: Rising college junior with above-average grades and a major in one of the disciplines related to Chrysler's business.

Requirements: Highly motivated, innovative and inspired students; competent in analysis and problem solving, communications, teamwork, interpersonal skills, and self-motivation. Interest in a career in the automotive business.

OVERVIEW

DaimlerChrysler is one of the world's leading automotive manufacturers and an international leader in the premium sector. The company is also the market leader for off-roaders and minivans and is the world's largest manufacturer of commercial vehicles. To maintain this market share, the company focuses on engineering, manufacturing, and the sale of innovative automobiles, as well auto service and vehicle financial services. With locations in Europe, North and South America, Africa, and Asia/Pacific, the company has transformed more than 100 years of experience in the automotive industry into a complete product range with a passion for technical innovation.

Interns have been working at Chrysler since the mid-1950s, in a variety of departments, including engineering, manufacturing, procurement, finance, human resources, and information services. An internship at Chrysler will give you an opportunity to become familiar with project assignments and daily business. Participants are assigned specific duties and goals to give them the best chance for learning, personal growth, and professional development. Assignments may last up to 17 weeks and will give you a chance to find out if Chrysler is the place you might like to work after graduation. After you graduate, participants in the program may be considered for full-time employment.

HOW TO APPLY

Representatives from the Chrysler Group visits select universities during the fall semester each year. If you're interested, you should review openings and apply for an interview through your college recruiting office. Also, check the preceding URL for a calendar of recruiting engagements at schools near you.

DUPONT SUMMER INTERNSHIP

DuPont
1007 Market Street
Wilmington, DE 19898
http://www1.dupont.com/dupontglobal/corp/
    careers/univ_internships.html

What You Can Earn: Competitive compensation depending on education.
Application Deadlines: January 1.
Educational Experience: Full-time rising college seniors with a minimum 3.0 GPA majoring in accounting/finance, logistics, marketing, or information technology; graduate students also welcome.
Requirements: U.S. citizens or resident aliens.

OVERVIEW

Operating in more than 70 countries, DuPont offers a wide range of innovative products and services for markets including agriculture, nutrition, electronics, communications, safety and protection, home and construction, transportation, and apparel.

When the company began in 1802, its primary product was explosives. A century ago, the company's focus enlarged to include chemicals, materials, and energy. Today, DuPont delivers science-based solutions designed to make real differences in people's lives in areas such as food and nutrition, healthcare, apparel, safety and security, construction, electronics, and transportation.

DuPont offers internships as a way of developing students into future leaders. As an intern in this company, you'll be given challenging work to stretch your capability and allow you to integrate classroom theory with the reality of industry.

If you're interested, you can apply for extended internships (that is, a summer plus the fall semester); these requests are considered on a case-by-case basis. You can contact the career services office at your school to see if DuPont is conducting interviews for internship opportunities at your school.

HOW TO APPLY

To fill out an application for a particular internship, first click "apply now" at http://www1.dupont.com/dupontglobal/corp/careers/univ_internships.html. This will bring up a window for you to search for internships. If there is a particular internship in which you're interested, you can then click it to bring up an application electronically.

ERNST & YOUNG INTERNSHIP

Ernst & Young
5 Times Square
New York, NY 10036-6530
(212) 773-3000
Fax: (212) 773-6350

What You Can Earn: $500 a week for undergraduate students; $700 for graduate students.
Application Deadlines: January 15 for the summer session.
Educational Experience: Business majors (juniors and above).
Requirements: None specified.

OVERVIEW

As a global leader in professional services, Ernst & Young pursues the highest level of integrity in providing clients with financial, transactional, and risk-management help for their core services of audit, tax, and transactions. Clients include Coca-Cola, Mobil, McDonald's, Reebok, TimeWarner, and the PGA Tour.

An Ernst & Young internship is the best way to find out whether a financial service career is what you want, before you make a full-time commitment. Typically, interns work in audit and tax and in management-consulting areas. As an intern here, you'll be exposed to clients, methods, and technologies that can give you an insider's view of how things work within a large international firm. As an intern, you can transfer the analytical and problem-solving skills you've acquired in school to the real world. Typical assignments include helping with audits, capital-sourcing efforts, company mergers, financial analysis, marketing strategies, research, tax obligations, and more.

HOW TO APPLY

Ernst & Young has an extensive campus recruiting program that includes career fairs, information sessions, interview opportunities, and other events. To interview at Ernst & Young, you must meet them when they are scheduled to interview at your college. Check your career counseling service for dates when they will be at your school.

FORD MOTOR COMPANY INTERNSHIP

Ford Motor Company
Internship Coordinator
PO Box 6248
Dearborn, MI 48126
(800) 392-3673
http://www.ford.com

What You Can Earn: Varies.
Application Deadlines: Rolling.
Educational Experience: Must have completed the sophomore year of an undergraduate program or the first year of a graduate program. (See specific internship areas for more precise educational requirements). Most opportunities are for students in business and technical fields, but students in other disciplines are sometimes considered.

Requirements: Exceptional leadership and communication skills; U.S. work authorization allowing you to work full time for an indefinite period.

OVERVIEW

Ford Motor Company needs interns in areas such as marketing, sales and service, and purchasing. Business students can find career opportunities at Ford in areas from finance to information technology. Interns receive a midterm and final performance evaluation. To provide practice interacting with managers and demonstrating business acumen, interns present work projects to a panel of managers in various organizations.

Those who excel in this program may be invited to return the following year or receive an offer for full-time employment in the Ford College Graduate program.

Finance

Summer internships in the finance department give you an outstanding opportunity to learn about Ford Motor Company, the finance team, and life in Michigan. Internships are project oriented and challenge you to demonstrate strong business acumen and technical skills in one of Ford's two finance programs: General Finance and Treasury.

General Finance
Interns in this area may work in product development, manufacturing, marketing, sales and service, treasury, purchasing, corporate finance, accounting, general auditor's office, Ford Financial Services, or Asia Pacific Operations and Associations.

Treasury
Interns in this area may work in financial markets, international financial management, banking relations, corporate financing, cash management, or risk management.

Preferred undergraduate summer intern candidates are juniors pursuing a bachelor's degree with a concentration in finance, accounting, business, economics, math, or statistics and have a GPA of at least 3.25.

Human Resources

Opportunities are available for first-year master's degree students in any discipline with a strong emphasis on business acumen and change management skills. Ford prefers a concentration in human resources management or human resources. Juris Doctorate candidates are considered as well. A GPA of 3.0 is strongly preferred. If you're accepted as an intern, you'll be assigned to one of Ford's HR teams and become a contributing member of its day-to-day operations. Recent Ford College Graduates will be available for guidance, mentoring, and consultation.

Information Technology

This program introduces you to Ford Motor Company's top-rated computer systems and how they're used throughout the company. As an intern here, you'll see firsthand how systems are developed and strategically implemented. Challenging assignments not only broaden your work experience but also help you understand the issues facing a global corporation.

The program also gives you the opportunity to apply academic knowledge to real-world business situations, learn more about information technology and process re-engineering, and make an informed decision on whether Ford Motor Company is the right place for you to start your career. As a summer intern, you'll take on assignments that build your skills in areas such as process re-engineering, systems design and development, Web development, systems maintenance and support, and hardware and infrastructure support. In addition, you'll gain experience working in a dynamic team environment with deliverables and deadlines. You'll also be given the chance to demonstrate innovation and creativity, oral and written communication skills, and negotiation skills.

The program is designed for students who have completed their sophomore year and are majoring in computer science, management information systems, or other technical areas. The company looks for strong academic credentials and a keen interest in applying information technology and process re-engineering in the automotive products and services industry. Strong communications skills and the ability to work on a team in a fast-past, ever-changing environment are pluses.

Your work will be measurable, so you can track your progress and see if you have accomplished your objectives. You'll have the opportunity to learn and contribute to the organization. Members of the Ford College Graduate program will be available to help you during your three-month assignment, to familiarize you with the company, its culture, and life in southeast Michigan. If you're graduating in the 12 months after your internship, you'll be considered for full-time employment as a Ford College Graduate.

Land Services

Three-month summer assignments are offered to a limited number of students, preferably MBA students with undergraduate degrees in real estate, engineering, architecture, finance, or construction management. Sample assignments include working in finance, marketing, facilities planning, facilities engineering, real estate development, or global plant engineering.

Facilities Engineering Intern

As an intern in this area, you'll help develop a five-year R&E Center facilities business plan, work on the facilities engineering Web page, and help with review of facilities projects.

Facilities Planning Intern

Assignments could include such projects as designing and overseeing the build of outdoor displays, facilitating the replacement of courtyard pavers or small concrete projects for office buildings, involvement in soft landscaping projects, and interacting with tenants/suppliers and other similar projects.

Finance

As an intern here, you'll help develop performance metrics for a facility-cost category such as scrap management, determine variables that influence performance against these metrics, complete a detailed financial analysis, and provide a complete analysis recommending inclusion or removal of properties from a real estate realignment project.

Global Plant Engineering Intern

As an intern in this department, you'll help organize internal work instruction/procedures documentation in support of ISO 9000 initiatives, as well as assist with the review of projects and/or implementation actions on small projects.

Marketing Intern

Here, you'll help with all planning and logistics for the annual Ford Senior Players Championship, including managing the transportation center, managing guest lists, working with volunteer schedules, and helping to manage the events leading up to the tournament.

Real Estate Department Intern

Here, you'll analyze corporate and dealership lease agreements to help with operating expense evaluations related to the lease audit program and verify real estate information and update databases. You might also help in various dealership real estate administrative functions, such as reviewing and adjusting dealership escrow accounts and helping to obtain completed customer service evaluations and commencement date agreements.

Marketing Sales and Service

This program runs from approximately mid-May through mid-August. Assignments exist both in the regional offices and in the general office in Dearborn, Michigan. Assignments include the following:

Field Operations

If you land an internship with "regional assignments," you'll work closely with field teams to implement corporate-wide marketing initiatives and help develop regional marketing plans. Many of these assignments also incorporate an e-commerce element. If you are assigned "general office,"

you can be placed in a variety of marketing assignments, such as franchising, vehicle brand development, and retail distribution. Many of these assignments also incorporate the growing e-commerce side of our business.

Candidates should have a bachelor's degree in a business-related field with a GPA of at least 3.0 on or be in the top 25 percent of their class.

Operations

In this area, you may work in engineering and production liaison, production supervision, or machine maintenance and repair coordination.

Parts, Supply & Logistics

Interns at the Detroit Parts Distribution Center and the National Parts Distribution Center work on meaningful projects that allow you to make a recognizable contribution during your summer.

Product Development

As an intern in product development, you'll help design and develop the highest-quality, world-class cars and light and commercial trucks. You'll use your engineering education to learn and use computer simulation skills and traditional empirical engineering methods to come up with the best designs before vehicles are produced.

Preferred applicants must have completed their junior year and have a minimum 3.0 GPA. Candidates must also be working toward a degree in mechanical or electrical/electronic engineering. Some opportunities also may be available for chemical, materials science, aeronautical, and biomedical engineers. Openings for this program are in southeastern Michigan.

Manufacturing

Meaningful summer internships are available in Materials Planning & Logistics (MP&L) and Component Design and Vehicle Operations. The MP&L intern program provides a three-month assignment in one of these areas: preproduction planning and change control; programming, scheduling and releasing; process leadership and systems; supply chain management; MP&L business office; engineering parts release; work plan development and maintenance; part scheduling coordination; project management analysis; material control coordination; or prototype material control and procurement.

The Component Design and Vehicle Operations program provides a three-month assignment in one of these areas: component and product system design; development engineering (electronics, plastics, climate control, electrical and fuel handling, glass, transmission, castings, engines, suspension and steering components); manufacturing process plant engineering (at assembly, stamping, powertrain, and components plants located throughout the U.S. and staff offices nationwide).

Purchasing

Potential summer intern assignments in the purchasing department include the following:

Core Purchasing
This group is the driving force behind Ford's goal to deliver a globally competitive supply base.

Facilities, Materials and Services Purchasing
This group is responsible for all of Ford Motor Company's worldwide purchases of goods and services other than vehicle component parts.

Purchasing Business Office
Interns are responsible for global strategic planning and supply-base analysis.

Purchasing Information Technology
This group identifies and develops improved processes and implements and oversees purchasing systems and procedures.

Strategic Planning and Process Improvement
This group identifies and develops improved processes.

Supplier Technical Assistance Group
Interns focus on quality, cost, and timing.

Vehicle/Product Center Purchasing
This group provides commodity and program-management expertise for products, delivering quality, cost, and timing targets at the component and systems level.

Candidates typically are junior undergraduates or first-year MBA students in mechanical or chemical engineering, finance, purchasing, procurement management, supply management, material planning and logistics, or an area such as technology.

HOW TO APPLY

To join the summer intern program, you can review openings and answer Ford's skills questionnaire to register your credentials on this Web site: http://www.careers.ford.com/matchingquestions.asp?AppID=98402. At this Web site, you may register for current internship openings and add your resume to the file. You should not e-mail your resume, however.

If Ford sends a recruiting team to your campus, you'll want to find out when they will be there. Visit this Web site to find out: http://www.careers.ford.com/HowWeHire.asp?CID=32.

GENERAL ELECTRIC INTERNSHIP

General Electric Internship
3135 Easton Turnpike
Fairfield, CT 06828-0001
http://www.gecareers.com

What You Can Earn: Stipend varies, plus relocation assistance or housing stipend and accrued vacation time.

Application Deadlines: Rolling.

Educational Experience: A full-time student enrolled in a four-year college or university. You must maintain a minimum GPA of 3.0; for master's students, a 3.2 GPA is the minimum.

Requirements: Must be authorized to work in the U.S. full time and without restriction. People with temporary work authorizations, such as students in practical training status (F1 visa), will be considered only for jobs where GE is experiencing a demonstrated shortage of candidates with particular skills. GE can't hire students from controlled countries and/or those who require export licensing.

OVERVIEW

GE is made up of a broad range of primary business units, each with its own number of divisions. GE is a diversified technology, media, and financial services company dedicated to creating products that make life better. From aircraft engines and power generation to financial services, medical imaging, television programming and plastics, GE operates in more than 100 countries and employs more than 300,000 people worldwide.

The company traces its beginnings to Thomas A. Edison, who established Edison Electric Light Company in 1878. In 1892, a merger of Edison General Electric Company and Thomson-Houston Electric Company created General Electric Company. GE is the only company listed in the Dow Jones Industrial Index today that was also included in the original index in 1896.

A GE internship can be just for the summer or as long as a couple of semesters. No matter how much time you spend, you're immediately plunged into meaningful assignments as you work side by side with experts in the business. Educational workshops and developmental seminars complement your on-the-job training. Many interns join GE after graduation, either through direct placement or as members of the company's Corporate Leadership Programs.

GE offers full-time, paid internships in a variety of areas, including engineering, human resources, information technology, and business. Qualified candidates can gain hands-on experience while working on challenging projects, network with professionals, and learn from some of the brightest minds in business. GE also offers co-ops to four-year college students who want to work more than 12 weeks while maintaining their college schedules. Co-ops allow students to contribute to and learn from exciting projects and network with GE professionals. Co-ops typically last between three and nine months and usually run from January to June or June to December.

HOW TO APPLY

GE recruits for internship positions by visiting a number of campuses each year. To see if GE is going to be interviewing on your campus, visit the following Web site: http://www.gecareers.com/GECAREERS/jsp/us/studentOpportunities/st//

If GE does have a schedule at your school, be sure to contact your local placement office for interviewing details.

HALLMARK CARDS INTERNSHIP

Hallmark Cards, Corporate Staffing
#112 Hallmark Cards Inc.
PO Box 419580
Kansas City, MO 64141-6580
(816) 274-5111
Hcolle1@hallmark.com

What You Can Earn: $2300 a month.
Application Deadlines: Rolling.
Educational Experience: An undergraduate senior or graduate degree in marketing, finance, accounting, human resources, business administration, engineering, or information technology.
Requirements: None specified.

OVERVIEW

Hallmark is the global leader in the greeting card industry and one of the world's most trusted brands. For nearly a century, Hallmark has believed in the very best of human nature, the desire to live a life that intertwines in meaningful ways with others.

Hallmark offers paid internships for both creative and corporate positions in the summer months only. Positions typically are located at the company's Kansas City headquarters, but operations/engineering internships may be available in other locations in Connecticut, Illinois, Kansas, Missouri, Pennsylvania, and Texas.

HOW TO APPLY

To apply, e-mail your resume and cover letter in Microsoft Word or PDF format to the e-mail address above.

HEWLETT-PACKARD SUMMER INTERNSHIP

Hewlett-Packard
Summer Internship Program
3000 Hanover Street
Palo Alto, CA 94304-1185
(650) 857-1501
http://www.hp.com

What You Can Earn: Varies.
Application Deadlines: Rolling.
Educational Experience: A variety of educational backgrounds, including engineering, computer science, information technology, materials science, marketing, finance, or business administration.
Requirements: Not specified.

OVERVIEW

Hewlett-Packard invents, engineers, and delivers technology solutions for business and personal areas throughout the world. HP co-founders Bill Hewlett and Dave Packard established the company in 1939 after successfully launching their first product (an audio oscillator) from a small garage in Palo Alto. Today, the company's solutions span IT infrastructure; personal computing and access devices; global services and imaging; and printing for consumers, enterprises, and small and medium businesses. Their $4 billion annual R&D investment fuels the invention of products, solutions, and new technologies. With more than 150,000 employees in 170 countries, HP does business in more than 40 currencies and more than 10 languages. HP offers internship opportunities in many areas. To find out what internships are available, visit http://h10055.www1.hp.com/jobsathp/content/search/search.asp?lang=Enen. This will allow you to find internship opportunities by region, location, and site, as well as function and duration.

HOW TO APPLY

To apply for internships or list your resume for future internships, submit a candidate profile at http://h10055.www1.hp.com/jobsathp/content/howtoapply/applyform.asp?lang=Enen. This profile should include your work preferences along with your cover letter and resume.

IMG INTERNATIONAL INTERNSHIP

Cleveland and Branch Office Internship Applications:
IMG Internship Program
1360 East 9th Street, #100
Cleveland, OH 44114
cleinterns@imgworld.com

New York Internship Applications:
IMG Internship Program
22 East 71st Street
New York, NY 10021
(212) 772-8900
Fax: (212) 772.2617
ny-interns@imgworld.com

What You Can Earn: Unpaid.

Application Deadlines: February 15.

Educational Experience: Should have interest in graphic design, management, fashion, and other creative fields as a career; should be bright, organized, and detail oriented, with excellent communications skills and the ability to take direction and follow through on projects. Computer literacy and proficiency important; knowledge of foreign languages helpful but not essential.

Requirements: IMG requires confirmation of academic credit eligibility before granting an applicant an interview; academic credit must be received for this internship from your university or graduate school (either a formal course credit or extra credit that a specific professor is willing to provide). Must be available to work at least 20 hours a week.

OVERVIEW

IMG is the world's premier sports and lifestyle management and marketing firm, with an international staff of more than 2,200 people in 30 countries. The company is commercially involved in an average of 11 major sports and cultural events around the world each day and represents the interests of major corporations. In addition, IMG is the world's largest noncharacter licensing firm and is a leading literary agency and book packager. It's also a performing arts management firm, and IMG Models is the world's number one international model management firm.

Interns work closely with all members of the staff, either on a project or ongoing basis. You may organize and mail publicity materials; maintain and print computer mailing lists; arrange appointments; assist with filing, typing, and other clerical and organizational duties; update the models look books; perform magazine research; or work on special promotional projects.

IMG has hired interns for the past 14 years and offers a very competitive program (typically more than 1,000 applications are received each year, and about 70 interns are placed in the company's North American offices annually).

Most IMG interns are located in Cleveland (the company's world headquarters) and in three New York City offices.

Interns are placed in various divisions of IMG based on their qualifications and IMG's current business needs. Areas of placement may include: accounting, human resources, tennis, investment advisors, tax, golf, or creative services. In New York, internships are offered in the following divisions: TWI Production, TWI Sales, Models, 7th on Sixth, Consulting, Business Development (sales and marketing), Licensing, or Speakers.

At IMG, you'll be exposed to the day-to-day operations of each specific department, as well as basic office procedures. Depending on the office location, you may also be involved in locally sponsored IMG events. In addition, you'll have several social activities scheduled throughout the summer. Speaker Days will include various department heads discussing their own IMG experiences, also allowing you to participate actively in group discussions with the executives.

IMG also offers part-time internships during the fall and spring semesters, which typically last four months. Applications for the fall and spring semesters are accepted throughout the year.

HOW TO APPLY

A cover letter and resume is the formal application to the program; resumes can be snail mailed or e-mailed to the preceding address. You should specify in your cover letter any preferences with regard to department placement or office location.

You'll be notified by mail in early March if you have been selected for an interview in March, in Cleveland, New York or via the telephone (for those unable to attend a personal interview in either city). Final decisions and selection notifications are made by late April.

Because IMG responds to all resume submissions, and as a result of the high volume of applications, you should not call IMG to follow up on your resume.

INROADS INTERNSHIP

INROADS Inc.
10 South Broadway, Suite 700
St. Louis, MO 63102
(314) 241-7488

What You Can Earn: Up to $1,000 a week, depending on sponsor.
Application Deadlines: January 31.
Educational Experience: Career interest in business, engineering, computers and information sciences, sales, marketing, allied healthcare, or healthcare management.
Requirements: Permanent U.S. residency; a 2.8 GPA and a high school 3.0 cumulative GPA and 1000 SAT or 20 ACT (some INROADS affiliates may have higher GPA and SAT/ACT requirements).

OVERVIEW

This organization is dedicated to developing and placing talented minority youth in business and industry to prepare them for corporate and community leadership. INROADS seeks high-performing African American, Hispanic, and Native American students for internship opportunities with some of the nation's largest companies. Their rigorous career development training process will challenge you to commit to excellence.

As an INROADS-sponsored intern, you'll have direct and immediate access to the global market via a paid multiyear internship with a Fortune 1000 company. You'll get an early start on your career, with unparalleled networking opportunities with others just like you. There will be plenty of professional and personal support, guidance, training and development, with corporate mentors who take a personal interest in you. Additional scholarship opportunities are available through corporate sponsors and INROADS affiliates.

INROADS recruits the brightest high school and college ethnically diverse students interested in pursuing careers in business, engineering, computer and information sciences, sales, marketing, allied healthcare, healthcare management, and retail management careers. Training and development incorporates interactive business simulations, seminars, and other opportunities to increase the intern's understanding of how to become a high-performing contributor in the workplace and develop new management skills for use in the classroom, the community, and beyond. From that point, INROADS places qualified college students in two-to-four-year internships with participating corporate sponsors and provides ongoing support and guidance to ensure their success.

Over the past five years, nearly 90 percent of graduating INROADS Interns accepted offers for full-time employment from their sponsoring companies. Most of the remaining INROADS graduates accepted offers from other INROADS corporate sponsors.

An INROADS Internship is a year-round experience that requires you to make a serious commitment to participate in and complete specific job readiness and leadership requirements while maintaining a 3.0 or better academic grade point average.

HOW TO APPLY

Fill out the four-part online application form, plus the INROADS Profile information. (You'll need a computer with MS Explorer 4.01 or higher, Netscape Navigator 5.0 or higher, or an equivalent browser.) You can save the application and return later to submit it to INROADS for processing.

Submit the application with an official transcript and official copies of SAT or ACT scores (demanded of high school and first-semester college students); these items can be submitted online. You will be asked to submit any other items via regular mail to your INROADS affiliate.

Once you've submitted your INROADS intern application, the staff will evaluate it and contact you for an interview if you qualify. If your interview is successful, you'll enter the INROADS "talent pool" and participate in mandatory training.

The INROADS staff at your affiliate office will arrange for you to have interviews with potential corporate sponsors and then notify you of any job offers and help you decide which offer is best suited to your goals.

KRAFT FOODS INTERNSHIP

Kraft Foods, University Relations
3 Lakes Drive
Northfield, IL 60093
(847) 646-2000
http://www.kraftfoods.com

What You Can Earn: $400 to $600 a week for undergrads; up to $1,000 a week for graduate students.
Application Deadlines: February 1.
Educational Experience: Most interns are college juniors or first-year graduate students.
Requirements: None specified.

OVERVIEW

For 100 years, Kraft has been at the forefront of innovation in every aspect of the food industry, including product development, packaging, branding, quality, and safety. The company's tradition of innovation began in 1906 with the introduction of the first decaffeinated coffee (Kaffee Hag) and continues into the present with modern-day breakthroughs such as Lunchables and Nabisco Go-Packs.

Kraft has identified key schools based on the quality of their academic programs, faculty, and students; the diversity of the student population; and the performance of alumni as current employees of Kraft. At Kraft, internships are available in all business functions and at many locations. This internship provides students with an opportunity to offer professional support and become an integral part of a business team, giving you the chance to learn while making a real contribution to the company. You'll become a part of key management meetings, receive meaningful projects, and have access to senior management.

Each intern is assigned a supervisor who designates projects, answers questions, and provides guidance. Throughout the experience, you'll receive feedback and informal mentoring, along with a midterm evaluation to assess your performance, review your goals, and discuss development activities. In addition, interns prepare a final presentation for members of senior-level management at the conclusion of their internship.

During the internship, interns get a chance to explore other aspects of the work environment at Kraft Foods. For example, they may tour the Kraft Kitchens, visit a manufacturing facility, spend time at a sales office, or participate in many other business activities. As an intern, you'll be welcomed by senior management throughout your internship.

You'll receive a formalized orientation, where you'll learn key information to succeed during and after your summer tenure, along with receptions and similar events to allow interns to meet their peers and Kraft professionals. You'll receive on-site training in areas that relate to your function or general management and presentation skills. A variety of social events are scheduled, including community-service events and field tour events.

INROADS Internship Program

The mission of INROADS is to develop and place talented minority youth in business and industry and prepare them for corporate and community leadership. INROADS internships are awarded to outstanding, bright, ethnically diverse students.

Candidates for these internships are graduating high school seniors applying or already admitted to an accredited college or college freshmen or sophomores, all of whom must have a B average and 1000 SAT or 20 ACT scores. You also must demonstrate leadership ability and have an interest in pursuing a bachelor's degree in business, engineering, computer and information sciences, sales, marketing, allied healthcare, healthcare management, or retail management.

HOW TO APPLY

Interviews for internships are usually conducted on campuses during September through February for summer positions. If you're interested in an internship with Kraft, you should contact your career placement office to learn when a Kraft representative will be on campus for interviews. Dates are advertised on campus in advance. Prior to interviews, the company typically conducts presentations to introduce students to its products and to discuss career opportunities at Kraft. Interns are usually selected and notified by early March.

For an INROADS internship, download an application at http://www.inroads.org/interns/internApply.jsp. The application consists of four parts, plus the INROADS Profile information. You will be asked to supply personal, educational, employment, and some additional information.

Once you've submitted your INROADS Intern Application, staff will evaluate it and contact you for an interview if you qualify. If your interview is successful, you'll enter the INROADS Talent Pool and participate in mandatory Talent Pool Training. The INROADS staff at your affiliate office will arrange for you to have interviews with potential corporate sponsors, and staff will notify you of any job offers and help you decide which offer is best suited to your goals.

LANDS' END INTERNSHIP

Lands' End
Code: LECLG
PO Box 549262
Suite 276
Waltham, MA 02454
careers@landsend.com
What You Can Earn: Competitive salaries, relocation assistance, free onsite activity center, and a 20 percent merchandise discount.
Application Deadlines: Spring internships: early November; summer internships: mid-January; fall internships: mid-April.

Educational Experience: Full-time students (juniors and above).
Requirements: None specified, but Lands' End encourages promising students to further their education by offering three $1000 scholarships. To be eligible, the student has to be enrolled on a full-time basis.

OVERVIEW

The goal of the internship program is to offer you a challenging learning opportunity and to enhance the company's pool of qualified candidates to help meet our growing needs. As an intern with Lands' End, you'll be given meaningful, hands-on projects that allow you to make a real contribution to the company. And you'll have access to some of the best resources and technology in the industry, as well as to all members of the senior management team.

Past participants have been assigned to teams with lots of different responsibilities in a number of different functions. Interns can work in a variety of areas, including advertising; apparel design; art direction; communication (corporate, employee, or operations); direct marketing; e-commerce (M.B.A. level); facilities distribution, logistics, engineering, environment health/safety, and planning CADD operator; health/fitness; information services; inventory; marketing; merchandising; operations management; quality; recruitment; and retail.

Advertising

As an advertising intern, you'll work with the ad team on all aspects of national ad campaigns, including strategic planning, execution, and tracking of all ads. Additional responsibilities include working through the ad process with several divisions of the company to develop a variety of campaigns. You will also help the team maintain a professional working relationship with external partners through accurate and timely communication.

You should be pursuing a bachelor's degree in advertising or marketing and have initiative, a strong sense of urgency, and the ability to adapt to change.

You also should be able to manage multiple tasks and meet and maintain timelines. Excellent communication skills are also important.

To ensure consideration for this position, you should indicate code LECLG in your resume and cover letter.

Apparel Design

As an Apparel Design intern, you'll work with seasoned designers to learn how to develop Lands' End products by interpreting concepts using color, fabrication, silhouettes, and mood for upcoming seasons. You will also learn how to work with manufacturers to develop original textiles and patterns and how to conduct raw material research. Additional responsibilities include conducting market research, drawing flat sketches and illustrations, detailing specifications and fabric/trim allocations, and participating in departmental meetings.

To apply, you should be pursuing a degree in apparel design, understand textile construction, color and printing techniques; do flat drawing/sketches for design and prototypes. You also should understand the industry and have a passion for apparel, have excellent organizational skills and strong attention to detail, and have the ability to work independently.

Creative (Art Direction)

As an intern in our Creative team, you will be working with a seasoned art director to learn how Lands' End develops a unified creative presentation across all catalogs. You'll learn the process behind designing, developing, and producing selling concepts and layouts, and you'll be responsible for editing film and working with layout revisions. Projects will include working with an internal electronic publishing group to produce catalog pages, as well as working with in-house photographers to gain exposure to the processes behind a photo shoot. For this internship, you'll need to be pursuing a degree in graphic design, commercial art or a related field, have excellent drawing skills, have the ability to conceptualize and implement ideas, and

have strong Mac and graphic design skills. You'll also need excellent organizational skills and strong attention to detail, as well as the ability to work independently.

Retail Store Management Internship

This internship may be offered in Lands' End stores in Chicago, Minneapolis, Madison, and Milwaukee. As an intern in a retail store, you'll work with managers to learn how to run a specialty retail store, including how to merchandise the store according to Lands' End standards, learning how to monitor inventory levels, and learn the store's overall operations. You'll be responsible for setting up an ad plan and overseeing its execution, as well as working on projects linked to sales and liquidation goals.

You should be majoring in retailing or merchandising and have prior retail experience and demonstrated leadership skills. You'll also need strong business skills, project management skills, and excellent communication skills.

HOUSING

Students intern with Lands' End from all over the United States, and many of them have never been to Wisconsin. The Employee Services group will work with all students to make sure they secure housing for the summer. Interns usually choose either to rent in Dodgeville or find places in Madison, about 45 minutes away. Madison is a university town with lots of housing options available during the summer. If you need to relocate from a distance of more than 50 miles, Lands' End will reimburse you for such travel expenses as mileage, U-Haul rental, and so on and will pick up security deposits on apartments for those needing to relocate.

HOW TO APPLY

Lands' End reviews intern resumes in two ways: during an on-campus recruitment visit to your school and when you send a resume via e-mail and/or snail mail. Resumes are reviewed and interviews are typically scheduled from October through March for all summer internships; all hiring decisions are usually made by early April.

If you mail or fax your resume, you should send an original because it will be scanned (all resumes are scanned at the Massachusetts address listed previously and then reviewed at corporate offices in Dodgeville, WI).

To ensure that your resume is scannable, use standard fonts (such as Arial, Courier, Helvetica, and Times New Roman); use a font size 10 points or larger; do not use shadows, italics, or underlining; avoid using graphics, horizontal and vertical lines, and boxes. Submit your resume referencing the job title along with a cover letter to the preceding address.

All applicants for spring internships will receive a response by the end of December, all applicants for summer internships will receive a response by early April, and all applicants for fall internships will receive a response by the end of June.

LIZ CLAIBORNE SUMMER INTERNSHIP

Liz Claiborne Summer Internship Program
1440 Broadway, 2nd Floor
New York, NY 10018
College_Recruiting@liz.com
http://www.lizclaiborneinc.com/careers/joblist.
  asp?section=internship_program

What You Can Earn: $9 to $11 an hour and a 40 percent discount on Liz Claiborne clothing.
Application Deadlines: March 1.
Educational Experience: Some internships require certain majors to apply (all other internships are open to any major). Design interns must be design majors; finance interns must be finance/accounting majors; information systems interns must MIS or computer science majors.
Requirements: Background checks and preemployment drug testing.

OVERVIEW

Liz Claiborne Inc. was founded in 1976 by Liz Claiborne and designs and markets an extensive range of women's and men's fashion apparel and accessories appropriate to occasions from casual to dressy. The company also markets fragrances for women and men. This Fortune 500 company is one of the largest marketers of women's clothing.

If you're interested in fashion and you'd like some real exposure to what it's all about, the Liz Claiborne Summer Internship Program may be what you're looking for. The Summer Internship program starts in mid-June and runs through mid-August (eight to ten weeks).

Internships are available in: design, merchandising/planning, production/manufacturing, sales, finance, information systems, human resources, and legal. You'll be given a summer project that will take six to eight weeks to finish, creating a hands-on experience for you to learn more about the area in which you've been placed. The Summer Internship Program also introduces you to different areas of the company as you complete your assignments.

Weekly activities include brown bag lunches, field trips, and other events to help you interact with other interns as well as gain more exposure to other areas of the organization.

HOW TO APPLY

Submit your resume with a cover letter to the preceding address.

LUCENT TECHNOLOGIES SUMMER INTERNSHIP

Lucent Technologies Summer Internship Program
600 Mountain Avenue
Murray Hill, NJ 07974-0636
(908) 582-3000
http://www.lucent.com/work/careerprograms.
  html#1

What You Can Earn: Unpaid.
Application Deadlines: Jan 15.
Educational Experience: Full-time students will be considered from any four- or five-year accredited U.S. college or university, ranging from first year through the master's level, Ph.D. level, and college faculty members. Students must be enrolled to return as a full-time student following the internship. Any of the following majors are acceptable: accounting; behavior science; business administration; chemical engineering; chemistry; computer engineering; computer science; economics; electrical engineering; engineering mechanics; finance; industrial engineering; journalism; management; manufacturing engineering; mathematics; mechanical engineering; operations research; physics; public relations; sales/marketing; statistics; systems engineering; and telecommunications.
Requirements: Overall GPA of 3.0/4.0 or above; U.S. citizen, permanent or conditional permanent resident, temporary resident, or refugee (Lucent will accept students on F-1 or J-1 visas).

OVERVIEW

Lucent Technologies designs and delivers the systems, services, and software that drive next-generation communications networks. Backed by Bell Labs research and development, Lucent is known for its mobility, optical, software, data, and voice-networking technologies as well as services. Lucent's customer base includes communications service providers, governments, and enterprises worldwide. The company hopes to create networks that deliver communications services that are simple, secure, and seamless (as personal and portable) for people at work, home, or anywhere in between.

Lucent's summer internship program provides valuable work experience within a corporate environment. The objective of the program is to provide summer employment with positive work/training experience, identify and track potential regular full-time employees, and establish "goodwill ambassadors" for Lucent on campuses. Interns receive project-focused assignments and challeng-

ing objectives consistent with their career goals, and they are assigned a mentor in addition to their supervisor/coach.

You'll receive a broad orientation to Lucent, the specific business unit and the individual work group to which you'll be contributing. Developmental opportunities may include meetings with corporate executives, various educational workshops, business unit information exchanges, networking events, and facility tours.

HOW TO APPLY

You may apply online at the following Web site: http://64.157.137.11/cgi-bin/parse-file?P_APP_TYPE=College&TEMPLATE=/htdocs/college/school-search-page.html.

MATTEL INTERNSHIP

Undergrad internships:
UndergradInterns@Mattel.com

M.B.A. internships:
MBAIntern@Mattel.com

What You Can Earn: $480 to $560 (undergrads); $1,150 weekly for grad students plus university credits.
Application Deadlines: February 28.
Educational Experience: M.B.A. interns must be enrolled in an accredited full-time M.B.A. program and complete the internship the summer between the first and second year of the program; undergraduate interns must be enrolled in an accredited undergraduate program.
Requirements: None specified other than those listed previously.

OVERVIEW

If you're still a kid at heart, imagine what fun you'll have working for a company that's provided toys to children all around the world for more than

50 years. Many of Mattel's products are classics, including Barbie, Hot Wheels, Fisher-Price, and the American Girl dolls. Mattel remains a leader in the design, manufacture, and marketing of children's products. Headquartered in El Segundo, California, Mattel sells its products in more than 150 nations throughout the world with more than 30,000 employees around the globe.

Mattel offers several types of summer internships for M.B.A.'s, college undergraduates, and high school students, coordinated through the Corporate Staffing Group, who work with the various divisions and departments within the company to recruit and select interns and plan and organize the events and activities held throughout the internship.

Internships are typically 12 weeks. Start and end dates will be determined prior to the beginning of the internship by the department and the intern.

M.B.A. Internships

Mattel offers challenging summer internships for first year M.B.A. students in either marketing or finance, as well as in other divisions or departments based on need. These unique opportunities provide project-based work that requires teamwork, ingenuity, and creativity, as well as tactical responsibilities that will help you learn what it's like to be a full-time employee. You'll learn the complexities of the department to which you're assigned, and you'll spend time with senior-level executives, attend brown bag presentations and seminars, take field trips to help increase your understanding of the company, and attend a few social events.

Undergrad Design Internships

The Design and Development group offers two types of unique internship opportunities: one in design and one in engineering.

Design internships will be ideal for you if you have a general understanding of design principles and practices and good problem solving skills. In this group, you'll be responsible for the design and development of medium-complexity projects.

Engineering internships are ideal for students who have a general understanding of common engineering principles and practices and who have skills in CAD/CAM, drafting, and mechanical schematics, along with good project management skills.

General Internships (Undergrad)

Also, general undergraduate internship opportunities are available in a variety of departments such as IT, legal, corporate communications, and human resources.

HOW TO APPLY

To be considered for an M.B.A. or undergrad internship, you should submit your resume with a cover letter to the preceding respective e-mail address.

MACY'S INTERNSHIP

Macy's Internship Program
151 West 34th Street, 17th floor
New York, NY 10001
(212) 494-5344
Jgreco@fds.com
http://www.macysjobs.com
http://www.retailology.com/college/internships

What You Can Earn: $200 to $500 a week, depending on the department; clothing discounts.
Application Deadlines: Rolling.
Educational Experience: Only college juniors and seniors considered.
Requirements: Leadership experience and solid academic achievement (3.0 GPA).

OVERVIEW

From the first dry goods store opened in the 1800s, Macy's envisioned itself as the biggest and the best. Macy's East is ranked as the largest operating division within the Federated Department Stores, with 95 stores spanning the East Coast from Maine to Puerto Rico. Moving to its current location at Herald Square in 1902, founder Rowland H. Macy made Macy's Herald Square the "World's Largest Store."

On the other side of the country, Macy's West combines Hollywood's glitz with the wizardry of Silicon Valley, the excitement of Las Vegas, and the wide-open style of Texas. Macy's West operates 144 stores in Arizona, California, Hawaii, Minnesota, Nevada, New Mexico, Texas, and Guam, with more than 29,900 employees. Macy's serves both Southern and northern California, with groups of stores in the Phoenix, Tucson, Las Vegas, Dallas, Hawaii, and Reno markets and single stores in the Houston, San Antonio, Albuquerque, Minneapolis/St. Paul, and Guam markets.

The company's nine-week summer internship program typically begins with a one-week introduction to the inner workings of this company, followed by four weeks spent selling in a branch store. You'll work with a department sales manager, observing and participating in the complexities of running a department.

The last four weeks of the program take place in the divisional buying offices in San Francisco, which gives you first-hand experience working with a buyer on marketing strategies, vendor relations, and special projects. Throughout the summer, you'll also participate in classroom training, discussing topics such as communication and management skills, selling techniques, and visual display.

Macy's also offers internship positions throughout the year at its stores around the country, at Macy's East, Macy's West, and macys.com. You'll have the chance to work in a variety of departments, including sales, store sales support, management, merchandising, and central offices.

Buying/Merchandising Internship

If you'd like to learn how and why specific merchandise is bought and distributed for a retail department store, this internship is for you. You'll have experiences in financial analysis, advertising, office management, professional development, and communication skills, helping you prepare for a career in either corporate buying or planning. You'll apply all aspects of your training in Macy's corporate buying and planning offices with merchant teams. This summer internship, located at division headquarters either in Atlanta, Miami, New York City, San Francisco, or Seattle, is designed to provide a view of the buying and planning functions, combining classroom instruction with on-the-job experience. You'll take core classes specific to each functional area of the business such as financial analysis, purchase order processing, and tracking and be exposed to stock analysis and competitive shopping. All interns are encouraged to get involved in the company's community initiatives, including the Partners In Time volunteerism program.

Any major is okay for this internship, but you should be looking for a dynamic, fast-paced, competitive environment.

Sales Management Internship

With experiences in customer service, merchandising, visual presentation, loss prevention, selling services, and human resources, a sales management internship can give you the backing for a successful career in retail management. This internship is available in selected Macy's stores.

Weekly learning objectives and classroom instruction are coordinated with projects and supervisory feedback to boost your understanding of business responsibilities. With this internship, you'll explore the dynamics of retailing in a supportive and challenging setting as you learn different aspects of the retail store environment, including customer service and selling strategies. You'll learn how to track sales performance and analyze business trends, manage inventory, and handle both visual merchandising and security. In addition, you'll participate on a team project and presentation that focuses on a particular business development strategy.

Sales Support

This internship (available in Macy's East only) exposes you to expense planning, human resources, advertising, divisional loss prevention, and information systems. You'll meet executives and associates from a variety of areas including advertising, production and marketing, expense planning, executive development, information systems, financial store operations, and human resources. You'll learn the role that each support area plays in a retail environment to ensure profitable sales growth, and you'll produce a project and presentation covering one of these areas. With this internship you'll have a detailed course guide and the opportunity to experience both individual and team-based problem solving.

HOW TO APPLY
Send resume and a cover letter to the preceding address.

MERCEDES-BENZ USA INTERNSHIP

Mercedes-Benz USA
Human Resources Department
One Mercedes Drive
Montvale, NJ 07645
aldicao@mbusa.com
http://www.mbusa.com

What You Can Earn: Competitive salary.
Application Deadlines: Six months before the desired start of the internship
Educational Experience: College student majoring in engineering, finance, marketing, human resources, computer science, or business administration.
Requirements: Advanced computer skills, related work experience, and excellent communication skills.

OVERVIEW
Mercedes-Benz USA (MBUSA) is a wholly-owned subsidiary of DaimlerChrysler and is responsible for the sales, service, and marketing of Mercedes-Benz and Maybach products in the United States. The company sold 221,610 vehicles in the U.S. during 2004, setting the highest sales volume in its history. MBUSA was founded in 1965 and moved to its current headquarters in Montvale, NJ, in 1972.

Prior to the founding of MBUSA, Mercedes-Benz cars were sold in the United States from 1957 to 1964 by Mercedes-Benz Sales Inc., a subsidiary of the Studebaker-Packard Corporation.

MBUSA internships last three to six months in the fields of engineering, finance, marketing, HR, computer science and business administration.

HOW TO APPLY
If you're interested in an internship with Mercedes, you should submit a cover letter including information about your expected time frame along with a resume and any details about earlier training or internships to the preceding address.

MERCK INTERNSHIP

Merck & Company
1 Merck Drive
Whitehouse Station, NJ 08889
(908) 423-1000
http://www.merck.com/mrkshared/careers/
    StudentSearch.jsp

What You Can Earn: $535 a week (undergrads); $600 a week (grad students). Interns also may obtain housing and transportation assistance as needed.
Application Deadlines: February 15.
Educational Experience: Undergraduate or graduate student.
Requirements: None specified.

OVERVIEW
Merck is a global research-driven pharmaceutical company that discovers, develops, manufactures, and markets a broad range of products to improve human and animal health. The world's largest drug company, Merck generates almost $11 billion in annual sales of products such as Varivax (chickenpox vaccine), Singulair (allergies), and Pepcid (ulcer medication).

Merck's intern program offers a meaningful work experience that can serve as a starting move to a prosperous career. The intern program usually lasts between 10 to 12 weeks and includes at least one project. Some interns have been a part of a research effort to develop life-saving drugs, while others have developed and helped administer market research studies for cardiovascular medicine.

Although Merck expects you to make a significant contribution, they also offer a lot in return. You can expect meaningful and challenging assignments based on your skills, experience and goals; mentors and coaches; seminars, presentations; exposure to senior management; and career development and guidance.

Depending upon your objectives, you may prepare a report, presentation, or final project describing the results you achieved during the assignment. After you've completed the program, you'll receive a thorough evaluation from your manager that will review your success in fulfilling both your personal goals and the project's objectives. If you're a recent graduate, this program could lead to a full-time career. And if you're still a college student, successful completion of your assignment could lead to an invitation to return the following summer.

Merck recruits at most college campuses during the fall and spring sessions. You can look in the University Recruiting Calendar of Events section for dates when Merck will be on your campus at http://www.merck.com/mrkshared/careers/StudentSearch.jsp.

HOW TO APPLY
Submit your resume and cover letter to the previous address.

PFIZER INTERNSHIP

Business technology internship:
Pfizer Inc.
Pfizer Global Pharmaceuticals
Attn: Business Technology Internships

235 East 42nd Street, 13th Floor
New York, NY 10017-5755

Global manufacturing internship:
Global Manufacturing Internship Coordinator
Pfizer Inc.
235 East 42nd Street, MS 13-4
New York, NY 10017-5755

Global pharmaceuticals finance internship:
Pfizer Inc., Human Resources
Pfizer Global Pharmaceuticals
Attn: PGP Finance Internships
235 East 42nd Street, 13th Floor
New York, NY 10017-5755

Global pharmaceuticals marketing internship:
Pfizer Inc., Human Resources
Pfizer Global Pharmaceuticals
Attn: Marketing Internships
235 East 42nd Street, 13th Floor
New York, NY 10017-5755

Global pharmaceuticals market research internship:
Pfizer Inc., Human Resources
Pfizer Global Pharmaceuticals
Attn: Market Analytics Internships
235 East 42nd Street, 13th Floor
New York, NY 10017-5755

What You Can Earn: $1350 weekly.
Application Deadlines: Rolling.
Educational Experience: Undergraduate or graduate student; see more specific educational requirements as follows.
Requirements: See specific program requirements as follows.

OVERVIEW
Pfizer Inc. discovers, develops, manufactures, and markets leading prescription medicines for humans and animals, producing many of the world's best-known consumer brands in more than 150 countries. The company has three busi-

ness segments: healthcare, animal health, and consumer healthcare.

Interns at Pfizer can choose to work in a variety of areas in the company, including research and development, marketing, finance, human resources, production, sales, and legal. Pfizer recruits from a diverse pool of top-ranked candidates currently enrolled in graduate and undergraduate programs in the United States. Some possible internship and co-op programs include Pfizer global research and development (see "Science"), finance, global manufacturing, global pharmaceuticals finance, global pharmaceuticals marketing, global pharmaceuticals market research, and business technology.

Business Technology

Members of this group work with internal clients to identify opportunities and solve problems through the strategic use of technology and computer applications.

As a summer intern, you'll be asked to take on projects that have the potential to make a significant impact on the department and throughout the company. Projects are designed to expose you to the workings of the organization, including areas such as marketing, sales, finance, human resources, and clinical operations.

You should have a quantitative undergraduate degree and be enrolled in an M.B.A. program. You also must be able to take responsibility and show initiative, think creatively, demonstrate leadership and professional expertise, communicate effectively, and have strong analytical skills.

Finance

Between 12 and 15 summer interns work on challenging assignments in areas such as shared financial services in Europe, Asia, or North or South America; operating divisions in pharmaceuticals, consumer health or animal health; internal audits; investor relations; strategic planning; or taxes.

If you're placed in the finance department, you'll work with senior management on your own short-term projects, and you'll be given orientation and visits to research and manufacturing facilities. In the past, interns have worked on a plant-wide audit in Switzerland, on an audit in New York City, and a project that focused on collecting and interpreting investment returns.

Global Manufacturing

Pfizer's Global Manufacturing Division, which is responsible for the manufacture of all Pfizer products, offers summer internships at its various manufacturing sites and world headquarters office. Here you'll have an opportunity to work on challenging projects as you learn about the pharmaceutical industry. Typically, interns interested in this area are majoring in chemical engineering, chemistry, environmental engineering, or industry pharmacy.

Global Pharmaceuticals Finance

Pfizer Pharmaceuticals Finance includes six areas: Disease Management Finance, Sales Finance, Headquarters Finance, Medical Finance, the Contracts Group, and the Trade Group. This department partners with each operating department within Pfizer Global Pharmaceuticals to provide financial support for their initiatives while managing the overall financial performance of Pfizer's pharmaceutical business.

You'll work in one or more of the six areas of the group on challenges facing Pfizer. Past interns have worked on projects such as the impact of proposed Medicaid legislation, sales force expansion, equipment financing and lease/buy options, product performance, and return on investment of various promotional activities.

To qualify for this internship, you must possess strong financial, analytical, organizational, and communication skills.

Global Pharmaceuticals Marketing

Employees of the Pfizer Global Pharmaceuticals Marketing department are responsible for successfully positioning the company's products in the highly competitive pharmaceutical marketplace. Pfizer marketing experts conduct market and product-specific research before launching a new product; after the product is introduced, its positioning is continually redirected to take advantage of market opportunities.

As a summer associate, you'll be a part of the marketing team and given assignments in marketing communications, market research, or business planning and budget presentations.

To apply for this internship, you'll need to be an M.B.A. candidate with emphasis in marketing and strategy. Previous consulting, pharmaceutical, or healthcare experience is helpful. You'll also need to be able to think strategically and be a good problem solver, have excellent qualitative and quantitative analytical skills, be a good team player, and show a willingness to take responsibility and initiative.

Global Pharmaceuticals Market Research

Pfizer Pharmaceutical's Market Analytics department operates as an internal consulting group to the pharmaceutical marketing and other teams, conducting research and analysis to develop marketing strategies and identify ways to measure the success of critical programs.

You'll be assigned to work with the market research manager on a specific marketing team based in New York to help with a variety of market research activities around the world. In addition, you'll have at least one project to complete and present at the end of the internship. You'll gain experience with both primary and secondary marketing research techniques, and you'll have the opportunity to help develop, assess, and recommend marketing strategies. Typical projects in which you may be involved include developing and evaluating marketing strategies with the marketing team, determining the appropriate positioning of Pfizer products, interpreting market trends, and evaluating concepts for new ad campaigns.

To apply for this internship, you should be a candidate for an M.B.A. or M.S. in marketing, statistics, or another relevant discipline, with a strong academic record. Market research experience and pharmaceutical industry experience are helpful but not required. You also should have strong analytical skills, be a creative thinker, and have exceptional communication and interpersonal skills.

HOW TO APPLY

Send a resume and cover letter to the appropriate preceding address.

RANDOM HOUSE INC. SUMMER INTERNSHIP

Random House
Attn: Summer Internship Coordinator
1745 Broadway
New York, NY 10019
http://www.randomhouse.com

What You Can Earn: $300 a week and discounted books.
Application Deadlines: March 1.
Educational Experience: Students between their junior and senior years of college.
Requirements: Bright, talented, analytical, customer-focused, and enthusiastic about process improvement.

OVERVIEW

Random House Inc. is the world's largest English-language general trade book publisher, a global house now owned by Bertelsmann, that includes a number of imprints, including Bantam Dell, Crown, Doubleday Broadway, Knopf, Random House Audio, and Random House Children's Books, among others. Together, these groups and their imprints publish fiction and nonfiction, both original and reprints, in a full range of formats—including hardcover, trade paperback, mass-market paperback, audio, electronic, and digital.

Internships are available at both the New York headquarters and in the operations center near Baltimore. As an intern for this 10-week session, you'll work on a variety of projects in different areas depending on your interests, including distribution operations, engineering, information technology, inventory management, customer service, data control, financial operations, and transportation.

Some of the projects completed by recent interns include making recommendations for productivity improvements in various departments, developing ways to reduce the incidence of damaged books, and managing existing application software.

On the first day of your internship, you'll have an orientation where you meet other interns and human resources staff; then you'll start your tour of duty in your assigned area. Although your internship is structured, it isn't rigid. About once a week, interns get together for lunch to hear key executives discuss their roles and the work within their divisions. Speakers may include experts in publishing, publicity, editorial, marketing, finance, production, and elsewhere. If you're interning in New York, you'll travel to the operations center in Maryland for a tour of the facilities and hear from key executives there.

Participating in the program could be your first step in a publishing career at Random House. Over the years, many former interns have joined the company after graduation.

Graduate student interns work with senior executives on a variety of projects designed to expose them to the company and to provide experience about what a permanent position at Random House might be like. Graduate-student projects in recent summers have included reviewing e-publishing business plans in corporate development, analyzing the company's advertising media buys for the purchasing area, recommending a new structure for the academic marketing department for the sales division, and implementing process improvements in operations areas.

HOW TO APPLY

Download and complete an application by clicking here: http://www.randomhouse.com/careers/cg_apply.html. After filling out the application, you should attach a resume and a letter explaining what you hope to gain from your internship and why you are interested. Submit it to the preceding address. Finalists are invited to New York for an interview in the spring (at their own expense).

RAYTHEON INTERNSHIP

Raytheon
870 Winter Street
Waltham, MA 02451
http://www.rayjobs.com/campus/index.
    cfm?Tool=Welcome

What You Can Earn: Varies.
Application Deadlines: Rolling.
Educational Experience: Currently attending an accredited university with at least a 3.0 GPA.
Requirements: Unspecified.

OVERVIEW

Raytheon is an industry leader in defense and government electronics, space, information technology, technical services, and business aviation and special mission aircraft. Its internship program is structured to maximize your hands-on experience as the company develops a lasting relationship with you. Internships are offered in a variety of areas during the spring, summer, or fall.

HOW TO APPLY

To apply for a summer internship, visit the Raytheon Web site at http://www.rayjobs.com/campus/CollegeJobSearch.html.

To find out when the company will be visiting certain campuses on recruiting visits, go to this Web site: http://www.rayjobs.com/campus/index.cfm?Tool=Events.

SAKS INCORPORATED INTERNSHIP

Saks Incorporated, Internship Coordinator
750 Lakeshore Parkway
Birmingham, AL 35211

(205) 940-4251
http:// www.saksincorporated.com

What You Can Earn: $15 an hour.
Application Deadlines: May for the fall session; November for the spring session; January for the summer session.
Educational Experience: A strong academic background in business, finance, marketing, human resources, liberal arts, or retail.
Requirements: Creative; analytical; decisive; confident; excellent communication skills; enthusiasm; strong leadership potential; success driven and goal oriented.

OVERVIEW

Saks is a Fortune 500 retail-merchandising and store-management organization. One of the country's premier retail enterprises, it operates 388 stores in 40 states, with more than $6 billion in annual revenues and nearly 55,000 associates. The company operates its Saks Department Store Group with department stores under the names of Parisian, Proffitt's, McRae's, Younkers, Herberger's, Carson Pirie Scott, Bergner's, Boston Store, and 47 mall-based Club Libby Lu specialty stores. The company also operates Saks Fifth Avenue Enterprises, which consists of 57 Saks Fifth Avenue stores and 52 Saks Off 5th stores. The company's mission is to be a great place to shop, a great place to work, and a great place to invest.

The internship program provides many facets of development for students, including business analysis and forecasting, sales promotion, retail management, vendor development, and planning and distribution. Internship programs are typically 10 to 12 weeks during the months of May through September and vary in content by area. Internship opportunities vary by division and are mainly in the areas of store management and merchandising.

HOW TO APPLY

To inquire about internship opportunities, visit one of the company's recruiters on campus. For a schedule of the college campuses where the company actively recruits, visit this Web site: http://www.saksincorporated.com/careers/campusrecruiting.html

To apply for an internship, you may submit a cover letter and your resume to the preceding address.

TOYOTA MOTOR NORTH AMERICA INTERNSHIP

Toyota Motor North America
Internship Coordinator
W. 57th Street, Suite 4900
New York, NY 10019-2701
(212) 223-0303

What You Can Earn: Minimum $13 an hour, depending on accumulated credit hours, plus the number of accumulated work hours at any Toyota facility, plus time-and-a-half overtime; if your permanent residence is outside a 50-mile radius of your work assignment, you're eligible for relocation assistance reimbursed at the current Toyota mileage rate for one relocation trip to the work site when you start work and for one return trip after your last day. Students traveling more than a 260-mile radius from the job site will either be reimbursed mileage as well as lodging, meals, and so on or given air transportation for the two one-way trips.
Application Deadlines: Rolling.
Educational Experience: Undergraduate students with a 3.0 GPA or better, which is confirmed each quarter/semester with grades. (Students with lower GPAs may be considered for assignments on an exception basis.)
Requirements: Curious and inquisitive; a "hands-on" person interested in making a difference.

OVERVIEW

Toyota is one of the largest automakers in North America. Toyota was founded in 1926 and was established in the United States in 1957. Today, it manufactures more than 4 million cars and trucks, half of which are sold outside Japan. Toyota Motor North America is headquartered in New York, with branch offices in Florida and Washington, D.C., and was established in 1996 as a wholly owned subsidiary of Toyota Motor Corporation (TMA). TMA is the holding company for Toyota's manufacturing, financing, sales, and marketing operations in Canada, Mexico, and the United States. Direct functions include corporate communications; investor relations; corporate advertising; federal government, industry, and regulatory affairs; market, economic, and auto industry research; and the Toyota USA Foundation. In addition, TMA coordinates the corporate planning, diversity, and business activities of all Toyota companies in North America.

HOW TO APPLY
To apply, you must create a job profile at Toyota's Web site: http://tmm.recruitsoft.com/servlets/CareerSection?art_ip_action=FlowDispatcher&flowTypeNo=3&alt=1&JServSessionIdtmm=5okxkouac1.RJS33932&art_servlet_language=en&csNo=10020.

Your electronic resume must be in plain text format, and you must have an active e-mail address available. Once you have applied for an in internship position, e-mail will be used as the primary method of communication. To receive correspondence from Toyota, you'll need to use an e-mail address that allows HTML attachments.

TYSON FOODS INTERNSHIP

Tyson Foods Internship
PO Box 2020
Springdale, AR 72765
(800) 643-3410
http://www.tyson.com

What You Can Earn: Varies.
Application Deadlines: August for the fall session; November for the spring session; March for the summer session.
Educational Experience: Engineering, computer science, business, marketing, accounting, human resources, or sciences.
Requirements: None specified.

OVERVIEW
Tyson Foods Inc. is the largest processor of beef, chicken, and pork in the world, after nearly seven decades of providing quality food products. The company is the country's second-largest producer of corn and flour tortilla products as well and produces and markets a broad variety of prepared foods, in addition to serving the pharmaceutical industry with quality ingredients. The company has more than 120,000 employees and more than 300 facilities in 26 states and 22 countries.

Intern experiences vary by department and location, but you'll be exposed to all facets of the industry. Areas of internships include production management, business management, quality assurance, human resources, information systems, accounting, and executive.

HOW TO APPLY
Apply by sending your resume and a cover letter to the preceding address.

VERIZON COLLEGE INTERNSHIP

Verizon Internship Coordinator
http://www22.verizon.com/about/careers/college/opportunities/internships.html

What You Can Earn: Unpaid.
Application Deadlines: Rolling.

Educational Experience: Completion of at least one year of studies at an accredited college/university with excellent academic preparation and achievement; most internships require an overall GPA of at least 3.0; technical internships: Pursuing B.S./M.S./Ph.D. with a major in electrical/computer engineering, computer science, telecommunications, DIS/MIS/CIS or operations research; business internships: Pursuing B.S./M.S./M.B.A. with a major in marketing/sales, finance, accounting, operations research, MIS, or human resources.
Requirements: Outstanding leadership, analytical, and interpersonal skills; superior oral and written communication skills.

OVERVIEW

Verizon is one of the country's top communications companies, with revenues of more than $67 billion. The company is a major local exchange carrier in the United States, a major wireless carrier in the U.S. and among the largest in the world, and a leader in the broadband business. Verizon is also the world's largest print and Internet directory provider.

The Verizon College Intern Program offers outstanding undergraduate and graduate business and technical majors the opportunity to apply professional skills and gain valuable practical experience in the dynamic telecommunications industry. Verizon internships are structured working assignments in Verizon business and staff units that will enable you to apply and develop your knowledge, skills, and abilities. The internships generally include formal performance appraisals, orientation, professional skills workshops, technology information sessions, online training opportunities, social events, and networking opportunities.

HOW TO APPLY

Visit the company Web site at http://www22.verizon.com/about/careers/ to apply for an internship online. To see current internship openings, visit http://www22.verizon.com/about/careers/jobsearch/results/?referrer=college.

WALT DISNEY WORLD CULINARY JOBS

College Recruiting
(800) 722-2930
wdw.college.recruiting@disney.com or wdw.college.education.program@disney.com

What You Can Earn: Starting pay is $6 an hour with time-and-a-half for overtime (any time over 40 hours per week).
Application Deadlines: Fall presentations are recruiting for spring and spring advantage programs only; spring presentations are recruiting for fall and fall advantage programs only.
Educational Experience: Culinary experience.
Requirements: Current college enrollment, with at least one semester completed and with a 2.0 average or higher. Participation requires unrestricted work authorization.

OVERVIEW

Cast members (all employees are called "cast members") in the business side of Walt Disney World could be working in many different locations at a variety of jobs. You're guaranteed a schedule of 30 hours per week with a maximum of 45 hours per week. During busy seasons, however, you could be requested to work more hours a week. You're expected to work the hours you're scheduled; additional hours or days may not be available or optional.

Culinary Assistant, Baking & Pastry

Students with a culinary-related education focused in baking and pastry arts make ideal candidates for this high-volume bakery, banquet, and restaurant environment. You'll learn food-cost control and product ordering as you learn the technical skills of muffin, bread, cake, petit fours, and dessert preparations.

Responsibilities may include: mixing, cutting, proofing, and baking while following standardized recipes and food sanitation guidelines.

Culinary Assistant, Cook II

WDS is looking for students with a culinary-related education to work in this high-volume and fast-paced environment. You'll be working with basic recipes and have the chance to learn advanced food preparation in à la carte or buffet environments. You also may be able to learn more in developmental workshops and seminars.

Responsibilities may include: deep-frying, cooking on a grill, preparing mixes, peeling and dicing vegetables, sandwich and salad preparation, and kitchen sanitation.

Full-Service Food & Beverage

Organizational skills and the ability to handle multiple tasks at once are important qualities to have in this position. You may work as a seating host/hostess in various restaurants across the property or as a door greeter at Downtown Disney Pleasure Island (no tips are involved here). Responsibilities may include greeting and seating guests, handling cash, rolling silverware, folding napkins, and keeping the work area clean and stocked.

Hospitality

Hospitality cast members may experience many different facets of the front office operations, including the usage of a computer-based system, working in an environment with a high level of guest interaction, resolving challenging guest situations, and handling cash. You must be willing to work in all areas, including the front desk, guest services, and luggage services, and you may be checking guests in and out of resorts, processing payments, assisting guests with itinerary planning and ticket sales, tagging and delivering luggage, answering guest phone calls, and providing information to guests.

HOW TO APPLY

Walt Disney World employees visit more than 350 schools each fall and spring, from all over the country. Campus visits consist of a presentation that provides detailed information followed by interviews. Students, parents, and faculty are encouraged to attend the presentation together. You must attend a presentation to be able to interview; you sign up for interviews at the presentation. The interview generally takes place within 24 hours of the presentation.

At the interview, you must bring your completed application that you've printed from the application section of the WDW internship Web site (http://www.wdwcollegeprogram.com/sap/its/mimes/zh_wdwcp/students/frameset/frameset_faqs.html) and submit your application to the recruiter.

You also can apply online, but once you have submitted your application, you must still attend a presentation. Students must bring a copy of their completed applications to their interviews. You don't need to bring a resume to apply, but you may bring one to your interview if you wish. After the interview, your application will be considered, and you'll receive a response within two to three weeks.

Everyone who interviews should receive notification. If you haven't heard something within four weeks, you should e-mail College Recruiting (wdw.college.recruiting@disney.com) with your full name, complete mailing address, and a description of your situation.

If you aren't accepted the first time, you can apply and interview the following semester; however, you can apply and interview only once per semester.

EDUCATION

ACADIA NATIONAL PARK EDUCATION INTERNSHIP

Education Coordinator
Acadia National Park
PO Box 177
Bar Harbor, ME 04609
(207) 288-8822
http://www.nps.gov/acad/eeweb/intern.htm

What You Can Earn: $100 a week for a 32-hour work week, housing included.
Application Deadlines: Rolling.
Educational Experience: College students in a related major.
Requirements: Strong communication skills, experience working with children in an educational outdoor setting, knowledge of/interest in the natural and cultural history of the Maine coast, valid driver's license, current first aid and CPR certification. Applicants must be in good physical condition.

OVERVIEW

Acadia National Park protects more than 47,000 acres of lakes, ponds, mountains, and miles of ocean shoreline along the coast of Maine—an area rich with plants and animals. Education is a primary mission of Acadia National Park, and the education staff provides high quality programs and services. Acadia's education staff offers a variety of curriculum-based programs in the spring and fall, which also provides excellent opportunities for students interested in education to work as interns.

Interns at the park work with the education staff in presenting programs for grades 3 through 8. Programs are curriculum based and focus on ecology or history. Custom programs and special projects related to environmental education are also possible. Park orientation and program training are provided.

Both outdoor and indoor work is involved. The outdoor work is subject to varying weather and terrain. Positions include 10-week spots open from April to mid-June, or from late August through October.

HOW TO APPLY

To apply, mail or e-mail a cover letter, resume, and three reference contacts to the address above.

AMERICAN FOLKLIFE CENTER INTERNSHIP

Ann Hoog, Reference Folklife Specialist
American Folklife Center
Library of Congress
101 Independence Avenue, SE
Washington DC 20540-4610
(202) 707-5510
Fax: (202) 707-2076
folklife@loc.gov
http://www.loc.gov/folklife/

What You Can Earn: Unpaid but academic credit can be earned.
Application Deadlines: Rolling.
Educational Experience: None specified.
Requirements: An interest in folklife, anthropology, ethnomusicology, or related disciplines; a willingness to work in a library/archive; a commitment to the 200-hour minimum; some prior experience with folk music or folklife materials, preferably in an archive or library.

OVERVIEW

Whether it's an ancient English ballad, the tales of "Bruh Rabbit," told in the Gullah dialect of the Georgia Sea Islands, or the stories of ex-slaves, the American Folklife Center has them all. The center was created in 1976 by the U.S. Congress to preserve and present this great heritage of American folklife through programs of research, documentation, archival preservation, reference service, live performance, exhibition, publication, and training. The center includes the Archive of Folk Culture, established in the Library of Congress in 1928, and is now one of the largest collections of ethnographic material from the United States and around the world.

The collections in the center's Archive of Folk Culture include folk cultural material from all 50 states, as well as U.S. trusts and territories. Most of these areas have been served by the American Folklife Center's cultural surveys, equipment loan program, publications, and other projects.

The center is working on the critical issues of digital preservation, web access, and archival management as a way of maintaining their extensive collections, which also includes Native American song and dance, an Appalachian fiddle tune, a Cambodian wedding in Lowell, MA, a Saint Joseph's Day Table tradition in Pueblo, CO, Balinese Gamelan music recorded shortly before the Second World War, and documentation from the lives of cowboys, farmers, fishermen, coal miners, shopkeepers, factory workers, quilt makers, professional and amateur musicians, and housewives throughout the United States. The collection includes firsthand accounts of community events from every state and international collections from every region of the world.

Folklife is an integral part of all American lives and an essential part of the National Library. The story of America is reflected in the cultural productions of the everyday lives of ordinary people, from cooking and eating meals, to the activities of work and play, to religious observances and seasonal celebration. Folklife includes the songs we sing, the stories we tell, and the crafts we make.

The American Folklife Center provides opportunities for students to work with these collections for course credit throughout the year. As an intern at the center, you'll gain educational experience and career training in the fields of folklore and folklife, ethnomusicology, archival studies, and library science. You'll be exposed to the field of folklife, the collections of the Archive of Folk Culture, and the processes of collection, preservation, and presenta-

tion as you structure a variety of activities at the center.

You'll get the chance to participate in a number of activities of the American Folklife Center, including reference, processing, acquisitions, special projects, and events. For example, you may compile aids to help find specific subject areas in the Archive's collections; organize and label collections for preservation and storage; and maintain a wide variety of subject and collections files. Other projects may include research for special projects and helping with public events. Occasionally, you may be asked to respond to requests from Congress, the public, or schools and universities.

Internships may range from just six weeks to more than a year (with a minimum of 200 hours). Part-time arrangements are possible, although a commitment of at least two full days a week is preferable.

HOW TO APPLY

To apply for an internship, submit a letter of application including a phone number where you can be reached, a resume or list of your interests and experience, a time when you can be interviewed, and an indication when you would like to schedule your internship. Because of security measures at the Library, U.S. mail and Federal Express may be delayed. The Center recommends that you fax your application.

AMERICAN GEOGRAPHICAL SOCIETY INTERNSHIP

The American Geographical Society
120 Wall Street, Suite 100
New York, NY 10005
(212) 422-5456
AGS@amergeog.org
http://www.amergeog.org/internships_program.htm

What You Can Earn: Unpaid.
Application Deadlines: Rolling.
Educational Experience: None specified.
Requirements: None specified.

OVERVIEW

Interns play an important part in activities at the American Geographical Society, working at the society at anytime of the year, either part time or full time, for a minimum of 10 weeks. Most assignments are for work in the AGS office in New York on Wall Street, but a few projects could be carried out elsewhere. Interns have been coming to the American Geographical Society since 1984, and in recent years most interns have come from abroad: Germany, Italy, Kazakhstan, Kenya, United Kingdom, Singapore, and Canada. Because of this, if you choose an internship at AGS, you'll probably meet a lot of young people from other countries, which can provide an interesting cross-cultural experience.

Interns get involved in everything from office work (stuffing envelopes, filing, and so on) to research, database development, compiling bibliographies, conducting an inventory of the archives, and much more.

Although you'll receive neither a stipend nor an expense allowance, the society will give you recommendations for future employment and for graduate school.

HOW TO APPLY

Send a copy of your resume with a cover letter to the preceding address.

AMERICAN SCHOOL FOR THE DEAF INTERNSHIP

Volunteer Coordinator
American School for the Deaf
139 North Main Street
West Hartford, CT 06107
(860) 570-2211 (Voice), (860)570-2229 (TTY)
maryann.coffey@asd-1817.org
http://www.asd-1817.org/index.html

What You Can Earn: Housing and meals provided.
Application Deadlines: Rolling.
Educational Experience: Pre- and post-college students accepted; knowledge of sign language helpful.
Requirements: None specified.

OVERVIEW

The American School for the Deaf provides a comprehensive program for the development of the intellect and the enhancement of the quality of life for the deaf community by providing educational and vocational programs for deaf and hard-of-hearing children ages three to 21 and their families. The school offers students a full range of programming from preschool to 12th grade, including those with additional disabilities, as well as offering alternative education for students with emotional/behavioral disorders. Instruction is conducted in small classes with a variety of approaches to meet the needs of diverse learners. Other special services may include instruction in communication skills (speech, auditory training, speech-reading and sign language); cochlear implant support; counseling (personal and guidance); occupational and physical therapy; sister school arrangements with local public schools; access to computer laboratories; enhanced literacy activities; and mainstream opportunities.

Interns play a vital part in the life of the American School for the Deaf. In a typical year, interns contribute more than 3,000 hours of volunteer assistance in all departments, from everyday service in the classroom to tutoring a child after school to special events such as Family Learning Weekend or the school's annual Golf Tournament.

In spring, summer, and fall terms (eight weeks minimum), you can get practical experience with deaf education and deaf culture by working in dorms and classrooms and by immersing yourself in a sign language environment. If you're interested in working with the deaf community, such long-term, in-depth involvement can help you develop your educational and career plans.

HOW TO APPLY

To apply for an internship, access the Volunteer Application Form at http://www.asd-1817.org/intern and return it to the preceding address.

ANASAZI HERITAGE CENTER INTERNSHIP

Internship Coordinator
BLM Anasazi Heritage Center
27501 Highway 184
Dolores, CO 81323
(970) 882-5622
Susan_Thomas@co.blm.gov
http://www.co.blm.gov/ahc/intern.htm

What You Can Earn: Stipend of $100 per week.; housing at a communal, three-bedroom house on six acres adjacent to the Anasazi Heritage Center; no travel reimbursement; college credit may be arranged depending upon policy of university.
Application Deadlines: None.
Educational Experience: Specific experience depends on intern area but in general should include students with an interest in museum collections, graphics, Native American cultures, archeology, anthropology, or applicants with prior background in archaeology, anthropology, and collections management.
Requirements: At least 18 years of age and one year of college.

OVERVIEW

The Anasazi Heritage Center includes a main archaeology gallery with artifact exhibits, a rep-lica pithouse, touchable and hands-on exhibits, computer-based explorations, a second gallery for temporary exhibitions, a movie theater, a room for special educational programs, and a 100-seat auditorium. On the museum grounds are two 12th century ruins (the Dominguez and Escalante Pueblos) and a nature walk through the forest up to a beautiful 360° view of the surrounding region (Mesa Verde, La Plata Mountains, Dolores River Valley, and Sleeping Ute Mountain). The AHC staff also manages a library, a conservation laboratory, and over 3 million artifacts, samples, and original documents.

The center periodically offers eight-week to 12-week student internships in three primary areas: collections management, exhibit and interpretive media, and museum education/interpretation.

Collections Management

As an intern in this area, you'll function as a general curatorial assistant and will therefore be involved in a variety of curatorial tasks. You'll be entering a considerable amount of data in the museum's ARGUS cataloging system and will help with various repackaging, reorganizing, and inventory projects of existing collections at the AHC. This position offers broad exposure to the curatorial operations of a federal repository.

This internship is open to anyone with an interest in museum collections management or curatorial activities; applicants with prior background in archaeology, anthropology and collections management will receive preference.

Education and Interpretation

As an education intern at the center, you'll be responsible for developing and presenting two educational and interpretive programs. Typically, the programs focus on the prehistoric culture of the Ancestral Puebloans, the Four Corners area natural history, Four Corners cultures, archaeological scientific methods, and land management practices. Program formats may include hiking tours, short art demonstrations, impromptu lectures, one- or two-hour children's classes, or preparation of an educational tool such as an artifact loan box or an activity booklet.

You'll also be responsible for providing information and collecting entry fees at the front desk and operating the museum shop cash register. However, this program is flexible and can be adapted to meet your needs and abilities. The job activities will vary according to seasonal audiences, with school programs presented in the spring and fall and general visitor programs in the summer.

This internship is usually available from March through October; a minimum of 40 hours a week is required, including some weekends and holidays.

You should be 18 years old or older, with one year of college studies in a related area and experience in education or museum programming. The ability to communicate with a wide variety of people including children is important, as is a background in Southwest archaeology, ethnology, and natural history.

Exhibit and Interpretive Media Design and Production

In this internship, you may work on improvements to the permanent exhibits in the main exhibits gallery, which are mainly based on materials available from AHC collections. The museum has a special interest in interactive and hands-on exhibit formats.

The AHC maintains a series of traveling exhibits for loan, and sometimes an internship is available involving administration of this program. Work may include loan tracking, marketing, repairs or enhancements to existing exhibits, and development of new exhibit offerings.

The AHC also hosts three to five temporary exhibitions annually in its special exhibit gallery, usually borrowed from other institutions but perhaps produced in-house or drawn from a combination of resources. Interns sometimes contribute to the installation or enhancement of these exhibitions, depending on circumstances and need.

You may wish to focus on the Chappell Collection, a private collection that includes nearly 1000 ceramic vessels plus organic and ornamental objects representing the Pueblo II and Pueblo III periods of Ancestral Puebloan occupation of this region. As the Chappell intern, you'll develop and install a thematic exhibit, working closely with the AHC curator and exhibit specialist; however, development and installation of the exhibit will be primarily your responsibility.

The AHC is the headquarters for Canyons of the Ancients National Monument, so other opportunities may involve creation of outdoor installations or interpretive literature for hikers and other nonmuseum recreational users.

These internships are open to students interested in the design and production of exhibits. Applicants with a background in exhibit development, interpretive writing, anthropology or archaeology, collections management, art, or art history will be given preference. Familiarity with principles of design, graphic, and desktop publishing software and ancestral Puebloan culture are all helpful.

HOW TO APPLY

Applications are accepted and most positions may be filled at any time of year, but the availability of internships varies. There is no specific form to be completed; applicants should mail a letter of interest and a resume to the preceding address.

BOSTON MUSEUM OF SCIENCE INTERNSHIP

Intern Program
Museum of Science
Science Park
Boston, MA 02114
Fax: (617) 589-0311
interncoordinator@mos.org

What You Can Earn: All internships earn $6.75 to $7 an hour except those marked "unpaid."
Application Deadlines: Mid-April for summer internships (check Web site for exact deadline).
Educational Experience: College and grad students in many different majors; high school students are

eligible to apply for some listed internships but only if they have completed 75 hours of volunteer work at the museum.

Requirements: Specific requirements are discussed as follows, according to department needs.

OVERVIEW

All of the following internships are three-month summer experiences beginning in June unless otherwise noted (a few are four months); most have fairly flexible start and end dates. All pay a stipend of $6.75 to $7 an hour unless otherwise noted.

Archival and Genealogical Research

This department provides information to support the fund-raising activities of the museum, reviewing internal documents to provide historical and biographical data and using external resources to help the museum learn about potential sources of funding. You'll help museum staff prepare a major building project and help to create the foundation for future space-naming opportunities at the museum. This internship offers a great opportunity to learn about the fund-raising field and research at an exciting nonprofit organization.

Applicants should have basic computer skills including Microsoft Word, Excel, and Internet and be able to learn how to use the department's fund-raising database. Applicants should be detail-oriented, accurate, and able to maintain confidentiality. Genealogical research experience is a plus. Also, you must be available to work Monday through Friday from 9:00 A.M. to 5:00 P.M.

Computer Clubhouse Network

The Computer Clubhouse is a safe, creative after-school learning environment where under-served youths explore high-end technology with the support of adult mentors, writing and recording music, making movies, building robots, creating Web sites, illustrating comic books, and filming music videos. Students learn to take a project from early concept to final product, to express the steps they have taken, and to help others follow the same path in more than 75 Clubhouses around the world, orches-

trated by The Computer Clubhouse Network based at the Museum of Science. This gives thousands of kids access to resources, skills, and experiences to help them succeed in their careers and contribute to their communities.

If you intern here, you'll work between 20 and 30 hours a week (unpaid) with Computer Clubhouse Network staff to collect information for Web pages describing new Clubhouse programs, design and program new pages on the Clubhouse Web site, and help update content. Applicants should enjoy working with a team in an informal educational environment and have skills in graphic design, Web programming, and Javascript (or other Web scripting languages). Hours are between 20 to 30 per week.

Design Challenges

This school field trip program introduces students in grades 4 through 10 to the engineering design process. Through 20-minute hands-on activities, students learn about the museum's new engineering and technology initiatives, linking the museum's exhibits to emerging technology. If you intern here, you'll work for three months during the summer with visitors, participating in developing new museum programming and helping with the week-long Design Challenges Summer Course. You'll also help develop some basic print materials that will be available for educators to download from the program Web site.

Applicants should have completed college-level coursework in education, science, or engineering and be interested in informally working with students, teachers, and museum educators. You should have basic skills in computers (MS Office) and digital photography software, with an interest and enthusiasm for working and interacting with diverse museum audiences. Salary is $6.75 to $7 an hour for between seven to 14 hours a week in a flexible schedule.

Exhibit Hall Interpretation

The Exhibit Hall Interpreter Program provides hands-on learning experiences for the public throughout the museum's exhibit halls. The core of the program consists of 80 volunteers who provide interpretations on science, engineering, and technology topics. During the summer, eight to 10 high school interns join the team of interpreters for four months beginning in early June. If you intern here, you'll help other Interpretation staff create unique, informal education experiences for visitors. As an interpreter, you'll try to stimulate enthusiasm about science and technology by presenting interpretations for museum visitors and help develop new interpretations. You'll help research daily educational briefings for volunteers and provide support to various special projects. Applicants should be interested in informal education and the sciences, have excellent verbal and written communication skills, and want to work with museum visitors. Education experience or experience working with school-aged children is helpful.

Exhibit Maintenance

As an intern here, you'll make sure that the exhibit halls are ready for visitors by checking the more than 600 interactive exhibits to identify problems and arrange for repairs when needed. As part of this internship, you'll receive hands-on training in many different areas, from repairing mechanical exhibits to rewiring electronic components. If you like, you can help in the exhibit-design process as well, working closely with staff to create new exhibits. Applicants should have had course work or experience in electronics and must have some soldering and electronics assembly experience and the ability to read schematics. You should be interested in electronics and repairs; knowledge of simple electrical circuits is a plus. You also should be interested in working in a science museum and have demonstrated the ability to work with people. This internship has a very flexible schedule, although you should be prepared to work one weekend day a week.

Facilities

If you love to fix things up and keep machines humming, this internship could be for you. Here, you'll work with the mechanical maintenance team, keeping track of HVAC, plumbing, and electrical services. In addition, you'll perform preventative maintenance work, repair work on mechanical systems, and other routine and emergency maintenance operations. Other jobs may include carpentry, painting, and grounds maintenance, and you'll need to help keep an orderly, properly stocked maintenance shop. You'll also perform maintenance routines on HVAC, plumbing, and steam systems including pumps, motors, air handling units, chillers, traps, valves, filters, water treatment systems, sewage ejector, and condensate pump systems and heat exchangers. Applicants should be enrolled in a degree program or be a career changer, with at least one year's educational experience in mechanical or facilities engineering or related work. Applicants should be able to perform or be willing to learn maintenance on mechanical and plumbing systems and be able to work well with others as well as independently. The internship lasts between seven and 35 hours a week, on a flexible schedule of Monday through Sunday.

Hear Our Voices (Girls in Technology)

Monday is "girls' day" at the Computer Clubhouse, a nation-wide after-school "drop in" environment where young people have complete access to computer technology and resources. The Clubhouse, whose headquarters are in the museum, offers a vibrant environment with state-of-the-art computers and a variety of software and technological tools for use on projects in the visual arts, video, robotics, music, and Web and graphic design. On Mondays, the Clubhouse is open only to girls and their mentors. "Hear Our Voices" is an initiative of the Clubhouse Network that will help 20 Clubhouses across the United States create new opportunities specifically for girls and young women.

As an intern here, you'll work with girls during the Monday Girls' Day program, helping to organize projects that have already been developed through the program. You'll also help update the Hear Our Voices Web site and help develop new projects that appeal specifically to girls and young women. Applicants should have completed college-level courses in math, science (any field), art, or education and have a strong commitment to help young women express their creative voices and develop self-confidence. Applicants should be comfortable working in an informal, creative learning environment and be sensitive to multicultural issues associated with working with inner-city youth. You'll need computer skills, and you should be familiar with Web design, Adobe Photoshop, Flash, Poser, and MS Office 2000. You should be able to work at least 10 hours a week (unpaid), and you must be available Mondays from 2:00 P.M. to 7:00 P.M.; the extra five hours each week are flexible.

Lectures and Special Programs, Research and Marketing (UNPAID)

In an attempt to attract new audiences and keep current fans happy, this department produces cutting-edge programming featuring high-profile academics, researchers, scientists, and technology developers. As intern, you'll need to be a versatile team player who'd love to work in the research, implementation, and promotion of lectures and special programs. This position will give you a chance to be involved in all aspects of event preparation, as well as the development of new adult audiences. Applicants must have good organizational abilities and excellent writing, computer/internet, and oral communication skills. Applicants also should be familiar with publicity, marketing communications, and promotional strategies and be organized, detail oriented, and responsible. You must be able to take initiative and be a problem solver, have a sense of adventure, and be energetic, articulate, friendly, creative, and a team player. This position lasts 10 hours a week from May to September, with some night and weekend work.

Planetarium

The Charles Hayden Planetarium has been educating families, school groups, and the general public about astronomy since 1958. The 240-seat round theater uses dozens of computer-controlled slide projectors and special lighting effects in planetarium programming. As an intern here, you'll join staff in presenting shows to the public, learning

how to explain scientific theory, understand the technical equipment in the Planetarium, and beef up your teaching skills. The three-month internship begins in June; you should be able to work between 21 to 35 hours a week.

Publications Graphics

This department is responsible for writing, editing, designing, and producing promotional and information projects, including the museum's annual report, newsletters, brochures, invitation packages, flyers, banners, and posters. As an intern here, you'll help staffers with various projects involving graphics design projects, help designers with photo and art research, and perform administrative tasks. Applicants should be college, art, or design school students or recent graduates with studies in graphic design or art and demonstrated experience in graphic design. Applicants should have experience with graphic layout and Macintosh computer-based graphic software tools such Quark, Illustrator, InDesign, and Photoshop and be creative, imaginative, and inventive. Interns should be able to work between 21 and 35 hours a week.

SciCORE Intern for Robotics

The SciCORE (Science, Careers, Opportunities, Research, Education) High School program is based on the idea that kids need to contribute to the community. This program's mission is to help high school interns, volunteers, and Computer Clubhouse members develop knowledge and confidence about science and technology and learn skills in critical thinking, public service, and job readiness. The SciCORE intern, who may NOT be a high school student, supports the high school interns and volunteers at the museum. Here, you'll work closely with the Youth Programs Coordinator and High School Program Manager as they work with the museum's young volunteers.

Participants in the Robotics SciCORE program meet twice a week, with two different teams of youth, for seven weeks, learning about the electronics of building robots or about simple programming languages robots (Lego Blocks, or Logo). Students will have workshops, activities, and projects around these areas, as well as a summer-long project that will develop their design skills and abilities.

As an intern here, you'll help staff develop the curriculum and implement the Robotics SciCORE Program while you guide SciCORE youth. Applicants must be undergraduates or graduate students or career changers interested in related fields and interested in working with and mentoring teens. Applicants should be interested in robotics and be experienced with either electrical configuration of robots or simple language programming; you should be flexible and dependable, able to work independently and with a team, and have good interpersonal and communication skills. Fluency in a second language is a plus.

Science Library Intern

The Harrison F. Lyman Library houses an extensive collection of books, journals, and videos that support the exploration of science and technology topics. As an intern here, you'll help maintain the collection, process new materials, staff the circulation desk, provide reference assistance, and help with special projects. Applicants should be college juniors with good attention to detail and the ability to work with a diverse audience. You must be responsible and self-motivated and be interested in museums, libraries, or education. This internship is unpaid.

Summer Courses Teaching Assistant

During the Summer Enrichment Program for school-aged children, kids are taught a variety of hands-on, minds-on science and technology courses. During this two-month internship beginning in July, you'll rotate among classrooms, supporting teachers and office staff on a preassigned schedule. You'll also serve as classroom teaching assistant for week-long courses, working with instructors to present quality educational programs and answer questions from adults before or after class. Working as a team directed by senior interns, you'll also help distribute supplies to teachers, greet children in the morning and help them get to class and take them to meet their parents after class. You'll also help supervise children during their lunch period, planning simple activities and games and preparing and serving simple mid-morning and mid-afternoon snacks. You also may help with the registration process and with other office tasks. You'll keep a journal of teaching observations and experiences and review it regularly with the summer course coordinator and read and discuss selected educational articles about science education. Applicants should be college or graduate students with previous experience working with children and enthusiasm for science education. Applicants should be problem solvers with the ability to multitask, with strong interpersonal and communication skills. Previous science teaching or recreation leadership is desirable, and technical expertise in computer graphics/Web design is required.

Technology Education

The staff, volunteers, and exhibits of Cahners ComputerPlace provide visitors the chance to learn about computer science topics such as robotics, artificial intelligence, and programming and to explore computers. The exhibit features an informal presentation area and a variety of themed computer activity clusters. As an intern here, you'll spend most of your time in Cahners ComputerPlace, teaching visitors about computer science and technology in an informal way. You'll also help develop new interactive educational components for the exhibit. Applicants should have a strong interest in teaching about technology and have basic experience as an educator, either in a formal or informal environment. Applicants should be energetic, independent, and enthusiastic, with creative instructional design skills, and enjoy working in an active environment. This internship lasts 11 weeks, from mid-June through the end of August (with flexible start and end dates). You should be prepared to work two days a week from 9:00 A.M. to 5:00 P.M. before July 4 and from 11:00 A.M. to 7:00 P.M. after July 4.

Technology Services

The technology services department at the museum is responsible for the upkeep of most of the organization's technical needs. As an intern here, you'll be responsible for desktop support, care of the automatic ticket machines, server and e-mail systems, and exhibit components. You'll help mostly with the technology services help desk, providing hands-on troubleshooting and maintenance. You'll also assess problems with nonfunctional workstations, update servers and workstations as new products become available, and keep everyone informed when network problems occur. Applicants should have some computer and network experience, with college-level coursework in computers or electronics. Applicants should be willing to work independently and as part of a team and have strong customer service skills and Macintosh computer skills. Stipend for this internship is $8 to $10 an hour.

HOW TO APPLY

To apply, submit a cover letter describing academic and career goals, personal interests, and why you would like to participate in the Intern Program at the Museum of Science, plus a resume that includes contact information for three references.

BROOKLYN CHILDREN'S MUSEUM INTERNSHIP

Brooklyn Children's Museum
145 Brooklyn Avenue
Brooklyn, NY 11213
(718) 735-4428
Fax: (718) 604-7442
gcones@brooklynkids.org
http://www.brooklynkids.org and http://www.
    brooklynexpedition.org

What You Can Earn: $230 weekly for 10 weeks.
Application Deadlines: Mid-April.
Educational Experience: Graduate students and college juniors and seniors.
Requirements: None specified.

OVERVIEW

The Brooklyn Children's Museum offers children active educational experiences with innovative exhibitions, programs, and collections. Founded in 1899, it's the world's first museum for children. Located in Brooklyn's Crown Heights neighborhood, the museum has a continuing tradition of community service and national leadership.

As an intern here, you'll have the opportunity to work in one of the following departments: exhibits (design and production skills); education (teaching, program preparation, and assessment); government (community outreach and public information); and collections (conservation, research, and documentation of cultural and natural science collections).

If you're accepted, you'll work on substantive projects, develop professional skills, and gain knowledge of the enormous societal impact of public service. Interns gather to attend exciting weekly events, both educational and social, and presentations by distinguished leaders from the public sector.

HOW TO APPLY

To apply, send a cover letter with your resume indicating the department in which you're interested in interning, and discuss your related skills and experiences. Submit the material to the preceding address.

CHICAGO CHILDREN'S MUSEUM INTERNSHIP

Chicago Children's Museum
Manager of Volunteer & Intern Services
700 E. Grand Ave., Suite 127
Chicago, IL 60611
Fax: (312) 832-7812
internships@ChiChildrensMuseum.org
http://www.chichildrensmuseum.org

What You Can Earn: Unpaid.
Application Deadlines: Rolling.
Educational Experience: Unspecified.
Requirements: Strong interpersonal skills, excellent written and verbal communication skills, the ability to work independently, and knowledge of computer systems (word processing, desktop publishing, and database management). See additional requirements below.

OVERVIEW

The Chicago Children's Museum tries to create a community where play and learning connect. The museum's primary audience is elementary age children and their families, along with the school and community groups that support and influence children's growth and development. Fifteen permanent exhibits and programming areas provide innovative learning experiences for more than 500,000 visitors each year. The museum also makes a significant investment in resources in neighborhoods across Chicago, particularly to children who might not otherwise have access to the museum.

The museum was founded in 1982 by a coalition led by The Junior League of Chicago in response to program cutbacks in the Chicago Public Schools, opening its doors in two hallways of the Chicago Public Library. In response to capacity crowds on-site, CCM developed trunk shows and exhibits which traveled to schools, branch libraries, and neighborhood centers.

The Chicago Children's Museum offers a wide variety of internship possibilities that can help students gain valuable experience. Interns will work with supervisors who have detailed knowledge in their fields.

A variety of internships are available, including :

Human Resources Intern

As an intern in the human resources department, you'll help both human resources and volunteer and intern services develop a museum-wide wellness program, creating and sending correspondence to prospective employment candidates, scheduling interviews, and checking references of final candidates. You'll also research other organizations regarding volunteer and internship programs and assist with the museum's internship program.

Candidates should have strong organizational skills and be creative, self-motivated, and flexible.

Special Events Intern

As an intern in the external affairs department, you'll help with all areas of planning for the museum's annual "Be A Kid Again" gala, including soliciting items for the silent auction, tracking contributions, writing acknowledgement letters, creating auction packages, and producing information for the auction book. You'll also work on other project development and implementation projects.

Candidates should be able to organize projects and events, pay attention to detail, prioritize multiple projects, and work effectively under pressure.

HOW TO APPLY

To apply, complete the internship application at http://www.chichildrensmuseum.org/form_intern_app.cfm. The application can be submitted electronically from the Web site.

CHILDREN'S MUSEUM OF INDIANAPOLIS INTERNSHIP

Intern Program Manager
Children's Museum of Indianapolis
PO Box 3000
Indianapolis, IN 46206
emilyc@childrensmuseum.org
Fax: (317) 920-2028
http://www.childrensmuseum.org

What You Can Earn: Unpaid but scholarship programs are available to qualified candidates to help with living and academic expenses; academic credit is available.

Application Deadlines: April 4 for summer. Other sessions are rolling. Candidates applying for the internship scholarship for any semester must submit applications according to this scholarship's deadline schedule.

Educational Experience: Qualified college students, recent graduates, or graduate students from all majors and interests; candidates must be at least 21 years of age.

Requirements: Interest in working with and for children, good interpersonal skills, and the ability to articulate goals.

OVERVIEW

Interns at The Children's Museum of Indianapolis work as part of a team, completing significant projects and providing input and seeing results. Whether working directly with children or within administrative departments, interns contribute to the museum's mission: to create extraordinary learning experiences that have the power to transform the lives of children and their families. Internships are available in a number of museum departments, including development, development grants, marketing, professional development, public relations, special events marketing, special events logistics, and Web site. Internships last the duration of a typical academic spring, summer, or fall semester.

There are a variety of education internships in different departments of the museum, including family programs, preschool programs, school services, the Biotechnology Learning Center, and the Dinosphere art gallery.

Biotechnology Learning Center

This two-part internship is divided into focusing on working in the museum's Biotechnology Learning Center and in creating teacher resources and other school-related opportunities in biotechnology. As an intern in this center, you may help implement biotechnology programming developed by curriculum specialists, using a variety of teaching strategies as you interact with visitors. You'll have practice using a variety of techniques to keep audiences interested. You'll also be responsible for preparing lab space for visitors, cleaning the lab space each day, and researching, planning, and helping to develop new teacher resource kits, lessons, the summer institute, and other opportunities for teachers. Occasionally, you'll help the science educator develop and plan activities and evaluate programs and special events that require the lab's space.

Candidates should have completed at least two years of undergraduate biology, with some knowledge of biotechnology; some experience working with children; good oral and communication skills; and the ability to complete tasks independently.

Dinosphere Art Gallery

The museum's new Dinosphere exhibit is designed to help children and their families discover and explore paleontology art and learn about dinosaurs through observation, discussion, and reflection. As an intern in the gallery, you'll help to develop and facilitate activities here, developing skills to interact with visitors and helping with art activities and general cleaning. You'll also educate visitors about artifacts in the gallery, and you'll develop and evaluate developmentally appropriate activities with opportunities to research and observe how children learn, develop, and behave.

Candidates should have completed at least one year of college with at least one semester of art education or related courses (art education majors are preferred). You should have experience working with children, the interest and ability to interact positively with children as well as adults, and a positive attitude when working with the public. Candidates should be able to resolve problems quickly and tactfully, have excellent oral and written communication skills and interpersonal skills, and be available between 9:00 A.M. to 5:00 P.M. at least three days a week.

Exhibit Production and Development Internships

There are several internships available in the production and development of exhibits, including internships for exhibit graphic designers and exhibit evaluation and researchers.

Exhibit Evaluation and Researchers

Working with exhibit developers, interns in this department will help analyze and interpret data using checklists, questionnaires, and visitor observations. Interns may also be involved in visitor interviews and focus groups and may participate in presenting collected data to exhibit teams. Interns will observe and interview visitors each day by unobtrusively following them and recording their exhibit interactions and coding visitor interviews and observation data.

Candidates should be majoring in museum studies, marketing and communications, anthropology, arts administration, education, or social and/or behavioral sciences. They also should have excellent oral and written communication skills, excellent time-management skills, and self-motivation. They should be proficient in Microsoft Word and able to record information accurately and be outgoing individuals who enjoy talking with museum visitors.

Exhibit Graphic Design

In this department, interns help design and produce signs and graphics to illustrate exhibits, daily programs, and events. You may be asked to help produce graphics and poster signs for activities, special events, and collection displays or scan images and mount graphics for final display.

Candidates should be juniors or seniors in college or graduate students with strong portfolios and good computer graphic skills in Adobe Illustrator and Photoshop. Candidates also should have strong composition and layout skills and good verbal communication skills. Interns should be good at multitasking, managing time, and producing art.

Family Programs

As an intern in this department, you'll help with the research, development, and implementation of family-oriented educational programs such as home-school programs, parent and child pro-

grams, school outreach programs, and family day trips. You may be asked to help develop family programs, including researching background for program topics, writing outlines for programs, and ordering supplies for programs, plus researching new and innovative approaches to family programming, childhood education, and family learning. Also, you may help coordinate effective programming and contribute to quality documentation. Finally, you may help organize inventory and maintain supplies.

Candidates should be majoring in education, child development, family studies, or other related fields; have experience working with children or families; have good writing and communication skills; have a positive attitude when working with children and families; be able to juggle several projects at once; and have basic computer skills (including Microsoft Word). Interns should be available some evenings and/or weekends to help with programs.

Gallery Interpretation

As an intern in this department, you'll help interpret the museum's exhibits to a wide variety of visitors in different programs.

Center for Arts Exploration

The Center for Arts Exploration offers experiences in dance, song, literature, and art, with special exhibits appearing every three to four months. As an intern here, you'll help interpret such activities.

Candidates should be college juniors with experience working with children and possess excellent oral and written communication skills. Candidates should be good at interacting with customers, be very organized and good at research, good at managing time and juggling tasks, and have a basic knowledge of Microsoft Word, Excel, and PowerPoint.

Mysteries in History/Passport to the World

As an intern in these areas, your job will be to introduce visitors to the past through hands-on exhibits and activities focusing on documents, photographs, architecture, and oral history. *Passport to the World* displays contemporary and traditional toys and folk objects from around the world. Your job will be to act as an interpreter in the gallery, creating learning experiences for museum visitors. You'll also help research and organize interpretive activities and programs for the gallery and help implement new adult-volunteer and youth-volunteer programs.

Candidates should be juniors in college with experience working with children and should possess excellent oral and written communication skills. Candidates should be organized, able to interact with the public, have good research skills, manage time well, and multitask effectively. Basic Microsoft Word, Excel, and PowerPoint skills are preferred.

Science Interpretation

As an intern in this department, you'll focus on mentoring adolescent volunteers as they develop projects in physical and natural sciences. You'll be expected to work closely with teens and help mentor specific teams. You'll also need to spend some time as a gallery interpreter in order to learn skills you'll be expected to teach to students. You'll be working closely with volunteers aged 12 to 16 on a variety of projects, helping with final projects for the science team and individual galleries and helping part-time staff work with youth volunteers. You'll use different teaching methods to remain flexible to the needs of various children and their families as you participate in the interpretation training program. You also may help plan activities and special events in the ScienceWorks, What if?. . ., and Dinosphere galleries.

Candidates should be majoring in secondary education, counseling, social work, psychology, or other related areas and have experience working with teens. Candidates also should have excellent communication skills, basic knowledge of the physical and natural sciences, and the ability to multitask and work on tasks independently.

Museum Administration

There are also a number of internships available in a number of departments related to museum administration, including development grants, marketing, professional development, public relations, special events marketing and logistics, and Web site development.

Development

If you intern in this department, you'll gain experience in annual campaign and special project fundraising, prospect research, relationship building, and solicitation. You'll also learn how to cultivate and retain clients as you discover the many facets of strategic development, including research, proposal writing, letter writing, cold calling, and sales-presentation collaborations and materials. You may need to help develop collateral materials for individuals and donor gift clubs, help maintain the client database and files, and help the staff create proposal budgets. You may research the latest studies in the arts, humanities, and sciences as they pertain to museum programs and exhibits, call museum donors, help write fund-raising letters, provide ongoing communication with new and existing clients, and implement ideas for core and lapsed donors. You also may provide promotional support at museum and outside events.

Candidates should be majoring in journalism, English, public administration, communications, or public relations and have excellent writing and verbal communication skills, a working knowledge of online research, respect for confidentiality of museum and client information, and the ability to work collaboratively in a diverse work environment. You also should be diplomatic, detail-oriented, self-motivated, and competent in Windows and MS Office applications such as Word and Excel. You should be able to interact positively with children and adults and be able to attend some after-hour and weekend events.

Development Grants Writer

With this internship position, you'll learn how to research, report, and write grants. You'll help in many aspects of grants writing, including research, identifying prospects, and writing proposals. You may help collect internal data about the museum's projects and programs to serve as templates for developing proposals to foundations. Templates would include program descriptions, budget information, statistical and demographic information of audiences served, and other support research as necessary. You also may help research the latest studies in the arts, sciences, humanities, and museums that support museum programs and exhibits. You may help the grants writer with prospect research and grant reporting and help with development events.

Candidates should be majoring in journalism, English, public administration, or nonprofit management and possess excellent writing, research, and verbal communication skills and excellent online research skills. Candidates also should be self-motivated, discreet, diplomatic, able to interact positively with children and adults, competent in Microsoft Word and Excel applications, able to work collaboratively in a diverse work environment, and able to attend some after-hour and weekend outside events and internal functions.

Marketing

As an intern in this area, you'll help support marketing programs and promotional activities for the museum as a way of boosting the audience base and increasing attendance and museum membership. You may find yourself helping develop marketing plans for a variety of areas, including museum membership, development, school services, special events, theater, the museum store, and programs.

You may also help manage print publications and promotional materials, help with community-event promotions, and help gather marketing materials for events. Occasionally, you may be asked to help work events with the marketing team. You also may help assemble and edit copy for the monthly e-newsletters for teachers, members, and the Early Discoveries Club, as well as work with the e-mail provider to get e-newsletter produced. You'll create ad concepts and submit work orders for a variety of publications under the supervision of the marketing manager, help with grassroots public relations and marketing efforts, and help

track attendance, coupon redemption, and advertising effectiveness of specific campaigns.

Candidates should have Windows software experience, excellent written and verbal communication skills, and strong organizational skills. Candidates also should be diplomatic, able to pay close attention to detail, able to manage multiple projects at one time, and able to work collaboratively.

Professional Development

This department is responsible for training museum staff, volunteers, and interns through a combination of class work, vendor training, and on-the-job training. All new staff members attend a core base of training classes, and then a customized training path is created to fit their position and responsibilities. As an intern in this department, you may help research information to be included in the curriculum, design course curriculum, evaluate the effectiveness of training and development, and assess the future needs of the department training.

Candidates should be university juniors or seniors with academic backgrounds or experience in related topics and have excellent interpersonal skills. You also should be self-motivated, willing to work independently or as part of a team, and willing to give presentations or help during training workshops.

Public Relations

As an intern in this department, you'll help promote programs and events of the museum, helping the marketing group publicize museum programs, galleries, and events and learning how to work with television, print, and radio media organizations. You'll also help write press releases, articles, and scripts for events and programs, compile data for inclusion in the quarterly media analysis, and attend outside media assignments, early-morning live coverage of the museum galleries, and after-hours public relations functions at the museum. You also may help oversee editing of master video tapes.

Candidates should have educational backgrounds or experience in public relations with strong communication, multitasking, and organizational skills. Candidates also should maintain a professional appearance and have good presentation skills, along with the ability to work well as part of a team.

Preschool Programs

If you're interning in this department, you'll learn how to create and evaluate developmentally appropriate activities and projects for preschoolers, in addition to observing how children learn and behave. You'll have the chance to work with fee-based preschool programs as well as develop activities in the Playscape gallery (the museum's early childhood education exhibit). Possible internship projects include helping prepare for preschool classes, organizing and creating materials for classes, and helping teachers during classes. You'll also help with the Playscape gallery, interacting with and educating visitors from age 18 months to five years. You'll play with children and their families, redirecting behavior when needed. You'll learn stories and finger plays and develop storytelling skills as you help with art activities and general cleaning. You'll also learn games to play with families and learn more about the artifacts so you can share with visitors. In addition, you'll help the early childhood educator and preschool teachers.

Candidates should have completed at least one semester in education or related courses; be studying early childhood, elementary education, or family studies; have experience with children; and be able to interact well with preschoolers as well as adults. Candidates also should have a positive attitude, professional behavior, and responsible work ethic; excellent oral communication and interpersonal skills; and the ability to work from 9:00 A.M. to 5:00 P.M. on Wednesdays, Thursdays, Fridays, and Saturdays.

School Services

As an intern in this department, you'll help implement programs and develop materials for the museum's school audiences. You'll work directly with children during the spring or fall, but you'll not usually work with children during the summer. Possible internship projects include researching topics for the teacher guides, developing writing resource materials for teachers that relate to the museum, and helping prepare programs for schools (during fall and spring semesters only). You'll also conduct a program or activity for the school and develop kit materials and correlate the kits to Indiana Academic Standards, while learning more about the scope of the museum's resources for educators. You'll also spend a lot of time in the galleries with school visitors during fall and spring semesters.

Candidates should have Web-research and word-processing skills; good writing and communication skills; and should be majoring in elementary education, child development, and family studies or library science, preferably with a background in history, art, science, or the humanities. Also important is experience working with children, customer service skills, and the ability to manage time and multitask.

Special Events Logistics

As an intern in this department, you'll handle logistics and coordination for museum events, working closely with the events staff in hosting and event planning at The Children's Museum. You may be asked to help set up and manage special events, attend client meetings with the logistics manager, and help with research.

Candidates should be able to commit to 25 hours a week during the internship and have completed three years of college with a major in advertising, public relations, marketing, or event planning/management. Candidates should have good oral and written communication skills, customer service skills, and organizational and research skills. Candidates should be good at multitasking and have experience with Word, Excel, and Access; maintain a professional appearance; and be able to attend at least 10 evening or weekend events.

Web Site Development Intern

As an intern in this department, you'll help develop and maintain museum Web sites, helping to write content for the volunteer page of The Children's

Museum's Web site and collaborating with museum staff in designing Web content.

Candidates should have strong technical skills and the ability to quickly learn new products and have excellent oral and written communication skills, strong organizational and planning skills, and excellent problem-solving, logic, analysis, and collaboration skills. Candidates should also have at least one year of experience with Web development technologies such as Dreamweaver, Paintshop Pro/Photoshop, Macromedia MX products (Flash, Director, Coldfusion), and HTML; and have database, graphic, design and HTML experience. Video editing/compression, animation, SQL, and XML experience is a plus.

Special Events Marketing

As an intern in this department, you'll help execute marketing projects for the events department as you help implement the marketing plan. Projects may include helping with direct mail pieces and research, working closely with the in-house caterer on effective marketing pieces, and attending some luncheons and evening events.

Candidates should be able to commit to 25 hours a week during the internship and have completed three years of college with a major in advertising, public relations, marketing, or event planning/management. Candidates should have good oral and written communication skills, customer service skills, and organizational and research skills. Candidates should be good at multitasking and have experience with Word, Excel, and Access; maintain a professional appearance; and be able to attend at least four evening and/or weekend events.

HOW TO APPLY

To apply for an internship at The Children's Museum, fill out an application form at http://www.childrensmuseum.org/generalinfo/interns_application.htm. Then mail, fax, or e-mail the form along with the following materials to the preceding address: a cover letter explaining why you are interested in interning at The Children's Museum

of Indianapolis, a resume, and a college transcript (required if applying for the scholarship).

For the exhibit graphic design internship, in addition to the preceding materials, you should submit one 8 ½ x 11 page with three or four examples of work (emphasizing creative text and image layout, use of color, and technical ability) with your resume or submit the materials electronically in PDF or JPEG format to the intern program manager.

DAUGHTERS OF THE AMERICAN REVOLUTION (DAR) MUSEUM INTERNSHIP

Internship Program

DAR Museum
1776 D Street, NW
Washington, DC 20006-5392
(202) 879-3240
Fax: (202) 628-0820
kscott@dar.org

What You Can Earn: Unpaid but academic credit can be arranged.
Application Deadlines: March 15 for summer session; August 15 for fall (priority given to those received by August 1); December 15 for spring.
Educational Experience: Rising college seniors and graduate students interested in gaining experience in American history, decorative and fine arts, education, collections management, and public relations.
Requirements: Organized and independent.

OVERVIEW

One of the most prominent American decorative arts museums in the country, the DAR Museum showcases the furnishings and decorative arts of preindustrial America with permanent and changing exhibitions in two galleries. Home to one of the most historic decorative arts collections in the United States, the DAR Museum was established in 1890, the year the Daughters of the American Revolution was founded. The collection includes 30,000 decorative and fine arts objects made or used in America before the Industrial Revolution (circa 1830). The items are displayed in two galleries and 31 period rooms, which trace the development of home, business, and social life in early America and reveal how lifestyles have changed over 300 years.

Interns generally work at least 20 hours a week, between three and four months. During your internship, you might help produce written materials, help with school tours and public programs, design new curricula for school programs, do research in preparation for exhibitions, and work on inventory, as well as cataloging objects in the museum's collection, writing press releases, assembling press kits, and maintaining media contacts.

HOW TO APPLY

To apply for an internship, download an application at http://www.dar.org/darnet/forms/CG-2004.pdf and mail or e-mail it (as a Word attachment) to the preceding address.

HISTORIC PRESERVATION INTERNSHIP TRAINING PROGRAM

National Council for Preservation Education
210 West Sibley Hall
Cornell University
Ithaca, NY 14853-6701
mat4@cornell.edu

What You Can Earn: $12 an hour for 10 weeks, 40 hours a week.
Application Deadlines: Mid-March for summer session (check Web site for exact dates).
Educational Experience: Undergraduate and graduate students in historic preservation programs and related disciplines, such as anthropology, archaeology, architectural history, architecture, ethnography, history, landscape architecture, museology, and planning.
Requirements: Computer and word processing skills; willing to travel throughout the metro Washington D.C. area (MD, VA, WV, DC, and PA).

OVERVIEW

If you'd much rather shore up than tear down, you might want to consider an internship with the Historic Preservation Internship Training Program, which offers interns the chance to undertake short-term research and administrative projects with the National Park Service either during the summer or the school year.

The Internship Training Program trains future historians, archeologists, architects, curators, planners, and archivists by fostering an awareness of the National Park Service cultural resource management activities and providing the opportunity to work under the direction of experienced professionals in the field of historic preservation. Operated jointly with the National Council for Preservation Education, the Internship Training Program places students in National Park Service cultural programs headquarters and field offices and in units of the park system with historic preservation and cultural resource management responsibilities. Here, you'll learn about the national historic preservation programs operated in partnership with state historic preservation offices and National Park Service efforts to preserve and manage historic properties.

Under the guidance of National Park Service professionals, you'll senior historical architects and other preservation craftspersons in ongoing historic preservation projects throughout the National Park System. Duties may include field inspection, documentation, fabric investigation, and condition assessments on a variety of historic structures; preparation of Condition Assessment Reports; and monitoring ongoing preservation treatments.

Applicants should be familiar with historic construction methodology, building-fabric investigation and analysis, and assessing building-fabric pathologies. Experience with field documentation, architectural drawing, and design skills are a bonus. A registered architect will supervise the position.

HOW TO APPLY

You can download the application at http://www.cr.nps.gov/hps/TPS/Intern/summer2005.doc. Submit all application materials in duplicate and mail to the preceding address.

INDEPENDENCE SEAPORT MUSEUM INTERNSHIP

Museum Intern Search
211 South Columbus Boulevard & Walnut Street
Penn's Landing
Philadelphia, PA 19106
(215) 925-5439
Fax: (215) 925-6713
seaport@phillyseaport.org
http://www.phillyseaport.org

What You Can Earn: Unpaid but college credit is available.
Application Deadlines: Rolling.
Educational Experience: Working toward a B.A. in public relations, marketing, communications, museum studies, or a related field.
Requirements: Organized, dependable, an eye for detail, strong writing and oral presentation skills, and a love of working with people in a professional, nonprofit environment.

OVERVIEW

Independence Seaport Museum is a nonprofit educational institution dedicated to collecting and exhibiting art, artifacts, and archival materials pertaining to the maritime history and traditions of the Delaware River, Bay and tributaries and to interpreting general themes related to civilization and the sea. International and national in scope but regional in emphasis, the museum is committed to enhancing an appreciation of the sea, exploring the impact of this history on commerce and culture that shaped this region, and helping people understand the continuing role of the waterways in contemporary life.

The museum uses interns to help with marketing, development, and public relations functions. As an intern here, you'll help maintain, update, and organize press clippings and advertising files; research media contacts; write and edit public relations material; help plan community events; help with development, membership, and group-sales mailings; and help with administrative duties.

HOW TO APPLY

Mail or e-mail your resume and a cover letter to the preceding address; if e-mailing, put "museum intern search" in the subject line.

JAPANESE AMERICAN NATIONAL MUSEUM INTERNSHIP

Japanese American National Museum
Attn: Human Resources
Re: Getty Internship (Specify Position)
369 East First Street
Los Angeles, CA 90012
(213) 830-5673
hr@janm.org

What You Can Earn: $3,500 for 10-week internship.

Application Deadlines: Early May for summer internships.

Educational Experience: Must be a currently enrolled undergraduate and have completed at least one semester of college by the time the summer internship starts but will not graduate before December of the year of the internship; must be a resident of or attend college in Los Angeles County.

Requirements: These internship opportunities are intended for members of groups underrepresented in the professions related to museums and the visual arts: individuals of African American, Asian, Latino/Hispanic, Native American, and Pacific Islander descent; specific requirements are listed below in individual internship categories.

OVERVIEW

The Japanese American National Museum is a new model for American museums dedicated to transforming lives and strengthening communities through the exploration of diverse histories, arts, and cultures. The mission of the Japanese American National Museum is to promote an understanding and appreciation of America's ethnic and cultural diversity by preserving, interpreting, and sharing the experiences of Japanese Americans. The National Museum believes in the importance of remembering history to better guard against the prejudice that threatens liberty and equality in a democratic society. It strives as a world-class museum to provide a voice and a forum that enable all people to explore their own heritage and culture. The institution promotes continual exploration of the meaning and value of ethnicity through programs that preserve individual dignity, strengthen communities, and increase respect among all people nationally and internationally.

Three types of internships are available from mid-June through late august: graphic designer/production intern, curatorial intern and media arts/public program intern.

Curatorial Internship

The curatorial intern for the National Center for the Preservation of Democracy will work with research and development-resource materials for the National Center's exhibition *Fighting for Democracy*. This includes supporting the implementation of these resources and related materials that will become part of the National Center's opening programs. These products will also be used to support the needs of teachers from a variety of educational institutions in Los Angeles and throughout the nation.

The intern will receive training with a variety of staff and volunteer trainers. Sessions will introduce the intern to the history and work culture of the National Museum and to the history of Americans of Japanese ancestry.

Interns should want to work in an educational institution; experience working in research is a plus. Candidates also should be familiar with MS Word and Excel and be interested in working in a nonprofit setting.

Graphic Designer/Production Internship

This intern will work closely with the art director, senior graphics designer, and production unit in developing and implementing printed materials primarily for exhibitions and public programs. Additional work will include developing printed materials for the annual courtyard kid's festival. The intern also will receive hands-on training with a variety of museum staff and volunteers. Sessions will introduce the intern to the history and work culture of the National Museum as well as to the history of Americans of Japanese ancestry.

Requirements: Fine arts, design, or architecture background; experience with Quark, Photoshop, and Illustrator; and an interest in learning about working in the arts.

Media Arts/Public Program Internship

This intern will participate in the development of media elements for the National Museum's public programs and will receive hands-on training in media-arts production with a variety of staff and volunteer trainers. Sessions will introduce the intern to the history and work culture of the National Museum and to the history of Americans of Japanese ancestry, as well as to the work of the National Center for the Preservation of Democracy.

Candidates should have strong writing and organizational skills and familiarity with diverse community-based cultural institutions. Familiarity with MS Word and Excel and experience with media editing tools are pluses.

HOW TO APPLY

Download an application at http://www.janm.org. Complete the application and submit it, along with a cover letter, resume, and two letters of reference, to the preceding address. No phone calls.

LITERACY PARTNERS INC. INTERNSHIP

Literacy Partners Inc.
30 E 33rd Street, 6th Floor
New York, NY 10016
(212) 725-9200
Fax: (212) 725-0414
volunteermanager@literacypartners.org
http://www.literacypartners.org

What You Can Earn: Unpaid but academic credit is possible.
Application Deadlines: July 30.
Educational Experience: High school or college student.
Requirements: Self-starter and independent worker; mature and dedicated; highly organized and detail oriented; great presentation skills.

OVERVIEW

Literacy Partners Inc. is a nonprofit organization that provides free community-based adult and family literacy programs to ensure that all adults have access to quality education needed to realize their potential as individuals, parents, and citizens.

About 90 million Americans lack adequate literacy skills, and 36 percent of all New York City adults can't read beyond the fifth-grade level.

This nonprofit organization tries to teach adults to read, write, and do mathematics in tutorial and family-literacy programs staffed by volunteers and professionals. For 30 years, the organization has been teaching thousands of New York City adults, in free classes, the basic literacy skills essential to a full life as individuals, parents, and citizens.

As an intern here, you'll be responsible for participating as a member of the Tech Team to maintain technology and information systems. You'll help maintain the hardware and software, both on site and off site; help assess staff knowledge and skills related to hardware and software and teach (when appropriate); help maintain computer inventory; troubleshoot and repair hardware and software, when possible; enter PC support forms into an Access database; update directory listings; conduct research for competitive bidding; and handle some clerical duties (copying, labeling, filing, and so on.)

Candidates should have excellent oral communication skills; expertise in MS Windows 2000, MS Office 2000/XP, (Blackbaud Raiser's Edge and Financial Edge a plus); fundamental knowledge of Microsoft Visio; and a positive and team-oriented attitude.

HOW TO APPLY

For the information-systems internship, send a resume and cover letter to literacypartnersTECH@gmail.com. No phone calls.

NATIONAL AIR AND SPACE MUSEUM INTERNSHIP

Summer Internship Program
Coordinator of Student Programs
PO Box 37012
National Air and Space Museum
Educational Services, Unit P-700, MRC 305
Washington, D.C. 20013-7012

What You Can Earn: $4500 stipend for full-time interns.

Application Deadlines: February 15 for the summer session.

Educational Experience: Undergrad or grad students in all fields of study with a strong academic record.

Requirements: A commitment of 10 weeks during the summer.

OVERVIEW

Since the Smithsonian's National Air and Space Museum opened in 1976, millions of people have visited the largest collection of historic aircraft and spacecraft in the world. The museum is not just a tourist destination but is also a vital center for research into the history, science, and technology of aviation and space flight. The museum is concerned with educational outreach and maintains a popular Web site that reaches millions of people all over the world.

If you're interested in aviation and history, you might enjoy this internship, where you'll work directly with museum staff conducting research, designing and building exhibits, preserving or restoring artifacts, or developing educational materials. Interns have a firsthand opportunity to learn about the historic artifacts and archival materials housed in the museum and to study the scientific and technological advances they represent. Each year, positions are available in a variety of museum departments such as aircraft restoration, aviation or space history, planetary science, collections management, exhibit design, public relations, and education.

When you're accepted for an internship, the museum tries to match your academic interests, abilities, and career goals with related projects. As an intern, you might find yourself helping geologists collect information on Mars in the Center for Earth and Planetary Studies or write press releases for the public affairs department. Or you might help create science activities for family programs or conduct detailed research into the history of new collections and integrate the information into the museum's records.

Full-time interns work 40 hours a week from about the first week in June until the second week in August; most interns work in the National Air and Space Museum on the National Mall in Washington, D.C., but others work in nearby Suitland, Maryland, at the Paul E. Garber Preservation, Restoration, and Storage Facility, which is accessible by shuttle bus from the museum.

HOW TO APPLY

Applications materials are posted online each fall; the museum accepts applications for summer internships from January 15 through February 15 during the calendar year of the internship. You will be notified of the status of your application no later than April 1.

To apply, submit an application package including a completed application form, official transcripts from all of your universities, two letters of academic recommendation, and a double-spaced typed letter of between 500 and 1,000 words indicating the type of internship you're interested in and explaining how an internship will contribute to your education and career goals.

NATIONAL ANTHROPOLOGICAL ARCHIVES INTERNSHIP

National Anthropological Archives
Smithsonian Museum Support Center
4210 Silver Hill Road
Suitland, MD 20746
(301) 238-3514
Fax: (301) 238-2883
leopold@si.edu
http://www.nmnh.si.edu/naa/volunteering.htm

What You Can Earn: Unpaid but academic credit is available.
Application Deadlines: Rolling.
Educational Experience: Graduate and undergraduate students interested in exploring a career in archives or the history of anthropology.
Requirements: A commitment of at least 10 hours a week.

OVERVIEW

The National Anthropological Archives collects and preserves historical and contemporary anthropological materials that document the world's cultures. The collections represent the four fields of anthropology (ethnology, linguistics, archaeology, and physical anthropology) and include manuscripts, field notes, correspondence, photographs, maps, sound recordings, film, and video created by Smithsonian anthropologists and other scholars. The collections include the Smithsonian's earliest attempts to document North American Indian cultures (begun in 1846); nearly 650,000 ethnological and archaeological photographs (including some of the earliest images of indigenous people worldwide); 20,000 works of native art (mainly North American, Asian, and Oceanic); 2,500 audio recordings; and more than 8 million feet of original film and video materials. The Smithsonian's broad collection policy and support of anthropological research for more than 150 years have made the NAA a great resource for scholars interested in the cultures of North America, Latin America, Oceania, Africa, Asia, and Europe.

To complete this work, the NAA needs interns to help staff with cataloging, preservation, and reference. Internships are available year round and vary in length; projects are carried out under the direct supervision of a professional archivist or anthropologist and vary depending on the background and experience of the student. Typically, you'll be involved in cataloging, preparing collections for use by researchers, digitizing collections, helping researchers in the reading room, or answering reference inquiries.

HOW TO APPLY

If you're interested in this internship, you can download an application at: http://www.nmnh.si.edu/naa/intern_application.pdf. Mail the completed form along with two references (or provide the requested information in an e-mail message) and send it to the preceding address.

A follow-up interview is required, but if you can't visit in person, you can make special arrangements for a telephone interview. If you'll be obtaining course credit for your internship, you should specify any paperwork NAA might be required to complete.

NATIONAL BUILDING MUSEUM INTERNSHIP

Intern Coordinator
National Building Museum
401 F Street NW
Washington, DC 20001
(202) 272-2448 ext. 3300
Fax: 202 376-3564
ehendricks@nbm.org
http://www.nbm.org/Support/intern.html

What You Can Earn: Unpaid; academic credit may be given, along with complimentary museum membership (includes subscription to *Blueprints* quarterly journal, invitations to exhibition openings, a discount in the museum shop, and reduced fees for programming), weekly enrichment programs.
Application Deadlines: March 15 for summer (June through August).
Educational Experience: Undergraduate and graduate students. No specific credentials or work experience is required.
Requirements: A strong interest in the subject areas covered by the National Building Museum's mission and in museum work in general.

OVERVIEW

The National Building Museum, created by an act of Congress in 1980, is America's premier institution dedicated to exploring and celebrating architecture, design, engineering, construction, and urban planning. A relatively young institution, the museum strives to give interns meaningful, hands-on activities that lead to tangible results.

You can apply any time of year, and schedules can be flexibly arranged depending on the museum's needs and your schedule. During the summer, you can learn about museum operations during a weekly enrichment program including behind-the-scenes visits to other cultural institutions in Washington, D.C. There are a variety of places in which to work, as the following descriptions show:

Collections

Here you'll help with the organization and documentation of the museum's staff library, which contains about 40,000 photographic images, 68,000 architectural prints and drawings, 100 linear feet of documents, and 2,100 objects documenting America's built environment.

Development

In this department, you'll help with fund-raising efforts (researching prospective donors using the Internet and other sources), help prepare grant proposals, draft membership appeal letters, assist during fund-raising events, and perform administrative tasks as necessary.

Education

Interns in this department help with the youth and family programs, tours of the museum, outreach programs, and adult programs.

Exhibitions

Interns here work with curators to research, plan, design, and construct permanent and short-term exhibitions.

Marketing and Communications

In this department, you'll write press releases, help with marketing and audience development strategies, help write articles for the quarterly magazine Blueprints, and other publications such as exhibition brochures and marketing pamphlets.

HOW TO APPLY

Download the application at http://www.nbm.org/Support/Intern_Registration_Form.pdf. Mail or fax the completed application, along with a recent writing sample (at least two pages), an interview in person or over the phone, two letters of recommendation from professors, and your most recent official academic transcript to the preceding address.

NATIONAL MUSEUM OF AMERICAN HISTORY INTERNSHIP

National Museum of American History, Intern Manager
12th St. and Constitution Ave., NW
National Museum of American History, Behring Center
Washington, D.. 20560
nmahintern@si.edu

What You Can Earn: Unpaid but stipends are available for a limited number of minority internships through the Smithsonian's Office of Fellowships.
Application Deadlines: November 1 for spring session (January to May); February 15 for summer session (June through August); July 15 for fall session (September through December).
Educational Experience: Must be at least 16 and have completed at least two years of high school; most interns are college undergrads or grad students, but student status isn't required. The museum welcomes diversity in age, occupation, nationality, and background.
Requirements: Ability to work at least 20 hours per week for eight weeks.

OVERVIEW

The National Museum of American History is all about history yet so much more! You don't have to be a student of history or American studies to take advantage of an internship here. If you explore the museum's Web site, you'll notice that the institution includes a wide range of disciplines, including graphic design, medicine, conservation, physical sciences, and music, in addition to history, archeology, and anthropology.

The internship program allows a diverse group of people with many different interests, strengths, and goals to work with and learn from professionals and scholars in related areas. Interns of various backgrounds have an incredible opportunity to study a variety of fields, from public relations to exhibition research to project design. Learning from knowledgeable mentors in the dynamic atmosphere of the museum and Washington, D.C., area, interns enjoy an intensive experience as multifaceted as the museum itself.

Some interns choose to devote up to 40 hours a week or stay for longer periods of time (from three months to a year). Your choices may depend on whether there's an appropriate project that coincides with what you want to learn and whether the staff is available to work with you. When choosing an area in which to work, don't overlook important museum-support positions such as administration, information technology, the library, and the archives. And don't forget that there are many opportunities to work with children of all ages in the museum's public programs.

HOW TO APPLY

First, download the application at http://www.americanhistory.si.edu/dynamic/downloads/interns/c_link_9_352.pdf. You can fill out the form online and then print it or print it and fill it out by hand. Write an essay of between 500 and 1,000 words discussing why you're seeking an internship and how it relates to your academic or professional development and goals. Indicate the types of areas of work you'd like to participate in, and explain why the Smithsonian staff or facilities are suited to your needs.

Submit five complete copies of the application, along with five copies of your resume and the essay, five copies of your unofficial college transcript, and letters of recommendation (five copies of each) to the preceding address.

After applying, e-mail the intern manager to confirm receipt of application, but remember that the application process takes several months to complete. Staff will interview selected candidates by phone or e-mail.

NATIONAL MUSEUM OF THE AMERICAN INDIAN INTERNSHIP

Internship Program
Cultural Resources Center
National Museum of the American Indian
Smithsonian Institution
4220 Silver Hill Road
Suitland, MD 20746
(301) 238-1541
Fax: (301) 238-3200
norwoodj@si.edu

What You Can Earn: Housing and stipends may be provided to Native and non-Native students on a limited basis; preference will be given to indigenous students currently enrolled in an academic program.

Application Deadlines: Early October for winter session (January to March); mid-November for spring session (March through May); early February for summer (June to August); early July for fall (September through December); check Web site for exact deadlines.

Educational Experience: Undergraduate and graduate students currently enrolled in a university program, as well as individuals who have completed studies in the past six months.

Requirements: Cumulative GPA of 3.0 or its equivalent is generally expected (with withdrawals and incompletes explained); a minimum of 20 hours per week is required for those not receiving a stipend. Students receiving internship stipends must work full-time (40 hours per week).

OVERVIEW

Opened on the National Mall in 2004, the National Museum of the American Indian in Washington, D.C., is a major exhibition space for Indian art and material culture as well as a center for educational activities, ceremonies, and performances. Internship opportunities are available in any of the four internship sessions throughout the year, lasting about 10 weeks each. You can choose to work in Administration; Collections; Exhibitions and Public Spaces; External Affairs and Development (which includes development, public affairs, membership, special events, and product licensing); Facilities Planning; Graphic Design; Information Technology; Public Programs; and Visitor Services.

For example, an intern working in visitor services might help maintain a welcoming environment in and around the museum, directing line queues, distributing and collecting timed-entry passes, providing visitor orientation, and providing information that reflects Native perspectives and sensitivities. This internship is ideal for students interested in museum or visitor studies.

Interns in public affairs, for example, might help work with news bureau staff to update media databases, pitch media stories, distribute press releases, monitor news coverage, and assemble clipping reports. You might write follow-up correspondence for both media and general public requests and help with photo needs, including shooting, selecting, captioning, and distributing images. This internship is ideal for students majoring in journalism, public affairs, public relations, or development.

If working outdoors is more your interest, you could work with museum horticulturists, helping to cultivate plants and maintain an ecologically balanced habitat. You might help plant and harvest crops and plants used in the museum's education program; students interested in working in a Native landscape are encouraged to apply. As you can see, the internship program here is designed to give you an educational opportunity through guided work/research experiences using the resources of the National Museum of the American Indian and other Smithsonian offices.

Intern projects vary by department, but most projects will give you museum practice and program development experience; some projects may be more research oriented.

HOW TO APPLY

Download an application at http://americanindian. si.edu/collaboration/files/internship_app_2005. pdf.

Submit one original and five copies of your application via U.S. mail or overnight delivery service (faxes will not be accepted), along with your resume and transcripts to the preceding address. Include an essay explaining what your interest is in the museum field, what you hope to accomplish through an internship, and how it would relate to your development, as well as what in particular about the NMAI interests you and has prompted you to apply.

PORTLAND CHILDREN'S MUSEUM INTERNSHIP

Portland Children's Museum
4015 SW Canyon Road
Portland, OR 97221
(503) 223-6500
volunteer@portlandcm.org

What You Can Earn: Unpaid, but college credit is possible.

Application Deadlines: Rolling.

Educational Experience: Not specified.

Requirements: Interest in working with and for children; good interpersonal skills; an enthusiasm for the mission of the museum; able to give a minimum 12-week time commitment, with 12 to 20 hours worked a week; background check required.

OVERVIEW

Founded in 1949, the nonprofit Portland Children's Museum is a hands-on museum for children 10 years old and younger. The museum's mission is to inspire imagination, creativity, and the wonder of learning in children and adults. The museum features changing exhibits, arts-based programs, and a public school.

A number of internships are available in different museum departments, including accounting, community partnership, development I, development II, exhibits, governance law, marketing/public relations, programs, studios, and textiles.

Accounting

As an intern here, you'll work with the accounting manager and director of finance to support the museum's financial objectives. You'll complete various accounting and bookkeeping tasks, work with multiple funds and departments, and help design and create various financial statement presentations.

Community Partnerships

The purpose of this program is to increase access and improve the quality of visits for all families. The museum's community partners (agencies and schools serving families with limited access) connect families with the museum's exhibit and program offerings. By working with more than 200 organizations in Oregon and Washington, the museum serves more than 15,000 people annually. As an intern here, you'll help the program developer and membership coordinator increase access for all children. You'll administer all aspects of the program including communicating with families and community organizations, maintaining databases, and coordinating mailings. You'll also represent the museum at community events, and you'll collaborate with the Program Developer to research, design and implement evaluation instruments.

Development I (Winter/Early Spring)

As an intern in this department, you'll work directly with the event coordinator and the Development Department to help with the annual fund-raiser award dinner and benefit. You'll help maintain and update the database with event attendees and prospects, compile table sales reports and other various reports as needed, help with mailings of invites and thank you letters, filing, e-mail correspondence, and helping with in-kind donations. Other projects may involve coordination of member-and-donor-only events, brainstorming for new campaigns and promotions, contributing to the museum newsletter, and communicating with current members or donors.

Development II

In this internship, you'll work with the development department on grant-related activities, including researching, writing proposals, reporting, and scheduling; researching public and private local, regional, and national funding sources; tracking progress of proposals for funding sources, and preparing progress summaries; helping with record-keeping, including donor and pledge tracking; acknowledging gifts; handling special mailings; coordinating promotional material for donor solicitations; and preparing the museum's list of gifts monthly report. Other projects may involve coordination of member- and donor-only events, brainstorming for new campaigns and promotions, contributing to the museum newsletter, and communicating with current members or donors.

Exhibits

As an intern here, you'll help the exhibit developer and fabricator maintain, improve, and renovate existing props, lighting, and signs, as well as fabricate new exhibit components and props. You'll be responsible for maintaining the highest safety standards at the museum, and you'll be expected to document your experience through words, drawings and photographs. You'll submit your final portfolio to the museum archives.

The Garage

As an intern here, you'll help the studio coordinator with ongoing planning, implementation, maintenance, documentation, and evaluation of the Garage environment and experience. You'll help make sure the creative space is physically and emotionally safe for young children and encourage open-ended exploration in positive and supportive ways. Internships are customized to meet your needs and interests, and you'll be expected to document your work through words, drawings, and photographs. You'll then submit your portfolio for the Museum archives.

Governance Law

As a governance intern in this area, you'll work with the human resources specialist and the governance committee reviewing museum governance documents, researching best practices, and presenting recommendations based on findings. You might help review current bylaws, Articles of Incorporation and board policies; research and make recommendations for revision based on findings; research and draft the charter for the Leadership Council; and incorporate the Leadership Council into the Children's Museum's bylaws.

Marketing/Public Relations

As a marketing/public relations intern, you'll support the public relations department by preparing press releases and other written materials, fielding and responding to requests for information, contributing to the membership newsletter, updating the Web site, handling office tasks, and helping plan and execute special events. Special study opportunities focusing on Web design, market

research, or individually designed original programs are possible.

Programs

As an intern here, you'll help provide administrative support with daily operations of exhibits and programs department, gaining nonprofit management experience in a dynamic environment. At the end of the internship, your supervisor will provide a written evaluation and, if requested, a letter of recommendation. You must be registered for academic credit from a college or university for this internship.

Studios

The Children's Museum operates two year-round studios for all ages (the Clay Studio and Wonder Corner) and one studio for children age 6 and up (the Garage). These studios are free with admission and provide families with opportunities to explore a variety of art media. Activities are facilitated by studio guides, who encourage play and learning through inquiry, demonstration, and interaction with families. As a studio intern, you'll help the studio coordinator with ongoing program preparation, implementation, maintenance, documentation, and evaluation. You'll ensure the environment is physically and emotionally safe for young children and encourage creative exploration in positive, open-ended ways.

Textile Internship

As a textile intern, you'll help design and construct costumes and backdrops and oversee fabric inventory and the sewing room. You'll also help solicit donations for equipment and supplies. Additional projects may include designing and building soft sculptures, managing textile projects, and reorganizing the sewing room. You'll then document your internship through words, completed textile projects and photographs, and submit your final portfolio to the museum archives.

HOW TO APPLY

E-mail your resume and a letter of interest in a specific internship opportunity to the preceding address. The applicant will be contacted if he/she is eligible and if a position is currently available.

SAN DIEGO MUSEUM OF ART—EDUCATION INTERNSHIP

San Diego Museum of Art
1450 El Prado
Balboa Park
San Diego, CA 92101
(619) 232-7931
http://www.sdmart.org

What You Can Earn: The museum offers both paid ($3500) and unpaid internships; you also can earn college credit.
Application Deadlines: Unpaid internships are rolling; paid summer internship deadline is March 2.
Educational Experience: Upper-level undergrad or grad students studying education, art history, studio art, art education, or museum education.
Requirements: None specified.

OVERVIEW

The San Diego Museum of Art has been the region's primary resource for exhibitions and collections of fine art for more than 75 years. Located in the heart of Balboa Park, the galleries offer opportunities for learning, introspection, and connection with cultures from around the world.

Education department internships are designed to provide students with opportunities to apply classroom skills in a real-world environment while critically thinking about how the museum functions as a contemporary educational tool.

Unpaid Internships

Unpaid internship positions are available at various times throughout the year in hands-on classroom instruction, curriculum development, art history research and application, exhibition and program evaluation, and special event planning, promotion, and production.

Paid Summer Internship

The San Diego Museum of Art's education department offers a 10-week paid summer internship position designed to provide practical experience in a museum setting. The summer intern will work in the education department for about 40 hours a week. The internship is designed to encourage the intern to critically think about how a museum serves as a contemporary educational tool and how patrons of all ages can learn from their experiences in museum galleries and programs. Meetings with department heads, administrators, curators, and staff are arranged to provide a complete overview of museum operations.

During this internship, from early June to mid-August, you'll work in the museum's studios and galleries with a third grade inner-city elementary class, help in summer art camps, participate as an instructor in SDMA's quarterly Family Festival, research SDMA's permanent collection, and develop lesson plans, gallery tours, and studio-based projects. Interns will also spend time examining various developments in art education relating to standards-based curriculum in California and around the country. Funds for the summer internship position are provided by the Carolyn Wolf Educational Internship Program.

HOW TO APPLY

To apply, visit: http://www.sdmart.org/education-intern-form.html and submit the online application, which requires you to include one academic reference and one professional or personal reference.

To apply for the paid summer internship, e-mail your resume to rhernandez@sdmart.org.

SAN DIEGO ZOO'S WILD ANIMAL PARK SUMMER CAMP TEEN INTERNSHIP

San Diego Zoo
PO Box 120551
San Diego, CA 92112-0551

What You Can Earn: Unpaid.
Application Deadlines: Positions are usually posted on the employment opportunities page (http://zoocf.console.net/jobs/jobSearch.cfm) about March of each year.
Educational Experience: None specified.
Requirements: Aged 16 to 19 and available to work during the hours listed as follows.

OVERVIEW

Can you imagine spending your summer interning at a Wild Animal Park? As a summer camp intern, you'll work in one of two versions of the internship: Safari Sleepover or Summer Camp. Safari Sleepover student interns work weekends as part of the zoo's overnight camp program. Summer Camp interns work Monday through Friday as part of a teaching team for campers ages five to 12. These positions do not involve any animal contact or animal care, but you'll see firsthand the inner workings of the park while helping the zoo teachers with summer classes.

In addition, you'll get great experience to add to a job or college application, plus have a terrific time visiting off-exhibit areas and seeing exotic animals closer than you ever thought possible!

HOW TO APPLY

You can request application by visiting this Web site: http://zoocf.console.net/mailform/contact.cfm?ID=5. The application can be submitted at the preceding address.

SOUTH STREET SEAPORT MUSEUM INTERNSHIP

School & Docent Programs Coordinator
207 Front Street
New York, NY 10038
(212) 748-8600
Fax: (212) 748-8610
schoolprograms@southstseaport.org
http://www.southstreetseaportmuseum.org

What You Can Earn: Unpaid.
Application Deadlines: May 31.
Educational Experience: Undergrad or grad students; high school students fulfilling community service requirements are welcome, space and supervision permitting.
Requirements: Strong interpersonal skills, computer skills, and organizational skills. Experience working with children is strongly preferred. Interest in museum or education fields is helpful.

OVERVIEW

The mission of the South Street Seaport Museum is to preserve and interpret New York City's history as a great world port through exhibitions, publications, and an extensive and diverse array of educational and social-service programs. The museum's programs range from on-site, one hour-and-a-half interactive tours in the galleries to multiweek in-school residencies; from educational sails aboard the museum schooners to free month-long summer camps.

College and post-graduate internships during the academic year are offered (without stipends) in many areas of the museum. In the internship in the museum's education department, you'll work from June to August from 9:30 A.M. to 3:00 P.M. You'll work with the museum's education staff to tell the dramatic story of New York's historic seaport through educational programs for families, children, and museum visitors. This position will be required to teach programs to visiting youth groups on board the ships, to help with daily administrative duties in the education department, and to work on an extended focus project within the museum to be designed by the intern and his or her supervisor.

HOW TO APPLY

To apply for this internship, fax or e-mail your resume and cover letter to the preceding address.

TEACH FOR AMERICA NATIONAL INTERNSHIP

Director of Operational Support, Teach for America
315 W. 9th Street, Suite 950
Los Angeles, CA 90015
(213) 489-9272, ext. 120
Fax: (213) 489-9383
http://www.teachforamerica.org

What You Can Earn: Development internships pay $15 to $17 per hour; program internships are unpaid.
Application Deadlines: Rolling.
Educational Experience: See specific internship qualifications below.
Requirements: See specific internship qualifications below.

OVERVIEW

Teach For America is building the movement to address the achievement gap that exists between children growing up in low-income and high-income areas by rallying the nation's most promising future leaders to commit two years to teaching in urban and rural public schools. Since 1990, Teach For America has grown into a $38 million organization with more than 300 full-time staff members and 3,000 corps members teaching in 22 urban and rural regions across the country. The 9,000 alumni are starting schools and nonprofit organizations, advising lawmakers on policy and social issues, providing healthcare and public health education in low-income communities, and marshalling the resources of major corporations and law firms to effect social change. Recognized for its measurable results and strong operating principles, Teach For America has served as a model for other nonprofits and has been the subject of documentaries on PBS and CNN.

Development Internship

This internship is a part-time, temporary position requiring between 10 and 20 hours of work a week to provide support to the national development team on special projects and initiatives. This internship is ideal for someone interested in working within a successful national nonprofit organization and on a team that has led Teach For America's efforts to increase revenues by more than 300 percent within the last four years. The development intern will gather, catalog, and collect information necessary for grant reports and update proposals and supplementary materials. The intern also will do office work (such as copying, filing, and mailing), update the funder database, conduct research on the giving history of individuals and organizations, and work with Teach For America's regionally based teams to help them conduct funding research.

Candidates for this internship should be organized, detail-oriented graduate students with excellent oral communication skills interested in performing a critical role while learning in a fast-paced environment. The intern should be a highly responsive, professional, motivated self-starter, conscientious and able to manage multiple projects concurrently and independently. The ideal candidate will be comfortable learning to use new software applications.

Program Intern—Los Angeles

Program interns in Los Angeles may help work on special research projects related to teacher testing, credentialing, and placement; maintain filing systems; update database information; help with phone calls and paperwork; and help with school mailings and event planning. Interns also will help program directors prepare for meetings and retreats, attend classroom visits, coordinate and track resources, and help with general office duties (such as phones, mail, and data entry).

Interns should have strong interpersonal and communication skills and the ability to build relationships with a broad range of constituents. This position requires strategic thinking and constant learning, as well as the ability to prioritize and organize different initiatives and to learn from results. Strong writing skills, attention to detail, and a passion for nonprofit work are key qualifications. Candidates should be invested in Teach For America's vision that one day all children in the United States will have the opportunity to attain an excellent education.

Interns should plan on working in the office each day, although some flexibility is possible.

HOW TO APPLY
Applicants should submit a cover letter and resume to the preceding address.

UNIVERSITY OF THE MIDDLE EAST PROJECT INTERNSHIP

University of the Middle East
Internship Program
66 Church Street
Cambridge, MA
(617) 876-6261
http://www.ume.org

What You Can Earn: $500 to $1000 for approximately eight weeks.
Application Deadlines: End of May.

Educational Experience: Boston-based graduate students with concentrations in conflict resolution, the Middle East, or education are preferred. Arabic, Hebrew, or French language skills are a plus.
Requirements: Interns must have an interest in the Middle East.

OVERVIEW
The University of the Middle East Project (UME) is an independent nonprofit and nongovernmental organization whose objective is to provide opportunities for higher education for all the people and communities of the Middle East and North Africa (MENA). UME's ultimate goal is to create a system of interconnected academic centers throughout the MENA region.

Since its founding in 1997, UME has been operating advanced academic institutes in the United States, Spain, and Morocco. To date, UME has offered 12 institutes and has more than 230 alumni. During 2004, institutes included: the Teacher Education Institute in Boston, the Institute in Sustainable Development in Spain, the Education Leadership Institute in Spain, and an alumni reunion for former participants of the Teacher Education Institutes. The long-term vision of the Center for Higher Education in the Middle East Inc. is the creation of a system of linked university campuses throughout the Middle East and North Africa, which will provide a permanent network of interconnected academic centers that foster free thought, education, and coexistence for all communities in the region.

During its seven years of existence, the University of the Middle East Project has implemented programs in the fields of teacher education, sustainable development, and governance in Boston, Casablanca, and Toledo (Spain). Program participants are from 12 nations in the Middle East and North Africa who engage in an intensive one-month educational experience. UME programs are designed to enhance academic and practical skills, as well as to promote open communication and mutual respect and understanding.

Interns for this summer program will work closely with the UME program director to implement a program focusing on teacher education for secondary-school teachers from Algeria, Egypt, Israel, Jordan, Lebanon, Morocco, Palestine, and Tunisia. The intern's duties will include program administration, conflict prevention/resolution, logistical support, event planning, and research. Interns here assume a lot of responsibility and can have a profound effect on the organization and its activities.

HOW TO APPLY

To apply, contact the internship coordinator at the preceding address.

U.S. DEPARTMENT OF EDUCATION INTERNSHIP

Office of the Deputy Secretary
U.S. Department of Education
400 Maryland Avenue, SW, Room 7E230
Washington, DC 20202
202-401-5344
Ann.Nawaz@ed.gov
http://www.ed.gov/students/prep/job/intern/
index.html

What You Can Earn: Unpaid
Application Deadlines: Rolling.
Educational Experience: Must be enrolled full time in a high school, trade school, technical or vocational institute, junior college, college, university or other accredited educational institution.
Requirements: Must be at least 16.

OVERVIEW

The U.S. Department of Education provides educationally related work assignments for student interns as a way of acquainting you with the department's mission and helping you figure out your future career plans. Internships are available in specific offices and programs as well as types of work. Some examples of types of work include:

- policy analysis
- evaluation and research
- project and program management
- finance
- public affairs and communications
- external affairs and Intergovernmental relations
- legislative affairs
- technology systems
- legal work

HOW TO APPLY

You can find links to the application, the student volunteer service agreement, and the recommendation form at http://www.ed.gov/students/prep/job/intern/index.html.

To apply, send to the above address the completed application form, service agreement, recommendation form, a resume, and a cover letter describing your interests, including an explanation of what you might want to do in the Department of Education. This need not be a job in a specific education topic or area but one in management, finance, public affairs, technology services, policy analysis, evaluation, project or program management, external affairs, legislation and many others. The letter should also include approximate dates that you will be available for internship. You also should include a signed volunteer agreement. A writing sample also would be helpful.

Once your materials have been submitted, someone from the department will contact you by telephone or e-mail as a follow up for a placement.

U.S. HOLOCAUST MEMORIAL MUSEUM INTERNSHIP

Office of Volunteer and Intern Services
United States Holocaust Memorial Museum
100 Raoul Wallenberg Place, SW

Washington, DC 20024-2126
(202) 479-9738
http://www.ushmm.org/museum/volunteer_intern

What You Can Earn: Most are unpaid; only a few paid internships are available, and they are highly competitive.
Application Deadlines: June 15 for fall session; October 15 for spring session; March 15 for summer session.
Educational Experience: None specified.
Requirements: Knowledge of German, Russian, Greek, Yiddish, or Eastern European languages necessary for some internships.

OVERVIEW
The U.S. Holocaust Memorial Museum is dedicated to presenting the history of the persecution and murder of 6 million Jews and millions of other victims of Nazi tyranny from 1933 to 1945. The museum's mission is to inform Americans about this tragedy, to commemorate those who suffered, and to inspire visitors to contemplate the moral implications of their civic responsibilities. Many individuals must work together to accomplish this mission, including a dedicated team of capable interns.

As an intern with this museum, you'll be able to learn about the Holocaust and about museum operations, either during a half-time or full-time semester internship. Included are hands-on projects and opportunities to work with Holocaust scholars and museum professionals to learn about their roles, responsibilities, and backgrounds.

In the past, interns in the archives division have translated original documents into finders' aids for future scholars and have translated personal correspondence. Photo archives interns have organized specific photographs into collections for public and scholarly access. Interns in the Collections Division maintain new or borrowed artifacts for future generations learning about the Holocaust, while those in the Exhibitions Division plan and install special exhibitions. Academic Publications interns work on editing

materials submitted for the Journal of Holocaust and Genocide Studies as well as books and monographs that the Museum publishes, while Outreach Technology interns work on design and maintenance of the museum's Web site. These are just a few of the many positions available at the museum for internships.

HOW TO APPLY
Interested candidates can apply online at: http://www.ushmm.org/museum/volunteer_intern/intern/online_form/application.php.

In addition to the completed application form, you must submit a resume, your most recent certified academic transcript, two letters of recommendation, and a brief personal statement in addition to a cover letter. Candidates whose skills and talents meet the requirements for available positions will be contacted for a telephone interview.

THE WASHINGTON CENTER FOR INTERNSHIPS AND ACADEMIC SEMINARS

The Washington Center for Internships and Academic Seminars
2301 M Street, NW
5th Floor
Washington, DC 20037
(202) 336-7600; (800) 486-8921
Fax: (202) 336-7609
info@twc.edu
http://www.twc.edu

What You Can Earn: Unpaid; college credit is given, and the program's tuition is similar to a college semester (around $4,000).
Application Deadlines: There are a variety of deadlines (security deadlines, competitive dead-

lines, regular deadlines) for spring, summer, fall, and winter quarters, which vary year to year. Visit http://www.twc.edu/students/deadlines.html to check specific deadlines.

Educational Experience: Must be enrolled in an accredited college or university as a graduate student or a second-semester sophomore or above during the term of your internship; must maintain a GPA of at least 2.75; if your GPA is below 2.75, you need a third recommendation letter. Higher GPAs (minimum 3.0) may be required for federal agencies such as the U.S. Departments of Justice and State, the U.S. Attorney's Office, and the Cable News Network (CNN).

Requirements: Must receive academic credit from your college or university for your participation in the internship program. The Washington Center does not grant academic credit.

OVERVIEW

For the past 30 years, the nonprofit Washington Center for Internships and Academic Seminars has provided challenging internships for selected students in Washington, D.C., a world capital rich in intellectual and cultural diversity that offers students an incredible range of internship opportunities. The nation's capital is home to thousands of corporations and businesses; embassies; volunteer organizations; interest groups; cultural and scientific organizations; law and lobbying firms; trade associations; and major media headquarters (not to mention the White House, the federal government, and congressional offices).

Students accepted by The Washington Center are assigned according to their interests to an internship program in one of these locations, guided by professional program advisors who counsel, place, supervise, and help evaluate students, as well as organize activities during the times when students are not at their internships.

Because of the wide variety of public, private, and nonprofit organizations located in Washington, D.C., The Washington Center can successfully place students from any academic major. Interested officials at possible placement sites contact students by phone to talk about the organization and the projects to which you would be assigned. The student then chooses the placement he or she wants. Interns become involved in a wide variety of projects, such as helping to write business plans for arts organizations; studying legislative proposals for tax incentives for renewable energy producers; supporting a health clinic director in a low-income neighborhood; planning a conference for an international food group; devising marketing strategies for professional sports teams; producing television broadcasts for Spanish-language stations; reviewing budget requests from federal agencies; and monitoring Congressional committees or creating databases for engineering firms.

The Main Program

This internship places students in many different areas, including health and human services, science and mathematics, the arts, and public administration. Students in the Main Program are assigned a program advisor and, like all Washington Center interns, take a class (one of 25 to 35 offered each semester). Placements for students in the Main Program have varied widely but have included the Kennedy Center for the Performing Arts, National Institutes of Health, District of Columbia Department of Health, Arena Stage, among hundreds of others. Internships last four or four and a half days a week.

Americas Leaders Program

This program gives students exposure to international trade agreements, multilateral organizations, cross-cultural communication, business relations and cooperation amongst nations, and international laws and regulations. Internships have been arranged at the Council of the Americas; Embassy of Canada; Embassy of Mexico; Hispanic Council on International Relations; General Electric; Business Administration; U.S.-Brazil Business Council; U.S. Chamber of Commerce; U.S. Trade Representative; and The World Bank, among many others. Internships in this program are four days a week. In addition, students in this program take courses related to international business and trade.

Banking and Finance Program

In this internship, students interested in banking and financial literacy learn how to become successful financial experts and leaders. Internships include Bank of America; Capital Partners; GE Capital; International Financial Corporation; International Monetary Fund; Legg Mason; Merrill Lynch; Morgan Stanley; Prudential Investments; Riggs Bank; and the U.S. Department of the Treasury. Internships in this program are four and a half days a week.

Business and Information Technology Program

This internship program prepares students for careers in finance, economics, accounting, human resource management, business administration, and information technology. Placements have included the U.S. Department of Commerce; U.S. Small Business Administration; U.S. Department of the Treasury; National Association of Manufacturers; Merrill Lynch; and Business Software Alliance and the Business/Industry Political Action Committee, among many others.

Congressional Leadership Program

In this internship, students intern with members of Congress, congressional committees, political party organizations, and interest groups. Students have the opportunity to work on a variety of issues, such as national defense, homeland security, environmental protection, tax policy, social security, healthcare, and the Middle East peace process. In this program, students meet policymakers and other influential figures as part of additional programming.

Environment and Energy Program

If you're interested in a career in the environmental field, this internship is for you. Participants learn about policy issues such as nuclear-waste disposal, pesticide management, and energy-resource development. Students in this program have interned with the National Wildlife Association, Friends of the Earth, Council on Environmental Quality, Environmental Health Center, Senate Committee on Natural Resources, U.S. Environmental Protection Agency, and the Chemical Manufacturers Association. Internships are four and a half days a week, and students are required to take a course on environmental policy. Some placements require a minimum 3.0 GPA; this program is not available to students whose schools run on a quarter basis.

International Affairs Program

This internship prepares students for careers in international affairs, specializing in human rights, national security, international trade, global women's rights, refugees, and conflict resolution. Placement sites have included the U.S. Department of State, Amnesty International, National Defense University, Embassy of Paraguay, the Center for Strategic and International Studies, and the United Nations Association, among many others. Internships are four and a half days a week. A minimum GPA of 3.0 is recommended for students who want a summer internship in this area.

Law and Criminal Justice Program

This program prepares students for careers in law, civil litigation, law enforcement, administration of justice, criminal defense and prosecution, and environmental law. The program introduces students to basic legal writing and research and provides training in public speaking. Placement sites have included the U.S. Department of Justice, Interpol, U.S. Attorney's Office, U.S. Marshals Service, Federal Bureau of Prisons, D.C. Office of the Public Defender, and various private law firms, among many others. Internships are four and a half days a week

Mass Communications Program

If you're interested in journalism and communication, this program prepares you for careers in print and broadcast journalism, production, advertising, public relations, photography, electronic communication, and graphic design. Placement sites have included the White House Media Affairs Office; congressional press offices, *USA Today*; CNN; *America's Most Wanted*; Tribune Broadcasting; C-SPAN; CBS News; National Press Club; *The Washington Times*; Tribune Broadcasting; Talk News Radio; BET; Univision; and many more. Internships are four and a half days a week. Applicants for the summer term should use the competitive deadline.

NAFTA Leaders Program

This program is open to students from the United States, Mexico, and Canada who want to understand and facilitate the opportunities of the North American Free Trade Agreement (NAFTA). Students have regular meetings with leading international policymakers to discuss issues related to North American trade integration. Internships have been obtained at the embassies of Canada and Mexico, the World Bank, U.S. Chamber of Commerce, Inter-American Development Bank, Canadian Business Council, office of The U.S. Trade Representative, NAFTA Secretariat, and many more agencies and organizations. Internships are four days a week. Candidates should have a minimum GPA of 3.5 and attend a university on the trimester system.

Nonprofit Leaders Program

This internship provides firsthand professional experience with the nonprofit sector, including trade associations and advocacy and social-action organizations. Interns also take part in a service project and learn how they can market themselves successfully to nonprofit organizations. Internship sites have included Amnesty International; U.S. Commission on Civil Rights; Oxfam America; Human Rights Campaign; Global Health Council; Share our Strength; U.S. Commission on Civil Rights; Points of Light Foundation; Physicians for Social Responsibility; and National Mental Health Association.

HOUSING

The Washington Center guarantees its interns excellent, upscale housing in apartment buildings in Northern Virginia, Washington, D.C, and suburban Maryland in well-lit, high-traffic neighborhoods that provide security and comfortable surroundings.

HOW TO APPLY

To apply online (which is preferred), visit this Web site to begin the process: http://www.twc.edu/students/online-application.html.

The application is available for download as a printable pdf at http://www.twc.edu/students/PDF/2005application.pdf. You are welcome to print the document, fill in your responses to questions, and mail the completed packet to the enrollment services office at the preceding address.

Your essays and your resume are important components of your application. The issues essay is a 750-word statement in which you discuss two topics that involve the field in which you hope to work. You should provide your personal views on at least one of these topics. This is not a research paper but rather an opportunity for you to demonstrate that you have a serious interest and some background knowledge about issues in the field in which you wish to work. In your 100-word internship-request statement, you should describe the types of activities in which you'd like to be involved during your internship and how these activities relate to your career goals. Your resume should clearly outline your educational, volunteer, leadership, and work experience to date.

ENTERTAINMENT

ACADEMY OF TELEVISION ARTS AND SCIENCES FOUNDATION INTERNSHIP

Academy Foundation—Internships
5220 Lankershim Boulevard
North Hollywood, CA 91601-3109
(818)754-2830
http://www.emmys.tv/foundation/education.php

What You Can Earn: Interns are paid a $4,000 stipend in three installments over the summer. Interns will be responsible for their own housing, transportation, and living expenses. Interns must have a car for transportation in Los Angeles. In most cases, it is not possible to rent a car without incurring a surcharge if you are under the age of 25. In all cases, a major credit card is required for rental.

Application Deadlines: March 15 for summer internship (selections are made in April); most internships start in late June or early July and end eight weeks after the start date. The music category usually starts in August.

Educational Experience: Full-time undergraduate or graduate college students with appropriate experience (see intern categories for experience requirements).

Requirements: Students who have completed college or graduate school prior to January 1, 2003 are not eligible. Non-U.S. citizens must submit an INS work authorization permit or CPT letter with application materials to be considered for an ATAS Foundation internship.

OVERVIEW

If the TV industry seems like a good career move to you, you may want to check out ATAS College Student Internship Program, which offers 38 eight-week paid summer internships in 29 categories of telecommunications work. The program is a national competition and for the last 10 years has been selected as one of the top 10 U.S. internship programs of any kind by the Princeton Review's "America's Top Internships." All internships are served during the summer in the Los Angeles area, and each intern is mentored by a former intern.

The Academy Foundation Internships are designed to provide qualified full-time undergraduate and graduate students pursuing degrees at U.S. universities with in-depth exposure to professional TV production, techniques, and practices, mostly in the Los Angeles area. Although administrative and production duties will be assigned to all interns, collective bargaining agreements within the industry mean some internships won't be able to have "hands-on" experience in certain areas.

The categories for which you could serve an internship include one of the following 29 areas: agency; animation (traditional); animation (nontraditional); art direction/production design; broadcast advertising and promotion; business affairs; casting; children's programming or development; cinematography; commercials; costume design; development (TV); documentary/nonfiction production; editing; entertainment news; episodic series; game shows; interactive media; made-for-TV movies; music; post-production; production management; public relations and publicity; sound; syndication/distribution; TV directing (multicamera); and TV directing (single camera).

Agency

This agency represents actors, directors, producers, or writers. Intern activities include handling phones, general office duties, script reading, and meetings. Minimum requirements include a liberal arts/business background, writing ability, and verbal and social skills. You should have a strong desire to enter agency or entertainment management.

Animation (Nontraditional)

This internship emphasizes computer-generated animation. Desirable background includes art, animated character development, computer skills, theatre arts, film, or writing. All applicants must submit a videocassette of an animation project (1/2" VHS) and a storyboard, preferably of work submitted. No slides.

Animation (Traditional)

With this emphasis on cel animation, interns ideally should have a background in art, theatre arts, film, or writing. All applicants must submit a drawing portfolio, a video cassette of animation projects, and a storyboard (with an emphasis on hand-drawing; cassette must be 1/2" VHS). No slides will be accepted.

Art Direction/Production Design

Located in an art department of a major studio or production company, interns will be exposed to set design, construction, dressing, painting, graphics, and practical locations adapted for TV production. Minimum requirements include theatre set design and/or architectural background, including drafting. All applicants must submit a portfolio of executed work, including set photographs, drafting, designs, renderings, sketches, or photographs of models. No slides will be accepted.

Broadcast Advertising and Promotion

Interns will work at a commercial television station, with exposure to all aspects of TV-station advertising, promotions, and publicity. There will be an emphasis on print advertising, on-air campaigns, and press-information relations. Minimum requirements include courses in broadcast advertising and promotion, advertising/marketing, and/or journalism, plus a demonstrated and creative interest in broadcast promotion.

Business Affairs

Interns will work in a studio, network or independent production company business/legal department, observing and participating in the negotiation for acquisition of material, employment of creative personnel, and license agreements between the network and program supplier. Minimum requirements include law or business major or TV/film major with business/management courses.

Casting

This opportunity will be located in a studio casting department or the office of a casting director and will include arranging readings and lots of phone work and clerical duties. Interns interested in casting should have great organizational skills, excellent people skills, and knowledge of television, movies, and theatre. A liberal arts/communications background is helpful.

Children's Programming/Development

This network/cable opportunity will include an overview of development and production of animated and live-action children's programs. Interns will review scripts and sell ideas to the networks and cable. Desirable background includes literature arts/communications.

Cinematography

Located at a TV/film studio, this internship opportunity will involve handling equipment and exposure to film production for prime-time TV. Minimum requirements include a strong motion picture/video/photography background; in addition, all applicants are required to submit a work sample on 1/2" VHS. Original work can be film or tape.

Commercials

This experience will take place in a commercial agency, production house, and post-production facility. Interns will participate in product conception, organization, production, and post-production of commercials. Students should have a TV/film production major/minor.

Costume Design

Interns will work in wardrobe departments at studios and independent companies, participating in preproduction meetings; prepping shows through to taping and filming; and helping a designer or costumer in wardrobe purchase, rental, and made-to-order. Interns should have a theatre costume design and/or fashion design background. All applicants must submit a sample of their work. (Photographs of portfolio contents are preferred but no more than 10.) No slides.

Development (TV)
At this studio or production company, interns will observe and participate in the evaluation of program ideas and literary materials, selection of writers, and oversight of script development. Interns should have a background in creative writing, literature, theatre arts, or liberal arts/communications.

Documentary/Nonfiction Production
At this production company or cable network, interns are exposed to the production of documentaries and/or reality specials, segments, or series. The job includes research, studio/location production, and post-production. Interns should have a background in documentary production, research, writing, and computer skills. There is the possibility of placement outside the Los Angeles area with this category.

Editing
At this studio or production company, interns will observe post-production of episodic, MOW or miniseries, with exposure to film/tape nonlinear systems. Interns should have taken film-editing and tape-editing courses. All applicants are required to submit a sample of film editing on 1/2" VHS (suggested length: 10 minutes).

Entertainment News
At a production facility, interns will observe and participate in day-to-day entertainment industry news-gathering and broadcasting activities. Minimum requirements include TV production and journalism courses and basic computer skills.

Episodic Series
At a studio or production company, interns will observe the production process of a current series, including script development, preproduction, filming/taping, and post-production. Interns should have a commitment to a career in television production.

Game Show
At offices and studios in the L.A. area, interns will help produce and develop original programming for the network, working with programming department staff and outside producers to manage creative and production issues. Minimum requirements include a passion for and knowledge of game shows; production and/or development experience is a plus. Interns must be able to work long hours, multitask, and be self-starters and team players.

Interactive Media
At this network, studio, production company, and interactive agency, interns will work on the creation and delivery of interactive content that enhances the television experience. Minimum requirements include courses in TV/film production and/or creative writing/storytelling, as well as familiarity with interactive technologies and platforms.

Made-for-TV Movies
Interns will handle preproduction, production, and production-assistant duties. Minimum requirements include a production background and a commitment to a career in TV production. Out-of-town placement is possible.

Music
At a production company and studios in August through September, interns will handle music production (electronic and orchestral), sound design, recording, editing, studio set-up, software, and hardware installation. Minimum requirements include a music background, a strong interest in music for TV/film, electronic aptitude, and familiarity with music-production software. All applicants must submit five short samples of original compositions on 1/2" VHS or audio cassettes.

Post-production

At a post-production facility, interns will be exposed to all aspects of post-production. Interns must have completed a videotape editing course; all candidates are required to submit a sample of videotape editing on 1/2"VHS only (suggested length: 10 minutes).

Production Management

At a studio or production company, interns will organize, schedule, and budget productions, with some production-assistant and general-office duties. Interns should be majoring in TV/film and have computer skills.

Programming Management

At a network or cable company, interns will be introduced to entertainment program development and current programming and attend pitch, notes and staff meetings, view production dailies, and visit sets. Minimum requirements include knowledge of TV. Interns should major in liberal arts, communications, or business. Finalists are required to submit script synopsis and evaluation upon notification.

Public relations and publicity

At a public relations firm or entertainment company in-house public relations department, interns will research and write news releases, help contact all media press, and attend meetings and news events. Minimum requirements include strong writing skills. Major or minor must be in public relations, journalism, communications, publicity, or English.

Sound

At an audio post-production facility, interns will be exposed to all aspects of production and post-production sound, along with sound editing, mixing, transfer and studio management techniques, sound effects, music, Foley, and dialogue. Minimum requirements include some music and/or sound effects editing and mixing experience, with a basic understanding of electronics, sound equipment, and computers. Interns should be committed to a career in audio production.

Syndication/Distribution

At a major studio, interns will observe all facets of sales, marketing, promotion, and program development/production in both domestic and international markets (emphasizing domestic). Interns should have a strong interest in marketing, communications, research, and/or sales.

TV Directing (Multi-camera)

At a TV station or production company, interns will get an overview of the directing process using multicamera videotape and/or film format, observing productions such as soaps, episodic, variety, and specials (but not news or sports.) Interns should have taken courses in directing and editing and have experience on electronic cameras. Only finalists are required to submit a work sample on 1/2 " cassette upon notification (VHS).

TV Directing (Single camera)

Interns will have an overview of the directing process using multicamera videotape and/or film format, observing on productions such as soaps, episodic, variety, specials (not news or sports). Minimum requirements include courses in directing and editing and experience on electronic cameras. Only finalists are required to submit a work sample on 1/2 " VHS.

TV Scriptwriting

Interns get an overview of comedy or drama writing process that may include idea inception, story meetings, revisions, and production. Minimum requirements: Strong writing background. Applicants must submit an original scene (approximately four pages) from a current comedy or drama series and a logline for the scene/episode they are submitting. Finalists must submit a complete original script (series episode, longform, or play) upon notification.

HOW TO APPLY

This is a rigorous program, so get prepared for some tough competition. To apply for an Academy Foundation internship, you may choose only one category and submit the following materials:

The cover page of your application must indicate your name; permanent home address and phone number; college or university and expected graduation date; address and phone while attending college; status (freshman, sophomore, junior, senior, or graduate student); major/minor and GPA; and the number and title of the category for which you're applying. (See categories above, in the overview section.) In addition, you should include a statement of 300 to 400 words discussing your professional objectives and the specific reasons for your choice of category, along with a copy of your resume and three letters of recommendation addressed to the Internship Committee (mailed with your entry, if possible). You'll also need to include transcripts of all college courses and grades (both college and graduate school, if applicable); unofficial photocopies will be accepted.

All finalists must submit a videotaped interview on 1/2" VHS in response to questions posed in the notice of final candidacy. Do not send any material other than as requested. No fax or e-mail entries will be accepted.

ACTORS THEATRE WORKSHOP INTERNSHIP

The Actors Theatre Workshop, Inc.
145 West 28th Street, Third Floor
New York, NY 10001
(212) 947-1386
(212) 947-0642
info@actorstheatreworkshop.com
http://www.actorstheatreworkshop.com

What You Can Earn: Unpaid.
Application Deadlines: Rolling.
Educational Experience: Background in theater or acting desirable.

Requirements: Current enrollment in college or university.

OVERVIEW

ATW's internship program provides young people with education in nonprofit theatre administration, programming, and production. The program is open to college undergraduates and recent graduates with a career interest in nonprofit arts management and to individuals considering a career change into the nonprofit arena. The program begins with a one-week training program in theatre operations conducted by senior staff members and enriched by reading essays written by ATW's artistic director and founder, Thurman E. Scott, and viewing videotape documentaries of past programs and productions. The training period allows interns to learn about ATW's mission and creative philosophy while learning about its operations. Interns are then assigned responsibility for focus areas within theatre administration, programming, and production.

In addition to hands-on work at the theatre, interns have the opportunity to develop creatively by participating in meetings, planning sessions, and discussions. ATW's goal for the internship program is to provide motivated individuals with the skills to manage nonprofit arts organizations, become part of New York's cultural community, and develop skills to develop their careers. Interns receive hands-on experience in both theater management and acting technique, working in theater administration, production, marketing, development, fund-raising, facility upkeep, video, and graphic design.

For example, an intern working in theatre management will manage the daily administrative operations of the organization and take a leadership role in programming. The intern will work closely with the artistic director and other members of the management team to produce classes and workshops for professional actors and community programs that serve at-risk youth and homeless children. Under the supervision of the ATW staff, interns in theatre management will be accountable for the completion of projects in management of ATW's studio rental business, theater administration, team management, marketing, development, sales, fund-raising, video production, event production, and graphic design.

Founded more than 20 years ago, ATW is an established pioneer in nonprofit theatre committed to producing classical and contemporary plays, developing new dramatic works, and training and developing actors, writers, and directors while making a difference in the lives of homeless children and the community at large. A creative development laboratory built by strong, experienced creative leadership, ATW's mission is to teach individuals from all walks of life original creative techniques that provide them with the tools to change, and to create new theatre that examines the conflicts that have emerged from today's cultural mix and create hope for fulfillment in the human experience.

ATW is open seven days a week from 10:00 A.M. to 10:00 P.M. and offers internships ranging from four months to a year or during the academic semesters of fall, winter, spring, and summer. This is a full-time internship (40 hours per week), but a limited number of part-time internships are available. ATW will work with each intern to determine a weekly schedule (including days, evenings, or a combination of both) that accommodates both need and availability. It's important that you make secure financial and living arrangements.

HOW TO APPLY

If you're interested in this internship, submit a letter of interest, your resume, and an internship application to the preceding address. In your letter, mention talents, skills, and resources that you feel could contribute to the management and vision of ATW. You can print an online application at http://www.actorstheatreworkshop.com/support/internship.html#. You also can fax your application to the preceding number.

Prior to the interview, ATW requires you to visit the Web site at and review the organization's background, creative leadership, and essays that articulate the creative foundation on which ATW is built.

AMERICAN CONSERVATORY THEATER INTERNSHIP

Internship Coordinator
American Conservatory Theater
30 Grant Avenue
San Francisco, CA 94108-5800

What You Can Earn: $6.75 an hour. All interns (except assistant directors) receive California minimum wage (currently $6.75/hour). Assistant director interns receive a competitive stipend. As a result of the high cost of living in the San Francisco area, all applicants must have additional independent funding for living expenses while living here. Production interns should be aware that, due to the variable hours of the program and the intense nature of the work, it's impossible to hold an outside job during the production internship period. However, while interns in the administrative and artistic departments require a professional level of commitment, hours are generally flexible, and work schedules that accommodate outside employment may be arranged with each department's intern supervisor.

Application Deadlines: April 15 (production positions); applicants will be notified by June 15. Administrative and artistic department internship applications are accepted year round.

Educational Experience: No particular degree is required for any of these internships, except the assistant director internship, which requires an MFA in directing or equivalent experience. Internships in the artistic and administrative departments also may be suited to those taking a break from college. These internships are not generally appropriate for high school students. A background that includes practical theater experience is preferred for all internships, although not required for the marketing/public relations internship.

Requirements: Specific requirements are listed below, depending on internship selected. In general, artistic and administrative department internships require a two-month commitment; however, an exceptional intern may be accepted for the duration of winter break. Most production department internships require a commitment of an entire season.

OVERVIEW

If you love to smell the greasepaint and hear the roar of the crowds, you may be interested in interning with the American Conservatory Theater (ACT), one of the nation's largest and most active resident professional theaters. Internships here include arts management, costume rental, costume shop, lighting design, makeup and wig construction, marketing/public relations, production management, sound design, technical design, and stage management.

ACT's internship program provides advanced training in both theater production and administration to students who want to work closely with top professionals in each field. ACT internships are springboards to a professional life in the theater.

As a result of the theater's schedule, there are no production internships during the summer; instead, these internships are seasonal positions that run approximately August through June. The theater does offer artistic and administrative internships during the summer months, however, depending on the needs of each department.

A monthly series of intern roundtables with guest speakers provides an overview of the creative work throughout the organization. Topics include a discussion of ACT's mission statement with the artistic director, a portfolio and resume workshop, and a tour of ACT's scene shop and costume shop. Interns receive complimentary tickets to all ACT productions, as well as the opportunity to attend other Bay Area theaters through reciprocal ticket agreements. Interns are also encouraged to attend student projects, brown-bag lunches with guest artists, and all audience events.

Artistic and Administrative

Several internships are available throughout the year in ACT's artistic and administrative departments for students interested in learning all aspects of managing a large repertory theater. These internships are suitable for students in many different majors seeking a professional life in the theater. You've got to have lots of energy and initiative, as well as the ability to focus on projects in many areas, along with excellent writing skills and some knowledge of computers. The length of the commitment and details of the daily schedule depend on your own availability and the department's needs, but a minimum two-month commitment is required.

Arts Management

In this area, you'll work with all aspects of the artistic and administrative departments, helping in casting, season planning, play development, budgeting, board relations, and visiting-artist support. This internship is designed for people interested in a career as an artistic manager or artistic or managing director. You must be sensitive, quick to learn, organized, and energetic and be willing to take initiative. You should have experience in theater production, a working knowledge of theater history, and good verbal/written communication skills. Experience with Microsoft Word, Excel, Outlook, and Filemaker Pro (for PC) is helpful. Candidates for this department internship must submit a writing sample with their applications.

Assistant Director Internship

Interns in this area may be invited to help direct a single ACT production. You'll also be given the chance to work closely with nationally known directors and actors, learning the directing job through the rehearsal process and previews to the opening-night performance. You also may participate in dramaturgical research, writing, or leading panel discussions. A full-time commitment of at least five weeks, corresponding with the rehearsal period for the production, is required. This internship requires a master's degree in drama, theater, or fine arts, with an emphasis on directing or equivalent related experience. You also may apply if you're currently enrolled in a graduate program similar to those listed above.

Costume Shop Intern

You'll work closely with the ACT costume staff in creating costumes for the stage, participating in meetings with the costume shop manager, directors, stage managers, and designers as the working plots for new productions are developed. You'll learn how to produce costumes from all time periods, including corsetry and millinery, and learn the ins and outs of the daily operation and maintenance of a full-season costume shop.

Costume Rentals Intern

Located in the same facility as the ACT costume shop, the costume rentals department maintains its own office and schedule, usually working a full 40-hour week. As an intern with the rental staff, you'll be responsible for maintaining ACT's large stock of period costumes as well as renting costumes to the public for business, personal, and theatrical use. Design ability is required, and you'll gain experience in period costume selection and identification, as well as the ability to create a unifying look by matching a variety of garments. You must have the ability to work well with people and also deal with the public as well as professional theater and film designers. You'll also get experience providing rehearsal costumes to mainstage ACT productions and creating new garments. The limited fabrication of accessories and hair is also usually a feature of the program. This position is seasonal and requires a commitment from August through May.

Development Intern

As a development intern, you'll help with fundraising activities and develop a thorough under-

standing of the essentials of nonprofit and performing arts fund-raising. Candidates must demonstrate strong organizational, writing, editing, and research skills and must submit a writing sample with their application. Experience with Microsoft Word and Excel is required.

Lighting Design Intern

You must have a strong background and experience in theatrical lighting for this internship, as you'll work as the assistant to the resident lighting designer in mounting each production. Your full-time responsibilities include attending all production meetings, maintaining records necessary for the upkeep of the light plot and inventory, drafting designs for special effects, and assisting the designers in the theater from focus calls to opening. A good sense of leadership is required, as it will occasionally be necessary to act in the resident designer's absence. The lighting intern must attend all technical and dress rehearsals for each of the mainstage productions of the season. This position parallels the production season.

Literary/Publications Internship

These interns help with dramaturgical research and evaluating and processing submitted scripts and also may become involved in readings. Interns also help the publications staff with dramaturgical research, writing, and editing of production study guides, as well as programs and subscriber newsletters. For this internship, you should demonstrate interest and experience in dramatic literature, criticism, and production (excellent writing skills and interest and experience in publishing are also helpful); you must submit a writing sample with the application.

Marketing/Public Relations Internship

In this position, you'll work closely with the communications staff, learning the essentials of arts marketing and public relations, developing promotions and helping to produce sales materials such as ads or brochures. In the public relations department, you'll learn the basics of public and press relations by helping in day-to-day operations and observing long-range strategy sessions. You also may participate in editing and proofing media releases, helping to maintain the press list, assembling press kits, staffing the opening night press table, archive maintenance, accompanying artists to and from press engagements, and handling information requests. You should be extremely detail oriented, with great general office skills, including a working knowledge of Microsoft Word, Excel, and Publisher. Experience in proofing and editing copy is highly desirable. The intern must be outgoing and have excellent written and verbal communication skills. A background in theater is preferred but not necessary.

Production Interns

ACT also offers production internships in each of the previous areas on a one-show-only basis. The time commitment is shorter, but the full-time nature of the position, duties, and experience required are the same as the seasonal internships. Dates of commitment vary depending on the production.

ACT is accredited by the Accrediting Commission of Senior Colleges and Universities of the Western Association of Schools and Colleges. Some schools translate the intern experience into academic units.

Production Management Intern

This intern works directly under the supervision of the production manager and is involved with the work of production department heads, stage managers, crews, and designers, as well as directors, actors, and other artists. You'll learn about season schedule and budget planning, contracts, design development, and the daily workings of the production department, developing a thorough understanding of the organization and operation of the production department. This is a good internship if you're interested in a career as a technical manager or as an artistic or managing director. A background in theater is required and technical training or stage management experience is very helpful. These full-time internships typically involve irregular schedules, depending on the needs of the production calendar.

Properties Intern

The properties intern works closely with the ACT properties staff in constructing properties for the stage and meeting with the properties master, directors, stage managers, and designers as the working plots for new productions are developed.

Sound Design Intern

You'll work with the resident sound designer in mounting each production, so experience with studio techniques is required and a familiarity with theater is highly recommended. You'll work closely with the designer in determining the artistic and technical needs for all shows, attending all technical and dress rehearsals and working in the sound studio to create each show's requirements.

Stage Management Interns

This area offers a training ground for a highly motivated student interested in getting some hands-on stage management experience in a professional theater. You'll become an integral member of the stage management team by working alongside the ACT stage management staff on productions, helping to develop and produce the shows to which you're assigned. Candidates must demonstrate lots of energy and initiative and maintain sensitivity to the demands and complexities of the rehearsal process. Stage management experience is required, and a background in acting and technical theater is helpful. Since you'll be working closely with the professional ACT staff, a full-time commitment is essential; working hours will be irregular with early morning rehearsal calls and evening performances. Interns are sometimes eligible to join the Actors' Equity Membership Candidacy Program.

Technical Design Intern

You'll work under the direction of the design associate and the technical supervisor to learn design techniques and construction methods developed by ACT staff. You'll concentrate on drafting and model building, so good skills in both areas are necessary. In addition, you'll maintain research files and have the opportunity to observe ACT's designers, scenic artists, and technicians at work.

Finalists will be asked to submit portfolios. This position requires a commitment concurrent with the production season.

Wig Construction/Makeup Intern

This intern will work under the supervision of the wigmaster, learning to construct hand-tied wigs and facial hair along with some special effects items. You'll also work backstage, maintaining wigs during performances and learning makeup techniques. Focus, concentration, and attention to detail are important. This position is seasonal and runs concurrently with the performing season.

HOUSING

The ACT Conservatory office and the production department have some information regarding housing, but finding a place to live is your responsibility. Rentals can be expensive, and most interns and students share rentals on a monthly basis.

Most areas of San Francisco and the Bay Area are easily accessible via public transportation. Parking in the city is difficult and expensive, and most interns find they can do without a car quite well.

HOW TO APPLY

If you're interested in an internship during the summer months, you should apply by the end of March, because these internships are quite popular.

To apply, first download an application (you'll need Adobe Acrobat to view the application). To request an application by mail, call the internship hotline (415-439-2447) and leave your name and address.

Submit the application and resume along with a personal statement of 500 words or less including your career objectives and how you expect to achieve them; what you expect from an ACT internship; your academic credentials; your experience and/or education in theater; and the qualities you possess that recommend you as a candidate

for an internship. Your personal statement should reveal information about yourself that may not be apparent in your resume or recommendations.

You also must include one short, nonfiction writing sample if you're applying for the arts management, literary/publications, or development internship (such as a college research paper or college newspaper article) together with three letters of recommendation from employers, professors, or mentors from different areas of your life who know you well and who can speak to your skills, abilities, and goals. These letters may be submitted separately, but they must be received by the April 15 deadline for production department internships.

Mail all of the materials, together with a $15 nonrefundable application fee, to the preceding address. A response is given within one month.

AMERICAN DANCE FESTIVAL INTERNSHIP

American Dance Festival Internship Program
Duke University, Box 90772
Durham, NC 27708
(919) 684-6402
adf@americandancefestival.org
http://www.americandancefestival.org

What You Can Earn: Between $950 and $1,100 for the summer, plus one free dance class daily and free tickets to many performances.
Application Deadlines: February 15.
Educational Experience: Experience in dance is helpful.
Requirements: None.

OVERVIEW

The American Dance Festival was founded in Bennington, Vermont, by dance enthusiasts Martha

Graham, Hanya Holm, Doris Humphrey, and Charles Weidman, eventually moving in 1978 to the sprawling green lawns, studios, offices, and dormitories of Duke University in Durham, North Carolina. Today the festival presents performances by a variety of leading dance companies and dancers and offers educational programs to an international group of more than 600 students in the summer.

Interns interested in dance can intern in a variety of situations with the dance festival and school, including archives, box office, press, finance, merchandising, performances, production, special projects, and support services. Depending on the area where you're interning, you might help put together press packets, help with performance productions, manage the ADF store, or publishing daily calendars of activities. You'll also get to participate in a weekly intern seminar with a special guest speaker, earn one free dance class each day, receive free tickets to a range of performances, and attend a variety of seminars and discussions.

HOW TO APPLY

You can download the application from the Web site; application information typically is posted to the Web site by Thanksgiving for the next summer's internship program. To apply, submit the application along with a resume and cover letter explaining your interests and what you hope to get out of the internship.

ARENA STAGE INTERNSHIP

Fellows and Interns Program Coordinator
Arena Stage
1101 Sixth Street, SW
Washington, DC 20024
(202) 554-9066

Fax: (202) 488-4056
interns@arenastage.org

What You Can Earn: Modest stipend and help in finding housing.

Application Deadlines: March 1 for summer (directing and technical production apprenticeships are not available during the summer); April 1 for fall and season internship and Allen Lee Hughes fellowship; October 1 for winter/spring internship.

Educational Experience: Undergraduate or graduate students, recent graduates, and career changers interested in pursuing a career in the professional theater; minority applicants are strongly encouraged; the Allen Lee Hughes fellow must be a minority college graduate with arts-related experience and training.

Requirements: A passion for the exploration of the human condition through dramatic forms.

OVERVIEW

The goal of the Arena Stage internship program is to cultivate the next generation of theater professionals by providing the highest standard of training through immersion in the art and business of producing theater. Arena Stage provides in-depth, hands-on experiences with seasoned professionals in the areas of artistic and technical production, arts administration, and community engagement.

Allen Lee Hughes Fellowship

This program was established to increase participation of people of color in professional theater. One of the first theater-run apprenticeships in the country dedicated exclusively to providing the highest standard of training to minorities, the program explains that it is trying to break the cycle of exclusion and disengagement that has created a severe shortage of trained minority arts administrators, artisans, and technicians. Fellowships require a 40- to 44-week commitment to working with seasoned professionals in artistic and technical production, arts administration, and community involvement.

Internship Program

The Arena Stage internship program demonstrates its dedication to quality training through the program's flexibility. Time periods for internships are flexible; however, all internships are full time. Internships are available on a semester or full-season schedule, although some may follow a production cycle of six to eight weeks. Consecutive internships in two departments, as well as summer internships, may be arranged.

INTERNSHIPS AND FELLOWSHIPS

The following departments are available for both internships and Allen Lee Hughes fellows. Because specific internships are not always available, you should call the stage to ask about the availability of particular openings.

Artistic Opportunities

Directing

This position (not available during the summer) provides an opportunity to observe and assist the director throughout the rehearsal period, attend production meetings, and support the artistic process. The selected applicant works on one or more shows of an eight-play season.

Literary

This is an opportunity to gain administrative and practical experience in dramaturgy and literary management, critiquing scripts, conducting research, preparing actor packets, and more.

Production/Casting

This position assists the producer, production office manager, company manager, and casting director. This is an opportunity to gain experience in contract information, casting, and the general operation of the production office.

Arts Administration Opportunities

AccessAbility/House Management

Here, you'll work with the house management coordinator/accessibility director to get experience in audience development and services that the Arena Stage offers for patrons with disabilities.

Development/Fund-raising

This position assists in all areas of fund-raising for a large not-for-profit theater and involves developing and maintaining corporate and individual donors; planning and implementing campaigns; and working on special events.

Executive Director

This opportunity encompasses gaining experience in areas such as general management; fund-raising; budget analysis and monitoring; contracts; board relations; and corporate and foundation research.

Finance/Personnel

This is an opportunity to gain experience in budget preparation and tracking; accounts payable; payroll; cash receipts; employee benefits; personnel; and internal and external financial reporting.

Graphic Design

This position supports the design and production of printed materials and advertising to support Arena's marketing efforts. It requires specific knowledge of graphic design software for Macintosh.

Information Systems

This opportunity involves working with the information systems department supporting Arena Stage's administrative and sales offices. Work will also include exposure to information systems work with Web design and maintenance, office work, help-desk procedures, and day-to-day operations in a production environment.

Marketing

This position offers you an opportunity to help the marketing staff help enlarge the audience, including a variety of administrative tasks and special projects.

Media Relations

In this position, you'll get the chance to help create and implement initiatives to garner press coverage for the theater's programs and productions, including a variety of administrative tasks and special projects.

Ticket Operations

This position is an opportunity to work with the inbound, outbound, and subscriptions staffs on a variety of sales and patron-oriented tasks. The selected applicant observes and assists with processing, reports, filing, problem resolution, and database maintenance.

Community Involvement Apprenticeships

This department helps cultivate future theater professionals, attracting new audiences and enriching theater education in schools and in the community. Interns in this area need to have excellent communication skills, computer literacy, attention to detail, knowledge of theater, and a passion for working with people.

Audience Enrichment

This intern will help the audience-enrichment manager implement a wide array of programs to heighten the experience of audiences.

Community and Schools

Selected applicants in this position will work with the community and school's manager to help manage the Students Playwrights Project, which instructs middle and high school teachers how to use playwriting and drama in the classroom as a way of developing a full range of literacy skills.

Education Program

The intern supports the director of education and the project-enrichment manager in maintaining relationships with program partners and participants and creating educational/performance related materials and curricula.

Technical Production Apprenticeships

The following internships are not available during the summer.

Costumes

This internship will help you gain experience in all areas of work in the costume shop, including sewing, shopping, pulling items from stock, and running crew. Applicants must have good sewing skills and a basic knowledge of costume history and costume vocabulary.

Lighting

The selected applicant will gain experience helping electricians implement and maintain lighting designs and equipment. Applicants must have a basic knowledge of theatrical lighting and lighting equipment.

Properties

This position supports the properties department in the construction and acquisition of props. Basic knowledge in several disciplines is required, including carpentry, upholstery, painting, crafts, graphics, sculpture, and blueprint-reading.

Set Construction/Paints

Here you'll work with the scenic department in building all scenery and set pieces. A basic knowledge of carpentry and welding and experience working with plastics, paint, fabrics, and other construction materials is necessary.

Sound

In this position, you'll help design, build, and run audio materials for rehearsals and performances and help set up and install related systems. A basic knowledge of audio electronics and recording materials is necessary.

Stage Management

Selected applicants in this area will help supervise rehearsals, performances, and other related activities. The intern will work on one or more shows of an eight-play season.

HOW TO APPLY

If you're interested in this internship, send a cover letter indicating your interest in either the Arena Stage internship or Allen Lee Hughes Fellowship and which discipline you are applying for and dates available (first and second choice), along with a resume with current, permanent, and summer phone numbers, addresses, and e-mail, one academic and one professional letter of recommendation, and a copy of your most recent academic transcript. Students interested in applying for an internship with directing or administrative and community involvement departments should also include a critical writing sample that discusses your eventual career goal in the theater, your reason for seeking an apprenticeship, and what you hope to gain from this apprenticeship. An interview is mandatory and can be handled in person or by telephone.

ATLANTA BALLET INTERNSHIP

Atlanta Ballet
1400 West Peachtree Street, NW
Atlanta, GA 30309
(404) 873-5811
tekholm@atlantaballet.com

What You Can Earn: Unpaid but includes free tickets to ballet, passes to local art group performances, free parking, and health club.
Application Deadlines: Rolling.
Educational Experience: None specified.
Requirements: Must be at least age 17; must be available a minimum of three months.

OVERVIEW

The Atlanta Ballet is one of the nation's premier professional ballet companies, recognized for the artistry of its dancers and innovative programming. For the past 75 years, Atlanta has had a ballet company of its own, which has embodied the spirit, resilience, and joy of this city. Today the ballet presents a full season of full-length ballets and also goes on tour.

The Atlanta Ballet offers internships in tech/production, public relations, marketing, development, and education, lasting from eight to 12 weeks in three sessions (summer, fall, and spring).

HOW TO APPLY

Call for more information at the preceding number. Submit a cover letter and resume via mail or e-mail to the preceding address. All applicants will be interviewed.

BALLETMET INTERNSHIP

Internship Coordinator
BalletMet
322 Mount Vernon Avenue
Columbus, OH 43215
(614) 229-4860

What You Can Earn: $200 a session, plus free tickets to all ballets and free parking.
Application Deadlines: Rolling.
Educational Experience: College juniors and seniors majoring in marketing.
Requirements: None specified.

OVERVIEW

BalletMet has provided artistic excellence in the field of dance to Central Ohio since 1978. The mission of BalletMet's education and community programs is to provide quality dance experiences that are informative, inspirational, accessible, and affordable so that the entire community may appreciate and enjoy the art of dance.

In May 2004 BalletMet made its critically acclaimed Manhattan debut at the renowned Joyce

Theater in New York. The company was one of 18 chosen from a field of 66 applicants internationally to perform.

BalletMet annually reaches a total audience of nearly 125,000 through performances at home and on tour, academy classes and activities, and extensive DanceReach educational/outreach programs.

As part of its commitment to education, Ballet-Met has been offering an internship program since 1991 that introduces college juniors and seniors to a professional marketing and public relations experience in a 10-week session (summer, fall, winter, or spring).

The BalletMet Dance Academy, founded in 1980, ranks among the five largest professional dance-training centers in the United States and offers a variety of classes to students ages four to 84.

HOW TO APPLY

Submit your resume and cover letter to the internship coordinator at the preceding address.

BERKSHIRE THEATER FESTIVAL INTERNSHIP

Berkshire Theatre Festival
Attn: Peter Durgin, General Manager
PO Box 797
Stockbridge, MA 01262-0797
(413) 298-5536, ext. 17
Fax: (413) 298-3368
pete@berkshiretheatre.org

What You Can Earn: Unpaid but room and board are included. (including breakfast, lunch, and dinner); college credit is available.
Application Deadlines: Rolling.
Educational Experience: None specified.
Requirements: None specified.

OVERVIEW

The Berkshire Theatre Festival (BTF) is the oldest performing-arts venue in Berkshire County, MA, and one of the oldest in the United States. The vast numbers of artists who have written, performed, directed, and designed here through its 77 years have given the BTF a unique perspective, with consistently high-quality productions on both the Main Stage and in the Unicorn Theatre. The festival's mission is to promote and produce theatre for its community through performance and educational activities. As part of that mission, the festival offers 20 to 25 internships each season.

The actual length of each internship varies from three to four months, depending on the position and your availability, but typically the season lasts from mid-May to Labor Day. During this time, you'll work on four Main Stage Equity productions and four productions on the Larry Vaber Stage in the Unicorn Theatre.

This isn't just a glorified office job; once you understand all the safety regulations, you'll be working closely with department heads on many different tasks. Administrative internships are available in public relations, marketing, development, accounting, company management, audience services, and general administration. Production internships are available in scenic art, carpentry, props, costumes, electric, sound, stage management, general production, and production management.

Although hours vary depending on departmental needs. They typically run from 9:00 A.M. to 6:00 P.M. with a lunch break. Because both theatres run simultaneously, crews work two shows at the same time. If your schedule includes participating in a run crew, you'd also need to work evenings. Otherwise, night work is limited wherever possible. Sundays are free, with the exception of changeovers.

Generally, each production runs three weeks. There are a total of four equity productions on the Main Stage, four productions on the second stage (the Unicorn Theatre), and one month-long production for young audiences performed by apprentices. Each week, there are eight performances on the Main Stage with matinees on Thursdays and Saturdays and six evening performances in the Unicorn. Both theatres are dark on Sundays. The Main Stage is housed in a 116-year-old, 415-seat proscenium theatre; the Unicorn theatre was remodeled in 1996 and has 122 seats and a small thrust stage. Many interns return to work as staff after their internship season.

HOUSING

The Lavan Center, the theatre's housing complex, is just over one mile from the two theatres. Interns and apprentices receive breakfast, lunch, and dinner daily. Although a car is certainly convenient, you don't need one. You'll usually have no problem getting a ride to and from Lavan, and the town of Stockbridge is less than a mile from the theatre complex.

HOW TO APPLY

Send a cover letter, resume, and three references to the general manager.

BOSTON BALLET INTERNSHIP

Boston Ballet
19 Clarendon Street
Boston, MA 02116
http://www.bostonballet.org/about/
    employment/internships.aspx

What You Can Earn: Unpaid but academic credit is available.
Application Deadlines: Rolling.
Educational Experience: Undergraduates and graduate students interested in arts administration.
Requirements: 12 to 15 hours a week; dedicated, responsible, and flexible, with excellent communications skills.

OVERVIEW

An internship with the Boston Ballet offers valuable experience working in the vibrant atmosphere of a world-class dance company. The repertory includes a mix of classic story ballets, contemporary ballets, and avant-garde works. Internships are available in a number of departments, including retail operations, Boston Ballet School, development/special events, administrative, production/stage management, wardrobe, or marketing/communications.

Administrative

In this department, interns will perform many different duties, as well as work on special projects in many different ballet departments.

Boston Ballet School

The ballet school, with more than 1,300 students, provides dance training for more than 1,300 students from ages three to adult. In this department, interns will provide support in maintaining student records, help with organizing student bulletin boards, and help in the day-to-day operation of the school. Interns should have good computer skills, be interested in customer service, and have a desire to work in a performing arts environment. As part of this department, the education and outreach office brings dance education to more than 5,000 Boston public school children; interns who enjoy working with children and who can help with general office duties may fit in well here.

Development/Special Events

This department is responsible for raising money for the ballet, by soliciting corporate, individual, government, and foundation donors and by organizing fund-raising events. In this department, interns will work on projects that may include proposal development, prospect identification, and preparation of news.

Marketing/Communications

The ballet marketing department is responsible for creating, organizing, and distributing all the ad-print materials, TV ads, season brochures, newspaper and magazine ads, flyers, programs, informational brochures, and other press materials about the ballet. Here interns will work on a variety of projects as directed by staffers.

Production/Stage Management

In this department, interns will gain direct backstage technical experience. Prospective interns must have significant preprofessional theater arts training.

Retail Operations

The ballet's retail and wholesale division offers Boston Ballet-related merchandise for sale as a way of raising money. In this department, interns will help staffers in many different aspects of product development and business.

Wardrobe

Here you'll gain direct experience in making costumes and professional shop operations. You must be a college sophomore, junior, or senior, and you must have strong stitching ability.

HOW TO APPLY

If you're interested, submit a resume and cover letter, indicating the internship of interest, the exact dates and hours a week you're available, and whether you're asking your college for academic credit. After the ballet reviews the applications, selected candidates will be contacted for an interview. No phone calls will be accepted.

CHICAGO SYMPHONY ORCHESTRA INTERNSHIP

Chicago Symphony Orchestra Association
Internship Programs, Rosenthal Archives
220 S. Michigan Avenue
Chicago, IL 60604-2508
Fax: (312) 294-3838
hr@cso.org

What You Can Earn: Unpaid.
Application Deadlines: Rolling.
Educational Experience: Bachelor's degree, preferably in music or history.
Requirements: Knowledge of classical music; familiarity with Microsoft Office: Word, Excel, Access, or similar databases; demonstrated research skills; and ability to work with attention to detail and limited supervision

OVERVIEW

Rich in tradition, innovative in vision, the Chicago Symphony Orchestra is a musical force that now, in its second century, enjoys an enviable position in the music world. Its best-selling recordings continue to win prestigious international awards, and its syndicated radio broadcasts are heard by millions nationwide.

As an intern in the Rosenthal Archives, you'll help staff with reference and research services for staff, media, and public, including handling requests for duplication of photographic and audio-visual materials in accordance with archival policies. You'll also help organize, process, and catalogue archival materials. Formed in 1990 during the CSO's centennial season, the Samuel R. and Marie Louise Rosenthal Archives of the Chicago Symphony Orchestra house an extensive collection of audio-visual materials, programs, photographs, newspaper clippings, and administrative records documenting the activities of the Chicago Symphony Orchestra, Chicago Symphony Chorus, Civic Orchestra, and Orchestra Hall and Symphony Center events.

Individuals can contact the Archives with reference questions and any other topics of historical nature or make appointments to conduct research in the Archives; to listen to recordings, radio broadcasts, preconcert lectures, and oral histories; or to watch videos.

HOW TO APPLY

Send your resume with a cover letter via e-mail as a Microsoft Word attachment or via regular mail to the preceding address. All resumes are acknowledged with postcard or e-mail upon receipt. No phone calls are accepted.

CHILDREN'S TELEVISION WORKSHOP INTERNSHIP

Children's Television Workshop
Education & Research Internship Program
1633 Broadway, 40th Floor
New York, NY 10019

What You Can Earn: Unpaid; $10 a day is paid to cover meals and transportation. In addition, expenses incurred while assisting with field work will be reimbursed.
Application Deadlines: July 15 for the fall session; November 15 for the spring session; March 15 for the summer session.
Educational Experience: Undergraduate juniors or seniors or graduate students.
Requirements: Individual areas below outline specific criteria

OVERVIEW
The Children's Television Workshop (CTW) was founded in 1969 to produce programs, products, and services that entertain and educate children and their families. Beginning with *Sesame Street,* and later following with *The Electric Company, 3-2-1 Contact, Square One TV, Ghostwriter, CRO, Big Bag, The New Ghostwriter Mysteries*, and *Dragon Tales*, CTW designs, researches, and produces programs as well as related materials.

Interns are selected to work in one of several areas of research at CTW, including international research, *Sesame Street* research, program research, and marketing and media research.

International Research
This department carries out the development of curricula and research for all CTW international co-productions. Interns qualify for this area if they're studying psychology, education, communications, and/or other social sciences; a special interest in research or international education is a plus. Flexibility and initiative are required; candidates should also be comfortable working independently. This internship does not include any field work, and you'll be expected to work two full days per week for a full semester.

Marketing and Media Research
This department conducts and analyzes research on audiences to better understand their attitudes and perceptions of CTW and *Sesame Street* brands, programs, and products. To intern here, you should have a strong interest in research and children's media, and you should be majoring in communications, marketing, or business. Some understanding of marketing research and basic knowledge of ratings is helpful. Here you'll help coordinate focus groups and surveys and work with outside consultants, analyzing magazine readership characteristics, tabulating ratings data and simple data analysis, and performing some general administrative tasks. Schedules are flexible.

Program Research
In this department, you'll help develop curricula and conduct research with children to support concept development, planning, and production for CTW's domestic TV other than *Sesame Street*, as well as online, magazine publishing, and outreach efforts. Potential interns should be studying education, focusing on a specific area among the current production roster, such as mathematics, history, literacy, or science. You should have experience in research and in working with young children. This group also seeks candidates who would like to gain experience in development and supervision of the educational content of CTW's projects and for whom field-work is not important. Schedules are flexible, but you'll be expected to work two days a week for a full semester.

Sesame Street Research

Interns in this area will help develop curricula and conduct research with children to support concept development, planning, and production for *Sesame Street* shows. To intern here, you should major in psychology, education, and/or communications with a special interest in research and children. If you're chosen, you may help with library research; stimuli development; interviewing children; collecting, coding, and verification of data; and screening show segments. You'll need to work Tuesdays, Wednesdays, and preferably Thursdays for the duration of the semester.

HOW TO APPLY

To apply, send a letter and resume to the preceding address, indicating the semester during which you'd like to participate and which group you would prefer. The placement of interns is determined by the needs of the groups and the qualifications of candidates. If the first-choice group does not need additional interns, candidates will be considered for other research groups. An in-person interview is part of the selection process and will be scheduled after resumes have been reviewed.

DALLAS THEATER CENTER INTERNSHIP

Dallas Theater Center/Internship Program
Attn: Lisa Lawrence Holland
3636 Turtle Creek Blvd.
Dallas, TX 75219
(214) 252-3918

What You Can Earn: Unpaid.
Application Deadlines: May 1.
Educational Experience: College undergraduates or graduate students.

Requirements: Full-time commitment of at least 40 hours a week; participation in the running crews for at least two mainstage productions.

OVERVIEW

The Dallas Theater Center (DTC), with its roots deeply implanted in the community, continues to grow in stature as one of the most exciting regional theaters in the country today, producing classic, contemporary, and new plays. DTC interns are involved in every area of the theater, from supporting nationally recognized artists on mainstage productions to working closely with the artistic, administrative, and production staffs on the theater's daily operation. It is DTC's goal that by the end of each season each intern will be fully equipped with the skills and knowledge to make informed choices about furthering his or her work in the theater.

You may choose to intern in any of the following areas: arts administration; company management; directing/literary management; education and community programs; production (individual internships are available in carpentry, electrics, sound, scenic art, costumes, wardrobe, properties, and stage operations); and stage management. Internships are full season, from August to May.

HOW TO APPLY

To apply, send a cover letter with your current and permanent addresses, e-mail address, name of school, dates available, and three internship areas of interest in order of preference. You also should include three letters of recommendation (two educational/professional and one personal). In addition, you should include a resume of your education, theater experience, and any related work, together with a brief statement (no longer than one typed page) including your long-range theater goals, why you should be chosen as an intern, and how you heard of the program. Finally, you should include a one-page description of a specific theater or artistic experience (music, art, literature, or dance), whether as an audience member or direct participant, that shaped your vision of theater.

Send all materials in one envelope to the preceding address. Applications are accepted beginning in February for the following season and are reviewed and processed as they arrive. Early applications will receive priority consideration.

DALLAS THEATER CENTER SUMMERSTAGE INTERNSHIP

Dallas Theater Center
3636 Turtle Creek Blvd.
Dallas, TX 75219
(214) 252-3916
education@dallastheatercenter.org

What You Can Earn: $2,000 for eight weeks.
Application Deadlines: April 1.
Educational Experience: Full-time undergraduates, returning to school full time in the fall after the internship; majoring in theater or education with a strong interest in theater arts.
Requirements: Full-time commitment of at least 40 hours a week (from 9:00 A.M. to 5:00 P.M. five days a week) from the beginning of June to the end of July.

OVERVIEW

If you'd like to combine an interest in education with the theater, the SummerStage internship at the Dallas Theater Center might be for you. SummerStage is the DTC's annual summer theater day camp and precollege actor-training program, which offers the area's best voice, movement, visual arts, and actor training. The theater center is the major regional theater serving North Texas, with a mainstage season of six plays, the Project Discovery arts-in-education program, and the DTC LAB: actor training for youths, teens, and adults.

If you're chosen as the SummerStage summer intern, you'll perform integral duties in the education and community programs department. You'll be responsible for helping teachers in daily theater classes for children ages four to 18 and directing lunchtime theater activities. The intern also will work with the director in general administration, including class scheduling, registration, and managing correspondence. The intern also will be exposed to all departments within the theater for educational purposes.

HOW TO APPLY

To apply, fax or mail your resume with a cover letter to the preceding address.

DANCE PLACE INTERNSHIP

Dance Place
Associate Director
3225 8th Street NE
Washington, DC 20017
(202) 269-1600
Fax: (202) 269-4103
deborahr@danceplace.org

What You Can Earn: Unpaid but all dance classes and performances are free; free housing in summer and fall.
Application Deadlines: Rolling.
Educational Experience: Dancers age 19 and older pursuing careers in dance in college, after college, or who are hoping to make a career transition to the field of dance.
Requirements: Good knowledge of Microsoft Word and Excel spreadsheets; experience in customer relations; able to work hard, have an open mind, and be ready for everything in a constantly changing setting.

OVERVIEW

Dance Place is a nationally recognized community arts organization and theater, school, and community resource that offers classes and presents contemporary and culturally specific performances in the Washington, D.C., metropolitan area.

Dance Place offers a multifocus internship especially helpful to dancers interested in sampling the real world of dance and exploring career options while in college or shortly after graduating. At Dance Place, interns will learn how a nonprofit community-arts center functions, what career opportunities there are in dance, and how to further their dance and teaching skills. As an intern here, you'll be expected to pitch in and do some administrative work, participate in professional dance classes, and help teach children's classes.

Internships are typically 12-weeks long, beginning each quarter in September, January, March, and June. You can expect to spend 20 hours a week doing administrative work as a Dance Place receptionist, studio manager, box office assistant, and administrative assistant. Responsibilities include interacting with the public, dealing with customers, selling and processing tickets, registering students for classes, selling merchandise, and providing information. In short, you'll play a prominent role in the everyday business of the organization.

But that's not all! You'll also participate in daily adult professional dance classes, including modern dance, West African dance, Dunham technique, and hip-hop. If you're interested, you'll also help teach children's classes. (Classes in creative movement, beginning ballet, modern, tap, and hip-hop for three to 13 year olds are held at Dance Place, and classes in Dance Place's methodology of kinesthetic learning are offered in public schools.) Teacher training in support of these classes is currently held on Friday mornings. Teaching assistantships are offered from October to May only.

HOUSING

Free housing for three interns is provided in a group intern house located across the street from the Dance Place facility in the summer and fall semesters only.

HOW TO APPLY

Fax or e-mail a letter of interest, a letter of support, and your resume detailing both dance and work experience to the associate director at the preceding address.

DREAMTIME FESTIVAL INTERNSHIP

Dreamtime Applications Process
38270 Stucker Mesa Road
Hotchkiss, CO 81419
(720) 272-5743
positions@dreamthefuture.org
http://www.dreamthefuture.org

What You Can Earn: Unpaid; housing included; tickets and meal tickets; college credit available.
Application Deadlines: Rolling.
Educational Experience: None specified; previous training in the area of interest is not required.
Requirements: The ability to present oneself professionally, a willingness to learn, a strong ability to work independently, a high level of creativity, and a can-do attitude.

OVERVIEW

Dreamtime is a nonprofit organization that aims to inspire, educate, connect and empower people to create positive change in themselves and the world through a dynamic blend of arts, entertainment, and education. The Dreamtime Festival is an annual outdoor event in Western Colorado, offering an open canvas for creative expression and blending entertainment, dance, learning, activism, and art. The event includes dancing, learning, creative expression, fire performances, theatre, multimedia, workshops, action, and more. Dreamtime tries to provide tools and opportunities to create positive change, offering opportunities for participants to explore new ideas, learn about transforming themselves and the world around them, and carry this learning back into their lives.

Internships at Dreamtime are designed to offer meaningful experience for those interested in performing arts, the environment, social change, media and film, communications, entertainment management, the nonprofit field, sustainability, and creative expression. Positions typically last one to six months, with immediate openings to work with Dreamtime on an individual project basis.

Dreamtime and the Dreamtime Festival are based in the Rocky Mountains, though some positions do not require travel to Colorado. As an intern here, you'll be responsible for helping with the artistic, administrative, promotional, and technical aspects of the Festival. You'll also interact with the audience, sponsors, instructors, performers, and guest artists. In return, you'll get on-the-job experience in technical event production, videography, art and creative performance, administration, promotion, funding, leadership, management, and education, while gaining valuable contacts and in-depth knowledge of contemporary nonprofit event management.

Positions are available in the following areas (most participants work in more than one area).

Administration

In this area, you'll work closely with the festival director; help the director/registrar and box office manager/artist liaison to support the day-to-day activities of the festival; help with general office management (phone, fax, copying, and data entry); create and prepare materials for participants, artists, outreach, and public events; program scheduling and logistics; and sales. You should have good computer, organizational, verbal, and writing skills.

Advertising/Fund Raising Coordinator

This intern will solicit sponsorships from larger organizations and businesses, advertising from local businesses, donations from local and national interests, and in-kind donations from appropriate sources. You'll also develop grants from local, regional, and national organizations supporting education and the arts and develop an individual donor base.

Event Coordinator

In this internship, you'll help the festival director coordinate the staff and volunteers before and during the event.

Guest Coordinator

This intern will coordinate housing, transportation, travel, events and food for visiting staff, interns, companies, instructors, performers, and artists.

Multimedia and Education Development

This intern will solicit and develop multimedia and educational content for the festival, including a multimedia film exhibition, and tabling materials, working closely with the workshop and educational coordinator.

Publicity and Marketing Coordinator

In this area, you'll coordinate communication with the media, developing press releases, information packets, and radio promotions. You'll also develop and distribute festival flyers, invitations and brochure, and develop or arrange for the design of the poster and the program. You'll also work to promote the festival to targeted audiences and provide material to update the Web page with current information pertinent to the festival.

Site Development

Here you'll help develop the festival grounds, directing volunteer and landscaping efforts and coordinating and assisting in structure construction and general site planning.

Technical Director

In this internship, you'll work with a designer to ensure practical, professional stage sets, art installations, and multimedia screening and coordinate lights and sound design and operation.

Technical Production/Lighting Design

Interns here work with technical lighting design, the production staff, visiting technical directors, and artists as part of the crew for the Dreamtime Festival. You'll be responsible for hanging, focusing, and operating lights, and you'll participate in ongoing lighting design and development, stage carpentry, and theatre maintenance.

Technical Production/Sound Design

Interns will work with technical sound design, the production staff, visiting technical directors, and artists as part of the crew for the Dreamtime Festival and will be responsible for equipment selection and setup, positioning, sound checks and monitoring, live broadcasts, providing filler, and coordination with multimedia productions. Interns also will participate in ongoing lighting development, sound booth carpentry, and maintenance.

Videography

Here interns will work directly with the festival videographers, recording all performances and gaining experience in all facets of archival documentation. You'll focus on artistic content, shooting techniques, concepts of documentation, proper titling, labeling and logging of material, use of editing programs, and the necessary editorial point of view for creation of an in-depth project. Candidates should have some experience with digital video.

Workshop and Educational Coordinator

Here you'll work with visiting instructors, lecturers, workshop hosts, guest artists, multimedia displays, and local participants to schedule a variety of workshops and educational opportunities for festival participants. You'll also select material for educational content during the festival and coordinate the casting and direction of the educational content.

Workshop Instructors

These interns will plan or solicit and execute or delegate site-specific curriculum for workshops that further Dreamtime's mission at the festival.

HOW TO APPLY

Fill out the application available on the Web site at http://www.dreamthefuture.org/intern.php and either e-mail it or mail it along with a resume documenting relevant work experience and a cover letter articulating your goals and expectations for the position to the preceding address.

DREAMWORKS SKG INTERNSHIP

DreamWorks Animation
Recruiting/Internship Coordinator
1000 Flower Street
Glendale, CA 91201
Fax: (818) 695-7199
animjobs@dreamworks.com

What You Can Earn: Unpaid; college credit only.
Application Deadlines: October 1 through 31 for spring; March 1 through 31 for summer; June 1 through 30 for summer.
Educational Experience: Enrolled full time in an accredited college or university, with an academic major related to the department of interest. Work experience (industry experience a plus). Specific experience is detailed below.
Requirements: Strong interest in film/TV; a positive attitude; strong work ethic; excellent communication and organizational skills; computer savvy; ability to multitask; organized; team player; and an ability to work in a fast-paced environment.

OVERVIEW

DreamWorks Animation develops and produces high-quality computer generated (CG) animated films. Utilizing world-class creative talent, a strong and experienced management team, and advanced CG film-making technology, DreamWorks Animation has produced a number of highly successful movies, including *Shrek*, the first-ever winner of the Academy Award for Best Animated Feature film, and *Shrek 2*, the third highest-grossing movie ever and the number one animated film of all time. Most recently, the company released *Shark Tale*. In 1994 Steven Spielberg, Jeffrey Katzenberg, and David Geffen formed DreamWorks SKG, a diversified entertainment company. Typically, internships are available in a variety of departments, including business affairs film/music, archives, worldwide technical services, and TV development.

Business Affairs Film Music Internship

In this department, your responsibilities include contract research and contract analysis, supervised contract drafting (once this level of responsibility has been proven), and letter drafting. You'll also learn about co-publishing agreements and composer and songwriter agreements, and you'll attend contract negotiations.

To qualify for this internship area, you should have an interest in music and entertainment law and be familiar with contract analysis, Word, and Excel. Law school students who have completed the first year of law school are strongly preferred.

Archives Internship

If you land this assignment, you'll be responsible for sorting, organizing, and describing assets related to studio collections. The main duties include imaging visual assets, cataloging, and storing items. While you're here, you'll learn all about corporate archives, plus how to inventory and process collections.

To intern here, you should have all the basic office and computer skills, plus you must be enrolled in a graduate program in archive studies, library information science, art history, or history.

Television Development Internship

In this department, interns read scripts, write coverage, meet and greet guests, dub tapes, and conduct research, as well as perform general office duties. Interns learn how a TV show is developed, from start to finish. Interns will learn about the elements that make a show successful, including writing, music, cast, budget, titles, and promotion, as well as learning the differences between single and multicamera shows, network, and cable. In addition, the intern will learn about programming and be exposed to the buying and selling process, while refining reading and writing skills to suit the style of a fast-paced production office.

For this internship, you must be proficient with Windows and Word programs, be a strong reader with the ability to grasp the main idea of a screenplay or film, write clearly and concisely, possess good listening skills, and be a quick learner.

Worldwide Technical Services Internship

Here, you'll provide general office support and maintain an active inventory database for film- and sound-based elements. You'll attend weekly production meetings, work with executives, and actively participate in day-to-day operations, ultimately gaining an in-depth understanding of the post-production process and an overview of international distribution.

For this internship, you must have a strong interest in film/TV, and a general understanding of audio post-production. You should have a positive attitude, a strong work ethic, excellent communication and organizational skills, be computer savvy and have the ability to multitask.

HOW TO APPLY

Submit your cover letter and resume with permanent contact information, either via e-mail (indicate your area of interest in the subject line) or by fax, addressed to the attention of the internship coordinator, at the preceding address. In your cover letter, identify your department and location of interest (either Glendale or Redwood City), what you hope to achieve from the internship, any special skills or experience you possess, and available days/hours. Indicate that the application is for an internship in the subject line.

Because of virus controls, only plain-text resumes can be received, within the body of the e-mail. Attached resumes or artwork will not be reviewed.

E! ENTERTAINMENT TALENT/CASTING INTERNSHIP

E! Entertainment
5750 Wilshire Blvd.
Los Angeles, CA 90036
Fax: (323) 954-2710

What You Can Earn: Unpaid.
Application Deadlines: Rolling.
Educational Experience: Check individual departments for specifics
Requirements: Must attend an accredited university and must be able to receive school credit; check individual departments for more specific requirements.

OVERVIEW

E! Networks tries to enhance and develop creative and hardworking students to better prepare for their desired career and is committed to promoting motivation and morale and helping interns develop their career goals.

Interns must be available for at least 15 hours per week for a minimum of two months. They may help the staff of the talent department by performing various administrative duties, including typing and/or sending correspondence, filing, faxing, photocopying, conducting Internet searches, returning tapes, and so on. They may copy and distribute all the entertainment news of the day to the talent department staff and help update and maintain pertinent celebrity information in the database. Interns may assemble the gift bags for celebrity guests, provide snacks and drinks, and prepare the Green Room for in-studio guests. Interns also may help organize and maintain talent-audition tapes and reels in the storage drawers and research talent information (biographies, TV show information, agent/manger contact information, and so on).

In addition, interns may help during auditions, help the talent staff with special projects, or support tasks as needed.

Advertising Sales

In this internship position, you'll be expected to support the Los Angeles advertising sales staff, providing support to account executives with advertising campaigns. You may help support tracking campaigns, send media kits and other correspondence to clients, summarize trade publications and monitor agency activities, manage staff travel, use research tools to prepare for sales calls, and help develop proposals for specific clients.

Facilities

This internship is designed to expose college students to hands-on work experience in a facilities and real estate department using AutoCAD and including miscellaneous commercial design responsibilities associated with an in-house department. As a facilities intern, you may help update E! AutoCAD floor plans with room/key code data and new build-out alterations; work on fabric selection/sample returns at the Pacific Design Center; help with systems furniture, case goods and storage selection, specification, and ordering; and help update specification books.

If you're interested in this position, you should have completed at least one semester in AutoCAD and be interested in pursuing a career in commercial interior design or facility management. You also should currently be enrolled in a college-level interior or architecture design program.

Information Technology

In this position, you'll work with the project manager and analysts on studying processes and systems, help draft user requirements and specification documents, develop Web-based UI prototypes, and report mock-ups. You also may work on software engineering based on coding capabilities and participate in quality assurance testing, application training, and implementation support.

For this intern position, you must have a minimum of two years of analysis and/or hands-on programming experience in an online or IT environment (or educational equivalent) and the ability to code in one or more programming languages (C, C++, or Java). You also must know relational database fundamentals, including SQL, have excellent people and communication skills, and be a team player with strong analytical and problem-solving skills. Web application development experience is preferred; entertainment or broadcast industry knowledge is desirable.

Marketing/Promotion

As an intern in this department, you'll help with guerilla marketing efforts by spreading news of new shows on the Internet; help research viable grass-roots methods to promote the network; help with strategically positioning original programming to targeted audiences; and help with quality control checks of E! Online and StyleNetwork.com. You'll also support managers in a variety of projects, including brainstorming, sourcing premium concepts, and so on; help with outreach mailings, premium shipments, and prize allocation; and help with research projects.

Music

Music intern positions offer students the opportunity to learn about the role of music in the television industry while earning course credit. In this position, you'll help answer phones and do light filing, copying, and typing. You may review data and create reports from library usage and show information; screen and log music submissions; provide research and support for music searches, including CD compiling, burning, and distribution; and photocopy, fax and/or distribute memos/reports.

You should have excellent people skills and verbal and written communication skills; a passion for music; a background or interest in music marketing and production; a working knowledge of the Internet, Windows, and Microsoft Office (Word, Excel, and so on) and Mac OS, iTunes, or other CD burning and music management applications. You'll also need to plan on spending at least 20 hours per week and occasionally may be required to lift and carry up to 10 pounds.

On-Air Design

This department internship can expose college students to hands-on work experience in the on-air design group at a cable channel. As an intern here, you'll help designers and producers in the daily production of on-air graphics. You'll observe designers create the on-air show package from initial concept through delivery and assist in research and image gathering under the supervision of a producer and help organize job binders, tape logs, and all materials associated with a project. You'll be able to watch and help producers in online, audio-sweetening, and smoke sessions and help designers in shoots for comps or storyboards. You'll become familiar with the daisy system and check out tapes from the E! Media Center.

Although no experience is required, course work in the area of design and/or television production is helpful.

Production

Internships are available in many shows within the production department including: *It's Good to Be, True Hollywood Story, Original Specials, E! News Live, Live Events, Howard Stern,* and shows on The Style Network, including *The Look For Less, How Do I Look?* and *Style Star.* As an intern here, you'll gather research for producers and associate producers, including written and taped material; acquire stills, slides, periodicals, and other visuals; arrange to have visual shots; transcribe interviews and remote tapes; and view and log b-roll.

Public Relations

This internship is designed to expose college students to hands-on work experience in entertainment public relations. As a public relations intern, you'll help write press releases and make press follow-up calls; assemble press kits and clipping books; create and distribute daily clip packets; organize and update the tape and publications library; and do general administrative tasks.

Recruitment

Interns in the recruitment office work closely with production recruiters to monitor job openings and help print and organize candidate resumes. You'll conduct professional telephone screenings for temporary and full-time production positions for assigned departments within E!; help in outreach efforts to a variety of universities and local high schools in an effort to develop a qualified and diverse pool of entry-level talent; help answer external candidate inquiries and respond via phone or e-mail in a timely and professional manner; and help check references and do background procedures for selected candidates. You also may draft and place advertising in college publications, with appropriate department faculty, and on the Internet to attract a qualified candidate pool and help with paperwork and administration related to new hires and terminations.

You should have a strong customer-service mentality and an interest in recruitment. Exceptional interpersonal, communication, writing, and organizational skills are required; you also must be proactive and detailed oriented and possess good follow-through. Strong computer skills, including proficiency in MS Word, Excel, and Outlook, are required.

Set Design

This internship is designed to expose college students to hands-on work experience in set design. Here you'll help designers and producers in set design and production. You'll observe set designers from initial concept through delivery and assist with props and the assembly of sets for various shows and help designers during shoots.

You must be able to lift items as needed while doing setups and working in set storage. A theater/film background is preferred; you also should be interested in pursing a career in television and/or film art department work.

Talent/Casting

In this area, you may help copy and distribute the entertainment news of the day to the talent department staff; update pertinent celebrity information in the talent database; assemble gift bags for celebrity guests; provide snacks/drinks for guests and prepare the Green Room; help organize and maintain talent audition tapes and reels in the storage drawers; research talent information (biographies, TV show info, agent/manger contact information,

and so on); help during auditions; and help the talent staff with special projects or support tasks as needed.

HOW TO APPLY

To apply to any of these internships, you should submit your resume and a cover letter to the preceding address, indicating the shows or areas of interest and semester you are applying for the internship. Resumes that provide this information will receive priority.

EUGENE O'NEILL THEATER INTERNSHIP

Producing Director's Office
Interns Program
O'Neill Theater Center
305 Great Neck Road
Waterford, CT 06385
(860) 443-5378, ext. 282
Fax: (860) 443-9653
info@theONEILL.org

What You Can Earn: Unpaid.
Application Deadlines: Rolling.
Educational Experience: None specified.
Requirements: None specified.

OVERVIEW

The Eugene O'Neill Theater Center, a Tony Award-winner for theatrical achievement, is dedicated to fostering new works for the stage and training theater artists. Each summer the O'Neill is home to the Playwrights Conference, Music Theater Conference, Critics Institute, and Puppetry Conference, with new conferences devoted to cabaret as well as film and television writing. Hundreds of actors, directors, playwrights, and people involved in every aspect of making theater come to the O'Neill during these conferences to share ideas, rehearse and perform new work, and examine what it means to be a writer.

Last year, more than 60 musicals, plays, and puppet shows were performed for the first time in front of an audience at the O'Neill, in the form of staged readings.

All internships take place at the Eugene O'Neill Theater Center in Waterford, CT. All interns participate in master classes and every conference event and present new work at various times throughout the summer. There's a ratio of three artists to every intern. Summer internships are available in many different areas, including box office; carpentry/crew; company management; electrics; house management; operations; props/crew; script office; sound; and stage management.

Box Office

If you intern here, you'll run the box office for the O'Neill conferences, answering phones, handling customer inquiries, preparing and distributing tickets for readings, and reconciling ticket sales.

Carpentry/Crew

Carpentry/crew interns are responsible for assembling basic modular scenery, performing light carpentry and painting, and participating in load-ins and strikes and serve as running crew when needed.

Company Management

If you work in company management, you'll help coordinate all housing, travel, transportation, and general administration of all the conferences.

Electronics

Electrics interns hang and cable lighting plots in all theaters, participate in focus calls, and program and run the light board during rehearsals, readings, and events.

House Management

This intern helps the house manager with all front-of-house activities for conference readings and events, including working with volunteer ushers, creating programs, and addressing patron needs.

Operations

If you intern here, you'll help run the O'Neill Puppetry, Playwrights, Critics, Film and Television, and Cabaret and Music Theater Conferences. Responsibilities include helping with housing preparation, transporting guests in conference vans, running errands, covering O'Neill Center phones, coordinating the O'Neill gift shop/merchandise sales, and working in the O'Neill Center Pub.

Production Assistants

These interns help stage managers, directors, playwrights, and dramaturgs with rehearsals and performances of selected staged readings during the conference.

Props/Crew

Props interns collect, assemble, and construct props for rehearsals and staged readings, participate in load-ins and strikes, and serve as running crew when needed.

Script Office

If you intern here, you'll participate in the daily operations of the conference script office, which may include helping with research, copying script changes and updates, maintaining a script library, and addressing participants' computer needs.

Sound

If you like the technical side of things, you may enjoy working as a sound intern, setting up sound systems and equipment in all theaters, providing basic maintenance of sound equipment, and running sound for all rehearsals, readings, and events.

Stage Management

Stage management interns (under the supervision of the production stage manager) run rehearsals, prepare schedules and reports, and call cues for assigned staged readings.

HOW TO APPLY

To apply, send a cover letter and resume including your theatrical experience to the preceding address. Your cover letter should discuss why you are applying for this internship and what you hope to gain from it. Alternatively, you can apply online at http://www.theoneill.org/involve/intapp.htm.

FOLGER SHAKESPEARE LIBRARY INTERNSHIP

Folger Shakespeare Library
Attn: Human Resources Manager
201 East Capitol Street, SE
Washington, DC 20003
Fax: (202) 544-4623
jobs@folger.edu

What You Can Earn: Unpaid.
Application Deadlines: Rolling.
Educational Experience: Undergraduate and graduate college students with a background in literature, English, journalism, communications, or theatre.
Requirements: None specified.

OVERVIEW

The Folger Shakespeare Library is an independent research library located on Capitol Hill in Washington, D.C., founded by Henry and Emily Folger in 1932 as a gift to the American people. A magnet for scholars from around the globe, the Folger is home to the world's largest collection of Shakespeare's printed works, as well as collections of other rare Renaissance books and manuscripts on history and politics, theology and exploration, and law and the arts.

The Folger is also devoted to Shakespeare's life and times, featuring changing exhibitions featuring items from the collections. Its striking architecture has earned the Folger a listing in the National Register of Historic Places.

The Folger is also a center for literary and performing arts, offering a full calendar of performances and programs from poetry readings and theatrical productions to early-music concerts and family activities. It is a renowned center for the revitalization of humanities education through precollege programs for students and teachers and provides seminars and colloquia on a wide range of early modern topics.

The Folger is not funded by the government but is an independent research library privately endowed and administered by the trustees of Amherst College in Massachusetts (the alma mater of Henry Clay Folger).

Two divisions at the Folger regularly accept students for unpaid internships, often where college credit is given for the experience. (Occasionally, an intern may be paid for an internship if the division's budget allows.) You may apply to work as an intern with the Folger's Academic Programs, which sponsors seminars, conferences, and workshops involving the Renaissance period for doctoral and postdoctoral level scholars and produces *The Shakespeare Quarterly*. Interns also are accepted for the summer with Public Programs, which produces events for the general public, including theatre productions, literary readings, concerts, and tours.

HOW TO APPLY

Potential interns are screened on an individual basis. If you're interested in interning at the Folger, you should send a résumé, a cover letter, and a letter from your college's internship office stating the requirements for credit (if it's offered). Three letters of recommendation are also required, preferably from faculty members who know your scholastic background or areas of interest. Mail or fax internship inquiries to the preceding Folger address.

GEDDES TALENT AGENCY INTERNSHIP

Geddes Talent Agency
8430 Santa Monica Blvd #200
West Hollywood, CA 90069
(323) 848-2700
ag@geddes.net
http://www.rsinternships.com/applications/
    posting.php3?ID=1407
For Chicago, e-mail: eg@geddes.net

What You Can Earn: Unpaid but college credit is available.
Application Deadlines: Rolling.
Educational Experience: None specified.
Requirements: Computer experience, Internet knowledge, typing ability, pleasant and easy-going demeanor, professional phone skills, multitasking ability.

OVERVIEW

The Geddes Agency represents actors in the entertainment industry. Its West Hollywood branch provides service for film, TV, and theater clients. The Chicago office works in the markets of voice-over, commercials, and theater, in addition to TV and film. Geddes is a family-owned business that started in Chicago and has been in operation for 35 years.

An internship position is available in both branches of Geddes Agency (in Chicago and West Hollywood). Although duties may vary depending on the season and the office, the daily tasks are related to basic office needs such as answering phones, routing calls, pulling pictures for submissions, typing letters, Internet downloading, Internet research, and so on.

HOW TO APPLY

If you're interested, send an e-mail describing why you'd like to intern at a talent agency to the preceding address.

GLIMMERGLASS OPERA INTERNSHIP

Intern Search Department D
Glimmerglass Opera
PO Box 191
Cooperstown, NY 13326
intern_info@glimmerglass.org
http://www.glimmerglass.org
What You Can Earn: Stipend available and housing provided.
Application Deadlines: March 18 for periods of seven to 18 weeks, with some positions beginning as early as late April; most begin mid-May or early June and continue through the end of August.
Educational Experience: Check individual internships for specifics.
Requirements: Individual departments below will outline requirements.

OVERVIEW

A number of different internships are available in different departments in administration, artistic administration, and production.

Administration
Accounting/Finance (Early May through late August)
This intern will help the accountant with accounts payable, accounts receivable, payroll and general finance office administration. Accounting or business administration focus is preferred. This internship also requires strong computer skills, including spreadsheet experience; excellent filing skills are a must.

Box Office (Mid-May through August)
Five interns will help with ticket, group, and special events sales; patron services; preparation of income reports; and gathering marketing data. Interns must be dedicated, enjoy assisting people, have excellent phone and personal manner, have customer service experience, and be computer literate.

Development (May through August)
This intern will help prepare and set up fundraising, audience development, and education programs and projects, including hosting, research, site arrangements, and scheduling; and provide clerical/office support. This position requires excellent communication, computer, and interpersonal skills.

General Administration (Late May through late August)
This intern will help the office manager in daily operations of administrative office, including mail processing and distribution, reception duties, and shipping and receiving. The intern must have a congenial personality, excellent phone manner, and sense of humor.

House Management (May through late August)
This intern will solicit and schedule volunteer ushers; assist with orientations, creating signage, opening and closing the theater; and assist house manager with patron comfort and safety at all performances. Prior house management experience is a plus. The intern also must have excellent communication and interpersonal skills.

Housing and Transportation (April/May through late August)
Three interns will help in a highly visible administrative department responsible for the housing, transportation, and other practical concerns of singers, directors, designers, and general personnel. Interns must be able to deal positively and tactfully with a variety of logistical arrangements vital to the company's smooth functioning and must be computer literate. A driver's license is required.

Marketing/Public Relations (Mid-May through late August)
Two interns will help the public relations department with preparation and distribution of press materials and other work with the press and public. They will also help distribute season promotions, advertising, and analysis of ticket sales data. Both positions help staff the audience services desk at all performances and require close attention to detail, a congenial public manner, and computer skills in Microsoft Office programs. Knowledge of Quark is a plus.

Operations/Special Events (May-August)
This intern will help with the planning, set-up and breakdown of special events such as dinners or symposia, and oversee the initiatives program. Attendance at every performance at audience services desk to assist patrons is required. The intern must have good communication and interpersonal skills.

Photography Intern (Mid-May through late August)
This intern will help the professional company photographer produce publicity and archival photographs of the season's productions; coordinate work with local photo supply shop; maintain photo files; and photograph special events. It requires proven photography skills, computer literacy, and a driver's license; photography career interest a plus.

Artistic Administration

Artistic Administration (Mid-May-late August)
This intern will help staff with copying, filing, basic data entry, and scheduling administration. The intern must possess common sense, practicality, a sense of humor, enthusiasm, sound judgment, initiative, and excellent communication skills. The intern should have excellent editing and computer skills.

Dramaturgy (June 6 through August 17)
This intern will provide research support for print materials, productions, lectures, and special programming; conduct, transcribe, and edit artist interviews for print and Web publication; and assist with special programming. This position offers an opportunity to closely observe the rehearsal/production process and to interact with renowned artists and professionals. Candidates should have excellent oral and written communication skills and a strong background in opera,

music and/or theater. Experience in preparing web pages is helpful, but not required.

Music (mid-May through late August)

Two interns will help locate and copy music; locate, hire and transport instruments, with heavy moving required; set up the rehearsal room and orchestra pit; and attend orchestra rehearsals and performances. The interns must be reliable and flexible, with good interpersonal and organizational skills and background in music. A driver's license is required.

Young American Artists Program Administration (Mid-May through late August)

Two interns will live at the Young Artist's residence and help set up, close down, and manage residences; interact with master class and audition personnel; schedule and provide transportation for Young Artists; produce programs and publicity materials for recitals and concerts; and act as liaison between Young Artists and the director of artistic operations. The interns should have excellent juggling skills, with levelheadedness under pressure a priority. Strong interpersonal and organizational skills allied with flexibility, reliability, and discretion are required, as are computer literacy and driver's license. Publishing/editing computer skills are a plus.

Production

Audio/Video/Projected Titles Engineering (Late May through August 27)

Two interns in this department will help install and maintain in-house audio and video monitoring/playback systems, a large wired and wireless intercom system, and a computer-controlled projection system for projected titles. This internship requires good basic experience with sound, video, intercom, and computer systems.

Costume Construction-Stitcher (Late May through early/late July)

Four interns will help with construction and/or alteration of costumes for four operas. This internship requires theatrical sewing skills and academic shop experience; professional experience is desirable.

Costume Construction-Crafts (Late May through July 30)

This intern will help with craftwork, including dying, distressing, millinery, and footwear for four operas. This internship requires theatrical sewing skills and skill in one or more crafts areas; professional experience is desirable.

Electrics (May 16/May 31 through August 27)

Five interns will help install, circuit and focus a 500+ unit plot; perform daily changeovers; run productions; strike, and load-out. This position requires thorough experience with stage electrics.

Hair and Make-up (June 20 through August 23)

This intern will help with daily maintenance of wigs; pre-performance application of make-up, wigs, and hairstyling for singers; and backstage quick changes. This position requires professional experience and a congenial and artist-oriented personality.

Production Administration (Early May through August 27)

This intern will help with office routines, scheduling, shopping, and staff support, including safety program implementation and crew meals. The job requires a basic knowledge of production procedures and terminology, computer literacy, and a driver's license.

Projected Titles (June 6 through August 23)

This intern will help the titles supervisor prepare scripts, scores, and a presentation system for titled productions; attend some rehearsals; and call titles for performances. The intern must be absolutely comfortable reading opera scores, detail-oriented, organized, and calm under pressure. General word processing and computer skills are required; training on presentation software will be provided.

Technical knowledge of projection equipment is not required.

Prop Construction (Mid-May through July 30)

This intern will help in the prop shop with creation of properties for four operas. It requires thorough shop knowledge, ability to work independently, and skill in one or more shop areas (wood, soft goods, paint, crafts, etc.).

Scene Design (May 24 through July 24)

During technical rehearsals, this intern will help scenic designers with notes, research, drafting, and help in the prop or paint shop as needed. This position requires attention to detail and the ability to work as part of a collaborative team. Experience with professional designers preferred.

Scenery Construction/Rigging (Mid-May through July 30)

Two interns will help carpentry staff with construction of new scenery, alterations to scenery built by contract shops, and initial load-in. They will also help rigging staff install hanging scenery and lighting equipment and with maintenance and upgrades to the rigging system. This job requires good stage and shop carpentry skills and basic knowledge of counterweight systems and rigging.

Scenic Art (May 23 through July 30)

This intern will help with in-house scenery and prop painting and with touch-ups and repaints of contract shop scenery. It requires excellent drawing, good layout, mixing and scenic craft skills; professional experience desirable.

Stage Management (May 23 through August 24)

This position will help with set up, maintaining and cleaning rehearsal halls, coordinating with shop heads and designers, overseeing and supervising the work of production rehearsal and running crews, and creating production books, scores and inventories. Interns do not call shows, but must read music proficiently and have considerable academic stage management experience.

Stage Operations (Mid/late May through August 27)

Eight interns will help install repertory scenery; run deck, rail and properties; perform daily scenery changeovers; build, install, and maintain rehearsal scenery and properties; and strike scenery at the end of the season. Some interns will have performance opportunities as supernumeraries. This is an excellent introduction to most aspects of production and requires only a basic familiarity with stage procedures.

Technical Direction (May 10 through August 27)

This intern will help create working drawings for archive and rental purposes; cataloguing and tracking rehearsal scenery; and organizing production archive books. The intern will also draft updated production ground plans and small projects for scene shop. The position requires good knowledge of scenery construction techniques. AutoCAD proficiency necessary.

Wardrobe (June 6 through August 27)

Three interns will help maintain large repertory costume inventory, dress chorus and principals, and assist with backstage quick changes. Interns also assist in costume shop for the first two to three weeks of the contract period and need basic theatrical sewing skills. A congenial and artist-oriented personality is essential.

HOW TO APPLY

To be considered for an internship, submit a current resume including present and permanent addresses, day and evening telephone numbers, education (post-high school), and dates of attendance, along with work experience, internships, and dates of employment. You also should include two references (stating relationship, address, and day/evening telephone numbers). In addition, you'll need to include a cover letter including your three choices of internships, in order of preference, along with your earliest date available and latest departure date. Scenic art and prop construction applicants should include examples of their work (color copies preferred).

JIM HENSON COMPANY INTERNSHIP

To apply for an internship in the archives department, send e-mail to
Karen Falk kfalk@henson.com

To apply for an internship in the creative department, fax, mail, or e-mail your resume to
The Jim Henson Company
1416 N. La Brea Avenue
Hollywood, CA 90028
Fax: (323) 802-1835
mlynch@henson.com

To apply for an internship in the design department, fax or e-mail your resume to
The Jim Henson Company
Maryanne Purdy
Fax: (323) 802-1836
mpurdy@henson.com

To apply for an internship in the media library, fax, mail, or e-mail your resume to
The Jim Henson Company
1416 N. La Brea Avenue
Hollywood, CA 90028
Fax: (323) 802-1835

To apply for an internship in the public relations department, e-mail your resume, making sure that subject heading reads PR INTERN, to
The Jim Henson Company
Nicole Goldman
ngoldman@henson.com

To apply for an internship in the marketing department, mail, fax, or e-mail your resume to
The Jim Henson Company
Jim Formanek
1416 N. La Brea Avenue
Hollywood, CA 90028
Fax: (323) 802-1836
jformanek@henson.com

What You Can Earn: Unpaid; course credit is available.

Application Deadlines: December 1 for spring semester: Internships typically begin in January; May 1 for summer semester: Internships typically begin in May; August 1 for fall semester: Internships typically begin in September.

Educational Experience: Minimum sophomore in college before beginning the internship. Check individual internships for other specifics.

Requirements: Course credit required (you'll need to provide proof of credit in the form of a transcript showing the internship or a letter from school); a high maturity level, a sense of humor, and a willingness to be flexible. The ability to write well is a strong asset. Good basic office skills (telephone, copying, and faxing) and computer literacy are a must. Applicants who will make a good fit with our staff and with the company as a whole are essential. The willingness to work quickly and juggle several projects at once is very important.

OVERVIEW

Over the past 50 years, The Jim Henson Company has become an international leader in family entertainment, with a commitment to continuing the late Jim Henson's legacy and mission.

The company, which is also a preeminent multimedia production company, is home of Jim Henson's Creature Shop, headquartered in Hollywood at the historic Charlie Chaplin studios.

In addition to The Muppets and Muppet Babies, the many timeless creations inspired by this vision include *Bear in the Big Blue House*, *Farscape*, *Fraggle Rock*, *Dark Crystal*, and *Labyrinth*. In 2002, after two years as part of EM.TV, a German-based TV merchandising and distribution company, The Jim Henson Company was reacquired by the five Henson children. The following year, the rights to the Muppet characters (along with *Bear in the Big Blue House*) were sold to The Walt Disney Company, thus realizing Henson's longtime dream that the Muppet characters would live on forever.

The company is looking for enthusiastic individuals willing to dedicate themselves to enhancing the company environment. The company seeks students who are organized, mature, and have a great sense of humor. You must have a positive attitude, a desire to learn, and a willingness to be flexible. This is a fun, relaxed place to work with a lot of creative energy and a good mix of hard work. You will see how the company functions from behind the scenes and play a large role in contributing to its goals. Please do not feel that you need to be a puppeteer, a puppet maker, or an arts and crafts buff to be considered for an internship. In fact, internships are primarily in an office atmosphere located in the Los Angeles or New York offices. However, all applicants are welcome who have a special interest in the company and its projects.

Internships are available in creative affairs, design department, media library, public relations, and marketing. The internship program aims to provide a great working opportunity as well as teach you about the business world. You'll be exposed to the company's projects and goals for the year and will be able to improve your business skills and learn new ones.

Keep in mind, however, that the company does not teach puppeteering or puppet making and that it does not provide any artistic internships in graphic design, animation, mold making, sculpting, animatronic construction, or foam latex construction.

Archives Department (New York)

If you intern with The Jim Henson Company Archives (located in Manhattan), you'll spend one or two days a week helping with collections management and organization of the company's historical collections. Duties include cataloguing and processing of materials, record-keeping, and some reference work. For this internship, you should be interested in archive, library, or museum work and have related course work.

Creative Affairs (Los Angeles)

In this department, you'll support the Jim Henson Company Creative Affairs team in developing sci-fi/fantasy genre films, while also helping on special projects. Your duties might include reading scripts and books, writing coverage, creative research, writer/director/design research, compiling artwork and pitch materials, general office support, helping executives, coordinating materials for meetings, and running occasional errands. Since you'll work directly with Henson executives in this small department, you'll have a unique opportunity to interact with the staff, share your thoughts on the material, and form valuable relationships.

In this department, you'll work primarily with the Creative Affairs team, but you'll also have the opportunity to work on projects with several other departments, such as new media, archives, administration, design, marketing, public relations, business and legal affairs, finance, the creature shop, and the president's office.

Design Department (Los Angeles)

This department is responsible for creating and maintaining the photographic archive of The Jim Henson Company. Here you'll compile artistic and photographic archival materials for current and upcoming productions. You'll help with image scanning and professional printing, work with professional printing services, run errands, handle general office duties, and work within artistic design platforms. Although most of the time you'll be working within the design department, you may get the chance to work on several projects within other departments.

You'll need to be familiar with Photoshop, Illustrator, and general Macintosh platforms for this internship. This is an excellent opportunity for students geared toward graphic design or other artistic venues within the television and film industry.

Marketing Department (Los Angeles)

Interns in this department support the Jim Henson Company marketing team in developing sci-fi/fantasy genre films and television. Here you'll help with creative research, developing presentations, and general office support including telephones and filing, helping executives, coordinating materials for meetings, running occasional errands, and so on. Working directly with the Henson executives in this small department will give you a unique opportunity to interact with the staff, share your thoughts on material, and form valuable relationships.

You'll primarily work very closely with the marketing team, but you'll also have the opportunity to work on projects with several of our other departments (new media; archives; administration; design; creative affairs; public relations; business and legal affairs; finance; the creature shop, and the president).

If you intern in this department, you must work three full days a week (weekdays only) from 9:30 A.M. to 6:00 P.M. Marketing or public relations majors are preferred, but these majors aren't required.

Media Library (Los Angeles)

In this internship, you'll help support the collections management/tape library team in managing the company's media assets. You'll help with project and property research; review of tape library materials; cataloguing; database entry and management; general office support; and fulfillment of duplication requests. You should demonstrate an interest in and have some experience in film archive or library work. Although you'll mostly work with the collections management and tape library team, you'll also have the chance to work on projects with several other departments. This is a great opportunity to work with a company's media library and could be a stepping stone for students looking to get into vault management/post-production.

Public Relations (Los Angeles)

In this internship, you'll help with all aspects of the company's worldwide communications and public outreach. In addition to performing standard office duties, you'll work directly with the director of corporate communications on a wide variety of projects, including press releases, media kits, interviews, pitches, appearances, and premiere strategies. You should be interested in media relations and entertainment.

HOW TO APPLY

To apply for these internships, you should send to the preceding contact addresses a one-page resume, a cover letter mentioning the position you're applying for, specifically stating reasons why you're interested in interning at Henson, and why you feel you'd be a good fit for this position and this company. You also should discuss work experience or college activities linked to your qualifications. You should be as creative as you wish with your application, but you should maintain professionalism.

As a result of the volume of resumes the company normally receives, they will only contact candidates they wish to consider for placement. These applicants will be called for an initial phone interview. If you have film, video, performance, or artistic skills, mention them in your cover letter and/or resume. Unsolicited materials become the property of The Jim Henson Company and will not be returned.

JUILLIARD SCHOOL PROFESSIONAL INTERNSHIP

The Juilliard School
60 Lincoln Center Plaza
New York, NY 10023

(212) 799-5000, ext. 7102
htaynton@juilliard.edu
http://www.juilliard.edu/about/profintern.html

What You Can Earn: $262 a week.
Application Deadlines: June 1.
Educational Experience: Specific educational requirements are detailed below and may differ depending on the specific internship desired.
Requirements: Specific requirements are detailed below and may differ depending on the specific internship desired.

OVERVIEW

An internship is a positive way to find out if a job in theater or arts administration is what you're looking for. To this end, the Juilliard School sponsors a professional intern program in both technical theater and arts administration designed to provide hands-on experience working with theater professionals and school administrators in respective fields. The program was created in 1977 and focused primarily on design; five years later, the program had expanded to focus on all aspects of technical theater. By the 1991-92 season, arts administration internships were introduced. Many former interns now work at Juilliard as administrators or as theater technicians. There is also a strong Intern Alumni Group providing support to those beginning their careers.

All Interns will participate in or attend professional drama, dance, and music productions. While technical interns learn the latest skills and techniques working with trained professionals, administrative interns get lots of practice operating one of the country's most prestigious performing arts schools.

An intern's performance is monitored and monthly group and individual meetings are held to evaluate progress and discuss your experiences. Seminars and discussions with alumni are held throughout the year on a variety of topics. You'll also get to participate in backstage tours of Broadway theaters, the Metropolitan Opera House, and other professional theater centers.

If you choose technical theater, your work will revolve around four performance spaces at Juilliard. In past seasons, the production department has produced two full stage operas, three opera workshops, five major drama productions, five Studio 301 drama workshop productions, a major dance concert, two dance workshops, and numerous concerts, recitals, and special events.

The Juilliard program is an internship, not a degree program. All internships are full time and usually begin in September and last through May. Although reasonable working hours are typically maintained, your weekly schedule will vary depending on your duties and the needs of the production schedules.

If you want academic credit for your participation in the internship program, you must do so through your sponsoring school. However, Juilliard will send an evaluation of your work and participation in the program to your school, if required.

Arts Administration

Arts administration internships are offered in building facilities, chamber music office, concert office, dance division, drama division, concert office, chamber music office, building, and facilities/maintenance/engineering.

Building Facilities

You'll work directly with the associate vice president for facilities management to provide an introduction to and involvement in all phases of managing a facility. This internship doesn't deal with theatrical production. It requires attention to detail and good follow-through skills; the ability to interact well with people is absolutely necessary.

Chamber Music Office

Here you'll help the assistant dean and director of chamber music primarily in the administration of the Chamber Music Program. You'll be responsible for maintaining the registration database of up to 120 chamber music ensembles, administering the January ChamberFest, and managing several ensembles (such as the spring semester chamber orchestra and Bach Aria ensemble). You'll also schedule chamber music ensembles in occasional performances outside of Juilliard, submit the monthly chamber music faculty payroll, and handle the details of counseling and interacting with many students, explaining chamber music policies and managing paperwork.

Imagination and personal initiative, along with the ability to manage routine administrative tasks, is important. You must be able to use Microsoft Office Suite and Microsoft Outlook and have excellent verbal and writing skills.

Concert Office

This internship is ideal if you're interested in producing events, since you'll be helping to produce the hundreds of recitals and activities that occur each year. Responsibilities range from preparing the printed program materials to stage managing master classes. The internship also will focus on front-of-house requirements for all major Juilliard productions, including house management and the daily supervision of the Juilliard box office.

The concert office intern must be a self-motivated individual with good follow-through and interpersonal skills and an eye for detail. Knowledge of music is helpful but not absolutely necessary.

Dance Division

This intern will help the production coordinator during preproduction of all Juilliard Dance Ensemble events, including main stage and studio workshops; Choreographers/Composers Concert; Winter Concert; Senior Production; and Outreach tours. You must attend production meetings and do scheduling, program layout, and follow up with other departments such as costumes, electrics, scenic, and so on. The intern will also work with the stage management team in running these events. Other duties include developing production elements with dance students for their independent and class choreographic projects; maintaining the video archives; organizing video recordings of dance events and classroom documentation; distributing video tape to students and faculty; and

overseeing audio recording and duplication of rehearsal and performance tapes. Stage management experience is preferred.

Drama Division

In this internship, you'll help the administrative director in the daily administrative and production operations associated with the division's four-year professional actor-training program. There is lots of interaction with faculty, guest artists, students, and prospective students, so diplomacy and excellent organizational and communication skills are required. Computer experience with MS Word and Outlook would be extremely helpful.

Costume Shop

Five internships are offered that involve assisting designers, fabric swatching, draping, and shopping. When helping the designers, you can expect to be responsible for executing the designer's sketches, costume research, budgeting, coordinating fitting schedules, and attending fittings. You'll also have hands-on experience in stitching, crafts, millinery painting, distressing, fabric manipulation, wardrobe stock maintenance, and running crew. A one-semester makeup class is offered. Sewing experience is required.

Electrics

In this internship, you'll experience many aspects of stage lighting, including reading a light plot; helping the master electrician; and hanging, focusing, and maintaining the inventory and spaces. You'll have the chance to act as master electrician and may have the opportunity to run light and sound boards for workshop productions. The sound intern will learn all aspects of sound for production by helping the house audio technician. You should have a practical knowledge of electrics and a basic understanding of electricity.

Production Assistant

There are two different production assistant internships. One is with the Juilliard theater events and music coordinator. Assignments will eventually lead to stage managing events in the Juilliard Theater. This intern also will help with the daily and long-term planning of these events, in addition to helping with the daily administrative and production operations associated with the production department. There may be opportunities to help with drama or opera productions as well.

The other intern will work with resident production stage managers and stage management interns, helping with drama and opera productions. Applicants for both production assistant internships are required to be organized, punctual, and flexible and have good interpersonal skills.

Props

This active shop needs committed interns who will learn many facets of prop design, procurement, and construction. You'll complete carpentry, soft good, sculpture, assemblage, and graphics projects as well as interpret designs through research and shopping in and around NYC and beyond. Budgeting, bookkeeping, and management skills will be addressed, as will interdepartmental communications and cooperation. Other duties include helping to maintain the props inventory and running crew assignments. You should be familiar with basic shop tools and a little curious.

Scene Painting

Successful candidates will work on all productions under the guidance of the scenic charge, helping with budgeting, layout, scene painting, faux finishes, and sculpturing, along with paint shop maintenance and safety. You should have some scene painting experience.

Stage Management

Six interns in this area will help production stage managers on opera, drama, and dance productions, starting with preproduction meetings and on through rehearsals and into performances. You'll need great organizational skills and the ability to work closely with students, directors, and choreographers, dealing with a wide variety of personalities. You must be flexible, take initiative, and be open to working with various production stage managers with different working styles.

Rehearsals occur in late afternoons and evenings, with many long hours. The ability to read music and stage management experience are highly desirable.

Technical Theater Internships

Internships are offered in costume shop, wigs and makeup, electrics, props, scene painting, stage management, and production assistant.

Wigs and Makeup

Two internships are offered to provide training in theatrical makeup, hair and wig styling, wig and facial hair construction, working with costume designers, and running crew skills. Experience in theater, cosmetology, or hair and makeup is helpful, but dexterity, a friendly personality, and a willingness to learn are the primary prerequisites.

HOUSING

Although Julliard offers a stipend of $262 a week, this is not enough to pay for your living expenses in New York. Since the internship is a full-time work commitment, you can't get a job on the side to supplement your income. Also remember that housing in New York is expensive and requires careful consideration; you should probably find housing before beginning your internship.

HOW TO APPLY

To apply to the program, you must submit a $15 fee with a completed application form that you can download in PDF form at www.juilliard.edu/about/profintern.html. Keep in mind that the earlier you apply, the better your chance of getting the internship you want. You should include a resume that includes your educational experience, an ID snapshot or photo, and three letters of reference describing your working style, an evaluation of skills, and, if applicable, an evaluation of design abilities. (These can be sent separately.) You also should include a 250-word personal statement describing your expectations about the internship and how it relates to your career goals.

Interviews are highly recommended, and you're encouraged to tour the facilities and arrange an interview whenever possible.

KENNEDY CENTER FOR THE PERFORMING ARTS MANAGEMENT INTERNSHIP

Vilar Institute for Arts Management Internships
The Kennedy Center
2700 F Street, NW
Washington, DC 20566
(202) 416-8821
http://www.kennedy-center.org/education/
vilarinstitute/internships/home.cfm

What You Can Earn: $800 monthly stipend, plus free tickets to center performances.

Application Deadlines: June 15 for fall semester (September through December); November 1 for winter/spring (January through April); March 1 for summer (May through August).

Educational Experience: College juniors/seniors, graduate students, and recent college graduates (within two years of graduation).

Requirements: Specific requirements are detailed below, depending on the area of the internship.

OVERVIEW

"I am certain that after the dust of centuries has passed over our cities," President John F. Kennedy once said, "we, too, will be remembered not for our victories or defeats in battle or in politics, but for our contribution to the human spirit." In its third decade, the Kennedy Center, the living memorial to this fallen president, continues its efforts to fulfill his vision by presenting a variety of theater and musicals; dance and ballet; orchestral, chamber, jazz, popular, and folk music; and multimedia performances. The Kennedy Center presents performers and performances from across America and around the world, nurturing new works and young artists and serving the nation as a leader in arts education.

Each year more than 6 million people nationwide take part in education programs initiated by the center, including performances; lectures; demonstrations; open rehearsals; dance and music residencies; master classes; competitions for young actors and musicians; backstage tours; and workshops for teachers.

If you're interested in beginning a career in performing arts management and/or arts education, an internship at the Kennedy Center in the nation's capital could be for you. Each semester, about 20 students are chosen to participate in a three- to four-month, full-time (40 hours a week) internship.

You may work either in advertising, development, education (local and national programs), press, National Symphony Orchestra, press relations, production, programming, technology, volunteer management, finance, or facilities.

At the start of your internship, you and your supervisor will develop a list of learning objectives and goals you'd like to accomplish; you'll also be assigned to a project to be completed during your time at the Kennedy Center. You'll submit a weekly journal, maintain a working portfolio, attend required intern events, and participate in mid-semester and final evaluations.

You'll also attend weekly sessions led by executives of the Kennedy Center and other major arts institutions in Washington, D.C. In addition, you may attend performances, workshops, and classes presented by the center for free (space available).

Advertising and Press Relations

These areas are designed to market and promote the Kennedy Center and its performances to the general public and to the local and international press. The in-house advertising agency works with the marketing and press departments to promote all activities at the Kennedy Center through print media, television and radio advertisements, and press conferences. Interns receive hands-on training in a variety of advertising, marketing, and press-related tasks and are exposed to the team-oriented process of determining the center's marketing and press needs. If you work here, you might coordinate all advertisements for the Kennedy Center and do copy editing; promotional event planning and management; assisting in the design of print material; developing new media contacts; writing press releases; pitching stories to press contacts; securing review coverage for performances; and various other marketing related projects.

Development
This department annually raises nearly $50 million for the ongoing work of the Kennedy Center and the National Symphony Orchestra. Here you'll help with many fund-raising activities, including membership fulfillment; corporate fund campaign; major gift donations; grants and sponsorships by corporations and foundations; planned giving; special events; and volunteer management.

Education
Through programs of the education department, people of all ages have the opportunity to learn in, through, and about the performing arts through the creation and presentation of quality works for young people and families; professional, resource, and leadership development opportunities for teachers, students, and artists and the general public and educational programming. If you intern here, you'll learn about local and national education reform issues and participate in many aspects of performing arts education.

Facilities
This department coordinates all aspects of strategic facilities planning at the Kennedy Center, including operations and maintenance, security, project/construction coordination, transportation, and contracting. The facilities internship will demystify what it takes to operate a performing arts facility.

Finance
With this internship opportunity, you'll gain an understanding of the center's financial activity, budgeting cycle, and systems and learn how the department interacts with and supports other Kennedy Center departments and programs.

General Counsel's Office
Through interning with the general counsel's office, you'll learn performing arts law (including dealing with standard artist and production contracts); federal programs (including the Federal Tort Claims Act); nonprofit tax; immigration law; labor law; insurance/risk management; and other legal issues that may arise in the day-to-day activities of a presidential memorial and performing arts center. You must be at least in your second year of law school; this placement is offered only during the summer semester.

National Symphony Orchestra
Via the NSO, you'll be given a chance to help with many aspects of symphony management, including the operation and administration of a 48-week season of performances with 100 musicians. As the orchestra of the capital of the United States, the NSO regularly participates in events of national and international importance, such as presidential inaugurations and annual Independence Day and Memorial Day celebrations with nationally televised, outdoor concerts at the U. S. Capitol.

Programming and Production
Each year the Kennedy Center commissions, produces, and presents performances in jazz, ballet, modern dance, classical music, comedy, theater, storytelling, puppetry, and musical theater for people of all ages. The center also presents and produces festivals, televised specials, radio programs, and cutting-edge and community-based programs. A number of internships

may be available with the administrative side of programming and production.

Technology

Technology continues to be more and more important in all aspects of managing the performing arts, from providing technical support to administrative staff and box office personnel, to the creation of Web-based projects and the development of Internet-based arts and education resources for teachers and students. The Kennedy Center is aggressively finding new ways to use technology, and you'll have the opportunity to work with leading professionals in the field of technology and performing arts.

HOW TO APPLY

You should submit all of the following materials in one complete package, including an internship application form downloaded from the preceding Web site; a cover letter discussing career goals, computer skills, and three internships of interest; your resume; an official university transcript; and two current letters of recommendation from people who can address your background and skills. Recommendation letters must arrive in sealed envelopes with the signature of the letter writer appearing across the envelope flap. You should also include a writing sample (no more than three pages).

Applicants from nonnative English-speaking countries must provide proof of English-speaking and writing competence through a minimum TOEFL score of 600. Applicants who have earned a bachelor's degree in an English-speaking country may request an exemption from this requirement. International applicants must have a valid visa. All materials must arrive in one package and must be written in English.

Telephone interviews will be conducted as part of the final selection process, and you'll be notified within six to eight weeks after the deadline has passed.

To prevent any delay in delivery of your application, you should send your materials by FedEx, UPS, or U.S. Priority Mail. The Kennedy Center also recommends that you follow up by phone to ensure receipt of all materials.

THE LATE SHOW WITH DAVID LETTERMAN INTERNSHIP

Late Show with David Letterman
Director of Human Resources
Fax: (212) 975-4734

What You Can Earn: Unpaid.
Application Deadlines: Fall (June 1); spring (October 1); summer (March 1).
Educational Experience: Any major but must receive college credit for participation in the program.
Requirements: Must be bright, energetic, and available to work Monday through Friday from 10:00 A.M. to 7:00 P.M.

OVERVIEW

The Late Show uses full-time interns in a variety of departments, including research, talent, production, writers, writers' production, and music. There is also a part-time production finance internship for finance or accounting majors. No matter where they work, interns work on projects specific to their departments and perform general office duties.

You may choose to apply to any of the three sessions offered year round: fall (August through December), spring (December through May), and summer (May through August).

HOW TO APPLY

If you're interested in applying for a *Late Show* internship, you should fax a resume and cover letter to the preceding number. The show will contact applicants they wish to interview shortly after each deadline date.

LONGWOOD GARDENS PERFORMING ARTS INTERNSHIP

Longwood Gardens
Student Programming
PO Box 501
Kennett Square, PA 19348
(610) 388-1000, ext. 508
studentprograms@longwoodgardens.org
General Web site: http://www.longwoodgardens.
   org
Application: http://www.longwoodgardens.
   org/Education/student%20programs/
   College%20Internship/CollegeInternship1.htm

What You Can Earn: $6.50 an hour for a 40-hour week, plus free housing and garden space.
Application Deadlines: February 1 for internships starting in June; May 1 for September; November 1 for January or March.
Educational Experience: Current arts administration, public relations, marketing, and journalism students; strong computer skills are helpful.
Requirements: A valid driver's license and the ability to work some weekends and to work independently; must have strong interest in and knowledge of the performing arts and news-writing skills.

OVERVIEW

Interning at Longwood Gardens offers excellent opportunities for you to gain practical experience, learn career skills, and study amid the world's premier horticulture display. The one-year performing arts internship offers an opportunity to work with a variety of the 400 performing arts events held at Longwood each year, and you'll learn how a performing arts office operates through hands-on involvement in the daily management of the office.

You'll write press releases, public-service announcements, calendar listings, and brochure copy; produce event flyers; and help with marketing events and mailings. You'll manage the performing arts coordinator's phone calls; create public-service announcements of all concert, theatre, and dance events; create and place in-house event publicity signs; create event fliers for mailing and posting in the community; contribute to schedule of events, Festival of Fountains brochure, Fun Days brochure, and Chamber Music brochures. You'll also help with performing arts payroll and mailings, check requests and paperwork for artists' checks, and maintain event files and artist files; work with employees in horticulture, maintenance, and services; act as a media contact for performing arts; and develop marketing of events plans for each event.

You'll also set up Excel spread sheets for events, meet and help visiting artists, and work some events as a performance attendant or manager.

HOUSING

If you wish, you may live rent-free (a taxable benefit) on the grounds of the former estate of industrialist Pierre S. du Pont. Student houses are furnished and include nearby garden space and are located on Red Lion Row. Each house has three or four bedrooms and comes fully furnished. At any given time, there are 20 to 40 students living on The Row.

Red Lion Row was originally built around the turn of the century by Pierre S. du Pont to house his employees and their families. The Row is within easy walking distance of Longwood Gardens.

To see pictures of what the houses look like, visit the Web site at http://www.longwoodgardens.org/Education/student%20programs/Housing%20and%20Activities/Housing/Housing.htm.

Directly south of the student houses is the student garden space, where you may have garden space. You're responsible for the upkeep of your garden, and you must return the plot to its original condition before leaving. Communal tools are available, as well as mulch, potting soil, and leaf mold. A greenhouse and head house are provided for the professional gardeners' class work. Any space they aren't using in the greenhouse may be used by interns.

HOW TO APPLY

The internship application is available online in PDF format, downloadable at the preceding Web site. To receive an application by mail, send a letter of request to the preceding address.

LOS ANGELES OPERA COMMUNITY PROGRAMS INTERNSHIP

Los Angeles Opera
135 N. Grand Avenue
Los Angeles, CA 90012
(213) 972-7498; (213) 972-8016
Fax: (213) 972-3007
jbabcock@laopera.com

What You Can Earn: Unpaid.
Application Deadlines: Rolling.
Educational Experience: Full-time, currently enrolled undergraduate students.
Requirements: Must be residents of or attend college in Los Angeles County; interest in opera is a plus.

OVERVIEW

Internships are available in community programs, development, and marketing.

Community Programs Internship

Intern will assist in the production of programs for youth, families, and adults both at the Music Center and throughout the community. Intern will organize department auditions; assist with volunteer training and management; coordinate youth Opera Camp auditions; registration and rehearsals; work with staff to create curriculum materials for various community productions; and research arts and social action organizations. Some phones, filing, record-keeping, and database management are also involved. Schedule to include some nights and weekends.

Development Intern

The intern will work on projects throughout the various program areas of the development department, including the annual fund, major gifts, institutional giving, research, and database management. The intern will assist with the preparation of direct mail solicitations, help to conceptualize the benefits program and materials, assist in the preparation of proposals, engage in donor prospect research, and assist with fund-raising-lead management, gift entry, and tracking.

Marketing Intern

The intern will work with members of the marketing team to learn how the entire department fits together. Responsibilities will include assisting with subscription and single-ticket sale campaigns, organizing archival materials, analysis and reporting, correspondence, general office projects, and interfacing with members of other departments. The intern will attend all marketing meetings and company meetings.

HOW TO APPLY

Send a resume and cover letter to the preceding address.

LUCAS DIGITAL INTERNSHIP

Lucas Digital, Intern Department
PO Box 2009
San Rafael, CA 94912

(415) 662-1999
http://www.ilm.com/employment.html

What You Can Earn: $10 an hour plus college credit.
Application Deadlines: Rolling.
Educational Experience: Currently enrolled as a junior or senior student at an accredited college or university and scheduled to return to an accredited college or university following the internship, with an overall GPA of at least 3.0 and a GPA of at least 3.5 in the major.
Requirements: Must be available to work the number of hours designated for the program session for which you're selected, and must provide your own housing and transportation. Applicants who have already completed a student internship with Lucas Digital Ltd. or any of the other Lucas companies are not eligible for a second student internship at another Lucas Company.

OVERVIEW

Lucas Digital Ltd. is an award-winning company dedicated to the digital needs of the entertainment and commercial production industries for visual effects, sound design, audio post-production, and editing for feature films, attractions, and television commercials. The company's two divisions, Industrial Light & Magic (ILM) and Skywalker Sound, offer internship opportunities for highly motivated students interested in pursuing technical and business careers in visual effects and sound design for feature films and commercials. An internship at ILM or Skywalker Sound is an opportunity to work with talented teams of artists and other professionals working on creative projects in a dynamic and highly collaborative atmosphere. Lucas Digital Ltd. was listed recently in *Fortune* magazine as one of the top 100 companies to work for in the United States.

The company typically offers two paid student internship program sessions a year: a summer session and a fall/winter session. The number of student internships and the areas in which they are available each session are determined by the projects in production. Internships for prior sessions have been offered in such areas as art, sound, editorial, computer graphics (CG) software and training, computer systems and software engineering, Web development, human resources, finance, accounting, media library, and video engineering.

Industrial Light and Magic (ILM)

Founded in 1975 by George Lucas, ILM is the largest, most advanced digital effects system and facility in the world. Beginning with a mastery of the traditional arts of blue-screen photography, matte painting, and model construction, ILM pioneered the development of motion-control cameras, optical compositing, and other advances in effects technology. It is a leader in the ability to merge photo-realistic digital images with live-action footage. ILM has played a key role in eight of the top 10 top box office hits of all time, winning 14 Academy Awards for Best Visual Effects and 16 Technical Achievement Awards. ILM has produced visual effects for more than 100 feature films, including the creation of wholly computer-generated characters in movies including *The Abyss, Terminator 2: Judgment Day,* the *Jurassic Park* film series, and *Star Wars: Episode I.* The company has also produced lifelike distortions of the human body in *Death Becomes Her, The Mask,* and *Forrest Gump* and came up with startling 3-D computer graphics in *Twister, The Perfect Storm,* and *Pearl Harbor.*

ILM currently employs a core group of more than 1,200 producers, art directors, model makers, stage technicians, computer graphics artists, computer engineers, editors, and camera operators.

As a student intern with Industrial Light & Magic, you'll work in San Rafael, California; student interns at Skywalker Sound will work at Skywaker Ranch in Nicasio, California. Both locations are in Marin County, which is approximately 20 miles north of San Francisco.

Skywalker Sound

Skywalker Sound is Lucas Digital's audio post-production facility, known for its sound design and advanced editing equipment. Skywalker Sound offers a full range of sound recording, editing and mixing services for film, video, music and theme park attractions. Skywalker Sound has a world-class scoring stage, six mix studios, ADR and Foley stages, 34 editing suites, and a 300 seat screening room. The company has won 15 Academy Awards for movies such as *Star Wars, Raiders of the Lost Ark, E.T. the Extra-Terrestrial,* and *Indiana Jones and the Last Crusade.*

As a student intern at Lucas Digital, you'll gain practical hands-on experience as you observe masters at work creating the spectacular sights and sounds of the screen. You'll also hear the inside story from award-winning artists and executives through scheduled presentations and informal get-togethers. The company's student internship program is an important part of its recruiting strategy; an internship could be the starting point for employment in a regular position with the company. However, while some student interns have been hired as regular employees following their internships, working as a student intern at Lucas Digital Ltd. is not a contract of employment and does not guarantee other employment with the company. The internship program is designed to provide an exciting educational supplement to your college career and to boost the company's relationships with colleges who teach the skills and talents the entertainment industry needs.

HOW TO APPLY

You can check to see what internships are available by visiting the Web site above. You can apply for an internship online at http://www.ilm.com/job_apply.html. You will not need to submit a transcript when applying; however, if you're selected to participate in the student internship program, you'll be required to submit transcripts.

If you are selected to participate in the student internship program, the company will notify you as soon as possible. All students selected to participate in a particular program session will be noti-

fied at least two weeks prior to the beginning of that program session.

LUCASFILM INTERNSHIP

Lucasfilm Ltd.
Human Resources
PO Box 29901
San Francisco, CA 94129-0901

Lucasfilm Animation Ltd.
Attn: Recruiting/The Carriage House
PO Box 10037
San Rafael, CA 94912

Lucasfilm Licensing
Human Resources
PO Box 29905
San Francisco, CA 94129-0905

What You Can Earn: $10 an hour plus college credit for 40 hours a week (9:00 A.M. to 6:00 P.M., Monday through Friday)
Application Deadlines: March 31.
Educational Experience: Must be a rising college junior or senior. Students from a variety of majors may apply, including business administration, marketing, communications, accounting, library science, museum studies, international relations, or economics; graduate students are also eligible. Students must be returning to class full time when the internship is over.
Requirements: For the part-time winter term (16 to 24 hours a week), you must be attending a local college or university within commuting distance to San Rafael, California.

OVERVIEW

Lucasfilm is one of the world's leading film and entertainment companies. Founded by George Lucas in 1971, it is a privately held entertainment company that includes a variety of global businesses in addition to motion picture and TV production. These include visual effects, sound, video games, licensing, and online activity.

Lucasfilm offers a part-time winter internship and a summer internship in various departments and disciplines based at either Skywalker or Big Rock Ranch facilities in Marin. The summer term is full time (40 hours a week) and is open to interns from across the United States. Assignments may be available in public relations, licensing, finance/accounting, Internet/online, archives, and library/research in any of the companies of Lucasfilm: Lucasfilm Ltd., Lucasfilm Licensing, or Lucasfilm Animation Ltd.

HOW TO APPLY

You may apply online at: http://www.lucasfilm.com/employment/apply, or you may send a resume to any one of the preceding addresses. For special information about Lucasanimation, visit their Web site at http://www.lucasfilm.com/employment/apply/anim_policy.html.

All applicants will be notified by no later than May 1 about their application status.

METRO-GOLDWYN-MAYER (MGM) INTERNSHIP

MGM Internships
10250 Constellation Boulevard
Los Angeles, CA 90067-6421
310-449-3000
http://mgmua.com/corp_career_internships.do

What You Can Earn: Paid or unpaid (unpaid internships must earn college credit)
Application Deadlines: Rolling.

Educational Experience: A registered student at a university eligible to earn academic credit and involved in a related course of study (such as theater, film and TV, business, and so on); preference will be given to juniors and seniors in a related field of study.
Requirements: Must have verification of legal right to work in the United States.

OVERVIEW

With a tradition of producing some of Hollywood's most beloved films at the core of its business, MGM has evolved into an integrated and diversified modern media company involved in film production, TV programming, interactive entertainment, music, animation, licensing, and more. Not surprising, there are many different areas that require interns at different times. For example, an intern in the MGM consumer products division might be responsible for creating and assembling press kits for select sci-fi and classic properties, doing field research, processing invoices, and maintaining certain aspects of the marketing budget. For this unpaid internship, the ideal candidate must be able to work 12 to 16 hours a week. Applicants for this position should have experience with Microsoft Word, Excel, and PowerPoint and must have excellent written and verbal communication skills, be organized and detail oriented, and be interested in promotions, marketing, and publicity.

An intern in post-production will get a good overview of the production process in the studio; during production, employees work to finalize a movie's budget, hire crew, secure product placement, manage daily paperwork while a movie is shooting (such as managing call sheets and production reports), and supervise post-production and the editing of a movie. If you work as an intern in production, you might copy, file, and distribute materials, help out with projects, and handle other general office work. You should be proficient in Microsoft Word and Excel for this internship.

To check which MGM internships are available, visit http://www.mgm.com/corp_career_internships.do and click the link to "current internships."

HOW TO APPLY
You can apply for an internship at MGM by visiting the preceding Web site.

Here you can copy and paste your resume into a form for submission. You will need to submit your resume only once, even though there might be several internship positions in which you're interested. MGM will review your qualifications and assess what position might be most appropriate.

MTV NETWORKS INTERNSHIP— NASHVILLE

Human Resources
Attn: Internship Program
CMT/MTVN Nashville
330 Commerce Street
Nashville, TN 37201
Fax: (615) 335-8614

What You Can Earn: Unpaid.
Application Deadlines: Specific majors are indicated in the application materials.
Educational Experience: Students in or entering their junior or senior year at an accredited college or university or students seeking a graduate degree.
Requirements: Motivated students who excel in a fast-paced environment; must provide proof of college-credit eligibility; must be energetic, creative, have a positive attitude, and a passion for country music.

OVERVIEW
How would you like to spend a semester with Kenny Chesney or Faith Hill? CMT (Country Music Television) and MTV Networks/Nashville invite you to apply for an internship with this top country music network that features a blend of cutting-edge music videos, creative original programming, and incredible concert events.

This internship is for you if you'd love to learn more about making ground-breaking TV and what it takes to write for and maintain one of the most visited Web sites (http://www.CMT.com).

HOW TO APPLY
To obtain an internship packet, send an e-mail to employment@cmt.com with "internship packet request" in the subject line. A few days after you send your e-mail, you'll receive a return e-mail containing an application, guidelines for the program, and a list of opportunities. Fax or mail your completed application (including all required documents) to the preceding address.

MTV NETWORKS INTERNSHIP— NEW YORK CITY

MTV Networks Internship Program
1515 Broadway, 30th floor
New York, NY 10036
Fax: (212) 846-1320
internships@mtvn.com

What You Can Earn: Unpaid.
Application Deadlines: Rolling (except for summer internships; resumes are accepted for summer on December 1, with a cut-off date of April 1).
Educational Experience: College upperclassmen (juniors/seniors) and eligible sophomores.

Requirements: Must be registered for an internship for academic credit with a college or university and must provide official documentation upon acceptance of this internship. Must be available at least two full days a week for a minimum of 10 weeks (no weekends).

OVERVIEW

MTV Networks in New York City has spring, summer, and fall internships available in affiliate sales/marketing; animation; business development; business and legal affairs; communications; consumer products; creative services; development; editorial; finance; human resources; home video; international; IS&T; marketing; national advertising sales; on-air graphics (motion graphics); planning and design; production; production management; programming; promotion; public affairs; radio network; research; special events; talent and artist relations; travel management; Web design; and wardrobe.

HOW TO APPLY

To apply, send a resume and cover letter indicating the semester for which you're applying and your areas of interest. You may e-mail your materials using MS Word attachments only or cut and paste your resume in an e-mail message.

MTV NETWORKS INTERNSHIP— SANTA MONICA

MTV Networks
Attn: Human Resources, Internship Program
2600 Colorado Avenue, 3rd Floor
Santa Monica, CA 90404

(310) 752-8811
sm.internships@mtvstaff.com

What You Can Earn: Unpaid.
Application Deadlines: Rolling.
Educational Experience: Freshmen to seniors or graduate students of all majors. Students must be registered in an internship credit course concurrently with the semester in which the internship will take place.
Requirements: Motivated interns who enjoy working in a fast-paced environment; team players; energetic; self-motivated; creative; responsible; a passion for music or entertainment and willingness to work hard. Must have general office and computer skills, strong verbal and written communication skills, and organizational and Internet skills. Should be able to intern two or three days (16 to 30 flexible hours) a week.

OVERVIEW

MTV Networks is a cutting-edge company that nurtures talent and encourages its interns to succeed by offering an excellent opportunity to get hands-on experience in the entertainment and animation industry. If you land an MTV Networks internship for the fall, spring, or summer session, you'll work in an innovative, progressive, fast-paced and professional environment. Students are exposed to all levels of MTV Networks, which can be an invaluable experience to anyone interested in pursuing a career in the entertainment industry.

You may choose an internship in ad sales; marketing; human resources; finance; legal; casting; animation; MTV series development; VH1 original programming and development; VH1 motion picture development; or music and talent relations. You may be asked to perform general office duties, projects, tape dubbing, script coverage, set work, and Internet research. Business hours for MTV Networks are Monday through Friday, 9:00 A.M. to 6:00 P.M., but hours are flexible.

HOW TO APPLY

Fax, e-mail, or mail your resume to the preceding address.

MTV NETWORKS LATIN AMERICA INTERNSHIP— MIAMI BEACH

MTV Networks Latin America
Internship Program
1111 Lincoln Road, 6th Floor
Miami Beach, FL 33139
Fax: (305) 535-3811
internship@mtvstaff.com

What You Can Earn: Unpaid; college credit.
Application Deadlines: Rolling.
Educational Experience: College students studying studio production and programming, on-air graphics, off-air print, wardrobe, marketing, communications, finance, information technologies, or law.
Requirements: Candidates must have strong Spanish written and verbal communication skills. Must be registered for an internship for academic credit with their college or university, and must provide official documentation on school letterhead confirming this information.

OVERVIEW

MTV Networks Latin America consists of three channels: MTV, Nickelodeon, and VH-1 Latin America. MTV Latin America is the world's first 24-hour Spanish-language network specifically for young adults whose roots are buried in both U.S. and Latin cultures. Nickelodeon is broadcast to kids in the United States, the United Kingdom, Australia, and Latin America. VH-1 targets the 25- to 49-year-old audience and celebrates pop culture and music through original programming hits.

The MTV networks are looking for bright, creative students to participate in the fall, spring, or summer internship program designed to offer an opportunity to gain insight into the TV industry. Interns obtain hands-on experience by working in jobs related to their career fields and by interacting with professionals in on-the-job situations.

Internships are available throughout the year, and MTV will work with you to determine how many days a week you can intern (usually two or three days a week for about 20 to 30 hours).

HOW TO APPLY

To apply, you should fax or mail a cover letter indicating the semester you're applying for and your areas of interest, along with your resume and a letter on school letterhead confirming you're registered for an internship class that provides academic credit. Include two letters of recommendation (from an employer, advisor, or professor) and an unofficial or official transcript. Fax or send all this information to the preceding address.

NATIONAL ENDOWMENT FOR THE ARTS INTERNSHIP

National Endowment for the Arts
The Nancy Hanks Center
Office of Human Resources, Room 627
1100 Pennsylvania Avenue, NW
Washington, DC 20506
(202) 682-5472
http://www.arts.gov/about/Jobs/Internships.html

What You Can Earn: Unpaid.
Application Deadlines: Four to six weeks before the date you want to start.

Educational Experience: None specified.
Requirements: None specified.

OVERVIEW

The National Endowment for the Arts is an independent federal agency and the largest annual funder of the arts in the United States. This public agency is dedicated to supporting excellence in the arts, bringing the arts to all Americans, and providing leadership in arts education. It has helped create regional theater, opera, ballet, symphony orchestras, museums, and other art, awarding more than 120,000 grants in four areas: Access to Artistic Excellence, Learning in the Arts, Challenge America, and Partnership Agreements.

In addition to the NEA Jazz Masters, the Arts Endowment awards fellowships in literature and the folk and traditional arts and solicits nominations from the public for the National Medal of Arts and forwards them to the president for a final decision.

Since 1990, 39 of the 58 recipients of National Book Awards, National Book Critics Circle Awards, and Pulitzer Prizes in fiction and poetry were awarded Arts Endowment Literature fellowships. The NEA also sponsored the design competition for the Vietnam Veterans Memorial and gave early, critical funding to The Sundance Film Festival, Minnesota Public Radio's *A Prairie Home Companion,* Spoleto Festival U.S.A., and PBS's *Great Performances* series. The NEA also created and funds the American Film Institute.

Undergraduate and graduate students and other volunteers who would like to gain work experience at the National Endowment for the Arts can apply for NEA internships throughout the year in many of the Endowment's offices. This internship offers a national overview of arts activities across the country.

If you're accepted, you'll help staffers with a variety of tasks related to the process of awarding federal grants. You'll be able to participate in a variety of resources, including an extensive arts library and meetings of advisory panels and the National Council on the Arts.

HOW TO APPLY

To apply, send a cover letter detailing the time period you'll be available (including days of the week, if you won't be available for all five days a week), your interest areas, and whether you'll be earning academic credit. You should also outline your experience and typing ability. Letters of recommendation, references, and college transcripts are suggested but not required. To ensure sufficient time for proper consideration of your application, you should send materials at least four to six weeks before the date you wish to begin your internship. Mail all materials to the preceding address.

NEW YORK STATE THEATRE INSTITUTE INTERNSHIP

New York State Theatre Institute
37 First Street
Troy, NY 12180
(518) 274-3573
aileff@nysti.org

What You Can Earn: Unpaid but academic credit is given.
Application Deadlines: Rolling.
Educational Experience: High school seniors, college students, and graduate students.
Requirements: Students must be affiliated with an accredited institution to participate.

OVERVIEW

The New York State Theatre Institute (NYSTI) was created by state legislation in 1974 and since then has provided training and opportunities for more than 1,000 students from the United States and 11 foreign countries. The NYSTI is not a college or university but a professional theatre with a wide range of educational programs. The institute does not offer degrees in theatre nor formal classes for the study of theatre in the traditional sense. NYSTI is located 150 miles north of New York City, in Troy, NY, on the Hudson River.

Highly individualized internships provide school-to-work transition experience for high-school seniors as well as college undergraduates and graduate students. Each intern is assigned a mentor who guides and assists the intern. Internships are individualized, combining academic studies with experiential learning alongside personnel.

You can earn academic credit as well as valuable practical experience. Semesters are divided into modules corresponding to the institute's season schedule. During each module, you'll be assigned to different departments, including box office, costumes, education, electrics, stage management, scenery, properties, performance, and public relations. You also may audition; interns are often cast in institute productions.

HOW TO APPLY

To apply, contact intern program director at the preceding address. If requesting information, please include a postal address.

NICKELODEON ANIMATION STUDIO INTERNSHIP

Nickelodeon Animation Studio
Recruitment Office
231 West Olive Avenue
Burbank, CA 91502
Fax: (818) 736-3539

What You Can Earn: Unpaid; academic credit is awarded.

Application Deadlines: Rolling.
Educational Experience: None specified.
Requirements: You must receive academic credit.

OVERVIEW

Located in Burbank, California, an internship at Nickelodeon's animation studio at Nicktoons can launch you on an exciting, fun-filled career in children's entertainment. Nicktoons produces such programs as *Dora the Explorer, Fairly Odd Parents, Chalk Zone, Danny Phantom, My Life as a Teenage Robot*, and the *Spike TV* series *Stripperella*. An internship in this studio is a hands-on experience. There are several opportunities for you to choose from, catering to every interest and talent. These internship areas include production, post-production, finance, casting, development, administration, artists, human resources, and paralegal.

HOW TO APPLY

To apply, send to the preceding address a resume and cover letter indicating the semester you're applying for and your areas of interest.

ONE REEL INTERNSHIP

One Reel
PO Box 9750
Seattle, WA 98109
Fax: (206) 281-7799
interns@onereel.org

What You Can Earn: $100 a month for part-time internships up to 20 hours per week; $200 a month for full-time internships (35 or more hours per week); complimentary event tickets when available; bus-pass reimbursement; college credit is possible.

Application Deadlines: Rolling.

Educational Experience: Most interns are college students or graduate students, although mature high school students may apply; nonstudents also may apply.

Requirements: Availability to work on July 4 and September 2–5, 2005, is mandatory for all internships except Teatro ZinZanni; younger applicants should be mature and confident enough to handle a variety of situations, including supervisory, customer service, independent problem solving, and decision-making; all applicants should be ready to handle the intense physical and mental demands of event work.

OVERVIEW

One Reel is a nonprofit arts, cultural, and special-events producer specializing in events that inform and entertain. One of the oldest and most unusual Northwest arts organizations, One Reel offers presentations of music, dance, theater, visual arts, literature, and cinema. From festivals to European cabaret to summer concerts, One Reel has created hundreds of unique and remarkable public celebrations around the United States, each with high production values, creative excellence, and a sense of celebration.

For the past 30 years, One Reel has created one-of-a-kind public celebrations, theatrical projects, spectacles, and festivals that combine ritual and road show, bringing people together from across town and around the globe to share moments of revelation and laughter.

An internship at One Reel is a once-in-a-lifetime opportunity to get hands-on arts and event-planning experience among a group of talented and dedicated professionals who respect hard work, creativity, and fun. Each internship will boost your knowledge and professional skills in a variety of areas.

For the most recent internship vacancies, check One Reel's Web site at http://www.onereel.org/internships. Examples of typical internships include the following:

Admissions and Ticketing

The intern in this area will gain firsthand experience in admissions operations, helping to manage high-volume sales, personnel, and customer service. Through projects such as ticket and sales inventory, tracking and reconciliation, and admissions-gate staffing, the intern will learn front- and back-end customer service.

Backstage Catering

Here you'll learn how to handle artists' catering orders and dressing room requests. By experiencing backstage catering operations at Bumbershoot, Family Fourth, and Summer Nights, the intern will gain broad exposure to varied catering practices tailored to different event formats.

Casting Internship, Teatro ZinZanni

The casting intern will learn the process and criteria upon which performers are competitively selected for Teatro ZinZanni's theatrical, cabaret, and culinary production. Through detailed, in-depth exposure to scouting, casting, contracting, travel, and accommodation, the intern will experience the behind-the-scenes work involved in casting for a fast-paced, international and nontraditional theatrical production. The intern will also learn how to process visa and immigration documents for international performers.

Family Fourth Event

This intern will be trained in planning, execution, and wrap-up of this one-day public event. An integral member of a three-person team, the intern will learn what goes into producing a large-scale public event and how to plan a one-day festival. This intern will oversee aspects of the event on site, and will also be invited to share in creative problem solving throughout the process.

Production

This intern will gain experience in festival and event production, including artist and venue logistics, site planning, security, public safety, communications, staffing, and credentialing. By attending all production meetings and taking notes for the department, the intern will contribute to the problem-solving process on various issues. Depending on availability and area of interest, the intern also may choose to shadow a role at the Summer Nights concert series, such as stage management, lighting, or soundboard operation.

Sponsorship

By tracking sponsorship agreements and taking the initiative to secure an in-kind sponsorship, this intern will learn about cross-promotion, fund-raising, and high-end customer service in the entertainment industry. This person will also have the opportunity to learn about pitching and promotions by shadowing the sponsorship director at presentations to potential sponsors.

Volunteer Program

This internship will provide hands-on experience in volunteer coordination and staffing in a nonprofit event setting. Perfect for a developing leader with compassion for others and an interest in event work, this person will learn how to recruit, screen, and manage volunteers, effectively matching volunteer resources with organizational needs in service to presenting the arts. In addition, involving self-directed research and providing valuable development experience, this person will solicit corporate donations for the year-end volunteer recognition event, as well as coordinate much of the event itself. The intern will receive specialized training in database use for management of volunteer resources.

HOW TO APPLY

After reading descriptions of currently available internships on the Web site, choose your top three and submit a cover letter, resume, and two writing samples via e-mail, fax, or mail to the preceding address. One Reel looks for well-organized ideas, a clear writing style, and the absence of spelling errors and typos. These qualities can be demonstrated in many types of written pieces (articles, school essays, fiction, and so on). One Reel welcome candidates to demonstrate their range and

creativity. Still, pieces of an intensely personal or controversial nature can raise red flags. It's always smart to pick a sample relevant to the internship you are applying for.

One Reel strongly prefers to meet you in person for an interview before offering placement in an internship. Selection for internships is competitive, and a great candidate met in person is more appealing than a great candidate on paper, who has been screened only on the phone.

OTHER HAND PRODUCTIONS PUPPET INTERNSHIP

Other Hand Productions
4836 NE 15th Avenue
Portland, OR 97211
internships@otherhandproductions.com
http://www.otherhandproductions.com

What You Can Earn: Unpaid.
Application Deadlines: Rolling.
Educational Experience: Unspecified.
Requirements: Time commitment equivalent to a full-time job, roughly 20 to 40 hours per week.

OVERVIEW

Other Hand Productions is an independent puppet theater based in Portland, OR, that performs across the United States as well as in Portland. Co-director Mary Robinette Kowal is an award-winning designer and directly oversees the internship program. Her partner, Jodi Eichelberger, is a critically acclaimed director, puppeteer, and writer and helps to guide interns in the creation of scripts for their independent projects.

This internship is ideal if you're interested in getting to know more about the field of professional puppetry. Activities in the program provide a fundamental understanding of the workings of a professional puppet theater in a hands-on fashion. Although every internship offers its own opportunities, each intern will experience hands-on building, daily interaction with and supervision by the production designer, creation of an individual project, and courses in manipulation of tabletop, hand, and marionette. While at the theater, you'll be treated like a member of the company and help the production designer with refurbishing existing shows and creating new ones.

HOUSING

You'll receive housing in a classic 1907 home 10 minutes from downtown Portland. (People with allergies should be aware that the home has two extremely friendly cats.)

HOW TO APPLY

To apply, mail a letter of interest explaining why you want this internship and a resume and two letters of recommendation to the preceding address.

must sign confidentiality agreements. Students should be available three or more days per week or at least 20 hours.

OVERVIEW

This internship program includes the following areas of specialty: On-set taping (control room, talent/guest coordination; audience coordination and wardrobe); research (assigned directly to a producer team for the semester); viewer services; and Web site. Interns are generally assigned to one of these areas or to a producer, for the semester (fall, spring, or summer).

On-set positions require the intern to be available on tape days (Tuesday, Wednesday, and Thursday) from 7: 00 A.M . to 2:30 P.M.

HOW TO APPLY

To apply, you should send your resume and cover letter, explaining your availability (days of week and hours per day), to the preceding address. If you e-mail your application, you may include your resume either as text in the body of the e-mail or as an attachment.

PARAMOUNT PICTURES/ *DR. PHIL SHOW* INTERNSHIP

Production Supervisor
Dr. Phil Show
Hollywood, CA
Fax: (323) 862-2195
laura_joslin@paramount.com
What You Can Earn: Unpaid.
Application Deadlines: Rolling.
Educational Experience: Media, radio/TV/film, communications, business, or related majors.
Requirements: Must receive college credit; most interns are college juniors or seniors and all interns

PHILADELPHIA ORCHESTRA ASSOCIATION INTERNSHIP

Director of Human Resources, Systems and Administration
The Philadelphia Orchestra Association
260 South Broad Street, 16th Floor
Philadelphia, PA 19102
humanresources@philorch.org

What You Can Earn: Unpaid but college credit is available.
Application Deadlines: Rolling.

Educational Experience: A music background is desirable but not required.

Requirements: Strong interpersonal and writing skills (writing samples may be required); strong organizational and analytical skills and proficiency in MS Office.

OVERVIEW

Founded in 1900, The Philadelphia Orchestra has distinguished itself as one of the leading orchestras in the world through a century of acclaimed performances, historic international tours, and best-selling recordings. Today the orchestra performs at the Kimmel Center, a regional performing arts center that provides modern performing space for a variety of arts groups from throughout the greater Philadelphia area. The 2500-seat Verizon Hall in the Kimmel Center was designed specifically for the orchestral sound of The Philadelphia Orchestra.

Summer internships are available in the administrative offices of the orchestra, including the departments of marketing; graphic design; public relations; education and community partnerships; development; artistic planning; orchestra personnel and production; information technology; and human resources. Internships may range from 20 to 35 hours per week and include the months of June, July, and August. The summer internship program is one of the ways in which The Philadelphia Orchestra Association is committed to training and mentoring students and young professionals in orchestra management, performing arts administration, and related fields.

Summer projects vary according to department and typically involve some degree of administrative support work but generally include the following.

Artistic Planning

In this internship, you'll update the artist history database, help in artist servicing, and help in production meetings and concert production.

Development

In this department, interns will help prepare gift acknowledgement letters, proposals, and other donor communications. Interns also will perform basic research on current and prospective funding sources and participate in the planning and execution of various fund-raising events.

Education/Community Partnerships

Interns in this area will help plan and market open dress rehearsals, help plan and implement neighborhood concerts, and help maintain the education Web site and the school concert database.

Graphic Design

In this department, you'll help produce design projects, scanning artwork and photography for design projects and the Web and organizing design portfolios for each season.

Human Resources

Interns will help update the candidate database for administrative staff positions, help prepare the updated employee handbook, and help enhance the employee orientation program.

Information Technology

In this department, you'll prepare and post pages for the orchestra Web sites, work with internal users to update the intranet site, and help in basic help desk support projects.

Marketing

Interns in this department will help maintain communication between the orchestra and members of Campus Classics, the orchestra's program for college students. Interns will participate in an analysis of single-ticket and subscription campaigns and help with concert support.

Orchestra Personnel and Production

Interns in this department produce the weekly orchestra schedules, help in weekly production meetings, and update musician and personnel office postings.

Public Relations

Here interns will update media lists and databases and help with some writing projects, as well as helping to maintain artist, photography, and musician and clippings files and helping with promotional events and concerts.

HOW TO APPLY

An application for these programs may be obtained by contacting the human resources office at the preceding address, either by mail or e-mail, for an application. Finalists will be invited for interviews in person or by telephone.

RADIO DISNEY— BOSTON INTERNSHIP

Radio Disney
Attn: Craig Matarazzo, Promotions Manager
226 Lincoln Street
Allston, MA 02134
(617) 787-0146, ext. 101
Fax: (617) 787-1236
http://www.radiodisney.com/wmkiam1260

What You Can Earn: Unpaid but college credit is possible.
Application Deadlines: Rolling.
Educational Experience: Unspecified.
Requirements: Local applicants only; must appreciate Disney traditions and values (strong work ethic, respect, independence, and so on).

OVERVIEW

Radio Disney AM1260 Boston is a 24-hour radio station specifically designed for a young listening audience (kids ages 6 to 14) with upbeat on-air personalities, pop music, and tons of contests and prizes. As a syndicated station, one of over 50 across the country, it is responsible for local marketing, local on-air spots, and promotions. It does not broadcast from the Boston location. This is a unique internship; the experience, while a great one, will be much different from a traditional radio station internship. The role of interns is to assist in the planning and execution of these tasks while living up to the station's high Disney standards.

As a Radio Disney intern, you'll help with promotions at local businesses, learn how to set up a DJ system, become comfortable on the mic at events, and understand how and what to pack for an event. You'll also interact with children and parents on site, run games for small and large crowds, assist production, and perhaps do voice work. You may work with clients on site and on the telephone, shadow marketing managers on sales calls/meetings, write spots for the radio, and create production orders and broadcast orders.

HOW TO APPLY

To apply for an internship here, submit a resume and cover letter to the preceding address.

RKO PICTURES INTERNSHIP

RKO Pictures Intern Program
jobs@rko.com

What You Can Earn: Unpaid.
Application Deadlines: Rolling.
Educational Experience: None specified.
Requirements: Must receive school credit; must commit to a minimum of 15 hours a week; be proficient in both Mac and PC and have a working knowledge of MS Word, Excel, PowerPoint (Photoshop proficiency is a plus), Outlook, and the Internet.

OVERVIEW

RKO Pictures is the oldest continuously operating movie studio and occupies a unique place in the history of filmmaking, founded in 1929 through the merger of the Keith Orpheum theater circuit, Joseph P. Kennedy's Film Booking Office, and Radio Corporation of America (RCA). In its heyday,

RKO released about 40 movies a year and in some years one film each week. The studio contracted with some of the industry's most talented artists, including Katherine Hepburn, Cary Grant, Ingrid Bergman, Orson Welles, Robert Mitchum, Bette Davis, Lucille Ball, John Ford, and Alfred Hitchcock. Its list of productions includes *King Kong*, *Citizen Kane*, *It's a Wonderful Life*, *The Hunchback of Notre Dame*, and *The Bells of St. Mary*, *The Best Years of Our Lives*, as well as a host of Astaire-Rogers musicals. Today, it retains an aggressive development slate and strong Hollywood relationships and produces, distributes, and finances new films and digital content.

Interns at RKO may find themselves watching old movies with an eye to remake, participating in creative meetings, script coverage, and special projects as assigned and being able to perform basic office tasks (phones, filing, copying, faxing, and so on). Qualified candidates should have a solid knowledge of foreign and independent filmmakers; have exceptional organizational and writing skills; and be detail oriented, self-motivated, and dependable.

HOW TO APPLY

E-mail your resume and cover letter (as an MS Word attachment) to the preceding address. Include "CREATIVE INTERN" in the subject line.

SACRAMENTO MUSIC CIRCUS SUMMER MUSICAL THEATER INTERNSHIP

California Musical Theatre
Outreach and Education Program Coordinator
1510 J Street, Suite 200
Sacramento, CA 95814
(916) 446-5880, ext. 147
Fax: (916) 446-1370
outreachandeducation@calmt.com

What You Can Earn: Unpaid; six college credits are available (paid jobs are offered to past interns who have proven themselves in nonpaid positions).
Application Deadlines: April 1 for the summer season.
Educational Experience: Graduating high school seniors (at least age 18) or those in their first two years of college; however, high school students starting their junior or senior year in the fall after the internship, who have a GPA of 3.0 or higher, are also eligible to apply.
Requirements: Full-time commitment of a six-day week with an average of 40 hours a week (you may volunteer for more); flexibility; theatre experience is preferred but not required.

OVERVIEW

This first-class summer stock season has become the predominant landmark on Sacramento's cultural landscape, attracting more than 125,000 patrons a year at the arena-style theatre. Truly a community event, the Music Circus employs a variety of professional and aspiring artists and theatre lovers. Creative staff (directors, choreographers, and designers) and lead actors and ensemble members are brought in from New York and Los Angeles to work with local actors, artisans, and students to produce seven shows in eight weeks.

If you love musical theater and you're serious about your theater training, the Music Circus internship, sponsored by the American River College, is geared toward the aspiring theatre artist. With this internship, you'll get valuable backstage experience in a variety of production areas in a professional theatrical setting. From June through August, as an intern here you'll have the opportunity to participate in seven theatrical productions. Throughout the summer you will be working in various assigned production areas, including properties, scenery, sound, stage management, costumes, wardrobe, and set/props run crew. Assignments will be rotated so that each intern will gain as much experience as possible. You'll also participate in weekly discussions with Music Circus staff and guest artists.

This is a demanding internship, due to the variable hours of the program and the intense nature of the work. It would be very difficult to hold an outside job while fulfilling an internship at Music Circus. Although the hours are long, the experience is invaluable. This is a chance to get your foot in the door and begin a career working in the theatre. As an intern, you'll be asked to give your best efforts for the good of the show and the company, which requires an intense commitment to a high standard of excellence and a tremendous amount of energy and enthusiasm.

HOW TO APPLY

You can request an application by phone or e-mail (see the preceding contact information) or you can stop by and pick up an application at American River College, Fine Arts Division Office or Admissions Office, 4700 College Oak Drive, Sacramento, CA 95841. You can find an application form online at http://www.californiamusicaltheatre.com.

After completing the application, attach a brief paragraph describing your future plans, your interest in theater, and why you want to be an intern at Music Circus. Also include a resume outlining your theatrical training and experience (technical and/or performing), along with information about your high school and/or college (include dates of attendance).

SAN FRANCISCO MIME TROUPE INTERNSHIP

SF Mime Troupe Internship Program
855 Treat Avenue
San Francisco, CA 94110

(415) 285-1717
http://www.sfmt.org

What You Can Earn: Sometimes a small stipend is paid; housing may be provided
Application Deadlines: Rolling.
Educational Experience: Check individual departments for specifics.
Requirements: Check individual departments for specifics.

OVERVIEW

The San Francisco Mime Troupe does not do pantomime but "mimes" in the ancient sense (to mimic). They consider themselves satirists, seeking to make their audience laugh at the absurdities of contemporary life. Since becoming a collective in l970, the troupe has done melodramas, spy thrillers, musical comedies, epic histories, sitcoms, and cartoon epics. Their trademark style draws from all these genres and is based on their common elements: strong story line, avowed point of view, larger-than-life characters, fantasy, and live music.

The San Francisco Mime Troupe is happy to take interns all year long, but artistic internships (design and so on) are offered only when a production is mounting, typically in May and June. Interns working on the summer production also may participate in the summer workshop but need to understand that they would be taking on a lot of work (the workshop is a 16-hour a week commitment.)

Interns may select from a variety of areas in which to work, including technical; assistant stage manager; scenic design; set design; assistants to the production manager; volunteer coordinator; costume and prop construction; and administrative.

Administrative

All year, the troupe needs interns to help the office run smoothly. Tasks range from making copies and answering the phones to data entry and special projects. If you're interested in seeing how a nonprofit theater functions, this is the internship for you.

Assistant Stage Manager

This internship typically begins during the last week in May, the first day of rehearsals for the summer show. The internship ends after the last show (usually Labor Day). You'll need to attend all rehearsals and production meetings. Rehearsals are typically from 10:00 A.M. to 6:00 P.M., Tuesday to Saturday, from the end of May through July 3.

Assistants to the Production Manager

If you intern here, you'll help the production manager with the administrative details of the summer production, including securing food donations and doing community outreach. Ideally, this internship starts the last week of May or in early June and ends Labor Day weekend, when the summer production ends. Sometimes production help is needed at other times of the year as well.

Costume and Prop Construction

Detail-oriented students with artistic ability are always needed to help make props and costumes. If you intern here, you'll be needed by mid-June until mid-July at the latest.

Scenic Design

For this internship, you'll begin the last week of May and end the second week of July, helping the scenic designer paint the set. The hours of this internship depend on whatever schedule is arranged with the designer.

Set Design

If the artistic side of entertainment appeals to you, you might be interested in this internship, where you'd help the set designer with set construction. These internships start the last week of May and end the second week of July; hours depend on whatever schedule is arranged with the designer.

Technical

For this internship, the Mime Troupe is seeking students interested in all areas of theater production but especially with experience in one or more of the following areas: stagecraft, woodworking, metal work, construction, painting, tool and machinery use, and rigging. You may be asked to take basic inventory of supplies and stock, research materials, and lift and tote the Mime Troupe stage. You would work directly with the technical director and learn to direct other volunteers in the construction of the summer set. The internship starts at the beginning of June and continues through the summer.

Volunteer Coordinator

This internship is responsible for organizing and overseeing the summer workshop participant work-exchange program. You'll need logistic and communication skills or the desire to develop them.

HOW TO APPLY

Apply for any of these opportunities by sending a cover letter and resume to the preceding address.

SECOND STAGE THEATRE INTERNSHIP

Second Stage Theatre Internship Coordinator
307 West 43rd Street
New York, NY 10036
Fax: (212) 397-7066
info@SecondStageTheatre.com

What You Can Earn: Unpaid but college credit is possible.
Application Deadlines: July 15 for fall (September to December); December 1 for spring (January to May); May 1 for summer (June to August).
Educational Experience: None specified.
Requirements: A minimum commitment of 15 hours per week; attendance at weekly staff meetings; willingness to work hard; high standards

of performance; reliable, conscientious, and energetic.

OVERVIEW

Second Stage Theatre offers internships in both production and administration. Interns work directly with individual department heads and staff to receive practical training in administrative management or technical theatre. Interns are selected by application and interview. In return, interns are treated as members of the professional staff and receive intensive hands-on experience. Interns are evaluated in face-to-face meetings with their supervisors before leaving Second Stage. These meetings provide a formal framework within which the intern's progress, future expectations, projects, and goals can be discussed.

Internships are available in a variety of departments, including second look, general management, development, marketing, literary management, production, and stage management.

Development

In this department, you'll maintain donor database and files, follow up on donor benefits, research funding sources, and help with mailings and special events. You'll also actively participate in all fund-raising activities, including the annual direct mail and telefunding campaigns, special events, funding research, special projects, and day-to-day booking and acknowledgement of gifts.

For this internship, you should be detail-oriented and self-motivated and have excellent writing and communication skills, basic familiarity with computers, the ability to work cooperatively, and the ability to keep sensitive information confidential.

General Management

This intern helps the general manager process artists' contracts, maintain management files, maintain the general ledger, and help with financial projects. You should have a warm personality, good communication skills, excellent organizational and time-management skills, discretion, and a great sense of humor.

Literary Management

Here you'll work with the associate artistic director on reading and evaluating new scripts, conducting dramaturgical research, helping with directing fellowships, attending rehearsals, and providing administrative support for various literary projects.

You should have excellent writing and communication skills, as well as a strong background in dramatic literature and practical theater.

Marketing

In this internship, you'll help do market research, help with subscription and single ticket promotions, distribute marketing materials, help write copy for newsletters and other promotional materials, help coordinate receptions and openings, and help develop single-ticket and subscription audiences through direct mail, print, and telemarketing. You'll also help with promotion via special events and outreach efforts.

You should have strong writing, verbal, and computer skills and the ability to handle multiple priorities and successfully meet deadlines.

Production

The production intern will help in all aspects of creating sets, props, sound, and lighting for Second Stage productions. You may be asked to help with carpentry, metal work, load in/out, set strikes, sewing, rigging, hanging and focusing lights, running shows, maintaining and installing equipment, and shadowing designers. This internship may be tailored to your specific interests and abilities.

Second Look

If you don't have a background in theater but you're interested in exploring the field, this internship is for you. Here you'll observe and experience both the artistic and the administrative functions of producing in an off-Broadway theater. Responsibilities cover a wide range of interrelated areas in the fields of company and artist relations, including weekly observation of rehearsals, helping develop specific projects and special events in marketing and fund-raising, helping the production team prepare sets, lighting, and sound for productions, and providing general support throughout the organization.

You'll be expected to interact with all departments to gain a well-rounded understanding of the theater industry. Strong organizational skills, excellent communication skills, and enthusiasm are required.

Stage Management

Interns here work with Equity stage managers, directors, and actors and are involved in the entire rehearsal and performance process of an off-Broadway production. Duties may include keeping track of props; preshow and post-show duties; helping at rehearsals and performances; and maintaining production paperwork. There are only a few internships here, and they require a commitment of 40 hours a week. This internship is tied directly to productions.

Production experience is required, and you should be organized and detail oriented. An outgoing and assertive personality is a plus.

HOW TO APPLY

To apply for an internship, download an application at http://www.secondstagetheatre.com/internapplication.doc. Mail or fax it with a resume, two letters of recommendation (professional or academic), and a brief personal statement (including what you expect to gain from an internship) to the preceding address.

Applications submitted after the deadline will receive full consideration only on a space-available basis.

Once the theatre has received your application materials, they will be in touch with you about the availability of internships or to request more information. They prefer in-person interviews, but phone interviews can be arranged.

SHAKESPEARE THEATRE INTERNSHIP

The Shakespeare Theatre Internships
516 8th Street, SE
Washington, DC 20003
(202) 547-5688
http://www.shakespearedc.org/intern.
  html#abo

What You Can Earn: Stipends are available; most internships include housing.
Application Deadlines: April 30.
Educational Experience: Undergraduates, graduate students, and young professionals with an interest in professional theatre.
Requirements: Strong interest in furthering professional development and a commitment to working in a regional theatre; solid computer experience, including familiarity with MS Office and the Internet. Additional requirements are listed in descriptions of specific internships.

OVERVIEW

The Shakespeare Theatre is a prominent, well-established Equity theatre in Washington, D.C., producing the works of Shakespeare and other classic playwrights during five mainstage productions as well as a two-week revival run in an outdoor amphitheater.

Interns are encouraged to complete an entire season's residency with the theater, which operates year round, July through June. Schedules are rigorous; production interns work between 40 to 60 hours a week and administration interns work at least 40 hours plus during special events.

The Shakespeare Theatre has forged an ongoing commitment to education, audience development, and professional training for theatre artists. An internship at the Shakespeare Theatre, the country's premier classical theatre, bridges the gap between academic theatre experience and a career in the professional theatre, providing opportunities in all aspects of theatre production and administration. Internships are available in administrative and production areas.

Artistic Administration

Interns here help the associate director and resident assistant director in casting, script preparation, production research, and other duties related to the smooth operation of a major theatre casting office. There is no directing involved in this internship, but you may be asked to help during rehearsal, with production research, and prompting actors during tech/preview week.

You should have a strong interest in directing, dramaturgy, or artistic management in Shakespeare and other classics; an MFA is preferred.

Costumes

Costume interns help in construction, shopping, stock maintenance, and running shows. The shop currently has four draping tables with a first hand and one stitcher on each team. There is also a craft department with a full-time crafts artisan supervisor. You'll work in several areas over the span of an internship. Costume work spans all eras and styles, with a range of work from corsetry to tailoring, chiffon to leather. A portfolio and/or examples of work are desirable.

Development

Development interns work in all aspects of development for a nonprofit arts organization, including fund-raising and cultivating donors as well as handling corporate, government, and foundation relations. You'll work closely with the annual fund director, the director of institutional advancement, donor officers, grant writers, and events planners. You'll help plan and carry out cultivation events (including evening events) and handle daily office tasks. Strong verbal and written skills are required.

Education

Education interns support the implementation of school, community, training, and audience-enrichment programs. You'll work with education staff and guest artists, helping to schedule workshops, develop educational outreach activities, handle event registration and marketing, and handle the daily administrative needs of the office.

General Management

General management internships are ideal if you're interested in the overall workings of a theatre, since the general manager deals with all departments including artistic, production, marketing, and business. Here you'll help the general manager and business manager with special projects in accounting and management, handling daily business functions, research/analysis, coordinating staff and board meetings, and special projects.

Graphic Design

Graphic design interns receive hands-on training in preparing publications for print, designing for a nonprofit organization, and four-color and two-color press. You'll handle projects ranging from newspaper ads to brochures to full-size posters. Knowledge of QuarkXPress, Adobe Photoshop, and Adobe Illustrator on a Mac platform is required; a portfolio and/or examples of work are required.

Lighting

Lighting interns help the master electrician and assistant master electrician hang, circuit, and focus lights for all productions. Experience trouble-shooting, programming light boards (ETC), maintaining instrument inventory, and building practicals and special effects is required. Understanding lighting design is helpful.

Production Management

Production management interns report to the production manager and work with the production management staff on contracts, production planning, and scheduling, as well as special research projects and presentations. You'll need strong administrative and organizational skills for this internship, as well as experience with spreadsheets and word processing and the ability to work with a broad range of people and handle numerous projects at the same time.

Public Relations/Marketing

PR/marketing interns help with audience development; subscription and single ticket marketing; call center strategy and management; press; publications; and group sales. You also may help with research, special events, direct mail campaigns, and special projects. Special requirements include strong written and verbal communication skills and strong organization skills.

Sound

Sound interns work with the resident sound designer to provide technical and creative support. Internships are designed around your interests and can include systems maintenance, installation, and engineering; helping with performance runs and changeovers; helping designers and composers; and design opportunities with outreach and internship projects. Experience with sound engineering for nonmusical theatre and examples of paperwork and recordings of designs/compositions are required.

Stage Management

Stage management interns work closely with stage managers, helping with stage management from preproduction preparation into rehearsal and through the run of the show as part of the running crew. You may have the opportunity to stage-manage special events and are eligible to receive EMC points.

Stage Properties

Stage properties interns help the property shop staff build and procure props for mainstage productions and outreach projects. Basic construction skills are required; you also must be willing to drive the company van and have a valid driver's license. Experience in painting, graphics, welding, upholstering, finish carpentry, or armory is preferred; a portfolio and/or examples of work are required.

Technical Direction

Technical direction interns help the technical director with budgeting, drafting, and scheduling for all shows produced by the scene shop, as well as load-in and strike. The scene shop works primarily with wood, steel, and aluminum and does extensive rigging and motion control, including hydraulics, pneumatics, and motors. Drafting experience is required; knowledge of automation is desirable.

HOW TO APPLY

Download an application from http://www.shakespearedc.org/pdf/internship_app06.pdf. To apply, send a completed application, resume, portfolio or writing samples, and two letters of recommendation to the preceding address.

SMITHSONIAN FOLKWAYS RECORDINGS INTERNSHIP

Smithsonian Folkways Recordings
Marketing Director
Smithsonian Institution
PO Box 37012
4100 Victor Building, MRC 0953
Washington, DC 20013-7012
Fax: (202) 275-1165
burgessr@si.edu

What You Can Earn: Unpaid but academic credit is available.
Application Deadlines: Rolling.
Educational Experience: Qualified students in college or university.
Requirements: None specified.

OVERVIEW

Folkways Records was founded in 1948 in New York City as a way of recording and documenting the entire world of sound, including traditional, ethnic, and contemporary music from around the world; poetry, spoken word, and instructional recordings in numerous languages; and documentary recordings of individuals, communities, current events, and natural sounds. In 1987, the Smithsonian Institution Center for Folklife and Cultural Heritage in Washington, D.C., acquired Folkways Recordings as well as the label's business papers and files to ensure that the sounds and genius of its artists would continue to be available to future generations. In the years since 1987, Smithsonian Folkways has added several other record labels to the collections and has released more recordings that document and celebrate the sounds of the world around us.

There are a number of opportunities for internships at Smithsonian Folkways Recordings. Internships can be from four weeks to one year, full time or part time, although the Smithsonian prefers that you work at least 15 to 20 hours a week. Intern projects are generally in the areas of marketing, recording production, mail order, and Web site production.

HOW TO APPLY

Download the intern application at http://www. folklife.si.edu/resources/2005Festival/intern_ application.doc. Then mail, e-mail, or fax the completed application and an essay of between 500 and 1,000 words discussing why you are seeking this internship, especially as it relates to your academic or professional development and goals. You also should indicate the types or areas of work in which you wish to participate and why this internship is suited to your needs. Send all materials to the preceding address.

SOUTH SHORE MUSIC CIRCUS INTERNSHIP

South Shore Music Circus
130 Sohier Street
Cohasset, MA 02025
(781) 383-9850

marketing@themusiccircus.org
http://www.themusiccircus.org

What You Can Earn: Unpaid.
Application Deadlines: April 1.
Educational Experience: None specified.
Requirements: Organized, motivated, and familiar with MS Outlook, Word, Excel, PowerPoint, Photoshop, and Quark.

OVERVIEW

For more than 50 years, the South Shore Music Circus and its sister venue, the Cape Cod Melody Tent, have been presenting world-class entertainment in the Massachusetts coastal communities of Cohasset and Hyannis on Cape Cod. The only two continuously operated tent theaters in the round in the United States, the Music Circus and Melody Tent are owned and operated by the South Shore Playhouse Associates, a nonprofit organization dedicated to encouraging and supporting the arts and cultural and educational organizations throughout the communities of the South Shore and Cape Cod. With a colorful history dating back to 1932 in Cohasset, the theaters today are popular summer entertainments providing a relaxed ambiance and intimate theatre experience where no seat is more than 50 feet from the stage.

Each summer, the Cape Cod Melody Tent and South Shore Music Circus present up to 55 shows at each venue, ranging from world-class entertainers to weekly children's theater and several summer festivals, including the Music, Food, and Wine Festival and the Cape Cod Chowder Festival. The theaters operate full time from Memorial Day weekend through Labor Day weekend and offer an excellent opportunity for anyone to become more familiar with theater life and the live concert experience.

In March 1990, the South Shore Playhouse Associates bought the Cape Cod Melody Tent in Hyannis. The resident theater has been replaced by touring performers of world-class caliber, including Tony Bennett; Linda Ronstadt; Bill Cosby; Moody Blues; Crosby, Stills and Nash; Carole King,

Melissa Etheridge; Johnny Mathis; Kenny Rogers; B.B. King; Alice Cooper; Willie Nelson; Hall & Oates; Hootie & the Blowfish; Doobie Brothers; Joe Cocker; Lyle Lovett; Huey Lewis; The Beach Boys; KC & the Sunshine Band; Indigo Girls; Aretha Franklin; Lisa Marie Presley; Hanson; and Boston Pops.

The Music Circus also offers an internship in the marketing/public relations department based at the South Shore Music Circus in Cohasset, Monday through Friday, from 9:00 A.M. to 6:00 P.M. Duties include helping the director in a variety of activities such as writing and distributing news releases, media advisories, and calendar listings; managing print production schedules; maintaining ongoing media relations, including responding to media inquiries, pitching, and arranging interviews; monitoring multiple radio promotions; and monitoring media coverage, including newspaper clippings.

HOW TO APPLY

You can obtain an application at the following Web site: http://64.233.179.104/search?q=cache:uQ_ fdioep74J:www.themusiccircus.org/employment. aspx+music+circus+internship&hl=en&ie=UTF-8. Interested candidates should send a resume and cover letter to the preceding e-mail address.

Applicants selected for an interview will be contacted at the number they provide.

SPOLETO FESTIVAL USA INTERNSHIP

Spoleto Festival USA
PO Box 157
Charleston, SC 29402
(843) 722-2764
Fax: (843) 723-6383
http://www.spoletousa.org/work/
apprenticeships.php

What You Can Earn: $250 per week, plus housing at the College of Charleston and $50 travel reimbursement.
Application Deadlines: Early February for summer session.
Educational Experience: Specific educational strengths are discussed in the overview.
Requirements: Specific requirements are detailed below in the overview.

OVERVIEW

For 17 days and nights each spring, Spoleto Festival USA fills Charleston, South Carolina's historic theaters, churches, and outdoor spaces with more than 120 performances by renowned artists as well as emerging performers in disciplines ranging from opera, theater, music theater, dance, and chamber, symphonic, choral, and jazz music, as well as the visual arts. Called "one of the best arts festivals in this country" by *The Washington Post*, Spoleto has presented 100 world premieres and 93 American premieres since its inception in 1977.

The apprentice program is a short-term intensive opportunity designed to offer a transition between academic and professional life. This program provides hands-on experience under the guidance of professional arts administrators and technicians in producing an international arts festival.

Interns work at least a 40-hour week, which may include long workdays and nights as well as weekends.

There are a number of apprenticeships available, including the following:

Artist Services

You'll assist with arrangements for artist housing; travel and hospitality; scheduling and setting up backstage hospitality; preparing mailings and artist welcome packets as well as various administrative tasks such as answering phones, filing, and correspondence. Positions may also involve providing special assistance to the music director. You should have excellent organizational and computer skills and the ability to work well with a variety of people.

Box Office

You'll handle incoming telephone sales orders, process mail orders, sell event tickets in the box office and at performance sites, disseminate program information, and reconcile daily ticket sales. This position requires an articulate, detail-oriented person with initiative, customer-service skills, and computer experience. Experience in phone sales, retail, or a hotel environment is a plus.

Development

You'll help with the logistics of more than 30 special events ranging from a black-tie gala to picnics, involving extensive phone work, managing invitation mailings, RSVPs, and helping with many last-minute details. This position requires excellent communication and basic computer skills.

Education

You'll help with logistics and coordination of all education events, including in-school activities, special school-day performances, workshops, and performances talks. You'll also help coordinate activities, mailings, and artist transportation. You should have good organizational skills and the ability to work well independently. Some backstage technical knowledge is preferred.

Finance

You'll help the business office compile and record information related to cash receipts, accounts payable, purchase orders, payroll, personnel, and accounts receivable. This position requires detail-oriented individuals with Excel spreadsheet skills and accounting education and/or experience. In addition to the apprentice term, part-time year-round hours in this position are available.

Media Relations

You'll staff the festival press room and help working press to obtain interviews, photos, and story information for print, radio, and television coverage of the festival. You'll write media alerts, create media kits/press packets, and maintain information, press clippings, and photo files, as well as handle the day-to-day operations of the press room. This apprenticeship requires strong computer, organizational, and interpersonal skills. Public relations, journalism, or photography experience or coursework is helpful. For this position, you must provide three writing samples with your application.

Merchandising

This apprenticeship focuses on retail sales, with an emphasis on official merchandise sold onsite at the various venues in Charleston. Duties include maintaining inventory, preparing bank deposits, and reconciliation. Candidates must be multitask oriented and attentive to detail and have excellent organizational and customer service skills. Sales experience is helpful.

Office Administration

Duties in this apprenticeship include answering multiline telephones, data entry, correspondence, and other office responsibilities. The position requires excellent customer service skills.

Orchestra Management

You'll help the orchestra managers in all phases of orchestra operations, including setup and transport of instruments, concert stage management, and library management. You must have the ability to lift large instruments, drive a cargo van, and work under tight deadlines. Knowledge of music and orchestras is helpful but not required.

Production

You'll work with professional theater staff in one of the following areas: stage carpentry, stage electrics, wardrobe, properties, sound, stage management, or production administration. You must have a willingness to work hard, a flexible and positive attitude, and a desire to pursue a career in technical theatre. Related experience in technical theater is required.

HOW TO APPLY

Submit completed applications and all materials including resume, cover letter, and two letters of recommendation (media relations applicants must also include three writing samples) to the preceding address.

THE STUDIO THEATRE INTERNSHIP

Spring or Summer Administrative Internships

The Studio Theatre
1501 14th Street, NW
Washington, DC 20005
Fax: (202) 588-5262
internship@studiotheatre.org

What You Can Earn: Unpaid but all interns can attend all first rehearsals, all staff run-throughs, and all opening nights of the Studio Theatre's performances.

Application Deadlines: Late April for summer internship (check Web site for exact dates).

Educational Experience: None specified.

Requirements: See individual internships for special qualification requirements.

OVERVIEW

The mission of The Studio Theatre is to produce the best in contemporary theatre and through its Secondstage and Acting Conservatory to provide opportunities for emerging artists and to offer rigorous training. The Studio Theatre has built a national reputation for the production of area premieres of bold American and European works, innovative revivals, and unusual performance art. This energetic urban theatre has received more than 180 Helen Hayes Award nominations for artistic excellence since the awards were founded in 1985. It offers daring, adventurous, unconventional productions committed to the highest artistic standards. Spring and summer internships are available in a variety of departments.

Spring Internship Program

The Studio Theatre has openings for administrative interns for 12 to 20 hours a week beginning in late March through late May. Administrative interns help with clerical duties, direct mail projects, and help distribute flyers.

Studio Theatre Secondstage Interns

These interns will work on The Studio Theatre Secondstage summer productions in one of the following positions.

Floor Manager

You'll help coordinate scene changes, costumes changes and maintenance, and prop tracking. This internship is ideal if you're interested in and have experience in stage management.

Light Board Operator

This intern will run the light board for all performances and help maintain the light design. You'll work as the assistant to the master electrician and help with hang and focus.

Sound Board Operator

This intern will help run the sound board for all performances and help maintain the sound design. You'll help in sound hangs and installs and assist the sound designer as needed.

Assistant Technical Director

Here you'll help with all show budgets and schedules and product and material research and ordering. You must be interested in shop management and have strong carpentry and office skills.

Scene Shop

Here you'll help the master carpenter in set construction for The Studio Theatre as well as The Studio Theatre Secondstage, helping the set and props designers.

Facilities

As an intern in this area, you'll help the facilities manager in theater maintenance and conduct an inventory of the theater's equipment and appliances, as well as renovate and maintain the theater's housing facilities.

Summer Internship Program
Administrative/Public Relations
In this department, you'll help with clerical duties, direct mail projects, receive guests, distribute flyers, assemble press packets, update media lists, and maintain a media library. You'll also help with the next season's planning, attend public relations department meetings, help with marketing projects, and help handle the day-to-day needs of the department.

Administrative/Conservatory
In this department, you'll help with clerical duties, direct mail projects, receive guests, distribute flyers, and class registrations. You'll also help host students' final scene presentations, help with the Arts Motivating Youth Program, update the school database, and help with the day-to-day needs of the administration and conservatory departments.

Development
In this department, you'll prepare grant materials, conduct donor research, update invitation and donor lists, and manage the database. Computer and research skills are required, and you must be organized, personable, self-motivated, and able to multitask.

Information Technology/Business
In this department, you'll help with the theater's computer systems, help maintain the central database; update the Web site; install and maintain hardware, software, and supplies; and help train personnel in software use. You'll also help with accounts payable activities, help with the budgeting process, and help prepare for the theatre's annual audit. Familiarity with HTML, PHP, and SQL is important.

Literary
In this department, you'll help research and prepare next season's performance and study guides, read and evaluate plays, help with correspondence to playwrights, organize script library, and update the literary database.

Production
In this department, you'll be working in technical areas that may require some previous training and/or experience. As an intern in production, you may choose to work in one of the following areas of production. You will help with casting, auditioning, and database and files maintenance, and work on building sets, painting, properties, lighting, electrics, sound, and theatre maintenance.

HOW TO APPLY
Download the application at the following Web site: http://www.studiotheatre.org/opportunities/APPLICATION_FOR_INTERNSHIP_sum_05.pdf. Then e-mail, fax, or mail the completed application and a resume and references to the preceding address.

TEXAS FILM COMMISSION INTERNSHIP

Texas Film Commission
PO Box 13246
Austin, TX 78711
Fax: (512) 463-4114
film@governor.state.tx.us
http://www.governor.state.tx.us/divisions/film/about/internships.htm

What You Can Earn: Unpaid but academic credit is possible.
Application Deadlines: Rolling.
Educational Experience: Sophomore, junior, or senior college students or graduate students currently enrolled in degree programs.
Requirements: Demonstrated professional interest in film/video production; excellent written and verbal communication skills; ability to work 10 to 20 hours per week.

OVERVIEW

The Texas Film Commission, a division of the Office of the Governor, has been assisting film-makers since 1971 with a complete range of film-related services. The commission can help with information on locations; crews; talent; state and local contacts; weather; laws; sales tax exemptions; housing; and anything filmmakers might need to know about filming in Texas. The commission offers details about locations. (Texas locations have doubled for the American Midwest, Mexico, Washington, D.C., Vietnam, Afghanistan, Bolivia, Africa, Florida, and a host of others. In the past year alone, Texas has been Morocco in three different features.) The Texas Film Commission also maintains an expansive list of qualified vendors and crews throughout Texas and can help with any necessary permits and financial incentives such as tax exemptions.

The commission's internship program offers college students the opportunity to develop a working knowledge of the film industry. The commission is seeking students with excellent communication skills who want to learn how the film industry works and who want to contribute to the film commission's efforts to promote and expand the Texas film industry.

As an intern here, you'll help prepare Texas location information for producers; help in the digital stitching, editing and printing of Texas location images; respond to information requests from film-industry professionals and the general public; and perform routine administrative/clerical tasks.

Interns have gone on to work on productions such as *Sin City*, *Friday Night Lights*, *The Alamo*, *The Texas Chainsaw Massacre*, and *Once Upon a Time in Mexico*. They have also landed positions at companies such as Miramax, Lucasfilm, NBC, CAA and the William Morris talent agency.

HOW TO APPLY

To apply, send a cover letter and resume to the preceding address.

WALT DISNEY WORLD SUMMER JOBS

Walk Disney World Summer Jobs
http://www.wdwcollegeprogram.com/sap/
    its/mimes/zh_wdwcp/students/frameset/
    frameset_faqs.html
(800) 722-2930
wdw.college.recruiting@disney.com
wdw.college.education.program@disney.com

What You Can Earn: Starting pay rate is $6 an hour with time-and-a-half for overtime (over 40 hours per week).

Application Deadlines: Fall presentations are recruiting for spring and spring advantage programs only; spring presentations are recruiting for fall and fall advantage programs only.

Educational Experience: All majors are welcome to apply.

Requirements: Current college enrollment, with at least one semester completed and a 2.0 GPA or higher. Participation requires unrestricted work authorization.

OVERVIEW

Cast members (all WDW employees are called "cast members") could be working in many different locations at Walt Disney World in a variety of jobs, including costuming, character greeters, character performers, or recreation workers.

You're guaranteed a schedule of 30 hours per week with a maximum of 45 hours per week. However, during busy seasons, you could be asked to work more hours a week. You're also expected to work the hours you're scheduled; additional hours or days may not be available.

Character Greeters

Character greeters provide guests with information about WDW, which could include show schedules, attraction information, character set locations, and set times. You should have a positive, friendly, helpful attitude and the flexibility to be able to work in multiple locations in WDW, including all four theme parks and any of the resorts.

Responsibilities may include maintaining show quality and character integrity; greeting and screening guests for appropriate attire and food and beverage items; providing audience control; setting up and removing stanchions and ropes and poles, retrieving and arranging strollers; and maintaining cleanliness and order.

This specialized role requires a separate interview process, so you should speak with the college program recruiter immediately after the presentation if you're interested in the character greeter role.

Character Performer

In this role, you bring the famous Disney characters to life! You'll have opportunities to interact with guests of all ages from around the world to create everlasting memories. This position is physically demanding, working in hot costumes in a fast-paced environment with lots of guest interaction.

You would be working in multiple locations across WDW, including all four theme parks and many of the resorts. You would be responsible for signing autographs, posing for photographs, attending restaurant dining experiences, and having the potential to perform in parade and puppeteer roles.

You must attend one of the auditions listed on the presentation schedule or any entertainment audition in Orlando, FL, to be considered for an entertainment role. Prior to auditioning, you must attend a campus presentation.

Costuming

If you're interested in working in costuming, you may find yourself at any of the many wardrobe departments throughout WDW, issuing costumes to fellow cast members. Costuming cast members are often the first persons other cast members interact with before they start their shifts. You may

be required to travel to work at any of the costuming destinations on or off property. This role can be physically demanding and requires heavy lifting and bending.

This is a backstage role with minimal guest interaction; responsibilities may include overhead reaching, bending and lifting, moving heavy costumes from location to location, issuing costumes to fellow cast members, operating basic laundry equipment, checking garments, transporting locker bags, and some light laundry.

Recreation

Cast members in this role may work in various areas, including resorts, towel rentals, watercraft rentals, marina operations, ticket sales, arcades, children's activities, and slide operations. There are additional certification requirements for some roles.

As a result of the nature of this role, you may spend a lot of time outdoors, and you should also have strong swimming skills. During off-peak seasons, recreation cast members may help in other operating areas throughout WDW. Responsibilities may include keeping recreation areas clean, maintaining safety standards, and helping guests.

HOW TO APPLY

WDW employees visit more than 350 schools each fall and spring, from all over the country. The campus visits consist of a presentation that provides more detailed information, followed by interviews. Students, parents, and faculty are encouraged to attend the presentation together. You must attend a presentation to be able to interview; you sign up for interviews at the presentation. The interview generally takes place within 24 hours of the presentation.

At the interview, you must bring your completed application, which you print from the application section of the WDW internship Web site (see preceding address), and submit it to the recruiter.

You also can apply online, but once you have submitted your application, you must attend a presentation. Students must bring a copy of their completed applications to their interviews. You don't need to bring a resume to apply, but you may bring one to your interview if you wish. After the interview, your application will be considered, and you'll receive a decision within two to three weeks.

Everyone who interviews should receive notification. If you haven't heard within four weeks, you should e-mail college recruiting (wdw.college.recruiting@disney.com) with your full name, complete mailing address, and an explanation of your situation.

If you aren't accepted the first time, you can apply and interview the following semester; however, you can apply and interview only once per semester.

WILMA THEATER INTERNSHIP

Education Director
The Wilma Theater
265 S. Broad Street
Philadelphia, PA 19107
(215) 893-0895
akh@wilmatheater.org

What You Can Earn: Unpaid; academic credit is given.
Application Deadlines: September 1 for fall (August through December); November 30 for winter/spring (January through May). April 30 for summer (June through August); starting dates are flexible.
Educational Experience: At least one year of college.
Requirements: None specified.

OVERVIEW

The Wilma Theater in Philadelphia has a reputation for freedom of thought, liberty of expression, and the celebration of the human spirit. The first new theater built in Philadelphia since 1928, its new home on the Avenue of the Arts reflects the pride that Philadelphians hold for this theater. In 1994, *The Philadelphia Inquirer* named the Wilma "Theater Company of the Year," and in 1995, Wilma productions swept the newly inaugurated Barrymore Awards. The Wilma's mission to ignite explosive theater in Philadelphia has extended beyond creating powerful works for the stage to training emerging artists through the Wilma Studio School and creating opportunities for audience members to join the creative conversation of the theater.

The Wilma Theater internship program enables college students to explore career paths in the administrative side of the arts, in literary, marketing/public relations, development, and education. Because the Wilma functions with a relatively small staff, interns will be able to manage individual assignments and receive individual attention from the department heads with whom they work. Typically, interns make a long-term commitment of at least 12 hours per week for eight weeks.

HOW TO APPLY

To apply for this internship, send your resume with a cover letter specifying the dates you're available and the position you are interested in obtaining to the education director at the preceding address. No phone applications will be accepted.

WOLF TRAP INTERNSHIP

Internship Program
Wolf Trap Foundation for the Performing Arts
1645 Trap Road
Vienna, VA 22182
(703) 255-1933 or 1(800) 404-8461
Fax: (703) 255-1924
internships@wolftrap.org

What You Can Earn: Unpaid.

Application Deadlines: March 1 for summer internships (May through August); July 1 for fall (September through December); November 1 for spring (January through April).

Educational Experience: Undergraduate students who have completed a minimum of one year of study (or the equivalent); graduate students; recent graduates (no more than two years out of school); and career-changers currently enrolled in a degree program.

Requirements: None specified. You must have a reliable mode of transit.

OVERVIEW

As America's national park for the performing arts, Wolf Trap plays a valuable leadership role in both the local and national performing-arts communities by offering a wide range of artistic and education programs. The late Catherine Filene Shouse founded Wolf Trap by donating 100 acres of her Virginia farmland (near Washington, D.C.) to the U.S. government, as well as funds for construction of a 6,800 seat indoor/outdoor theater. Wolf Trap's larger venue (the Filene Center) opened in 1971 as a public/private partnership between the Wolf Trap Foundation and the U.S. Department of the Interior, National Park Service. The foundation is a nonprofit organization that creates and selects programming; develops all education programs; handles ticket sales, marketing, publicity, and public relations; and raises funds. The National Park Service maintains the grounds and buildings of Wolf Trap National Park for the Performing Arts and provides technical theater assistance for the Filene Center.

In 1981, Mrs. Shouse also donated the land and funds for an indoor theater constructed of two adjacent 18th-century barns, each moved from upstate New York and rebuilt on its present site. The addition of The Barns at Wolf Trap created a year-round center for the performing arts and related education programs.

A typical season at Wolf Trap includes performances ranging from pop, country, folk, and blues to orchestra, dance, theater, and opera, as well as innovative performance art and multimedia presentations. The Filene Center season usually runs from the end of May to the beginning of September, with an average of 90 performances each year. From October to early May, Wolf Trap's 382-seat indoor The Barns at Wolf Trap continues to present diverse artists in a casual and more intimate atmosphere. The Barns are also summer home to the Wolf Trap Opera Company.

In addition to year-round performances, Wolf Trap offers a variety of education programs, including the Wolf Trap Institute for Early Learning through the Arts. In classroom residencies, these artists use drama, music, and movement to teach basic skills and encourage active participation and self-esteem in the earliest stages of learning. Wolf Trap Institute artists also conduct workshops and presentations throughout the country to demonstrate to teachers and parents how the arts can bring new life to learning and literature.

Wolf Trap internships offer the practical opportunity to become an integral member of the staff and to work side by side with professionals, producing, promoting, and administering the full spectrum of the performing arts. Wolf Trap internships provide meaningful hands-on training and experience in the areas of arts administration, education, and technical theater.

Wolf Trap's internship program also offers interns professional development opportunities through a guest speaker series, field trips, presentations by department heads, performance facility tours, a mentorship program, and professional development training workshops.

Internships are 12 weeks long, full time in the summer and part time (24 hours a week) in the fall and spring; however, the duration and hours required may vary. College credit may be available through your university.

You may choose an internship in a wide variety of areas at Wolf Trap, including directing; administrative; stage management; technical theater; scenic/prop painting; costuming; education; development; communications and marketing; advertising; graphic design; publications; media relations; photography; program and production; human resources; accounting; box office/group sales; information systems; Internet programs; special events; national partnerships; President's Committee on the Arts and Humanities; or Arts Education Partnership.

HOUSING

Wolf Trap offers a stipend to help offset housing and transportation expenses, since housing is your responsibility (although guidance is available). You're also required to have a reliable mode of transportation, since the Wolf Trap Foundation is not accessible by public transit. Summer interns have the opportunity to receive complimentary tickets to performances.

HOW TO APPLY

To apply for an internship, you should submit a cover letter with a brief personal statement and an outline of career goals, specifying which departmental internship you want, a resume listing relevant courses, previous experience, and special skills (no transcripts) and two academic and/or professional letters of reference. You also should submit two contrasting samples of writing, no more than three pages each (unless you are applying for a technical, scenic painting, costuming, stage management, accounting, graphic design, information systems, or photography position). Graphic design applicants should also include three desktop publishing/design samples.

If you choose to submit internship applications via e-mail, you must format your materials as text (.txt) or Microsoft Word (.doc) documents and attach them to an e-mail message sent to the preceding e-mail address. Provided your application is complete, Wolf Trap will confirm receipt of your application via e-mail or mail.

GOVERNMENT

AMERICAN ENTERPRISE INSTITUTE INTERNSHIP

The American Enterprise Institute
1150 17th Street, NW
Washington, DC 20036
(202) 862-5800
Internships@aei.org
http://www.aei.org

What You Can Earn: Unpaid, but college credit is possible. Benefits include complimentary breakfast and lunch prepared by AEI's own in-house gourmet chef, served in the institute dining room, plus free attendance at the many conferences and seminars that AEI hosts.

Application Deadlines: April 1 for summer (May through August); September 30 for fall (September through December); December 1 for spring (January through May). Applications are processed on a rolling basis, so apply early as positions fill quickly. The dates of internships are flexible in order to accommodate various school schedules.

Educational Experience: Advanced undergraduate students, graduate students, and recent graduates. Upperclassmen and graduate students are preferred; you should apply once you have taken college coursework in your area of interest.

Requirements: A minimum of a 3.0 GPA on a 4.0 scale is required, however, most successful candidates have at least a 3.5 GPA on a 4.0 scale. In the summer, almost all internships are full time. In the fall and the spring, offices are more flexible in that they are working with various academic programs, and intern hours vary greatly, but require a minimum commitment of at least three days a week.

OVERVIEW

The American Enterprise Institute (AEI) for Public Policy Research is dedicated to preserving and strengthening the foundations of government, private enterprise, vital cultural and political institutions, and a strong foreign policy and national defense through scholarly research, open debate, and publications. Founded in 1943 and located in Washington, D.C., AEI is one of America's largest "think tanks," covering research in economics and trade; social welfare; government tax, spending, regulatory, and legal policies; U.S. politics; international affairs; and U.S. defense and foreign policies.

The institute publishes dozens of books and hundreds of articles and reports each year, and a policy magazine, *The American Enterprise*. AEI publications are distributed to government officials and legislators, business executives, journalists, and academics, and offers conferences, seminars, and lectures.

The institute's 50 resident scholars and fellows include some of America's foremost economists, legal scholars, political scientists, and foreign policy experts, in addition to a network of more than 100 adjunct scholars at universities and policy institutes throughout the United States and abroad. AEI scholars testify frequently before congressional committees, provide expert consultation to all branches of government, and are cited and reprinted in the national media more often than those of any other think tank. The institute is an independent, nonprofit organization supported primarily by grants and contributions from foundations, corporations, and individuals. It is strictly nonpartisan and takes no institutional positions on pending legislation or other policy questions.

AEI internships provide students with an opportunity to work with some of America's most renowned scholars, economists, legal scholars, political scientists, and foreign policy specialists doing research on current public policy questions. Internship opportunities are available to undergraduates, graduate students, and postgraduates. About 50 internship opportunities are available in the fall, winter, and summer in economic policy, foreign and defense studies, social and political studies, public relations, *The American Enterprise* magazine, communications, seminars and conferences, publications, publications marketing, information systems, marketing, and human resources. An internship with AEI offers opportunities for extensive interaction on an everyday basis in an arena with more than 50 of America's most cited experts in the fields of politics and public policy.

Internships on the research side of the organization consist in all aspects of research, writing, event planning, and administrative tasks. As an intern here, you can typically expect 80 percent substantive work with less than 20 percent purely administrative duties. On the business side of the organization, interns will participate in the life of the department in which they work, meaning that the level of administrative elements varies depending on the role of the department, time of year, and so on. Hours and days are flexible, either part or full time.

As an intern here, you'll be paired with a scholar or business director whose area of expertise coincides with your interests. You'll also be able to attend conferences and lectures hosted by AEI featuring top experts on the most up-to-date issues, along with a series of policy lectures from scholars and career talks from business directors for the interns each term.

Frequent intern happenings provide an informal environment for interns to interact with scholars, staff, and other interns. In addition, a formal intern dinner is given every semester to honor you for your hard work. Interns also participate in tours to places of interest in the D.C. area such as the Pentagon, Capitol Building, White House, and State Department. What's more, working as an intern here might lead to full-time employment; in the past 10 years, nearly 50 former interns were hired as full-time staff members.

HOW TO APPLY

All applications for these internships and supporting documents must be submitted through the institute's online system. They no longer accept e-mail, fax, or paper applications.

To apply, you'll need to know which scholars or offices you're interested in working with. All available internships are posted under the "Current Internship Opportunities" page at http://www.aei.

org/about/contentID.20050825161402905/default. asp.

In the profile section of the online application, enter your basic contact information; you can save your information at the conclusion of the profile and come back later, or you may continue to the main application. The main application must be completed in one session.

In order to complete the application, you will need to have a cover letter detailing your areas of interest and background, an up-to-date resume, and an approximately 500-word writing sample on a relevant topic. This may be an excerpt from a larger paper or a piece written specifically for this application. This is an opportunity to showcase your analytical abilities as well as your background in your areas of interest. You'll also need an unofficial electronic copy of your transcripts (this can be information copied from your registrar's Web site, or a scanned .pdf file of your paper transcripts). Transcripts must be submitted through our online system or your application will not be considered complete. You can apply online at http://www.aei. org/about/filter.,contentID.20038142214000060/default.asp.

You'll receive an e-mail notification when your application is complete, and updates by e-mail as your application is reviewed. Your status will also be reflected under the internships tab when you are logged into the institute's system. Online information is the most up to date, so all questions about your application status can be answered by logging into the application system. If you are selected for an interview, you will be contacted directly.

ARIZONA LEGISLATIVE INTERNSHIP

Office of the Associate Provost—Academic Administration
Northern Arizona University
NAU Box 6052

Flagstaff, AZ 86011
(928) 523-5291
http://www2.nau.edu/academicadmin/Intern.
htm

What You Can Earn: Stipend of $4,200 paid in biweekly checks; 12 units of upper-division undergraduate credit or nine units of graduate credit (PASS/FAIL); assistance with locating housing is available. Students moving from schools outside Maricopa County are eligible for up to $500 relocation expenses.

Application Deadlines: September 28.

Educational Experience: Any candidate for a bachelor or master's degree at an Arizona university who will have completed 75 credit hours at the end of the fall semester, with a 3.0 GPA. Students from all academic disciplines are eligible and encouraged to apply.

Requirements: Communication and writing skills, the ability to work in a team setting, and self-starting independence. Most important, this internship demands a strong desire to learn the legislative process through hands-on experience.

OVERVIEW

The Arizona Legislative Internship Program is co-sponsored by the Arizona State Senate/Arizona State House of Representatives and Arizona universities and offers selected college students an opportunity to participate in the Arizona Legislative process, work in the governor's or Supreme Court offices, or work with the Arizona Senate broadcasting sessions via the Internet.

About 50 interns serve in the House and Senate. Many former interns have succeeded in getting jobs at various state agencies, with lobbying groups, and law firms. Several former interns are currently on permanent staff with the House of Representatives and the Senate and some have gone to various federal agencies in Washington, D.C.

The program is designed to broaden the scope of undergraduate and graduate curricula by offering students a unique type of learning experience: participating in the legislative internship and also helping the state legislature with extra legislative research and specific project research. The internship also provides service opportunities for college students who want to participate in helping to solve problems facing the citizens of Arizona and encourages students to evaluate career goals, consider citizen leadership in public programs, and let the legislature and state agencies get to know possible future employees.

As an intern here, you'll help analyze bills and write bill summaries, answer constituent letters and handle constituent casework, write speeches, track the current status of bills, and present information to caucuses and committees. Committees cover topics including appropriations and budget; taxes and finance; health and welfare; legal and law enforcement; education; insurance and banking; natural resources; business or labor; Republican leadership staff; constituent services; state and local government; transportation; and Democrat leadership staff.

Interns may also be selected to work in the governor's office or with the Supreme Court.

Arizona Supreme Court Internship

One temporary, full-time, paid intern position is available at the Arizona Supreme Court administrative office in Phoenix. The Arizona Constitution charges the Supreme Court with the responsibility for providing administrative supervision over all the courts of the state. This is done through the administrative office and includes adult and juvenile probation, juvenile detention, diversion programs, child support, child custody, adoption, domestic relations, restitution, substance abuse treatment, administrative and personnel matters; and issues affecting municipal, justice, superior, and appellate courts. The intern will work in the executive division of the administrative office, assisting with judicial department legislation and other administrative responsibilities.

The Supreme Court has two main responsibilities: hearing cases on appeal from the lower courts and statewide administration of the court system. The intern's work focuses exclusively on the court's administrative responsibility. This means that you may be involved in preparing information for the chief justice about legislative proposals, but researching cases pending before the court and writing legal briefs would not be one of your duties.

Because the Arizona Supreme Court has administrative responsibility for the state court system, this internship exposes you to all aspects of the judicial department. Part of your responsibilities will be informing judges and court administrators about proposed legislation and obtaining feedback from the courts on introduced legislation.

As an intern here, you'll attend court and legislative committee meetings and hearings; help the administrative director and legislative officers prepare, research, and track legislation with impact on the courts; act as a liaison to the legislature; and communicate with judges and administrative staff on legislative activity. You'll also be required to prepare written materials (such as fact sheets, legislative summaries, and letters) and make oral presentations on legislation to court committees and staff. You may also lobby legislators on select proposals.

The term of the intern position is from early January to early May between 8:00 A.M. to 5:00 P.M.; however, legislative activity and other job duties will require extended hours and attendance at early morning or evening meetings. There are no holidays or semester breaks.

Candidates should have good basic research, word processing, and strong communication and organizational skills and be able to work independently. Preference will be given to applicants with experience and demonstrated interest or academic studies in public administration, the justice system, political science, or law. Both undergraduate and graduate students are encouraged to apply, but you do not need to be a law student. Prior interns have had educational backgrounds in justice studies, English, business, accounting, public administration, social work, and political science. A demonstrated interest in public administration or the judicial system through course work, future career plans, or volunteer or work experience is preferred.

Many prior interns have gone on to law school and other graduate programs. In addition to the submission requirements that follow, candidates for this internship should also include a written statement identifying current issues of interest to the student that effect Arizona Courts and stating their reasons for and interest in applying for the Supreme Court internship.

Senate Broadcast Internship

The Arizona State Senate's Broadcast Internship offers qualified students a rare opportunity to learn about the legislative process while producing daily video coverage of committee meetings and floor debate for the Internet and cable television. A background in journalism and/or experience with video equipment is preferred but not required.

HOW TO APPLY

Download the completed application at http://www2.nau.edu/academicadmin/applink.html.

Submit the completed application, two letters of recommendation, and a statement of purpose to the above address. After the submission, students will be interviewed on campus with faculty and legislature representatives. Top candidates are referred to the legislature for interviewing; successful candidates will be notified by the legislature by early December.

ASIAN PACIFIC AMERICAN INSTITUTE FOR CONGRESSIONAL STUDIES INTERNSHIP

Summer Internship Program
1001 Connecticut Avenue, NW
Suite 835

Washington, DC 20036
(202) 296-9200
http://www.apaics.org

What You Can Earn: $2,500 for interns attending continental U.S. schools; $3,000 for interns attending Hawaii schools, or who live in Hawaii, to cover additional transportation costs.
Application Deadlines: January 31.
Educational Experience: Currently enrolled in an accredited undergraduate educational institution. (Those who graduated within 90 days of the start of the summer session are also welcome to apply.)
Requirements: Must be interested in the political process, public-policy issues, and Asian American and Pacific Islander community affairs; have excellent leadership abilities and excellent oral and written communication skills; possess U.S. citizenship or legal permanent residency; must be 18 years of age by the start of the internship.

OVERVIEW

APAICS is a nonpartisan, nonprofit educational organization dedicated to promoting the participation of Asian American and Pacific Islanders in the political process. Through its internship program, APAICS hopes to encourage the political and civic involvement of young Asian American and Pacific Islanders, fostering their interest in political and public policy careers and developing their leadership skills.

Every summer, APAICS invites a group of exceptional college students from across the nation to experience working in Congress and federal agencies. In addition, interns attend briefings with members of Congress, networking events with other interns from other national Asian Pacific Islander American organizations, and also participate in joint activities with the Congressional Black and Hispanic Caucus Institutes. APAICS places its interns in the U.S. Congress, federal agencies, and institutions that further APAICS' mission. All interns will be required to complete weekly journals and a program evaluation at the end of the internship.

HOW TO APPLY

You can find an application at http://www.apaics.org/downloads/2005_Summer_Internship_app.pdf.

To apply, mail the application to the preceding address (do not fax or e-mail), along with the following information:

- an official copy of your most current transcript
- a cover letter discussing why you should be selected for the internship, how you selected your internship placement preference, and how participating in this particular program will further your personal goals
- a resume listing your education, work experience, extracurricular activities, community involvement and honors/awards
- two separate letters of recommendation (from people not related to you) who can evaluate your potential as an intern (such as an employer, community leader and/or campus organization sponsor or professor)
- a writing sample consisting of three essays addressing the following questions in three pages or fewer using Arial, 12-point font for all three essays (The answers to the questions do not have to be equal lengths, so if you choose, you may use more space for one question, than the others):

  - How did you become interested in politics, and what have you done to further that interest?
  - Select a publicly elected official whom you consider to be a role model, and explain why you believe this person is a role model.
  - How do you see yourself participating in politics in the future?

Finalists may be contacted for a telephone interview, and successful applicants will be notified in

March. APAICS will give preference to students who have not previously had an internship in Washington, D.C.

CALIFORNIA GOVERNOR'S INTERNSHIP

California Governor's Internship Coordinator
State Capitol Building
Sacramento, CA 95814
(916) 445-2841
Fax: (916) 323-9991
Internships@gov.ca.gov

What You Can Earn: Unpaid.
Application Deadlines: Summer internships application deadline is April 1. Fall internships application deadline is August 15. Spring internships application deadline is December 1.
Educational Experience: Must be enrolled in an accredited U.S. college, with a 2.8 or higher GPA and be at least 18 years of age.
Requirements: Must be able to work a minimum of 20 hours a week.

OVERVIEW

The governor's internship program provides an excellent opportunity to learn about state government and the political process. Internships last 12 to 16 weeks in the spring, summer, and fall semesters; approximately 40 interns are chosen each semester. You and your supervisor will determine the hours and days that are best for you and the office of your internship, but if you're interning for college credit, most programs require you to intern between 20 to 25 hours a week to be eligible for credit.

Several areas within the governor's office need interns: advance, office of the first lady, scheduling, communications, press, appointments, legislative unit, constituent affairs, cabinet affairs, legal affairs, and executive writers. Interns are encouraged to indicate on the application a specific area where they would like to be placed.

Each office has different needs and requirements, but some responsibilities may include answering phones, taking messages, gathering information on groups or organizations, performing general clerical duties, and helping plan special events.

Advance
The advance office coordinates all logistical arrangements for offsite visits by the governor.

Appointments
This unit helps the governor find the highest caliber of talent to serve in the administration.

Cabinet Affairs
This is the primary point of contact and liaison between the governor's office and the governor's cabinet. The cabinet office is responsible for developing, coordinating, and implementing public policy.

Communications
This office is responsible for communicating the governor's policies and actions to the press and the public. The governor's press office is the liaison to the media.

Constituent Affairs
This office is concerned with the people of California; staffers and interns here take constituent calls, answer their correspondence, and offer help.

First Lady's Office
The first lady's office works on community and statewide projects such as the California Women's History Museum, California History Center, and California Governor's Conference on Women and Families.

Legal Affairs
This office provides legal counsel to the governor and the governor's staff.

Legislative Affairs

The office of legislative affairs provides strategic planning and guidance to the governor and senior staff on all matters related to legislation.

Executive Writers

This office is responsible for composing the governor's public remarks including the State of the State.

Scheduling

The scheduling office is responsible for the organization and implementation of the governor's daily and long-term schedule. All requests for appointments, meetings, or events with the governor are directed through this office.

HOW TO APPLY

Download an application at http://www.governor.ca.gov/state/govsite/gov_htmldisplay.jsp?sCatTitle=%20&sFilePath=/govsite/appointments/InternshipApplicationProcess.html.

E-mail or fax the completed application along with a current resume and letter of recommendation to the internship coordinator at the preceding address. For summer internships, you'll be contacted no later than May 1 to be informed whether your application has been accepted or denied. Start date for summer internships will be May 1. For fall internships, you'll be contacted no later then September 1. The start date will be September 26. For spring internships, you'll be contacted no later then January 6 with a start date of January 23.

If you aren't selected for the semester in which you are applying, you are welcome to apply again for the following semester.

CAPITOL HILL INTERNSHIP

For a listing of Web sites of all senators and congresspeople plus committee Web sites, go to http://www.politixgroup.com/dcintern/congress.htm

What You Can Earn: Mostly unpaid.
Application Deadlines: Early fall for spring and summer internships; mid-spring for fall internships.
Educational Experience: Graduate or undergrad students with a strong academic record and interest in civics, such as involvement in student government or community service, plus leadership skills and extracurricular activities.
Requirements: Good scholastic and personal record.

OVERVIEW

Ever since Congress was established in 1789, interns have been walking the historic halls helping to serve senators and House members in a variety of tasks. Today the historic halls are swarming with interns, especially in summer. You'll find most interns working in the personal offices of Senate and House members, either on the Hill or in their home districts.

In general, internships on the Hill are quite competitive; many students apply to 10 or 15 internships in hopes of getting one or two. You don't need to restrict your search to a congressperson from your own district or state; it may be a better idea to apply with someone whose party or positions mimic your own. The state you choose can play a big role in how selective the internship is; states such as Wyoming, where few D.C. college students (who apply for many internships) come from, are less selective. Many applicants assume it's easier to land an internship with a House member, since there are more of them and hence less competition for positions. Spring and fall tend to be less competitive times for intern applicants to find work than during the busy summer season. And keep in mind that in addition to their D.C. offices, many members of Congress offer internships in their state district offices.

To find a likely candidate to intern for, you can search for the offices of House and Senate members on the Internet; you may want to begin with the Library of Congress "Thomas" Web site.

When you visit a member's Web site, you can usually find details on possible internships by clicking the "services" section of the Web site. Insiders suggest you may want to consider more than one program, since competition is stiff and there are usually many more applicants than open positions.

As a Capitol Hill intern, you'll have unparalleled access to the power centers of Washington, D.C. While these internships can provide terrific experiences, be prepared to do some taxing work; don't expect to sit down daily with the Congressperson to discuss policy. And while you may spend days copying or faxing, at other times you *will* get to do policy research or attend congressional hearings or Capitol Hill receptions. If you've got a special interest in a particular topic, you may be assigned to work closely with the full-time employee assigned to that subject. Many offices also offer structured programs including mentoring, educational sessions with government officials, and tours of agency buildings. Daily experiences provide valuable lessons in the workings of Capitol Hill, too.

When applying, keep in mind that committee office internships tend to allow interns to work more on issue-oriented projects, while members' personal office interns tend to work more on constituent and media-oriented issues. But no matter where you work, if you think you'd like to pursue a career in federal government, many former interns agree that the contacts you can make can create an inside track for future jobs and that this internship is really the best way to prepare for getting a job in Washington after graduation.

HOW TO APPLY

The first step in securing a Capitol Hill internship is to send a cover letter along with your resume and some writing samples to the office's intern coordinator, who will perform the initial screening. Applicants with excellent skills in writing, computer, and Internet research stand the best chance. Several weeks after you submit your letter, follow up with a phone call to try to get an interview. The final approval may rest with the administrative assistant (or chief of staff). You should not send a mass mailing to every office; be sure to individualize each letter.

CENTRAL INTELLIGENCE AGENCY INTERNSHIP

CIA Recruitment Center
PO Box 4090
Reston, VA 20195

What You Can Earn: Stipend is available; students also are eligible for employee benefits including health and life insurance, retirement investment options, paid federal holidays, annual and sick leave, and possible tuition assistance.

Application Deadlines: Applications for winter, spring, and fall internships should be sent six to nine months before the desired start date.

Educational Experience: Undergraduate students (particularly minorities and people with disabilities) majoring in engineering, computer science, mathematics, economics, physical sciences, foreign languages, area studies, business administration, accounting, international relations, finance, logistics, human resources, geography, national security studies, military and foreign affairs, political science, and graphic design. You'll need a strong academic record (3.0 GPA or better). Foreign language skills, previous international residency, and military experience are pluses. Graduate students should check out requirements listed below.

Requirements: Outstanding interpersonal skills, the ability to write clearly and accurately, and a strong interest in foreign affairs are necessary. As part of the hiring process, you must successfully complete medical and polygraph examinations as well as a background investigation. To be considered suitable for agency employment, applicants must generally not have used illegal drugs within the last 12 months. The issue of illegal drug use in the prior to 12 months is carefully evaluated during the medical and security processing. You're also required to work either a combination of one semester and one summer internship, or two 90-day summer internships.

OVERVIEW

If you're interested in foreign affairs and you'd like to make a difference, you might be interested in checking out the CIA's undergraduate internship program. The George Bush Center for Intelligence is located in suburban McLean, Virginia, on the west bank of the Potomac River, just seven miles from downtown Washington, D.C. The CIA, charged with guarding our country's security, was created in 1947 with the signing of the National Security Act by President Harry S. Truman. The act also created a director of central intelligence (DCI) to serve as head of the United States intelligence community; act as the principal adviser to the president for intelligence matters related to the national security; and serve as head of the Central Intelligence Agency. The Intelligence Reform and Terrorism Prevention Act of 2004 amended the National Security Act to provide for a director of national intelligence who would assume some of the roles formerly fulfilled by the DCI, with a separate director of the Central Intelligence Agency.

College undergraduates and graduate students can apply to either the CIA internship program or the graduate studies program, earning promising undergrads the chance to gain practical work experience in an area of interest. As an intern with the CIA, you'll be given the opportunity to work with highly skilled professionals and to see exactly how the CIA supports U.S. officials who make foreign policy. The CIA offers both student internships and graduate studies programs. As an intern at the CIA, you'll help with substantive and meaningful work assignments, while earning a competitive income and gaining invaluable practical experience. These internship programs can help prepare you for careers at the CIA. Based on the CIA's needs and your performance during your internship, the CIA might offer you a job when you graduate.

Graduate students may want to apply for an internship in the graduate studies program, which looks for bright graduate students focusing on international affairs, languages, economics, geography, cartography, physical sciences, and engineering. Other majors may be accepted on a case-by-case basis. Students selected for this program should be entering either their first or second year of graduate studies following this assignment. In this program, graduate interns will become acquainted with the work of professional intelligence analysts through active participation in agency projects. If you do well, selected pieces of your work may be distributed throughout the intelligence community.

HOW TO APPLY

It's a good idea to discuss CIA opportunities with your on-campus career adviser or internship program coordinator, and to check your school's schedule for recruiting events. Eligible applicants can submit a resume online at http://www.cia.gov/employment/resume.html.

CONNECTICUT GOVERNOR'S PREVENTION PARTNERSHIP INTERNSHIP

The Governor's Prevention Partnership
Campus Coordinator
30 Arbor Street
Hartford, CT 06106
(860) 523-8042

Fax: (860) 236-9412
http://www.preventionworksct.org/Internships/
cmp1.html

What You Can Earn: Unpaid.
Application Deadlines: Rolling.
Educational Experience: College undergraduate,
any major.
Requirements: Interest in prevention and youth
issues, good organizational skills, and excellent
written and oral communication skills. Must be
able to commit a minimum of 10 hours a week and
a maximum of 25 hours a week.

OVERVIEW

The Governor's Prevention Partnership is a nonprofit
public-private partnership trying to reduce drug and
alcohol use and its related impact on health, safety,
and violence in Connecticut. The organization's
work is based on six factors that protect children:
parent involvement; mentoring; success at school;
youth leadership; anti-drug, anti-violence messages
delivered through the media; and safe and drug-free
communities. The organization is co-chaired by the
governor and a business leader.

The staff of the Connecticut Mentoring Partnership of The Governor's Prevention Partnership
provides resources to schools, businesses, and community groups throughout the state to develop
school-based mentoring programs. Interns in this
program would help conduct a survey to determine
how many mentoring matches in Connecticut there
would be; respond to requests for information and
technical assistance from mentoring programs
throughout the state; update mentoring resource
material to include latest state and national research;
create a mentoring resource library and update the
Web site with available resources; and help with
organizing activities and planning for National Mentoring Month (January) recruitment campaign.

HOW TO APPLY

For more information or to set up an interview,
contact the office at the preceding address.

DEMOCRATIC NATIONAL COMMITTEE INTERNSHIP

Internship Office
430 South Capitol Street SE
Washington, DC 20003
(202) 863-8000
Fax: (202) 479-5125
staffinterns@dnc.org
http://www.democrats.org/a/2005/07/dnc_
internshi.php

What You Can Earn: Unpaid.
Application Deadlines: March 15 for summer; fall
and spring are rolling.
Educational Experience: Unspecified.
Requirements: The DNC expects all interns to be
Democrats.

OVERVIEW

The Democratic National Committee plans the
Democratic Party's presidential nominating con-
vention, which occurs every four years, promotes
the election of party candidates with both technical and financial support, and works with national,
state, and local party organizations, elected officials, and candidates to respond to the needs and
views of Democrats and the nation.

If you're a Democrat and you're interested in
learning more about Democratic campaigns, this
could be the internship for you. Interns with the
DNC are involved in the election of Democrats
from the state legislature to the White House,
working in every department of the DNC. Most
interns work in the political, communications, and
research departments or the office of the secretary.
In addition, you should expect to do your share of
pouring coffee and handling administrative tasks,
because everyone at the DNC makes copies and
sends faxes. However, interns who prove that they
can be trusted to work responsibly, accurately, and
promptly are often given more substantive work as
the semester progresses.

As an intern in the political department, you might help the Midwestern desk gather information on Midwestern states, check newspapers for Midwestern political events, help out with special events, or compile contact numbers for county Democratic chairs in Midwestern states. As an intern in communications, you'll try to publicize the Democratic message, setting up press conferences, helping write press releases and Op-Ed pieces, and helping with the morning clips. As an intern in the office of the secretary, you might help plan committee meetings, contact members for conference calls with the chair, and compile biographical information on membership.

Typically, you'll work full time during the summer or between 15 and 20 hours during the fall and spring.

HOW TO APPLY

You can download a copy of the application in PDF format at http://a9.g.akamai.net/7/9/8082/v002/democratic1.download.akamai.com/8082/pdfs/internapplication.pdf.

FEDERAL BUREAU OF INVESTIGATION (FBI) WASHINGTON INTERNSHIPS FOR NATIVE STUDENTS (WINS)

FBI WINS
4400 Massachusetts Avenue, NW
Washington, DC 20016-8083
(202) 895-4900
wins@american.edu
http://www.american.edu/wins/wins_
    participation.html

What You Can Earn: Weekly stipend plus all expenses paid. The program pays for your travel to Washington, D.C., plus all books, tuition, housing, meals, metro fare, insurance, scheduled social and cultural activities, and a weekly stipend. Funding is provided by governmental agencies, Native organizations, tribes, foundations, American University, and corporations. Incidental expenses for nonprogram activities, including medical care and independent social activities, are the responsibility of the student.

Application Deadlines: Late November for next summer's internship beginning in June (check for firm deadline date).

Educational Experience: Sophomores, juniors, seniors, and grad students with a minimum 3.0 GPA are eligible to apply. Preferred candidates will have Web experience and a journalism, creative writing, or English major or minor.

Requirements: This internship is open to Native Americans and Alaskan Natives currently enrolled in college.

OVERVIEW

This internship enables Native American students an opportunity to intern with the FBI as a guest of the federal government and also take a course at American University during the summer term. If you're selected, you'll live on the American University campus; all expenses are paid by a government grant and American University.

The academic course covers topics important to Native communities such as tribal sovereignty; trust responsibilities; health and social welfare issues; and gaming and economic development concerns. You'll also intern at the FBI for 36 hours a week and prepare a prescribed portfolio on your work experience and research.

You'll live in a university dorm on the Tenley campus of American University, just two blocks from the Tenleytown/AU Metro station in northwest Washington, D.C. All of your meals will be prepared at the Tenley Café, located on campus.

Members of the WINS Native Advisory Council provide advice and counsel to make sure that the traditional values and practices of the nations and tribes throughout Indian country are maintained.

The WINS program also offers a special summer program and a fall and spring internship.

HOW TO APPLY

If you're interested, you must submit a completed WINS application form; an FD 140 form (you'll find one at https://www.fbijobs.com/FBIEmployment.asp); an essay of at least 500 words about why you would like to participate; a nomination letter from a member of your nation or tribal council or from an official of the applicant's nation or tribal education department; a recommendation letter from a faculty member at your university; a resume detailing your work experience; and an official copy of your most recent transcript.

You may obtain a copy of the application online at (https://my.american.edu/cgi/mvi.exe/A26. APPL.LOGIN?SCH=WINS) or call the WINS headquarters at the preceding number to ask that an application be mailed to you. You also may request an application via e-mail (see preceding address).

FLORIDA GOVERNOR'S INTERNSHIP

Internship Program
Executive Office of the Governor
The Capitol
Room PL-05
Tallahassee, FL 32399-0005

What You Can Earn: Unpaid but academic credit is available.
Application Deadlines: Application deadline July 1 for fall session (August 30 to December 10); deadline November 1 for spring session (January 10 to April 29); deadline March 1 for summer session (May 10 to August 30).

Educational Experience: Must be enrolled as a full-time student or have recently graduated from an accredited college or university and have a GPA of at least 3.0.
Requirements: Minimum of 15 to 30 hours a week on a schedule designed around your academic classes or outside employment.

OVERVIEW

The Florida governor's internship program is designed to provide students with an opportunity to gain hands-on experience in the executive branch of Florida government. It was created to provide exceptional college students and recent graduates with the opportunity to learn more about the role of the executive branch in Florida's government but also to experience firsthand what it's like to work in the highest office in the state.

For 13 weeks, interns will gain practical knowledge and experience in one of several departments within the Executive Office of the Governor. Internships are available during the three academic semesters: fall, spring, and summer.

Once selected, interns will be assigned to specific offices based on their preferences, availability, academic and employment experience, and the number of open positions.

HOW TO APPLY

For more information, log on to http://www.myflorida.com/myflorida/government/bushteam/internships.html.

Interested students should download an official internship program application at http://www.myflorida.com/myflorida/government/bushteam/application.pdf and submit it (along with a certified transcript, a complete resume including education, employment, and volunteer history; a letter of recommendation from a major professor or teacher; and a letter of personal recommendation) to the preceding address.

Applicants should read the Executive Summary of Functions document at http://www.myflorida.

com/myflorida/government/bushteam/positions. pdf. This outlines the roles and responsibilities of each department within the executive office of the governor. This document will help you select the office that interests you. You should note your preferences on the application.

GEORGIA GOVERNOR'S INTERNSHIP

Office of the Governor
Georgia State Capitol
Atlanta, GA 30334
(404) 656-1776
http://www.ganet.org/governor/intern/index. html

What You Can Earn: Ranges from a $1,690 summer stipend for 20 hours a week to a $3380 summer stipend for 40 hours a week; the fall/spring stipend ranges from $2340 to $4680. The stipend is paid in three installments during the term of your internship. The amount you receive depends on the number of hours you work per week, the term of your internship, and your academic status. Academic credit is also available.

Application Deadlines: Spring, September 23; summer, March 3; fall, July 1.

Educational Experience: Currently enrolled junior, senior, or graduate student with at least a 2.75 GPA (grad students must have 3.0 GPA); must be a Georgia resident or attending a Georgia college or university; must have passed both parts of the regents exam.

Requirements: None specified.

OVERVIEW
The Governor's Intern Program, initiated in 1971, provides the best, brightest, and most ambitious college students with practical professional experience before they enter the working world.

Entering the 34th year of operation, the governor's intern program offers invaluable work experience each semester in numerous state agencies throughout Georgia. The intern serves as a staff member with professionals in a career of interest to the student. A great deal of emphasis is placed on merging classroom learning with practical application.

The governor's intern program offers invaluable work experience in a state or nonprofit agency and creates a mutually beneficial arrangement for college students, their respective schools, and participating agencies. The intern serves as a staff member with professionals in a career of interest to the student. A great deal of emphasis is placed on merging classroom learning with practical application. College juniors, seniors, and master's-level students in any academic discipline are encouraged to participate. Internships are available throughout the state of Georgia in all fields of academic interest.

Internships last 18 weeks in the fall and spring semesters and 13 weeks in the summer. The governor's intern program strives to schedule the dates and deadlines for the internships in accordance with the academic schedule of most Georgia colleges, universities, and law schools.

At the end of the internship, you'll be invited to a reception with the governor, where you'll be able to meet and mingle with the other interns and their supervisors from respective agencies. A photograph will be taken of you and the governor and will be sent to you as a memento.

HOW TO APPLY
You can fill out an application online at https:// www.ganet.org/governor_intern/application.

After submitting an application and resume, students are selected for an interview with the governor's intern program staff. After a preliminary interview, the student can be selected for a second round of interviews with one or more agencies that will best utilize their talents and interests. This process is very effective in determining the best placement and provides an excellent opportunity for college students to improve their interviewing and job-search skills. Students will be confirmed an internship before the school year concludes each semester. (In the case of the fall semester, students will be notified before school begins.)

IDAHO LIEUTENANT GOVERNOR'S INTERNSHIP

Intern Coordinator
Office of the Lieutenant Governor
State Capitol
Room 225
Boise, ID 83720-0057
http://lgo.idaho.gov/intern.html

What You Can Earn: Small stipend or academic credit is available.
Application Deadlines: Rolling.
Educational Experience: College juniors, seniors, or graduate students.
Requirements: Good written and verbal English skills and good computer skills; ability to take notes and organize them; ability to conduct research on proposed legislation or other pertinent issues; ability to write letters and listen to constituents; willingness to assist policy advisors and constituent services representatives; good telephone skills; and willingness to become familiar with issues, state agencies, staff, and staff assignments. Candidates should have a helpful, pleasant attitude, be willing to do basic office work, and be familiar with Microsoft Word and Excel. Some familiarity with a Web browser and the Internet is highly desirable.

OVERVIEW

There are many internship opportunities in policy areas such as natural resources, education, social/welfare services, criminal justice, business and industry, state finance and budgeting, press/public relations, and communications.

As an intern for the lieutenant governor, you'll be involved in the political process, attending committee meetings, researching current and proposed legislation, and so on, and learning or improving office and computer skills. You may be asked to attend and take notes on legislative hearings or other meetings and prepare them for reporting to the governor and other staff members. At other times, your duties will be more routine, and you may be asked to run errands, recycle paper, make copies, send faxes, and help with mail, office filing, and so on. You'll also spend some time writing letters, reports, minutes, documents, charts, press releases, and so on.

Internships are available during the fall, spring, and summer.

HOW TO APPLY

You can download and print out the application at http://lgo.idaho.gov/Intern/app_form.pdf (or submit it online). E-mail or mail the completed application, along with a brief essay explaining your reasons for wanting to intern in the office of the governor, a current resume, and a written recommendation from a faculty member or a teacher who is familiar with your qualifications, to the preceding address.

ILLINOIS GOVERNOR'S INTERNSHIP

Intern Coordinator, Illinois Governor's Office
100 West Randolph, Suite 16
Chicago, IL 60601
(312) 814-2121

What You Can Earn: Blagojevich internships are unpaid, but academic credit is available. Curry interns receive $1200 a month.

Application Deadlines: January 31.
Educational Experience: College or graduate students with a minimum GPA of 3.0; see specific internship descriptions for more information.
Requirements: Organized, self-motivated, and energetic individuals who possess strong writing and research skills.

OVERVIEW
The office of the governor provides internship opportunities for undergraduate and graduate students interested in experiencing the day-to-day operations of the chief executive's office. The governor's office is responsible for overseeing the administration of state departments, agencies, and boards and commissions. Working with the legislature, the governor's office coordinates policy initiatives and the overall agenda for the state. The governor's office offers two summer internships: The Michael Curry Summer Internship Program and the new Rod R. Blagojevich Governmental Internship are for college and graduate students.

Michael Curry Summer Internship
This program offers college juniors, seniors, and graduate students in all disciplines (including law) an opportunity to work in one of the agencies under the jurisdiction of the governor full time for 10 weeks during the summer. Positions are available in Springfield and Chicago. Eligible applicants must be Illinois residents who have not previously participated in the Curry Internship Program.

Rod R. Blagojevich Governmental Internship
As an intern here, you'll have the opportunity to become familiar with all aspects of the operation of the governor's office. More specifically, interns will assist administratively, aid in media relations, and, where appropriate, respond to correspondence from Illinois citizens. Interns will be given as much substantive work as possible and will interact directly with staff and assist in state government. Internships are available year-round on a semester/quarter length basis. Intern schedules are based on each student's hours of availability.

HOW TO APPLY
Michael Curry Summer Internship
Download a copy of the application at http://www.illinois.gov/gov/pdfdocs/2005_curry.pdf. Candidates must submit a completed application, college transcript(s) and a brief essay to: Office of the Governor, Michael Curry Summer Internship Program, 107 William G. Stratton Building, Springfield, IL 62706.

Rod R. Blagojevich Governmental Internship
Download a copy of the application at http://www.illinois.gov/Gov/pdfdocs/2003govint.pdf. Send a completed internship application, a resume, and a cover letter explaining your interest in being an intern in the governor's office to the preceding address

LIBRARY OF CONGRESS INTERNSHIP

Library of Congress
101 Independence Avenue, SE
Washington, DC 20540-4500
(202) 707-5213
Fax: (202) 707-3434

What You Can Earn: Varies with specific internships; see individual programs below.
Application Deadlines: See individual programs below for specific deadlines.
Educational Experience: See individual programs below for specific educational requirements.
Requirements: See individual programs below for specific requirements.

OVERVIEW

There are many internship, fellowship, and volunteer program opportunities throughout the library, as follows:

Ability Internship Program

This one- or two-semester internship program is designed for high school, college, and vocational students with disabilities seeking job experience at the Library of Congress. As an intern here, you may choose to work with geography and maps; collections conservation and preservation; government and business administration; humanities, arts, and culture; information technology; law; library sciences; policy analysis; or public relations. The stipend varies with competitive job status and application qualifications.

Candidates must be U.S. citizens.

The George Washington University, Columbian School of Arts and Sciences, Museum Studies Internship Program

This internship program is a cooperative effort among the various universities and the Library of Congress. This internship is designed to give students a sense of the complexities of a library-based exhibit program, while allowing the intern to help develop and execute a scheduled Library of Congress exhibition. As an intern here, you'll be expected to offer a weekly report of your activities and assignments, participate in staff meetings, help with at least two exhibitions, research items to be included in the American Treasures of the Library of Congress exhibition (a changing, ongoing exhibition), and participate in programs such as Treasure Talks, docent training, and exhibition tours.

High School Work-Study Program

This program is open to high school seniors who are allowed to work at the library on a paid and volunteer basis. If you're interested, you must obtain a recommendation from someone at your school and be available to work during the school year on a part-time basis. Work-study employees are selected on a competitive basis.

You'll be given a one-year appointment at the GS-1 grade level. At the end of this temporary appointment, you may be extended or promoted (permanent or temporary).

Hispanic Association of Colleges and Universities Internship

Under this program, Hispanic and other undergraduate and graduate students participate in internships (15 weeks in the spring, 10 weeks in the summer, and 15 weeks in the fall) in various sections throughout the library, including human resources, the office of workforce diversity, and the copyright division. HACU interns aren't official library employees during the internship, but they may be given a temporary appointment and possibly a permanent position at the end of the internship.

Hispanic Division Junior Fellowship Program

This program offers on-the-job experience working on programs in the Hispanic Division, for a $1200 monthly stipend. Candidates should be recent college graduates with real work experience in a research environment, with degrees in the humanities, social sciences, or library science. If you are accepted, you will participate in this program for one summer.

Information Systems and Web Design Internship

This program is designed for current or former students with recent experience in any programming language to earn credit hours for field work.

Library of Congress Coca-Cola Fellowship for the Study of Advertising and World Cultures

Awards for a fellowship of six months to a year will be made to researchers studying the interrelationships among advertising, culture, commerce, and the media in the 20th century. Administered by the Library of Congress Motion Picture, Broadcasting, and Recorded Sound Division (M/B/RS) in collaboration with the Library of Congress Office of Scholarly Programs, the fellowship will provide recipients with access to resources for an extended period of in-depth research into the library's broadcast advertising and other audio-visual collections. The program carries a $20,000 stipend.

Preservation Directorate Book Conservation Internship

This internship is designed to offer an educational opportunity in book conservation and provides a stipend. As an intern here, you'll focus on conservation problems in a research-library context and be challenged to develop solutions for a broad range of book structures and historic styles. You'll have the chance to work in a variety of areas, including documentation, examination, treatment, housing, preventive conservation, and research. In addition to practical exercises and projects, you may expand your knowledge in fundamental areas of book conservation, such as book theory, book identification, deterioration mechanisms, storage environments, and emergency preparedness and recovery.

Interns are given the chance to participate in lab tours and public inquiries and are encouraged to participate in the Washington Conservation Guild by attending meetings and giving lectures. Interns will meet with curators and historians to discuss individual objects and their treatment. The Washington area is home to many museums and other institutions with conservation facilities available for visits.

The library may accept one or more advanced-level interns per year in the book-conservation specialization, typically for an internship of 11 to 12 months (generally following the academic year). Other options are possible, depending on time available, current library staffing and work load, and your interests and qualifications.

Candidates will be selected on the basis of conservation knowledge, skills, and abilities, an active commitment to professional ethics, effective communication skills, and an understanding of library and archival collections.

Preservation Directorate Multicultural Fellowship

This is an educational opportunity for students with experience in preservation seeking further training.

Preservation Directorate Paper Conservation Internship

The goal of this internship is to provide an educational opportunity for conservation graduate students seeking training in paper conservation. Interns focus on conservation problems in a research library context and are challenged to develop solutions for a broad range of formats and collections. Interns may have opportunities in variety of areas: documentation, examination, treatment, housing, preventive conservation, and research. In addition to practical exercises and projects, interns may develop and expand their knowledge in fundamental areas of works of art and manuscripts on paper, including identification of drawing and printing techniques and processes, connoisseurship issues, deterioration mechanisms, storage environments, and emergency preparedness and recovery.

The library may accept one or more advanced-level interns per year in the paper-conservation specialization for a year-long internship. Other options are possible, depending on time available, current library staffing and work load, and your interests and qualifications.

Preservation Directorate Photograph Conservation Internship

The goal of this internship is to provide an educational opportunity for conservation graduate students who want more training in photograph conservation. As an intern in this program, you'll focus on conservation problems in a research-library context, and you'll be challenged to develop solutions for a broad range of photographs and collections. You may have opportunities in a variety of areas, including documentation, examination, treatment, housing, preventive conservation, and research. In addition to practical exercises and projects, you may expand your knowledge in fundamental areas of photograph conservation such as photographic theory, process identification, deterioration mechanisms, storage environments, and emergency preparedness and recovery. A limited stipend may be available for this internship.

Preservation Directorate Preventive Conservation Internship

Interns will focus on institution-wide conservation problems in context and be challenged to develop practical and theoretical solutions for a broad range of formats and collections. Interns will learn how to assess collections, develop conservation strategies, apply preventive treatments, develop treatment work plans, monitor and manage work in conservation, and contribute generally to the conservation of library and archival collections through participation in education and training initiatives. In addition to practical exercises and projects, interns will develop their theoretical knowledge in key conservation areas, including the selection of materials for treatment, environmental monitoring and control, the application of microenvironments, disaster preparedness, response and recovery, program administration, and the development of strategies for the long-term preservation of collections.

The Washington Center Native American Leadership Program

Interns will be assigned to one of 12 policy-research divisions or support offices.

HOW TO APPLY
Ability Internship Program

You should submit a resume and a personal cover letter indicating the type of work and work schedule you're interested in performing to Eric Eldritch at (202) 707-0698, fax: 202-252-2045, e-mail: eeld@loc.gov.

The George Washington University, Columbian School of Arts and Sciences, Museum Studies Internship

To apply, contact L. Johnson at (202) 707-5223, fax (202) 707-9063, or e-mail: cajo@loc.gov. Applications are accepted at any time.

High School Work-Study Program

Application deadline is February 1. To apply, contact Leon Turner at (202) 707-2087, fax: 202-252-2045, or e-mail: letu@loc.gov.

Hispanic Association of Colleges and Universities

Go to http://www.hnip.net for an online application and more information; apply between mid-June and early November to David Christopher at (202) 707-8825 or e-mail: dchristopher@crs.loc.gov.

Hispanic Division Junior Fellowship Program

To apply, contact Georgette Dorn at (202) 707-2003, fax (202) 707-5400, or e-mail: gdor@loc.gov.

Library of Congress Coca-Cola Fellowship for the Study of Advertising and World Cultures

Application dates are unspecified. To apply, contact Coca-Cola Fellowship Selection Committee at (202) 707-3302 or e-mail: cokefellow@loc.gov. For application information, go to http://www.loc.gov/rr/mopic/cokefellowship.

Preservation Directorate Book Conservation Internship

To apply, complete and submit an application to the Preservation Directorate at the preceding address. Applications can be obtained at http://www.loc.gov/preserv/internapp.pdf. In addition to the application, you should provide a resume, two letters of recommendation, and a formal letter of interest. Those applicants most qualified for this fellowship will be scheduled for an interview with fellowship coordinators. Applications will be accepted after January 3 and until February 1 each year; announcement of selection will be made by April 15.

Preservation Directorate Paper Conservation Internship

You should complete the application form at http://www.loc.gov/preserv/internapp.pdf and submit it to the preceding address, along with a resume, two letters of recommendation, and a formal letter of interest. Those applicants most qualified for this fellowship will be scheduled for an interview with fellowship coordinators. Applications will be accepted after January 3 and until February 1 each year; announcement of selection will be made by April 15 for the internship, which begins in the summer.

Preservation Directorate Photograph Conservation Internship

You should complete the application form at http://www.loc.gov/preserv/internapp.pdf and submit it to the preceding address, along with a resume, two letters of recommendation, and a formal letter of interest. Those applicants most qualified for this fellowship will be scheduled for an interview with fellowship coordinators. Applications are due by February 1; announcement of selection will be made by April 15 for the internship, which begins in the summer.

MAINE STATE GOVERNOR'S INTERNSHIP

Office of the Governor
#1 State House Station
Augusta, ME 04333-0001
(207) 287-3531
Fax: (207) 287-1034
governor@maine.gov
http://www.maine.gov/governor/baldacci/
    contact/index.html

What You Can Earn: Unpaid but college credit is possible.
Application Deadlines: Rolling.
Educational Experience: High school or college student.
Requirements: None specified.

OVERVIEW

The Maine governor's office is looking for highly motivated Maine residents with an interest in politics to work as interns in the governor's office. Internships are a great way to gain valuable work experience, serve the state, and possibly earn college credit. A resume and short application must be submitted.

HOW TO APPLY

A resume and short application must be submitted to the preceding address.

MARYLAND GOVERNOR'S SUMMER INTERNSHIP

The Shriver Center at UMBC
Attn: GSIP Selection
1000 Hilltop Circle
Baltimore, MD 21250
(410) 455-2493
routzahn@umbc.edu

What You Can Earn: $2500 stipend.
Application Deadlines: March 18.
Educational Experience: Must be rising juniors or seniors attending a two-year or four-year college or university in Maryland or Maryland residents attending an out-of-state college or university. Students must have a GPA of 3.0 or higher; all majors are strongly encouraged to apply.
Requirements: None specified.

OVERVIEW

The Governor's Summer Internship Program was created to introduce college students to the unique challenges and rewards of working within Maryland State Government. For 10 weeks beginning in June, interns will work on substantive projects with senior-level public administrators and policy makers, in departments or policy areas that closely correspond with their fields of study or career interests. Duties often include attending meetings, drafting correspondence, tracking legislation, and researching policy options.

You'll also develop policy papers that address significant issues facing Maryland today. These papers, researched in teams, are presented to the governor and other senior staff members at the end of the program. You'll attend site visits and seminars designed to introduce interns to specific challenges of public administration and gain valuable exposure to the tremendous talents and resources of the Maryland State Government.

Placements may include the Office of the Governor, Office of the Lieutenant Governor, Office of the Secretary of State, Comptroller of Maryland, Governor's Office for Children, Youth and Families, Governor's Office of Crime Control and Prevention, and many more state agencies and departments.

HOW TO APPLY

The presidents of all colleges and universities in Maryland nominate three to five candidates to the governor's summer internship program. A selection committee will then review the application materials of all nominees, and 20 candidates will be invited to participate in the program.

If you're interested, you should contact the designated on-campus coordinator (for a list of coordinators, visit this Web site: http://shrivercenter.org/gsip/coordinators.html) or the president's office at your university to learn more about specific application deadlines.

You'll also need to fill out an application, which you download from this Web site: http://shrivercenter.org/documents/GSIP.application.05.doc.

If you are a Maryland resident but are attending an out-of-state institution, send a completed application with essays, a current resume, an official transcript, and two sealed letters of recommendation to the preceding address.

MICHIGAN EXECUTIVE OFFICE INTERNSHIP

Internship Program Coordinator
Office of the Governor
PO Box 30013
Lansing, Michigan, 48909

(517) 373-3400
Fax: (517) 241-2910

What You Can Earn: Unpaid, but college credit available.
Application Deadlines: August 31.
Educational Experience: College juniors or seniors majoring in economics, political science, public policy and public administration, sociology, social work, business, or one of the following majors with a demonstrated interest in the public-policy aspects of each field: agriculture and natural resources, criminal justice, labor and industrial relations, urban planning, education, public health, nursing or medicine, women's studies, African-American studies, Asian American studies, and similar programs.
Requirements: Excellent writing, communication, and proofreading skills; a desire to learn; the ability to ask questions; high degree of integrity and ethical conduct; punctuality and dependability; professional demeanor; strong individual initiative/work ethic; basic computer skills, as well as knowledge of or willingness to learn other computer skills (Word, Excel, PowerPoint); ability to work both independently and as a team member; interpersonal skills; and interest in public service.

OVERVIEW

The office of Governor Jennifer M. Granholm encourages students and recent graduates from all disciplines to apply for the Executive Office Internship Program. Participants will gain exposure to all divisions within the governor's executive office. Through meaningful, hands-on work experience, seminars featuring guest speakers, community-service projects, and other activities coordinated specifically for interns, the Executive Office Internship Program provides insight into the workings of state government, as well as a window through which to view potential careers.

The 10- to 12-week program will begin during the second week of September and conclude in December. Participants will be able to work a part- or full-time schedule and may be eligible to earn school credit for their participation (depending upon their educational institution). Positions are primarily based in Lansing; however, limited placements are also available within satellite offices in Northern Michigan (Marquette), Southeast Michigan (Detroit), and Washington, D.C. There are a number of divisions in which interns can work, as follows:

Appointments Division

This division recommends people to the governor for appointment to state boards, commissions, judicial vacancies, and boards of certain public universities.

Office of the Chief Operating Officer

This division oversees the day-to-day operations of the office of the governor. It also directs and coordinates state departments, supervises community and statewide liaison efforts, and oversees legislative, public policy, constituent services, and communication responsibilities of the office of the governor.

Communications Division

This division works with the media to inform the public of the governor's goals, actions, and ideas. Information is provided through the preparation and coordination of news releases, news conferences, and audio and video presentations. This division also prepares a large volume of speeches and issues papers for the governor.

Constituent Services Division

This division reviews constituent correspondence, drafts replies, coordinates agency support, and issues gubernatorial tributes, proclamations, and letters recognizing special events and noteworthy achievements. It is also responsible for responding to constituent visits and phone calls to the governor's office.

Governor's Residence

The governor's residence staff provides logistical planning and coordination of events ranging from large-scale public occasions to small dinner parties. In addition, this staff ensures the upkeep and presentation of the residence grounds and the preparation and presentation of cuisine.

Intern candidates interested in a position within the governor's residence should have a background in hospitality\business, horticulture, or culinary arts. Depending on candidates' backgrounds, interested applicants should expect to work closely with the hospitality coordinator, the residence manager, the head chef, or the resident horticulturist.

Office of the First Gentleman/First Lady

Staff within this office is responsible for reviewing and responding to all requests for event attendance and speaking engagements, managing the first gentleman's/first lady's calendar and constituent correspondence, coordinating all communication to state employees, and heading up the Mentor Michigan initiative and first man's/lady's Forums.

Legal Counsel

This division provides legal counsel to the governor. It also reviews legislation; drafts and negotiates compacts; reviews charters, inter-local agreements, resolutions created by local units of government, extraditions, pardons, commutations, certificates of good conduct for prisoners within Michigan's penal system, and administrative and emergency rules submitted by each state department; confers with the attorney general on significant litigation; and supervises the judicial selection and appointment process. In addition, the division drafts executive orders, directives, and proclamations.

Office of the Lieutenant Governor

The lieutenant governor constitutionally serves as governor in the absence of the governor and serves as president of the state senate. Also, the lieutenant governor is a voting member of the state administrative board and serves as chair in the absence of the governor. Some additional responsibilities are to serve as the point person for Bay, Genesee, and Saginaw counties and to take a leadership role in conservation issues.

Operations Division

This division provides the day-to-day business needs of the office of the governor. This involves the coordination of facilities, personnel, budget, and information technology.

Public Policy Division

The policy division assists state officials in the development and implementation of executive initiatives and provides policy advice to the governor. If you're interested in placement with public policy, the writing sample submitted must be a paper written for an academic class on any public-policy topic. Writing samples for public policy can be longer than five pages if necessary.

Scheduling Division

This division is responsible for developing the governor's long-term and day-to-day calendar and coordinating participants of scheduled events, including the governor's security detail.

Satellite Offices

Positions are primarily based in Lansing; however, limited placements are also available within satellite offices in Northern Michigan (Marquette), Southeast Michigan (Detroit), and Washington, D.C.

The Northern Michigan office is located in the city of Marquette and serves as the governor's liaison to the residents of Northern Michigan on issues including rural public policy, special projects, and coordination with public officials.

The Southeast Michigan office is located in Detroit and serves as the governor's liaison for the counties of Wayne, Oakland, Macomb, Monroe, and Washtenaw.

The Washington, D.C., office serves as the governor's liaison to the nation's capitol, seeking to maximize Michigan's influence on legislation and the regulatory and policy process at the federal level. It is also responsible for advising the governor on issues of national importance.

HOW TO APPLY

To apply, interested candidates must complete the application form at http://www.michigan.gov/documents/Internship_Application__Summer_2004__79252_7.pdf.

You must submit a copy of your resume and a three-to-five-page writing sample along with your completed application to the preceding address.

Applications for the Executive Office Internship Program are reviewed on a rolling basis; as soon as an application is complete, it is reviewed. This means that candidate-selection decisions are made quickly. It also means that the program may fill prior to the published application deadline of August 31. Consequently, you should apply as early as possible.

You'll be notified as to the status of your application (whether you will be invited to interview or not) after your submission has been processed. After completion of candidate interviews, invitations to join the Executive Office Internship Program will be extended.

To apply for placement in the Southeast Michigan or Northern Michigan offices, complete the application and specify your satellite office of interest in the division placement preference section. To apply for placement in Washington, D.C., please submit a cover letter and resume to the contact listed on http://www.michigan.gov/mldp. You can visit http://www.michigan.gov/mldp for additional information on placements in any of these locations.

NEW JERSEY GOVERNOR'S INTERNSHIP

Governor's Office of Administration and Personnel
PO Box 001
Trenton, NJ 08625
Fax: (609) 292-5212
Carolyn.Ross@gov.state.nj.us
http://www.state.nj.us/governor/intern.html

What You Can Earn: Unpaid but college credit is possible.
Application Deadlines: Rolling.
Educational Experience: Any college student.

Requirements: Minimum of 12 hours per week; New Jersey residents only.

OVERVIEW

This year-round internship program places students in many different offices throughout state government and is designed for college students interested in careers in state government. These internships provide an excellent opportunity to gain valuable work experience.

Possible agencies include agriculture; health and senior services; banking and insurance; human services; board of public utilities; labor, commerce, and economic development; law and public safety; community affairs; military and veterans affairs; corrections; personnel; education; environmental protection; transportation; governor's office; and the treasury.

HOW TO APPLY

To apply, fax or mail an application, your resume, a writing sample, and a cover letter stating how many and what days you will be able to work, as well as how many hours a week, to the preceding address. Do not submit an application by e-mail. Students are encouraged to earn credits, but doing so is not required.

It will take between four and six weeks to complete the placement process. You'll receive an acknowledgment e-mail once your application is received. Students are placed on a first-come, first-serve basis. If you're selected for the program, you'll be contacted for an interview.

NEW YORK CITY SUMMER INTERNSHIP

New York City Department of Citywide Administrative Services
One Centre Street, 17th Floor South
New York, NY 10007

(212) 669-7000
http://www.nyc.gov/html/dcas/html/employment/summerintern.shtml#acs

What You Can Earn: Some internship positions are unpaid, and some offer academic credit for work experience; others may provide a travel stipend. Refer to the specific internship descriptions for details.
Application Deadlines: See individual descriptions.
Educational Experience: Graduate students must be currently enrolled or accepted into a graduate program, and undergraduate students must be enrolled in college or university.
Requirements: See individual descriptions.

OVERVIEW

City government internships allow students to make important contributions to the city while participating in a challenging and rewarding work experience.

To complement the work experience, all summer graduate and undergraduate interns participate in a special seminar series that features top city officials presenting overviews of municipal government, specific agencies, and the latest issues confronting the city. There are no uniform start or end dates for internship assignments. Internships are available between May and September for a maximum of 13 weeks. Individual agencies determine the actual length and start/end dates for their internship assignments.

Participating agencies include the administration for children's services; office of administrative trials and hearings; department of citywide administrative services; economic development corporation; department of environmental protection; New York City fire department; New York City housing authority; department of investigation; office of the mayor; department of parks and recreation; department of probation; Queens Borough Public Library; department of small business services; taxi and limousine commission; department of transportation;

and the department of youth and community development.

Administration for Children's Services

This agency is responsible for the protection of New York City's children. ACS investigates reports of abuse and neglect provides, foster care and adoption services to families, and provides head start and daycare services.

Intern opportunities are available in a variety of divisions with the ACS, including: childcare at head start; curriculum department; assessment and evaluation; professional development; community education; office management; training; video unit; deputy commissioner's office; office for family and children health; collaboration and client services; office of advocacy; office of placement; child evaluation/family assessment; division of child protection; childcare program; and financial services.

Department of Citywide Administrative Services

This department's primary responsibility is to ensure that other city agencies have the resources and support they need to provide the best services to the public. To assist city agencies, DCAS handles the civil service administration for all New York City employees; makes all citywide purchases over the amount of $25,000; and administers the City's portfolio of 53 public buildings, including City Hall, the Manhattan and Brooklyn Municipal Buildings, and all borough halls and city and state courts. DCAS also purchases, sells, and leases property and locates space for city agencies.

A wide variety of internships are available in this agency, including lease compliance unit; audit unit; certification unit; unemployment insurance unit; investigation unit; acquisitions and construction; lease administration; auction sales unit; purchasing unit; appraisal unit; central storehouse; office of surplus activities; food procurement; contract compliance; vendor performance; management services; IT procurement; and the office of contracts.

Economic Development Corporation

New York City Economic Development Corporation (NYCEDC) is the city's primary vehicle for promoting economic growth in each of the five boroughs. Its mission is to stimulate job growth through expansion and redevelopment programs that encourage investment and strengthen the city's competitive position. NYCEDC builds relationships with companies that allow them to take advantage of New York City's many opportunities.

Internships are available in budget office, internal audit unit, and the workouts and compliance unit.

Department of Environmental Protection

This department manages and preserves the city's water supply, cleans its waterways, and manages the environment by protecting major investments in the water and sewer infrastructure. To maintain the integrity of these systems, DEP has also undertaken an ambitious program of reconstruction and replacement.

Interns may be responsible for many projects, which may include helping to prepare public service announcements used by radio and television stations; developing computer programs to analyze fire and arson trends; performing legal research and drafting legal programs to analyze fire and arson trends; performing legal research and drafting legal reports; compiling statistical and financial data related to revenue collection and projection; and conducting statistical analyses to determine the factors that influence various trends.

Department of Investigation

The New York City Department of Investigation's (DOI) primary mission is to promote the integrity, effectiveness, and efficiency of city government by investigating allegations of corruption and criminal misconduct by city employees and those doing business with the city.

Assignments may vary. Investigative, legal, and auditing interns are assigned throughout the city. Interns help collect data and analyze white-collar criminal cases, as well as study mismanagement and waste in New York City government. They help interview witnesses regarding organizational records and procedures, review subpoenaed and seized documents for evidence and leads; prepare transcripts of undercover tape recording; participate with attorneys, investigators, and investigative auditors in creating and executing investigative strategies; organize evidence and material in case files; and prepare written factual presentations of gathered evidence. DOI hires both graduate and undergraduate investigative interns during the summer, fall, and spring semesters. Students with any major may apply for investigative internships. DOI also accepts first-year, second-year, and third-year law students. Auditing interns must be accounting majors. Because of the sensitive nature of the agency's work, all interns must pass a fingerprint screening (at the agency's expense) before they can begin working at the DOI.

Department of Parks and Recreation

This department hires more than 3,000 employees (8,000 at the summer peak) to keep the parks, playgrounds, and sitting areas clean and safe. It also offers quality facilities, programs, and events to meet the needs of all New Yorkers.

Interns may work at the Greenbelt summer camp; ecological research; forest restoration; natural resources; mapping; field internships; Manhattan events and permits; office of video production; monuments field crew; Forever Wild; plant ecology; street tree inventory; tree census; Americorps program intern; central recreation; photo archive; map file; historic houses trust; operations; partnerships for the parks; the Dyckman Farmhouse; or the office of public information.

Department of Probation

This department promotes public safety in New York City by providing community-oriented justice sanctions. It fulfills its responsibilities by supplying criminal and family courts with information and recommendations, supervising offenders through the monitoring and enforcing of their counseling and access to rehabilitative services, and giving victims and their communities a voice in the justice process. Interns may work in either the adult operations bureau or the general counsel's office.

Department of Small Business Services

This department makes it easier for companies in New York City to form, operate, and grow. It provides direct assistance to business owners, fostering neighborhood development in commercial districts, promoting financial and economic opportunity among minority- and women-owned businesses, preparing New Yorkers for jobs, and linking employers with a skilled and qualified workforce.

Interns in this department work in a variety of areas, including the commercial revitalization program, the division of economic and financial opportunity, or the office of communications and media relations.

Department of Transportation

The department's mission is to provide for the safe, efficient, and environmentally responsible movement of people and goods in New York City and to maintain the transportation infrastructure. The department regulates traffic, builds and maintains roadways, sidewalks, bridges, and municipal parking facilities, maintains and operates municipal ferry systems, and monitors private ferry systems. It also serves as an advocate for better transportation.

Interns may work in traffic operations, division of bridges, or a variety of other positions to help fulfill this mission.

Department of Youth and Community Development

This department awards contracts to a broad network of community-based organizations throughout New York City that support a variety of youth services and activities, including leadership development, runaway and homeless programs, structured recreation and athletics, tutoring and remedial education, cultural enrichment, and delinquency prevention. In fostering the development of communities, DYCD also administers contracts to support programs and services that address their unique needs, including lessening the impact of poverty, helping families and neighborhoods become more self-sufficient, and providing services to youth, senior citizens, families, and recent immigrants.

Interns work in the Planning, Research, and Program Development Division, helping the assistant commissioner develop requests for proposals for services for runaway and homeless youth and develop adolescent-literacy and adult-literacy initiatives. Interns may help gather and present data, draft research memoranda, interview existing service providers or experts, participate in community forums, and prepare for NYC council hearings.

Candidates should be graduate students pursuing a degree in liberal arts, public affairs, or government, with strong writing and analytical skills and good consensus-building skills. The intern should be detail oriented yet flexible; familiarity with program budgets and spreadsheet software is desirable. Stipend is up to $500 a week, not to exceed 12 weeks.

Fire Department

The mission of the fire department is to protect the lives and property of the city from fire and to promote fire prevention and fire-safety education, as well as to provide emergency medical services to those in need.

Interns may be responsible for many projects, including helping to prepare public service announcements used by radio and television stations; developing computer programs to analyze fire and arson trends; performing legal research and drafting legal programs to analyze fire and arson trends; performing legal research and drafting legal reports; and compiling statistical and financial data.

Candidates should have completed at least one year of law school or be majoring in quantitative or financial analysis, business management, economics, computer science, or journalism. A working knowledge of PC applications is required.

New York City Housing Authority

The New York City Housing Authority provides decent and affordable housing in a safe and secure living environment for low-income and moderate-income residents throughout the five boroughs. The largest public-housing authority in North America, its Conventional Public Housing Program has more than 181,000 apartments in 345 developments throughout the city in 2,698 residential buildings. Its 15,000 employees serve about 175,159 families.

Interns in this agency may help plan, solve problems, and do research and general administration, as well as help analyze agency programs and develop alternative proposals.

Candidates should have an undergraduate degree and be enrolled in a graduate program. Some positions require a major or minor in business, project management, or program review and assessment and a general understanding of technology (but not necessarily a technical background). Some positions require excellent analytical and writing skills, experience in systems analysis, project management, or programming, and knowledge of Microsoft Office, Word, Excel, Access, PowerPoint, and other computer applications. Summer graduate interns earn between $400 and $500 per week.

Office of Administrative Trials and Hearings

This is New York City's central administrative tribunal. OATH conducts adversarial trials and related proceedings in a wide variety of matters, including employee disciplinary and medical disability actions, license revocation and other regulatory proceedings, zoning matters, conflicts of interest cases, contract disputes, and other cases. OATH functions as a central tribunal with the authority to conduct administrative hearings for any agency, board, or commission of the city. OATH was established in 1979 to professionalize the administrative hearing system serving city government, acting as an independent agency of government so that its judges would not be unduly influenced by prosecutors or petitioning agencies.

The law intern, under the supervision of the senior law clerk, will perform legal research, write legal research memoranda, and assist the administrative law judges as needed on case-related matters. Candidates should be currently enrolled in an accredited law school and have completed at least one year of study at an accredited law school. Strong legal research and writing skills is required. Stipend is $500 a week.

Office of the Mayor

This office is the city agency that houses the mayor, the deputy mayors, the advisors and assistants to the mayor, and their support staffs. Their function is mainly to develop and implement the mayor's policies.

Under guidance and supervision, interns in the mayor's office will work in a very broad range of professional work assignments. Strong consideration will be given to the student's field of education, areas of interest, and work experience as to where they would be assigned. If a candidate's background makes him or her a better candidate for another city agency, the resume will be forwarded to that agency for consideration. Qualifications vary according to unit assignment and specific tasks.

Interns may work in any of the varied outreach offices, such as the community assistance unit and the mayor's office of special projects and community events. Some units are more involved with service provision, such as the office to combat domestic violence office of immigrant affairs, office for people with disabilities, New York City loft board, office of veterans' affairs, mayor's volunteer center and the New York City commission for the united nations, and the consular corps and protocol. Interns also may be assigned to work in units that provide support services, such as administrative operations, fiscal operations, management information systems, payroll/timekeeping, and personnel division.

Queens Borough Public Library

The library serves 2 million people from 63 library locations plus six Adult Learning Centers. It circulates more books and other library materials than any other library system in the country. Established in 1995, the Queens Library Gallery is an adjunct to the Queens Borough Public Library in Jamaica, Queens. The gallery hosts four museum-quality exhibits per year, including a children's exhibit every summer.

Gallery interns would help with planning and giving tours of the exhibit to school-age children, teaching related news themes and craft activities to children, maintaining exhibits, and performing various administrative duties.

The ideal candidate is an undergraduate student studying education, museum studies, or fine art and who enjoys working with children and young adults. Candidates must be responsible, punctual, creative, flexible, and able to work as part of a team. Teaching experience is a plus.

Taxi and Limousine Commission

This commission (TLC) is the city agency responsible for oversight of the for-hire vehicle industries in New York City, including yellow medallion taxis, community car services and livery cars, black cars services, luxury limousines, commuter vans, and paratransit services. Combined, TLC regulates industries responsible for more than 500,000 daily trips, serving more than a million passengers. Its role is to ensure that each passenger's riding experience is safe, comfortable, and convenient.

Interns here work in a variety of areas, including legal affairs, licensing division, human resources, public affairs, or management information systems.

HOW TO APPLY

Visit http://www.nyc.gov/html/dcas/html/employment/summerintern.shtml#acs for details on applying for specific internships, which are administered by staffers at individual agencies. There is no centralized internship application processing center.

Each agency requires that applicants forward a cover letter and resume to the agency contact person. The agency contact person or assigned staff member will respond to questions about agency internship programs.

NORTH CAROLINA GOVERNOR'S INTERNSHIP

North Carolina Governor's Internship
217 West Jones Street, 2nd Floor
Raleigh, NC 27699
(919)733-9296
Fax: (919)733-1461
http://www.doa.state.nc.us/yaio/intern.htm

What You Can Earn: $8.25 an hour.
Application Deadlines: January 20.
Educational Experience: Must be North Carolina resident attending a university, college, law school, community college, or technical institute in or out of North Carolina; must be enrolled for the semester after the internship, have completed the first year of college, and have a cumulative GPA of at least 2.5.
Requirements: Applicants who have previously served a paid internship with the Youth Advocacy and Involvement Office or with the Legislative Program are not eligible.

OVERVIEW

Since 1969, more than 3,300 college and law students have worked with the state government internship program. it may be the oldest and largest paid internship program of any state government in the United States!

An internship with the North Carolina state government internship program will let you assert initiative and creativity through hands-on involvement and problem solving as you gain essential work experience, improve your resume, and use what you've learned at school. Some of the program's internships have included introducing visitors to reptiles at the Museum of Natural Sciences, working in the governor's office, tracking the nesting patterns of loggerhead turtles on Bear Island, and clerking at the N.C. Court of Appeals.

Internships are offered in virtually all areas of state government through the North Carolina youth advocacy and involvement office; 75 paid internships are available for 10 weeks each summer for undergraduates, graduate students, and those in professional schools. Unpaid internships during the academic year can be arranged periodically, and part-time paid spring internships are sometimes offered.

The makeup of the North Carolina internship council, which oversees the program, is also unique. The council includes former interns, a legislator, a judge (who is a former intern), several college professors, and college-placement professionals. The internship council chooses the projects and interns, thus keeping the program fair.

Many interns have accepted full-time state jobs at their internship sites after graduation; even some state legislators were interns in this program!

HOW TO APPLY

All application materials (application form, cover letter, academic transcript, and resume) should be mailed in one envelope to the YAIO office at the preceding address. It must be postmarked by the deadline and all materials must be typed or computer printed.

You'll need to download and complete the application form in Microsoft Word or RTF format at http://www.doa.state.nc.us/forms/intern. doc. Remember to provide an e-mail address on the application form, as all applicants will be notified of their status by e-mail.

If you're applying for several different projects, you don't need several different cover letters. The supervisors understand that you may be applying to several different projects, so your cover letter may be general; however, you should provide a bulleted list of the projects to which you are applying in the body of your letter.

State government agencies submit project proposals by mid-August, and the approved projects and program information are placed online by mid-October. Applications can be submitted as soon as project descriptions and application information are posted. The firm deadline for applications to be postmarked is mid-January.

Applications are screened and approved or rejected by mid-February; supervisors conduct interviews by the end of February. Applicants are informed of placement in the first week or two of March, and internships begin after Memorial Day.

OKLAHOMA GOVERNOR'S INTERNSHIP

Office of the Governor
State Capitol Building
2300 N. Lincoln Blvd., Suite 212
Oklahoma City, OK 73105
Fax: (405) 521-3353
Nelda.Kirk@gov.state.ok.us
http://www.governor.state.ok.us/internships.php

What You Can Earn: Unpaid but academic credit is available
Application Deadlines: Rolling.
Educational Experience: Juniors, seniors, or graduate students.
Requirements: Good communication skills and the ability to work independently.

OVERVIEW

The Office of Governor Brad Henry offers an internship program in which interns get the chance to become acquainted with the political process and work in a state agency while serving the people of Oklahoma.

If you're chosen, you'll help various staff members in a variety of tasks and projects, responding to inquiries and requests from constituents, opening and sorting mail, answering phones, greeting visitors to the office, copying documents, and working on various special projects.

HOW TO APPLY

Send a copy of your resume, references, and times of availability to the preceding address.

OREGON GOVERNOR'S INTERNSHIP

Internship Program
Attn: Office Administrator
Office of the Governor
900 Court Street NE
Salem, OR 97301-4047
http://governor.oregon.gov/Gov/internships.shtml

What You Can Earn: Unpaid but academic credit is available.
Application Deadlines: Rolling.
Educational Experience: College or community college students; however, exemplary high school students also may be considered.
Requirements: Strongly prefer interns to commit to an internship of at least one academic quarter or 10 weeks.

OVERVIEW

The governor's internship program is designed to provide young people with the opportunity to gain experience and knowledge in state government. We are seeking highly motivated individuals interested in a hands-on learning experience. Interns will serve as staff members alongside professionals who are experts in the fields of public policy, communications, legislation, and/or scheduling and constituent services. The following are two typical types of internships available:

Media Clips Internship

As a media clip intern, you'll track, collect, and file newspaper clips of interest to the governor's office. This means you'll review daily newspapers in print and online for stories related to the governor's office, clip or print appropriate newspaper articles, set up and managing the media clips filing system for the communications office, and retrieve, copy, and distribute clips from the filing system upon request from the governor's senior staff.

The schedule and number of hours worked per week will be arranged between you and your intern sponsor prior to the beginning of the work period.

Office of Education, Workforce, and Revenue Policy

This office works with state, local, and federal governmental agencies as well as with the private and nonprofit sector to address issues involving education, workforce development, and revenue. As an intern in this office, you'll do research on education, workforce, and revenue issues, help track policy and legislative issues, and help the office respond to citizen and government questions. In addition to the general application materials, you should include a description of how your education and experience would be helpful to the office, and add two references and a recent writing sample of two to four pages.

HOW TO APPLY

To apply for an internship with the governor's office, send a resume and cover letter to the preceding address. The cover letter should include your preferred contact information (phone and e-mail address); any computer experience you have; any honors, achievements, or special qualifications for the position; your areas of interest and your career goals; why you want to intern for the governor's office; and the time period and hours you are available to work. If there is a need for your services, you may expect to be contacted by a staff member within several weeks. If you are interested in other opportunities that may become available, you can download an interest form at http://governor. oregon.gov/Gov/pdf/internship/Internship_interest_form.pdf. Submit it to the preceding address.

REPUBLICAN NATIONAL COMMITTEE INTERNSHIP

Republican National Internship Programs
310 First Street, SE
Washington, DC 20003
(202) 863-8500
http://www.rnc.org

What You Can Earn: Unpaid but academic credit is available.
Application Deadlines: Rolling.
Educational Experience: College students majoring in business, communications, history, political science, or government.
Requirements: Loyal Republicans available for the duration of the internship, able to commit to a 30 hour/week schedule; strong computer and communications skills; an interest in learning about our nation's current political environment.

OVERVIEW

The Republican National Committee is the official Republican organization, whose objective is to expand and maintain the Republican Party. The organization provides fund-raising, research, and press-related resources and offers candidates political strategy and advice.

Interns can learn about campaign organization and management through hands-on experience. Internships are excellent opportunities to develop fund-raising, communication, and political skills; make valuable political contacts; and become familiar with the political landscape. Interns conduct research, analyze reports, and assemble data. In addition, they assist in drafting press releases and media advisories.

HOW TO APPLY

For information on internships at the Republican Party's National Headquarters, call and ask for the internship office or send a letter expressing interest to the preceding address.

SOUTH CAROLINA GOVERNOR'S INTERNSHIP

Office of the Governor
PO Box 12267
Columbia, SC 29211
(803) 734-2100
Fax: (803) 734-5167

What You Can Earn: Unpaid but credit is available.
Application Deadlines: Rolling.
Educational Experience: Unspecified.
Requirements: A minimum commitment of 10 to 20 hours a week.

OVERVIEW

Interns will have the opportunity to experience many areas of state government through working directly with senior-level staff members, visiting various agencies, and observing the preparations for the next legislative session.

Daily intern duties include assisting the press office and correspondence office, as well as addressing a variety of constituent needs. Interns are often exposed to high-level meetings and officials in an environment where questions and input are highly encouraged.

Office schedules are created around class schedules and can be flexible throughout the semester.

HOW TO APPLY

Call Morgan Harrell at (803) 734-2100 for an application or to receive further information.

U.S. SUPREME COURT INTERNSHIP

Supreme Court Fellow
Office of the Administrative Assistant to the Chief Justice
Supreme Court of the United States
Room 5
1 First Street, NE
Washington, DC 20543
(202) 479-3415

What You Can Earn: Unpaid, but $1,000 scholarships may be available if the student successfully completes the internship and within one year returns to an undergraduate program or enrolls in a graduate or professional degree program. Interns may receive academic credit through special arrangement with their college or university and consultation with the Supreme Court Fellow.
Application Deadlines: June 10 for fall (September through December); October 20 for spring (January through May); March 10 for summer (June through August).
Educational Experience: Rising college juniors or seniors and graduating seniors who have interests in law, management, and social sciences. High intellectual development, including an ability to think clearly, speak articulately, and write cogently; substantial research experience; some course work on constitutional law or the Supreme Court; a demonstrated capacity to absorb extensive information and to analyze, summarize, and derive conclusions from it.
Requirements: Experience with office and library resources, the ability to work under time constraints, strict attention to detail, creative thinking, and editorial skills. Ability and willingness to work closely with others in a complex and sensitive organization. Capacity to undertake a variety of tasks as assigned and a willingness to handle less glamorous tasks; an ability to function with a low profile in a hierarchical institution, unusual

trustworthiness and discretion, maturity, and a nondoctrinaire approach to projects and issues. Good judgment is critical. Self-sustaining motivation and initiative. Consultation with staff on specific questions and ideas is expected, but interns should carry research as far as possible and present their findings in succinctly written memoranda. If accepted, you must complete fingerprinting and a background check before starting work. Since interns often have access to sensitive information, anything you write about your experience must be reviewed by the Court's Public Information Officer; no papers or copies may be taken from the office except by express written permission.

OVERVIEW

The judicial internship program at the Supreme Court offers a unique opportunity to gain exposure to the field of judicial administration by working in the Office of the Administrative Assistant to the Chief Justice. The program's location within the country's highest court, combined with the intimacy of having only two judicial interns each term, creates an environment of substantial responsibility, learning, and collegiality. Interns work eight-hour days, five days a week, so don't plan to work at any other job during this time.

Judicial interns perform several routine but important office tasks, which include summarizing news articles and preparing memoranda and correspondence. Interns also conduct background research for speeches and briefings provided to visiting foreign dignitaries. Additionally, interns may participate in the diverse research projects conducted by the Supreme Court fellow and the administrative assistant. These projects require interns to gather, assemble, and synthesize information from a wide range of sources.

However, keep in mind that office research is completely unrelated to the case work of the Supreme Court. You won't do any work on cases pending before the Court or with the justices. However, circumstances permitting and with approval, you may also take advantage of the Court's extensive resources to work on your own academic or other research projects.

Participants usually find the internship both interesting and educational. Since the judicial branch operates on a fraction of the scale of the executive and legislative branches, you'll quickly become familiar with the way the Court functions. The program also enables you to become familiar with the various internal offices that support the Court.

Recent interns have received tours of the marshal's office, the clerk's office, data systems, and the library. When time permits, you may observe Court sessions and take advantage of outside lectures and conferences. The office also sometimes holds educational luncheon meetings with individuals from government, academia, and private institutions. In recent years, interns have attended luncheons with associate justices, the counsel to the president, and the solicitor general.

Interns selected for the fall and spring should plan to work for 16 weeks. Summer interns are expected to work for 12 weeks.

HOW TO APPLY

Application materials may be submitted in hard copy to the address above, or online at http://www.supremecourtus.gov. All incoming mail must go through a security screening process that can delay receipt of application materials by several days or even weeks. Therefore, to ensure that all applications are processed, intern candidates are urged to send application materials via a commercial delivery service such as Fed-Ex, UPS, DHL, etc.

To apply to the Judicial Internship Program, you must submit the following application materials:

- a resume
- an official transcript, sealed and sent directly by the institution
- three letters of recommendation from a variety of references, sealed and sent directly by the recommender to the Supreme Court Fellow
- a written statement (double-spaced and labeled "candidate's statement") presenting your reasons for seeking this internship

and demonstrating that your experiences (scholastic and non-scholastic), skills, and personality meet the program's criteria

- a writing sample (such as a short term paper) no longer than 10 double-spaced pages labeled "Writing Sample")
- an essay of not less than two double-spaced pages giving your view of the importance of the American constitutional system from a personal, historical, national, or international perspective (labeled "Constitutional Essay")

You should apply well before the internship begins. Because candidates are not notified automatically about the completeness of the application, you are responsible for figuring out if all portions of the application have been received.

To help schedule internships, you should list preferred alternative times when you'll be available to participate in the program. Telephone interviews may be conducted after your complete application is received.

VERMONT GOVERNOR'S INTERNSHIP

Office of the Governor
109 State Street
Montpelier, VT 05609-0101
802-828-3333;toll-free in Vermont: 1-800-649-6825
Fax: (802) 828-3339

What You Can Earn: Unpaid.
Application Deadlines: Fall term, September-November, application due by August 1; spring term, January-April, application due by December 1; summer term, May-August, application due by April 1.
Educational Experience: Must have completed two full years of college. Candidates majoring in English, political science, business management, public administration, government, or a related field are preferred.

Requirements: Excellent writing skills, research experience, good communication skills, punctuality, reliability, and professionalism. A minimum commitment of 15 hours per week and a maximum of 30 hours per week.

OVERVIEW

The executive office offers a number of internship opportunities to college students interested in governmental affairs. Internships are part-time positions offered during fall, spring, and summer terms.

Each intern should expect to complete the following tasks: constituent services, including drafting correspondence and answering phones; researching legislative issues; and offering general support to the senior staff (to include special projects, research, and general office duties).

HOW TO APPLY

Download the application at http://www.vermont.gov/governor/priorities/Intern-Application.doc.

Fax or mail the completed application, your resume, a writing sample, and a letter of recommendation to the preceding address.

WASHINGTON INTERNSHIPS FOR NATIVE STUDENTS (WINS)

WINS
4400 Massachusetts Avenue, NW
Washington, DC 20016-8083
(202) 895-4900
wins@american.edu
http://www.american.edu/wins/wins_participation.html

What You Can Earn: Weekly stipend plus all expenses paid. The program pays for your travel to Washington, D.C., plus all books, tuition, housing, meals, metro fare, insurance, scheduled social and cultural activities, and a weekly stipend. Funding is provided by governmental agencies, Native organizations, tribes, foundations, American University, and corporations. Incidental expenses for nonprogram activities, including medical care and independent social activities, are the responsibility of the student.

Application Deadlines: Fall semester: first Friday of June; spring semester: first Friday of October.

Educational Experience: Sophomores, juniors, seniors, and grad students in good academic standing at their university are eligible to apply.

Requirements: This internship is open to Native Americans and Alaskan Natives currently enrolled in college.

OVERVIEW

This internship enables Native American students an opportunity to intern with government agencies and take two courses at American University during the spring or fall as a guest of the federal government. If you're selected, you'll live on the American University campus while earning 12 hours of college credit you can transfer to your home school. All expenses are paid for by a government grant and American University.

There are a variety of Washington, D.C., organizations you can choose; recent WINS participants have interned with the departments of agriculture, labor, energy, the treasury, and veterans affairs; the Bureau of Indian Affairs; the National Institutes of Health; the Social Security Administration; the Federal Aviation Administration; and the Federal Communications Commission.

Here's how it works: You select two courses from the multiple course offerings at American University, selecting classes to match your interests and home school requirements. You'll also intern at an agency for 36 hours a week and prepare a prescribed portfolio on your work experience and research.

You'll live in a university dorm on the Tenley campus of American University, just two blocks from the Tenleytown/AU Metro station in north-

west Washington, D.C. All of your meals will be prepared at the Tenley Café, located on the campus.

Members of the WINS Native Advisory Council provide advice and counsel to make sure that the traditional values and practices of the nations and tribes throughout Indian country are maintained.

The WINS program also offers a special summer program and a special internship with the FBI.

HOW TO APPLY

If you're interested, you must submit a completed WINS application form; an essay of at least 500 words about why you would like to participate; a nomination letter from a member of your nation or tribal council or from an official of the applicant's nation or tribal education department; a recommendation letter from a faculty member at your university; a resume detailing your work experience; and an official copy of your most recent transcript.

You may obtain a copy of the application online at (https://my.american.edu/cgi/mvi.exe/A26.APPL.LOGIN?SCH=WINS) or call the WINS headquarters at the preceding number to ask that an application be mailed to you. You also may request an application via e-mail (see preceding address).

WASHINGTON LEADERSHIP SUMMER INTERNSHIP SEMINAR FOR NATIVE AMERICAN STUDENTS

WINS Leadership
4400 Massachusetts Avenue, NW
Washington, DC 20016-8083
(202) 895-4900
wins@american.edu
http://www.american.edu/wins/wins_
    participation.html

What You Can Earn: Weekly stipend plus all expenses paid. The program pays for your travel to Washington, D.C., plus all books, tuition, housing, meals, metro fare, insurance, scheduled social and cultural activities, and a weekly stipend. Funding is provided by governmental agencies, Native organizations, tribes, foundations, American University, and corporations. Incidental expenses for nonprogram activities, including medical care and independent social activities, are the responsibility of the student.

Application Deadlines: First Friday of February preceding the summer session.

Educational Experience: Sophomores, juniors, seniors, and grad students in good academic standing at their university are eligible to apply.

Requirements: This internship is open to Native Americans and Alaskan Natives currently enrolled in college.

OVERVIEW

If you're a Native American and you've dreamed of working and studying in Washington, D.C., over the summer, this internship is for you! The six-credit summer Washington Leadership Seminar for interns is designed specifically for Native students. It's part of the Washington Internship for Native Students (WINS) and offers three credits for the internship and three credits for the academic course. The academic course covers topics important to Native communities such as tribal sovereignty; trust responsibilities; health and social welfare issues; and gaming and economic development concerns. Special arrangements are made with a wide range of federal agencies, congressional offices, and Native organizations to provide a focused internship experience for WINS participants.

If you're selected, you'll live on the American University campus; all expenses are paid by a government grant and American University.

There are a variety of Washington, D.C., organizations you can choose; recent WINS participants have interned with the departments of agriculture, labor, energy, the treasury, and veterans affairs; the Bureau of Indian Affairs; the National Institutes of Health; the Social Security Administration; the Federal Aviation Administration; and the Federal Communications Commission.

Several major cultural and social activities are planned throughout the program. Recent activities have included a welcoming picnic, a theatrical performance at the John F. Kennedy Center for the Performing Arts, a Powwow hosted by local Native organizations, a tour of the National Museum of the American Indian (NMAI) in New York City, and a farewell banquet.

Here's how it works: You select courses from the multiple course offerings at American University, selecting classes to match your interests and home school requirements. You'll also intern at an agency for 36 hours a week and prepare a prescribed portfolio on your work experience and research.

You'll live in a university dorm on the Tenley campus of American University, just two blocks away from the Tenleytown/AU Metro station in northwest Washington, D.C. All of your meals will be prepared at the Tenley Café, located on the campus.

Members of the WINS Native Advisory Council provide advice and counsel to make sure that the traditional values and practices of the nations and tribes throughout Indian country are maintained.

The WINS program also offers a special fall and spring program and a special internship with the FBI.

HOW TO APPLY

If you're interested, you must submit a completed WINS application; an essay of at least 500 words about why you would like to participate; a nomination letter from a member of your nation or tribal council or from an official of the applicant's nation or tribal education department; a recommendation letter from a faculty member at your university; a resume detailing your work experience; and an official copy of your most recent transcript.

You may obtain a copy of the application online at https://my.american.edu/cgi/mvi.exe/A26.APPL.

LOGIN?SCH=WINS or call the WINS headquarters at the preceding number to ask that an application be mailed to you. You also may request an application via e-mail (see preceding address).

WASHINGTON STATE GOVERNOR'S INTERNSHIP

Program Coordinator
Division of Vocational Rehabilitation
612 Woodland Square Loop S.E.
Building C
Lacey, WA 98504
(360) 725-3641
murphnj@dshs.wa.gov

What You Can Earn: $1,873-$2,148 per session, plus sick leave at a rate of eight hours for each full-time month worked and retirement credits.
Application Deadlines: Rolling.
Educational Experience: Those who have completed one term (quarter or semester) of college enrollment and are actively pursuing a four-year degree. Students are not considered eligible if a degree was obtained prior to the time of hire or prior to completing the first half of the internship.
Requirements: None specified.

OVERVIEW

The governor's internship program provides college students an opportunity through internships to gain valuable work experience and knowledge in various areas of state government, leading to a potential career in public service. Student interns are also encouraged to seek academic credit for the internship experience with their college or university. Undergraduate internships are three to six months.

The governor's internship program strives to attract, develop, and ultimately retain highly capable program participants as state employees. Program participants will receive work experi-ence, hands-on training, and the opportunity to observe the various roles and duties within state government. Participants are expected to leave the program as competent, prepared, and experienced public-sector employees whose skills and talents can lead to a career in state government.

Current internship positions are listed at http://hr.dop.wa.gov/gip/examples.htm. Undergraduate internships are three- to six-month appointments and may begin at any time throughout the year. Undergraduate interns will receive a performance evaluation prior to the conclusion of their internship.

HOW TO APPLY

Download and complete the supplemental questionnaire at http://hr.dop.wa.gov/forms/gipsupqu.doc. Submit the completed questionnaire along with a letter of interest (include the UG # of the position for which you are applying), a resume, a copy of school transcripts (these need not be official), and two to three letters of recommendation to the preceding address. Application contents should not be together.

WEST VIRGINIA GOVERNOR'S INTERNSHIP

Governor's Internship Program
WV Division of Personnel
1900 Kanawha Blvd., East
Bldg. 6, Room 420
Charleston, WV 25305
(304) 558-3950, ext. 260
Fax: (304) 558-1399
chambers@wvadmin.gov

What You Can Earn: At least minimum wage.
Application Deadlines: April 30.
Educational Experience: Must be a student at a West Virginia university or a West Virginia resi-

dent attending an accredited college or university elsewhere; must have completed at least one academic year of study at an accredited college or university by the start of the internship and must have a cumulative GPA of at least 3.0.

Requirements: None specified.

OVERVIEW

The governor's internship program is an extraordinary learning experience for college students in West Virginia. Since its creation in 1989, more than 1,200 talented students have participated in rewarding internship experiences in West Virginia. Private businesses, nonprofit organizations, and government agencies may host interns.

The governor's internship program offers high-achieving college students the opportunity to step beyond the classroom into the world of experiential learning by participating in coordinated internships in private businesses, nonprofit organizations, and government agencies. Students gain knowledge of the real-world work environment, learn valuable communication and leadership skills, obtain experience, and gain references for the future. Students may also use the internship experience to evaluate current and future career choices.

The governor's internship program strives to place students in internships by matching their interests with the needs of the agencies, businesses, or organizations seeking to host interns. Internships generally last nine to 13 weeks.

The Governor's Internship Program sponsors semiweekly academic seminars for interns. Interns working in the Charleston area are strongly encouraged to attend the academic seminars. Topics may range from graduate scholarship programs to resume-writing skills and much more.

Many government jobs are located in Charleston. While the governor's internship program does strive to open job opportunities across the state for college students, most have traditionally found internships for state government agencies in the Charleston area. If you don't have a car or aren't willing to travel, you can still get an internship; few jobs have required a student to have a car or to be willing to travel.

HOW TO APPLY

Download an application at http://www.wvgip.org/internshipApp.cfm. You must complete and submit the application online. When you come for an interview, you must bring a current copy of your college transcript (the copy of your transcript does NOT have to be official) and two letters of recommendation from people who can evaluate your suitability for this program.

The selection of interns is competitive. Your application materials, including transcripts and letters of recommendations, are reviewed by the agency, business, or organization that will interview and ultimately select the summer intern that best suits its needs. The number of students applying usually exceeds the number of positions available; therefore, not all candidates submitting an application will be interviewed or selected to participate in the program.

WHITE HOUSE INTERNSHIP

The White House Internship Program
1600 Pennsylvania Avenue, NW
Washington, DC 20500
(202) 456-1414 (ask for the White House
    Internship Program Office)
Fax: (202) 456-7966
intern_application@whitehouse.gov
http://www.whitehouse.gov/government/wh-
    intern.html

What You Can Earn: Unpaid.
Application Deadlines: Spring term (January to May): applications due October 15; candidates notified mid-November. Summer term (May to August): applications due March 1; candidates notified mid-April.
Educational Experience: No specific major.
Requirements: U.S. citizenship; age 18 on or before the first day of the internship; college enrollment; security clearance prior to start date; random drug test.

OVERVIEW

The White House Internship Program provides students enrolled in college with a unique opportunity to learn more about the daily operations of the White House and observe government officials. Interns learn how the federal government functions and how they can become a part of it. About 100 interns are chosen each spring, summer, and fall to participate in this highly competitive program. Interns are selected based on their application and demonstrated interest in public service.

As glorious and exciting as it may sound, of course, the reality of working as a White House intern is far more pedestrian. If you get an internship at any of the 23 White House offices, you'll spend weeks working at a variety of unpaid tasks and projects. Most White House interns work in the Old Executive Office Building, which is next door to the White House.

Despite this, the competition is intense for the 200 internships offered each year, so don't be disappointed if you don't make it on your first try.

Consider carefully which White House department you would like to work in. You will be asked for your top four preferences (the complete list follows). Try to choose those that will give you valuable experience for your future career, although your preferences aren't guaranteed.

Cabinet Affairs

The Office of Cabinet Affairs is the liaison between the White House and the president's cabinet and agency heads, acting as an advocate within the White House for the cabinet agencies; an early warning system of agency initiatives and late-breaking issues for the president and senior White House staff; the primary information source of White House and Administration policy and directives for the Cabinet; and an impartial mediator and policy broker, when needed, among departments and the White House.

Comment Line and Greeting Line

This office is responsible for filling requests from the public and congressional offices for greeting cards from the president acknowledging special occasions. The Comment Line takes calls from the public who wish to convey their opinions and ideas to the president.

Communications

This office is responsible for the production and planning of the president's media events, coordinating with the advance office to handle the president's public appearances and formal visits outside the White House.

Communications Director's Office

This office oversees the activities of the press secretary, communications, speechwriting, media affairs, and global communications, helping to formulate White House policy and manage the daily operation of communicating the president's messages.

Fellows Office

The White House Fellows Program Office is responsible for the selection process of each class of White House Fellows, as well as the day-to-day management of the program. The office plans, coordinates, and hosts activities for the White House Fellows, including domestic and international policy study trips, an ongoing speaker series, and any social or educational events the Fellows are invited to attend.

First Lady's Correspondence

This office processes all mail sent by the public to the first lady and to the first family, including all first lady's scheduling requests and e-mail. The office also prepares messages of greeting from the first lady for events throughout the country.

First Lady's Press Office

This office manages the first lady's day-to-day media relations, promotes her projects, and publicizes White House social activities to the national and international media. The office works closely with the first lady's scheduling and advance teams to coordinate events and appearances.

Gift Office

This office values and records all gifts received by the first family and members of the White House staff.

Global Communications

This office provides strategic direction and themes to the government agencies that promote America's interests, prevent misunderstanding and conflict, build support for and among United States coalition partners, and inform and persuade international audiences.

Intergovernmental Affairs

This office serves as the liaison between the White House and state and local governments and represents the views of state and local elected officials within the administration. As part of this work, the office works closely with organizations representing state and local elected officials such as the National Governors' Association and the United States Conference of Mayors.

Legislative Affairs

The office serves as the liaison between the White House and the legislative branch, developing the strategies used to promote and defend the president's legislative agenda. Legislative Affairs also acts as a contact through which members of Congress can forward their concerns and priorities to the president and engage in dialogue with the White House.

Mail Analysis

This office analyzes, routes, and processes certain correspondence addressed to the president.

Media Affairs

This office works with local TV stations, regional daily newspapers, and national and local radio outlets, along with the Spanish language media, religious press, and special interest publications such as sports media and business news outlets. They are also responsible for the design and content of the White House Web site.

Office of Counsel to the President

This office is responsible for advising on all legal aspects of policy questions, legal issues arising in connection with the president's decision to sign or veto legislation, ethical questions, financial disclosures, conflicts of interest during employment and post employment, and defining lines between official and political activities. The Counsel's Office also oversees executive appointments and judicial selection, handles presidential pardons, reviews legislation and presidential statements, and handles lawsuits against the president, as well as serving as the White House contact for the Department of Justice.

Office of Policy Development (OPD)

This office includes domestic policy council and the national economic council. Both of these offices accept intern applications, and both are responsible for advising and helping the president formulate, coordinate, and implement economic and domestic policy. The two groups are responsible for ensuring coordination in the development and implementation of executive branch policy.

Office of Presidential Correspondence Agency Liaison

This office helps members of the public who request help from the president or first lady in resolving a problem, such as a complaint about failure to receive veteran's benefits. The office refers many requests to established contacts in federal agencies or with private-sector organizations, depending on the nature of the casework, to assist these people.

Photo Office

This office documents the official events of the president, vice president, and first lady; interns help place and track the status of orders for photographs through each stage of the process. There are general duties such as telephone coverage and assisting staff with specific photo requests.

Political Affairs

This office ensures that the executive branch and the president are aware of the concerns of American citizens.

Presidential Advance

This office is responsible for the organization and implementation of the president and first lady's visits outside of the White House complex and helps structure activities at each location the president and first lady visit. For most trips, advance staff members serve as the primary coordinators between the White House Military Office, the Secret Service, and the local communities to be visited.

Presidential Messages and Proclamations

This office drafts and reviews some individual letters and all messages and proclamations signed by the president. Message requests are provided only for milestone occasions (such as anniversaries of cities, churches, civic groups, and so on) in five-year increments, for annual national observances, for prestigious awards and testimonials, and special events of national organizations.

Presidential Personnel

This office is responsible for recruiting, screening, and recommending qualified candidates for presidential appointments to federal departments and agencies.

Presidential Student Correspondence

This office responds to all letters and requests received from students through high-school age and produces publications for the use by teachers in classrooms.

Press Secretary

This office handles all national press inquiries and issues press releases to the country's major newspapers, major radio services, major news magazines, the wire services, and all of the major television networks.

Presidential Scheduling

The Scheduling Office is responsible for the planning, organization, and implementation of the president's daily and long-range schedules, handling all requests for appointments, meetings, or time with the president.

Public Liaison

This office promotes presidential priorities through outreach to concerned constituencies and public interest groups, including planning briefings, meetings, and large events with the president, vice president and other White House staff and coordinating national, state, and local activities on behalf of presidential initiatives.

Records Management

The Office of Records Management (ORM) is responsible for maintaining the records of the president and the White House staff, ensuring access and preserving them as a historical record of the administration's activities.

Speechwriting

This office crafts the president's speeches; writers in this office compose everything from talking points to the State of the Union Address.

Strategic Initiatives

This office coordinates the planning and development of a long-range strategy for achieving presidential priorities, conducting research, and helping to develop messages in conjunction with the Office of Public Liaison and the Office of Political Affairs.

Travel Office

This office provides airline and train tickets, rental cars, and hotel accommodations for all officially approved travel and provides logistical support for the White House Press Corps travel in conjunction with the president's travel.

USA Freedom Corps

This group was born out of the response to the terrorist attacks of September 11, 2001, in communities around the country. The USA Freedom Corps is a coordinating council responsible for encouraging and helping Americans to answer President Bush's two-year Call to Service. The policies and programs coordinated by the council include The Citizen Corps initiative, The AmeriCorps, Senior Corps and Learn and Serve America programs, and The Peace Corps. The USA Freedom Corps is also connecting Americans with service organizations large and small in communities across the country by serving as a resource for individuals, nonprofit organizations, foundations, corporations, and government at all levels.

Vice President, Office of
The Vice President's staff helps the vice president carry out executive and legislative duties, providing support on domestic policy, national security affairs, legislative affairs, communications, scheduling, advance, military support, protective matters, administration, and legal matters. The office also supports the vice president's spouse.

Visitors Office
The primary responsibility of the Visitors Office is scheduling White House tours, but duties extend beyond daily tours to include coordination of the White House Easter Egg Roll, Holiday Open Houses, Spring and Fall Garden Tours, State Arrival Ceremonies, Presidential Marine One Arrivals and Departures, and other special events.

White House Management
This office provides daily administrative support to the White House staff.

White House Office of Personnel
This office helps with the placement process for all White House staff.

HOW TO APPLY
To apply for a White House internship, you must fill out the internship application form available online as a downloadable application (go to http://www.whitehouse.gov/government/wh-intern-appl.pdf). Submit this application along with a current resume and three letters of recommendation by e-mail or fax. (See the preceding contact information.)

WISCONSIN GOVERNOR'S INTERNSHIP

Wisconsin Governor's Internship Program
Office of Gov. Jim Doyle
State Capitol
115 East
Madison, WI 53702
http://www.wisgov.state.wi.us/section_detail.asp?linkcatid=420&linkid=211&locid=19&sname=Internship%20Program

What You Can Earn: Unpaid.
Application Deadlines: April 15.
Educational Experience: Undergraduate students, graduate students, and recent graduates.
Requirements: Professional appearance and attitude; strong communication skills (phone etiquette, writing, conversation); the ability to work independently as well as in group settings; proficiency in computer skills and computer research; flexibility and an openness to new and different tasks at all levels; patience and well-developed interpersonal skills; the ability to multitask in a fast-paced environment; and diligence and dependability.

OVERVIEW
There are many diverse opportunities for interns in the governor's office. This specialized program allows interns to work in either the governor's office in Madison, Milwaukee, or Washington, D.C., in an area of your interest, enabling you to have a meaningful, hands-on experience and to work as a contributing member of a team.

Interns are involved in a wide assortment of activities. Responsibilities include assisting the following departments: appointments (boards, councils, and commissions); constituent relations; executive residence; external relations; first lady projects; legal; legislative; operations/information technology; outreach; policy; press; and scheduling.

As an intern, you'll be involved in constituent casework, processing constituent correspondence, monitoring media sources, researching legislative matters and policy issues, supporting administrative services, and processing applications to serve on boards, councils, or commissions.

HOW TO APPLY

Apply online or send a cover letter and resume, including your GPA and a list ranking your departmental preference, to the governor's office, via hand delivery, fax, or e-mail. After submitting application materials, prospective intern candidates will be contacted by the governor's office by late April.

INDEXES

INTERNSHIPS AND SUMMER JOBS BY APPLICATION DEADLINE

JANUARY

Asian Pacific American Institute for Congressional Studies Internship	1:320–322
Boeing Internship	1:168–169
Callaway Gardens Internship	2:201
Carnegie Endowment for International Peace Internship	2:97–98
CBS-4 (KCNC-TV) Sports Department Internship	2:302–303
Chincoteague National Wildlife Refuge Internship	2:201–203
DuPont Summer Internship	1:173
The Economist Internship	2:103–104
Ernst & Young Internship	1:173–174
Fossil Rim Wildlife Center Internship	1:94–95
Genesis Animal Sanctuary Summer Internship	1:95–96
Hansard Society Scholars Program	2:104–105
Illinois Governor's Internship	1:330–331
INROADS Internship	1:181–182
Jackson Laboratory Summer Student Program	2:250–251
Kaiser Media Minority Internship in Urban Health Reporting	2:155–156
Knight Ridder Internship for Native American Journalists	2:157–158
Lands' End Internship	1:183–185
Lucent Technologies Summer Internship	1:185–186
Lunar and Planetary Institute Internship	2:252–253
Lunar and Planetary Institute Summer Intern Program	2:348
Marathon Oil Corporation/UNCF Corporate Scholars Program	2:350
Metropolitan Museum of Art Internship	1:138–140
Mount Desert Island Biological Lab Research Fellowships for Undergraduates	2:255–256
Museum of Modern Art Internship	1:142–146
NASA Kennedy Space Center Space Flight and Life Sciences Training Program	2:256–259
National Gallery of Art Internship	1:148–150
National Zoo Beaver Valley Internship	1:102–103
NCR Internship	2:357
North Carolina Governor's Internship	1:344–345
Nuclear Regulatory Commission Historically Black Colleges and Universities Student Research Internship	2:267–268
Saks Incorporated Internship	1:193–194
Smithsonian Architectural History and Historic Preservation Division Internship	2:71

FEBRUARY

The Aark Wildlife Rehabilitation Internship	1:81
ABC *Good Morning America* Internship	2:117
Advertising Club Internship	2:124–125
American Dance Festival Internship	1:250–251
American Society for Microbiology Research Internship	2:228–229
Amnesty International—Washington, D.C. Internship	1:30–32
Anchorage Daily News Internship	2:128–129
Arnold Arboretum of Harvard University Internship	2:197–198
Atlantic Monthly Internship	2:132–133

Buffalo Bill Historical Center Internship 2:40–43
California Academy of Science A. Crawford Cooley Internship in California Botany 2:230–231
California Academy of Science Internship in Biological Illustration 2:231
California Academy of Science Robert T. Wallace Undergraduate Research Internship 2:231–232
Callaway Gardens Internship 2:201
CBS News Internship 2:137–140
Chicago Zoological Society Brookfield Zoo Internship 1:85–87
Cold Spring Harbor Lab Summer Internship 2:235–236
Cooperative Center for Study Abroad: Ireland Internship 2:99
Cooper-Hewitt, National Design Museum Internship 1:126–127
Cornell University Plant Genome Research Program Internship 2:237
Dolphin Institute Internship 1:91–92
The Economist Internship 2:103–104
Entertainment Weekly Internship 2:150–151
Fermilab Summer Internship in Science and Technology 2:339–340
Fossil Rim Wildlife Center Internship 1:94–95
Genentech Internship 2:239–240
Guggenheim Museum Internship 1:133–135
Harper's Internship 2:152–153
Harvard School of Public Health Minority Internship 2:22–23
Harvard University Four Directions Summer Research Program 2:241–242
Harvard University Summer Honors Undergraduate Research Program 2:242–243
Historic Deerfield Summer Fellowship 2:52–54
Howard Hughes Honors Summer Institute 2:245–246
IMG International Internship 1:179–180
Institute of Ecosystem Studies Internship 2:246–250
Kraft Foods Internship 1:182–183
Leadership Alliance Summer Internship 2:251–252
Lockheed Martin Internship 2:344–345
Longwood Gardens Internship 2:208–214
Longwood Gardens Performing Arts Internship 1:283–284
Mattel Internship 1:186–187
Merck Internship 1:189–190
Mickey Leland Energy Fellowships 2:254–255
Morris Arboretum of the University of Pennsylvania Internship 2:214–217
Mount Vernon Summer Internship 2:60–61
Mystic Aquarium Internship 1:99–101
National Air and Space Museum Internship 1:221–222
National Museum of African Art Internship 1:150
National Museum of American History Internship 1:224–225
National Museum of Natural History Internship 2:261–262
National Museum of the American Indian Internship 1:225–226
Naval Research Lab Science and Engineering Apprenticeship Program 2:264–265
New York Daily News Graphics Designer Internship 2:169
New York Daily News Internship 2:169–170
New York University School of Medicine Summer Undergraduate Research Program (SURP) 2:266–267
Nightline Internship 2:172–173
Office of Naval Research Internship 2:268–273
Oregon Zoo Internship 1:104–105
Orlando Magic Internship 2:316–321
Philadelphia Museum of Art Internship 1:157–158
Rockefeller University Summer Undergraduate Research Fellowship 2:275–276
Rocky Mountain Biological Laboratory Summer Internship 2:276–277
Roswell Park Cancer Institute Summer College Internship 2:277
Roswell Park Cancer Institute Summer High School Internship 2:277–278
Santa Fe Institute Internship 2:361–362
Science News Internship 2:180–181
Smithsonian Astrophysical Observatory Internship 2:279–280
Spoleto Festival USA Internship 1:306–308
St. Petersburg Times Summer Internship 2:182–183

St. Petersburg Times Yearlong
  Newsroom Internship 2:183
SUNY Albany Summer Research
  Experience for Undergraduates 2:281–282
Teen People Summer Internship 2:184–185
Toledo Mud Hens Baseball Club
  Internship 2:325
University of California-Davis
  Undergraduate Summer Training in
  Environmental Toxicology 2:282
University of Colorado at Boulder
  Summer Minority Access to
  Research Training 2:283–284
University of Massachusetts Medical
  School Summer Enrichment Program .. 2:287–288
University of Texas-Houston Health
  Science Center Summer Research
  Program 2:288–289
Virginia Institute of Marine Science
  Internship 2:294–296
Washington Leadership Summer
  Internship Seminar for Native
  American Students 1:350–352
Wellesley College Biological Sciences
  Internship 2:296
Whitney Laboratory Marine
  Biomedical Research Experience
  for Undergraduates 2:296–297

MARCH

Abbott Laboratories Environmental,
  Health, and Safety Internship 2:5
ABC John Stossel Specials Internship 2:117
ABC News Internship 2:117–120
ABC News *PrimeTime Live* Internship 2:120
ABC News Radio Internship 2:120–121
ABC News Special Events Internship 2:121
ABC News Washington Bureau
  Internship 2:121–122
ABC *Weekend News* Internship 2:122–123
ABC *World News Tonight* Internship 2:123
Academy of Television Arts and
  Sciences Foundation Internship 1:241–245
Akron Beacon Journal Internship 2:125
Archives of American Art Internship 1:121–122

Arena Stage Internship 1:251–254
Art Institute of Chicago Internship 1:122–123
Art Museum of the Americas Internship 1:123
Aspen Center for Environmental
  Studies Internship 2:198–199
Atlantic Monthly Web Site Content
  Internship 2:133
AT&T Undergraduate Research Program 2:333
Axle Alliance Group Internship 1:167
Blethen Maine Newspapers Minority
  Summer Internship 2:136
Boston University Internship Abroad—
  Auckland Internship 2:83–84
Boston University Internship Abroad—
  Dresden Internship 2:85–86
Boston University Internship Abroad—
  Dublin Internship 2:86–87
Boston University Internship Abroad—
  Geneva Internship 2:87
Boston University Internship Abroad—
  Haifa Internship 2:88
Boston University Internship Abroad—
  London Internship 2:88–90
Boston University Internship Abroad—
  Madrid Internship 2:90–91
Boston University Internship Abroad—
  Paris Internship 2:91–92
Boston University Internship Abroad—
  Sydney Internship 2:92–93
Buchanan/Burnham Internship 2:39–40
The Carter Center Internship 1:35–43
Children's Television Workshop
  Internship 1:258–259
Chincoteague National Wildlife Refuge
  Internship 2:201–203
Chronicle of Higher Education Internship 2:142–143
CIIT Centers for Health Research
  Internship 2:15–16
Columbia Journalism Review Internship 2:145
Cooper-Hewitt, National Design
  Museum Internship 1:126–127
Daughters of the American Revolution
  (DAR) Museum Internship 1:217–218
Democratic National Committee
  Internship 1:326–327
Denver Zoo Internship 1:87–88

DreamWorks SKG Internship   1:263–264
Elizabeth Glaser Pediatric AIDS
    Foundation Internship   2:18–19
Field Museum Internship   1:129–130
Florida Governor's Internship   1:328–329
Fossil Rim Wildlife Center Internship   1:94–95
Freer Gallery of Art/Arthur M. Sackler
    Gallery Internship   1:130–131
Friends Committee on National
    Legislation (FCNL) Internship   1:45–46
Georgia Governor's Internship   1:329–330
GlaxoSmithKline Internship   2:240–241
Glimmerglass Opera Internship   1:270–274
Harvard University Summer Research
    Program in Ecology   2:243–245
HBO Internship   2:153–155
Hirshhorn Museum and Sculpture
    Garden Internship   1:135–136
Historic Preservation Internship
    Training Program   1:218–219, 2:54–55
Kennedy Center for the Performing
    Arts Management Internship   1:280–282
KFSK-Southeast Alaska Public Radio
    Internship   2:156–157
The Late Show with David Letterman
    Internship   1:282–283
Living History Farms Internship   2:55–56
Liz Claiborne Summer Internship   1:185
Lucasfilm Internship   1:286–287
Marine Biology Lab at Woods Hole
    Marine Models in Biological Research
    Internship   2:253–254
Maryland Governor's Summer Internship   1:335–336
MSNBC Multimedia Internship   2:166
Museum of Contemporary Art San
    Diego Internship   1:140–142
NASCAR Diversity Internship   2:314–315
National Building Museum Internship   1:223–224
National Council for Preservation
    Education Internship   2:61–68
National Institutes of Health Summer
    Internship Programs in Biomedical
    Research   2:259–261
National Museum of Women in the
    Arts Internship   1:150–152
National Portrait Gallery Internship   1:152–155

New York Rangers Internship   2:316
New York University Center for Neural
    Science Undergraduate Summer
    Research Program   2:265
Nightline Internship   2:172–173
Oracle Corporation Internship   2:357–358
Philadelphia Junior Zoo Apprentice
    Internship   1:106–108
Preservation Action Internship   2:70–71
Random House Inc. Summer Internship   1:192–193
Rocky Mountain PBS-TV Studio and
    Production Internship   2:176–177
San Diego Museum of Art—Education
    Internship (summer session only)   1:229
San Diego Zoo's Wild Animal Park
    Summer Camp Teen Internship   1:230
SeaWorld Adventure Camp Internship   1:109–111
Sierra Magazine Internship   2:181–182
Stanford Linear Accelerator Center
    Summer Fellowship   2:280–281
Tiger Creek Wildlife Refuge Internship   1:112–113
20/20 Vision Internship   1:73
Tyson Foods Internship   1:195
University of Massachusetts Medical
    School Undergraduate Summer NIH
    Research Fellowship Program   2:288
U.S. Holocaust Memorial Museum
    Internship   1:233–234
U.S. Supreme Court Internship   1:347–349
Washingtonian Editorial Internship   2:189
White House Internship   1:353–357
Whitney Museum of American Art
    Internship   1:159–160
Wolfsong Ranch Foundation Internship   1:114–115
Wolf Trap Internship   1:312–314

APRIL

ABC *Good Morning America* Internship   2:117
American Conservatory Theater
    Internship   1:246–250
American Public Health Association Internship   2:9
Amnesty International—Washington,
    D.C. Internship   1:30–32
Arena Stage Internship   1:251–254
Boston Museum of Science Internship   1:205–210

Brooklyn Children's Museum Internship   1:210
California Governor's Internship   1:322–323
Capitol Hill Internship   1:323–324
CBS-4 (KCNC-TV) Sports Department
   Internship   2:302–303
Center for Arts and Culture Internship   1:123–124
Cessna Internship   1:169
Children's Museum of Indianapolis
   Internship   1:211–217
Cornell University Materials Science
   Research Internship   2:236–237
Dallas Theater Center SummerStage
   Internship   1:260
Doctors Without Borders Internship   2:16–18
Duke University Neurosciences
   Summer Research Program in
   Mechanisms of Behavior   2:238
Hansard Society Scholars Program   2:104–105
The Hermitage (Home of Andrew
   Jackson) Internship   2:51–52
KPNX-TV (Phoenix) Internship   2:158
Kroenke Sports Enterprises Internship   2:312–314
Lands' End Internship   1:183–185
Los Alamos National Laboratory
   High School Co-Op Program   2:345–346
Los Alamos National Laboratory
   Internship   2:346–348
MTV Networks Internship—
   New York City   1:288–289
National Aquarium in Baltimore
   Internship   1:101–102
National Gallery of Art High School
   Internship   1:147–148
National Gallery of Art Internship   1:148–150
National Zoo Beaver Valley Internship   1:102–103
New England Healthcare Institute
   Internship   2:28–29
New Museum of Contemporary Art
   Internship   1:155–157
Oregon Zoo Internship   1:104–105
Population Institute Internship   2:30
Sacramento Music Circus Summer
   Musical Theater Internship   1:298–299
San Diego Chargers Internship   2:324–325
San Diego Zoo Internquest   1:109
Science Magazine Internship   2:179–180

Shakespeare Theatre Internship   1:302–304
Smithsonian Architectural History
   and Historic Preservation Division
   Internship   2:71
South Shore Music Circus Internship   1:305–306
The Studio Theatre Internship   1:308–309
University of Massachusetts
   Undergraduate Research in Ecology
   and Conservation Biology   2:284–286
Vermont Governor's Internship   1:349
WakeMed Health and Hospitals
   Internship   2:33–34
Washingtonian Art Department
   Internship   2:188–189
West Virginia Governor's Internship   1:352–353
Wilma Theater Internship   1:312
Wisconsin Governor's Internship   1:357–358
Women's International League for Peace
   and Freedom Internship   2:108–111

MAY

ACCION International Internship   1:27
American Civil Liberties Union
   Immigrants Rights Project Internship   1:28–29
American Institute for Foreign Study—
   Cannes Internship   2:78–79
American Institute for Foreign Study—
   Florence Internship   2:79–80
American Institute for Foreign Study—
   London Internship   2:80–81
American Institute for Foreign Study—
   Sydney Internship   2:81–82
Bread for the City Legal Clinic Internship   1:34
Center for Adolescent Health and the
   Law Internship   2:14–15
Center for Food Safety Internship   2:15
Chicago Bears Graphic Design
   Internship   2:303
Dallas Theater Center Internship   1:259–260
EarthTrends Summer Internship   1:44–45
El Pueblo de Los Angeles Historical
   Monument Multicultural Summer
   Internship   2:47–48
Grey Towers National Historic Site
   Internship   2:49–50

Initiative for a Competitive Inner City
Internship   1:51
International Center for Tolerance
Education Internship   1:51–52
Japanese American National Museum
Internship   1:219–221
Jim Henson Company Internship   1:274–276
Longwood Gardens Internship   2:208–214
Longwood Gardens Performing Arts
Internship   1:283–284
Museum of Modern Art Internship   1:142–146
National Campaign to Prevent Teen
Pregnancy Internship   1:56–57
New American Dream
Communications Internship   1:58–59
Peaceworks Foundation Internship   1:61
Population Services International
Internship   1:63–64
Pratt & Whitney Co-op and Internship   2:360–361
Prison Activist Resource Center
Internship   1:65–66
Public Leadership Education Network
Internship   1:66–67
Pulmonary Hypertension Association
Internship   2:31–32
Rainforest Action Network Internship   1:67–68
Robert F. Kennedy Memorial Center for
Human Rights Internship   1:68
Saks Incorporated Internship   1:193–194
Second Stage Theatre Internship   1:300–302
Share Our Strength Internship   1:70–71
South Street Seaport Museum Internship   1:230–231
United Nations Association of the USA
Internship   1:74
University of the Middle East Project
Internship   1:232–233
Vermont Folklife Center Internship   2:72–73
Washingtonian Advertising Internship   2:188
Women's International League for
Peace and Freedom Internship   2:108–111

JUNE

Art Museum of the Americas Internship   1:123
Atlantic Monthly Internship   2:132–133
The Carter Center Internship   1:35–43

DreamWorks SKG Internship   1:263–264
Entertainment Weekly Internship   2:150–151
Fossil Rim Wildlife Center Internship   1:94–95
Guggenheim Museum Internship   1:133–135
Hansard Society Scholars Program   2:104–105
HBO Internship   2:153–155
Heifer International Internship   1:49–50
Hirshhorn Museum and Sculpture
Garden Internship   1:135–136
Juilliard School Professional Internship 1:276–280
Kennedy Center for the Performing
Arts Management Internship   1:280–282
The Late Show with David Letterman
Internship   1:282–283
Los Angeles Times Internship   2:159–160
Mystic Aquarium Internship   1:99–101
National Museum of African Art
Internship   1:150
National Museum of Women in the
Arts Internship   1:150–152
New York Rangers Internship   2:316
Orlando Magic Internship   2:316–321
Science News Internship   2:180–181
Strong Women, Strong Girls Internship   1:72–73
Tiger Creek Wildlife Refuge Internship   1:112–113
U.S. Holocaust Memorial Museum
Internship   1:233–234
U.S. Supreme Court Internship   1:347–349
Washingtonian Advertising Internship   2:188
Washingtonian Art Department
Internship   2:188–189
Washington Internship for Native
Students (WINS)   1:349–350
World Affairs Council Internship   1:77

JULY

ABC *Good Morning America* Internship   2:117
American Civil Liberties Union Internship 1:29–30
American Public Health Association
Internship   2:9
Atlantic Monthly Web Site Content Internship 2:133
Cessna Internship   1:169
Children's Television Workshop
Internship   1:258–259

Chincoteague National Wildlife Refuge
Internship   2:201–203
Cooper-Hewitt, National Design
Museum Internship   1:126–127
Doctors Without Borders Internship   2:16–18
Florida Governor's Internship   1:328–329
Freer Gallery of Art/Arthur M. Sackler
Gallery Internship   1:130–131
Georgia Governor's Internship   1:329–330
KPNX-TV (Phoenix) Internship   2:158
Literacy Partners Inc. Internship   1:221
National Museum of American History
Internship   1:224–225
National Museum of the American
Indian Internship   1:225–226
Nightline Internship   2:172–173
Second Stage Theatre Internship   1:300–302
Sierra Magazine Internship   2:181–182
Smithsonian Architectural History
and Historic Preservation Division
Internship   2:71
Washingtonian Editorial Internship   2:189
Wolf Trap Internship   1:312–314
Women's International League for
Peace and Freedom Internship   2:108–111

AUGUST

Amnesty International—Washington,
D.C. Internship   1:30–32
Art Institute of Chicago Internship   1:122–123
California Governor's Internship   1:322–323
CBS-4 (KCNC-TV) Sports Department
Internship   2:302–303
Center for Arts and Culture Internship   1:123–124
Chicago Zoological Society Brookfield
Zoo Internship   1:85–87
Chincoteague National Wildlife Refuge
Internship   2:201–203
Daughters of the American Revolution
(DAR) Museum Internship   1:217–218
Dolphin Institute Internship   1:91–92
Great Dog Obedience Training Internship 1:96
Jim Henson Company Internship   1:274–276
Michigan Executive Office Internship   1:336–338

New Museum of Contemporary Art
Internship   1:155–157
Oregon Zoo Internship   1:104–105
Prison Activist Resource Center
Internship   1:65–66
20/20 Vision Internship   1:73
Tyson Foods Internship   1:195
Vermont Governor's Internship   1:349

SEPTEMBER

Arizona Legislative Internship   1:318–320
Axle Alliance Group Internship   1:167
Bettis Atomic Power Lab Internship   2:229–230
Buffalo Bill Historical Center Internship   2:40–43
Capitol Hill Internship   1:323–324
Georgia Governor's Internship   1:329–330
National Zoo Beaver Valley Internship   1:102–103
Rocky Mountain PBS-TV Studio and
Production Internship   2:176–177
Tiger Creek Wildlife Refuge Internship   1:112–113
Wilma Theater Internship   1:312

OCTOBER

ABC *Good Morning America* Internship   2:117
American Civil Liberties Union
Internship   1:29–30
American Institute for Foreign Study—
Cannes Internship   2:78–79
American Institute for Foreign Study—
Florence Internship   2:79–80
American Institute for Foreign Study—
London Internship   2:80–81
American Institute for Foreign Study—
Sydney Internship   2:81–82
Arena Stage Internship   1:251–254
Boston University Internship Abroad—
Auckland Internship   2:83–84
Boston University Internship Abroad—
Beijing Internship   2:84–85
Boston University Internship Abroad—
Dresden Internship   2:85–86
Boston University Internship Abroad—
Dublin Internship   2:86–87

Boston University Internship Abroad—
Geneva Internship   2:87
Boston University Internship Abroad—
Haifa Internship   2:88
Boston University Internship Abroad—
London Internship   2:88–90
Boston University Internship Abroad—
Madrid Internship   2:90–91
Boston University Internship Abroad—
Paris Internship   2:91–92
Boston University Internship Abroad—
Sydney Internship   2:92–93
The Carter Center Internship   1:35–43
Denver Post Reporting/Photography
Internship   2:148
DreamWorks SKG Internship   1:263–264
Entertainment Weekly Internship   2:150–151
The Late Show with David Letterman
Internship   1:282–283
Los Angeles Times Internship   2:159–160
Miami Herald Internship   2:161–162
Museum of Modern Art Internship   1:142–146
Mystic Aquarium Internship   1:99–101
National Museum of African Art
Internship   1:150
National Museum of the American
Indian Internship   1:225–226
National Museum of Women in the
Arts Internship   1:150–152
Nightline Internship   2:172–173
Orlando Sentinel Internship   2:173–174
Science News Internship   2:180–181
U.S. Holocaust Memorial Museum
Internship   1:233–234
U.S. Supreme Court Internship   1:347–349
Washingtonian Art Department
Internship   2:188–189
Washington Internship for Native
Students (WINS)   1:349–350
White House Internship   1:353–357

NOVEMBER

ABC Good Morning America Internship   2:117
Akron Beacon Journal Internship   2:125

American Society of Magazine Editors
Internship   2:127–128
Amnesty International—Washington,
D.C. Internship   1:30–32
Art Institute of Chicago Internship   1:122–123
Art Museum of the Americas Internship   1:123
Associated Press Broadcast News
Internship   2:130–131
Associated Press Internship   2:129–130
Atlantic Monthly Internship   2:132–133
Austin American-Statesman Internship   2:134–135
Baltimore Sun Two-Year Internship   2:135
Boston Globe Internship   2:136–137
Cessna Internship   1:169
Chicago Tribune Internship   2:142
Children's Television Workshop
Internship   1:258–259
Dallas Morning News Internship   2:147–148
Des Moines Register Internship   2:148–149
Dow Jones Newspaper Fund Minority
Summer Internship   2:149–150
Federal Bureau of Investigation (FBI)
Washington Internship for Native
Students (WINS)   1:327–328
Florida Governor's Internship   1:328–329
Fossil Rim Wildlife Center Internship   1:94–95
Freer Gallery of Art/Arthur M. Sackler
Gallery Internship   1:130–131
Guggenheim Museum Internship   1:133–135
HBO Internship   2:153–155
Hirshhorn Museum and Sculpture
Garden Internship   1:135–136
Kennedy Center for the Performing
Arts Management Internship   1:280–282
KPNX-TV (Phoenix) Internship   2:158
Lands' End Internship   1:183–185
Longwood Gardens Internship   2:208–214
Longwood Gardens Performing Arts
Internship   1:283–284
Modesto Bee Internship   2:162–163
National Aquarium in Baltimore
Internship   1:101–102
National Association of Black
Journalists Summer Journalism
Internship   2:166–168

National Museum of American History
  Internship   1:224–225
National Museum of the American
  Indian Internship   1:225–226
New York Rangers Internship   2:316
New York Times Copyediting Internship   2:170
New York Times Graphics, Design and
  Photography Internship   2:171–172
New York Times Reporting Fellowship   2:172
Nightline Internship   2:172–173
Oregon Zoo Internship   1:104–105
Orlando Sentinel Internship   2:173–174
Philadelphia Inquirer Minority Internship   2:174–175
Philadelphia Inquirer Nonminority
  Copyediting and Graphics Arts
  Internship   2:175
Pratt & Whitney Co-op and Internship   2:360–361
Prison Activist Resource Center
  Internship   1:65–66
Sacramento Bee Internship   2:177
Saks Incorporated Internship   1:193–194
San Francisco Chronicle Summer
  Internship   2:177–178
Science Magazine Internship   2:179–180
Sierra Magazine Internship   2:181–182
Tyson Foods Internship   1:195
U.S. Department of Energy's Science
  Undergraduate Lab Internship (SULI)   2:289–294
Wall Street Journal Internship   2:187
Washingtonian Editorial Internship   2:189
Washington Post Internship   2:189–190
Wilma Theater Internship   1:312
Wolf Trap Internship   1:312–314
Women's International League for Peace
  and Freedom Internship   2:108–111

DECEMBER

American Public Health Association Internship   2:9
Anchorage Daily News Internship   2:128–129
Atlanta Journal Constitution Internship   2:131–132
Atlantic Monthly Web Site Content
  Internship   2:133
Audubon Internship   2:133–134
Bangor Daily News Internship   2:135–136

Bay Nature Magazine Internship   2:200–201
Boston Environment Department
  Internship   1:33–34
California Governor's Internship   1:322–323
Center for Arts and Culture Internship   1:123–124
Charlotte Observer Internship   2:141
Chicago Sun-Times Minority
  Scholarship and Internship Program   2:141–142
Chicago Zoological Society Brookfield
  Zoo Internship   1:85–87
Cleveland Plain Dealer Internship   2:143
CNN News Internship   2:143–144
Cooper-Hewitt, National Design
  Museum Internship   1:126–127
Daughters of the American Revolution
  (DAR) Museum Internship   1:217–218
Detroit Free Press Internship   2:149
Doctors Without Borders Internship   2:16–18
Fresno Bee Internship   2:152
Getty Foundation Internship   1:131–133
Jim Henson Company Internship   1:274–276
Kaiser Media Minority Internship in
  Urban Health Reporting   2:155–156
Los Angeles Times Internship   2:159–160
Museum of Modern Art Internship   1:142–146
New Museum of Contemporary Art
  Internship   1:155–157
Newsweek Internship   2:168–169
Prison Activist Resource Center
  Internship   1:65–66
Reuters Internship   2:175–176
Rocky Mountain PBS-TV Studio and
  Production Internship   2:176–177
San Francisco Chronicle Two-Year
  Internship   2:178–179
Second Stage Theatre Internship   1:300–302
St. Petersburg Times Summer Internship   2:182–183
Tampa Tribune Internship   2:183–184
Tiger Creek Wildlife Refuge Internship   1:112–113
Time Inc. Summer Internship   2:185–186
20/20 Vision Internship   1:73
USA Today Summer Internship   2:186
U.S. News & World Report Internship   2:186–187
Vermont Governor's Internship   1:349
Washingtonian Advertising Internship   2:188

UNSPECIFIED

ABC-TV Channel 7 (Los Angeles) Internship 2:122
Anasazi Heritage Center Internship 1:204–205
Indiana Pacers Internship 2:306–311
KOCE Public TV (Huntington Beach,
    Calif.) Internship 2:158
Library of Congress Internship 1:331–335
Mother Jones Internship 2:163
MTV Networks Internship—Nashville 1:288
Walt Disney World Culinary Internship 1:196–197
Walt Disney World Summer Jobs 1:310–312
The Washington Center for Internship
    and Academic Seminars 1:234–237
Women for Peace Internship 1:75

ROLLING

Abbott Laboratories Internship 1:165–166
Acadia National Park Education Internship 1:201
Actors Theatre Workshop Internship 1:245–246
The Ad Club (Boston) Internship 2:124
Administration on Aging Internship 2:6
Advocates for Youth Internship 1:27–28
Aerospace Corporation Internship 2:329
Agilent Technologies Internship 2:329–330
AIESEC Internship 2:77
Amazon.com Software Development
    Engineer Internship 2:330–331
Amelia Island Internship 1:166–167
American Association for the
    Advancement of Science Entry
    Point Internship 2:226–227
American Association for the
    Advancement of Science Internship 2:225–226
American Cancer Society Internship 2:6–7
American Enterprise Institute Internship 1:317–318
American Farmland Trust Internship 2:193
American Folklife Center Internship 1:201–202
American Forests Internship 2:193–195
American Foundation for the Blind Internship 2:7
American Friends Service Committee
    International Internship 2:77–78
American Geographical Society
    Internship 1:202–203, 2:227–228
American Lung Association Internship 2:8

American Red Cross Internship 2:9–13
American Red Cross Media Internship 2:126
American Rivers Internship 2:195–197
American-Scandinavian Foundation
    Internship 2:82–83
American School for the Deaf Internship 1:203–204
Anacostia Museum and Center for
    African American History and Culture
    Internship 2:39
The Antarctica Project Internship 2:197
Apple Computer Internship 2:331–333
Archives of American Art Internship 1:121–122
Atlanta Ballet Internship 1:254
Aullwood *Audubon* Center and Farm
    Internship 2:199–200
Australian Embassy Internship 2:83
Ball Aerospace Internship 2:334
BalletMet Internship 1:254–255
Beaver Dam Farm Equine Internship 1:81–83
Bechtel Corporation Internship 1:167–168
Bechtel Internship 2:334–335
Berkshire Theater Festival Internship 1:255–256
Best Friends Animal Society Internship 1:83–84
Beyond Pesticides Internship 1:32–33
Big Cat Rescue Internship 1:84–85
Boston Ballet Internship 1:256–257
Boston Celtics Internship 2:301–302
Boys Hope, Girls Hope Internship 2:13–14
Brooklyn Parents for Peace Internship 1:34–35
Callaway Advanced Technology
    Internship 2:335–336
Camp Counselors USA—European Day
    Camps 2:93–95
Camp Counselors USA—Russia 2:95
Camp Counselors USA—United Kingdom 2:96
Canadian Embassy Internship 2:96–97
Center for Science in the Public Interest
    Internship 2:232–235
Center for Women in Politics and
    Public Policy Internship 1:43
Center for World Indigenous Studies
    Internship 2:98–99
Central Intelligence Agency Internship 1:324–325
ChevronTexaco Engineering Internship 1:170–172
Chicago Bulls Ticket Sales
    Representative Internship 2:303–304

Chicago Children's Museum Internship 1:210–211
Chicago Historical Society Internship 1:124–125
Chicago Symphony Orchestra Internship 1:257–258
Children's Museum of Indianapolis
    Internship 1:211–217
Christie's Internship 1:125–126
Chrysler Group Internship 1:172
Cisco Systems Internship 2:336–337
Colonial Williamsburg Internship 2:43–46
Colorado Springs Sky Sox Internship 2:304–306
Common Cause Internship 1:43–44
Connecticut Governor's Prevention
    Partnership Internship 1:325–326
Corcoran Gallery of Art Internship 1:128–129
Costa Rica Internship Institute Internship 2:100
Council on Foreign Relations Internship 2:100–101
Council on Hemispheric Affairs
    (COHA) Internship 2:101–103
C-SPAN TV (Washington, D.C.)
    Internship 2:145–147
Dance Place Internship 1:260–261
D. C. Booth Historic Fish Hatchery
    Internship 2:46
Dell Computer Internship 2:337–338
Democratic National Committee
    Internship 1:326–327
Disney's Animal Kingdom Advanced
    Internship 1:88–91
Dow Chemical Company Internship 2:338
Dreamtime Festival Internship 1:261–263
DuPont Engineering Internship 2:238–239
Eastman Kodak Internship 2:338–339
E! Entertainment Talent/Casting
    Internship 1:265–267
Eisenhower National Historic Site
    Internship 2:46–47
Eugene O'Neill Theater Internship 1:267–269
EurekAlert! Web Site Internship 2:151–152
Farm Sanctuary Internship 1:92–93
Folger Shakespeare Library Internship 1:269
Ford Motor Company Internship 1:174–177
Fort Wayne Children's Zoo Veterinary
    Medicine Internship 1:93–94
Friends of the Earth Internship 2:203–205
Frontier Nursing Service Internship 2:19–20
Gay Men's Health Crisis Internship 2:20–21

Geddes Talent Agency Internship 1:270
General Electric Internship 1:177–178
Georgia State Park and Historic Sites
    Internship 2:48–49
Gould Farm Internship 2:21–22
Government Accountability Project
    Internship 1:47
Greenbelt Alliance Internship 1:47–48
Habitat for Humanity—New York City
    Internship 1:49
Hallmark Cards Internship 1:178–179
Hawk Mountain Sanctuary Internship 2:204–206
Head Start National Internship 2:23–24
Healthy Mothers, Healthy Babies
    Coalition of Washington Internship 2:24
Hermitage Foundation Museum Internship 2:51
Hewlett-Packard Internship 1:179
Hilltop Farm Inc. Internship 1:97
Houston Zoo Internship 1:97–98
IBM Extreme Blue Internship 2:340–342
Idaho Lieutenant Governor's Internship 1:330
Independence Seaport Museum Internship 1:219
Injury Center Internship 2:24–25
Intel Internship 2:342–343
International Atomic Energy Agency
    Internship 2:105–107
International Child Art Foundation
    Internship 1:136–137
International Diplomacy Council
    Internship 1:52–53
Jane Goodall Institute Internship 2:206–208
Julia Morgan Center for the Arts
    Internship 1:137–138
Kansas City Blades Internship 2:311–312
KTTV-TV (Los Angeles) Internship 2:159
Lam Research Internship 2:343
Lexmark Internship 2:343–344
Los Alamos National Laboratory
    Internship 2:346–348
Los Angeles Lakers Internship 2:314
Los Angeles Opera Community
    Programs Internship 1:284
Lucas Digital Internship 1:284–286
Macy's Internship 1:187–189
Maine State Governor's Internship 1:335
Marathon Oil Corporation Internship 2:349–350

Marvel Comics Internship 2:160–161
MediaRights Internship 1:53–55
Mercedes-Benz USA Internship 1:189
Merck Family Fund Internship 1:55–56
Metro-Goldwyn-Mayer (MGM)
Internship 1:287–288
Michael Perez Gallery Internship 1:140
Microsoft Internship 2:350–353
Minnesota Historical Society Internship 2:56–60
Motorola Internship 2:353–354
MSNBC Internship 2:164–166
MTV Networks Internship—
New York City 1:288–289
MTV Networks Internship—Santa Monica 1:289–290
MTV Networks Latin America
Internship—Miami Beach 1:290
NASCAR Internship 2:315–316
National Anthropological Archives
Internship 1:222–223
National Endowment for the Arts
Internship 1:146–147, 1:290–291
National Environmental Law Center
Internship 1:57
National Healthy Mothers, Healthy
Babies Coalition Internship 2:25–26
National Instruments Internship 2:354–355
National Mental Health Association
Internship 2:26–28
National Organization for Women
(NOW) Internship 1:58
National Park Foundation Internship 2:217–218
National Renewable Energy Laboratory
Internship 2:355–356
National Science Foundation Research
Experience for Undergraduates (REU) 2:263–264
National Semiconductor Internship 2:356–357
National Trust for Historic Preservation
Internship 2:68–69
NBC Internship 2:168
New England Wildlife Center Internship 1:103–104
New Jersey Governor's Internship 1:338–339
The New Press Internship 1:60
New York City Summer Internship 1:339–343
New York State Theatre Institute
Internship 1:291–292

Nickelodeon Animation Studio
Internship 1:292
Oklahoma Governor's Internship 1:345
Old Sturbridge Village Internship 2:69–70
One Reel Internship 1:292–294
Oregon Governor's Internship 1:345–346
Other Hand Productions Puppet
Internship 1:294–295
Pacific Gas and Electric Company
Internship 2:358–359
Packer Foundation Engineering
Internship 2:359–360
Paramount Pictures/Dr. Phil Show
Internship 1:295
Paws Companion Animal Internship 1:105–106
Pendle Hill Social Justice Internship 1:61–62
Pennsylvania Department of Public
Health Internship 2:29
Performance Research Internship 2:321–322
Pfizer Internship 1:190–192
Pfizer Research and Development
Internship 2:273–274
Philadelphia Orchestra Association
Internship 1:295–297
Philadelphia Phantoms Internship 2:322–323
Philadelphia 76ers Internship 2:323–324
Philadelphia Zoo Internship 1:108–109
Physicians for Social Responsibility
Internship 1:62–63
Portland Children's Museum Internship 1:226–229
Project HOPE (Health Opportunities
for People Everywhere) Internship 2:30–31
Radio Disney—Boston Internship 1:297
Raytheon Internship 1:193
Republican National Committee
Internship 1:346–347
RKO Pictures Internship 1:297–298
San Diego Museum of Art—Education
Internship 1:229
San Francisco Mime Troupe Internship 1:299–300
Santé Group Internship 1:69
Seattle Art Museum Internship 1:158–159
Seattle Times Internship 2:181
Seeds of Peace Internship 1:69–70
Sierra Club Internship 1:71–72

Silent Spring Institute Internship   2:32–33
Silicon Graphics Inc. (SGI) Internship   2:362–363
Smithsonian Folkways Recording
    Internship   1:304–305
South Carolina Governor's Internship   1:347
Strides Therapeutic Riding Center
    Internship   1:111–112
Student Climate Outreach Internship   2:218–219
Student Conservation Association
    Internship   2:219–221
Surgeons of Hope Foundation Internship   2:33
Teach for America National Internship   1:231–232
Texas Film Commission Internship   1:309–310
Texas Instruments Internship   2:363–364
Toyota Motor North America Internship   1:194–195
UNICEF Graduate Student Internship   2:107
U.S. Capitol Historical Society Internship   2:71–72
U.S. Department of Education Internship   1:233

Verizon College Internship   1:195–196
Very Special Arts (VSA) Internship   1:159
Washington, D.C., Department of
    Health Internship   2:34–35
Washington Food Coalition Internship   1:74–75
Washington State Governor's Internship   1:352
Wild Horse Sanctuary Internship   1:113–114
Wildlife Rescue and Rehabilitation
    Internship   1:114
Women Work Internship   1:75–77
Work Canada   2:111–113
World Bird Sanctuary Internship   1:115–116
WVSA Arts Connection Internship   1:160–162
Wyckoff Farmhouse Museum Internship   2:73–74
Xerox Internship   2:364–365
YAI National Institute for People with
    Disabilities Internship   2:35
Zoo Atlanta Internship   1:116–117

INTERNSHIPS AND SUMMER JOBS BY EDUCATION LEVEL

HIGH SCHOOL STUDENTS

American Red Cross Internship	2:9–13
American Red Cross Media Internship	2:126
Boston Museum of Science Internship	1:205–210
Brooklyn Parents for Peace Internship	1:34–35
Cornell University Plant Genome Research Program Internship	2:237
Elizabeth Glaser Pediatric AIDS Foundation Internship	2:18–19
Freer Gallery of Art/Arthur M. Sackler Gallery Internship	1:130–131
Gay Men's Health Crisis Internship	2:20–21
Great Dog Obedience Training Internship	1:96
International Child Art Foundation Internship	1:136–137
Jackson Laboratory Summer Student Program	2:250–251
Library of Congress Internship	1:331–335
Literacy Partners Inc. Internship	1:221
Los Alamos National Laboratory High School Co-Op Program	2:345–346
Maine State Governor's Internship	1:335
Marathon Oil Corporation Internship	2:349–350
National Gallery of Art High School Internship	1:147–148
National Museum of American History Internship	1:224–225
Naval Research Lab Science and Engineering Apprenticeship Program	2:264–265
New York State Theatre Institute Internship	1:291–292
One Reel Internship	1:292–294
Oregon Governor's Internship	1:345–346
Packer Foundation Engineering Internship	2:359–360
Paws Companion Animal Internship	1:105–106
Philadelphia Junior Zoo Apprentice Internship	1:106–108
Roswell Park Cancer Institute Summer High School Internship	2:277–278
Sacramento Music Circus Summer Musical Theater Internship	1:298–299
San Diego Zoo Internquest	1:109
San Diego Zoo's Wild Animal Park Summer Camp Teen Internship	1:230
South Street Seaport Museum Internship	1:230–231
Student Conservation Association Internship	2:219–221
U.S. Department of Education Internship	1:233

COLLEGE STUDENTS
Freshmen

Academy of Television Arts and Sciences Foundation Internship	1:241–245
American Institute for Foreign Study—Cannes Internship	2:78–79
American Institute for Foreign Study—Florence Internship	2:79–80
American Institute for Foreign Study—London Internship	2:80–81
American Institute for Foreign Study—Sydney Internship	2:81–81
American School for the Deaf Internship	1:203–204
American Society for Microbiology Research Internship	2:228–229
Apple Computer Internship	2:331–333
Archives of American Art Internship	1:121–122
Arena Stage Internship	1:251–254
Axle Alliance Group Internship	1:167
Boston Ballet Internship	1:256–257
Boston Museum of Science Internship	1:205–210

Brooklyn Parents for Peace Internship   1:34–35
Callaway Advanced Technology
    Internship   2:335–336
Center for Arts and Culture Internship   1:123–124
Chicago Bears Graphic Design Internship   2:303
Chicago Historical Society Internship   1:124–125
Children's Museum of Indianapolis
    Internship   1:211–217
Chincoteague National Wildlife Refuge
    Internship   2:202–203
Cooperative Center for Study Abroad:
    Ireland Internship   2:99
Cooper-Hewitt, National Design
    Museum Internship   1:126–127
Corcoran Gallery of Art Internship   1:128–129
Dallas Theater Center Internship   1:259–260
Dallas Theater Center SummerStage
    Internship   1:260
Dance Place Internship   1:260–261
DreamWorks SKG Internship   1:263–264
DuPont Engineering Internship   2:238–239
EarthTrends Summer Internship   1:44–45
Field Museum Internship   1:129–130
Fort Wayne Children's Zoo Veterinary
    Medicine Internship   1:93–94
Freer Gallery of Art/Arthur M. Sackler
    Gallery Internship   1:130–131
General Electric Internship   1:177–178
Genesis Animal Sanctuary Summer
    Internship   1:95–96
Guggenheim Museum Internship   1:133–135
Habitat for Humanity—New York City
    Internship   1:49
Harvard University Summer Research
    Program in Ecology   2:243–245
HBO Internship   2:153–155
Hilltop Farm Inc. Internship   1:97
Historic Preservation Internship
    Training Program   1:218–219
Independence Seaport Museum Internship   1:219
Institute of Ecosystem Studies Internship   2:246–250
Intel Internship   2:342–343
Japanese American National Museum
    Internship   1:219–221
Lexmark Internship   2:343–344
Literacy Partners Inc. Internship   1:221

Los Alamos National Laboratory
    Internship   2:346–348
Los Angeles Lakers Internship   2:314
Los Angeles Opera Community
    Programs Internship   1:284
Lucent Technologies Summer Internship   1:185–186
Marathon Oil Corporation Internship   2:349–350
Mercedes-Benz USA Internship   1:189
Merck Family Fund Internship   1:55–56
Merck Internship   1:189–190
Mickey Leland Energy Fellowships   2:254–255
Microsoft Internship   2:350–353
Motorola Internship   2:353–354
Mystic Aquarium Internship   1:99–101
NASA Kennedy Space Center Space
    Flight and Life Sciences Training
    Program   2:256–259
NASCAR Diversity Internship   2:314–315
National Air and Space Museum
    Internship   1:221–222
National Anthropological Archives
    Internship   1:222–223
National Aquarium in Baltimore
    Internship   1:101–102
National Building Museum Internship   1:223–224
National Endowment for the Arts
    Internship   1:146–147
National Environmental Law Center
    Internship   1:57
National Instruments Internship   2:354–355
National Museum of African Art
    Internship   1:150
National Museum of American History
    Internship   1:224–225
National Museum of Natural History
    Internship   2:261–262
National Museum of the American
    Indian Internship   1:225–226
National Portrait Gallery Internship   1:152–155
National Science Foundation Research
    Experience for Undergraduates (REU)   2:263–264
National Semiconductor Internship   2:356–357
National Zoo Beaver Valley Internship   1:103–104
NCR Internship   2:357
New American Dream
    Communications Internship   1:58–59

Nuclear Regulatory Commission
Historically Black Colleges and
Universities Student Research
Internship   2:267–268
Oracle Corporation Internship   2:357–358
Pacific Gas and Electric Company
Internship   2:358–359
Packer Foundation Engineering
Internship   2:359–360
Pfizer Internship   1:190–192
Pfizer Research and Development
Internship   2:273–274
Philadelphia Zoo Internship   1:108–109
Physicians for Social Responsibility
Internship   1:62–63
Pratt & Whitney Co-op and Internship   2:360–361
Public Leadership Education Network
Internship   1:66–67
Rocky Mountain Biological Laboratory
Summer Internship   2:276–277
Santa Fe Institute Internship   2:361–362
Santé Group Internship   1:69
Smithsonian Astrophysical Observatory
Internship   2:279–280
South Street Seaport Museum Internship 1:230–231
Strong Women, Strong Girls Internship   1:72–73
SUNY Albany Summer Research
Experience for Undergraduates   2:281–282
Texas Instruments Internship   2:363–364
Toyota Motor North America Internship 1:194–195
University of Massachusetts Medical
School Undergraduate Summer NIH
Research Fellowship Program   2:288
U.S. Department of Energy's Science
Undergraduate Lab Internship (SULI) 2:289–294
Washington State Governor's Internship   1:352

Sophomores

Abbott Laboratories Environmental,
Health, and Safety Internship   2:5
Abbott Laboratories Internship   1:165–166
Academy of Television Arts and
Sciences Foundation Internship   1:241–245
Aerospace Corporation Internship   2:329
Agilent Technologies Internship   2:329–330
American Forests Internship   1:193–195

American Friends Service Committee
International Internship   2:77–78
American Institute for Foreign Study—
Cannes Internship   2:78–79
American Institute for Foreign Study—
Florence Internship   2:79–80
American Institute for Foreign Study—
London Internship   2:80–81
American Institute for Foreign Study—
Sydney Internship   2:81–81
American Public Health Association
Internship   2:9
American School for the Deaf Internship 1:203–204
American Society for Microbiology
Research Internship   2:228–229
Apple Computer Internship   2:331–333
Archives of American Art Internship   1:121–122
Arena Stage Internship   1:251–254
Axle Alliance Group Internship   1:167
Boston Ballet Internship   1:256–257
Boston Museum of Science Internship   1:205–210
Brooklyn Parents for Peace Internship   1:34–35
Callaway Advanced Technology
Internship   2:335–336
Center for Arts and Culture Internship   1:123–124
Chicago Bears Graphic Design Internship   2:303
Chicago Historical Society Internship   1:124–125
Children's Museum of Indianapolis
Internship   1:211–217
Chincoteague National Wildlife Refuge
Internship   2:202–203
Cold Spring Harbor Lab Summer
Internship   2:235–235
Cooperative Center for Study Abroad:
Ireland Internship   2:99
Cooper-Hewitt, National Design
Museum Internship   1:126–127
Corcoran Gallery of Art Internship   1:128–129
Dallas Theater Center Internship   1:259–260
Dallas Theater Center SummerStage
Internship   1:260
Dance Place Internship   1:260–261
Dell Computer Internship   2:337–338
Disney's Animal Kingdom Advanced
Internship   1:88–91
Dow Chemical Company Internship   2:338

DreamWorks SKG Internship 1:263–264
Duke University Neurosciences Summer Research Program in Mechanisms of Behavior 2:238
DuPont Engineering Internship 2:238–239
EarthTrends Summer Internship 1:44–45
Eastman Kodak Internship 2:338–339
E! Entertainment Talent/Casting Internship 1:265–267
Federal Bureau of Investigation (FBI) Washington Internship for Native Students (WINS) 1:327–328
Fermilab Summer Internship in Science and Technology 2:339–340
Field Museum Internship 1:129–130
Fort Wayne Children's Zoo Veterinary Medicine Internship 1:93–94
Freer Gallery of Art/Arthur M. Sackler Gallery Internship 1:130–131
General Electric Internship 1:177–178
Genesis Animal Sanctuary Summer Internship 1:95–96
Grey Towers National Historic Site Internship 2:49–50
Guggenheim Museum Internship 1:133–135
Harvard University Summer Research Program in Ecology 2:243–245
HBO Internship 2:153–155
Hilltop Farm Inc. Internship 1:97
Historic Preservation Internship Training Program 1:218–219
IBM Extreme Blue Internship 2:340–342
Independence Seaport Museum Internship 1:219
Institute of Ecosystem Studies Internship 2:246–250
Intel Internship 2:342–343
Japanese American National Museum Internship 1:219–221
Jim Henson Company Internship 1:274–276
Lam Research Internship 2:343
Lexmark Internship 2:343–344
Literacy Partners Inc. Internship 1:221
Living History Farms Internship 2:55–56
Los Alamos National Laboratory Internship 2:346–348
Los Angeles Lakers Internship 2:314

Los Angeles Opera Community Programs Internship 1:284
Lunar and Planetary Institute Summer Intern Program 2:348
Marathon Oil Corporation Internship 2:349–350
Marathon Oil Corporation/UNCF Corporate Scholars Program 2:350
Mercedes-Benz USA Internship 1:189
Merck Family Fund Internship 1:55–56
Merck Internship 1:189–190
Mickey Leland Energy Fellowships 2:254–255
Microsoft Internship 2:350–353
Motorola Internship 2:353–354
Mount Desert Island Biological Lab Research Fellowships for Undergraduates 2:255––256
MSNBC Internship 2:164–166
Mystic Aquarium Internship 1:99–101
NASA Kennedy Space Center Space Flight and Life Sciences Training Program 2:256–259
NASCAR Diversity Internship 2:314–315
National Air and Space Museum Internship 1:221–222
National Anthropological Archives Internship 1:222–223
National Aquarium in Baltimore Internship 1:101–102
National Building Museum Internship 1:223–224
National Endowment for the Arts Internship 1:146–147
National Environmental Law Center Internship 1:57
National Instruments Internship 2:354–355
National Museum of African Art Internship 1:150
National Museum of American History Internship 1:224–225
National Museum of Natural History Internship 2:261–262
National Museum of the American Indian Internship 1:225–226
National Portrait Gallery Internship 1:152–155
National Science Foundation Research Experience for Undergraduates (REU) 2:263–264
National Semiconductor Internship 2:356–357

National Trust for Historic Preservation
  Internship   2:68–69
National Zoo Beaver Valley Internship   1:103–104
NBC Internship   2:168
NCR Internship   2:357
New American Dream
  Communications Internship   1:58–59
Nuclear Regulatory Commission
  Historically Black Colleges and
  Universities Student Research
  Internship   2:267–268
Oracle Corporation Internship   2:357–358
Pacific Gas and Electric Company
  Internship   2:358–359
Packer Foundation Engineering
  Internship   2:359–360
Pfizer Internship   1:190–192
Pfizer Research and Development
  Internship   2:273–274
Philadelphia Zoo Internship   1:108–109
Physicians for Social Responsibility
  Internship   1:62–63
Pratt & Whitney Co-op and Internship   2:360–361
Public Leadership Education Network
  Internship   1:66–67
Rockefeller University Summer
  Undergraduate Research Fellowship   2:275–276
Rocky Mountain Biological Laboratory
  Summer Internship   2:276–277
Santa Fe Institute Internship   2:361–362
Santé Group Internship   1:69
Seattle Times Internship   2:181
Seeds of Peace Internship   1:69–70
Share Our Strength Internship   1:70–71
Silicon Graphics Inc. (SGI) Internship   2:362–363
Smithsonian Astrophysical Observatory
  Internship   2:279–280
South Street Seaport Museum Internship   1:230–231
Stanford Linear Accelerator Center
  Summer Fellowship   2:280–281
St. Petersburg Times Summer Internship   2:182–183
Strong Women, Strong Girls Internship   1:72–73
SUNY Albany Summer Research
  Experience for Undergraduates   2:281–282
Texas Film Commission Internship   1:309–310
Texas Instruments Internship   2:363–364

Toyota Motor North America Internship   1:194–195
University of California-Davis
  Undergraduate Summer Training in
  Environmental Toxicology   2:282
University of Colorado at Boulder
  Summer Minority Access to Research
  Training   2:283–285
University of Massachusetts Medical
  School Summer Enrichment Program   2:287–288
University of Massachusetts Medical
  School Undergraduate Summer NIH
  Research Fellowship Program   2:288
University of Texas-Houston Health
  Science Center Summer Research
  Program   2:288–289
USA Today Summer Internship   2:186
U.S. Department of Energy's Science
  Undergraduate Lab Internship (SULI)   2:289–294
Verizon College Internship   1:195–196
Washington Internship for Native
  Students (WINS)   1:349–350
Washington Leadership Summer
  Internship Seminar for Native
  American Students   1:350–352
Washington State Governor's Internship   1:352
West Virginia Governor's Internship   1:353
Wilma Theater Internship   1:312
Wolf Trap Internship   1:312–314
Zoo Atlanta Internship   1:116–117

Juniors

Abbott Laboratories Environmental,
  Health, and Safety Internship   2:5
Abbott Laboratories Internship   1:165–166
ABC John Stossel Specials Internship   2:117
ABC News Internship   2:118–120
ABC News *PrimeTime Live* Internship   2:120
ABC News Radio Internship   2:120–121
ABC News Special Events Internship   2:121
ABC News Washington Bureau
  Internship   2:121–122
ABC *Weekend News* Internship   2:122–123
ABC *World News Tonight* Internship   2:123
Academy of Television Arts and
  Sciences Foundation Internship   1:241–245
Aerospace Corporation Internship   2:329

Agilent Technologies Internship   2:329–330

AIESEC Internship   2:77

Amazon.com Software Development Engineer Internship   2:330–331

American Enterprise Institute Internship   1:317–318

American Farmland Trust Internship   2:193

American Forests Internship   2:193–195

American Friends Service Committee International Internship   2:77–78

American Institute for Foreign Study— Cannes Internship   2:78–79

American Institute for Foreign Study— Florence Internship   2:79–80

American Institute for Foreign Study— London Internship   2:80–81

American Institute for Foreign Study— Sydney Internship   2:81–81

American Public Health Association Internship   2:9

American-Scandinavian Foundation Internship   2:82–83

American School for the Deaf Internship   1:203–204

American Society for Microbiology Research Internship   2:228–229

Amnesty International—Washington, D.C. Internship   1:30–32

Apple Computer Internship   2:331–333

Archives of American Art Internship   1:121–122

Arena Stage Internship   1:251–254

Art Institute of Chicago Internship   1:122–123

Associated Press Broadcast News Internship   2:130–131

Associated Press Internship   2:129–130

Atlanta Journal Constitution Internship   2:131–132

Atlantic Monthly Internship   2:132–133

Atlantic Monthly Web Site Content Internship   2:133

AT&T Undergraduate Research Program   2:333

Audubon Internship   2:133–132

Aullwood *Audubon* Center and Farm Internship   2:199–200

Austin American-Statesman Internship   2:134–135

Australian Embassy Internship   2:83

Axle Alliance Group Internship   1:167

Ball Aerospace Internship   2:334

BalletMet Internship   1:254–255

Bettis Atomic Power Lab Internship   2:229–230

Boston Ballet Internship   1:256–257

Boston Celtics Internship   2:301–302

Boston Museum of Science Internship   1:205–210

Brooklyn Children's Museum Internship   1:210

Brooklyn Parents for Peace Internship   1:34–35

Buffalo Bill Historical Center Internship   2:40–43

California Academy of Science A. Crawford Cooley Internship in California Botany   2:230–231

California Academy of Science Robert T. Wallace Undergraduate Research Internship   2:231–232

Callaway Advanced Technology Internship   2:335–336

The Carter Center Internship   1:35–43

CBS-4 (KCNC-TV) Sports Department Internship   2:302–303

CBS News Internship   2:137–140

Center for Arts and Culture Internship   1:123–124

Chicago Bears Graphic Design Internship   2:303

Chicago Historical Society Internship   1:124–125

Chicago Tribune Internship   2:142

Chicago Zoological Society Brookfield Zoo Internship   1:85–87

Children's Museum of Indianapolis Internship   1:211–217

Children's Television Workshop Internship   1:258–259

Chincoteague National Wildlife Refuge Internship   2:202–203

Chrysler Group Internship   1:172

CIIT Centers for Health Research Internship   2:15–16

Cleveland Plain Dealer Internship   2:143

CNN News Internship   2:143–145

Cold Spring Harbor Lab Summer Internship   2:235–236

Cooperative Center for Study Abroad: Ireland Internship   2:99

Cooper-Hewitt, National Design Museum Internship   1:126–127

Corcoran Gallery of Art Internship   1:128–129

Dallas Theater Center Internship   1:259–260

Dallas Theater Center SummerStage Internship   1:260

Dance Place Internship — 1:260–261

D. C. Booth Historic Fish Hatchery Internship — 2:46

Dell Computer Internship — 2:337–338

Disney's Animal Kingdom Advanced Internship — 1:88–91

Dolphin Institute Internship — 1:91–92

Dow Chemical Company Internship — 2:338

DreamWorks SKG Internship — 1:263–264

Duke University Neurosciences Summer Research Program in Mechanisms of Behavior — 2:238

DuPont Engineering Internship — 2:238–239

DuPont Summer Internship — 1:173

EarthTrends Summer Internship — 1:44–45

Eastman Kodak Internship — 2:338–339

E! Entertainment Talent/Casting Internship — 1:265–267

Entertainment Weekly Internship — 2:150–151

Ernst & Young Internship — 1:173–174

Federal Bureau of Investigation (FBI) Washington Internship for Native Students (WINS) — 1:327–328

Fermilab Summer Internship in Science and Technology — 2:339–340

Field Museum Internship — 1:129–130

Ford Motor Company Internship — 1:174–177

Fort Wayne Children's Zoo Veterinary Medicine Internship — 1:93–94

Fossil Rim Wildlife Center Internship — 1:94–95

Freer Gallery of Art/Arthur M. Sackler Gallery Internship — 1:130–131

Genentech Internship — 2:239–240

General Electric Internship — 1:177–178

Genesis Animal Sanctuary Summer Internship — 1:95–96

Georgia Governor's Internship — 1:329–330

GlaxoSmithKline Internship — 2:240–241

Grey Towers National Historic Site Internship — 2:49–50

Guggenheim Museum Internship — 1:133–135

Harvard School of Public Health Minority Internship — 2:22–23

Harvard University Summer Research Program in Ecology — 2:243–245

HBO Internship — 2:153–155

The Hermitage (Home of Andrew Jackson) Internship — 2:51–52

Hilltop Farm Inc. Internship — 1:97

Historic Preservation Internship Training Program — 1:218–219

Howard Hughes Honors Summer Institute — 2:245–246

IBM Extreme Blue Internship — 2:340–342

Idaho Lieutenant Governor's Internship — 1:330

Independence Seaport Museum Internship — 1:219

Institute of Ecosystem Studies Internship — 2:246–250

Intel Internship — 2:342–343

Japanese American National Museum Internship — 1:219–221

Jim Henson Company Internship — 1:274–276

Kennedy Center for the Performing Arts Management Internship — 1:280–282

Kraft Foods Internship — 1:182–183

KTTV-TV (Los Angeles) Internship — 2:159

Lam Research Internship — 2:343

Lands' End Internship — 1:183–185

Leadership Alliance Summer Internship — 2:251–252

Lexmark Internship — 2:343–344

Literacy Partners Inc. Internship — 1:221

Living History Farms Internship — 2:55–56

Lockheed Martin Internship — 2:344–345

Los Alamos National Laboratory Internship — 2:346–348

Los Angeles Lakers Internship — 2:314

Los Angeles Opera Community Programs Internship — 1:284

Lucas Digital Internship — 1:284–286

Lucasfilm Internship — 1:286–287

Lucent Technologies Summer Internship — 1:185–186

Lunar and Planetary Institute Summer Intern Program — 2:348

Macy's Internship — 1:187–189

Marathon Oil Corporation Internship — 2:349–350

Mercedes-Benz USA Internship — 1:189

Merck Family Fund Internship — 1:55–56

Merck Internship — 1:189–190

Metropolitan Museum of Art Internship — 1:139–140

Miami Herald Internship — 2:161–162

Michael Perez Gallery Internship — 1:140

Michigan Executive Office Internship — 1:336–338

Mickey Leland Energy Fellowships — 2:254–255

Microsoft Internship   2:350–353
Minnesota Historical Society Internship   2:56–60
Motorola Internship   2:353–354
Mount Desert Island Biological
  Lab Research Fellowships for
  Undergraduates   2:255––256
MSNBC Internship   2:164–166
MTV Networks Internship—Nashville   1:288
MTV Networks Internship—New York
  City   1:288–289
Museum of Contemporary Art San
  Diego Internship   1:140–142
Museum of Modern Art Internship   1:142–146
Mystic Aquarium Internship   1:99–101
NASA Kennedy Space Center Space
  Flight and Life Sciences Training
  Program   2:256–259
NASCAR Diversity Internship   2:314–315
NASCAR Internship   2:315–316
National Air and Space Museum
  Internship   1:221–222
National Anthropological Archives
  Internship   1:222–223
National Aquarium in Baltimore
  Internship   1:101–102
National Building Museum Internship   1:223–224
National Endowment for the Arts
  Internship   1:146–147
National Environmental Law Center
  Internship   1:57
National Instruments Internship   2:354–355
National Museum of African Art Internship   1:150
National Museum of American History
  Internship   1:224–225
National Museum of Natural History
  Internship   2:261–262
National Museum of the American
  Indian Internship   1:225–226
National Museum of Women in the
  Arts Internship   1:150–152
National Portrait Gallery Internship   1:152–155
National Renewable Energy Laboratory
  Internship   2:355–356
National Science Foundation Research
  Experience for Undergraduates (REU)   2:263–264
National Semiconductor Internship   2:356–357

National Trust for Historic Preservation
  Internship   2:68–69
National Zoo Beaver Valley Internship   1:103–104
NBC Internship   2:168
NCR Internship   2:357
New American Dream
  Communications Internship   1:58–59
New York Daily News Graphics
  Designer Internship   2:169
New York Daily News Internship   2:169–170
New York Rangers Internship   2:316
New York Times Copyediting Internship   2:170
New York Times Graphics, Design, and
  Photography Internship   2:171–172
New York University School of
  Medicine Summer Undergraduate
  Research Program (SURP)   2:266–267
Nightline Internship   2:172–173
Nuclear Regulatory Commission
  Historically Black Colleges and
  Universities Student Research
  Internship   2:267–268
Office of Naval Research Internship   2:268–273
Oklahoma Governor's Internship   1:345
Oracle Corporation Internship   2:357–358
Orlando Magic Internship   2:316–321
Orlando Sentinel Internship   2:173–174
Pacific Gas and Electric Company
  Internship   2:358–359
Packer Foundation Engineering
  Internship   2:359–360
Pfizer Internship   1:190–192
Pfizer Research and Development
  Internship   2:273–274
Philadelphia Inquirer Minority Internship   2:174–175
Philadelphia Inquirer Nonminority
  Copyediting and Graphics Arts
  Internship   2:175
Philadelphia Museum of Art Internship   1:157–158
Philadelphia Phantoms Internship   2:322–323
Philadelphia 76ers Internship   2:323–324
Philadelphia Zoo Internship   1:108–109
Population Institute Internship   2:30
Pratt & Whitney Co-op and Internship   2:360–361
Public Leadership Education Network
  Internship   1:66–67

Random House Inc. Summer Internship 1:192–193
Reuters Internship 2:175–176
Rockefeller University Summer
  Undergraduate Research Fellowship 2:275–276
Rocky Mountain Biological Laboratory
  Summer Internship 2:276–277
Roswell Park Cancer Institute Summer
  College Internship 2:277
San Diego Museum of Art—Education
  Internship 1:229
Santa Fe Institute Internship 2:361–362
Santé Group Internship 1:69
Seattle Times Internship 2:181
SeaWorld Adventure Camp Internship 1:109–111
Seeds of Peace Internship 1:69–70
Share Our Strength Internship 1:70–71
Silicon Graphics Inc. (SGI) Internship 2:362–363
Smithsonian Astrophysical Observatory
  Internship 2:279–280
South Street Seaport Museum
  Internship 1:230–231
Stanford Linear Accelerator Center
  Summer Fellowship 2:280–281
St. Petersburg Times Summer Internship 2:182–183
Strong Women, Strong Girls Internship 1:72–73
SUNY Albany Summer Research
  Experience for Undergraduates 2:281–282
Texas Film Commission Internship 1:309–310
Texas Instruments Internship 2:363–364
Tiger Creek Wildlife Refuge Internship 1:112–113
Time Inc. Summer Internship 2:185–186
Toyota Motor North America Internship 1:194–195
University of California-Davis
  Undergraduate Summer Training in
  Environmental Toxicology 2:282
University of Colorado at Boulder
  Summer Minority Access to Research
  Training 2:283–285
University of Massachusetts Medical
  School Summer Enrichment Program 2:287–288
University of Massachusetts Medical
  School Undergraduate Summer NIH
  Research Fellowship Program 2:288
University of Massachusetts
  Undergraduate Research in Ecology
  and Conservation Biology 2:284–286

University of Texas-Houston Health
  Science Center Summer Research
  Program 2:288–289
USA Today Summer Internship 2:186
U.S. Department of Energy's Science
  Undergraduate Lab Internship (SULI) 2:289–294
U.S. News & World Report Internship 2:186–187
U.S. Supreme Court Internship 1:347–349
Vermont Governor's Internship 1:349
Very Special Arts (VSA) Internship 1:159
Virginia Institute of Marine Science
  Internship 2:294–296
WakeMed Health and Hospitals Internship 2:33–34
Washington Internship for Native
  Students (WINS) 1:349–350
Washington Leadership Summer
  Internship Seminar for Native
  American Students 1:350–352
Washington Post Internship 2:189–190
Washington State Governor's Internship 1:352
Wellesley College Biological Sciences
  Internship 2:296
West Virginia Governor's Internship 1:353
Whitney Museum of American Art
  Internship 1:159–160
Wild Horse Sanctuary Internship 1:113–114
Wilma Theater Internship 1:312
Wolf Trap Internship 1:312–314
WVSA Arts Connection Internship 1:160–162
Xerox Internship 2:364–365

Seniors

Abbott Laboratories Environmental,
  Health, and Safety Internship 2:5
Abbott Laboratories Internship 1:165–166
ABC John Stossel Specials Internship 2:117
ABC News Internship 2:118–120
ABC News PrimeTime Live Internship 2:120
ABC News Radio Internship 2:120–121
ABC News Special Events Internship 2:121
ABC News Washington Bureau
  Internship 2:121–122
ABC Weekend News Internship 2:122–123
ABC World News Tonight Internship 2:123
Academy of Television Arts and
  Sciences Foundation Internship 1:241–245

Aerospace Corporation Internship 2:329
Agilent Technologies Internship 2:329–330
AIESEC Internship 2:77
Amazon.com Software Development
  Engineer Internship 2:330–331
American Enterprise Institute Internship 1:317–318
American Farmland Trust Internship 2:193
American Forests Internship 2:193–195
American Friends Service Committee
  International Internship 2:77–78
American Institute for Foreign Study—
  Cannes Internship 2:78–79
American Institute for Foreign Study—
  Florence Internship 2:79–80
American Institute for Foreign Study—
  London Internship 2:80–81
American Institute for Foreign Study—
  Sydney Internship 2:81–81
American Public Health Association
  Internship 2:9
American-Scandinavian Foundation
  Internship 2:82–83
American School for the Deaf Internship 1:203–204
American Society for Microbiology
  Research Internship 2:228–229
American Society of Magazine Editors
  Internship 2:127–128
Amnesty International—Washington,
  D.C. Internship 1:30–32
Apple Computer Internship 2:331–333
Archives of American Art Internship 1:121–122
Arena Stage Internship 1:251–254
Art Institute of Chicago Internship 1:122–123
Associated Press Broadcast News
  Internship 2:130–131
Associated Press Internship 2:129–130
Atlanta Journal Constitution Internship 2:131–132
Atlantic Monthly Internship 2:132–133
Atlantic Monthly Web Site Content Internship 2:133
AT&T Undergraduate Research Program 2:333
Audubon Internship 2:133–132
Aullwood Audubon Center and Farm
  Internship 2:199–200
Austin American-Statesman Internship 2:134–135
Australian Embassy Internship 2:83
Axle Alliance Group Internship 1:167

Ball Aerospace Internship 2:334
BalletMet Internship 1:254–255
Baltimore Sun Two-Year Internship 2:135
Bettis Atomic Power Lab Internship 2:229–230
Boston Ballet Internship 1:256–257
Boston Celtics Internship 2:301–302
Boston Museum of Science Internship 1:205–210
Brooklyn Children's Museum Internship 1:210
Brooklyn Parents for Peace Internship 1:34–35
Buffalo Bill Historical Center Internship 2:40–43
California Academy of Science A.
  Crawford Cooley Internship in
  California Botany 2:230–231
California Academy of Science Robert
  T. Wallace Undergraduate Research
  Internship 2:231–232
Callaway Advanced Technology
  Internship 2:335–336
Carnegie Endowment for International
  Peace Internship 2:97–98
The Carter Center Internship 1:35–43
CBS-4 (KCNC-TV) Sports Department
  Internship 2:302–303
CBS News Internship 2:137–140
Center for Arts and Culture Internship 1:123–124
Charlotte Observer Internship 2:141
Chicago Bears Graphic Design Internship 2:303
Chicago Historical Society Internship 1:124–125
Chicago Tribune Internship 2:142
Chicago Zoological Society Brookfield
  Zoo Internship 1:85–87
Children's Museum of Indianapolis
  Internship 1:211–217
Children's Television Workshop
  Internship 1:258–259
Chincoteague National Wildlife Refuge
  Internship 2:202–203
CIIT Centers for Health Research
  Internship 2:15–16
Cleveland Plain Dealer Internship 2:143
CNN News Internship 2:143–145
Cooperative Center for Study Abroad:
  Ireland Internship 2:99
Cooper-Hewitt, National Design
  Museum Internship 1:126–127
Corcoran Gallery of Art Internship 1:128–129

Costa Rica Internship Institute
Internship   2:100
Dallas Theater Center Internship   1:259–260
Dallas Theater Center SummerStage
Internship   1:260
Dance Place Internship   1:260–261
Daughters of the American Revolution
(DAR) Museum Internship   1:217–218
D. C. Booth Historic Fish Hatchery
Internship   2:46
Dell Computer Internship   2:337–338
Denver Post Reporting/Photography
Internship   2:148
Disney's Animal Kingdom Advanced
Internship   1:88–91
Dolphin Institute Internship   1:91–92
Dow Chemical Company Internship   2:338
DreamWorks SKG Internship   1:263–264
Duke University Neurosciences
Summer Research Program in
Mechanisms of Behavior   2:238
DuPont Engineering Internship   2:238–239
EarthTrends Summer Internship   1:44–45
Eastman Kodak Internship   2:338–339
E! Entertainment Talent/Casting
Internship   1:265–267
Entertainment Weekly Internship   2:150–151
Ernst & Young Internship   1:173–174
Federal Bureau of Investigation (FBI)
Washington Internship for Native
Students (WINS)   1:327–328
Fermilab Summer Internship in Science
and Technology   2:339–340
Field Museum Internship   1:129–130
Ford Motor Company Internship   1:174–177
Fort Wayne Children's Zoo Veterinary
Medicine Internship   1:93–94
Fossil Rim Wildlife Center Internship 1:94–95
Freer Gallery of Art/Arthur M. Sackler
Gallery Internship   1:130–131
Fresno Bee Internship   2:152
Friends of the Earth Internship   2:203–204
Genentech Internship   2:239–240
General Electric Internship   1:177–178
Georgia Governor's Internship   1:329–330
GlaxoSmithKline Internship   2:240–241

Grey Towers National Historic Site
Internship   2:49–50
Guggenheim Museum Internship   1:133–135
Hallmark Cards Internship   1:178–179
Harvard School of Public Health
Minority Internship   2:22–23
Harvard University Summer Research
Program in Ecology   2:243–245
HBO Internship   2:153–155
The Hermitage (Home of Andrew
Jackson) Internship   2:51–52
Hilltop Farm Inc. Internship   1:97
Historic Preservation Internship
Training Program   1:218–219
Howard Hughes Honors Summer
Institute   2:245–246
IBM Extreme Blue Internship   2:340–342
Idaho Lieutenant Governor's Internship 1:330
Independence Seaport Museum Internship 1:219
Institute of Ecosystem Studies
Internship   2:246–250
Intel Internship   2:342–343
Japanese American National Museum
Internship   1:219–221
Jim Henson Company Internship   1:274–276
Kennedy Center for the Performing
Arts Management Internship   1:280–282
KTTV-TV (Los Angeles) Internship   2:159
Lam Research Internship   2:343
Lands' End Internship   1:183–185
Leadership Alliance Summer Internship 2:251–252
Lexmark Internship   2:343–344
Literacy Partners Inc. Internship   1:221
Living History Farms Internship   2:55–56
Lockheed Martin Internship   2:344–345
Los Alamos National Laboratory
Internship   2:346–348
Los Angeles Lakers Internship   2:314
Los Angeles Opera Community
Programs Internship   1:284
Lucas Digital Internship   1:284–286
Lucasfilm Internship   1:286–287
Lucent Technologies Summer Internship 1:185–186
Lunar and Planetary Institute Internship 2:252–253
Lunar and Planetary Institute Summer
Intern Program   2:348

Macy's Internship 1:187–189
Marathon Oil Corporation Internship 2:349–350
Marine Biology Lab at Woods Hole
Marine Models in Biological Research
Internship 2:253–254
Maryland Governor's Summer Internship 1:335–336
Mercedes-Benz USA Internship 1:189
Merck Family Fund Internship 1:55–56
Merck Internship 1:189–190
Metropolitan Museum of Art Internship 1:139–140
Michael Perez Gallery Internship 1:140
Michigan Executive Office Internship 1:336–338
Mickey Leland Energy Fellowships 2:254–255
Microsoft Internship 2:350–353
Minnesota Historical Society Internship 2:56–60
Modesto Bee Internship 2:162–163
Motorola Internship 2:353–354
Mount Desert Island Biological
Lab Research Fellowships for
Undergraduates 2:255––256
MSNBC Internship 2:164–166
MTV Networks Internship—Nashville 1:288
MTV Networks Internship—
New York City 1:288–289
Museum of Contemporary Art San
Diego Internship 1:140–142
Museum of Modern Art Internship 1:142–146
Mystic Aquarium Internship 1:99–101
NASA Kennedy Space Center Space
Flight and Life Sciences Training
Program 2:256–259
NASCAR Diversity Internship 2:314–315
NASCAR Internship 2:315–316
National Air and Space Museum
Internship 1:221–222
National Anthropological Archives
Internship 1:222–223
National Aquarium in Baltimore
Internship 1:101–102
National Building Museum Internship 1:223–224
National Council for Preservation
Education Internship 2:61–68
National Endowment for the Arts
Internship 1:146–147
National Environmental Law Center
Internship 1:57

National Instruments Internship 2:354–355
National Museum of African Art Internship 1:150
National Museum of American History
Internship 1:224–225
National Museum of Natural History
Internship 2:261–262
National Museum of the American
Indian Internship 1:225–226
National Museum of Women in the
Arts Internship 1:150–152
National Portrait Gallery Internship 1:152–155
National Renewable Energy Laboratory
Internship 2:355–356
National Science Foundation Research
Experience for Undergraduates (REU) 2:263–264
National Semiconductor Internship 2:356–357
National Trust for Historic Preservation
Internship 2:68–69
National Zoo Beaver Valley Internship 1:103–104
NBC Internship 2:168
NCR Internship 2:357
New American Dream
Communications Internship 1:58–59
Newsweek Internship 2:168–169
New York Daily News Graphics
Designer Internship 2:169
New York Daily News Internship 2:169–170
New York Rangers Internship 2:316
New York Times Copyediting Internship 2:170
New York Times Graphics, Design and
Photography Internship 2:171–172
New York University Center for Neural
Science Undergraduate Summer
Research Program 2:265
New York University School of
Medicine Summer Undergraduate
Research Program (SURP) 2:266–267
Nightline Internship 2:172–173
Nuclear Regulatory Commission
Historically Black Colleges and
Universities Student Research
Internship 2:267–268
Office of Naval Research Internship 2:268–273
Oklahoma Governor's Internship 1:345
Oracle Corporation Internship 2:357–358
Orlando Magic Internship 2:316–321

Orlando Sentinel Internship   2:173–174
Pacific Gas and Electric Company
  Internship   2:358–359
Packer Foundation Engineering
  Internship   2:359–360
Pfizer Internship   1:190–192
Pfizer Research and Development
  Internship   2:273–274
Philadelphia Inquirer Minority
  Internship   2:174–175
Philadelphia Inquirer Nonminority
  Copyediting and Graphics Arts
  Internship   2:175
Philadelphia Museum of Art Internship   1:157–158
Philadelphia Phantoms Internship   2:322–323
Philadelphia 76ers Internship   2:323–324
Philadelphia Zoo Internship   1:108–109
Physicians for Social Responsibility
  Internship   1:62–63
Population Institute Internship   2:30
Pratt & Whitney Co-op and Internship   2:360–361
Public Leadership Education Network
  Internship   1:66–67
Reuters Internship   2:175–176
Rocky Mountain Biological Laboratory
  Summer Internship   2:276–277
Roswell Park Cancer Institute Summer
  College Internship   2:277
San Diego Chargers Internship   2:324–325
San Diego Museum of Art—Education
  Internship   1:229
Santé Group Internship   1:69
Science Magazine Internship   2:179–180
Science News Internship   2:180–181
Seattle Times Internship   2:181
Seeds of Peace Internship   1:69–70
Share Our Strength Internship   1:70–71
Silicon Graphics Inc. (SGI) Internship   2:362–363
Smithsonian Astrophysical Observatory
  Internship   2:279–280
South Street Seaport Museum
  Internship   1:230–231
Stanford Linear Accelerator Center
  Summer Fellowship   2:280–281
St. Petersburg Times Summer Internship   2:182–183
Strong Women, Strong Girls Internship   1:72–73

SUNY Albany Summer Research
  Experience for Undergraduates   2:281–282
Texas Film Commission Internship   1:309–310
Texas Instruments Internship   2:363–364
Tiger Creek Wildlife Refuge Internship   1:112–113
Time Inc. Summer Internship   2:185–186
Toyota Motor North America Internship   1:194–195
University of California-Davis
  Undergraduate Summer Training in
  Environmental Toxicology   2:282
University of Colorado at Boulder
  Summer Minority Access to Research
  Training   2:283–285
University of Massachusetts Medical
  School Undergraduate Summer NIH
  Research Fellowship Program   2:288
University of Massachusetts
  Undergraduate Research in Ecology
  and Conservation Biology   2:284–286
University of Texas-Houston Health
  Science Center Summer Research
  Program   2:288–289
USA Today Summer Internship   2:186
U.S. Department of Energy's Science
  Undergraduate Lab Internship (SULI)   2:289–294
U.S. News & World Report Internship   2:186–187
U.S. Supreme Court Internship   1:347–349
Vermont Governor's Internship   1:349
Very Special Arts (VSA) Internship   1:159
Virginia Institute of Marine Science
  Internship   2:294–296
WakeMed Health and Hospitals
  Internship   2:33–34
Washington Internship for Native
  Students (WINS)   1:349–350
Washington Leadership Summer
  Internship Seminar for Native
  American Students   1:350–352
Washington Post Internship   2:189–190
Washington State Governor's Internship   1:352
Wellesley College Biological Sciences
  Internship   2:296
West Virginia Governor's Internship   1:353
Whitney Museum of American Art
  Internship   1:159–160
Wild Horse Sanctuary Internship   1:113–114

Wilma Theater Internship   1:312
Wolf Trap Internship   1:312–314
WVSA Arts Connection Internship   1:160–162
Xerox Internship   2:364–365

UNSPECIFIED
FOR COLLEGE STUDENTS

The Aark Wildlife Rehabilitation Internship   1:81
ABC *Good Morning America* Internship   2:117
ABC-TV Channel 7 (Los Angeles) Internship   2:122
Acadia National Park Education Internship   1:201
ACCION International Internship   1:27
Actors Theatre Workshop Internship   1:245–246
The Ad Club (Boston) Internship   2:124
Administration on Aging Internship   2:6
Advertising Club Internship   2:124–125
Advocates for Youth Internship   1:27–28
Akron Beacon Journal Internship   2:125
Amelia Island Internship   1:166–167
American Association for the Advancement of Science Entry Point Internship   2:226–227
American Association for the Advancement of Science Internship   2:225–226
American Cancer Society Internship   2:6–7
American Civil Liberties Union Immigrants Rights Project Internship   1:28–29
American Civil Liberties Union Internship   1:29–30
American Conservatory Theater Internship   1:246–250
American Dance Festival Internship   1:250–251
American Folklife Center Internship   1:201–202
American Foundation for the Blind Internship   2:7
American Geographical Society Internship   1:202–203, 2:227–228
American Lung Association Internship   2:8
American Red Cross Internship   2:9–13
American Red Cross Media Internship   2:126
American Rivers Internship   2:195–197
Anacostia Museum and Center for African American History and Culture Internship   2:39
Anasazi Heritage Center Internship   1:204–205
Anchorage Daily News Internship   2:128–129
The Antarctica Project Internship   2:197

Arizona Legislative Internship   1:318–320
Arnold Arboretum of Harvard University Internship   2:197–198
Art Museum of the Americas Internship   1:123
Asian Pacific American Institute for Congressional Studies Internship   1:320–322
Aspen Center for Environmental Studies Internship   2:198–199
Atlanta Ballet Internship   1:254
Bangor Daily News Internship   2:135–136
Bay Nature Magazine Internship   2:200–201
Beaver Dam Farm Equine Internship   1:81–83
Bechtel Corporation Internship   1:167
Bechtel Internship   2:334–335
Berkshire Theater Festival Internship   1:255–256
Best Friends Animal Society Internship   1:83–84
Beyond Pesticides Internship   1:32–33
Big Cat Rescue Internship   1:84–85
Blethen Maine Newspapers Minority Summer Internship   2:136
Boeing Internship   1:168–169
Boston Environment Department Internship   1:33–34
Boston Globe Internship   2:136–137
Boston University Internship Abroad—Auckland Internship   2:83–84
Boston University Internship Abroad—Beijing Internship   2:84–85
Boston University Internship Abroad—Dresden Internship   2:85–86
Boston University Internship Abroad—Dublin Internship   2:86–87
Boston University Internship Abroad—Geneva Internship   2:87
Boston University Internship Abroad—Haifa Internship   2:88
Boston University Internship Abroad—London Internship   2:88–90
Boston University Internship Abroad—Madrid Internship   2:90–91
Boston University Internship Abroad—Paris Internship   2:91–92
Boston University Internship Abroad—Sydney Internship   2:92–93
Brooklyn Parents for Peace Internship   1:34–35
Buchanan/Burnham Internship   2:39–40

California Academy of Science
   Internship in Biological Illustration   2:231
California Governor's Internship   1:322–323
Callaway Gardens Internship   2:201
Camp Counselors USA—European Day
   Camps   2:93–95
Camp Counselors USA—Russia   2:95
Camp Counselors USA—United Kingdom   2:96
Canadian Embassy Internship   2:96–97
Capitol Hill Internship   1:323–324
Center for Food Safety Internship   2:15
Center for Science in the Public Interest
   Internship   2:232–235
Center for Women in Politics and
   Public Policy Internship   1:43
Center for World Indigenous Studies
   Internship   2:98–99
Central Intelligence Agency Internship   1:324–325
Cessna Internship   1:169
ChevronTexaco Engineering Internship   1:170–172
Chicago Children's Museum Internship   1:210–211
Chicago Sun-Times Minority
   Scholarship and Internship Program   2:141–142
Chicago Symphony Orchestra Internship   1:257–258
Christie's Internship   1:125–126
Chronicle of Higher Education Internship   2:142–143
Cisco Systems Internship   2:336–337
Colonial Williamsburg Internship   2:43–46
Colorado Springs Sky Sox Internship   2:304–306
Columbia Journalism Review Internship   2:145
Common Cause Internship   1:43–44
Connecticut Governor's Prevention
   Partnership Internship   1:325–326
Cornell University Materials Science
   Research Internship   2:236–237
Cornell University Plant Genome
   Research Program Internship   2:237
Council on Foreign Relations Internship   2:100–101
Council on Hemispheric Affairs
   (COHA) Internship   2:101–103
C-SPAN TV (Washington, D.C.)
   Internship   2:145–147
Dallas Morning News Internship   2:147–148
Democratic National Committee
   Internship   1:326–327
Denver Zoo Internship   1:87–88

Des Moines Register Internship   2:148–149
Detroit Free Press Internship   2:149
Doctors Without Borders Internship   2:16–18
Dow Jones Newspaper Fund Minority
   Summer Internship   2:149–150
Dreamtime Festival Internship   1:261–263
The Economist Internship   2:103–104
Eisenhower National Historic Site
   Internship   2:46–47
Elizabeth Glaser Pediatric AIDS
   Foundation Internship   2:18–19
El Pueblo de Los Angeles Historical
   Monument Multicultural Summer
   Internship   2:47–48
Eugene O'Neill Theater Internship   1:267–269
EurekAlert! Web Site Internship   2:151–152
Farm Sanctuary Internship   1:92–93
Florida Governor's Internship   1:328–329
Folger Shakespeare Library Internship   1:269
Friends Committee on National
   Legislation (FCNL) Internship   1:45–46
Frontier Nursing Service Internship   2:19–20
Gay Men's Health Crisis Internship   2:20–21
Geddes Talent Agency Internship   1:270
Georgia State Park and Historic Sites
   Internship   2:48–49
Glimmerglass Opera Internship   1:270–274
Gould Farm Internship   2:21–22
Government Accountability Project
   Internship   1:47
Greenbelt Alliance Internship   1:47–48
Hansard Society Scholars Program   2:104–105
Harvard University Summer Honors
   Undergraduate Research Program   2:242–243
Hawk Mountain Sanctuary Internship   2:204–206
Head Start National Internship   2:23–24
Hermitage Foundation Museum
   Internship   2:51
Hewlett-Packard Internship   1:179
Hirshhorn Museum and Sculpture
   Garden Internship   1:135–136
Historic Deerfield Summer Fellowship   2:52–54
Historic Preservation Internship
   Training Program   2:54–55
Houston Zoo Internship   1:97–98
Illinois Governor's Internship   1:330–331

IMG International Internship   1:179–180
Indiana Pacers Internship   2:306–311
Initiative for a Competitive Inner City
    Internship   1:51
INROADS Internship   1:181–182
International Atomic Energy Agency
    Internship   2:105–107
International Center for Tolerance
    Education Internship   1:51–52
International Child Art Foundation
    Internship   1:136–137
International Diplomacy Council
    Internship   1:52–53
Jackson Laboratory Summer Student
    Program   2:250–251
Jane Goodall Institute Internship   2:206–208
Juilliard School Professional Internship   1:276–280
Julia Morgan Center for the Arts
    Internship   1:137–138
Kaiser Media Minority Internship in
    Urban Health Reporting   2:155–156
Kansas City Blades Internship   2:311–312
Knight Ridder Internship for Native
    American Journalists   2:157–158
KOCE Public TV (Huntington Beach,
    Calif.) Internship   2:158
KPNX-TV (Phoenix) Internship   2:158
Kroenke Sports Enterprises Internship   2:312–314
The Late Show with David Letterman
    Internship   1:282–283
Library of Congress Internship   1:331–335
Liz Claiborne Summer Internship   1:185
Longwood Gardens Internship   2:208–214
Longwood Gardens Performing Arts
    Internship   1:283–284
Los Angeles Times Internship   2:159–160
Maine State Governor's Internship   1:335
Marvel Comics Internship   2:160–161
Mattel Internship   1:186–187
MediaRights Internship   1:53–55
Metro-Goldwyn-Mayer (MGM)
    Internship   1:287–288
Morris Arboretum of the University
    of Pennsylvania Internship   2:214–217
Mother Jones Internship   2:163
Mount Vernon Summer Internship   2:60–61
MSNBC Multimedia Internship   2:166

MTV Networks Internship—
    Santa Monica   1:289–290
MTV Networks Latin America
    Internship—Miami Beach   1:290
National Association of Black
    Journalists Summer Journalism
    Internship   2:166–168
National Campaign to Prevent Teen
    Pregnancy Internship   1:56–57
National Endowment for the Arts
    Internship   1:290–291
National Healthy Mothers, Healthy
    Babies Coalition Internship   2:25–26
National Institutes of Health Summer
    Internship Programs in Biomedical
    Research   2:259–261
National Mental Health Association
    Internship   2:26–28
National Organization for Women
    (NOW) Internship   1:58
National Park Foundation Internship   2:217–218
New England Wildlife Center Internship   1:103–104
New Jersey Governor's Internship   1:338–339
New Museum of Contemporary Art
    Internship   1:155–157
The New Press Internship   1:60
New York City Summer Internship   1:339–343
New York State Theatre Institute
    Internship   1:291–292
New York Times Reporting Fellowship   2:172
Nickelodeon Animation Studio Internship   1:292
North Carolina Governor's Internship   1:344–345
Old Sturbridge Village Internship   2:69–70
One Reel Internship   1:292–294
Oregon Governor's Internship   1:345–346
Oregon Zoo Internship   1:105–106
Other Hand Productions Puppet
    Internship   1:294–295
Paramount Pictures/Dr. Phil Show
    Internship   1:295
Peaceworks Foundation Internship   1:61
Pendle Hill Social Justice Internship   1:61–62
Pennsylvania Department of Public
    Health Internship   2:29
Performance Research Internship   2:321–322
Philadelphia Orchestra Association
    Internship   1:295–297

Portland Children's Museum Internship   1:226–229
Preservation Action Internship   2:70–71
Prison Activist Resource Center Internship   1:65–66
Pulmonary Hypertension Association
   Internship   2:31–32
Radio Disney—Boston Internship   1:297
Rainforest Action Network Internship   1:67–68
Raytheon Internship   1:193
Republican National Committee
   Internship   1:346–347
RKO Pictures Internship   1:297–298
Rocky Mountain PBS-TV Studio and
   Production Internship   2:176–177
Sacramento Bee Internship   2:177
San Francisco Chronicle Summer
   Internship   2:177–178
San Francisco Chronicle Two-Year
   Internship   2:178–179
San Francisco Mime Troupe Internship   1:299–300
Seattle Art Museum Internship   1:158–159
Second Stage Theatre Internship   1:300–302
Seeds of Peace Internship   1:69–70
Shakespeare Theatre Internship   1:302–304
Sierra Club Internship   1:71–72
Sierra Magazine Internship   2:181–182
Silent Spring Institute Internship   2:32–33
Smithsonian Architectural History
   and Historic Preservation Division
   Internship   2:71
Smithsonian Folkways Recording
   Internship   1:304–305
South Carolina Governor's Internship   1:347
South Shore Music Circus Internship   1:305–306
Spoleto Festival USA Internship   1:306–308
Strides Therapeutic Riding Center
   Internship   1:111–112
Student Climate Outreach Internship   2:218–219
Student Conservation Association
   Internship   2:219–221
The Studio Theatre Internship   1:308–309
Surgeons of Hope Foundation Internship   2:33
Tampa Tribune Internship   2:183–184
Teach for America National Internship   1:231–232
Teen People Summer Internship   2:184–185
Toledo Mud Hens Baseball Club Internship   2:325
20/20 Vision Internship   1:73
Tyson Foods Internship   1:195

United Nations Association of the USA
   Internship   1:74
U.S. Capitol Historical Society Internship   2:71–72
U.S. Department of Education Internship   1:233
U.S. Holocaust Memorial Museum
   Internship   1:233–234
Wall Street Journal Internship   2:187
Walt Disney World Culinary Internship   1:196–197
Walt Disney World Summer Jobs   1:310–312
Washington, D.C., Department of
   Health Internship   2:34–35
Washington Food Coalition Internship   1:74–75
Washingtonian Advertising Internship   2:188
Washingtonian Art Department
   Internship   2:188–1889
Washingtonian Editorial Internship   2:189
White House Internship   1:353–357
Whitney Laboratory Marine
   Biomedical Research Experience for
   Undergraduates   2:296–297
Wildlife Rescue and Rehabilitation
   Internship   1:114
Wisconsin Governor's Internship   1:357–358
Wolfsong Ranch Foundation Internship   1:114–115
Women for Peace Internship   1:75
Women's International League for Peace
   and Freedom Internship   2:108–111
Women Work Internship   1:75–77
Work Canada   2:111–113
World Affairs Council Internship   1:77
Wyckoff Farmhouse Museum Internship   2:73–74

GRADUATE STUDENTS

Academy of Television Arts and
   Sciences Foundation Internship   1:241–245
Administration on Aging Internship   2:6
American Association for the
   Advancement of Science Entry Point
   Internship   2:226–227
American Association for the
   Advancement of Science Internship   2:225–226
American Cancer Society Internship   2:6–7
American Conservatory Theater
   Internship   1:246–250
American Enterprise Institute Internship   1:317–318

American Geographical Society
Internship   2:227–228
American Public Health Association
Internship   2:9
American Red Cross Internship   2:9–13
American Red Cross Media Internship   2:126
American Rivers Internship   2:195–197
American School for the Deaf Internship 1:203–204
Amnesty International—Washington,
D.C. Internship   1:30–32
Anacostia Museum and Center for
African American History and
Culture Internship   2:39
The Antarctica Project Internship   2:197
Apple Computer Internship   2:331–333
Arizona Legislative Internship   1:318–320
Art Institute of Chicago Internship   1:122–123
Associated Press Broadcast News
Internship   2:130–131
Associated Press Internship   2:129–130
Atlanta Journal Constitution Internship 2:131–132
Atlantic Monthly Internship   2:132–133
Atlantic Monthly Web Site Content Internship   2:133
AT&T Undergraduate Research Program   2:333
Audubon Internship   2:133–132
Axle Alliance Group Internship   1:167
Bangor Daily News Internship   2:135–136
Bettis Atomic Power Lab Internship   2:229–230
Blethen Maine Newspapers Minority
Summer Internship   2:136
Boston Ballet Internship   1:256–257
Boston Celtics Internship   2:301–302
Boston Museum of Science Internship   1:205–210
Boys Hope, Girls Hope Internship   2:13–14
Bread for the City Legal Clinic Internship   1:34
Brooklyn Children's Museum Internship   1:210
Buchanan/Burnham Internship   2:39–40
Buffalo Bill Historical Center Internship 2:40–43
California Academy of Science
Internship in Biological Illustration   2:231
Callaway Advanced Technology
Internship   2:335–336
Canadian Embassy Internship   2:96–97
Capitol Hill Internship   1:323–324
The Carter Center Internship   1:35–43

Center for Adolescent Health and the
Law Internship   2:14–15
Center for Arts and Culture Internship 1:123–124
Center for Science in the Public Interest
Internship   2:232–235
Central Intelligence Agency Internship 1:324–325
Chicago Bulls Ticket Sales
Representative Internship   2:303–304
Chicago Historical Society Internship   1:124–125
Chicago Tribune Internship   2:142
Children's Museum of Indianapolis
Internship   1:211–217
Children's Television Workshop
Internship   1:258–259
CIIT Centers for Health Research
Internship   2:15–16
Cleveland Plain Dealer Internship   2:143
CNN News Internship   2:143–145
Columbia Journalism Review Internship   2:145
Cooper-Hewitt, National Design
Museum Internship   1:126–127
Corcoran Gallery of Art Internship   1:128–129
Costa Rica Internship Institute Internship 2:100
Council on Foreign Relations Internship 2:100–101
Dallas Theater Center Internship   1:259–260
Dance Place Internship   1:260–261
Daughters of the American Revolution
(DAR) Museum Internship   1:217–218
D. C. Booth Historic Fish Hatchery Internship   2:46
Dell Computer Internship   2:337–338
Denver Post Reporting/Photography
Internship   2:148
Dow Chemical Company Internship   2:338
Dow Jones Newspaper Fund Minority
Summer Internship   2:149–150
DuPont Summer Internship   1:173
EarthTrends Summer Internship   1:44–45
Eastman Kodak Internship   2:338–339
Elizabeth Glaser Pediatric AIDS
Foundation Internship   2:18–19
Entertainment Weekly Internship   2:150–151
Eugene O'Neill Theater Internship   1:267–269
Federal Bureau of Investigation (FBI)
Washington Internship for Native
Students (WINS)   1:327–328
Field Museum Internship   1:129–130

Folger Shakespeare Library Internship	1:269
Ford Motor Company Internship	1:174–177
Fresno Bee Internship	2:152
Friends of the Earth Internship	2:203–204
Gay Men's Health Crisis Internship	2:20–21
General Electric Internship	1:177–178
Georgia Governor's Internship	1:329–330
Getty Foundation Internship	1:131–133
GlaxoSmithKline Internship	2:240–241
Glimmerglass Opera Internship	1:270–274
Guggenheim Museum Internship	1:133–135
Hallmark Cards Internship	1:178–179
Harper's Internship	2:152–153
Harvard University Four Directions Summer Research Program	2:241–242
Hawk Mountain Sanctuary Internship	2:204–206
Head Start National Internship	2:23–24
Healthy Mothers, Healthy Babies Coalition of Washington Internship	2:24
Heifer International Internship	1:49–50
The Hermitage (Home of Andrew Jackson) Internship	2:51–52
Historic Preservation Internship Training Program	1:218–219
IBM Extreme Blue Internship	2:340–342
Idaho Lieutenant Governor's Internship	1:330
Illinois Governor's Internship	1:330–331
IMG International Internship	1:179–180
Injury Center Internship	2:24–25
International Atomic Energy Agency Internship	2:105–107
International Child Art Foundation Internship	1:136–137
Jim Henson Company Internship	1:274–276
Juilliard School Professional Internship	1:276–280
Kennedy Center for the Performing Arts Management Internship	1:280–282
KFSK-Southeast Alaska Public Radio Internship	2:156–157
Kraft Foods Internship	1:182–183
Library of Congress Internship	1:331–335
Lucasfilm Internship	1:286–287
Lucent Technologies Summer Internship	1:185–186
Lunar and Planetary Institute Internship	2:252–253
Mattel Internship	1:186–187
Merck Internship	1:189–190
Metropolitan Museum of Art Internship	1:139–140
Miami Herald Internship	2:161–162
Michael Perez Gallery Internship	1:140
Minnesota Historical Society Internship	2:56–60
Modesto Bee Internship	2:162–163
Motorola Internship	2:353–354
MTV Networks Internship—Nashville	1:288
MTV Networks Internship—Santa Monica	1:289–290
Museum of Contemporary Art San Diego Internship	1:140–142
Museum of Modern Art Internship	1:142–146
Mystic Aquarium Internship	1:99–101
NASCAR Internship	2:315–316
National Air and Space Museum Internship	1:221–222
National Anthropological Archives Internship	1:222–223
National Building Museum Internship	1:223–224
National Council for Preservation Education Internship	2:61–68
National Endowment for the Arts Internship	1:146–147, 1:290–291
National Gallery of Art Internship	1:148–150
National Healthy Mothers, Healthy Babies Coalition Internship	2:25–26
National Mental Health Association Internship	2:26–28
National Museum of African Art Internship	1:150
National Museum of American History Internship	1:224–225
National Museum of the American Indian Internship	1:225–226
National Museum of Women in the Arts Internship	1:150–152
National Portrait Gallery Internship	1:152–155
National Renewable Energy Laboratory Internship	2:355–356
National Science Foundation Research Experience for Undergraduates (REU)	2:263–264
National Trust for Historic Preservation Internship	2:68–69
New American Dream Communications Internship	1:58–59
New England Healthcare Institute Internship	2:28–29

Newsweek Internship   2:168–169
New York City Summer Internship   1:339–343
New York Rangers Internship   2:316
New York State Theatre Institute
   Internship   1:291–292
New York Times Copyediting Internship   2:170
North Carolina Governor's Internship   1:344–345
Nuclear Regulatory Commission
   Historically Black Colleges and
   Universities Student Research
   Internship   2:267–268
Office of Naval Research Internship   2:268–273
Oklahoma Governor's Internship   1:345
Old Sturbridge Village Internship   2:69–70
One Reel Internship   1:292–294
Orlando Magic Internship   2:316–321
Orlando Sentinel Internship   2:173–174
Pennsylvania Department of Public
   Health Internship   2:29
Pfizer Internship   1:190–192
Pfizer Research and Development
   Internship   2:273–274
Philadelphia Inquirer Minority
   Internship   2:174–175
Philadelphia Inquirer Nonminority
   Copyediting and Graphics Arts
   Internship   2:175
Philadelphia Phantoms Internship   2:322–323
Philadelphia 76ers Internship   2:323–324
Philadelphia Zoo Internship   1:108–109
Physicians for Social Responsibility
   Internship   1:62–63
Population Institute Internship   2:30
Population Services International
   Internship   1:63–65
Preservation Action Internship   2:70–71
Project HOPE (Health Opportunities
   for People Everywhere) Internship   2:31
Public Leadership Education Network
   Internship   1:66–67
Reuters Internship   2:175–176
Robert F. Kennedy Memorial Center
   for Human Rights Internship   1:68
San Diego Chargers Internship   2:324–325
San Diego Museum of Art—Education
   Internship   1:229

San Francisco Mime Troupe Internship   1:299–300
Seattle Times Internship   2:181
Second Stage Theatre Internship   1:300–302
Shakespeare Theatre Internship   1:302–304
Silent Spring Institute Internship   2:32–33
Silicon Graphics Inc. (SGI) Internship   2:362–363
Smithsonian Architectural History
   and Historic Preservation Division
   Internship   2:71
South Street Seaport Museum Internship   1:230–231
St. Petersburg Times Summer Internship   2:182–183
St. Petersburg Times Yearlong
   Newsroom Internship   2:183
Texas Film Commission Internship   1:309–310
Texas Instruments Internship   2:363–364
Time Inc. Summer Internship   2:185–186
UNICEF Graduate Student Internship   2:107–108
United Nations Association of the USA
   Internship   1:74
University of the Middle East Project
   Internship   1:232–233
USA Today Summer Internship   2:186
U.S. Capitol Historical Society Internship   2:71–72
Verizon College Internship   1:195–196
Vermont Folklife Center Internship   2:72–73
Very Special Arts (VSA) Internship   1:159
WakeMed Health and Hospitals
   Internship   2:33–34
Wall Street Journal Internship   2:187
The Washington Center for Internship
   and Academic Seminars   1:234–237
Washington Internship for Native
   Students (WINS)   1:349–350
Washington Leadership Summer
   Internship Seminar for Native
   American Students   1:350–352
Washington Post Internship   2:189–190
Wisconsin Governor's Internship   1:357–358
Wolf Trap Internship   1:312–314
Women's International League for Peace
   and Freedom Internship   2:108–111
World Bird Sanctuary Internship   1:115–116
WVSA Arts Connection Internship   1:160–162
YAI National Institute for People with
   Disabilities Internship   2:35

INTERNSHIPS AND
SUMMER JOBS BY SALARY

UNPAID

The Aark Wildlife Rehabilitation Internship   1:81

ABC *Good Morning America* Internship   2:117

ABC John Stossel Specials Internship   2:117

ABC News Internship   2:117–120

ABC News *PrimeTime Live* Internship   2:120

ABC News Radio Internship   2:120–121

ABC News Special Events Internship   2:121

ABC News Washington Bureau
Internship   2:121–122

ABC-TV Channel 7 (Los Angeles)
Internship   2:122

ABC *Weekend News* Internship   2:122–123

ABC *World News Tonight* Internship   2:123

Actors Theatre Workshop Internship   1:245–246

Administration on Aging Internship   2:6

Amazon.com Software Development
Engineer Internship   2:330–331

American Association for the
Advancement of Science Internship   2:225–226

American Civil Liberties Union
Immigrants Rights Project Internship   1:28–29

American Civil Liberties Union Internship   1:29–30

American Enterprise Institute Internship   1:317–318

American Folklife Center Internship   1:201–202

American Foundation for the Blind
Internship   2:7

American Friends Service Committee
International Internship   2:77–78

American Geographical Society
Internship   1:202–203, 2:227–228

American Institute for Foreign Study—
Cannes Internship   2:78–79

American Institute for Foreign Study—
Florence Internship   2:79–80

American Institute for Foreign Study—
London Internship   2:80–81

American Institute for Foreign Study—
Sydney Internship   2:81–82

American Lung Association Internship   2:8

American Public Health Association
Internship   2:9

American Red Cross Internship   2:9–13

American Red Cross Media Internship   2:126

American Rivers Internship   2:195–197

American School for the Deaf Internship   1:203–204

Amnesty International—Washington,
D.C. Internship   1:30–32

Anacostia Museum and Center for
African American History and
Culture Internship   2:39

The Antarctica Project Internship   2:197

Archives of American Art Internship   1:121–122

Arena Stage Internship   1:251–254

Art Institute of Chicago Internship   1:122–123

Art Museum of the Americas Internship   1:123

Associated Press Broadcast News
Internship   2:130–131

Associated Press Internship   2:129–130

Atlanta Ballet Internship   1:254

Atlantic Monthly Internship   2:132–133

Atlantic Monthly Web Site Content
Internship   2:133

Australian Embassy Internship   2:83

Bay Nature Magazine Internship   2:200–201

Beaver Dam Farm Equine Internship   1:81–83

Berkshire Theater Festival Internship   1:255–256

Best Friends Animal Society Internship   1:83–84

Big Cat Rescue Internship   1:84–85

Boston Ballet Internship   1:256–257

Boston Celtics Internship   2:301–302

Boston Environment Department
  Internship   1:33–34
Boston Museum of Science Internship   1:205–210
Boston University Internship Abroad—
  Auckland Internship   2:83–84
Boston University Internship Abroad—
  Beijing Internship   2:84–85
Boston University Internship Abroad—
  Dresden Internship   2:85–86
Boston University Internship Abroad—
  Dublin Internship   2:86–87
Boston University Internship Abroad—
  Geneva Internship   2:87
Boston University Internship Abroad—
  Haifa Internship   2:88
Boston University Internship Abroad—
  London Internship   2:88–90
Boston University Internship Abroad—
  Madrid Internship   2:90–91
Boston University Internship Abroad—
  Paris Internship   2:91–92
Boston University Internship Abroad—
  Sydney Internship   2:92–93
Bread for the City Legal Clinic Internship   1:34
California Governor's Internship   1:322–323
Callaway Advanced Technology
  Internship   2:335–336
Canadian Embassy Internship   2:96–97
Capitol Hill Internship   1:323–324
The Carter Center Internship   1:35–43
CBS-4 (KCNC-TV) Sports Department
  Internship   2:302–303
CBS News Internship   2:137–140
Center for Adolescent Health and the
  Law Internship   2:14–15
Center for Arts and Culture Internship   1:123–124
Center for World Indigenous Studies
  Internship   2:98–99
Chicago Bears Graphic Design Internship   2:303
Chicago Children's Museum Internship   1:210–211
Chicago Historical Society Internship   1:124–125
Chicago Symphony Orchestra Internship 1:257–258
Chicago Zoological Society Brookfield
  Zoo Internship   1:85–87
Children's Museum of Indianapolis
  Internship   1:211–217

Children's Television Workshop
  Internship   1:258–259
Christie's Internship   1:125–126
CNN News Internship   2:143–144
Colonial Williamsburg Internship   2:43–46
Colorado Springs Sky Sox Internship   2:304–306
Common Cause Internship   1:43–44
Connecticut Governor's Prevention
  Partnership Internship   1:325–326
Cooperative Center for Study Abroad:
  Ireland Internship   2:99
Cooper-Hewitt, National Design
  Museum Internship   1:126–127
Corcoran Gallery of Art Internship   1:128–129
Costa Rica Internship Institute Internship   2:100
Council on Foreign Relations Internship 2:100–101
Council on Hemispheric Affairs
  (COHA) Internship   2:101–103
C-SPAN TV (Washington, D.C.)
  Internship   2:145–147
Dallas Theater Center Internship   1:259–260
Dance Place Internship   1:260–261
Daughters of the American Revolution
  (DAR) Museum Internship   1:217–218
Democratic National Committee
  Internship   1:326–327
Denver Zoo Internship   1:87–88
Doctors Without Borders Internship   2:16–18
Dolphin Institute Internship   1:91–92
Dreamtime Festival Internship   1:261–263
DreamWorks SKG Internship   1:263–264
E! Entertainment Talent/Casting
  Internship   1:265–267
Eugene O'Neill Theater Internship   1:267–269
Farm Sanctuary Internship   1:92–93
Federal Bureau of Investigation (FBI)
  Washington Internship for Native
  Students (WINS)   1:327–328
Florida Governor's Internship   1:328–329
Folger Shakespeare Library Internship   1:269
Fort Wayne Children's Zoo Veterinary
  Medicine Internship   1:93–94
Fossil Rim Wildlife Center Internship   1:94–95
Freer Gallery of Art/Arthur M. Sackler
  Gallery Internship   1:130–131
Friends of the Earth Internship   2:203–204

Frontier Nursing Service Internship 2:19–20
Gay Men's Health Crisis Internship 2:20–21
Geddes Talent Agency Internship 1:270
Government Accountability Project
   Internship 1:47
Great Dog Obedience Training Internship 1:96
Greenbelt Alliance Internship 1:47–48
Habitat for Humanity—New York City
   Internship 1:49
Hansard Society Scholars Program 2:104–105
Harper's Internship 2:152–153
Head Start National Internship 2:23–24
Healthy Mothers, Healthy Babies
   Coalition of Washington Internship 2:24
Hermitage Foundation Museum Internship 2:51
Hilltop Farm Inc. Internship 1:97
Hirshhorn Museum and Sculpture
   Garden Internship 1:135–136
Houston Zoo Internship 1:97–98
Idaho Lieutenant Governor's Internship 1:330
Illinois Governor's Internship 1:330–331
IMG International Internship 1:179–180
Independence Seaport Museum
   Internship 1:219
Indiana Pacers Internship 2:306–311
International Center for Tolerance
   Education Internship 1:51–52
International Child Art Foundation
   Internship 1:136–137
International Diplomacy Council
   Internship 1:52–53
Jim Henson Company Internship 1:274–276
Julia Morgan Center for the Arts
   Internship 1:137–138
Kansas City Blades Internship 2:311–312
KPNX-TV (Phoenix) Internship 2:158
Kroenke Sports Enterprises Internship 2:312–314
KTTV-TV (Los Angeles) Internship 2:159
The Late Show with David Letterman
   Internship 1:282–283
Literacy Partners Inc. Internship 1:221
Los Angeles Lakers Internship 2:314
Los Angeles Opera Community
   Programs Internship 1:284
Lucent Technologies Summer Internship 1:185–186
Maine State Governor's Internship 1:335

Marvel Comics Internship 2:160–161
MediaRights Internship 1:53–55
Metro-Goldwyn-Mayer (MGM)
   Internship 1:287–288
Michael Perez Gallery Internship 1:140
Michigan Executive Office Internship 1:336–338
Mickey Leland Energy Fellowships 2:254–255
Minnesota Historical Society Internship 2:56–60
MSNBC Internship 2:164–166
MTV Networks Internship—Nashville 1:288
MTV Networks Internship—
   New York City 1:288–289
MTV Networks Internship—
   Santa Monica 1:289–290
MTV Networks Latin America
   Internship—Miami Beach 1:290
Museum of Contemporary Art San
   Diego Internship 1:140–142
Mystic Aquarium Internship 1:98–101
NASCAR Diversity Internship 2:314–315
NASCAR Internship 2:315–316
National Anthropological Archives
   Internship 1:222–223
National Aquarium in Baltimore
   Internship 1:101–102
National Building Museum Internship 1:223–224
National Campaign to Prevent Teen
   Pregnancy Internship 1:56–57
National Endowment for the Arts
   Internship 1:146–147, 1:290–291
National Environmental Law Center
   Internship 1:57
National Healthy Mothers, Healthy
   Babies Coalition Internship 2:25–26
National Mental Health Association
   Internship 2:26–28
National Museum of African Art Internship 1:150
National Museum of American History
   Internship 1:224–225
National Museum of the American
   Indian Internship 1:225–226
National Museum of Women in the
   Arts Internship 1:150–152
National Organization for Women
   (NOW) Internship 1:58
National Portrait Gallery Internship 1:152–155

National Trust for Historic Preservation
  Internship   2:68–69
National Zoo Beaver Valley Internship   1:102–103
NBC Internship   2:168
New American Dream
  Communications Internship   1:58–59
New England Wildlife Center Internship   1:103–104
New Jersey Governor's Internship   1:338–339
New Museum of Contemporary Art
  Internship   1:155–157
New York City Summer Internship   1:339–343
New York Daily News Graphics
  Designer Internship   2:169
New York Daily News Internship   2:169–170
New York State Theatre Institute
  Internship   1:291–292
Nickelodeon Animation Studio
  Internship   1:292
Nightline Internship   2:172–173
Oklahoma Governor's Internship   1:345
Old Sturbridge Village Internship   2:69–70
Oregon Governor's Internship   1:345–346
Oregon Zoo Internship   1:104–105
Other Hand Productions Puppet
  Internship   1:294–295
Paramount Pictures/Dr. Phil Show
  Internship   1:295
Paws Companion Animal Internship   1:105–106
Peaceworks Foundation Internship   1:61
Philadelphia Junior Zoo Apprentice
  Internship   1:106–108
Philadelphia Museum of Art Internship   1:157–158
Philadelphia Orchestra Association
  Internship   1:295–297
Philadelphia Phantoms Internship   2:322–323
Philadelphia 76ers Internship   2:323–324
Philadelphia Zoo Internship   1:108–109
Physicians for Social Responsibility
  Internship   1:62–63
Portland Children's Museum Internship   1:226–229
Prison Activist Resource Center Internship 1:65–66
Project HOPE (Health Opportunities
  for People Everywhere) Internship   2:30–31
Public Leadership Education Network
  Internship   1:66–67
Radio Disney—Boston Internship   1:297

Rainforest Action Network Internship   1:67–68
Republican National Committee
  Internship   1:346–347
RKO Pictures Internship   1:297–298
Robert F. Kennedy Memorial Center for
  Human Rights Internship   1:68
Rocky Mountain PBS-TV Studio and
  Production Internship   2:176–177
Sacramento Music Circus Summer
  Musical Theater Internship   1:298–299
San Diego Chargers Internship   2:324–325
San Diego Museum of Art—Education
  Internship   1:229
San Diego Zoo's Wild Animal Park
  Summer Camp Teen Internship   1:230
San Francisco Mime Troupe Internship   1:299–300
Santé Group Internship   1:69
Seattle Art Museum Internship   1:158–159
Second Stage Theatre Internship   1:300–302
Shakespeare Theatre Internship   1:302–304
Share Our Strength Internship   1:70–71
Sierra Club Internship   1:71–72
Silent Spring Institute Internship   2:32–33
Smithsonian Folkways Recording
  Internship   1:304–305
South Carolina Governor's Internship   1:347
South Shore Music Circus Internship   1:305–306
South Street Seaport Museum Internship 1:230–231
Strides Therapeutic Riding Center
  Internship   1:111–112
Strong Women, Strong Girls Internship   1:72–73
The Studio Theatre Internship   1:308–309
Surgeons of Hope Foundation Internship   2:33
Texas Film Commission Internship   1:309–310
Tiger Creek Wildlife Refuge Internship   1:112–113
Toledo Mud Hens Baseball Club Internship   2:325
20/20 Vision Internship   1:73
UNICEF Graduate Student Internship   2:107–108
United Nations Association of the USA
  Internship   1:74
USA Today Summer Internship   2:186
U.S. Capitol Historical Society Internship   2:71–72
U.S. Department of Education Internship   1:233
U.S. Holocaust Memorial Museum
  Internship   1:233–234
U.S. Supreme Court Internship   1:347–349

Verizon College Internship   1:195–196
Vermont Governor's Internship   1:349
The Washington Center for Internship
    and Academic Seminars   1:234–237
Washington Food Coalition Internship   1:74–75
Washingtonian Art Department
    Internship   2:188–189
Washington Internship for Native
    Students (WINS)   1:349–350
Washington Leadership Summer
    Internship Seminar for Native
    American Students   1:350–352
White House Internship   1:353–357
Wild Horse Sanctuary Internship   1:113–114
Wilma Theater Internship   1:312
Wisconsin Governor's Internship   1:357–358
Wolfsong Ranch Foundation Internship   1:114–115
Wolf Trap Internship   1:312–314
Women for Peace Internship   1:75
World Affairs Council Internship   1:77
WVSA Arts Connection Internship   1:160–162
YAI National Institute for People with
    Disabilities Internship   2:35
Zoo Atlanta Internship   1:116–117

$1 TO $999

Advertising Club Internship   2:124–125
American Dance Festival Internship   1:250–251
American Farmland Trust Internship   2:193
American Forests Internship   2:193–195
BalletMet Internship   1:254–255
Center for Women in Politics and
    Public Policy Internship   1:43
Christie's Internship   1:125–126
Chrysler Group Internship   1:172
Gould Farm Internship   2:21–22
HBO Internship   2:153–155
Mattel Internship   1:186–187
Mother Jones Internship   2:163
National Gallery of Art High School
    Internship   1:147–148
One Reel Internship   1:292–294
Performance Research Internship   2:321–322
Pulmonary Hypertension Association
    Internship   2:31–32

SeaWorld Adventure Camp Internship   1:109–111
Sierra Magazine Internship   2:181–182
University of the Middle East Project
    Internship   1:232–233
Very Special Arts (VSA) Internship   1:159
West Virginia Governor's Internship   1:352–353
Whitney Museum of American Art
    Internship   1:159–160
Wildlife Rescue and Rehabilitation
    Internship   1:114
World Bird Sanctuary Internship   1:115–116

$1,000 +

Abbott Laboratories Environmental,
    Health, and Safety Internship   2:5
Abbott Laboratories Internship   1:165–166
Academy of Television Arts and
    Sciences Foundation Internship   1:241–245
Acadia National Park Education
    Internship   1:201
ACCION International Internship   1:27
The Ad Club (Boston) Internship   2:124
Akron Beacon Journal Internship   2:125
Amelia Island Internship   1:166–167
American Cancer Society Internship   2:6–7
American Conservatory Theater
    Internship   1:246–250
American-Scandinavian Foundation
    Internship   2:82–83
American Society for Microbiology
    Research Internship   2:228–229
American Society of Magazine Editors
    Internship   2:127–128
Anasazi Heritage Center Internship   1:204–205
Anchorage Daily News Internship   2:128–129
Apple Computer Internship   2:331–333
Arizona Legislative Internship   1:318–320
Arnold Arboretum of Harvard
    University Internship   2:197–198
Asian Pacific American Institute for
    Congressional Studies Internship   1:320–322
Aspen Center for Environmental
    Studies Internship   2:198–199
Atlanta Journal Constitution Internship   2:131–132
Audubon Internship   2:133–134

Aullwood Audubon Center and Farm
  Internship   2:199–200
Austin American-Statesman Internship   2:134–135
Baltimore Sun Two-year Internship   2:135
Bangor Daily News Internship   2:135–136
Boston Globe Internship   2:136–137
Boston Museum of Science Internship   1:205–210
Boys Hope, Girls Hope Internship   2:13–14
Brooklyn Children's Museum Internship   1:210
Buchanan/Burnham Internship   2:39–40
Buffalo Bill Historical Center Internship   2:40–43
California Academy of Science A.
  Crawford Cooley Internship in
  California Botany   2:230–231
California Academy of Science
  Internship in Biological Illustration   2:231
California Academy of Science Robert
  T. Wallace Undergraduate Research
  Internship   2:231–232
Callaway Gardens Internship   2:201
Camp Counselors USA—European Day
  Camps   2:93–95
Camp Counselors USA—United Kingdom   2:96
Carnegie Endowment for International
  Peace Internship   2:97–98
Center for Food Safety Internship   2:15
Center for Science in the Public Interest
  Internship   2:232–235
Charlotte Observer Internship   2:141
Chicago Bulls Ticket Sales
  Representative Internship   2:303–304
Chicago Sun-Times Minority
  Scholarship and Internship Program   2:141–142
Chicago Tribune Internship   2:142
Chincoteague National Wildlife Refuge
  Internship   2:201–203
Chronicle of Higher Education Internship 2:142–143
Chrysler Group Internship   1:172
CIIT Centers for Health Research
  Internship   2:15–16
Cleveland Plain Dealer Internship   2:143
Cold Spring Harbor Lab Summer
  Internship   2:235–236
Columbia Journalism Review Internship   2:145
Cooper-Hewitt, National Design
  Museum Internship   1:126–127

Cornell University Materials Science
  Research Internship   2:236–237
Cornell University Plant Genome
  Research Program Internship   2:237
Dallas Morning News Internship   2:147–148
Dallas Theater Center SummerStage
  Internship   1:260
Denver Post Reporting/Photography
  Internship   2:148
Denver Zoo Internship   1:87–88
Des Moines Register Internship   2:148–149
Detroit Free Press Internship   2:149
Dow Jones Newspaper Fund Minority
  Summer Internship   2:149–150
Duke University Neurosciences
  Summer Research Program in
  Mechanisms of Behavior   2:238
EarthTrends Summer Internship   1:44–45
Eisenhower National Historic Site
  Internship   2:46–47
Elizabeth Glaser Pediatric AIDS
  Foundation Internship   2:18–19
El Pueblo de Los Angeles Historical
  Monument Multicultural Summer
  Internship   2:47–48
Entertainment Weekly Internship   2:150–151
Ernst & Young Internship   1:173–174
Freer Gallery of Art/Arthur M. Sackler
  Gallery Internship   1:130–131
Fresno Bee Internship   2:152
Friends Committee on National
  Legislation (FCNL) Internship   1:45–46
Genesis Animal Sanctuary Summer
  Internship   1:95–96
Georgia Governor's Internship   1:329–330
Georgia State Park and Historic Sites
  Internship   2:48–49
Getty Foundation Internship   1:131–133
Grey Towers National Historic Site
  Internship   2:49–51
Guggenheim Museum Internship   1:133–135
Hallmark Cards Internship   1:178–179
Harvard School of Public Health
  Minority Internship   2:22–23
Harvard University Summer Honors
  Undergraduate Research Program   2:242–243

Harvard University Summer Research Program in Ecology   2:243–245

Hawk Mountain Sanctuary Internship   2:204–206

Heifer International Internship   1:49–50

The Hermitage (Home of Andrew Jackson) Internship   2:51–52

Historic Deerfield Summer Fellowship   2:52–54

Historic Preservation Internship Training Program   1:218–219, 2:54–55

Howard Hughes Honors Summer Institute   2:245–246

Illinois Governor's Internship   1:330–331

Injury Center Internship   2:24–25

INROADS Internship   1:181–182

Institute of Ecosystem Studies Internship   2:246–250

Jackson Laboratory Summer Student Program   2:250–251

Jane Goodall Institute Internship   2:206–208

Japanese American National Museum Internship   1:219–221

Juilliard School Professional Internship   1:276–280

Kaiser Media Minority Internship in Urban Health Reporting   2:155–156

Kennedy Center for the Performing Arts Management Internship   1:280–282

KFSK-Southeast Alaska Public Radio Internship   2:156–157

Knight Ridder Internship for Native American Journalists   2:157–158

Kraft Foods Internship   1:182–183

Lands' End Internship   1:183–185

Library of Congress Internship   1:331–335

Living History Farms Internship   2:55–56

Liz Claiborne Summer Internship   1:185

Longwood Gardens Internship   2:208–214

Longwood Gardens Performing Arts Internship   1:283–284

Los Alamos National Laboratory High School Co-Op Program   2:345–346

Los Alamos National Laboratory Internship   2:346–348

Los Angeles Times Internship   2:159–160

Lucas Digital Internship   1:284–286

Lucasfilm Internship   1:286–287

Lunar and Planetary Institute Internship   2:252–253

Lunar and Planetary Institute Summer Intern Program   2:348

Macy's Internship   1:187–189

Marathon Oil Corporation/UNCF Corporate Scholars Program   2:350

Marine Biology Lab at Woods Hole Marine Models in Biological Research Internship   2:253–254

Maryland Governor's Summer Internship   1:335–336

Mattel Internship   1:186–187

Merck Family Fund Internship   1:55–56

Merck Internship   1:189–190

Metropolitan Museum of Art Internship   1:138–140

Miami Herald Internship   2:161–162

Modesto Bee Internship   2:162–163

Morris Arboretum of the University of Pennsylvania Internship   2:214–217

Mount Desert Island Biological Lab Research Fellowships for Undergraduates   2:255–256

Mount Vernon Summer Internship   2:60–61

Museum of Modern Art Internship   1:142–146

National Air and Space Museum Internship   1:221–222

National Association of Black Journalists Summer Journalism Internship   2:166–168

National Council for Preservation Education Internship   2:61–68

National Gallery of Art Internship   1:148–150

National Institutes of Health Summer Internship Programs in Biomedical Research   2:259–261

National Museum of Natural History Internship   2:261–262

National Museum of Women in the Arts Internship   1:150–152

National Park Foundation Internship   2:217–218

Naval Research Lab Science and Engineering Apprenticeship Program   2:264–265

New American Dream Communications Internship   1:58–59

New York Rangers Internship   2:316

New York Times Copyediting Internship   2:170

New York Times Graphics, Design, and
Photography Internship   2:171–172
New York Times Reporting Fellowship   2:172
New York University School of
Medicine Summer Undergraduate
Research Program (SURP)   2:266–267
North Carolina Governor's Internship   1:344–345
Nuclear Regulatory Commission
Historically Black Colleges and
Universities Student Research
Internship   2:267–268
Office of Naval Research Internship   2:268–273
Orlando Magic Internship   2:316–321
Orlando Sentinel Internship   2:173–174
Pendle Hill Social Justice Internship   1:61–62
Pennsylvania Department of Public
Health Internship   2:29
Pfizer Internship   1:190–192
Pfizer Research and Development
Internship   2:273–274
Philadelphia Inquirer Minority
Internship   2:174–175
Philadelphia Inquirer Nonminority
Copyediting and Graphics Arts Internship   2:175
Population Institute Internship   2:30
Preservation Action Internship   2:70–71
Random House Inc. Summer Internship   1:192–193
Rockefeller University Summer
Undergraduate Research Fellowship   2:275–276
Rocky Mountain Biological Laboratory
Summer Internship   2:276–277
Roswell Park Cancer Institute Summer
College Internship   2:277
Sacramento Bee Internship   2:177
Saks Incorporated Internship   1:193–194
San Diego Museum of Art—Education
Internship (summer session only)   1:229
San Francisco Chronicle Summer
Internship   2:177–178
San Francisco Chronicle Two-Year
Internship   2:178–179
Science News Internship   2:180–181
Smithsonian Architectural History and
Historic Preservation Division Internship   2:71
Smithsonian Astrophysical Observatory
Internship   2:279–280

Spoleto Festival USA Internship   1:306–308
Stanford Linear Accelerator Center
Summer Fellowship   2:280–281
St. Petersburg Times Summer Internship 2:182–183
St. Petersburg Times Yearlong
Newsroom Internship   2:183
Student Climate Outreach Internship   2:218–219
Student Conservation Association
Internship   2:219–221
SUNY Albany Summer Research
Experience for Undergraduates   2:281–282
Tampa Tribune Internship   2:183–184
Teach for America National Internship   1:231–232
Teen People Summer Internship   2:184–185
Time Inc. Summer Internship   2:185–186
Toyota Motor North America Internship   1:194–195
University of California-Davis
Undergraduate Summer Training in
Environmental Toxicology   2:282
University of Colorado at Boulder
Summer Minority Access to Research
Training   2:283–284
University of Massachusetts Medical
School Undergraduate Summer NIH
Research Fellowship Program   2:288
University of Massachusetts
Undergraduate Research in Ecology
and Conservation Biology   2:284–286
University of Texas-Houston Health
Science Center Summer Research
Program   2:288–289
U.S. Department of Energy's Science
Undergraduate Lab Internship (SULI)   2:289–294
U.S. News & World Report Internship   2:186–187
Vermont Folklife Center Internship   2:72–73
Virginia Institute of Marine Science
Internship   2:294–296
WakeMed Health and Hospitals Internship   2:33–34
Wall Street Journal Internship   2:187
Walt Disney World Culinary Internship   1:196–197
Walt Disney World Summer Jobs   1:310–312
Washington, D.C., Department of
Health Internship   2:34–35
Washingtonian Advertising Internship   2:188
Washingtonian Editorial Internship   2:189
Washington Post Internship   2:189–190

Washington State Governor's Internship 1:352
Women's International League for Peace
and Freedom Internship 2:108–111
Women Work Internship 1:75–77
Xerox Internship 2:364–365

UNSPECIFIED

Abbott Laboratories Environmental,
Health, and Safety Internship 2:5
Advocates for Youth Internship 1:27–28
Aerospace Corporation Internship 2:329
Agilent Technologies Internship 2:329–330
AIESEC Internship 2:77
American Association for the
Advancement of Science Entry Point
Internship 2:226–227
American Association for the
Advancement of Science Internship 2:225–226
American Red Cross Internship 2:9–13
American Red Cross Media Internship 2:126
AT&T Undergraduate Research Program 2:333
Axle Alliance Group Internship 1:167
Ball Aerospace Internship 2:334
Bechtel Corporation Internship 1:167–168
Bechtel Internship 2:334–335
Bettis Atomic Power Lab Internship 2:229–230
Beyond Pesticides Internship 1:32–33
Blethen Maine Newspapers Minority
Summer Internship 2:136
Boeing Internship 1:168–169
Brooklyn Parents for Peace Internship 1:34–35
Camp Counselors USA—Russia 2:95
Central Intelligence Agency Internship 1:324–325
Cessna Internship 1:169
ChevronTexaco Engineering Internship 1:170–172
Cisco Systems Internship 2:336–337
D. C. Booth Historic Fish Hatchery
Internship 2:46
Dell Computer Internship 2:337–338
Disney's Animal Kingdom Advanced
Internship 1:88–91
Dow Chemical Company Internship 2:338
DuPont Engineering Internship 2:238–239
DuPont Summer Internship 1:173
Eastman Kodak Internship 2:338–339

The Economist Internship 2:103–104
EurekAlert! Web Site Internship 2:151–152
Fermilab Summer Internship in Science
and Technology 2:339–340
Field Museum Internship 1:129–130
Ford Motor Company Internship 1:174–177
Genentech Internship 2:239–240
General Electric Internship 1:177–178
GlaxoSmithKline Internship 2:240–241
Glimmerglass Opera Internship 1:270–274
Harvard University Four Directions
Summer Research Program 2:241–242
Hewlett-Packard Internship 1:179
Historic Deerfield Summer Fellowship 2:52–54
IBM Extreme Blue Internship 2:340–342
Initiative for a Competitive Inner City
Internship 1:51
Intel Internship 2:342–343
International Atomic Energy Agency
Internship 2:105–107
KOCE Public TV (Huntington Beach,
Calif.) Internship 2:158
Lam Research Internship 2:343
Leadership Alliance Summer Internship 2:251–252
Lexmark Internship 2:343–344
Library of Congress Internship 1:331–335
Lockheed Martin Internship 2:344–345
Marathon Oil Corporation Internship 2:349–350
Mercedes-Benz USA Internship 1:189
Metro-Goldwyn-Mayer (MGM)
Internship 1:287–288
Microsoft Internship 2:350–353
Motorola Internship 2:353–354
MSNBC Multimedia Internship 2:166
NASA Kennedy Space Center Space
Flight and Life Sciences Training
Program 2:256–259
National Instruments Internship 2:354–355
National Renewable Energy Laboratory
Internship 2:355–356
National Science Foundation Research
Experience for Undergraduates (REU) 2:263–264
National Semiconductor Internship 2:356–357
NCR Internship 2:357
New England Healthcare Institute
Internship 2:28–29

The New Press Internship   1:60
Newsweek Internship   2:168–169
New York University Center for Neural
    Science Undergraduate Summer
    Research Program   2:265
Oracle Corporation Internship   2:357–358
Pacific Gas and Electric Company
    Internship   2:358–359
Packer Foundation Engineering
    Internship   2:359–360
Physicians for Social Responsibility
    Internship   1:62–63
Population Services International
    Internship   1:63–64
Pratt & Whitney Co-op and Internship   2:360–361
Raytheon Internship   1:193
Reuters Internship   2:175–176
Roswell Park Cancer Institute Summer
    High School Internship   2:277–278

San Diego Zoo Internquest   1:109
Santa Fe Institute Internship   2:361–362
Science Magazine Internship   2:179–180
Seattle Times Internship   2:181
Seeds of Peace Internship   1:69–70
Silicon Graphics Inc. (SGI) Internship   2:362–363
Texas Instruments Internship   2:363–364
Tyson Foods Internship   1:195
University of Massachusetts Medical
    School Summer Enrichment Program   2:287–288
U.S. Holocaust Memorial Museum
    Internship   1:233–234
Wellesley College Biological Sciences
    Internship   2:296
Whitney Laboratory Marine
    Biomedical Research Experience for
    Undergraduates   2:296–297
Work Canada   2:111–113
Wyckoff Farmhouse Museum Internship   2:73–74

INTERNSHIPS AND SUMMER JOBS BY COUNTRY (NON-U.S.)

AUSTRALIA

American Institute for Foreign Study—
Sydney Internship   2:81–82
Australian Embassy Internship   2:83
Bechtel Internship   2:334–335
Boston University Internship Abroad—
Sydney Internship   2:92–93

AUSTRIA

Camp Counselors USA—European Day
Camps   2:93–95
International Atomic Energy Agency
Internship   2:105–107

CANADA

Beaver Dam Farm Equine Internship   1:81–83
Canadian Embassy Internship   2:96–97
Work Canada   2:111–113

CHINA

Boston University Internship Abroad—
Beijing Internship   2:84–85

COSTA RICA

Costa Rica Internship Institute Internship   2:100

DENMARK

American-Scandinavian Foundation
Internship   2:82–83

FINLAND

American-Scandinavian Foundation
Internship   2:82–83

FRANCE

American Institute for Foreign Study—
Cannes Internship   2:78–79
Boston University Internship Abroad—
Paris Internship   2:91–92

GERMANY

Boston University Internship Abroad—
Dresden Internship   2:85–86
Camp Counselors USA—European Day
Camps   2:93–95

GREAT BRITAIN

American Institute for Foreign Study—
London Internship   2:80–81
Boston University Internship Abroad—
London Internship   2:88–90
The Economist Internship   2:103–104
Hansard Society Scholars Program   2:104–105

HONG KONG

Bechtel Internship   2:334–335

HUNGARY

Camp Counselors USA—European Day
Camps   2:93–95

ICELAND

American-Scandinavian Foundation
 Internship   2:82–83

IRELAND

Boston University Internship Abroad—
 Dublin Internship   2:86–87
Cooperative Center for Study Abroad:
 Ireland Internship   2:99

ISRAEL

Boston University Internship Abroad—
 Haifa Internship   2:88

ITALY

American Institute for Foreign Study—
 Florence Internship   2:79–80

MEXICO

Center for World Indigenous Studies
 Internship   2:98–99

NEW ZEALAND

Boston University Internship Abroad—
 Auckland Internship   2:83–84

NORWAY

American-Scandinavian Foundation
 Internship   2:82–83

RUSSIA

Camp Counselors USA—Russia   2:95

SINGAPORE

Bechtel Internship   2:334–335

SPAIN

Boston University Internship Abroad—
 Madrid Internship   2:90–91

SWEDEN

American-Scandinavian Foundation
 Internship   2:82–83

SWITZERLAND

Boston University Internship Abroad—
 Geneva Internship   2:87
Women's International League for Peace
 and Freedom Internship   2:108–111

UNITED KINGDOM

Bechtel Internship   2:334–335
Camp Counselors USA—United Kingdom   2:96

INTERNSHIPS AND SUMMER JOBS BY STATE

ALABAMA
Saks Incorporated Internship   1:193–194

ALASKA
Anchorage Daily News Internship   2:128–129
KFSK-Southeast Alaska Public Radio
    Internship   2:156–157

ARIZONA
Arizona Legislative Internship   1:318–320
Bechtel Corporation Internship   1:167–168
Bechtel Internship   2:334–335
KPNX-TV (Phoenix) Internship   2:158
National Institutes of Health Summer
    Internship Programs in Biomedical
    Research   2:259–261

ARKANSAS
Heifer International Internship   1:49–50
Tyson Foods Internship   1:195

CALIFORNIA
ABC-TV Channel 7 (Los Angeles) Internship 2:122
Academy of Television Arts and
    Sciences Foundation Internship   1:241–245
Aerospace Corporation Internship   2:329
Agilent Technologies Internship   2:329–330
American Conservatory Theater
    Internship   1:246–250
Apple Computer Internship   2:331–333
Bay Nature Magazine Internship   2:200–201
California Academy of Science A.
    Crawford Cooley Internship in
    California Botany   2:230–231
California Academy of Science
    Internship in Biological Illustration   2:231
California Academy of Science Robert
    T. Wallace Undergraduate Research
    Internship   2:231–232
California Governor's Internship   1:322–323
ChevronTexaco Engineering Internship   1:170–172
Cisco Systems Internship   2:336–337
DreamWorks SKG Internship   1:263–264
E! Entertainment Talent/Casting
    Internship   1:265–267
Elizabeth Glaser Pediatric AIDS
    Foundation Internship   2:18–19
El Pueblo de Los Angeles Historical
    Monument Multicultural Summer
    Internship   2:47–48
Fresno Bee Internship   2:152
Geddes Talent Agency Internship   1:270
Genentech Internship   2:239–240
Getty Foundation Internship   1:131–133
Greenbelt Alliance Internship   1:47–48
Hewlett-Packard Internship   1:179
Intel Internship   2:342–343
International Diplomacy Council
    Internship   1:52–53
Japanese American National Museum
    Internship   1:219–221
Jim Henson Company Internship   1:274–276
Julia Morgan Center for the Arts
    Internship   1:137–138
Kaiser Media Minority Internship in
    Urban Health Reporting   2:155–156
KOCE Public TV (Huntington Beach,
    Calif.) Internship   2:158

KTTV-TV (Los Angeles) Internship 2:159
Lam Research Internship 2:343
Los Angeles Lakers Internship 2:314
Los Angeles Opera Community
  Programs Internship 1:284
Los Angeles Times Internship 2:159–160
Lucas Digital Internship 1:284–286
Lucasfilm Internship 1:286–287
Mattel Internship 1:186–187
Metro-Goldwyn-Mayer (MGM)
  Internship 1:287–288
Modesto Bee Internship 2:162–163
Mother Jones Internship 2:163
MTV Networks Internship—Santa
  Monica 1:289–290
Museum of Contemporary Art San
  Diego Internship 1:140–142
National Semiconductor Internship 2:356–357
NBC Internship 2:168
Nickelodeon Animation Studio Internship 1:292
Oracle Corporation Internship 2:357–358
Pacific Gas and Electric Company
  Internship 2:358–359
Paramount Pictures/Dr. Phil Show
  Internship 1:295
Prison Activist Resource Center Internship 1:65–66
Rainforest Action Network Internship 1:67–68
RKO Pictures Internship 1:297–298
Sacramento Bee Internship 2:177
Sacramento Music Circus Summer
  Musical Theater Internship 1:298–299
San Diego Chargers Internship 2:324–325
San Diego Museum of Art—Education
  Internship 1:229
San Diego Zoo Internquest 1:109
San Diego Zoo's Wild Animal Park
  Summer Camp Teen Internship 1:230
San Francisco Chronicle Summer
  Internship 2:177–178
San Francisco Chronicle Two-Year
  Internship 2:178–179
San Francisco Mime Troupe Internship 1:299–300
Sierra Magazine Internship 2:181–182
Silicon Graphics Inc. (SGI) Internship 2:362–363
Stanford Linear Accelerator Center
  Summer Fellowship 2:280–281

Strides Therapeutic Riding Center
  Internship 1:111–112
Teach for America National Internship 1:231–232
University of California-Davis
  Undergraduate Summer Training in
  Environmental Toxicology 2:282
Wild Horse Sanctuary Internship 1:113–114
Women for Peace Internship 1:75

COLORADO

Anasazi Heritage Center Internship 1:204–205
Aspen Center for Environmental
  Studies Internship 2:198–199
Ball Aerospace Internship 2:334
CBS-4 (KCNC-TV) Sports Department
  Internship 2:302–303
Colorado Springs Sky Sox Internship 2:304–306
Denver Post Reporting/Photography
  Internship 2:148
Denver Zoo Internship 1:87–88
Dreamtime Festival Internship 1:261–263
Kroenke Sports Enterprises Internship 2:312–314
National Renewable Energy Laboratory
  Internship 2:355–356
Rocky Mountain Biological Laboratory
  Summer Internship 2:276–277
Rocky Mountain PBS-TV Studio and
  Production Internship 2:176–177
University of Colorado at Boulder
  Summer Minority Access to Research
  Training 2:283–284

CONNECTICUT

American School for the Deaf
  Internship 1:203–204
Callaway Advanced Technology
  Internship 2:335–336
Connecticut Governor's Prevention
  Partnership Internship 1:325–326
Eugene O'Neill Theater Internship 1:267–269
General Electric Internship 1:177–178
Mystic Aquarium Internship 1:99–101
Pratt & Whitney Co-op and Internship 2:360–361
Xerox Internship 2:364–365

DELAWARE

DuPont Engineering Internship   2:238–239
DuPont Summer Internship   1:173

DISTRICT OF COLUMBIA

ABC News Washington Bureau
  Internship   2:121–122
Administration on Aging Internship   2:6
Advocates for Youth Internship   1:27–28
American Association for the
  Advancement of Science Entry Point
  Internship   2:226–227
American Association for the
  Advancement of Science Internship   2:225–226
American Civil Liberties Union Internship   1:29–30
American Enterprise Institute Internship   1:317–318
American Farmland Trust Internship   2:193
American Folklife Center Internship   1:201–202
American Forests Internship   2:193–195
American Public Health Association
  Internship   2:9
American Rivers Internship   2:195–197
American Society for Microbiology
  Research Internship   2:228–229
Amnesty International—Washington,
  D.C. Internship   1:30–32
Anacostia Museum and Center for
  African American History and
  Culture Internship   2:39
The Antarctica Project Internship   2:197
Archives of American Art Internship   1:121–122
Arena Stage Internship   1:251–254
Art Museum of the Americas Internship   1:123
Asian Pacific American Institute for
  Congressional Studies Internship   1:320–322
Beyond Pesticides Internship   1:32–33
Bread for the City Legal Clinic Internship   1:34
Capitol Hill Internship   1:323–324
Carnegie Endowment for International
  Peace Internship   2:97–98
Center for Food Safety Internship   2:15
Center for Science in the Public Interest
  Internship   2:232–235
Chronicle of Higher Education Internship   2:142–143

Corcoran Gallery of Art Internship   1:128–129
Council on Foreign Relations Internship   2:100–101
Council on Hemispheric Affairs
  (COHA) Internship   2:101–103
C-SPAN TV (Washington, D.C.)
  Internship   2:145–147
Dance Place Internship   1:260–261
Daughters of the American Revolution
  (DAR) Museum Internship   1:217–218
Democratic National Committee
  Internship   1:326–327
EarthTrends Summer Internship   1:44–45
EurekAlert! Web Site Internship   2:151–152
Federal Bureau of Investigation (FBI)
  Washington Internship for Native
  Students (WINS)   1:327–328
Folger Shakespeare Library Internship   1:269
Freer Gallery of Art/Arthur M. Sackler
  Gallery Internship   1:130–131
Friends Committee on National
  Legislation (FCNL) Internship   1:45–46
Friends of the Earth Internship   2:203–204
Government Accountability Project
  Internship   1:47
Hirshhorn Museum and Sculpture
  Garden Internship   1:135–136
Historic Preservation Internship
  Training Program   2:54–55
Injury Center Internship   2:24–25
International Child Art Foundation
  Internship   1:136–137
Kennedy Center for the Performing
  Arts Management Internship   1:280–282
Library of Congress Internship   1:331–335
Mickey Leland Energy Fellowships   2:254–255
National Air and Space Museum
  Internship   1:221–222
National Building Museum Internship   1:223–224
National Campaign to Prevent Teen
  Pregnancy Internship   1:56–57
National Endowment for the Arts
  Internship   1:146–147, 1:290–291
National Museum of African Art Internship   1:150
National Museum of American History
  Internship   1:224–225

National Museum of Natural History
Internship 2:261–262
National Museum of Women in the
Arts Internship 1:150–152
National Park Foundation Internship 2:217–218
National Portrait Gallery Internship 1:152–155
National Trust for Historic Preservation
Internship 2:68–69
National Zoo Beaver Valley Internship 1:102–103
Nightline Internship 2:172–173
Population Institute Internship 2:30
Population Services International
Internship 1:63–64
Preservation Action Internship 2:70–71
Public Leadership Education Network
Internship 1:66–67
Republican National Committee
Internship 1:346–347
Reuters Internship 2:175–176
Robert F. Kennedy Memorial Center
for Human Rights Internship 1:68
Science Magazine Internship 2:179–180
Science News Internship 2:180–181
Shakespeare Theatre Internship 1:302–304
Share Our Strength Internship 1:70–71
Sierra Club Internship 1:71–72
Smithsonian Architectural History and
Historic Preservation Division Internship 2:71
Smithsonian Folkways Recording
Internship 1:304–305
The Studio Theatre Internship 1:308–309
20/20 Vision Internship 1:73
U.S. Capitol Historical Society Internship 2:71–72
U.S. Department of Education Internship 1:233
U.S. Holocaust Memorial Museum
Internship 1:233–234
U.S. News & World Report Internship 2:186–187
U.S. Supreme Court Internship 1:347–349
Very Special Arts (VSA) Internship 1:159
The Washington Center for Internship
and Academic Seminars 1:234–237
Washington, D.C., Department of
Health Internship 2:34–35
Washingtonian Advertising Internship 2:188
Washingtonian Art Department
Internship 2:188–189
Washingtonian Editorial Internship 2:189

Washington Internship for Native
Students (WINS) 1:349–350
Washington Leadership Summer
Internship Seminar for Native
American Students 1:350–352
Washington Post Internship 2:189–190
White House Internship 1:353–357
Women's International League for Peace
and Freedom Internship 2:108–111
Women Work Internship 1:75–77
World Affairs Council Internship 1:77
WVSA Arts Connection Internship 1:160–162

FLORIDA

Amelia Island Internship 1:166–167
Big Cat Rescue Internship 1:84–85
Disney's Animal Kingdom Advanced
Internship 1:88–91
Florida Governor's Internship 1:328–329
Miami Herald Internship 2:161–162
MTV Networks Latin America
Internship—Miami Beach 1:290
NASA Kennedy Space Center Space
Flight and Life Sciences Training
Program 2:256–259
NASCAR Diversity Internship 2:314–315
NASCAR Internship 2:315–316
Orlando Magic Internship 2:316–321
Orlando Sentinel Internship 2:173–174
SeaWorld Adventure Camp Internship 1:109–111
St. Petersburg Times Summer Internship 2:182–183
St. Petersburg Times Yearlong
Newsroom Internship 2:183
Tampa Tribune Internship 2:183–184
Walt Disney World Culinary Internship 1:196–197
Walt Disney World Summer Jobs 1:310–312
Whitney Laboratory Marine
Biomedical Research Experience for
Undergraduates 2:296–297

GEORGIA

American Cancer Society Internship 2:6–7
Atlanta Ballet Internship 1:254
Atlanta Journal Constitution Internship 2:131–132
Callaway Gardens Internship 2:201

The Carter Center Internship 1:35–43
Georgia Governor's Internship 1:329–330
Georgia State Park and Historic Sites
    Internship 2:48–49
Zoo Atlanta Internship 1:116–117

HAWAII
Dolphin Institute Internship 1:91–92

IDAHO
Idaho Lieutenant Governor's Internship 1:330

ILLINOIS
Abbott Laboratories Environmental,
    Health, and Safety Internship 2:5
Abbott Laboratories Internship 1:165–166
Art Institute of Chicago Internship 1:122–123
Chicago Bears Graphic Design Internship 2:303
Chicago Bulls Ticket Sales
    Representative Internship 2:303–304
Chicago Children's Museum Internship 1:210–211
Chicago Historical Society Internship 1:124–125
Chicago Sun-Times Minority
    Scholarship and Internship Program 2:141–142
Chicago Symphony Orchestra Internship 1:257–258
Chicago Tribune Internship 2:142
Chicago Zoological Society Brookfield
    Zoo Internship 1:85–87
Fermilab Summer Internship in Science
    and Technology 2:339–340
Field Museum Internship 1:129–130
Illinois Governor's Internship 1:330–331
Kraft Foods Internship 1:182–183
Motorola Internship 2:353–354
Packer Foundation Engineering
    Internship 2:359–360

INDIANA
Children's Museum of Indianapolis
    Internship 1:211–217
Fort Wayne Children's Zoo Veterinary
    Medicine Internship 1:93–94
Indiana Pacers Internship 2:306–311

IOWA
Des Moines Register Internship 2:148–149
Living History Farms Internship 2:55–56

KANSAS
Cessna Internship 1:169

KENTUCKY
Frontier Nursing Service Internship 2:19–20
Lexmark Internship 2:343–344

LOUISIANA
Lockheed Martin Internship 2:344–345

MAINE
Acadia National Park Education Internship 1:201
Bangor Daily News Internship 2:135–136
Blethen Maine Newspapers Minority
    Summer Internship 2:136
Jackson Laboratory Summer Student
    Program 2:250–251
Maine State Governor's Internship 1:335
Mount Desert Island Biological
    Lab Research Fellowships for
    Undergraduates 2:255–256

MARYLAND
Baltimore Sun Two-year Internship 2:135
Bechtel Internship 2:334–335
Hilltop Farm Inc. Internship 1:97
Jane Goodall Institute Internship 2:206–208
Maryland Governor's Summer
    Internship 1:335–336
National Anthropological Archives
    Internship 1:222–223
National Aquarium in Baltimore
    Internship 1:101–102
National Association of Black Journalists
    Summer Journalism Internship 2:166–168
National Gallery of Art High School
    Internship 1:147–148

National Gallery of Art Internship   1:148–150
National Institutes of Health Summer
   Internship Programs in Biomedical
   Research   2:259–261
National Museum of the American
   Indian Internship   1:225–226
New American Dream
   Communications Internship   1:58–59
Pulmonary Hypertension Association
   Internship   2:31–32
Random House Inc. Summer Internship   1:192–193
Santé Group Internship   1:69
Student Climate Outreach Internship   2:218–219

MASSACHUSETTS

ACCION International Internship   1:27
The Ad Club (Boston) Internship   2:124
Arnold Arboretum of Harvard
   University Internship   2:197–198
Atlantic Monthly Internship   2:132–133
Atlantic Monthly Web Site Content
   Internship   2:133
Berkshire Theater Festival Internship   1:255–256
Boston Ballet Internship   1:256–257
Boston Celtics Internship   2:301–302
Boston Environment Department
   Internship   1:33–34
Boston Globe Internship   2:136–137
Boston Museum of Science Internship   1:205–210
Center for Women in Politics and
   Public Policy Internship   1:43
CNN News Internship   2:143–144
Gould Farm Internship   2:21–22
Harvard School of Public Health
   Minority Internship   2:22–23
Harvard University Four Directions
   Summer Research Program   2:241–242
Harvard University Summer Honors
   Undergraduate Research Program   2:242–243
Harvard University Summer Research
   Program in Ecology   2:243–245
Historic Deerfield Summer Fellowship   2:52–54
Initiative for a Competitive Inner City
   Internship   1:51
Lands' End Internship   1:183–185

Merck Family Fund Internship   1:55–56
National Environmental Law Center
   Internship   1:57
New England Healthcare Institute
   Internship   2:28–29
New England Wildlife Center Internship 1:103–104
Old Sturbridge Village Internship   2:69–70
Radio Disney—Boston Internship   1:297
Raytheon Internship   1:193
Silent Spring Institute Internship   2:32–33
Smithsonian Astrophysical Observatory
   Internship   2:279–280
South Shore Music Circus Internship   1:305–306
Strong Women, Strong Girls Internship   1:72–73
University of Massachusetts Medical
   School Summer Enrichment Program   2:287–288
University of Massachusetts Medical
   School Undergraduate Summer NIH
   Research Fellowship Program   2:288
University of Massachusetts
   Undergraduate Research in Ecology
   and Conservation Biology   2:284–286
University of the Middle East Project
   Internship   1:232–233
Wellesley College Biological Sciences
   Internship   2:296

MICHIGAN

Axle Alliance Group Internship   1:167
Chrysler Group Internship   1:172
Detroit Free Press Internship   2:149
Dow Chemical Company Internship   2:338
Ford Motor Company Internship   1:174–177
Michigan Executive Office Internship   1:336–338

MINNESOTA

Knight Ridder Internship for Native
   American Journalists   2:157–158
Minnesota Historical Society Internship   2:56–60

MISSOURI

Boys Hope, Girls Hope Internship   2:13–14
Hallmark Cards Internship   1:178–179

INROADS Internship 1:181–182
Kansas City Blades Internship 2:311–312
World Bird Sanctuary Internship 1:115–116

MONTANA
National Institutes of Health Summer
Internship Programs in Biomedical
Research 2:259–261

NEW HAMPSHIRE
Student Conservation Association
Internship 2:219–221

NEW JERSEY
Dow Jones Newspaper Fund Minority
Summer Internship 2:149–150
Lucent Technologies Summer Internship 1:185–186
Mercedes-Benz USA Internship 1:189
Merck Internship 1:189–190
MSNBC Internship 2:164–166
New Jersey Governor's Internship 1:338–339
Wall Street Journal Internship 2:187

NEW MEXICO
Los Alamos National Laboratory High
School Co-Op Program 2:345–346
Los Alamos National Laboratory
Internship 2:346–348
Santa Fe Institute Internship 2:361–362
Wolfsong Ranch Foundation Internship 1:114–115

NEW YORK
ABC *Good Morning America* Internship 2:117
ABC John Stossel Specials Internship 2:117
ABC News Internship 2:117–120
ABC News *PrimeTime Live* Internship 2:120
ABC News Radio Internship 2:120–121
ABC News Special Events Internship 2:121
ABC *Weekend News* Internship 2:122–123
ABC *World News Tonight* Internship 2:123
Actors Theatre Workshop Internship 1:245–246

Advertising Club Internship 2:124–125
AIESEC Internship 2:77
American Civil Liberties Union
Immigrants Rights Project Internship 1:28–29
American Foundation for the Blind Internship 2:7
American Geographical Society
Internship 1:202–203, 2:227–228
American Lung Association Internship 2:8
American Society of Magazine Editors
Internship 2:127–128
Associated Press Broadcast News
Internship 2:130–131
Associated Press Internship 2:129–130
AT&T Undergraduate Research Program 2:333
Audubon Internship 2:133–134
Brooklyn Children's Museum Internship 1:210
Brooklyn Parents for Peace Internship 1:34–35
CBS News Internship 2:137–140
Children's Television Workshop
Internship 1:258–259
Christie's Internship 1:125–126
Cold Spring Harbor Lab Summer
Internship 2:235–236
Columbia Journalism Review Internship 2:145
Common Cause Internship 1:43–44
Cooper-Hewitt, National Design
Museum Internship 1:126–127
Cornell University Materials Science
Research Internship 2:236–237
Cornell University Plant Genome
Research Program Internship 2:237
Council on Foreign Relations Internship 2:100–101
Doctors Without Borders Internship 2:16–18
Eastman Kodak Internship 2:338–339
Entertainment Weekly Internship 2:150–151
Ernst & Young Internship 1:173–174
Farm Sanctuary Internship 1:92–93
Gay Men's Health Crisis Internship 2:20–21
Glimmerglass Opera Internship 1:270–274
Guggenheim Museum Internship 1:133–135
Habitat for Humanity—New York City
Internship 1:49
Harper's Internship 2:152–153
HBO Internship 2:153–155
Historic Preservation Internship
Training Program 1:218–219

Howard Hughes Honors Summer
Institute   2:245–246
IBM Extreme Blue Internship   2:340–342
Institute of Ecosystem Studies Internship 2:246–250
International Center for Tolerance
Education Internship   1:51–52
Juilliard School Professional Internship 1:276–280
The Late Show with David Letterman
Internship   1:282–283
Literacy Partners Inc. Internship   1:221
Liz Claiborne Summer Internship   1:185
Macy's Internship   1:187–189
Marvel Comics Internship   2:160–161
MediaRights Internship   1:53–55
Metropolitan Museum of Art Internship 1:138–140
Michael Perez Gallery Internship   1:140
MTV Networks Internship—
New York City   1:288–289
Museum of Modern Art Internship   1:142–146
National Council for Preservation
Education Internship   2:61–68
National Organization for Women
(NOW) Internship   1:58
NBC Internship   2:168
New Museum of Contemporary Art
Internship   1:155–157
The New Press Internship   1:60
Newsweek Internship   2:168–169
New York City Summer Internship   1:339–343
New York Daily News Graphics
Designer Internship   2:169
New York Daily News Internship   2:169–170
New York Rangers Internship   2:316
New York State Theatre Institute
Internship   1:291–292
New York Times Copyediting Internship 2:170
New York Times Graphics, Design, and
Photography Internship   2:171–172
New York Times Reporting Fellowship 2:172
New York University Center for Neural
Science Undergraduate Summer
Research Program   2:265
New York University School of
Medicine Summer Undergraduate
Research Program (SURP)   2:266–267

Peaceworks Foundation Internship   1:61
Pfizer Internship   1:190–192
Pfizer Research and Development
Internship   2:273–274
Random House Inc. Summer Internship 1:192–193
Rockefeller University Summer
Undergraduate Research Fellowship 2:275–276
Roswell Park Cancer Institute Summer
College Internship   2:277
Roswell Park Cancer Institute Summer
High School Internship   2:277–278
Second Stage Theatre Internship   1:300–302
Seeds of Peace Internship   1:69–70
South Street Seaport Museum Internship 1:230–231
SUNY Albany Summer Research
Experience for Undergraduates   2:281–282
Surgeons of Hope Foundation Internship 2:33
Teen People Summer Internship   2:184–185
Time Inc. Summer Internship   2:185–186
Toyota Motor North America Internship 1:194–195
UNICEF Graduate Student Internship 2:107–108
United Nations Association of the USA
Internship   1:74
Whitney Museum of American Art
Internship   1:159–160
Women's International League for Peace
and Freedom Internship   2:108–111
Wyckoff Farmhouse Museum Internship 2:73–74
YAI National Institute for People with
Disabilities Internship   2:35

NORTH CAROLINA

American Dance Festival Internship   1:250–251
Center for Adolescent Health and the
Law Internship   2:14–15
Charlotte Observer Internship   2:141
CIIT Centers for Health Research
Internship   2:15–16
Duke University Neurosciences
Summer Research Program in
Mechanisms of Behavior   2:238
Genesis Animal Sanctuary Summer
Internship   1:95–96
GlaxoSmithKline Internship   2:240–241

Marine Biology Lab at Woods Hole
Marine Models in Biological Research
Internship   2:253–254
National Institutes of Health Summer
Internship Programs in Biomedical
Research   2:259–261
North Carolina Governor's Internship   1:344–345
WakeMed Health and Hospitals
Internship   2:33–34

OHIO
Akron Beacon Journal Internship   2:125
Aullwood *Audubon* Center and Farm
Internship   2:199–200
BalletMet Internship   1:254–255
Cleveland Plain Dealer Internship   2:143
IMG International Internship   1:179–180
NCR Internship   2:357
Toledo Mud Hens Baseball Club Internship   2:325

OKLAHOMA
Oklahoma Governor's Internship   1:345

OREGON
Oregon Governor's Internship   1:345–346
Oregon Zoo Internship   1:104–105
Other Hand Productions Puppet
Internship   1:294–295
Portland Children's Museum Internship   1:226–229

PENNSYLVANIA
The Aark Wildlife Rehabilitation Internship   1:81
American Friends Service Committee
International Internship   2:77–78
Bettis Atomic Power Lab Internship   2:229–230
Eisenhower National Historic Site
Internship   2:46–47
GlaxoSmithKline Internship   2:240–241
Grey Towers National Historic Site
Internship   2:49–51
Hawk Mountain Sanctuary Internship   2:204–206

Independence Seaport Museum Internship   1:219
Longwood Gardens Internship   2:208–214
Longwood Gardens Performing Arts
Internship   1:283–284
Morris Arboretum of the University
of Pennsylvania Internship   2:214–217
Pendle Hill Social Justice Internship   1:61–62
Pennsylvania Department of Public
Health Internship   2:29
Philadelphia Inquirer Minority
Internship   2:174–175
Philadelphia Inquirer Nonminority
Copyediting and Graphics Arts Internship   2:175
Philadelphia Junior Zoo Apprentice
Internship   1:106–108
Philadelphia Museum of Art Internship   1:157–158
Philadelphia Orchestra Association
Internship   1:295–297
Philadelphia Phantoms Internship   2:322–323
Philadelphia 76ers Internship   2:323–324
Philadelphia Zoo Internship   1:108–109
Wilma Theater Internship   1:312
Women's International League for Peace
and Freedom Internship   2:108–111

RHODE ISLAND
Buchanan/Burnham Internship   2:39–40
Leadership Alliance Summer Internship   2:251–252
Performance Research Internship   2:321–322

SOUTH CAROLINA
South Carolina Governor's Internship   1:347
Spoleto Festival USA Internship   1:306–308

SOUTH DAKOTA
D. C. Booth Historic Fish Hatchery Internship   2:46

TENNESSEE
The Hermitage (Home of Andrew
Jackson) Internship   2:51–52
MTV Networks Internship—Nashville   1:288

Nuclear Regulatory Commission Historically Black Colleges and Universities Student Research Internship 2:267–268

TEXAS
Austin American-Statesman Internship 2:134–135
Bechtel Internship 2:334–335
Dallas Morning News Internship 2:147–148
Dallas Theater Center Internship 1:259–260
Dallas Theater Center SummerStage Internship 1:260
Dell Computer Internship 2:337–338
Fossil Rim Wildlife Center Internship 1:94–95
Houston Zoo Internship 1:97–98
Lunar and Planetary Institute Internship 2:252–253
Lunar and Planetary Institute Summer Intern Program 2:348
Marathon Oil Corporation Internship 2:349–350
National Instruments Internship 2:354–355
Texas Film Commission Internship 1:309–310
Texas Instruments Internship 2:363–364
Tiger Creek Wildlife Refuge Internship 1:112–113
University of Texas-Houston Health Science Center Summer Research Program 2:288–289
Wildlife Rescue and Rehabilitation Internship 1:114

UTAH
Best Friends Animal Society Internship 1:83–84
Naval Research Lab Science and Engineering Apprenticeship Program 2:264–265
Office of Naval Research Internship 2:268–273

VERMONT
Vermont Folklife Center Internship 2:72–73
Vermont Governor's Internship 1:349

VIRGINIA
American Red Cross Internship 2:9–13
American Red Cross Media Internship 2:126
Center for Arts and Culture Internship 1:123–124
Central Intelligence Agency Internship 1:324–325
Chincoteague National Wildlife Refuge Internship 2:201–203
Colonial Williamsburg Internship 2:43–46
Head Start National Internship 2:23–24
Hermitage Foundation Museum Internship 2:51
Marathon Oil Corporation/UNCF Corporate Scholars Program 2:350
Mount Vernon Summer Internship 2:60–61
National Healthy Mothers, Healthy Babies Coalition Internship 2:25–26
National Mental Health Association Internship 2:26–28
National Science Foundation Research Experience for Undergraduates (REU) 2:263–264
Project HOPE (Health Opportunities for People Everywhere) Internship 2:30–31
USA Today Summer Internship 2:186
Virginia Institute of Marine Science Internship 2:294–296
Wolf Trap Internship 1:312–314

WASHINGTON
Amazon.com Software Development Engineer Internship 2:330–331
Boeing Internship 1:168–169
Great Dog Obedience Training Internship 1:96
Healthy Mothers, Healthy Babies Coalition of Washington Internship 2:24
Microsoft Internship 2:350–353
MSNBC Multimedia Internship 2:166
One Reel Internship 1:292–294
Paws Companion Animal Internship 1:105–106
Seattle Art Museum Internship 1:158–159
Seattle Times Internship 2:181
Washington Food Coalition Internship 1:74–75
Washington State Governor's Internship 1:352

WEST VIRGINIA
West Virginia Governor's Internship 1:352–353

WISCONSIN

Wisconsin Governor's Internship   1:357–358

WYOMING

Buffalo Bill Historical Center Internship   2:40–43

STATE NOT SPECIFIED

U.S. Department of Energy's Science
     Undergraduate Lab Internship (SULI)   2:289–294
Verizon College Internship   1:195–196

ORGANIZATION INDEX

A

The Aark Wildlife Rehabilitation 1:81
Abbott Laboratories 1:165–166, 2:5
ABC *Good Morning America* 2:117
ABC John Stossel Specials 2:117
ABC 7 Los Angeles 2:122
ABC News 2:117–120
ABC News *PrimeTime Live* 2:120
ABC News Radio 2:120–121
ABC News Special Events 2:121
ABC News Washington Bureau 2:121–122
ABC *Weekend News* 2:122–123
ABC *World News Tonight* 2:123
Academy of Television Arts and Sciences 1:241–245
Acadia National Park 1:201
ACCION International 1:27
ACLU (American Civil Liberties Union) 1:28–30
The Actors Theatre Workshop, Inc. 1:245–246
The Ad Club (Boston) 2:124
Administration on Aging 2:6
Advertising Club 2:124–125
Advocates for Youth 1:27–28
Aerospace Corporation 2:329
AFSC (American Friends Service
    Committee) International 2:77–78
Agilent Technologies 2:329–330
AIESEC United States 2:77
Akron Beacon Journal 2:125
Amazon.com 2:330–331
Amelia Island 1:166–167
American Association for the
    Advancement of Science 2:225–227
American Cancer Society 2:6–7
American Civil Liberties Union (ACLU) 1:28–30
American Conservatory Theater 1:246–250

American Dance Festival 1:250–251
American Enterprise Institute 1:317–318
American Farmland Trust 2:193
American Folklife Center 1:201–202
American Forests 2:193–195
American Foundation for the Blind 2:7
American Friends Service Committee
    (AFSC) International 2:77–78
American Geographical Society
    1:202–203, 2:227–228
American Institute for Foreign Study 2:78–82
American Lung Association 2:8
American Public Health Association 2:9
American Red Cross 2:9–13, 2:126
American Rivers 2:195–197
American-Scandinavian Foundation 2:82–83
American School for the Deaf 1:203–204
American Society for Microbiology 2:228–229
American Society of Magazine Editors 2:127–128
Amnesty International 1:30–32
Anacostia Museum and Center for
    African American History and Culture 2:39–40
Anasazi Heritage Center 1:204–205
Anchorage Daily News 2:128–129
Antarctica Project 2:197
Apple Computer 2:331–333
Archives of American Art, Smithsonian
    Institution 1:121–122
Arena Stage 1:251–254
Arizona Legislative 1:318–320
Arnold Arboretum of Harvard University 2:197–198
Art Institute of Chicago 1:122–123
Art Museum of the Americas 1:123
Asian Pacific American Institute for
    Congressional Studies 1:320–322

Aspen Center for Environmental
  Studies   2:198–199
The Associated Press   2:129–131
Association of Schools of Public Health   2:24–25
Atlanta Ballet   1:254
Atlanta Journal Constitution   2:131–132
Atlantic Monthly   2:132–133
AT&T Undergraduate Research   2:333
Audubon magazine   2:133–134
Aullwood Audubon Center and Farm   2:199–200
Austin American-Statesman   2:134–135
Australian Embassy   2:83
Axle Alliance Group   1:167

B

Ball Aerospace   2:334
BalletMet   1:254–255
Baltimore Sun   2:135
Bangor Daily News   2:135–136
Bay Nature Magazine   2:200–201
Beaver Dam Farm   1:81–83
Bechtel Corporation   1:167–168, 2:334–335
Berkshire Theater Festival   1:255–256
Best Friends Animal Society   1:83–84
Bettis Atomic Power Lab   2:229–230
Beyond Pesticides   1:32–33
Big Cat Rescue Educational Sanctuary   1:84–85
Blethen Maine Newspapers   2:136
Boeing   1:168–169
Boston Ballet   1:256–257
Boston Celtics   2:301–302
Boston Environment Department   1:32–34
Boston Globe   2:136–137
Boston Museum of Science   1:205–210
Boston University Division of
  International Programs   2:83–93
Boys Hope, Girls Hope   2:13–14
Bread for the City   1:34
Brooklyn Children's Museum   1:210
Brooklyn Parents for Peace   1:34–35
Buffalo Bill Historical Center   2:40–43

C

California Academy of Science   2:230–232
California Governor's Office   1:322–323

California Musical Theatre Sacramento
  Music Circus   1:298–299
Callaway Advanced Technology   2:335–336
Callaway Gardens   2:201
Camp Counselors USA—European Day
  Camps   2:93–96
Canadian Embassy   2:96–97
Carnegie Endowment for International
  Peace   2:97–98
Carter Center   1:34–43
CBS News   2:137–140
Center for Adolescent Health and the Law   2:14–15
Center for Arts and Culture   1:123–124
Center for Food Safety   2:15
Center for Science in the Public Interest   2:232–235
Center for Women in Politics and Public Policy   1:43
Center for World Indigenous Studies   2:98–99
Central Intelligence Agency (CIA)   1:324–325
Cessna Aircraft Company   1:169
Charlotte Observer   2:141
ChevronTexaco Engineering   1:170–172
Chicago Bears   2:303
Chicago Bulls Ticket Sales
  Representative   2:303–304
Chicago Children's Museum   1:210–211
Chicago Historical Society   1:124–125
Chicago Sun-Times   2:141–142
Chicago Symphony Orchestra
  Association   1:257–258
Chicago Tribune   2:142
Chicago Zoological Society   1:85–87
Children's Museum of Indianapolis   1:211–217
Children's Television Workshop   1:258–259
Chincoteague National Wildlife Refuge   2:201–203
Christie's   1:125–126
Chronicle of Higher Education   2:142–143
Chrysler Group   1:172
CIA (Central Intelligence Agency)   1:324–325
CIIT Centers for Health Research   2:15–16
Cisco Systems, Inc.   2:336–337
City of Boston Environment Department   1:32–34
Cleveland Plain Dealer   2:143
CNN News   2:143–144
COHA (Council on Hemispheric Affairs)   2:101–103
Cold Spring Harbor Lab   2:235–236
Colonial Williamsburg Foundation   2:43–46
Colorado Spring Sky Sox   2:304–co6

Columbia Journalism Review 2:145
Common Cause 1:43–44
Connecticut Governor's Prevention
 Partnership 1:325–326
Cooper-Hewitt, National Design
 Museum of the Smithsonian
 Institution 1:126–127
Corcoran Gallery of Art 1:128–129
Cornell University Center for Materials
 Research 2:236–237
Cornell University Plant Genome
 Research Program 2:237–238
Costa Rica Internship Institute 2:100
Council on Foreign Relations 2:100–101
Council on Hemispheric Affairs (COHA) 2:101–103
C-Span 2:145–147

D

Dallas Morning News 2:147–148
Dallas Theater Center 1:259–260
Dance Place 1:260–261
Daughters of the American Revolution
 (DAR) Museum 1:217–218
D. C. Booth Historic Fish Hatchery 2:46
Dell Computer Corporation 2:337–338
Democratic National Committee 1:326–327
Denver Post 2:148
Denver Zoo 1:87–88
Des Moines Register 2:148–149
Detroit Free Press 2:149
Doctors Without Borders 2:16–18
Dolphin Institute (Kewalo Basin Marine
 Mammal Laboratory) 1:91–92
Dow Chemical Company 2:338
Dow Jones Newspaper Fund 2:149–150
Dreamtime Festival 1:261–263
DreamWorks SKG 1:263–264
Duke Undergraduate Neurosciences Program 2:238
DuPont 1:173, 2:238–239

E

EarthTrends (World Resources Institute) 1:44–45
Eastman Kodak Company 2:338–339
The Economist 2:103–104
E! Entertainment 1:265–267

Eisenhower National Historic Site 2:46–47
Elizabeth Glaser Pediatric AIDS
 Foundation 2:18–19
El Pueblo de Los Angeles Historical
 Monument 2:47–48
Entertainment Weekly 2:150–151
Ernst & Young 1:173–174
Eugene O'Neill Theater 1:267–269
EurekAlert! 2:151–152

F

Farm Sanctuary 1:92–93
FCNL (Friends Committee On National
 Legislation) 1:45–46
Federal Bureau of Investigation
 Washington Internships for Native
 Students (FBI WINS) 1:327–328
Fermilab 2:339–340
Field Museum 1:129–130
Florida Governor's Office 1:328–329
Folger Shakespeare Library 1:269
Ford Motor company 1:174–177
Fort Wayne Children's Zoo 1:93–94
Fossil Rim Wildlife Center 1:94–95
Freer Gallery of Art/Arthur M. Sackler
 Gallery 1:130–131
Fresno Bee 2:152
Friends Committee On National
 Legislation (FCNL) 1:45–46
Friends of the Earth 2:203–204
Frontier Nursing Service 2:19–20

G

Gay Men's Health Crisis 2:20–21
Geddes Talent Agency 1:270
Genentech 2:239–240
General Electric 1:177–178
Genesis Animal Sanctuary 1:95–96
Georgia Governor's Office 1:329–330
Georgia State Park and Historic Sites 2:48–49
Getty Foundation 1:131–133
GlaxoSmithKline 2:240–241
Glimmerglass Opera 1:270–274
Gould Farm 2:21–22
Government Accountability Project 1:47

Governors' offices. *See specific state, e.g.:*
   Oregon Governor's Office
The Governor's Prevention Partnership
   (Connecticut)   1:325–326
Great Dog Obedience Training   1:96
Greenbelt Alliance   1:48
Grey Towers National Historic Site   2:49–50
Guggenheim Museum   1:133–135

H

Habitat for Humanity   1:49
Hallmark Cards   1:178–179
The Hansard Society   2:104–105
Harper's   2:152–153
Harvard School of Public Health   2:22–23
Harvard Summer Research Program
   in Ecology   2:243–245
Harvard University Arnold Arboretum   2:197–198
Harvard University Four Directions
   Summer Research Program   2:241–242
Harvard University Summer Honors
   Undergraduate Research Program   2:242–243
Hawk Mountain Sanctuary   2:204–206
HBO   2:153–155
Healthy Mothers, Healthy Babies
   Coalition of Washington   2:24
Heifer International   1:49–50
Hermitage Foundation Museum   2:51
The Hermitage (Home of Andrew
   Jackson)   2:51–52
Hewlett-Packard   1:179
Hilltop Farm Inc.   1:97
Hirshhorn Museum and Sculpture
   Garden   1:135–136
Historic Deerfield, Inc.   2:52–54
Historic Mount Vernon   2:60–61
Historic Preservation   2:54–55
Houston Zoo   1:97–98
Howard Hughes Honors Summer
   Institute   2:245–246

I

IBM Corporation   2:340–342
Idaho Lieutenant Governor's Office   1:330

Illinois Governor's Office   1:330–331
IMG International   1:179–181
Independence Seaport Museum   1:219
Indiana Pacers   2:306–311
Initiative for a Competitive Inner City   1:51
Inroads, Inc.   1:181–182
Institute of Ecosystem Studies   2:246–250
Intel   2:342–343
International Atomic Energy Agency   2:105–107
International Center for Tolerance
   Education   1:51–52
International Child Art Foundation   1:136–137
International Diplomacy Council   1:52–53

J

The Jackson Laboratory   2:250–251
Jane Goodall Institute   2:206–208
Japanese American National Museum   1:219–221
Jim Henson Company   1:274–276
The Juilliard School   1:276–280
Julia Morgan Center for the Arts   1:137–138

K

Kaiser Family Foundation   2:155–156
Kansas City Blades   2:311–312
KCNC-TV   2:302–303
Kennedy Center for the Performing Arts   1:280–282
Kewalo Basin Marine Mammal Laboratory   1:91–92
KFSK-Southeast Alaska Public Radio   2:156–157
Knight Ridder Newspapers   2:157–158
KOCE Public TV   2:158
KPNX-TV   2:158
Kraft Foods   1:182–183
Kroenke Sports Enterprises   2:312–314
KTTV-TV   2:159

L

Lam Research Corporation   2:343
Lands' End   1:183–185
The Late Show with David Letterman   1:282–283
Leadership Alliance   2:251–252
Lexmark International, Inc.   2:343–344
Library of Congress   1:331–335

Literacy Partners Inc.   1:221
Living History Farms   2:55–56
Liz Claiborne   1:185
Lockheed Martin   2:344–345
Longwood Gardens   1:283–284, 2:208–214
Los Alamos National Laboratory   2:345–348
Los Angeles Lakers   2:314
Los Angeles Opera   1:284
Los Angeles Times   2:159–160
Lucas Digital   1:284–286
Lucasfilm, Ltd.   1:286–287
Lucent Technologies   1:185–186
Lunar and Planetary Institute 2:252–253, 2:348–349

M

Macy's   1:187–189
Maine State Governor's Office   1:335
Marathon Oil Corporation   2:349–350
Marine Biology Lab at Woods Hole   2:253–254
Marvel Enterprises, Inc.   2:160–161
Maryland Governor's Office   1:335–336
Mattel   1:186–187
MediaRights   1:53–55
Mercedes-Benz USA   1:189
Merck & Company   1:189–190
Merck Family Fund   1:55–56
Metro-Goldwyn-Mayer (MGM)   1:287–288
Metropolitan Museum of Art   1:138–140
Miami Herald   2:161–162
Michael Perez Gallery   1:140
Michigan Executive Office   1:336–338
Mickey Leland Energy Fellowships   2:254–255
Microsoft Corporation   2:350–353
Minnesota Historical Society   2:56–60
Modesto Bee   2:162–163
Morris Arboretum of the University of
    Pennsylvania   2:214–217
Mother Jones   2:163–164
Motorola   2:353–354
Mount Desert Island Biological Lab   2:255–256
Mount Vernon (Historic Mount Vernon)   2:60–61
MSNBC   2:164–166
MSNBC Multimedia   2:166
MTV Networks   1:288–290
Museum of Contemporary Art   1:140–142

Museum of Modern Art   1:142–146
Mystic Aquarium   1:98–101

N

NASA Kennedy Space Center Space
    Flight and Life Sciences   2:256–259
NASCAR   2:315–316
National Air and Space Museum   1:221–222
National Anthropological Archives   1:222–223
National Aquarium in Baltimore   1:101–102
National Association of Black
    Journalists   2:166–168
National Building Museum   1:223–224
National Campaign to Prevent Teen
    Pregnancy   1:56–57
National Council for Preservation
    Education   1:218–219, 2:61–68
National Endowment for the Arts
    1:146–147, 1:290–291
National Environmental Law Center   1:57
National Gallery of Art   1:148–150
National Gallery of Art High School
    Summer Institute   1:147–148
National Head Start Association   2:23–24
National Healthy Mothers, Healthy
    Babies Coalition   2:25–26
National Institutes of Health (NIH)   2:259–261
National Instruments   2:354–355
National Mental Health Association   2:26–28
National Museum of African Art   1:150
National Museum of American History   1:224–225
National Museum of Natural History   2:261–262
National Museum of the American
    Indian   1:225–226
National Museum of Women in the Arts 1:150–152
National Organization for Women (NOW)   1:58
National Park Foundation   2:217–218
National Portrait Gallery   1:152–155
National Renewable Energy Laboratory 2:355–356
National Science Foundation (NSF)   2:263–264
National Semiconductor   2:356–357
National Trust for Historic Preservation 2:68–69
National Zoo Beaver Valley   1:102–103
Naval Research Lab Science and
    Engineering   2:264–265

NBC   2:168
NCR   2:357
New American Dream Communications   1:58–59
New England Healthcare Institute   2:28–29
New England Wildlife Center   1:103–104
New Jersey Governor's Office   1:338–339
New Museum of Contemporary Art   1:155–157
Newport Historical Society   2:39–40
The New Press   1:60
Newsweek   2:168–169
New York City Department of Citywide
    Administrative Services   1:339–344
New York Daily News   2:169–170
New York Rangers   2:316
New York State Theatre Institute   1:291–292
New York Times   2:170–172
New York University Center for Neural
    Science   2:265
New York University Howard Hughes
    Honors Summer Institute   2:245–246
New York University School of
    Medicine   2:266–267
Nickelodeon Animation Studio   1:292
Nightline   2:172–173
NIH (National Institutes of Health)   2:259–261
North Carolina Governor's Office   1:344–345
Northern Kentucky University
    Cooperative Center for Study
    Abroad--Ireland   2:99
NOW (National Organization for Women)   1:58
NSF (National Science Foundation)   2:263–264
Nuclear Regulatory Commission   2:267–268

O

Office of Naval Research   2:268–273
Oklahoma Governor's Office   1:345
Old Sturbridge Village   2:69–70
One Reel   1:292–295
Oracle Corporation   2:357–358
Oregon Governor's Office   1:345–346
Oregon Zoo   1:104–105
Orlando Magic   2:316–321
Orlando Sentinel   2:173–174

P

Pacific Gas and Electric Company   2:358–359
Packer Foundation Engineering   2:359–360
Paramount Pictures/Dr. Phil Show   1:295
Paws Companion Animal   1:105–106
Peaceworks Foundation   1:61
Pendle Hill Quaker Center for
    Contemplation and Study   1:61–62
Pennsylvania Department of Public Health   2:29
Performance Research   2:321–322
Pfizer Inc.   1:190–192, 2:273–274
Philadelphia Inquirer   2:174–175
Philadelphia Museum of Art   1:157–158
Philadelphia Orchestra Association   1:295–297
Philadelphia Phantoms   2:322–323
Philadelphia 76ers   2:323–324
Philadelphia Zoo   1:106–109
Physicians for Social Responsibility   1:62–63
Population Institute   2:30
Population Services International   1:63–64
Portland Children's Museum   1:226–229
Pratt & Whitney   2:360–361
Preservation Action   2:70–71
Prison Activist Resource Center   1:65–66
Project HOPE (Health Opportunities
    for People Everywhere)   2:30–31
Public Leadership Education Network   1:66–67
Pulmonary Hypertension Association   2:31–32

R

Radio Disney   1:297
Rainforest Action Network   1:67–68
Random House, Inc.   1:192–193
Republican National Committee   1:346–347
Reuters America Inc.   2:175–176
RKO Pictures   1:297–298
Robert F. Kennedy Memorial Center for
    Human Rights   1:68
Rockefeller University   2:275–276
Rocky Mountain Biological Laboratory   2:276–277
Rocky Mountain PBS   2:176–177
Roswell Park Cancer Institute   2:277–278

S

Sacramento Bee	2:177
Saks Incorporated	1:193–194
San Diego Chargers	2:324–325
San Diego Museum of Art	1:229
San Diego Zoo	1:109, 1:230
San Francisco Chronicle	2:177–179
San Francisco Mime Troupe	1:299–300
Santa Fe Institute	2:361–362
The Santé Group	1:69
Science Magazine	2:179–180
Science News	2:180–181
Seattle Art Museum	1:158–159
Seattle Times	2:181
SeaWorld Adventure Camp	1:109–111
Second Stage Theatre	1:300–302
Seeds of Peace	1:69–70
Shakespeare Theatre	1:302–304
Share Our Strength	1:70–71
Sierra Club	1:71–72
Sierra Magazine	2:181–182
Silent Spring Institute	2:32–33
Silicon Graphics Inc. (SGI)	2:362–363
Smithsonian Architectural History and Historic Preservation Division	2:71
Smithsonian Astrophysical Observatory	2:279–280
Smithsonian Folkways Recordings	1:304–305
Smithsonian Institution Archives of American Art	1:121–122
Solomon R. Guggenheim Museum	1:133–135
South Carolina Governor's Office	1:347
South Shore Music Circus	1:305–306
South Street Seaport Museum	1:230–231
Spoleto Festival USA	1:306–307
Stanford Linear Accelerator Center	2:280–281
State governors' offices. See specific state, e.g.: Oregon Governor's Office	
St. Petersburg Times	2:182–183
Strides Therapeutic Riding Center	1:111–112
Strong Women, Strong Girls	1:72–73
Student Climate Outreach	2:218–219
Student Conservation Association	2:219–221
Studio Theatre	1:308–309

SUNY Albany Department of Biomedical Sciences	2:281–282
Surgeons of Hope Foundation	2:33

T

Tampa Tribune	2:183–184
Teach for America	1:231–232
Teen People	2:184–185
Texas Film Commission	1:309–310
Texas Instruments Incorporated	2:363–364
Tiger Creek Wildlife Refuge	1:112–113
Time Inc.	2:185–186
Toledo Mud Hens	2:325
Toyota Motor North America	1:194–195
20/20 Vision	1:73
Tyson Foods	1:195

U

United Nations Association of the USA	1:74
United Nations Children's Fund (UNICEF)	2:107
University of California - Davis Department of Environmental Toxicology	2:282
University of Colorado at Boulder SMART Program	2:283–284
University of Florida—Whitney Laboratory	2:296–297
University of Massachusetts Department of Biology	2:284–286
University of Massachusetts Medical School	2:287–288
University of the Middle East	1:232–233
USA Today	2:186
U.S. Capitol Historical Society	2:71–72
U.S. Department of Education	1:233
U.S. Department of Energy Science Undergraduate Laboratory	2:289–294
U.S. Holocaust Memorial Museum	1:233–234
U.S. News & World Report	2:186–187
U.S. Supreme Court	1:347–349

V

Verizon	1:195–196
Vermont Folklife Center	2:72–73

Vermont Governor's Office   1:349
Virginia Institute of Marine Science   2:294–296
VSA Arts   1:159

W

Wake Forest University Department
    of Biology   2:253–254
WakeMed Health and Hospital   2:33–34
Wall Street Journal   2:187
Walt Disney World   1:196–197, 1:310–312
Walt Disney World Animal Kingdom   1:88–91
Washington, D.C., Department of Health   2:34–35
The Washington Center for Internships
    and Academic Seminars   1:234–237
Washington Food Coalition   1:74–75
The *Washingtonian*   2:188–190
Washington Internships for Native
    Students (WINS)   1:349–352
Washington State Governor's Office   1:352
Wellesley College Department of
    Biological Sciences   2:296
West Virginia Governor's Office   1:352–353
The White House   1:353–357
The Whitney Laboratory (University
    of Florida)   2:296–297
Whitney Museum of American Art   1:159–160
Wild Horse Sanctuary   1:113–114
Wildlife Rescue and Rehabilitation, Inc.   1:114
The Wilma Theater   1:312
WINS (Washington Internships for
    Native Students) *See also* Federal
    Bureau of Investigation Washington
    Internships for Native Students   1:349–352

Wisconsin Governor's Office   1:357–358
Wolfsong Ranch Foundation   1:114–115
Wolf Trap Foundation for the
    Performing Arts   1:312–314
Women for Peace   1:75
Women's International League for Peace
    and Freedom   2:108–111
Women Work   1:76–77
Woods Hole Marine Biology Lab   2:253–254
Work Canada   2:111–113
World Affairs Council   1:77
World Bird Sanctuary   1:115–116
World Resources Institute (WRI)   1:44–45
WVSA Arts Connection   1:160–162
Wyckoff Farmhouse Museum   2:73–74

X

Xerox   2:364–365

Y

YAI National Institute for People with
    Disabilities   2:35

Z

Zoo Atlanta   1:116–117